Introduction to Media Production: From Analog to Digital

Introduction to Media Production: From Analog to Digital

GORHAM KINDEM

ROBERT MUSBURGER

Focal Press

Boston • Oxford • Johannesburg • Melbourne • New Delhi • Singapore

Focal Press is an imprint of Butterworth–Heinemann.

Recognizing the importance of preserving what has been written, Butterworth–Heinemann prints its books on acid-free paper whenever possible.

Library of Congress Cataloging-in-Publication Data

Kindem, Gorham Anders.
Introduction to media production : from analog to digital / Gorham Kindem, Robert Musburger.
p. cm.
Includes bibliographical references and index.
ISBN 0-240-80239-X (alk. paper)
1. Motion pictures—Production and direction. 2. Television—Production and direction. 3. Analog electronic systems. 4. Digital electronics. I. Musburger, Robert B.
PN1995.9.P7K538 1997
791.43′0232—dc20 96-38611
CIP

British Library Cataloguing-in-Publication Data

A catalogue record for this book is available from the British Library.

The publisher offers special discounts on bulk orders of this book.
For information, please contact:
Manager of Special Sales
Butterworth–Heinemann
313 Washington Street
Newton, MA 02158–1626
Tel: 617-928-2500
Fax: 617-928-2620

For information on all Focal Press publications available, contact our World Wide Web home page at: http://www.bh.com/fp

10 9 8 7 6 5 4 3 2 1

Printed in the United States of America

For Nancy and Pat
in return for their patience, understanding, and support.

Table of Contents

Preface

Introduction to Media Production: From Analog to Digital introduces students and others to the exciting and challenging world of media production as media technology moves from analog to digital. As a basic textbook, it bridges a transitional period during which both types of technology will be in common use. Schools that teach media production will continue to use analog equipment for some time, making the transition to digital a relatively slow and gradual process.

Introduction to Media Production provides a practical framework for approaching a diverse set of production problems and helps future media artists and professionals learn to make good decisions and choices, whether they will be using analog or digital equipment, or a combination of the two. The text is intended not only as a basic college textbook, but also as a handy reference for anyone involved with media production, including those who are not required to handle or operate equipment, such as writers, producers, directors, and even salespeople. Many people who are or will be directly or indirectly involved in media production need a basic knowledge of the techniques required to carry out the requirements of their portion of the production process. Within an academic context, the text can be used in either a lecture-only class or for the first semester or quarter of a hands-on production class.

Introduction to Media Production offers an analytical approach to production, one that provides both a historical and aesthetic background as well as an emphasis on preplanning and conceptualization skills that must accompany a knowledge of practical production techniques and technology.

Focusing on the similarities and differences between video, film, and audio, and the role that computers play in the production process, is an efficient and effective way to learn about media production. It provides the reader with a variety of options that can be pursued depending on the types and availability of equipment for a particular production. Presenting concepts and information applicable to different media in a single textbook offers an alternate approach to more equipment-oriented production manuals. Readers learn to consider a full range of options and in so doing become better prepared to function successfully in a dynamic and rapidly changing field during a transition period from analog to digital technology.

The one certainty that readers must prepare themselves for is the certainty that media technology will continue to change but that these changes will not occur overnight. Newer and older methods, as well as digital and analog technologies, will continue for some time to occupy important places in our media environment and in the production of moving images and sounds.

1

The Production Process: Analog and Digital Technologies

Introduction

Analog and digital technologies are used in media production. The advent of digital technologies has stimulated a number of important developments in media production. This chapter explores the continuing importance of analog technologies and some of significant changes stimulated by digital technologies, and it provides an overview of the media production process.

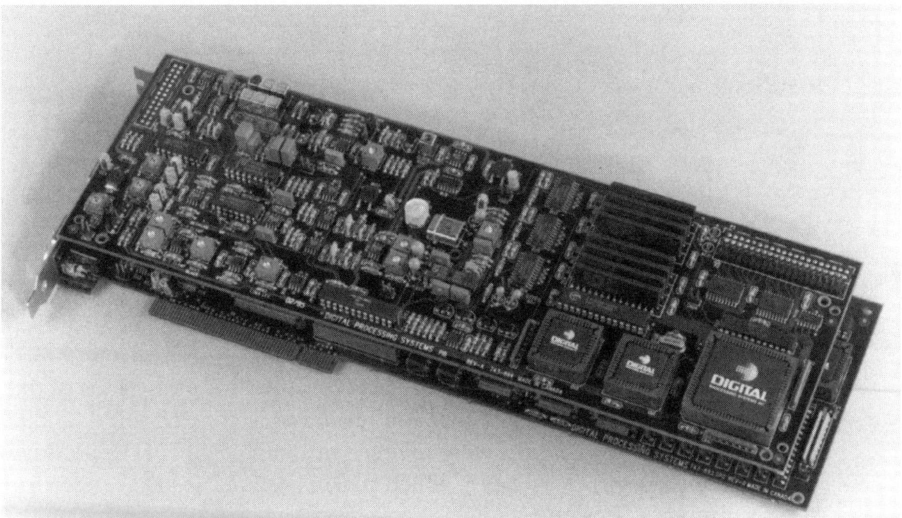

(Courtesy of Digital Processing Systems, Inc.)

Stages of Production

The production process can be organized into three consecutive stages: preproduction, production, and postproduction. Everything from the inception of the project idea to setting up for actual recording is part of the preproduction stage. This includes the writing of a proposal, treatment, and script, and the breakdown of the script in terms of production scheduling and budgeting. The second major phase of production is the production stage. Everything involved in the setup and recording of visual images and sounds—from performer, camera, and microphone placement and movement, to lighting and set design—is part of the production stage. Postproduction consists of the editing of the recorded images and sounds, and all of the procedures needed to complete a project.

Preproduction

Preproduction consists of the preparation of project proposals, premises, synopses, treatments, scripts, script breakdowns, production schedules, budgets, and storyboards. A *proposal* is a market summary, which is used to promote or sell a project. A *premise* is a concise statement or assertion that sums up the story or subject matter. For example, the basic premise of Joan Didion's film *The Panic in Needle Park* (1971) is "Romeo and Juliet on drugs in New York's Central Park." A *synopsis* is a short paragraph that describes the basic story line. *Treatments* are longer plot or subject-matter summaries in short-story form, while *scripts* are virtually complete production guides on paper, specifying what will be seen and heard in the finished product. Scripts can be broken down by listing all equipment and personnel needs for each scene, so that a production can be scheduled and budgeted. A *budget* describes how funds will be spent in each production category. A *storyboard* provides a graphic visualization of important shots, which will eventually be recorded by a camera.

Production

Production begins with setup and rehearsal. The film or video director stages and plots the action by rehearsing scenes in preparation for actual recording. Charting the movement of talent on the set is known as *performer blocking*, while charting the movements of the cameras is called *camera blocking*. Every camera placement and movement of the talent must be carefully worked out prior to recording. If the action cannot be controlled, as in the live transmission of a sporting event or the production of a documentary, the director must be able to anticipate exactly where the action is likely to go and place the camera or cameras accordingly. During actual production the entire project is essentially in the hands of the director. In multiple-camera studio or location production, for example, the director often selects the shots by commanding the technical director (TD) to press certain buttons on a device called a *switcher*, which makes instantaneous changes from one camera to another. In single-camera production, the director remains on the set and communicates directly with the talent and crew. The script supervisor or continuity person watches the actual recording session with a sharp eye to ensure that every segment in the script has been recorded. Perfect continuity between shots, in such details as a consistent left-to-right or right-to-left direction and identical flow of performer movements (matched action) from one shot to the next, must be maintained so that these shots can be properly combined during editing.

In an audio production or recording session, the producer maintains the same authority and responsibilities as a video or film director: rehearsing the musicians, instructing the engineer, and supervising the actual recording session.

Postproduction

Postproduction begins after the visual images and sounds have been recorded. Possible edit points can be determined during the preview stage, when the recorded images and sounds are initially viewed. Pictures and accompanying sounds are examined and reexamined to find exact edit points before various shots are combined. Separate sound tracks can be added later to the edited images, or the sounds can be edited at the same time as the pictures. The postproduction stage ties together the audio and visual elements of production and smooths out all the rough edges. The visual and audio elements must be properly balanced and controlled. Sophisticated analog and digital devices help editors and technical specialists mold sounds and images into their final form.

In audio postproduction the emphasis is placed on choosing the best of the many sound takes and the combining of the various tracks onto one, or in the case of stereo, two, finished tracks. Signal processing, including equalization, adding effects, and balancing tracks against each other, is often performed during the sound mix, that is, during the final process of combining various sound tracks.

The three stages of production are separate only in a chronological sense. Proficiency in one stage of the production process necessarily requires some knowledge of all other stages. A director or writer cannot visualize the possibilities for recording a particular scene without having some awareness of how images can be combined during editing. In short, while the overall organization of this text into three stages (preproduction, production, and postproduction) follows a logical progression, mastery of any one stage demands some familiarity with other stages as well.

Digital versus Analog Technology

While all three stages of media production have been affected by the advent of digital technologies, analog technologies continue to play important roles in each stage as well. For many years equipment used in media production was exclusively analog, and many analog technologies, including motion picture film, are still widely used today. In fact, the size and quality of images recorded by some film technologies have never been surpassed. The potential screen size and image detail or resolution of projected large-format film images, such as IMAX, Omnivision, and even standard 35mm film, is still superior to video projection systems, including digital high definition television (HDTV) projection systems, and it is likely to remain so for some time. The look of film, the softness of the film image, the intense saturation of colors, and its superior reflectance contrast range (from bright white to dark black) over electronic media (100:1 vs. 30:1) translate into a very sophisticated and subtle visual medium. As MIT Media Lab founder and author of *Being Digital,*

Professor Nicholas Negroponte, has said, " . . . the subtlety and nuance of film is so far out of reach right now. Film is still by far the highest, best-resolution medium we have." (*American Cinematographer,* May 1995, p. 79).

New media technologies rarely eliminate older technologies, although they often make the use of older technologies more specialized. The use of film has become more and more specialized with every advance in electronic imaging technology. For example, advances in videotape recording and editing made it less advantageous for television news operations to use news film during the 1970s, but most prime-time dramatic programs used film and have continued to do so. Today digital editing systems offer a number of advantages over conventional film editing, and digital technologies have virtually replaced analog audiotape and videotape recording and editing technologies in certain situations as well.

Digital systems encode audio and video information as a series of ones and zeros or "on" and "off" signals. A full range of sounds (from loud to soft and from high pitch to low) and images (from bright to dark and from high color saturation to low) can be digitally encoded as a series of zeros and ones. Analog audio and video information, on the other hand, contains a vast range of incremental electrical or photochemical values that are analogous to the sound and image spectrum.

Digital recordings are more permanent and are much less likely to experience a loss in quality when they are copied from one generation to the next than are analog recordings, because only one value is used for encoding, "on" or "off," one or zero. Digital encoding also offers increased flexibility and efficiency in terms of manipulating and shaping recorded sounds and visual images during postproduction editing and special effects, because it is easier to manipulate a single value (one or zero) than a vast range of incremental values (Figure 1.1).

Digital technologies have increased the speed, efficiency, and flexibility of film and TV production, and it is important to recognize some of the contributions that digital technologies have made to each stage of media production, including preproduction writing, producing, and storyboarding, production recording and lighting, and postproduction editing and special effects. Overall, digital technologies have significantly increased production efficiency in each of these areas, and they have also begun to alter conventional notions of reality and history through a proliferation of imaginative and realistic special effects.

Digital Technologies Used in Preproduction

Digital computers are widely used in film and TV preproduction. Scriptwriting and word processing computer software programs help writers efficiently format and revise scripts. Producers and production managers use scheduling and budgeting software programs to quickly break down scripts and preplan their productions. Breakdown sheets list all equipment and personnel needs for each scene in a film or TV script. The cost of each of these items can quickly be totaled up to produce an overall budget, while the duration and sequence of recording each scene can be used to create an overall production schedule. Changes that need to be made in a script, a budget, or a schedule can be made quickly and efficiently on a digital computer.

Computer graphics software facilitates the creation of storyboards, which can provide visual guidelines for camera shots, editing, and overall storytelling. A story-

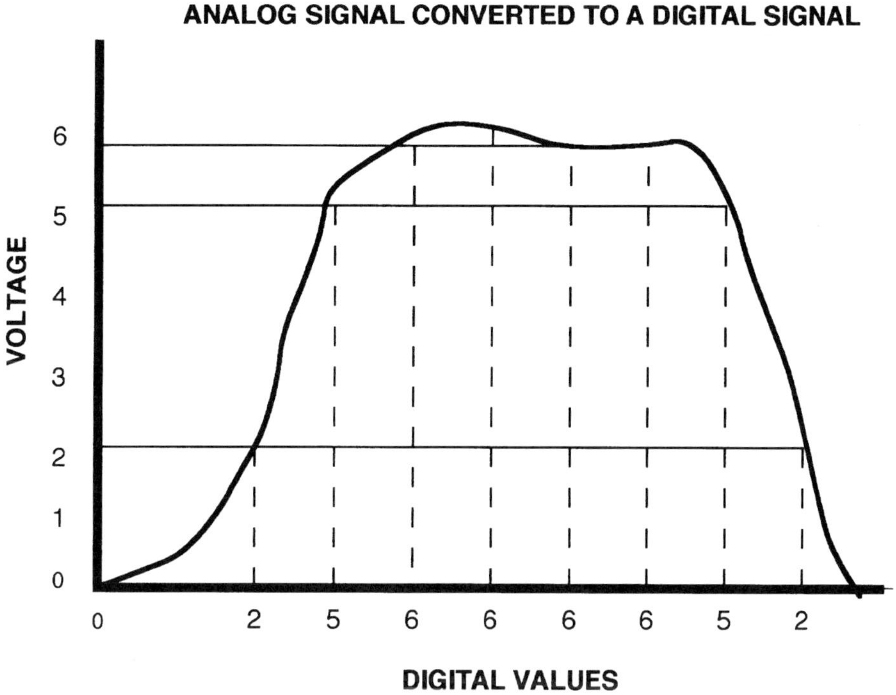

Figure 1.1 Digital signals are determined by periodically sampling the values of comparable analog signals. The greater the number of samples per second, the higher the quality of the digital signal.

board consists of a series of graphic images that indicate the camera framing and composition for each shot in a film or TV program. Other graphics programs allow sets and costumes to be visualized and coordinated before they are actually made. Lighting plots can be quickly revised when computer programs offer the potential to visualize the lighting effects on simulated characters and settings prior to actually hanging the lights.

Computerized casting networks and performer databases help talent agencies to promote actors they represent and casting directors to find them. Location scouting has been facilitated by computer databases, and the World Wide Web's ability to provide pictures of possible locations via computer networks offers the potential to both cut down on travel expenses and shorten preproduction schedules. The ability to capture and send images and sounds as well as text around the world via digital computer networks, such as the Internet and the World Wide Web, offers tremendous potential regarding the international flow of information. The Internet also offers a new means of marketing motion pictures, and as Nicholas Negroponte at MIT has suggested, " . . . the net will perhaps be the primary form of world commerce. . . . And the cinematography community will enjoy an extraordinary new marketplace." (*American Cinematographer,* May 1995, p. 80).

Digital Technologies Used in Production

New digital recording devices for video cameras offer a number of advantages for news recording. For example, a computer hard disk can be attached to a portable video camera to record news stories for television. Dockable (camera-attachable) hard disks allow up to 25 minutes or more of professional quality video to be recorded. Digital images and sounds can be edited immediately on a digital nonlinear editing system since they do not need to be "captured," or transferred in "real time" from videotape to digital hard disk, greatly speeding up the production of news stories. Just as videotape recording and editing offered significant advantages over news film in the 1970s, today digital recording and editing devices offer potential advantages over conventional videotape recording and editing news stories.

Computerized digital lighting boards facilitate production by allowing a cinematographer or lighting director to preprogram a lighting setup and hang several lighting setups simultaneously using different computer files on the same lighting board program. Special lighting effects, such as projecting images and graphics on the walls of sets to add atmosphere or create laser light shows, can also be preprogrammed into a computerized lighting board and software program.

For example, the lighting director for a popular American film, *Batman Forever* (1995), made extensive use of digital lighting techniques and equipment during production in order to control more complicated lighting setups and changes than would be possible using conventional analog technology. This film returned to the original 1939 comic-book source of the mythical crime fighter, the Caped Crusader, to create a more active and action-oriented hero as well as comic-book villains. In one scene at a circus, where the villain, Two-Face (played by Tommy Lee Jones) staged a deadly threat to Batman (played by Val Kilmer), over 225 Xenon lamps were controlled by a computerized lighting board so that they could do color changes and chases. In another "pan-Asian" sequence within Gotham City, they used computer-controlled lighting to project saturated colors and Chinese motifs onto the side of the buildings, which was filmed on Figueroa Street in downtown Los Angeles. The lighting director's extensive experience with rock and roll concerts and theatrical shows greatly facilitated his use of computerized lighting equipment on the film.

Sound recording has been greatly facilitated by Digital Audio Tape (DAT) recording processes and equipment. Digitally recorded sounds can be filtered more effectively and efficiently on location than analog recordings, for example, to remove unwanted background sounds. Digital sound recordings also minimize hiss as well as generational loss in sound quality when they are copied and dubbed for editing purposes, and blend well with digitally recorded sound effects, music, and Automatic Dialogue Replacement (ADR) recorded in a sound studio during postproduction.

Digital Technologies Used in Postproduction

Some of the most significant contributions of digital technology to film and TV production have come in the postproduction area. Digital videotape recorders, such as D1, D2, D3, and D5, facilitate the creation of special effects during final or on-line editing by allowing images to be layered on top of one another in successive recordings.

Digital editing systems make editing and revising a film or video as simple and quick as operating a computer word processor. In addition to increasing postproduction efficiency, digital editing systems allow an editor to visualize a final edited program, including many special effects, prior to the final stages of film or video postproduction, including conforming and answer printing or on-line videotape editing.

Digital editing systems are now widely used in both film and TV postproduction. Most digital editing systems employ computer hardware that is capable of processing and storing vast amounts of visual and audio information. A digital editing system usually includes a computer processing unit (CPU) with a 60+ megahertz (MHz) processing system, 30+ megabytes (MB) of random access memory (RAM), a keyboard, a mouse, one or two computer monitors, a videotape recorder, an amplifier and loudspeakers, and a large hard disk drive designed for audiovisual (AV) use.

Digital editing software offers several advantages over conventional means of editing film, audiotape, and videotape, including increased flexibility, as well as potential time and cost savings. A common cliché is that digital editing is the equivalent of word processing and desktop publishing for audio, film, and video postproduction. The analogy holds for many aspects of editing that are shared by word processing and various digital editing software programs. For example, most word processing software allow a writer to cut, copy, paste, and delete words, paragraphs, and pages of text. Digital editing affords an editor similar flexibility in terms of instantaneously changing the order and duration of sounds and images. For example, clips of video or audio information can be cut, trimmed, copied, pasted, inserted, and deleted along a time line (Figure 1.2).

A clip is usually the smallest unit of digital video (or audio) information that can be stored and manipulated during editing. It can range from just one frame to an entire movie in duration, but it often consists of a single shot, that is, a continuous camera recording or take. Digitized clips are usually imported (or copied) into a particular editing project file, where they are edited along a time line with other images and sounds. Images and sounds from each clip are often displayed as a series of representative still frames along the time line. Clips can be copied and inserted at various points along the time line, and they can also be deleted from the time line and the remaining images and sounds attached to one another.

Every edit made using a digital software program is usually a virtual edit. No digitized material is discarded when clips are trimmed, cut, or deleted along an editing time line, since each clip is usually stored separately outside the time line window. Every clip stored on a disk drive is instantaneously accessible in its entirety and can be grabbed in the project or clip window and reinserted at any point along the time line. Many alternative versions of a scene or sequence can thus be quickly edited and examined without prematurely eliminating material that may be needed later. Transitions from one shot to another can be previewed, as can the superimposition of titles and various digital video effects without ever actually cutting, discarding, eliminating, or deleting any originally digitized video or audio.

The ability to manipulate clips of video and sound along a time line not only adds flexibility to the editing process, it can also make editing more efficient and cost effective. Clips can be very rapidly trimmed, cut, inserted, and deleted. Digital editing is extremely fast compared with physically cutting and splicing a conventional feature film, for example, and the time it takes to find and insert videotape

Figure 1.2 Digital equipment may be used to record, control, or edit audio, video, or lighting signals. (Courtesy Akai, Lexicon, Nagra, Colortran, and Yamaha.)

images and sounds from a source onto a master videotape can be dramatically reduced by using instantaneously accessible digital clips along a time line. The amount of time scheduled for postproduction editing can be significantly diminished, facilitating the editing of projects that require a short turnaround time, such as topical news magazine segments and minidocumentaries. Increased editing efficiency can also translate into cost savings that affect the overall budget of longer term projects when an editor's time and salary can be reduced. Clearly, digital editing offers a number of advantages in terms of flexibility and efficiency over conventional videotape and film editing.

Digital editing systems can be used at many different production levels. Some low-end digital editing systems are designed for use on home computers, and the range of graphics and special effects that are available on relatively inexpensive consumer programs to edit home videos is truly remarkable. Inexpensive digital editing systems also provide an excellent means of teaching video and sound editing, graphics, and special effects to students at a variety of educational levels. High-end professional systems can be used to efficiently edit feature films, relying upon Kodak film Keykode numbers and SMPTE time code numbers (discussed later in Chapter 12) as references for film conforming and/or on-line editing. Large corporations whose video production units use high-end digital editing system sometimes finish their programs in digital form, avoiding the added time and cost of on-line videotape editing. A large number of audio tracks can usually be edited initially using digital editing software and additional editing, mixing, and sound "sweetening" can be done later using a compatible digital audio workstation.

Special effects techniques have been greatly expanded and enhanced by digital technologies, and the Academy of Motion Picture Arts and Sciences recently granted full branch status (similar to the acting and cinematography branches of the Academy) to visual effects supervisors and artists. Digital effects are often combined with miniatures (smaller copies of objects) and models (full-size mockups) to produce startlingly realistic special effects in Hollywood feature films, such as *Jurassic Park* (miniatures and models are discussed more fully in Chapter 14). Computer graphics hardware and software have played an important role in the creation of special effects.

Many of the special effects used in the Hollywood film *Apollo 13* (1995), for example, were achieved by compositing (combining digital images) miniatures and models using computer graphics and digital video effects. *Apollo 13* focuses upon the nearly tragic story of the Apollo 13 astronauts after an accident occurred on board their spacecraft in April of 1970 that forced their moon landing to be aborted and nearly left them stranded in space. These events took place at the height of the space race and the Cold War competition between the United States and the Soviet Union.

The ability to manipulate and control individual pixels (single dots of colored light on a monitor that collectively creates an image) on a computer screen and to animate three-dimensional graphic images has led to a proliferation of effects that challenge conventional conceptions of history and reality. For example, the NASA space program astronaut who advised the producers of *Apollo 13* regarding the authenticity of various space launch procedures and restagings asked the producers where they had obtained actual documentary footage of the launch of the Apollo 13 spacecraft, when in fact the images were digital special effects created on a computer.

The Hollywood film *Forrest Gump* (1994) placed the fictitious main character inside the frame of an actual documentary recording of former President Lyndon B. Johnson, while President Johnson's lips were animated and he appeared to speak to Forrest Gump. These examples illustrate the power of digital special effects to potentially rewrite history and to create artificial worlds that sometimes seem more real than authentic documentary recordings. Film history has itself been revised and manipulated through the digital colorization of old black-and-white feature films. While colorizing old (and sometimes new) Hollywood films has clearly distorted the original artist's intentions and has altered film history, in the hands of media moguls, such as Ted Turner, who acquired the MGM library for use on Turner Network television, it has also significantly added to the television markets and viewing audiences for older films. Digital film and TV technologies have had a significant impact upon conventional notions of history and reality, and they have challenged traditional legal, ethical, and aesthetic conceptions as well.

A relatively new digital technology that offers potential connections to film and video is CD-ROM, especially computer games and other interactive software. Many Hollywood film companies work with CD-ROM producers to create interactive computer games in conjunction with the release of feature films to theaters. The same settings or locations used in a feature film can be recorded in virtual 360-degree space using several film cameras, and these images can then be mapped three dimensionally via various computer programs so that a CD-ROM player can move throughout the space, interacting with characters and situations from the film. CD-ROMs that incorporate film and video material also offer tremendous potential in education, including interactive film and TV production training, such as learning how to operate specific pieces of equipment.

Digital technologies have clearly increased the speed, efficiency, and flexibility of media production in all three stages of film and TV production—preproduction, production, and postproduction. While they have not yet eliminated superior analog technologies, such as film recording and theater screenings, digital devices have made the use of traditional analog technologies more specialized. In addition, digital technologies have begun to alter conventional notions of history and reality through the use of sophisticated computer graphics and special effects, including the colorization of old black-and-white films. Finally, as we look to the 21st century, new digital technologies, such as CD-ROMs, the Internet, and the World Wide Web, will undoubtedly provide new markets for films and videos and new educational opportunities for film and TV students and scholars.

The advent of digital technology has blurred many traditional distinctions in media production, such as off-line versus on-line editing, film versus video production, and (active) artists versus (passive) viewers. Traditionally, videotape editing occurs in two stages, often referred to as off-line and on-line editing. During *off-line editing,* the sequential order of visual images and sounds is arranged and rearranged using small-format dubs or copies of the original videotape recordings. During *on-line editing,* the final decisions resulting from off-line editing are performed again using the original, high quality videotape recordings and more sophisticated equipment. Today a high quality digital editing system can perform both functions, that is, it can be used for both (preliminary) off-line editing and for (final) on-line editing, making the passage from one stage to the next less distinct. In addition, the flexibility afforded by digital editing systems often seems much closer to traditional techniques of film editing than to somewhat more restrictive off-line videotape editing systems. For example, a digital editing system allows an editor to reduce the overall length or duration of a program by deleting or removing images and sounds along a time line and simply bringing the remaining images and sounds together so that they directly precede and follow one another. This technique is similar to the removal of frames of film or a shot and accompanying sound from the middle of a film. The potential to change the overall program duration at will is often referred to as a "nonlinear" approach to editing because the order of shots and sounds can be reordered at any time. The overall program length or duration cannot be shortened or lengthened at will in "linear" videotape analog editing systems without re-editing the entire program from the point at which something is removed. Digital systems can be used to edit productions that were originally recorded on either film or videotape using a nonlinear approach. In so doing, digital editing equipment has brought film and video editing closer together.

Digital HDTV cameras capture electronic images that have an aspect ratio (width to height ratio) and resolution (clarity and amount of detail in the image) that in some ways more closely approximates theatrical film than it does traditional video images. Finally, computers and interactive multimedia software allow traditionally passive media viewers and listeners to analyze and manipulate audio, video, and film productions and to actively recreate their own versions of existing media texts, as well as to learn new skills interactively or play computer games. Traditional distinctions between (active) artists versus (passive) viewers/listeners, film versus video production, and off-line versus on-line editing are becoming less and less meaningful as digital technologies bring traditional forms of media production closer together.

A Short History of Audio, Film, and Video Production Technology

The basic technology for the eventual development of radio and audio recording, motion pictures, and television was available as early as the beginning of the 19th century. The predecessors of motion pictures may be considered to be still photography, audio systems, the telegraph, television, and the electrical discharge of light-sensitive materials. Each of these was discovered or invented before 1840 (Figure 1.3).

From 1839 to the end of the 19th century, experiments and practical models of both selenium-based electrical systems and rotating disc-based systems were developed to convert and transmit visual images. By 1870 Thomas Edison had produced a primitive mechanical cylindrical audio recording device called the Gramaphone. During the last half of the 19th century, a variety of toylike machines, such as the Thaumatrope, Phenakistoscope, and Zoetrope and lantern shows, with delightful titles such as Phantasmagoria and Magasin Pittoresque were used to display projected pictures that appeared to move.

The perceptual mechanism or illusion on which motion pictures depend was labeled an instance of the phi phenomenon by perceptual psychologists well after the introduction of film. Gestalt psychologists were fascinated by perceptual tricks and illusions because they provided a convenient means of studying the way our brains process sensory information. The phi phenomenon produces apparent motion out of stationary lights or objects. It occurs when two lights, separated by a short distance, are flashed or strobed very rapidly. Above a certain threshold of flashes per second, the human eye is deluded into thinking that one light is moving, rather than that two stationary lights flashing. This same phenomenon helps to

Figure 1.3
Early media production equipment by today's standards was primitive and ineffective. But production techniques developed to produce shows on that early equipment still provides the basis for today's digital media production. (An early Technicolor camera.)

explain the perception of apparent motion from rapidly flashed still photographs. The mind's eye fills in the gaps between frames and produces apparent, not real, motion.

The Age of Invention brought about the telephone; the electric telescope, designed to convert moving images into an electrical signal; and early carbon, crystal, and ceramic microphones. Before the turn of the century, the disc record player and recorder were improved, Edison and W.K.L. Dickson developed a workable motion picture camera and projector, and George Eastman invented the flexible film base that made motion pictures possible. The century ended with the first "wireless" broadcasts, film projected on a screen for an audience, and a working model of a wire recorder.

Television experiments continued into the early 20th century, alternating between rotating disc and electrical systems. Motion picture sound systems at the turn of the century utilized sound recorded on discs with primitive methods designed to maintain synchronization between picture and sound. Many of the frustrations of workers in all three industries were partially solved by deForest's invention of the amplifying vacuum tube, the Audion. This invention provided the means for Fessenden to send voices over the air for the first time and for the motion picture industry to use sound-reinforcing systems for theatres.

In 1908 the all electrical television system now in use was described, but it took 17 years before a practical model became operational. Television technology is based on light coming through a camera lens and striking a light-sensitive surface on a camera pickup tube or surface of a CCD chip. Fluctuations in current on the face of the tube or the surface of the chip are read by the circuitry of the camera as direct variations in the light striking the surfaces. These fluctuations in electrical current are then fed to a television picture tube, which reverses the process. Bright light striking specific points on the camera pickup tube correspond to bright light emitted by the phosphors of the television receiver's picture tube. A television screen is scanned completely thirty times every second; thus the images move at a speed of thirty frames per second, rather than the twenty-four frames per second of sound film. Television, like film, depends on the phi phenomenon to produce apparent motion, but it also relies on persistence of vision to fuse the continuous scanning of the picture tube into complete frames of picture. *Persistence of vision* refers to the temporary lag in the eye's retention of an image, which can fuse one image with those that immediately precede or follow. This phenomenon does not explain apparent motion, because the fusion of images in the same position within the frame would result in a confused blur, rather than the coherent motion of objects.

The first two-color, two-negative Technicolor film process was developed in 1917 and was followed three years later by the first AM radio stations in the United States receiving licenses and 21 television stations being licensed to use the spinning disc system. By the early 1920s the Hollywood motion picture industry had become pervasive enough to dominate foreign screens and to be threatened with domestic censorship. The first sound-on-film system was developed by deForest the same year that Zworykin invented the iconoscope television camera tube, which opened the way for an all-electronic television system. Within that same decade, the recording industry moved from acoustical recording to electronic methods and RCA started the first radio network. Fox first used the Movietone sound on film system for newsreels. Warner Bros. used the Vitaphone disc system for their first sound features.

During the 1930s modern dynamic and ribbon microphones were invented, and both British and American inventors continued to toy with audio wire recorders. By 1932 Technicolor introduced their three-color, three-negative film process and FM radio was developed. German scientists perfected an audiotape recording system based on paper coated with iron oxide, and Eastman Kodak introduced 16mm film as an amateur format. The format quickly became popular with professional military, educational, and industrial filmmakers, as well as documentary producers.

Immediately preceding the entry of the United States into World War II, RCA promoted their all-electronic television system with the FCC approving that system over the CBS rotating disc system in 1941.

Although World War II interrupted the rapidly expanding field of electronics, many developments in communication technology came from the war effort. The use of higher frequencies, miniaturization of equipment and circuits, and advances in radar that were used in television, and eventually computers, were all perfected. Following the war, magnetic tape became a standard for recording audio, television stations and receivers increased in number rapidly, and motion picture studios experimented with theatre TV and close relationships with television stations and networks. The Paramount decrees divorced motion picture production and distribution from theater exhibition, bringing an end to the major studio era and stimulating greater independent production. The transistor was invented, CBS developed the 33⅓ Long Playing (LP) record and RCA followed with the 45 rpm. The inception of cable television brought television to many rural areas out of reach of the TV stations of the time.

Television saved the record business by forcing radio stations to turn to all-music formats, and the motion picture industry felt compelled to turn to wide-screen, 3-D, and all-color films to compete with the small-screen, black-and-white television systems of the 1950s. Eventually greater interaction occurred between film and television as television series were produced by film studios and feature films were shown on television. By the middle of the decade, the FCC approved the NTSC color TV standard and stereo recordings on tape were marketed, leading to the development of multitrack recording techniques. Within the next two years, all three industries moved forward: television with the invention of the quadraplex videotape recorder, motion pictures with the Panavision camera and lens systems, and audio with the perfection of stereo discs.

The beginning of the rapid acceleration of technical developments occurred in 1959, when the integrated circuit (computer chip) was invented. Within the next 10 years professional helical videotape recorders and electronic editing of videotape were developed; satellites were launched to permit transmission of audio, visual, and digital information instantaneously worldwide; the FCC approved a stereo standard for FM; quadraphonic and digital sound systems were developed; and cable moved from the country to the cities. During the period of these great advancements in the electronic communication fields, motion pictures also utilized the same inventions to improve sound recording, lighting and editing systems, and theatre exhibition systems.

During the 1970s miniaturization produced smaller cameras, recorders, and receivers, leading to new production techniques in both radio and television. Videotape formats began to proliferate, with both systems for the home (BetaMax and VHS) and for the professional (U-matic and 1 inch). Cable became a major player in distributing both films and video productions as pay channels took to the satellites. HBO provided movies, ESPN sports, and CNN 24-hour news.

Technical advances continued through the 1980s, with two events setting the stage for massive changes in all communication fields: In 1981 High Definition TV (HDTV) was first demonstrated, and a Supreme Court decree ordered the divestiture of American Telegraph and Telephone (AT&T), separating the long distance and equipment supply portions of the corporation from the individual local telephone systems. Less earth shattering, but still important, developments were the authorization of Lower Power TV (LPTV) stations, Direct Broadcast Satellite (DBS) systems, the invention and rapid spread of compact discs (CD), and the agreement on a Musical Instrument Digital Interface (MIDI) standard. The FCC approved a stereo TV standard, and RCA introduced the Charge Coupled Device (CCD) camera, which used computer chips in place of camera tubes. By the middle of the decade digital systems were being used in new videotape formats, motion picture editing and synchronizing systems, and digital audio decks and editing systems.

The Fox television network began operation as the other three networks changed ownership. Experiments with teletext and videotext found limited use, and a once-failed system, videodisc, returned and began making inroads in the home market. Professional videotape formats shrunk in size as half-inch BetaCam and Recam were followed by BetaSP and M-II, which become the standards of the production and broadcast studios before digital cameras and recording formats were developed.

In the 1990s computer workstations and DAT integrated audio production into a complete digital world and nonlinear digital editing systems for video programs became the standard. The motion picture industry turned to digitized video for postproduction and special effects, as the two visual industries began to share many more technologies. Black-and-white movies were colorized, and graphics were created through the expanded use of digital systems. Interactive multimedia production of CDs incorporated audio, video, text, and graphics into interactive computer programs. The computer slowly encompassed virtually the entire field of communications in rapid sequences of developing technologies.

Production Terminology

Acquiring basic media production terminology is crucial to understanding the entire production process. The use of production technology and techniques requires a rather specialized vocabulary. As key words are introduced in this text, they are usually defined. When chapters are read out of sequence, the reader can refer to the glossary and index at the end of the book to find a specific definition or the initial mention of a term. We almost intuitively understand the meaning of such words as television, video, audio, and film, but it is important to be as precise as possible when using these and other terms in a production context. *Television* refers to the electronic transmission and reception of visual images of moving and stationary objects, usually with accompanying sound. The term *television* has traditionally referred to images and sounds that are broadcast through the air waves. Electronic television signals can be broadcast by impressing them on a carrier wave of electromagnetic energy, which radiates in all directions from a television tower and is picked up by home receivers. Electrical energy travels in waves, much like ocean waves that crash on the surf at the beach. A carrier wave is usually rated in thousands of watts of power channeled through a television transmitter (Figure 1.4).

Electromagnetic energy ranges from long radio waves to very short light waves. These waves can travel through the atmosphere and be picked up by home receivers. Television signals can also be sent through closed-circuit television systems, that is, along electrical wires rather than through the air waves. Prior to the 1930s, television was primarily closed circuit, but the commercial exploitation of this technology as a mass medium and as a means of distributing television to large numbers of private homes, known as *cable television,* did not occur until much later. Since the 1960s it has been possible to transmit television signals via satellites across continents and around the world. *Satellites* are communications relay stations that orbit the globe. Line-of-sight microwave (i.e., high-frequency) transmissions of television signals is frequently used for live, nondelayed, real-time news

BROADCAST ELECTROMAGNETIC SPECTRUM

LONG WAVES LOW FREQUENCIES	MEDIUM WAVES MEDIUM FREQUENCIES	SHORT WAVES HIGH FREQUENCIES
Navigation Amatuer (Ham) Operators AM Radio	International Comm. Aviation VHF-TV FM Radio	UHF-TV Ham Operators Government Comm. Microwave

Figure 1.4 The frequencies which carry broadcast signals share space on the international electromagnetic spectrum with a variety of other signals and frequency uses.

reports in the field and for sending signals to outlying areas where broadcast signals are not well received.

The terms *television* and *video* are sometimes used interchangeably, but it is generally agreed that television is a means of distributing and exhibiting video signals, usually over the air. Video, on the other hand, is a production term. Sometimes the term *video* is used very narrowly to refer to the visual portion of the television signal, as distinguished from the audio or sound. The more general definition of *video* as a production term refers to all forms of electronic production of moving images and sounds. This is the preferred use in this text. The term *video* can refer to a 3- to 5-minute popular song with accompanying visuals on a videotape or a CD-ROM, which is actually a shortened form of the term *music video.* A *video* can also refer to a videotape copy of a feature film available at video rental stores. *Videotape* refers to magnetic tape, which is used to record both the video and the audio portions of the television signal. Videotape allows television signals to be transmitted on a time-delayed basis, rather than live, and when used with various electronic editing devices, it allows recorded images and sounds to be changed and rearranged after they have been recorded. Videotape also allows feature films to be played at home on a *VCR* (Video Cassette Recorder).

Film has a variety of meanings in production. Defined very narrowly, it simply refers to the light-sensitive material that runs through a motion picture camera and records visual images. When film is properly exposed to light, developed chemically, and run through a motion picture projector, moving objects recorded on the film appear to move across a movie screen. In a more general sense, the term *film* can be used interchangeably with such words as *motion picture(s), movie(s),* and *cinema.* The first two words in the singular refer to specific products or works of art that have been recorded on film, while in the plural they can also refer to the whole process of recording, distributing, and viewing visual images produced by photochemical and mechanical, that is, nonelectronic, means.

Audiotape refers to magnetic tape that is used to record sounds. *Digital Audio Tape* or *DAT* is used to record audio signals in digital form on high density magnetic tape in a DAT recorder. *Compact Discs* or *CDs* are digital audio recordings that are "read" by a laser in a CD player for high quality audio reproduction.

Making clear-cut distinctions between video and film is becoming increasingly difficult, especially in the context of new digital technologies. For example, when a feature film, a television series, a music video, or a commercial advertisement is initially recorded on film but edited in digital form and distributed on videotape, broadcast on television, satellite transmitted, or sold or rented as a CD-ROM or videodisc, is this a video, a film, or a new type of digital hybrid? Using a single video camera to record a program in segments, rather than using multiple video cameras to transmit it live or to record it live on tape has frequently been called *film-style video production* because the techniques used in single-camera video production are often closer to traditional film practice than to those of multiple-camera studio or remote video production. On the other hand, the techniques of multiple-camera film production used to record stunts in feature films are often closer to traditional multiple-camera studio television practice than to traditional single-camera film practice. As mentioned earlier, digital editing techniques often combine traditional film and videotape editing techniques at the same time that they mimic computer word processing. All of these developments make it difficult to make firm distinctions between film, video, and digital media today.

Multimedia refers to the creation of works that combine video, audio, graphics, and written text. Combining these media necessarily involves digitizing all of the various elements so that they can be computer controlled and stored in a variety of forms, such as on hard disk drives and CD-ROMs. *Interactive media* refers to various forms of viewer/reader/listener manipulation of and interaction with computer-controlled multimedia forms. Multimedia and interactive media have both been widely used in training and education, as well as computer games, but they are also developing into important new art forms and means of personal expression. These terms are often used in combination, with *interactive multimedia* referring to works that are interactive and involve the use of multimedia.

New forms of media are constantly being developed, and existing media forms are constantly changing. Thus, while it is important to be as precise as possible in the use of media terms, it is equally important to realize that the meanings of these terms can change over time, reflecting changes in the technology on which these media are based and the ways in which that technology is used.

Single-Camera versus Multiple-Camera and Studio versus Location Production

A producer or director of a "live action" production must make two basic decisions before production begins. First, he or she must decide whether one or more than one camera should be used to record or transmit images. Using one camera is called *single-camera production,* while using more than one camera is referred to as *multiple-camera production.* Second, a decision must be made about whether the images should be recorded inside or outside the studio. Recording inside the studio is known as *studio production,* while recording outside the studio is called *location production* in film and *remote production* (involving cable/microwave links to the studio) or *field production* in video.

Multiple-camera production techniques are used to record continuous action quickly and efficiently without interruption. Such techniques are the basis for television news programs, entertainment programs involving a studio audience, as well as much corporate, educational, and religious programming. Remote coverage of sporting events almost always requires multiple cameras. Multiple film cameras are frequently used to record dangerous stunts simultaneously from a variety of angles for feature films.

In single-camera production, each separate shot is set up and recorded individually. The main artistic advantage of single-camera production is that few compromises have to be made in lighting or microphone placement in order to accommodate the viewing requirements of several different cameras. Logistically, only one camera needs to be set up or carried into the field at a time. Single-camera production of dramatic fiction usually begins with the recording of a master shot, which covers as much of the action in a scene as possible from a single camera position. Then the same actions are repeated and recorded again with the camera placed closer to the action. The resulting material is combined during postproduction editing. Single-camera production techniques are used to record feature films, documentaries, and television commercials, as well as in news recording. Except for live coverage of sports events, single-camera production is the norm for location and remote production situations.

In some production situations it is simply impossible to record events inside a studio, even though studio production facilities and techniques are usually more efficient and economical. Lighting and sound recording are more easily controlled in a studio than at a remote location. Most production studios are designed to provide ideal recording conditions by insulating the recording space from outside sounds, reducing the echo of interior sounds, and allowing easy overhead or floor positioning of lights and access to power supplies. Location production can give a film or television production a greater sense of realism or illusion of reality. Exterior locations often create a sense of authenticity and actuality. But location settings rarely provide ideal lighting and acoustical environments. Extraneous sounds can easily disrupt a production. Confined settings often create sound echo and make it difficult to position lights and to control the shadows they create. Inclement weather conditions outdoors can delay the completion of a project. Since location production sometimes increases production risks and costs, a producer must have strong justification for recording outside the studio. Of course, the construction of sets inside a studio can also be extremely expensive, in addition to creating an inappropriate atmosphere, and location production in this case is easily justified on the basis of both costs and aesthetics.

Planning for Positive Production Experiences

Everyone wants to have positive production experiences. While there probably is no secret formula for success, a thorough understanding of production principles and a positive attitude toward the overall production process is certainly helpful. Exuding confidence in a project enlists the support of others. This requires knowing what is needed and how to get it. Making good creative choices demands careful advance planning of every logistical and conceptual aspect of production.

Many production techniques can be mastered through practice exercises, such as those recommended at the end of each chapter in this book, and through actual production experience. Truly benefitting from these experiences requires taking risks and learning from one's mistakes. Learning to work within present levels of ability, avoiding unnecessary or repeated errors through careful planning, and the development of strong conceptualization skills are also essential.

Avoiding Negative Production Experiences

The first law of production is Murphy's Law: **Anything that can go wrong, will go wrong**. Every production person has vivid memories of his or her first encounter with Murphy's Law, such as an essential piece of equipment that the camera crew forgot to take on location or one that failed to work properly. The second law of production is an antidote to Murphy's Law: **Proper prior planning prevents poor productions**.

Many production problems are preventable. Ignoring conceptual and aesthetic considerations, failing to learn how to operate a camera properly, forgetting to bring necessary equipment, and having no backup or replacement equipment are preventable mistakes. No one is beyond the point of needing to think carefully about what he or she is doing or learning how to use new equipment. Everyone should use detailed equipment checkoff lists, specifying every necessary piece of equipment, which are checked and rechecked prior to going into the field. Every production needs to have some backup equipment and contingency plan to turn to when things start to go other than planned.

Some production problems are not preventable. No one can precisely predict the weather or when a camera will stop working. But everyone must have an alternative or contingency plan if such a problem occurs. Equipment should be properly maintained, but not everyone can or should try to repair equipment in the field. Certainly, the option to record another day, if major problems should occur, must be available. Good quality productions are rarely made in a panic atmosphere, and careful planning is the best antidote to panic, Murphy's Law, and negative production experiences.

Quality productions are shaped and reshaped many times on paper before they are recorded and edited. Preproduction planning is extremely important. It is always cheaper and easier to modify a project before actual recording takes place than to do so after production is under way. The organization of this text reflects the importance of preproduction planning and the development of conceptualization skills. The first section is devoted entirely to preproduction planning. Some degree of advance planning and conceptualization is implicit in later stages of production and postproduction as well (Figure 1.5).

The Production Team in Audio, Video, and Film Production

The production team can be organized hierarchically or cooperatively. In a hierarchical situation, the commands flow downward from the producer to the director, and from her to the rest of the creative staff or production crew. In a cooperatively organized production, every member of the production team has equal authority and control, and decisions are made collectively. Most production situations combine aspects of both the hierarchical and the cooperative models, although the for-

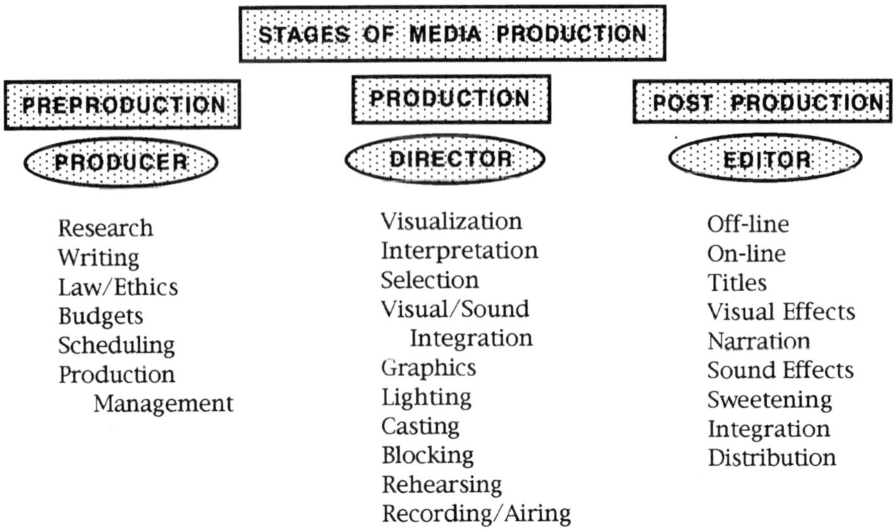

Figure 1.5 Each of the three stages of media production fulfill critical facets of the production process. Each of the three stages rely upon the professional completion of the other two stages. No one stage is more important than any other.

mer approach is clearly dominant in the commercial world. Combining approaches, the producer and/or director makes most of the important decisions, but the help, support, guidance, and input of all the creative staff and some of the technical crew is actively sought and obtained. Production is rarely a purely democratic process, but it is almost always a collective process that requires the support and cooperation of large numbers of people (Figure 1.6).

The members of any television or film production team can usually be divided into two distinct groups: the creative staff and the technical crew. This basic division is often used for budgeting purposes. Dividing the team and costs into above-the-line creative aspects and below-the-line technical aspects allows for a quick financial comparison between investments in the creative and technical sides of a production. The costs of paying the producer, director, scriptwriter, and performers are considered above-the-line, while those for equipment and the crew are below-the-line. The two should be roughly equivalent in terms of the allocation of financial support to ensure that neither the creative nor the technical side of the production is being overemphasized.

Creative Staff in Media Production

The creative staff in audio, video, and film production includes the producer, director, assistant director, scriptwriter, and the talent or performers.

The Producer

There are many different types of television and film producers: executive producers, independent producers, staff producers, line producers, and producer hyphen-

COMPARISONS OF MEDIA PRODUCTION TEAMS			
PERSONNEL CLASSIFICATIONS	**MOTION PICTURES**	**AUDIO**	**VIDEO**
ABOVE THE LINE			
EXECUTIVE	Executive Producer Producer Production Manager	Producer	Executive Producer Producer Production Manager
CREATIVE	Director Writer Art Director	Arranger	Director Writer Art Director
PERFORMANCE	Actor Narrator	Musician	Actor Announcer
BELOW THE LINE			
TECHNICAL	Stage Manager Lab Technician Sound Designer	Operator	Technical Director Technician Audio Director Lighting Director
PRODUCTION	Director of Photography Camera Operator Recordist Editor Mixer Grip-Gaffer	Mixer Board Assistant Machine Operator	Camera Operator CG/ESS/Graphics Operator Audio Operator Assistant Director Editor Stage Manager Stage Crew

Figure 1.6 Parallels exist between the organization of production teams, depending upon the media used, but each medium has unique personnel categories for each level depending on whether the classification is above the line or below the line.

ates (e.g., producer-writer-directors). The exact responsibilities of the producer vary greatly between different commercial and noncommercial production categories and levels. In general, the producer is responsible for turning creative ideas into practical or marketable concepts. The producer secures financial backing for a television or film production, and manages the entire production process, including budgeting and scheduling, although production managers often handle many of these tasks at major studios. Some producers become directly involved in day-to-day production decisions, while others function as executive managers, who largely delegate production responsibilities to others. The producer ensures that the financial support for a production is maintained and usually represents the views of his or her clients, investors, or superiors, as well as those of prospective audiences throughout the production process (Figure 1.7).

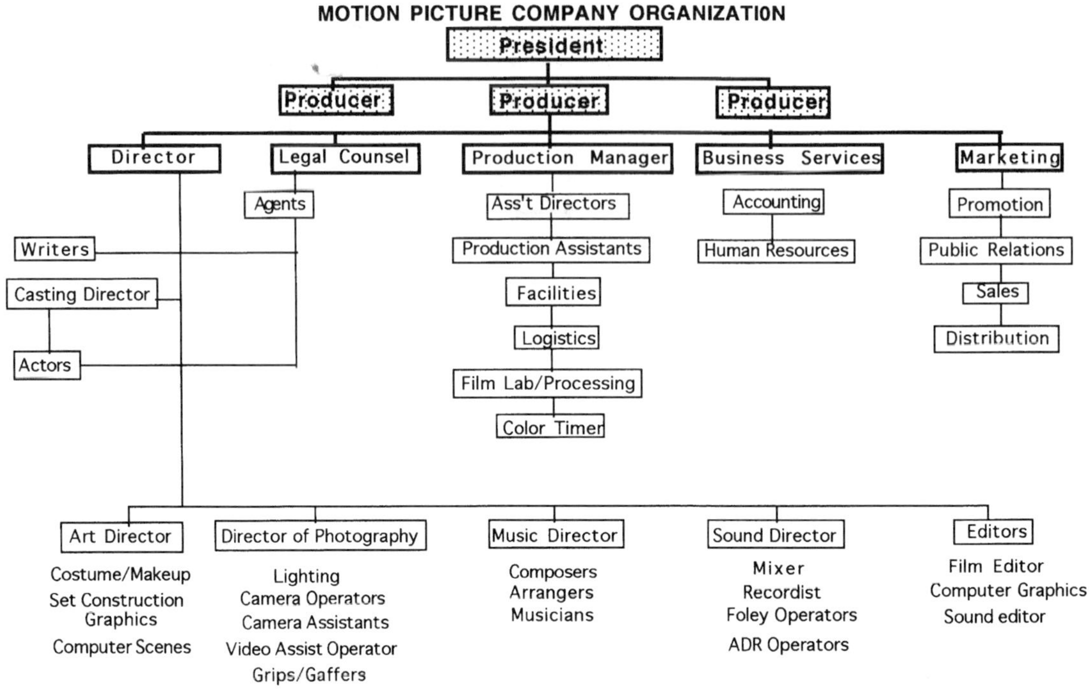

Figure 1.7 The organization of motion picture companies varies with the number of films in production at any one time. Some company services are shared between productions, others are unique to each individual production.

The Director

The director creatively translates the written word or script into specific sounds and images. He or she visualizes the script by giving abstract concepts concrete form. The director establishes a point of view on the action that helps to determine the selection of shots, camera placements and movements, and the staging of the action. The director is responsible for the dramatic structure, pace, and directional flow of the sounds and visual images. He or she must maintain viewer interest. The director works with the talent and crew, staging and plotting action, refining the master shooting script, supervising setups and rehearsals, as well as giving commands and suggestions throughout the recording and editing.

The director's role changes with different types of production situations. In live, multiple-camera video, the director usually is separated from the talent and crew during actual production, remaining inside a control room. In the control room, the director supervises the operation of the switcher, a live television editing device that controls which picture and sound sources are being recorded or transmitted. The director also gives commands to the camera operators from the control room. A stage manager or floor manager (FM) acts as the live television director's representative in the studio, cueing the talent and relaying a director's commands. In single-camera production, the director remains in the studio or on the set or location, and works closely with the talent and the director of photography.

The Assistant/Associate Director

The assistant or associate director helps the television or film director concentrate on his or her major function, controlling the creative aspects of production. In feature film production, the assistant director (AD) helps break down the script into its component parts prior to actual production for scheduling and budgeting purposes. The AD then reports to the production manager, who supervises the use of studio facilities and personnel. During actual production, the AD becomes involved in the day-to-day paperwork and recordkeeping, sometimes actually taking charge of a shooting unit, but always making sure that the talent and the crew are confident, well informed, and generally happy. In studio video production the associate director (AD) keeps track of the time, alerts the crew members and performers of upcoming events, and sometimes relays the director's commands to the camera operators, video switcher, and other crew members.

The Scriptwriter

The scriptwriter is a key member of the production team, particularly during preproduction. A scriptwriter outlines and, in large part, determines the overall structural form of a production project. He or she writes a preliminary summary of a production project, called a *treatment.* A treatment lays the groundwork for the script and is written in the third person, present tense, much like a short story. The script provides a scene-by-scene description of settings, actions, and dialogue or narration, and functions as a blueprint that guides the actual production (Figure 1.8).

The Production Crew in Media Production

The production crew in media production includes the director of photography, camera operator, lighting director, art director or scenic designer, editors, and perhaps a number of specialized engineers and technicians, depending on the size and sophistication of the production. Figures 1.7 and 1.8 illustrate a more complete breakdown of the organization of a motion picture company and of a television station.

The Director of Photography

The overall control of film lighting and cinematography, or the creative use of a movie camera, is usually given to one individual, the director of photography (DP). A DP supervises the camera crew, who are sometimes called *cameramen* (referred to as *camera operators* in this text), assistant cameramen, grips, and the electrical crew, who are sometimes called *engineers* or *gaffers,* and actually control the lighting setup. The DP works very closely with the director to create the proper lighting mood and camera coverage for each shot.

The DP is considered an artist who paints with light. He or she is intimately familiar with composition as well as all technical aspects of camera control, and is

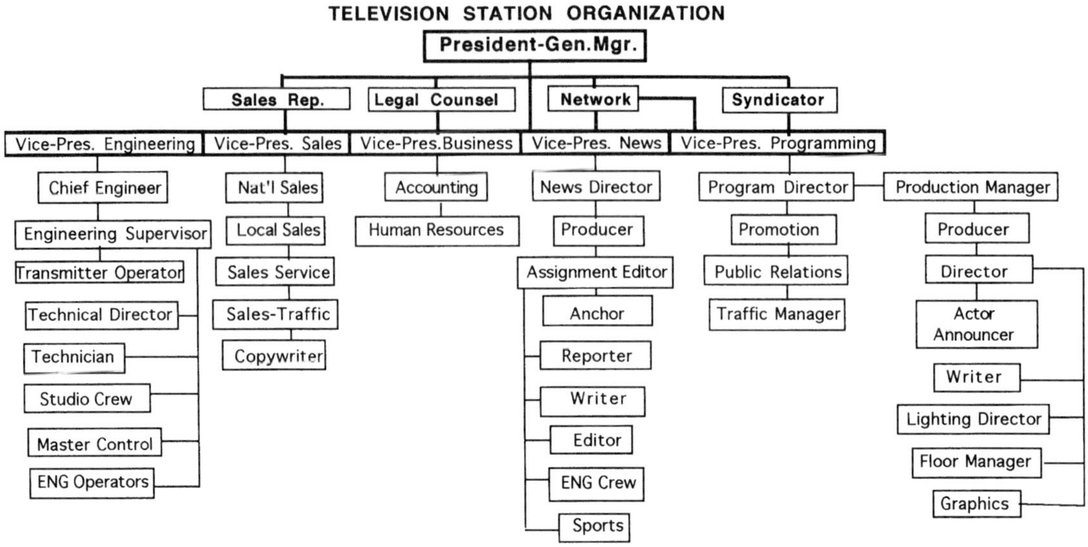

Figure 1.8 The organization of a television station varies considerably depending on the size of the market and whether the station is a network affiliate, network owned and operated, or a totally independent operation.

frequently called on to solve many of the technical and aesthetic problems that arise during film recording. The DP rarely, if ever, actually operates the camera.

The Lighting Director

In video production the camera recording and lighting functions are usually kept separate. The lighting director is responsible for arranging and adjusting the lights in the studio or on location according to the director's wishes or specifications. The lighting director supervises the lighting crew, which hangs and adjusts the various lighting instruments.

The Camera Operator

The camera operator controls the operation of the video camera. Many adjustments of the video camera must be made instantaneously in response to movements of the subject or commands from the director, such as changing the positioning of the camera or the focus and field of view of the image. The director's commands come to the camera operator in the studio via an intercom system connected to the camera operator's headset. The camera operator must smoothly, quietly, and efficiently control the movement of the support to which the camera is attached in the studio and avoid any problems with the cable, which connects the camera to the switcher and/or videotape recorder.

The Art Director or Scenic Designer

The art director (film) or scenic designer (video) supervises the overall production design. He or she determines the color and shape of sets, props, and backgrounds.

Art directors frequently work very closely with costume designers and carpenters to ensure that costumes and sets properly harmonize or contrast with each other. In feature films, the art director delegates the supervision of set construction and carpentry to the set designer, while in video the scenic designer often supervises both the abstract design of a set on paper and its actual construction.

The Technical Director

The technical director (TD) operates the switcher, a multiple video camera editing device, in the control room. At the director's command, the TD presses the buttons that change the television picture from one camera or playback device to another. In some television studios, the technical director supervises the entire technical crew, including relaying the director's commands to the camera operators, while also operating the switcher.

The Editor

In video postproduction, the editor operates an editing system that electronically connects the individually recorded segments into a sequential order. A film editor physically cuts together various pieces of film into a single visual track and an accompanying sound track. The sound editor is a specialist who constructs and organizes all the various sound elements so that they can be properly blended or mixed together into a final soundtrack. In film the sound segments can be physically spliced together, while in video they are edited electronically. Film and film audio can also be transferred to videotape and audiotape for electronic editing.

The Audio Engineer or Mixer

In video production the individual responsible for all aspects of initial audio recording is called the *audio engineer*. In film production this person is referred to as the *mixer* or *audio recordist*. In studio video production the audio engineer sits behind a large audio console in the control room, where he or she controls the sound from the microphones and playback units. The audio engineer also supervises the placement of microphones in the studio. The film mixer or audio recordist, like the audio engineer in video, adjusts and controls the various audio recording devices, but unlike the audio engineer, remains on the set rather than in the control room. The film mixer usually operates an audiotape recorder that runs synchronously with the film camera. The mixer tries to record a consistent, balanced audio signal throughout all the different single-camera setups, so that a smooth, even sound track can be created during subsequent editing and mixing (Figure 1.7).

The Video Engineer or Laboratory Color Timer

The quality of video and film images depends on technical specialists who can control image, color, brightness, and contrast levels. In video production the setting and adjustment (shading) of camera recording and transmission levels is usually controlled by a video engineer. The engineer is responsible for ensuring that all cameras are functioning properly and that multiple cameras all have comparable image qualities. A video engineer can also make color corrections to individual shots during postproduction. The color timer at a film laboratory performs a similar role, but does so after the film has been edited and before copies are made. In

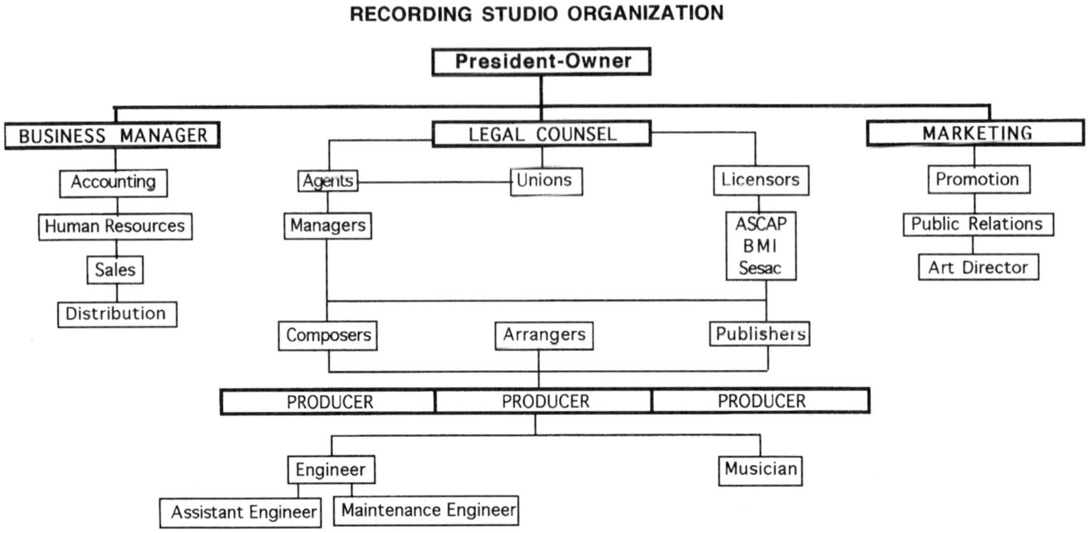

Figure 1.9 The organization of a recording studio varies depending on the size of the studio, the type of recordings that are made in that facility, and the number of artists using the facility on a regular basis.

video postproduction and in film that has been transferred to video, the color in each shot can be adjusted using special equipment, such as a DaVinci color control. Color can also be adjusted within individual frames using computer-controlled colorizing equipment, which digitizes images and allows a colorist to control individual pixels in the frame. This is the same process that has been used to colorize entire black-and-white feature films for television and videocassette distribution.

The Production Team in Interactive Multimedia Production

The interactive multimedia creative staff and production team includes the developer, publisher, producer, designer, writer, video director, graphic artist/animator, and programmer.

The Developer

The developer is the individual or corporation that creates a interactive multimedia product. The developer oversees program content and programming, and delivers the product to the publisher. Developers are analogous to the production side of the film and video business. Production companies are developers.

The Publisher

The publisher provides financial backing and ensures that the product will be successfully distributed. Publishers are analogous to the distribution side of the film and video business.

The Producer

The producer manages and oversees a project, interacts with the marketing people and executives in the publishing company, and coordinates the production team. The producer is sometimes referred to as a project director, project leader, project manager, or a director.

The Designer

The designer is basically a writer who visualizes the overall interactive multimedia experience and then creates the design document that specifies its structure, that is, a product's necessary and unique attributes. In an interactive computer game, for example, the design document may include the basic elements of the story, locations, and problems to be solved by the person playing the game. Animation, music, and sound effects are included in the design document, which is then handed over to a producer, who coordinates the creation of the design elements into a product.

The Writer

The writer may consult with the designer who initially envisioned a particular product but is usually hired by the producer to help create and develop design elements and to shape them into their final form. The writer may flesh out the characters, dialogue (which may appear as text in one platform but be spoken in another), music, sound effects, and possible scenarios envisioned by the designer, or he or she may invent entirely new material. Interactive multimedia writers are generally very skilled at nonlinear storytelling.

The Video Director

If a video recording is needed to add live action material to an interactive multimedia experience, a video director is brought in to handle staging the action, actors, and crew.

The Graphic Artist/Animator

The graphic artist and/or animator draws and animates characters, backgrounds, and computer environments, which make up the visual elements of an interactive multimedia product.

The Programmer

The programmer is the person who develops computer programs that integrate the various aspects of a multimedia product and/or facilitate interaction with it on various computer platforms, such as on a Macintosh computer. Several computer programmers may be involved in the creation of interactive multimedia, which will be used on different platforms or computer environments, such as Windows, Mac, and PowerMac. Programmers are sometimes referred to as engineers.

Visualization: Images, Sounds, and the Creative Process

Visualization can be defined as the creative process of translating abstract thoughts, ideas, and feelings into concrete sounds and images. This demands strong conceptualization skills and a thorough understanding of media production methods and techniques. Scriptwriters and directors must have something significant to say and the technical means to say it. Quality production work requires an ability to organize one's creative thoughts and to select and control many devices that record, edit, and transmit visual images and sounds. Scriptwriters and directors must acquire a basic understanding of the overall production process before they can fully develop their visualization skills. A knowledge of production principles and practices stimulates the search for innovative ways to translate abstract ideas into concrete sounds and images. It also sets limits on a writer's creative imagination. A scriptwriter must be practical and realistic about production costs and logistics. An imaginative script may be too difficult or expensive to produce. A scriptwriter must also have some knowledge of camera placement and editing, even though his or her work is basically completed during the preproduction stage.

To visualize means to utilize the full potential of audio, video, and film for creative expression. Film, video, and audio communicators must be constantly open to new ideas, technologies, and techniques because these media are constantly changing. But they cannot ignore traditional communicative practices and ways of structuring messages. Other media and older forms of communication provide a wealth of information about the communication process.

In a sense, the attempt to use visual images and/or sounds to communicate with others is as old as the human species itself. Early human beings, for example, drew pictures of animals on the walls of caves. Cave drawings may have been created out of a desire to record a successful hunt for posterity, to magically influence the outcome of future hunts by controlling symbolic images, or to express the feelings and thoughts of an artist toward an animal or hunt. These three purposes of communication can be summarized as conveying information, rhetorical persuasion, and artistic expression. To some extent, these explanations are also applicable to contemporary uses of video, film, and audio.

Conveying Information

Communicating with pictures and sounds may have a single purpose—to convey information. What is communicated, the specific content or meaning of the message, consists of informative signs and symbols, images and sounds, which are transmitted from one person to another. We tend to think of certain types of films and television programs, such as documentaries, educational films, videotapes and audio recordings, and news programs, as primarily intended to convey information. Few media messages are exclusively informational, however. Other types of communication are needed to arouse and maintain audience interest and to enliven an otherwise dull recitation of facts.

Rhetorical Persuasion

Rhetoric is the art of waging a successful argument. Persuasive devices and strategies are designed to shape opinions, change attitudes, or modify behavior. The term *rhetoric* has been applied to the use of stylistic as well as persuasive devices and techniques in artistic works, such as novels. An artist can select a rhetorical device, such as the point of view of a specific character, to tell or stage a story, so that the reader or audience becomes more emotionally involved. Rhetorical devices often stimulate emotions. They can make a logical argument more persuasive and a work of fiction more engaging and emotionally effective. In television, radio, and film we tend to think of editorials, commercials, political documentaries, and propaganda as rhetorical forms of communication. Many fictional dramas can also be thought of as rhetorical in structure and intent.

Artistic Expression

Artistic works often communicate an artist's feelings and thoughts toward a person, object, event, or idea. Sometimes artistic expressions are extremely personal, and it is difficult for general audiences to understand them. At other times the artist's thoughts and feelings are widely shared within or even between cultures. An artistically expressive film or television program can convey a culture's ethos and ideology, its shared values and common experiences, in unequaled and innovative ways. Works of art can communicate an artist's unique insight into his or her own self, culture, and/or medium of expression. Artists often experiment with new expressive techniques and devices, presenting ordinary experiences in new and provocative ways. They can challenge a viewer's prior preconceptions and stimulate a serious and profound reexamination of personal or cultural goals and values. They can also reinforce traditional conceptions and cultural values.

Production Aesthetics

Media production requires more than a mastery of technology and techniques. It is also an artistic process that demands creative thinking and the ability to make sound aesthetic judgments. How should you approach a specific topic? What techniques should you use? Important aesthetic choices have to be made. To make these decisions you must be aware of many different possibilities and approaches. Every production choice implicitly or explicitly involves aesthetics. Some production techniques go unnoticed and enhance an illusion of reality, for example, while others are devices that call attention to themselves and the production process. The aesthetic alternatives from which you must choose at each stage of the production process can be divided into three basic categories: realism, modernism, and postmodernism.

Realism

A realist approach to production creates and sustains an illusion of reality. Realist techniques rarely call attention to themselves. Spaces seem to be contiguous to one another within a specific scene, and time seems to flow continuously and without interruption, similar to our experience of the everyday world.

Figure 1.10 A realist production strives to create the illusion of real people living a real life as Meryl Streep and Clint Eastwood are depicted in Warner Bros.' production of *The Bridges of Madison County.* (Courtesy of Warner Bros.)

A standard Hollywood film, for example, sustains an illusion of reality and usually makes us forget that we are watching a movie. This illusion of reality in Hollywood films is based on stylistic conventions that audiences readily accept as "real," however. Conventional editing techniques, such as matching a character's action over a cut from one shot to the next shot in traditional Hollywood films, for example, help to sustain an illusion of reality, and are often referred to as realist conventions of Classical Hollywood cinema (Figure 1.10).

As William Earl has suggested in his cogent description of modernism as a revolt against realism in films, realist films, which include many Classical Hollywood films, define reality as familiar, recognizable, and comprehensible. Realist art "feels most at home living among familiar things in their familiar places, or among persons with recognizable characters acting or suffering in comprehensible ways." (William Earl, "Revolt Against Realism in the Films," *The Journal of Aesthetics and Art Criticism,* Winter, 1968, Volume 27, #2.)

Modernism

A modernist approach to production, which is reflected by many avant-garde works of video and film, often calls attention to forms and techniques themselves. Modernist works fail to create a realistic world that is familiar, recognizable, and comprehensible. A modernist media artist instead feels free to explore the possibilities and limitations of the audio, video, or film medium itself without sustaining an illusion of reality (Figure 1.11).

Figure 1.11 A semi-modernist production goes beyond realism to create a world that might have been or might be in the future as depicted by Kevin Costner in Universal Pictures' production of *Waterworld.* (Courtesy of Universal Pictures.)

As viewers of modernist works, we often see familiar objects and events portrayed in a new light through the use of their innovative techniques. Modernist art often appears less objective than realist art. Modernist works sometimes probe the subjectivity or inner psychological world of the individual artist/creator. In addition to self-expression, modernist productions often reflect feelings of ambiguity, as opposed to objective certainty. Time is not always continuous, and space is not always contiguous. Modernist art tends to be more elitist and private, as opposed to popular and public. The surrealist, dreamlike images in paintings by Salvador Dali and early avant-garde films, such as Salvador Dali's and Luis Buñuel's *Un Chien Andalou* or *Andalusian Dog* (1929), illustrate these aspects of modernism, as do some of the experimental dramatic films of Swedish film director, Ingmar Bergman, such as *Persona* (1966). Many other European art films and some contemporary music videos are distinctly modernist in approach as well.

Postmodernism

The emergence of digital technologies coincides with the rise of postmodernist films, videos, and audio art. Postmodernism literally means "after" or "beyond" modernism. While modernist art emphasizes the individual artist's self-expression and the purity of artistic form, postmodernist art is anything but pure. It is often characterized by a collage or grab bag of past styles and techniques, rather than a pure or simple form. What emerges from this menagerie of styles and grab bag of techniques is not an individual artist's self-expression but rather a hodgepodge of different expressive forms by different artists from different periods. The absence of a single artist as a controlling presence (controlling what a piece of art means or how it should be viewed) encourages the viewer or listener to interact with the artwork, to play with it, and reshape it into another form. The artist doesn't control the meaning of a postmodernist text, the viewer or listener does (Figure 1.12).

Postmodernist films and television programs often combine popular culture with classical and elite art, mixing a variety of traditionally distinct genres or modes, such as documentary and dramatic fiction, and encouraging viewer and listener interaction with (if not the actual recreation of) art works. Postmodernist art borrows images and sounds from previous popular and classical works of art with which most viewers and listeners are often already familiar. Rather than inventing entirely new and perplexing original forms (modernism) or trying to establish explicit connections to the real world (realism), postmodernist art plays with previously developed images and sounds and recreates a self-contained, playfully unreal world of unoriginal forms, genres, and modes of expression. Interactive multimedia works, such as Peter Gabriel's CD-ROM music videos, allow viewers and listeners to adjust the volume and remix separate music tracks, creating their own versions of his music. A modernist piece of music would never allow the viewer/listener to freely play in this way with the work of art, since the artwork is presumed to been perfected and completed by the artist.

Figure 1.12 A post modernist production far exceeds realism to the point that the audience must contribute to the production by mixing styles to the point of forcing the audience to pick and choose the impressions they may gain from watching a production such as depicted by Harrison Ford in The Ladd Company's production of *Blade Runner.* (Courtesy of The Ladd Company.)

Postmodernism may be more difficult to define than realism or modernism because it is a more recent development, and it is still evolving. Nonetheless, some of the main characteristics associated with postmodernism are already apparent. These include the production of open-ended works that encourage viewer participation and play, rather than a concern for the subjectivity of the individual artist. Postmodernist art frequently offers a pastiche or collage of simulated images and sounds drawn from a variety of different modes and genres (both fiction and nonfiction, for example), a feeling of nostalgia for the past, a plundering of old images and sounds from previous works, a mixture of classical and contemporary forms, as well as popular and elite culture.

Combining Aesthetic Approaches

Obviously the three aesthetic movements and choices that have just been described—realism, modernism, and postmodernism—are neither definitive nor exhaustive. Many projects combine aesthetic approaches in various ways. Modernist sequences can be incorporated into realist movies, for example dream sequences in Classical Hollywood cinema. Some Hollywood movies, such as Ridley Scott's *Blade Runner* (1982) and *Thelma and Louise* (1991), seem to combine realism with postmodernism. The choice of one aesthetic approach is neither absolute nor irreconcilable with other approaches. But while different approaches can be combined, the decision to combine them should be a matter of conscious choice.

Because aesthetic decisions are basic to different stages of the production process, many of the chapters in this text begin with a discussion of realist, modernist, and postmodernist approaches. This is followed by a discussion of production practices that are relevant to the use of digital and analog technologies. Combined with actual hands-on production experience, this text provides basic information needed to make sound production decisions with the confidence that many possible alternatives have been explored and the best possible approach and techniques have been selected.

Summary

Production is divided into three stages: preproduction, production, and postproduction. Preproduction designates all forms of planning that take place prior to actual recording, including producing, production management, and writing. The producer tries to attract investors and sponsors, and tries to organize and solve many financial problems involved in production. Logistical and personnel problems are resolved through effective production management. Scriptwriting occurs in distinct stages, from writing a proposal, which helps to attract sponsors, to treatments and scripts. Production begins with the director's preparations to record sounds and images. It includes all aspects of sound and image recording, from camera operation to lighting, set design, and graphics. Postproduction refers to the last stage of production, when the editing of recorded images and sounds begins and the completed project is distributed and exhibited.

Digital technology is replacing analog technology in a number of media production areas, but analog technologies such as film continue to play important roles in each stage of production. Large-screen film technologies continue to provide the highest resolution images with the widest contrast range. Digital video and audio allow for somewhat greater control and manipulation of images and sounds in all three stages of production. Digital computers are used for writing and revising scripts, schedules, and budgets, as well as to preplan lighting and even to scout locations through the Internet and the World Wide Web during preproduction. Digital recording devices can record images on sounds directly on a hard disk during production, which can be efficiently edited using a digital nonlinear editing system in postproduction. Digital technology has opened up a wide range of fascinating special effects and has begun to alter conventional notions of history and reality. Digital technology significantly reduces, if not eliminates, the degradation of sounds and images when copies are made. It has also blurred traditional distinctions and has brought media technologies closer together. Digital nonlinear editing, for example, is conceptually closer to traditional film editing than it is to linear off-line videotape editing, and it significantly speeds up the editing process.

The histories of film, television, and audio technology are interrelated and overlap. Film is based on photochemical means, discovered in the 19th century, of recording light. Television and video technology, which developed commercially somewhat later, reproduce images by electronic means. Audio technology developed simultaneously with film and television because both visual media eventually required sound to match their pictures. All three media have undergone substantial changes during the 20th century. From the late 1940s to the present day, the three media have been economically interdependent.

To have positive production experiences you must have a positive attitude toward the entire production process. You must know what you want and how to get it. You must develop strong conceptualization skills and plan your production carefully. Careful advance planning during the preproduction stages is the best way of avoiding negative production experiences, and technologies have increased production efficiency in certain areas (i.e., postproduction editing) and have spawned innovative approaches to production in others (i.e., interactive multimedia). Digital computer technologies are now used in every stage and area of film and video production, from preproduction to production or recording and postproduction, but older analog technologies continue to perform important roles throughout the production process as well.

A producer initiates a project by drafting a proposal, obtaining financial support, and assembling the circumventing of operation of Murphy's Law: Anything that can go wrong, will go wrong.

Visualization is the creative process of image and sound construction. Video and film record moving images and sounds. These recordings can be edited. Writers and directors must be skilled at visualization. They must understand the relation between abstract words in a script and the concrete sounds and images that are recorded and edited. Ever since early humans painted pictures on the walls of caves, the human race has used images and sounds for informational, rhetorical, and aesthetic purposes. Rhetoric is the art of waging a successful argument, but it also refers to the use of persuasive and artistic devices and techniques in fictional as well as expository or nonfictional writing and media production. Aesthetics refers to the use of artistic forms and devices, which can be conventional or inventive and original. Strictly informational programs will be dull and lifeless if they are completely lacking in rhetorical and aesthetic techniques.

Visual recording can be done with multiple cameras or a single camera, depending on the demands of the situation. Production can take place either in a studio or on location, again depending on the nature of the events to be recorded. The production team is usually organized somewhat hierarchically, in the sense that a producer or director is in charge, and everyone is accountable to a staff head, who specializes in a particular area. But to work together effectively, a production team should also be cooperatively organized, so that individual specialists function collectively as a team. The production team in audio, video, and film production can be divided into the creative staff and the production crew. The creative staff consists of the producer, director, assistant director, and scriptwriter. The production crew includes all the various technical specialists, from camera operators to audio engineers or mixers and scenic designers. The creative staff and production team in interactive multimedia production include the developer, publisher, producer, designer, writer, video director, graphic artist/animator, and programmer.

There are three basic aesthetic approaches to media production: realism, modernism, and postmodernism. A realist approach relies on techniques that enhance an illusion of reality. Time and space are relatively continuous, and images and sounds are recorded so that they do not call attention to the recording process. A modernist approach emphasizes the artist's active shaping and manipulation of his or her material. Modernist works seem more subjective and ambiguous than realist works. Time and space is often discontinuous. A postmodernist approach offers a pastiche of simulated images and sounds that are both classic and contemporary, reflecting a nostalgia for the past, and mixing traditionally distinct categories, such as fiction and nonfiction. The choice of an aesthetic approach guides the selection of specific production techniques.

Additional Readings

Bordwell, David and Kristin Thompson. *Film Art,* 5th ed. New York: McGraw-Hill, 1996.

Cook, David A. *A History of Narrative Film,* 3rd ed. New York: W.W. Norton & Company, 1996.

Ellis, Jack C. *The Documentary Idea: A Critical History of English-language Documentary Film and Video.* Englewood Cliffs, NJ: Prentice-Hall, 1989.

Mast, Gerald, Marshall Cohen, and Leo Braudy. *Film Theory and Criticism,* 4th ed. New York: Oxford University Press, 1992.

Udelson, Joseph H. *The Great Television Race: A History of the American Television Industry, 1925-1941.* Tuscaloosa, AL: University of Alabama Press, 1982.

Wasko, Janet. *Hollywood in the Information Age.* Cambridge: Polity Press, 1994.

Yager, Tom. *Multimedia Production Handbook for the PC, Macintosh, and Amiga.* Boston: Academic Press Professional, 1993.

2

Producing and Production Management

Introduction

A producer is often the only key member of the production team who guides a project through all phases of production from preproduction planning through postproduction editing and distribution. A producer initiates a project by drafting a proposal, obtaining financial support, assembling the necessary personnel, and then managing and overseeing the entire production process. He or she also ensures that the completed project reaches its target audience and satisfies people who have financially supported it. A producer provides necessary continuity between one stage of production and the next, and tries to ensure consistency in the final product. While the producer plays an important part in all three production stages, this chapter focuses on the producer's role during preproduction and production. The producer's role during postproduction is covered in the final chapter of this book on distribution and exhibition.

Producing

The Role of the Producer

A producer is a risk taker, someone who seizes an idea, runs with it, and convinces others to participate in a project. Producers are creative administrators who act as links between the corporate executives, managers, financial concerns, investors, or distributors who finance video and film productions and the artists who create them. Such productions can require large sums of money, which come in the form of bank loans, outright grants, risk capital, and governmental or corporate "in-house" budget allocations. These productions also require a great deal of logistical planning and administration. Creative artists rarely have the time or the desire to deal with many of these administrative tasks, such as financing, budgeting, scheduling, and overall production management. Producers try to create high quality products as efficiently as possible. They know how to turn unappealing or extravagant ideas into workable material and marketable concepts. They understand the diverse needs of creative people, corporate executives, investors, product buyers, and audiences. Producers tread a fine line between the creative talent's need for artistic expression and the necessity of providing concrete returns on production investments.

Good producers are effective decision makers and people managers. A producer's ability to understand and work with many different individuals is constantly tested throughout the entire production process. Ultimately, the production buck stops with the producer, who assumes responsibility for the successful completion of the project. If the production is running over schedule or over budget, that is, beyond the initial guidelines in terms of production time or money, it is the producer who must step in and decide what to do. Should production be terminated, a key individual replaced, or additional time and funds allocated to complete the project? These decisions can be extremely difficult. If a problem develops with a particularly unruly and disruptive actor or staff member, the producer or the director must try to resolve the dispute amicably or take disciplinary action.

Producers often specialize in particular types of programs. Specialists who work with television commercials, dramas, sports news, or interactive multimedia, for example, rarely work outside of their program type because success in one type of production does not guarantee success in another. Producers are further typed into at least four different categories according to the nature and extent of their responsibilities: staff producers, independent producers, executive producers, and producer hyphenates.

Staff producers are employed on a continuing basis by a production company or organization. Producers are often assigned to specific projects in a small video or film production company. Local television station staff producers often work in several areas simultaneously, sometimes floating from news to sports to public affairs. At the network television level, staff producers are assigned to specific divisions, such as news or sports, and they work exclusively within these domains. Staff producers in film often specialize in the production of feature films, educational films, commercials, documentaries, sports films, or industrial films. Staff producers of interactive multimedia productions and computer games coordinate a team of artists, designers, programmers, and writers for a developer or publisher.

Independent producers put together and sell production ideas to studios, film distributors, network and cable television executives, syndicators, and publishers. Independent producers are responsible for the bulk of all theatrically released entertainment films and prime-time television programming. They put together marketable story, staff, and talent packages. An independent producer is not employed on a continuing basis by a film studio or a television network or station. She or he works on a specific project or freelance basis.

Executive producers are often less involved in day-to-day production decisions than other types of producers. They may delegate many production tasks to others and focus on project development and evaluation instead. They sometimes supervise several productions simultaneously and are constantly developing and promoting new concepts and ideas.

Finally, producer "hyphenates" combine the role of producer with those of writer and/or director. Writer-producer-directors immerse themselves in preplanning and the day-to-day production process, almost totally controlling the quality of the final product and preserving the integrity of their original idea.

Production Strategies

Producers often rely upon production strategies to help ensure that a project is successful in obtaining necessary funding, fulfilling its purposes, and reaching an audience. The development of a production strategy involves at least four steps: (1) turning a provocative idea into a funded and/or marketable media package, (2) defining the goals and objectives of the project, (3) researching the topic, and (4) assessing the potential audience. While adopting an effective production strategy does not ensure that a project will be artistically creative or innovative, it does provide an organizational framework with which creative energies can be effectively channeled.

Where do media production ideas come from? Creative minds? Obviously creativity is a necessary asset in production, but it is not sufficient in itself to guarantee success. Producers must also be sensitive to the needs, preferences, and desires of potential funding sources, investors, executives, managers, buyers, distribution channels, and audiences. Project ideas can arise from a variety of sources, including personal experiences, such as a chance encounter with an impressive human being, an unusually committed or effective organization, or a compelling social problem. An idea might be generated by a current event in a newspaper; a presold property, such as a successful book or play that suddenly becomes available; a desire to make a statement or to explore a specific issue for the public good; a need expressed by a corporate executive, government administrator, or a consumer or labor group; or a previously successful television program, film, or computer game. Exactly where an idea comes from is not as important (unless it involves copyrighted material whose media rights have already been secured and are unavailable) as what is done with that idea to make it appeal to potential funding sources, distribution channels, and audiences. Successful producers are people who not only develop or recognize good ideas but also know how to package, promote, and execute their ideas and to communicate them to others.

To transform good ideas into funded, marketable, and doable material, producers put together marketable packages featuring components of known or presumed value to reduce the uncertainty that sponsors and investors feel about whether or not a proposed project will be successful. Many people believe that the prior success of a similar venture or previous productions by members of the creative staff enhances the chances of success for a new project. According to this view, a producer, writer, director, or star performer who has recently had successful films or television programs is likely to be successful again. Obtaining production financing for proven talent is always easier than for unproven talent. The prior success or notoriety of the subject of a documentary or of a novel or play upon which a dramatic film or television program is based is also presumed to provide some guarantee of success. Noncommercial projects initiated by people who have been previously successful are also more likely to receive funding than those undertaken by neophytes, but inexperienced producers can overcome this problem by involving at least a few experienced creative staff members in their project. Previous success in production can be defined in terms of awards, published reviews, specialized showings, and satisfied clients, as well as in terms of profits. In any case, an attractive media idea and package plays on prior success to appease sponsors and partially reduce financial risks inherent in production support and investments.

Unfortunately, producers rarely have the luxury of waiting for prior success of a similar project or property to be amply demonstrated before they initiate a project. Screen rights to novels and plays are often secured prior to publication or staging. A hot topic may have lost its popularity before a project is actually completed due to the long lead time between project initiation and completion. Successful producers anticipate trends almost before they happen, but they are also able to package these new concepts and ideas in traditional ways that help a sponsor or investor see how appealing and/or marketable a new concept can be.

Defining the goals and objectives for a project begins with the formation of a project idea, which must be refined as it is transformed into workable material. The importance of defining the goals and objectives of a project cannot be overestimated. Members of the production team need to be aware of a program's overall objectives and to share common goals to prevent unnecessary conflicts from arising during the production process. Obtaining financial support for a project is much easier when the goals and objectives of the project are clearly specified. Any potential sponsor or funding source wants to know what you are trying to accomplish. If your goals and objectives remain vague and unspecified, your project is unlikely to generate much support.

While the goal or objective of a project may be primarily a commercial one, it is rarely exclusively to make money. Project goals may be quite specific, such as winning a particular award, or they may be more general, such as reaching a new level of artistic expression. They may involve a political agenda, such as changing people's minds about an important issue or problem, or motivating concrete actions, including voting for a particular candidate or buying a specific product. The goal might be primarily educational, such as teaching students to use a new computer program through the production of an interactive CD. On the other hand, the goal might be to produce pleasure by allowing someone to play a challenging computer game, listen to emotive music on an audio CD, or view a compelling or exciting story on videotape. It might be to increase public appreciation of work undertaken by a fascinating person or a highly committed organization. It might also be to increase public awareness about compelling social problems, such as hunger, disease, and violent conflict at home or abroad, or to serve the needs of children or a minority group for nonviolent entertainment and educational programming.

Whatever the goals and objectives of a project may be, it is important to write them down so that they can be clarified, carefully considered, and discussed prior to developing a script or recording and editing a project. Enumerating the goals and objectives of a project will help to galvanize support and to ensure that everyone on the production team is using the same playbook. It will help to reduce future conflicts and to increase the appeal of a project to potential funding sources.

Researching a topic is another important step in the development of a production strategy. Topic research allows a producer to gather accurate information about a specific film or television topic. Careful research ensures that productions do not misinform. The quality of the research directly affects the integrity of the entire project. A hastily produced, poorly researched production can generate a great deal of antipathy from its audience. Sometimes pressure groups are aroused and legal actions, such as libel suits, are taken against the producer or production company. Careful research can make the difference between promoting misinformation versus carefully examining the key issues and stimulating a reasonable debate. Exciting action and intense, well-acted performances contribute a great deal to the impact and success of any dramatic production, but thorough topic research gives a project significance, depth, and lasting value and promotes the long-term interests of the producer.

Topic research requires imagination and determination. New sources of information are only uncovered with extreme diligence and persistence. Research can involve the collection and inspection of at least four different types of data or material records: written, visual, oral, and digital. Data banks of information are produced daily as vast quantities of information of all types are collected and released in digital form, either on disc, CD-ROM, or through the Internet or web sites. Producers or their researchers can save many hours traditionally spent in libraries by using digitized sources. Books, magazines, newspapers, diaries, and private correspondence are written materials that often need to be uncovered, read, and analyzed. Good producers read extensively about their subject in preparation for production. Unlike scholars, producers may perform their research with a broad brush and with little attention to footnotes and minute details in order to get an overall understanding of their topic, which will facilitate the presentation of information in an accessible and logical manner.

Visual records may include photographs; drawings of relevant settings, props, and costumes may also need to be examined. Actual locations may need to be visited as well. Historical visual and audio records and stock footage may need to be examined. Performing research in archives often requires considerable time and effort. Location scouts may use the World Wide Web (WWW) and electronic mail (e-mail) to provide a rapid method of corresponding with location sources and interviewing subjects without waiting for mail service and a telephone response. Stock footage of historical events is expensive since rights to duplicate this material must be obtained.

It is often important to examine or conduct oral interviews with people who are knowledgeable about a specific topic. Interviews might be conducted with actual participants in events or recognized experts in a field. Interview questions should be written down and carefully planned, but the interviewer should not read them, but rather remember them as a guide so that a more lively and spontaneous interview can be recorded. In some cases experts who are interviewed during preproduction may be retained as consultants throughout the production phase. Sometimes consultants are supplied by specific organizations, such as the American Medical Association, which do not want to be slighted by improper or inaccurate medical treatment. In any case, extensive topic research often helps a producer make intelligent production decisions, while impressing potential sponsors and funding sources with her or his knowledge of the subject, adding program depth, and avoiding a variety of ethical pitfalls and problems.

An accurate estimate of the size, demographic makeup, and needs of a prospective audience is essential for the development of workable, funded projects and marketable media ideas. What media should a producer use to reach a specific audience? How large is the potential audience? What size budget is justified? What needs and expectations does a particular audience have? What film or television format should be used? These questions can only be answered when the prospective audience is clearly defined. Even in noncommercial productions, the overall budget must be justified to some degree on the basis of the potential size and demographics of the audience.

Audiences differ in size and demographics. The age and sex of the members of an audience is often just as important as the overall number of people who will see it. Television advertisers, for example, often design television commercials to reach specific demographic groups. Even documentary filmmakers, such as George Stoney, who has headed the undergraduate production program at New York University, often pretests films on audiences to see how effective they are in generating and maintaining interest and waging arguments. The process of assessing audience preferences for and interest in specific projects has become more scientific in recent years, but it inevitably requires an experienced and knowledgeable producer to interpret and implement research findings.

Detailed audience information can facilitate later stages of the production process by giving the audience an input into production decisions. The nature and preferences of the audience can be used to determine a project's format, subject matter, and structure, as well as its budget. For example, the feature film *The Life and Times of Grizzly Adams* (1975) was targeted specifically for working-class families interested in outdoor-adventure dramas. Everything from the actual locations to specific character types was selected on the basis of audience pretesting. While the artistic merit of using audience-survey research to make production decisions may be questionable, since it can produce a hodgepodge of styles and content rather than a unified work, its success has to some degree validated the technique in the commercial marketplace. It has also proved vital for noncommercial productions, where audience response is a primary measure of program effectiveness. Research can also be used during postproduction to assess the impact and effectiveness of a project. While audience research is no substitute for professional experience, it can give scientific, statistical validity to production decisions that might otherwise be based solely upon less reliable hunches and guesses.

Estimating the size and demographics, for example, the age, sex, and other characteristics, of the potential audience for a prospective media project can be quite complicated. Sometimes a project's potential audience can be estimated from the prior success of similar productions. For example, the A.C. Nielsen and Arbitron ratings for television audiences drawn to previous programming of the same type can be consulted. Television ratings provide audience information in the form of program ratings, shares, and demographic breakdowns for national and regional television markets. *Ratings* refer to the percent of all television households, that is of all households with a television set regardless of whether that set is on or off at a particular time, that are tuned to a specific program. If there are 80 million television households and 20 million of them are tuned to a specific program, then that program has a rating of 25, which represents 25 percent of the total television population.

Shares indicate the percent of television households with the set on at a specific time that are actually watching a specific program. Thus if 20 million households are watching something on television at a particular time and 10 million of those 20 million households are watching the same program, then that program has an audience share of 50, which represents 50 percent of the viewing audience. Demographic breakdowns of the television audience help advertisers and media-time buyers and sellers to target programs for specific audiences. Consulting ratings data about earlier programs of the same general type provides only a rough estimate of the potential drawing power of a future program, since audience interest in that type of programming can increase or decrease with time and repetitive presentations.

Commercial producers and distributors often rely on market research to estimate audience size and the preferences of audiences that might be drawn to a particular project. The title of the project, a list of the key talent, the nature of the subject matter, a synopsis of the story line, for example, might be given to a test audience, and their responses recorded and evaluated. Research has shown that by far the best predictor of feature film success is advertising penetration, that is, the number of people who have heard about a project, usually through advertising in a variety of media. Other significant predictors of success appear to be the financial success of the director's prior work, the current popularity of specific performers or stars, and interest generated by basic story lines pretested in written form.

Audience research has been used for a variety of purposes in commercial production. Sometimes prior to production, researchers statistically compare the level of audience interest ("want-to-see" index) generated by a synopsis, title, or credits of a production to the amount of audience satisfaction resulting from viewing the completed project. A marketing and advertising strategy is often chosen on the basis of this research. A film that generates a great deal of audience interest prior to production, but little audience satisfaction after viewing a prerelease screening of the completed film, might be marketed somewhat differently from a film that generates little interest initially but is well received in completed form. The former might be marketed with an advertising blitz and released to many theaters before "word of mouth" destroys it at the box office, while the latter might be marketed more slowly to allow word of mouth to build gradually.

Some television programs and commercials will be dropped and others aired solely on the basis of audience pretesting. Story lines, character portrayals, and editing are sometimes changed after audience testing. Advertising agencies often test several versions of a commercial on sample audiences before selecting the version to be aired. A local news program may be continuously subjected to audience survey research in an attempt to discover ways to increase its ratings or share. A sponsor or executive administrator may desire concrete evidence of communication effectiveness and positive viewer reaction after a noncommercial production has been completed.

Audience research has to be recognized as an important element in the production process. While it is no substitute for professional experience and artistic ability, research nonetheless can provide some insurance against undertaking expensive projects that have no likelihood of reaching target audiences or generating profits. Informal assessments of viewer responses to media products, such as viewer letters of praise or interest, or having audiences fill out questionnaires after viewing, can provide some index of success. Even a film or video project whose main purpose is self-expression and aesthetic pleasure can benefit from or be harmed by audience response in the form of published criticism.

Noncommercial audience research often focuses on assessments of audience needs and program effectiveness. A project that is not designed to make money often justifies production costs on the basis of corporate, government, or cultural needs as well as audience preferences and size. Sponsors need to have some assurance that the program will effectively reach the target audience and convey its message. Audience pretesting can help to determine the best format for conveying information and reaching the audience. Successful children's programs are often based on audience research that assures program effectiveness. For example, the fast-paced, humorous instructional style of "Sesame Street," which mirrors television commercials and comedy programs, was based on exhaustive audience research. Whether it is used during preproduction and/or postproduction, audience research can strengthen a program and widen its appeal.

Proposal Writing

A proposal is a written document designed to help raise money and obtain other kinds of support for a project. It may be submitted to a group of investors, a private foundation, or a government agency, such as the National Endowment for the Arts or a regional, state, or local arts council. An effective proposal generates enthusiastic support. It should be clearly and engagingly written in language that any nonspecialist can understand, but it should also be sufficiently thorough to meet the expectations of media and subject area specialists.

Good proposals usually contain the following elements: a provocative opening statement of purpose; a rationale of the need for such a project; its structure, organization, and approach; a preliminary budget and schedule; specific information concerning the anticipated audiences and means of reaching them; and short paragraph-length summaries of the producer's, director's, and other key creative personnel's careers. Proposals are sometimes accompanied by videotape "show reels" containing clips from previously successful works by members of the creative staff (Figure 2.1).

The opening statement of purpose for any proposal is extremely important. It should provide a concise summary of the goals and objectives of your project. It should also generate interest and enthusiastic support. Try to imagine that you have just read about 100 proposals, and, while some of them are stimulating, you are becoming quite bored with the whole process. Suddenly something hits you like a breath of fresh air. One proposal stands out above the others. The writer is particularly clever, insightful, and/or committed. The proposal generates a contagious feeling of excitement. This is what you must try to accomplish in your opening statement of purpose. What is it that has stimulated your own interest and involvement in this project? Now encapsulate this feeling and communicate it to someone else by putting it into powerful prose that relies upon active rather than passive verbs in every sentence.

The opening statement usually includes a tentative title for the project. It also identifies the subject matter and convinces the reader of its importance and impact, often by providing a taste and flavor of the story that will unfold, including at least a hint of the conflicting forces and elements of dramatic structure that stimulate and propel it. Try to specify what you want your project to accomplish and who you hope will be moved by it.

What important need justifies the expenditure of the money and resources required to undertake and complete your project? Will it serve the public good?

SAMPLE PROPOSAL FORMAT

TITLE:	Safety Training	PAGE: 1
WRITER:	T. Bartlett	LENGTH: 10 mins
CLIENT:	Mountain Industries	DATE: 10-10-96

Rivers and Streams Productions, Inc. will produce a ten minute, color videotape to be used as a training medium for new and present employees of Mountain Industries. The tape will target specific safety procedures necessary to be followed in the unique operation of logging in the mountains of Montana. The tape will emphasize personal safety actions and procedures required by the Occupational Safety and Health Administration.

The shooting schedule will last for ten days, weather and other acts of nature not withstanding. Postproduction will last for four weeks following the completion of principle videography. Taping will start within two weeks of final script approval. Research and preparing of the treatment will last three weeks following the acceptance of the proposal. The final script will be prepared within three weeks of acceptance of the proposed treatment.

The budget will be approximately $35,000.00, depending on specific technical requirements of the script. Because the script calls for a series of dangerous actions requiring stunt actors and technicians, some allowances for costs and shooting overruns may be required.

The format will be semi-documentary/instructional with the tape narrated and techniques explained by an actor representing a skilled and knowledgeable logger. Both incorrect and correct operational procedures will be illustrated. Employees, equipment, and facilities of Mountain Industries logging operation will be required for the production of this tape.

Figure 2.1 A proposal is a sales tool that needs to be written clearly and completely describe the intended project including all critical or unusual aspects of the production.

How? Will it be commercially successful? Why? Does it help to solve a social problem or promote greater understanding among and between different groups of people? Does it have a particular appeal to young or old people?

Proposal writers often provide some essential background information so that nonspecialists can begin to understand why that need is so compelling. Background statements provide the reader with sufficient grounding in a subject area to be able to understand and accept a basic premise and to make informed judgments concerning the importance, feasibility, and effectiveness of your project. They should be very concise, providing basic and essential information. Writers use computers to access data and information sources during proposal writing stages to gather accurate and comprehensive information. Two of the resources are LEXIS and NEXIS. LEXIS is a legal database, containing court cases and other legal information in the United States. NEXIS is a news retrieval system, listing most major newspaper, magazine, and newsletter contents. Both systems are designed for searching under a variety of methods to quickly reach the specific information that the research requires.

The approach, organization, and structure of a proposal indicate how you plan to tell your story and from whose point of view. For example, you might classify your project as a serious drama about an imminent separation and divorce told from a child's view or as a documentary portrait of an artist exploring an upbeat former stage designer's views on his pending blindness as he creates wall hangings and fabric designs that are enriched by his newly stimulated tactile senses. A documentary may consist of verite sequences, "talking-head" interviews, and traditional voice-over narration, or it may present dramatic re-enactments of what "witnesses" convinced themselves happened at a violent crime scene, such as those presented in Errol Morris' *Thin Blue Line*. Each of these descriptions of a project characterizes its approach and structure.

The anticipated audience may be quite narrow or very broad, but it should be described in specific terms. The primary audience for a documentary might be a specific ethnic group, such as African-American communities in northern urban areas. A dramatic Appalachian folktale might be aimed at young Anglo-American teenage girls. In the latter case, the means of reaching that audience, that is, the specific distribution channel, might be motion picture theaters, prime-time public television, or afternoon commercial television. The former project might be designed for prime-time commercial or public television broadcast, as well as for rental to schools and universities through a nontheatrical distributor.

A proposal should also contain short biographies of the primary creative staff, written in paragraph form. These should highlight previous productions that are most closely related in content and approach to the project being proposed. Citing earlier works that have received major awards or national distribution will encourage potential funding sources to believe that prior success will ensure continued success. If you have a limited track record yourself, you should enlist the participation and/or support of creative staff members who have extensive experience and impressive track records, if at all possible. Letters of endorsement and support from highly regarded individuals, especially from people with whom the funding source is already familiar, should also be included with a proposal whenever possible. You should also try to make personal contact with the funding source, which may eventually lead to a project presentation. Writers use computers to prepare all written preproduction materials; such as proposals, treatments, and scripts. A computer allows the writer flexibility to make changes, deletions, and additions quickly and efficiently. Work in digital form allows distribution of information to all involved personnel in either digital or hard copy form.

Project Presentations

A producer who has interested a potential funding source usually tries to make a personal, face-to-face presentation to the investor, sponsor, or executive who is considering funding the project. Sometimes the presentation will be made over lunch or dinner. At other times it will be a more formal presentation in an office. At the very least, it will consist of a telephone conversation. Regardless of the setting, it is essential that the producer capitalize on any interest generated by a written proposal during the presentation. A producer who lacks enthusiasm in presenting his or her project to a prospective sponsor or investor is destined to fail. Sometimes the acceptance of a dramatic project hinges on the availability of a well-known creative staff member or star performer. If a producer has some well-known talent under contract before the face-to-face presentation, that presentation is more likely to solidify funding support. The presentation also offers a producer the opportunity to present additional, less fully developed, future project ideas to a funding source, to gauge his or her interest, and to make adjustments later based on some of the funding source's reactions and recommendations. You should always go to a "pitch" or presentation with another idea in your back pocket just in case you are given the opportunity to present it.

Law

Producers are often involved in legal matters, many of which require the involvement of a qualified entertainment lawyer. Music and written materials are usually protected by copyright. Any use of copyrighted materials is usually secured on the basis of a royalty fee that is paid to the owner of this property. Legal releases free the producer from threat of lawsuits from people who appear in a film or television program, and must be secured before that work is publicly exhibited. Private citizens can sue for libel, slander, invasion of privacy, or defamation of character if they believe they have been unfairly portrayed. The law is somewhat different for public figures, but they are still protected to some extent, and, as noted earlier, producers must exercise great care in the treatment of human subjects to avoid lengthy and expensive legal actions. The large number of legal services that are often required for commercial production has resulted in legal specialists, known as *entertainment lawyers,* who cater to the specific needs of the industry.

Some producers maintain their own music libraries, so that they do not have to commission expensive original music for every production need. These music libraries are collections of musical recordings that are available from organizations such as the American Society of Composers, Authors, and Publishers (ASCAP) and Broadcast Music Incorporated (BMI). These music recordings on phonograph records require royalty payments in the form of needle drop fees, which simply means that every time the phonograph needle is dropped on one of these records, a specific fee must be paid, regardless of how long the record or recording runs. Production music libraries are also available on tape, although the needle drop fee still applies.

Unions, Guilds, and Nonunion Working Conditions

Talent and technicians in many states are protected by union or guild contracts that have been worked out with major producers and production companies. Union or guild-negotiated contracts specify salary scales, working conditions and policies, and many other factors, such as residual payments. The unions or guilds with which a producer may work, or at least honor in terms of salary and working conditions, include AFTRA (American Federation of Radio and Television Artists), SAG (Screen Actors Guild), WGA (Writers' Guild of America), DGA (Directors' Guild of America), AFM (American Federation of Musicians), IATSE (International Alliance of Theatrical and Stage Employees), NABET (National Association of Broadcast Employees and Technicians), and IBEW (International Brotherhood of Electrical Workers). Some states, of course, have right-to-work laws, which prohibit the formation of completely closed shops; that is, they prevent unions from requiring all workers to join their union, pay dues, and abide by union-negotiated contracts.

Production in most metropolitan areas is heavily unionized, especially at the highest levels of production, such as network and broadcast station television, feature films, and 35mm film commercials. In these areas salary levels must meet or exceed certain specified minimum levels. A union member who fails to abide by these conditions and works for less pay is vulnerable to disciplinary fines or expulsion from the union, while the producer or production company may have to renegotiate a union contract, since its violation of the agreement makes the document null and void. In right-to-work states union contracts of this type do not always exist, and salaries and working conditions are often negotiated on an individual basis.

Nonunion productions are often difficult to distribute or air at the highest, most lucrative levels. It is well known that the major Hollywood feature film distributors cannot purchase or distribute more than one nonunion produced film per year without jeopardizing their union contracts, for example. Most producers of feature films and network television programs must face the added costs of union salary scales during production or accept the added difficulties of finding an effective means of national distribution. While the highest levels of television and film production are heavily unionized, except in right-to-work states, a great deal of commercial and noncommercial production is accomplished without union talent and crews throughout the country. Much public, cable, local, corporate, government, educational, and religious television and film production takes place in nonunion or partially unionized work environments. It is often easier to obtain initial production experience and employment in these nonunionized production settings.

Ethics

The "illusion of reality" inherent in nonfiction programming and films, it has been argued, gives television and film producers the power to shape as well as reflect public opinion. Some nonfiction programming, such as network news broadcasts, function as a primary source of public information about current events. Since nonfiction media producers can influence public opinion, they have an ethical responsibility not to intentionally mislead the public. The fact that many nonfiction film and television producers are concerned with making a profit as well as performing a useful social function often means that individuals will be tempted to compromise their ethical responsibilities. While it is true that nonfiction works must have entertainment or dramatic value to attract audiences and prove cost effective, there is a point at which a shortsighted pursuit of profit forces abandonment of long-term social goals and values. Self-serving creators of nonfiction programming have the potential to do harm to individuals and our democratic institutions. The Federal Communications Commission (FCC) attempts to ensure that broadcasters operate in "the public interest, convenience, and necessity." The concept of *equal time*, requiring broadcasters to provide equal time for presenting alternative points of view, is an attempt to compensate for limited channels of television information.

Private citizens are protected from media abuse by the possibility of bringing libel, slander, or invasion of privacy suits. Documentary filmmakers, for example, must obtain written permission (releases) from private citizens before they can publicly exhibit television or film recordings of them. Public figures are less well protected than private citizens, and even private citizens who are involved in bona fide, public news events may legally be filmed or taped without their permission.

Beyond the legal and public policy limitations, writers and producers of films and television programs have an ethical responsibility to use the "illusion of reality" inherent in nonfiction and fiction formats wisely and to treat their human and non-human subjects fairly. From a production standpoint, documentary and news people must be concerned about the potentially negative effects a publicly exhibited work may have on the people who are photographed or recorded. What is done to a human being when his or her picture is shown to thousands or millions of viewers, especially when that person is a private citizen rather than a public figure?

Lance Loud, the gay son who appeared along with the rest of his family before a national public television audience when "An American Family" (1972) was broadcast, made a public exhibition of "coming out of the closet." Is he still laboring under the impact of this program over ten years later? The same could be asked about Edie Beale, the reclusive cousin of Jacqueline Kennedy Onassis who was featured along with her mother in the Maysles' *Grey Gardens* (1975). Was she exploited by the filmmakers, or did she try to use the film to further her own career as a would-be performer? She was offered a singing engagement at a New York nightclub as a result of her participation in this film. Who was using whom? Are we talking about exploitation or the pursuit of mutual self-interest?

How are releases or permissions to use the images of private citizens obtained? Are people coerced into signing a release, or do they freely choose to be publicly exhibited? Does the unannounced appearance of a news or documentary camera crew at a private citizen's home or office constitute a form of coercion? Does the subject's initial permission allow the producer or editor to use the recordings in any manner that he or she sees fit, or does a writer, editor, director, or producer have some responsibility to show the completed work to the subject before it is publicly shown, so that a follow-up permission can be obtained? These are ethical questions that should concern documentary and news writers, directors, and producers, who must weigh the public's right to know against the citizen's right to privacy. They frequently arise in many different types of nonfiction programming, not only documentaries and news stories, but also commercials and educational programming.

Production Management

Producers are usually responsible for production management. Production management includes the supervision, acquisition, use, and scheduling of the production staff, equipment, and facilities. The producer, or another member of the staff under the producer's direction, such as a production manager for a major film studio, breaks a script down according to its component locations and settings. The personnel and facilities needed for each scene are easily specified by an experienced individual who is intimately familiar with essential production equipment needs, budget limitations, personnel contracts, and salary scales.

Script Breakdown

A script breakdown helps a producer estimate and follow realistic schedules and budgets by providing a complete record of all equipment, personnel, and facilities needed for every scene or sequence. It also makes it possible to shoot the production efficiently out of continuity, that is, by ignoring the chronology of sequences in the script and shooting all the scenes that take place in one setting at the same time, regardless of where they will appear in the finished product. This procedure is obviously more efficient than returning to the same settings or locations several times in the course of production. After the script has been broken down according to its settings and locations, breakdown sheets are filled out. Each sheet lists the cast members, staff, sets, props, costumes, and equipment needed at one setting or location. An overall shooting schedule and equipment and personnel list can be made and total costs estimated from all the breakdown sheets put together. All of the production management forms are now available as computer programs, allowing for such forms to be manipulated as easily as any word processing program. Shooting schedules, script breakdowns, production reports, and budgets all may be processed in a digital format (Figure 2.2).

Shooting Schedule

A shooting schedule indicates the total number of days of recording that will actually be required to complete the project. Shooting schedule information is often assembled using a computer program that segments a schedule into units of one day's shooting at a specific location or studio. An individual segment indicates all major personnel and equipment needs for one day at one place. The segments can be moved around if the production schedule must be altered. Since shooting is scheduled primarily on the basis of scenes and locations, the segments for all the days of shooting of the same scene or location usually appear sequentially on a schedule board.

The expense or lack of availability of key production personnel at a certain period can complicate scheduling, sometimes forcing a producer to return to a location or studio more than once during actual production. Once the shooting schedule is finalized, the production schedule for a feature film at a major studio, for example, can be fitted into a master production schedule governing a production company's overall use of facilities and personnel for several simultaneous or overlapping projects. Scheduling computer software can generate as many hard copies as needed and allow instantaneous changes to be made in production scheduling (Figure 2.3).

SCRIPT BREAKDOWN

PRODUCTION TITLE ______________________ PAGE: ________

SET: ______________________ SEQUENCE: ________

SOUND: ________ SILENT: ________ LOCATION ________ DAY/NIGHT: ________

CAST	SCENE NUMBERS & SYNOPSIS
WARDROBE	
SPECIAL EFFECTS & CONSTRUCTION	SET DRESSING & PROPS
MUSIC	MISCELLANEOUS

Figure 2.2 The script breakdown form needs to indicate everything that will be used on a production during a specific shooting period, usually a day or single location.

SHOOTING SCHEDULE

DATE:______

DIRECTOR: PROD.NO.: PROD. TITLE:

Date	No. of Days	Name of Set & Scene Numbers	Cast	Location

Figure 2.3 The shooting schedule form lists the key requirements for an entire production broken down by shooting days or portions of days if more than one location is scheduled in any one day.

Production Budget

Production budgets are usually divided into above-the-line and below-the-line costs. *Above-the-line costs* include the salaries of the creative staff members, such as the producer, the director, the designer (in interactive multimedia production), and the scriptwriter, and fees paid to performers or talent, such as actors or narrators. *Below-the-line costs* cover technical facilities, equipment, and personnel, such as production engineers and crew. When below-the-line costs are approximately equal to above-the-line costs, the production values, or overall level of sophistication of the equipment and crew, are usually appropriate for the investment in creative talent.

Running time, the total duration (as well as the complexity) of a completed project, is an important determinant of overall budget. While it is generally true that longer running times require larger budgets, the case of high-budget network-level television commercials suggests that there are some exceptions to this rule. Running times for specific types of programs are often standardized. A public television program might run for about twenty-seven or fifty-six minutes, whereas the same program would be only about twenty-three or forty-six minutes long if it were to be commercially broadcast, to allow time for the commercials. Theatrical films, those that are shown in commercial theaters, are rarely more than three hours in duration, because it is difficult for a theater owner to show films longer than this more than twice a day—once in the afternoon and once in the evening. Film length can directly affect box-office revenues.

Shooting ratios represent the ratio of footage shot during production to footage actually used in the final edited version. Such ratios vary considerably from format to format. Shooting ratios for a cinema verité, a documentary approach in which a single camera is used to record unstaged events, can range anywhere from 20:1 to more than 100:1 of recorded material shot to material used. An efficiently produced sponsored film or videotape, on the other hand, may be produced at a 4:1 or 5:1 shooting ratio of footage shot to footage used. An average feature film or television action drama requires a shooting ratio of 15:1 or more. Television commercials can easily run up shooting ratios as high as 50:1 or more. In some categories, such as certain soft drink commercials, as much as 50,000 feet of 35mm film may be originally exposed in order to produce just 45 feet (thirty seconds) of final product.

Producers must determine the exact cost of almost every production item, from equipment rental or purchase to union salary scales, talent residuals, and copyright royalty fees. Television and film equipment can be rented from businesses that specialize in these services, or it can be purchased by a studio or individual and amortized, that is, depreciated in value for tax purposes on a yearly basis over the period of time that it is actually used. *Residuals* are payments made to performers and talent for repeat uses of productions in which they appear that continue to earn money (Figure 2.4).

Every final budget should include a contingency fund that represents from 10 percent to 30 percent of the estimated budget. The contingency fund permits some latitude for error, which can arise in a number of areas, for unpredictable circumstances such as inclement weather that delays production, and for talent or labor difficulties. A budget that does not include a contingency fund is unlikely to attract any but the most naive sponsors or investors.

There are many different ways to organize and structure production personnel and the production process, but most approaches can be placed somewhere along a continuum from a strict hierarchy to a loose cooperative. A hierarchical model is basically a pyramid structure. Authority flows downward from the producer to the director and other members of the production team. In short, everyone has an immediate supervisor who is responsible for making production decisions. These decisions flow downward from the top. A cooperative model divides production tasks and responsibilities equally among each of the various areas of specialization. A different individual or group is responsible for each aspect of production, and all decisions are made cooperatively and collectively within and between different divisions.

Few actual production situations are exclusively hierarchical or cooperative in approach. Television and film production is necessarily a cooperative, collective process to some extent. In large-scale productions specialization forces producers and directors to delegate responsibility to experts, whose cooperation and creative innovation is essential to the completion of a quality product. But media produc-

PRODUCTION BUDGET

TITLE:	DATE:	
PRODUCER:	DIRECTOR:	
CLIENT:	PHONE:	
ADDRESS:	MEDIUM:	FORMAT:
CONTACT:	PHONE:	
ALTERNATE:	PHONE:	

1. SCRIPT (Rights, research, writing, duplication) ________

2. STAGING (Sets, costumes, location fees, props) ________

3. EQUIPMENT (Rental, lease, use fees) ________

4. SPECIAL EQUIPMENT (Mounts, aerials, submarine) ________

5. RAWSTOCK ________

6. DUPING (Time code copies, off-line copies) ________

7. AUDIO (Effects, fees, rights, sweetening, looping, etc.) ________

8. MUSIC (Fees, rights, performance) ________

9. GRAPHICS (Titles, animation, art) ________

10. EDITING ________

11. PERSONNEL: Staff ________
    Crew ________
    Talent ________ ________

12. TRAVEL (Transportation, lodging, per diem) ________

13. DISTRIBUTION (Dubs, promotion) ________

14. POSTAGE/INSURANCE ________

15. OTHER ________

SUB-TOTAL ________

OVERHEAD ________ 0

CONTINGENCY ________ 0

GRAND TOTAL ________

Figure 2.4 The production budget form must indicate all costs, regardless of how small, and if unknown, a professional estimate must be made. This figure is the summary page, each of the categories indicated above require one or more pages to include each category of funds required for the production.

tion is rarely a purely democratic art. Most productions are organized somewhat hierarchically around the funding source or the producer, who represents that source. Responsibility for daily decisions is frequently delegated to the director, and by the director to specialists in each area, such as the stage manager, the art director, and the lighting director. The producer and the director must coordinate and supervise the overall production. They must create an effective communication network that ensures information flows freely from the bottom up as well as the top down.

One means of ensuring adequate communication among the various staff and crew members is to schedule regular production meetings before, during, and after actual production. Coordinating the overall production minimizes the risk that continuity will be lost, that costumes will clash with sets, that lighting will be inappropriate to the mood of a particular scene, or that staff members will simply misunderstand the overall purpose and design of the production. Involving people in production decision making encourages their support and cooperation. A production meeting may also require some exercise of authority on the part of the producer or director to ensure production efficiency and consistency. In general, the more time allocated to production meetings, provided that these are not simply drink fests or "bull sessions," the less time and money the production team will later need to spend on costly reshooting.

Producers must constantly evaluate the efficacy of procedures being used in production. Short-term evaluations focus on gathering daily information. The producer fills out daily production reports, based on information received from each production area. Accurate records are kept for financial purposes, and some secretarial or clerical skills are essential. The forms to be filled out concerning a feature film production, for example, are almost endless. There are daily call sheets, weekly budget summaries, revised shooting schedules, lab reports, and work orders. The producer must supervise a staff of assistants and secretaries who are able to organize and maintain production records and quickly respond to daily production needs. Long-term evaluations focus on applications to future projects.

The producer often works in consort with the director in casting the major talent for a specific production. Many variables must be considered before casting decisions are made. Selections from the available talent pool are sometimes suggested by individual agents, but actors are finally selected and tested at auditions, in which they read segments of the script in the presence of the director, the producer, and sometimes the casting director. The actor's appearance, voice quality, talent, and salary have to be carefully considered. Sometimes an inexperienced actor or "real" person from the actual locale will offer a more authentic portrayal than a professional actor.

Producers often consider the box-office appeal (theatrical film popularity) or TVQ (television quotient, an index of popularity based on the star's fame and popularity that is used by television networks) of specific star performers as a means of justifying the added expense of acquiring proven talent. Directors are often more concerned about aesthetic values, such as whether or not a particular actor or individual is perfectly right or natural for the role, than is the producer, who also worries about salaries and box-office appeal. The producer is often the funding source's sole representative during production and must therefore consider many financial, as well as aesthetic, factors.

Staff producers in small corporate, government, educational, and local cable television production units function much the same way as other producers. Their budgets may be smaller and the people they work with are fewer in number, but the same basic skills are required. To illustrate the fact that all producers perform essentially the same role, let us consider a student production made in an academic setting. A student who is producing an assigned project for a grade must obtain funding for the project, either by earning the money, negotiating with parents, or finding a sponsor who can use the finished product. The student producer must procure the necessary equipment, supplies, and personnel to make the best possible film or video project with limited resources. Scheduling the production and acquiring talent within an academic environment is often extremely difficult, since students have different class schedules and responsibilities.

Once the actual shooting is scheduled, the weather may not cooperate and the shoot may have to be rescheduled. Perhaps special costumes or props are needed, and the student must undertake delicate negotiations with the drama department or the head of buildings and grounds on campus. If the work is to be publicly screened or used on a local cable channel, the producer must be sure to pay all copyright fees for prerecorded music or commission original music from a friend in the music department. Release forms should be obtained from people who appear in a work that will be publicly exhibited. Finally, when the project is finished, the student must evaluate feedback from a number of people, including an instructor's unexpectedly high or low grade.

The producer, then, has to be an effective supervisor of people, an administrator, a salesman, a sensitive but objective critic, and above all, a good fund-raiser and money manager. These diverse skills, which combine business acumen and organizational ability with creativity and sensitivity to people, are not plentiful in the profession, nor are they easily acquired. Good producers should be recognized for their unique value to both the artistic and the business sides of the production process.

Summary

Producers plan, organize, and supervise the production process from the initial idea to its eventual distribution and exhibition. There are four different types of producers: staff producers, independent producers, executive producers, and producer hyphenates. Producers provide an important link between investors and creative talent. Producers adopt conscious production strategies to turn creative ideas into marketable concepts. A production strategy involves at least four steps: generating funded and workable ideas, defining the goals and objectives of the project, researching the topic, and assessing the potential audience. Producers must also estimate the production budget and make a proposal to a potential source of funding, during a face-to-face presentation of the project's ideas and goals. Production management involves breaking the script down into its component parts so that the project can be shot cost effectively out of continuity. Script breakdown sheets also aid in the preparation of a budget and the scheduling of production facilities and personnel. Production team interaction can be structured in two different ways: hierarchically or cooperatively. Few actual production situations are organized exclusively according to just one of these models. Effective producers possess a variety of supervisory skills, from the ability to manage people and resolve disputes, to strong organizational skills, which facilitate the flow and recording of information as well as budgetary decisions. Together with the director, the producer becomes involved in casting decisions. The producer is frequently the sponsor's or investor's sole representative during actual production. The role of the producer is essentially the same in high-level and low-level production situations. The budgets may be smaller, and fewer numbers of people may have to be supervised and managed, but the requisite skills are essentially the same for both levels of producing and production management.

Additional Readings

Barnouw, Erik. *The Sponsor.* New York: Oxford University Press, 1978.

Bluem, A. William, and Jason Squire, eds. *The Movie Business.* New York: Hastings House, 1972.

Blum, Richard A. and Richard D. Lindheim. *Inside Television Producing.* Boston: Focal Press, 1991.

Curran, Trisha. *Financing Your Film: A Guide for Independent Filmmakers and Producers.* New York: Praeger, 1986.

Gayeski, Diane M. *Corporate and Industrial Video.* Englewood Cliffs, NJ: Prentice-Hall, 1983.

Kindem, Gorham, ed. *The American Movie Industry: The Business of Motion Pictures.* Carbondale, IL: Southern Illinois University Press, 1982.

Lazarus, Paul N. *The Film Producer: A Handbook for Producing,* 2nd ed. New York: St. Martin's Press, 1992.

Pryluck, Calvin. "Ultimately We Are All Outsiders: The Ethics of Documentary Filming." *Journal of Film and Video* 28, no. 1:21-29.

Rosenthal, Alan. *Writing, Directing & Producing Documentary Films,* 2nd ed. Carbondale, IL: Southern Illinois University Press, 1996.

Singleton, Ralph S. *Film Scheduling, Film Budgeting.* Los Angeles, CA: Lone Eagle Publishing, 1989.

Squire, Jason, ed. *The Movie Business Book.* Englewood Cliffs, NJ: Prentice-Hall, 1983.

3

Scriptwriting

Introduction

Scriptwriting can be divided into two basic categories: fiction and nonfiction. Many feature films, television series, miniseries, serials, made-for-TV movies, and interactive games are works of fiction, and most documentaries, news programs, commercials, corporate videos, and interactive educational or training productions are works of nonfiction. Fiction scripts generally present dramatic stories that are imaginatively invented by the scriptwriter. Nonfiction scripts often convey information and/or rhetorical arguments concerning various topics of issues and actual historical events.

The line separating fiction from nonfiction is not always clear and distinct, however. Some projects fall into a gray area between the two. For example, historical dramas and docudramas are often based upon actual events, and some documentaries involve staged or dramatized re-enactments. Dramatic and narrative structures associated with fiction are sometimes relevant to the presentation of historical or contemporary events in works of nonfiction, and rhetorical structures associated with nonfiction are sometimes relevant to the presentation of characters and themes in fiction.

Every scriptwriter should be familiar with basic elements of both fiction and nonfiction writing. Principles of dramatic structure used in fiction may also be applicable to the development of audience interest in a documentary or news story. Principles of rhetorical persuasion and expository structures used in documentaries and commercials can be helpful in terms of presenting a social issue or problem in a dramatic production, such as a children's afternoon special program or a made-for-TV movie.

This chapter provides an introduction to visual thinking and a sequence overview of the scriptwriting process. It also examines some of the ways in which fiction and nonfiction scripts can be effectively organized. The focus is on elements of dramatic, narrative, rhetorical, and expository structure, which are of practical value to scriptwriters working in a variety of areas and formats.

Visual Thinking

A script that guides the production of a film, video, audio, or interactive multimedia program can be compared with an architectural drawing or blueprint. A script orients the director and other key members of the creative staff to the overall story or topic. It provides a preliminary sketch or outline for a project that is to be constructed and given concrete form. Just as an architect must be knowledgeable about building construction methods and materials, a scriptwriter must understand the entire production process. Scriptwriting cannot be completely divorced from other preproduction, production, and postproduction activities discussed in this book.

A scriptwriter should only write what he or she is confident can actually be staged and recorded. Abstract concepts and ideas have a more limited place in scriptwriting than they do in forms of writing that are not intended to be performed or pictorially rendered. Thinking visually demands that a scriptwriter think in practical terms of actual settings, concrete actions, and specific dialogue that will actually be performed or observed and recorded. A good feature film scriptwriter or screenwriter, for example, often begins a script visually with an image that will give the audience a strong sense of place, atmosphere, mood, and even the theme of the picture.

Television, film, audio, and interactive multimedia are visual and acoustic media. A fiction scriptwriter establishes settings, describes actions, and defines characters through concrete sounds and visual images. Settings are established very economically as specific buildings, locations, and/or props. Characters are defined by their actions and reactions, as well as by what they say to other characters. The emotional texture of settings, actions, and characters is developed through the actual performance and recording of concrete sounds and visual images. A sound or image does not speak in terms of "people" or "screams" in general, but of this specific person and this specific scream.

Unlike a playwright, a scriptwriter does not need to rely exclusively or even primarily upon dialogue or just a few settings to tell a story. Dialogue can be substantial or it can be practically nonexistent. A scriptwriter can use a variety of settings to reflect different moods, atmospheres, and aspects of a character, or just one setting to provoke a feeling of confinement. Actions can occur outdoors or indoors, in quick succession at different times and at a variety of geographic locations, or slowly at one time and place. A stage play is usually restricted to just a few settings, which must be set up quickly between different scenes or acts. Time is usually continuous within each scene. Time and place in a film, television program, audio recording, or interactive game can be continuous or discontinuous. A media production can depict many existing settings around the world, reconstruct them in a studio, or create a purely imaginative acoustic or animated environment. Actions occurring in a character's past can be intercut with those in the present or future.

Economy of expression is one of the hallmarks of good scriptwriting. Every setting, prop, or character in a fictional story, for example, can only be briefly described. Its presence in the script indicates that it is an essential and integral part of the story or topic, rather than a peripheral detail. Unlike a novelist or short story writer, a scriptwriter rarely writes long passages describing the setting or a character's state of mind and feelings.

One of the skills that scriptwriters must develop is visual thinking. A script facilitates the recording of specific moving images and sounds, and is based on a firm understanding of the production process. By reading the production and postproduction sections of this book, especially those chapters that focus on the aesthetics of generating, recording, and/or editing sounds and images, a beginning scriptwriter can acquire some understanding of the creative potential of moving images and sounds, or visual thinking. Quality scriptwriting demands a firm grasp of production aesthetics and the entire production process.

Preparation for Scriptwriting

The scriptwriting process has several distinct stages, beginning with the research phase. Before a script is written, considerable research must be carried out. Research provides insurance against presenting implausible stories or conveying factually incorrect information. It also provides a source of inspiration and creative ideas.

A premise, synopsis, and several story outlines may be drafted after the research phase before a treatment is prepared. A treatment is a plot description in short-story form and is used primarily as part of a proposal submitted to a potential funding source. It also provides a guide for the writing of a complete script.

The next stage in the scriptwriting process is the writing of the script itself. A script may go through several drafts and involve the participation of several writers before it is completed and production can begin. The final stage is the preparation of a shooting script, which indicates all camera placements, transition devices, and various types of effects. These are usually added by the director (or the designer in multimedia production).

Research

The first stage of scriptwriting is the research phase. Every aspect of the topic should be carefully and thoroughly researched before the script is written. Whether the project is to be primarily entertaining, informative, or persuasive, its overall quality directly depends on the quality of research that has gone into the development of the script. The more carefully documented the information contained in a script is, the more realistic, authentic, accurate, and responsible the finished product will seem to be. A digital word processing program is the most efficient method to research and write proposals, treatments, and scripts.

Careful research is both a form of insurance and a source of inspiration. Carefully documenting sources of information can protect a producer from legal prosecution. News and documentary writers, for example, have an obligation to research their stories carefully. It is often necessary to find hard evidence from reliable sources in order to support a basic statement or argument. Thorough investigation of a subject frequently leads to the revelation of information that stimulates the creative process and challenges and excites the viewer.

Research is a creative process of uncovering new sources of information. A project researcher or scriptwriter begins by acquiring a general background in the area on which the project will focus. She collects as many books and articles as possible that deal with the general topic area and reads those that seem to be most helpful and pertinent to the specific issues at hand. Searching computer files and systems such as LEXIS and NEXIS, as well as other databases, is one of the fastest and most accurate methods of acquiring the basic information needed when researching a project. Armed with this general knowledge, the researcher progresses by focusing more narrowly on specific problems and concerns. General understanding of the topic stimulates the creation of insightful questions that can be raised during interviews with an expert or a participant in the events. The more knowledgeable a writer or researcher becomes, the more information she will elicit from additional sources of information. Like a good detective, a writer learns that one piece of evidence leads to the discovery of another.

Production research is usually either novelistic or journalistic in approach. A fiction writer or novelist conducts research in order to find details that stimulate reader interest and authenticate events and settings. A fictional film, television program, or computer game is often researched in this manner. Strict authenticity is sometimes sacrificed for dramatic interest and action. Journalistic research, on the other hand, aims at uncovering sources of documentary evidence that can be used to support the presentation of information and editorial arguments (Figure 3.1).

Premise, Synopsis, and Outline

Every good treatment is preceded by the writing of a simple idea or concept, called a *premise.* A premise is basically a "what if" statement, which describes the basic story idea. For example, "what if" Romeo and Juliet sang and danced, and were

Figure 3.1 The beginning of any media production is the research stage. Information must be gathered, facts checked, and information documented before the script is written.

caught between rival gangs and ethnic groups in New York City? This is the basic premise of *West Side Story* (1961). "What if" Romeo and Juliet were involved with drugs in Central Park? A feature film entitled *The Panic in Needle Park* (1971) operates on the basis of this simple premise. A good treatment is always based on a simple, but interesting concept. The premise can be used later as a strong opening "pitch" of a script or screenplay to a producer by providing a concise label for the project.

The next preparatory step prior to writing of a treatment is to compose a synopsis, which consists of one or more paragraphs that describe the basic *story line*: "Tony and Maria fall in love but because they are associated with rival gangs, the Sharks and the Jets, there are many obstacles placed in the path of their love. After Maria's brother is accidentally killed by Tony in a fight, their relationship is filled with suffering and frustration."

On the basis of this synopsis of *West Side Story*, an *outline* could be written, developing the major plot lines and characters in the story. This outline also defines all major actions and character reactions. Usually several outlines are written and revised before the treatment is created.

Treatments

A treatment is an important step in the development of a script. Usually written in the third person, present tense, it provides a narrative summary of the basic story lines. A treatment visualizes the story as it will unfold on the screen and gives a play-by-play of all major actions and scenes in reduced form. A writer composes a treatment so that he or she can receive an approval or commission to write a fictional script or undertake a documentary project. When a producer initiates a project, the treatment sometimes accompanies a proposal, which is submitted to a funding source. Scriptwriters (and their agents) often initiate a film or television project by writing a treatment.

The major portion of the treatment is devoted to a highly visual, but concise, narrative presentation of characters and events. Some examples of dialogue spoken by characters are usually included, and the treatment adopts a short-story format. A good treatment adopts a lively prose style that dramatizes the basic premise and effectively communicates the tone and flavor of a piece. Camera directions and shot descriptions are used very sparingly, if at all. Resonant images are conveyed by highly visual nouns or adjectives and action verbs. A treatment is not a legal document fashioned with dry regularity and precision. It must excite and interest a producer or funding source, and serve as a thorough and helpful guide for the writing of a script or screenplay. A treatment provides some protection against future writing problems by forcing the writer to resolve many difficulties prior to actual scriptwriting.

How long should a treatment be? A treatment for a feature-length film screenplay, which will run about two hours, usually has about twenty to seventy double-spaced, typewritten pages. The finished screenplay will be 100 to 140 pages, since each page of a screenplay usually translates into about one minute of actual screen time. A treatment for a work of short fiction should probably be from five to ten pages in length. It is always preferable to err on the side of brevity, since verbose, overwritten treatments are not likely to be read with interest and enthusiasm.

SAMPLE TREATMENT FORMAT

TITLE:	Safety Training	PAGE:	1
WRITER:	T. Bartlett	LENGTH:	10 mins
CLIENT:	Mountain Industries	DATE:	10-10-96

The ten-minute training tape will open with a montage of incorrect logging operations followed in each case by the possible disastrous and life-threatening results of such actions. Examples of such scenes are:

A logger without a safety belt steps back and falls from a tree stand.

A chainsaw jams and flips back into the logger.

A tractor tips over on the driver because it exceeded its tilt limit.

A logging truck driven too fast forces an on-coming car from the road.

A log falls from a truck being loaded and strikes a logger who was standing too close to the truck.

A logger refuels his saw improperly, causing a fire.

A truck or tractor becomes a runaway when left improperly locked down.

A logger dumped into the river and crushed by logs.

A log avalanche occurs because of careless blocking of a log stack.

This series of accidents will be enhanced with sound effects and dramatic music as well as the actual sound of each accident.

Following this montage, the narrator will walk into the scene and describe in general the dangers and reasons for following OSHA safety requirements for those working in dangerous occupations such as the

(continued)

Figure 3.2 The treatment of a production is a second sales tool, along with the proposal. A funding source needs to be able to accurately visualize in their mind while reading the treatment exactly what the producer has in mind. If the treatment is not clear and complete, funding is highly unlikely.

Nonfiction treatments, such as a documentary treatment that is included in a proposal submitted to a potential funding source, are concise narrative descriptions of what the viewer will see and hear written in the present tense. Like dramatic fiction treatments, the purpose is to evoke interest, excitement, and, if possible, the same emotional response from the reader that you hope your production will elicit from the viewer or listener. A separate paragraph is usually devoted to each sequence that will appear in the completed project (Figure 3.2).

Scriptwriting Formats

After the preliminary stages of scriptwriting have been completed, a writer or group of writers begins to write a full script. The script conforms to one of the following formats: split-page, full-page, or a semi-scripted format, such as a script outline. Scriptwriters rely on a basic set of terms as well as these common formats in order to effectively communicate with other members of the creative staff, such as the director. A discussion of three standard scriptwriting formats, full-page, split-page, and semi-scripted, is presented below.

Full-Page Master Scene Script Format

A full-page master scene script format is frequently used in dramatic fiction programs, including single-camera film and video productions, such as live action dramas and feature films, and multiple-camera live-on-tape productions, such as television situation comedies. In a full-page master scene script format, a single column, which is devoted to both visuals and audio, fills the entire page. The script is organized into scenes, which are numbered in consecutive order. The location and time of day of each scene are specified. Actions and camera movements are described in full paragraphs. Script writing computer programs are available for all computer operating systems. These programs format the script in a professional layout, relieving the script writer of the tedium of worrying about margins and spacing while attempting to create a workable script (Figure 3.3).

Because a full-page master scene script is organized by scenes, it can easily be reorganized so that all the scenes requiring a single set or location can be shot consecutively. As we noted in the previous chapter, producers and production managers try to organize production so that all the scenes at a specific location can be shot at one time because it is usually more efficient and cost effective than recording the scenes in chronological order as they appear in the script.

Every scene presented in a master scene script usually begins with a "scene heading," indicating an indoor/interior (INT.) or outdoor/exterior (EXT.) setting, the name of the specific location, and the time of day. There may be a number of different setups, dialogue sequences, and descriptions of actions and characters until the location, time of day, and interior or exterior setting change.

EXT. XANADU — NIGHT — EXTREME LONG SHOT — FENCE AND MANSION

The full-page master scene script describes few, if any, camera movements and shots. It is much more common for the director to select and indicate specific shots during the preparation of the final shooting script immediately prior to production. A director's shot descriptions often specify camera-to-subject distance, angle of view, and/or camera movement when they are incorporated into the stage directions following the scene heading. Rather than providing shot descriptions, a scriptwriter can artfully visualize the scene in prose following the header without specifying camera-to-subject distances, angles, etc. In any case, camera shots, angles, movements, transition devices, times of day, interior and exterior settings,

MASTER SCENE SCRIPT FORMAT

(Margins and tabs set as indicated below. assuming 80 space wide paper)
5 10 20 25 55 60 70 75

FADE IN:
1. INT./EXT. DAY/NIGHT 1.
BRIEF SCENE OR SHOT DESCRIPTION, CAM. ANGLE.

In upper and lower case, a more detailed description of the scene giving setting, props, and CHARACTERS position if needed with margins set at 10/70.

CHARACTER
(Mode of delivery, upper and lower case, margins at 25/55)

The dialog is typed in upper and lower case centered within 20/60 margins.

Any other descriptions of shot framing, movement of CAMERA or CHARACTER is at margins set at 10/70.

(TRANSITION)

2. INT WS UNIVERSITY CLASSROOM DAY 2.

Classroom is full of students, some wide awake, gossiping, others sleeping or nodding off as they wait for the professor to arrive.

JANE
(Quietly so only Jack can hear her.)
Are you sure there isn't going to be an exam during tomorrow's class?

JACK
(With a bravado, all-knowing tone)
Of course not, have I ever lied to you?

The professor enters the room, downstage right, walks to the lecturn and the room becomes quiet.

PROFESSOR
(Emphatically as a reminder)
If I am forced to repeat myself again, I WILL be forced to give you your first examination in tomorrow's class.

(DISSOLVE TO)
3. EXT WS CAMPUS DAY 3.

The clouds suddenly darken the sky as rain, thunder and lightning start and the lights go out plunging the room into darkness.

(A scene script describes the entire scene in very general terms, a shooting script contains much more detailed descriptions and shot instructions)

Figure 3.3 A master scene script gives the screenwriter the opportunity to notify the director the writer's intent without limiting the director to specific shots. But the script must include enough information so that the director understands what the writer had in mind and wants the actors to say and do.

specific character names, and sound effects are generally typed in uppercase letters, while actions, events, and specific stage directions, including sets, props, characters, and actions, as well as dialogue, are usually in lowercase letters. Dialogue to be spoken by a specific character normally follows the stage directions and has the character's name listed in the middle of the page immediately above his or her lines of dialogue, which are slightly indented from the paragraph descriptions of actions and camera movements. The end of a scene is usually indicated by a "scene close," such as CUT TO: or DISSOLVE TO:, which indicates the transition to the next scene.

The information highlighted in UPPERCASE LETTERS throughout a master scene script is emphasized for the convenience of the producer or production manager, who will break down the script into its component parts for scheduling and budgeting. Each scene is numbered for easy reference, and each revision of a master scene script is dated, to ensure that all performers, creative staff, and crew members are using identical copies of the script during production.

Split-Page Script Format

In a split-page script, the visual information appears in one column on a sheet of paper and the audio information in the other column. The split-page script format is often used for commercials and other forms of nonfiction production, such as documentaries. The dialogue and narration are written out fully on the audio side of the page. Visual images are indicated on the opposite side of the page. The latter are sometimes described quite sparingly in live multicamera productions, such as awards ceremonies and performances, leaving wide margins, so that the director or assistant director can make copious notes about specific cameras and shots in these blank areas. Visual cues and segment durations are written in full uppercase letters in the visual column, and any information in the script that should not be read on-air is circled (Figure 3.4).

The obvious advantage of the split-page format is that visual and audio elements can be directly compared and coordinated. An empty column suggests that one aspect is being focused on to the exclusion of the other. A rough equality in terms of space devoted to these two tracks or creative elements ensures that both will be fully utilized in the completed project.

Semi-Scripted Formats

Many types of nonfiction television programs and films do not need to be fully scripted in advance of production. A talk show, game show, or even a documentary film or videotape may only be partially or semi-scripted. A semi-scripted format may consist of a simple rundown sheet, which is a basic outline of the show from beginning to end, indicating what material or performer is needed at specific times. It is organized on the basis of the running time of each segment and of the entire program. Different electronic sources of material, such as remote feeds and VTR playbacks, are also specified (Figure 3.5).

A script outline is another semi-scripted format. Portions of a script outline may be fully scripted, such as the opening or closing segments of a news, talk, or game show, which remain the same from show to show. Other elements are simply

DUAL COLUMN SCRIPT FORMAT

TITLE:	PAGE:
WRITER:	LENGTH:
CLIENT:	DATE:

VIDEO	AUDIO
1. SINGLE SPACE VIDEO INSTRUCTIONS	1. ANNCR: Audio copy is lined up directly across the page from its matching video.
2. TRIPLE SPACE BETWEEN EACH SHOT	2. Double space between each line of audio copy.
3. EACH SHOT MUST BE NUMBERED ON THE SCRIPT	3. The audio column's number must match that of its video.
4. EVERYTHING THE VIEWER IS TO SEE; ALL VISUALS, VIDEO TAPES, CG, CAMERA SHOTS, ARE INCLUDED IN THE LEFT-HAND COLUMN.	4. Everything the viewer is to hear; all sounds, music, voices, sound effects, narration and all audio cues are included in the right-hand column.
5. EVERYTHING ON THE VIDEO SIDE IS TYPED IN CAPITOL LETTERS.	5. Everything spoken by the talent is typed in upper and lower case letters. All instructions in the audio column are typed in capitol letters.
6. THE TALENT'S NAME STARTS EACH NEW LINE, BUT DOES NOT HAVE TO BE REPEATED IF THE SAME PERSON OR SOUND SOURCE CONTINUES.	6. SAM: Note--the name is in caps, what Sam says is in upper and lower case.
7. AVOID SPLITTING SHOTS AT BOTTOM OF THE PAGE.	7. Avoid splitting words or thoughts at the end of the line.

Figure 3.4 A split-page format defines clearly how each shot is to be framed, action within that shot along with the accompanying audio.

Client:	WEMPLE'S DUTCH MILL	DATE:	7-7-94
JOB:	#WDM-94-7-3	MEDIA:	TV

SCENE 1:

SCENE:	Kitchen, middle class	MOM: A little more mustard?
TALENT:	Mom and Male kid	
ACTION:	Mom busily fixing lunch	KID: That's great, you make the best cheeseburgers in the whole world

SCENE 2:

SCENE:	Backyard	KID: But I'd rather be eating at Wemple's
TALENT:	Male kid	
ACTION:	Kid runs out of back door	

SCENE 3:

SCENE:	Mom in kitchen	
TALENT:	Mom	MOM: Never mind burgers, I'd rather be eating at Wemple's
ACTION:	Mom puts away lunch, hurries out front door	

□
SCENE 4:

Key logo & tag	VO: Everybody'd rather be eating at Wemple's

Figure 3.5 A semi-script provides the director with a rough outline of the production, allowing much greater freedom for deciding on shots. The form also is used for productions that cannot be scripted: sporting events, games shows, and special events.

outlined in rough form, either because they must be ad-libbed during recording or because the exact information to be read may not, in fact, be available until just prior to air or recording time, such as with quiz and game shows. Documentary, sports, and talk show directors often use a script outline, as it is difficult to precisely script live or uncontrolled events. The questions to be asked during an interview show can be written down in advance, but the answers cannot, unless the interview is staged. A director or camera operator must be able to respond instantly to unpredictable events as they happen. The actual selection of shots to be used may be delayed to later stages of production, such as postproduction editing. Only the general type of shot or action may be specified in a script outline.

Fiction Scriptwriting

Drama and narrative are fictional art forms that have a basis in everyday life. A drama is basically a series of actions performed by actors, such as a stage play. A narrative is a chain of events, which is told or narrated, such as a novel or short story. While most dramas and narratives draw upon everyday life and experience, effective works of fiction are often shaped and refined by carefully organizing and structuring these actions and events, and removing the dull moments of life so that viewer, listener, or reader interest can be intensified. The organization of dramatic actions and narrative events is often referred to as the *elements* of dramatic and narrative structure. Fiction scriptwriting has the potential to combine certain elements of dramatic and narrative structure, and a successful work of fiction, be it a film, video, audio, or multimedia production, is usually one that makes effective use of these basic structural elements.

Dramatic Structure

Dramatic films and television programs can be plotted into a framework that consists of a basic three-act structure and a series of rising and falling actions, which culminate in a climax and resolution. Act One of a drama usually sets up the main plot by establishing the central characters, their goals and conflicts, as well as the basic time, place, and situation of the story. Act Two and Act Three each begin with a turning point, such as a major shift in the main plot, which moves the drama in a different direction from the previous act, generating audience interest and maintaining story momentum. Secondary as well as primary characters and themes are usually more fully developed through both main plot and subplot actions in Act Two. Conflicts and problems eventually reach a climax and are resolved as the main plot and subplot are brought together near the end of Act Three.

Rising actions include build sections, where conflicts build into a series of crises, and a final climax. Falling and horizontal actions include temporary resolutions or pauses in the action following crises, which allow the audience to catch its breath before proceeding to the next crisis or climax and a final resolution of the conflicting elements that led to the climax.

These classic forms of dramatic structure ensure that actions build in a logical and exciting way on the basis of major conflicts that must be resolved. A drama may have very limited or extensive expositions of characters, situations, and settings; few or many complications, reversals, and crises; but it almost always relies upon internal or external conflicts, which build toward a climax and resolution, if it is to sustain interest, arouse excitement, and evoke a sense of fulfillment. Mystery programs such as "Murder She Wrote" and medical dramas such "ER" illustrate classic dramatic structure.

Act One

Act One usually begins with powerful images that convey the essential focus, pace, and style of the film or television program. We not only sense the time and place of the story, but we are often introduced to a major theme as well. Generally without writing any dialogue, the scriptwriter is able to convey the basic ideas, thoughts, and feelings that the unfolding story will eventually develop in great detail through character actions, dialogue, and/or interior monologue.

The main plot action is usually initiated and propelled by a precipitating event or catalyst in Act One. The precipitating event may consist of an action, such as a murder; a piece of dialogue, such as one character informing another that they have found the secret to eternal life; or a situation, such as the appearance of a young unmarried woman who is obviously pregnant. The precipitating event helps to establish the basic spin or direction of the main plot.

Learning more about the characters in Act One might require some back story, such as flashbacks into a character's past or some discussion of a particular character's life by other characters. The plot unfolds in Act One as a series of dramatic beats or actions that reveal who characters are by what they do and say. A dramatic scene, that is, a series of actions or events occurring at one time and place, may consist of several beats or dramatic moments.

Act Two

Act Two usually begins with the first turning point. A turning point substantially changes or reverses the direction of the plot. For example, one character may believe that another character is her best friend, but new information reverses her opinion and suggests that her supposed friend is really someone to be feared and avoided. During Act Two the subplot is more fully developed than in Act One. For example, the main plot of the story may focus on a woman whose career objective is to succeed as an executive in a major corporation, while the subplot may focus upon her romantic involvement with the chief executive at a rival company. In Hollywood films, subplots often focus upon romantic love and develop important themes, while main plots often focus upon characters' pursuit of material goals, actions, and concrete objectives.

During Act Two secondary as well as primary characters are more fully developed, along with resulting conflicts between characters. Subsequent events, such as the eventual death of a particular character, are often foreshadowed, although the payoff may not occur until Act Three. Complications develop, which sometimes act as barriers to a character's successful accomplishment of his or her goals. For example, a long distance runner who is very religious may discover that a major competition is scheduled to take place on an important religious holiday and his participation in that event violates his own ethical and religious standards.

Act Three

The second turning point usually initiates Act Three and speeds up the action. Act Three provides a sense of urgency and propels the story toward its conclusion. Actions build toward a climax, where the conflicts originating in Act One are resolved and the main plot and the subplot come together.

Rising Action: Crises and Climax

Dramatic action that has progressed through several complications inevitably builds to a crisis. A drama may have several crises, in which the conflict that has stimulated the action intensifies to the point that something or someone is threatened. We all encounter crises in our lives, but drama removes most of the dull moments between these crises, so that character actions and emotions, and viewer interest and involvement, are intensified. The major character or characters may have to make an important decision. Perhaps it is a life and death situation. Should a risky surgical procedure be performed? Can a murderer be identified and sacrificed? Should a character choose between a lover or a spouse? The dramatic action usually builds through several important crises that finally culminate in a major crisis or climax.

A climax is the most decisive point of confrontation in a drama. It simply demands some form of resolution. One side must win or a compromise must be reached. The climax brings the major conflicting forces together so that they may be openly confronted and resolved. The climax is usually the highest, most intense emotional peak of the drama.

Falling Action: Resolution

Overcoming the basic conflict or fulfilling the goals and motivations that have stimulated the dramatic action is known as a resolution. The defeat of the antagonist, the death of the hero, the marriage of the loving couple, or the attainment of the major goal may each represent the culmination of the action. A resolution is considered a falling action compared with the rising action of a crisis or climax. The resolution section of the drama considers the implications of the climactic actions and gives the audience time to contemplate what has just transpired before new actions are initiated or the drama ends. Emotionally, the audience may need sufficient time to recuperate from the emotional experience of the climax. A drama that ended immediately after the climax might leave some of the audience's expectations unfulfilled.

The resolution of a drama can be ambiguous or unambiguous. An ending can appear to resolve all major conflicts or allow the hero to achieve his or her major goals. In a mystery story the discovery of a secret can answer all questions. But an ending can also be ambiguous. Conflicts can persist and goals remain unachieved. Some dramatic forms have virtually no resolution at all. Soap operas rarely, if ever, reach any resolution. They consist of a series of crises. Any apparent solution, such as a marriage, is usually the source of another conflict. The absence of any resolution establishes a new convention that is unique to the open-ended, serial dramatic form. A closed dramatic form uses resolution to enforce a sense of finality or closure at the end. The drama is essentially self-contained, although the dramatic action may continue in the form of a sequel.

Text and Subtext

A good writer not only plays with the surface text of the dialogue while telling a story but often develops a subtext through character actions and reactions. The subtext defines what the characters are really feeling, that is, the feelings that underlie their dialogue. For example, a man and a woman may be discussing something rather innocuous, such as the weather. Their dialogue defines the text. "Don't you think that it's getting warmer?" "Yes, but my hands are freezing." "There's still a touch of winter in the air, but the ice is melting." The text indicates that the characters are aware that spring is coming and the weather outside is getting warmer, but by staging the action so that the characters gradually get closer together and begin holding hands and touching one another the subtext (and double entendre of the dialogue) is that they are gradually warming up to each other romantically.

Narrative Structure

In addition to having dramatic structure, the structure of action, scripts also have narrative structure, the structure of time and point of view. A story can follow an uninterrupted chronological structure from beginning to end, or it can have flashbacks and flashforwards, which disrupt the continuous flow of time. A great deal of screen time can be devoted to some events and very little to others. For example, a character in a soap opera can go upstairs in one scene and come down in the next, having aged several years (and sometimes having been replaced by another actor). On the other hand, it may take several episodes or even several weeks of episodes to develop all the intrigues occurring at a party that supposedly lasted for only two hours on one day. The difference between the actual screen time and the supposed story or historical time devoted to specific events is sometimes referred to as *narrative duration,* and the difference between the actual order of presentation and the supposed historical chronology of specific events in the story is sometimes referred to as *narrative order.* Scriptwriters can manipulate narrative order and duration to effectively relate one event to another, such as providing character back story by using a flashback to break the chronological order of the narrative and to relate a character's past history to his or her present actions.

A fictional work can be narrated by someone. A story can be told from a specific point of view. An omniscient or effaced (hidden) narrator tells the story but does not appear as a character within it, while a dramatized narrator is a specific character who also tells the story. In media production the director can use the camera to enhance the point of view of a specific character whom the scriptwriter is using to tell the story by placing the camera in that character's approximate physical position on the set. We, the audience, then see and understand what that character sees and understands from their point of view throughout the story. An effaced or omniscient narrator acts a substitute for the scriptwriter. He or she is an unseen person who presents the story when no character takes responsibility for it. An effaced narrator selects what we will see and understand by adopting a more "objective" point of view, and a director can use the camera more "jectively" by not placing it in the approximate spatial position of any specific character.

Narrative point of view is an extremely important structural component. How something is presented is just as important as what is presented. If we experience a series of events through the eyes of a character as opposed to omnisciently through an effaced narrator, our experience of these events is quite different. Adopting the point of view of a particular character makes a difference in terms of how actions, events, and their meanings are perceived. Imagine, for example, the presentation of the Battle of the Little Big Horn through the eyes of a Sioux warrior versus those of a U.S. Cavalryman. Arthur Penn's film *Little Big Man* (1970) presents a shifting point of view on General Custer through the ambiguous cultural identity and affiliation of its main character/narrator. The adoption of a specific point of view colors and even distorts events in a particular way, and such a perspective must be carefully and thoughtfully selected.

A well-known short film called *An Occurrence at Owl Creek Bridge* (1964), based on the short story of the same name by Ambrose Bierce, illustrates most major aspects of narrative structure. It tells the story of a southerner during the Civil War who is about to be hanged from a bridge by Union soldiers. The story is generally presented from the victim's point of view. The victim dreams about his wife as he is about to be hanged, and the images intercut pleasant memories of the past with the present horror of imminent death as he watches the Union soldiers prepare for his execution. We are shown his memories of his wife as the victim narrates past historical time. Cutting back to his present predicament, the camera often assumes his physical position within the setting at the bridge. Just when he seems about to die, the rope snaps and he falls into the river. Writer-director Robert Enrico expands historical time underwater. It takes the victim over three minutes of film time to free himself underwater from the ropes that bind him and swim to the surface. Enrico then condenses the time it takes him to swim away down the river, eluding the gunfire of the soldiers along the shore. But when he gets home and is about to embrace his wife, the scene cuts directly to his hanging at the bridge again. In retrospect, the escape scenes can be interpreted by the audience as a wish fulfillment of the victim's hope of escaping death, which is shattered by the reality of his death. The events of the escape have only occurred in the victim's mind. They have been narrated by the victim and exist as a dream outside of the normal "present" time of the dramatic scenes of the hanging (Figure 3.6).

Characterization and Theme

There are almost as many ways to initiate the writing of an original piece of fiction as there are works of fiction. Some writers begin with specific characters. Once they have these characters firmly in mind, they begin to imagine specific, exciting situations within which these people find themselves. Conflicts arise from interactions among characters who have different goals and values. Certain themes begin to emerge as the characters initiate or become involved in specific actions. This "organic" approach to fiction writing tries to ensure that actions and themes flow "naturally" out of "real" characters.

Another approach to writing fiction begins with a basic theme, idea, or message. In some ways it is more difficult to begin with the theme and then find three-dimensional characters who can initiate actions to reinforce the theme. There is a real danger that the theme will become overbearing. The opposite danger faced by the "character-first" approach is that the actions undertaken by certain characters will not be thematically significant or interesting.

A third way to initiate a fictional script is to begin with the plot or story structure, and then work in both directions, that is, toward characters who can carry out those actions and the themes that those actions reflect or represent. In using this method, there is a danger that characters will simply become pawns to carry out actions and that themes will be tacked on from the outside.

Where a scriptwriter begins is probably less important than paying attention to the development of all three fictional aspects: plot, characters, and themes. Plot, that is, the telling or presentation of specific actions and events, has already been discussed in terms of dramatic and narrative structure, but characterization and theme need further consideration.

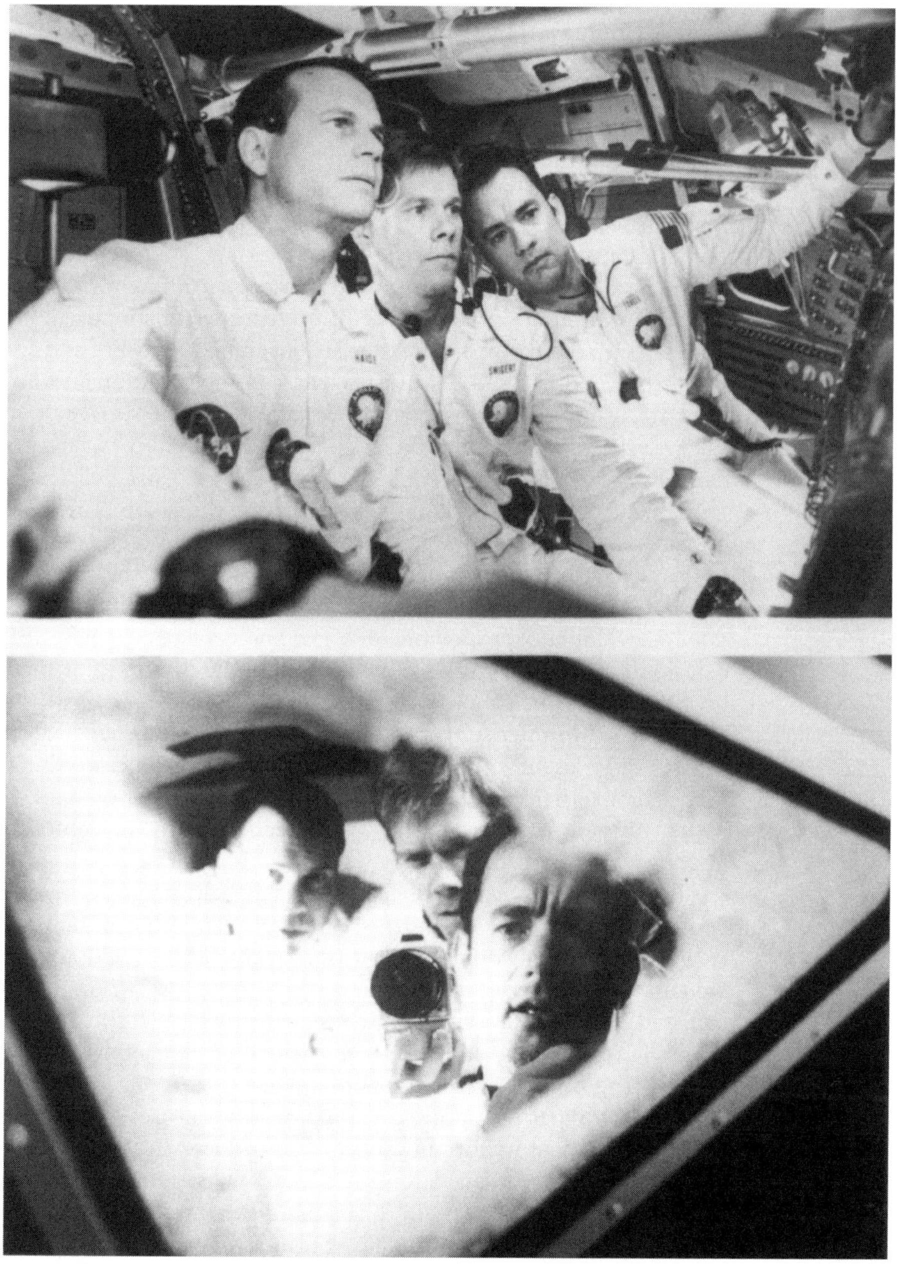

Figure 3.6 A dramatic production should draw the audience into the story through a combination of quality acting, directing, and production vales. Universal Pictures' production of *Apollo 13* provided the audience with such an experience. (Courtesy of Universal Pictures.)

Developing strong, believable, and interesting characters is just as important as creating an exciting series of actions and events. Complex characters give a story depth and three dimensionality. A character's values and beliefs lead to conflicts with other characters who hold opposing values. If these values are significant and strongly held, the entire fictional experience is enhanced.

Character can be revealed through two primary vehicles: actions and words. What characters do and say reveals in large part who they are. But actions and behavior are usually more important than dialogue. Characters should show us what they believe through their actions. The important thing for the writer to remember is that communication takes place through concrete sounds and images. A character is largely created through external appearances, actions, and speech. But the external surface of a character must reflect a complex internal value system and a set of abstract thoughts, beliefs, and feelings. An external surface that is not based on a solid psychological foundation lacks depth, understanding, and true artistic potential.

Characters can be roughly divided into three categories: central characters, principal characters, and secondary or incidental characters. The central character or characters figure prominently in a story. They are the primary sources of audience satisfaction, interest, and identification. The decisions they make and the actions they initiate propel the drama. Their values, beliefs, feelings, and goals determine, to a great extent, how meaningful and significant the entire drama will become. The principal characters are usually friends or foils to the central character(s). They can offer support to the actions and thoughts of the central character, or they can present significant obstacles to the attainment of his or her goals. In a longer drama there is usually enough time to give most or all of the principal characters sufficient depth so that their interactions with the central character become important and convincing.

Secondary and incidental characters may help create a situation that provokes a conflict, but they are contributors to, rather than initiators of, major actions. There is rarely time to fully develop all the minor characters in a drama into complex individuals. They have certain traits and mannerisms that distinguish them in a crowd and add spice to the drama, but these can easily deteriorate into stereotypes or clichés. Stereotyping secondary or incidental characters often runs the risk of stereotyping certain occupational or ethnic groups and minorities. Some reliance on character types (as opposed to stereotypes) ensures immediate audience recognition of the most important aspect of a character and contributes to the drama as a whole. What minor characters say about any major character helps to develop the latter's characterization. A good deal of information about the central character can be communicated to the audience through the words of secondary and incidental characters, sometimes reinforcing and sometimes contradicting the central character's own speech and actions.

A *theme* is basically a significant statement that a work of fiction asserts or an important issue that it raises. Themes generally emanate from the values, beliefs, and goals of the central characters, but a general theme may be much broader and universal than the attitudes of any single character. The film *Citizen Kane* (1941) has several broad themes, for example. The portrayal of Kane's life focuses on such issues as the absence of love in his life and his pursuit of fame, fortune, and power. Images, symbols, and motifs, such as "Rosebud" suggest, perhaps, that the absence of a happy childhood or family or parental love and guidance can lead to an inability to love and a meaningless pursuit of money and power. This film also develops other themes concerning democracy, politics, and the press, including, perhaps, a criticism of American society and capitalism in general. Of course, not all films are so heavily thematic, but the greatness of this film is that it does not sacrifice characterization and dramatic structure in order to make meaningful statements. Important themes coexist with strong characters and a complex plot. The themes are not the sole interest of the story (Figure 3.7).

Adaptation

An adaptation is a relatively faithful translation of a play, short story, or novel into a film or television program. The scriptwriter is usually very familiar with the original literary work and makes every attempt to translate it into a different medium with the central characters and themes virtually intact. A television or film script that is less faithful to the original is frequently said to be based on that source, while a work that uses the original written piece as a springboard for essentially new ideas is said to be freely adapted or simply suggested by the original (Figure 3.8).

Figure 3.7 *Citizen Kane*'s acclaim is based in part upon its strong characters, complex plot, and important themes. (Courtesy of Rico Pictures.)

Figure 3.8 The *Batman* series of films produced by Warner Bros. were adapted from the original Batman cartoon strip and an animated television series. (Courtesy of Warner Bros.)

The adaptation process usually begins with a consideration of the author's intent. What is the basic theme and point of view from which the story is told? Which characters are particularly memorable and/or attractive, disturbing and/or sympathetic? The plot must be analyzed in detail, using some of the basic elements of dramatic and narrative structure discussed earlier as a guide to good storytelling technique in media production. Does the story have a basic three-act structure? Does it build logically and dramatically toward a climax and resolution? Does the story have a plot and a subplot, and do the two coalesce at the denouement, that is, at the point of their final solution and clarification? Are there dead spots that can be eliminated or conflicts that need to be intensified? How many different scenes and settings are required? Is the story told from an omniscient or a specific character's point of view? Is there substantial dialogue and action, or will a character's interior monologue need to be dramatized and shown rather than simply told? Does the story follow a chronological structure, or does it involve flashbacks and/or flash-forwards in time?

After completing a careful analysis of the basic plot, subplot, characters, and themes, the scriptwriter who is adapting a work from one medium to another will write a treatment and then a screenplay that usually provides a number of changes from the original work. These changes may include the following: creating or eliminating subplots; eliminating, combining, adding, or altering (usually secondary or minor) characters; cutting, shortening, or expanding and enhancing specific scenes; adding, subtracting, or altering settings. The scriptwriter makes these changes to hopefully improve a story's dramatic and narrative structure; to enhance the characterization and theme of the original novel, play, or short story; and to increase the efficiency and often decrease the cost of actual production.

A full and complete adaptation of a lengthy novel, for example, could substantially exceed the normal time restrictions of most media productions. A scriptwriter must then decide which elements are crucial to the story, which will be the most dramatic, what scenes or portions of the plot can be eliminated entirely, and how others can be shortened. Sometimes characters can be combined, so that the ideas and values they espouse are not lost but simply condensed. Dialogue or action scenes may have to be added, however, in order to dramatize information that was presented in the novel as pure description or characters' inner thoughts. The story should be shown not just told. Literary dialogue must work well as spoken dialogue, and dialogue should not become so lengthy and informative that it substitutes for action. An adaptation scriptwriter must understand the production problems and costs involved in composing a faithful adaptation of an original piece of writing. He or she must also understand the needs and expectations of the audience so that an effective, exciting, and interesting presentation of characters, actions, and themes will be created on the screen.

Before the adaptation process commences, the rights to a published and/or copyrighted work, of course, must be secured. An original novel, short story, play, history, or biography may be protected by copyright for up to seventy-five years, and any television or film producer who attempts to adapt it, however freely, without paying for the right to do so can be held liable for damages to the value of that property.

Short Fiction Forms and Formats

Some short fiction forms, such as television situation comedies, may require different treatment, including the use of alternative dramatic and narrative structures and story construction, from that of longer forms, such as feature films. For example, half-hour episodes in a television situation comedy series present the same set of characters in a slightly different situation each week. The relatively short duration of an individual episode encourages a different organization and approach.

A sitcom episode is usually organized into two acts with three scenes per act and a tag or epilogue after the last commercial to keep the audience tuned in and to reinforce any message or theme. The opening of an episode must grab the attention of the audience to prevent them from switching channels. A major conflict or problem must be presented in the first five minutes (Act One, Scene One), prior to the first commercial break. The dramatic device that grabs the audience is called a *hook.* It often takes the form of a problem or conflict that excites the viewer and foreshadows events that occur later in the story. A specific object or idea introduced early in a drama, which becomes an important factor during the final resolution, is called a *plant.* Planting and foreshadowing are effective devices in terms of hooking the audience. The conflict builds through a series of complications or misunderstandings until the end of Act One, where a new complication is introduced. In Act Two things begin to get sorted out and the main conflict is resolved in Act Two, Scene Three. With the opening credits, closing tag, and commercials between scenes, a series episode writer only has about twenty minutes to quickly develop the basic conflict or situation, add a few complications, and then neatly resolve it. The structure of a situation comedy follows this basic formula, regardless of the exact setting and characters. There is a constant need for imagination and creativity within this tight, somewhat restrictive format.

Other types of short fiction are not as formulaic as situation comedy, but they nonetheless demand tight dramatic structure. There simply isn't enough time to develop many minor characters or a complicated subplot. A short drama usually has a short exposition section. New characters and situations must be developed very quickly and efficiently. A few lines of dialogue can establish who new characters are and their basic motivations. The plot must develop several complications to promote interest and variation, but it must also build toward a climax. Loose ends are quickly tied up and resolved.

Interactive Stories and Games

Interactive scripts differ from traditional dramatic and narrative scripts in a number of ways. Traditional noninteractive scripts tend to be linear in terms of narrative structure. There may be flashbacks and flashforwards in time, but dramatic narratives follow a relatively fixed linear progression. Interactive stories and game scripts, on the other hand, are distinctly nonlinear. Players can select characters and a variety of story paths to pursue during a game.

Scriptwriters and programmers use one of two types of logic systems for interactive story construction: branching and artificial intelligence. *Branching* refers to a structure that is similar to the structure of a tree or a series of highways that intersect. Choosing a specific action sends the player character along a path that consists of a series of branches off the initial road or tree trunk. Branches may intersect bringing the character back towards the center, or they may send the character further and further away from the center. A scriptwriter specifies various branches by placing single words in brackets, such as [ATTACK] or [RETREAT], which indicate actions the player or "PC" ("player character") has chosen. Actors and computer characters (CCs) then respond to the player character's actions with various forms of text-based or spoken dialogue, and in so doing the story proceeds along various paths or branches.

Artificial intelligence (AI) refers to the ability to insert variables into a text so that a wide variety of text-based dialogue can be created and displayed very efficiently. Using standard terms, such as computer character (CC) and player character (PC), the scriptwriter uses a % mark to indicate a variable set of dialogue that can be accessed elsewhere. A # mark is used to locate the name of a set of dialogue and instructions, and a series of "if/then" statements indicate actions and dialogue that will be inserted as the PC makes various choices and the CC responds.

One method of organizing scenes for interactive stories is a flow chart, which is also discussed in more detail later in this chapter in reference to interactive educational scriptwriting. Flow charts allow writers and programmers to visualize various branches and/or variables that can be followed throughout a game. Computer programs are available, which allow a standard full-page master scene script to be married to a flowchart program.

An interactive script consists of a series of instructions to programmers concerning player characters, computer characters, text-based and spoken dialogue, actions, and responses, which follow a branching or artificial intelligence logic system for story construction. An interactive story or game may be designed for one or more platforms, including CD-ROM, Sega, Genesis, floppy disk, and/or online. Dialogue is usually written as text or spoken dialogue to be recorded using actors. In either case it is usually very brief. Writers need to be conscious of the limitations of various platforms, such as CD-ROM, in terms of storage space for both graphics and text.

Every line of dialogue needs to have a specific purpose in terms of moving the story forward, and this restriction makes it somewhat more difficult to build character through dialogue in interactive than in motion picture and television scripts. There should be enough variety that a player is not bored by endless repetitions of the same line of dialogue. If the dialogue will appear on the screen in written form, remember that the screen is generally restricted to eighty characters of twelve-point type per line or less. Scripts are often written in ASCII unformatted style so that they can be directly input into the computer. Full caps are used to emphasize the most important information, such as if/then statements, character names, and actions the player character may choose. Notation and style are generally based upon a standard computer programming language known as C++.

Nonfiction Scriptwriting

Many different types of nonfiction programs and films are used as informative or persuasive media devices. Documentaries, news stories, instructional programs, and commercials are examples of nonfiction films and television programming. These types of products seem to share some common characteristics. There is usually an emphasis on actuality or the presentation of real people, things, situations, actions, and problems. They are often structured or organized to transmit information or to motivate people to change their attitudes or behavior. They make frequent use of expository and rhetorical structures to convey information and to make persuasive appeals to an audience.

Nonfiction shares certain characteristics with dramatic fiction. All scriptwriters attempt to stimulate viewer interest through the portrayal of dramatic conflicts. Theorist Kenneth Burke has argued that all media presentations (both fictional and nonfictional) are essentially dramatic social devices. Reuven Frank, as executive producer of the NBC Evening News in the 1960s, sent the following memorandum to his news staff: "Every news story should, without any sacrifice of probity or responsibility, display the attributes of fiction, of drama. It should have structure and conflict, problem and denouement, rising action and falling action, a beginning, a middle and an end. These are not only the essentials of drama; they are the essentials of narrative." In short, elements of dramatic and narrative structure are important to nonfiction scriptwriters, and the material presented earlier concerning fiction scriptwriting is relevant to nonfiction scriptwriting as well. In addition, nonfiction scriptwriters utilize rhetorical and expository structure to present arguments and convey information.

Rhetorical and Expository Structure

Nonfiction scriptwriters know how to wage effective arguments and to present information in a logical manner that facilitates understanding. Arguments are fashioned on the basis of rhetorical strategies. An argument can take the form of inartistic or artistic proof. Inartistic proofs are dependent upon factual material available to the writer, editor, or speaker, such as interviews with various participants, witnesses, and observers. There are three main types of artistic proof: ethical, emotional, and demonstrative. An ethical proof relies quite heavily on the moral integrity and credibility of the speaker. An emotional proof relies on the appeal to audience emotions and feelings. A demonstrative proof relies on a series of expositions (showing, not just telling), which have recourse to actual events or oppositional points of view. A specific script might rely on all of these different forms of proof and argument.

We can also distinguish rhetorical strategies and approaches on the basis of whether the argument focuses upon its source, its subject, or the viewer. The credibility of the source of an argument in part determines its effectiveness. For example, a highly trusted or reliable person, such as a news anchor or a narrator with a commanding voice, carries a certain persuasive power. Invoking widely shared beliefs about a subject can also be highly persuasive, such as the idea that all politicians are corrupt or that many large corporations are insensitive to environmental issues. Other arguments focusing on the subject include leaving out various alternative solutions to a problem and implying that the solution presented is the only one possible. This form of argument conceals its basic premise. Emotional arguments, such as waving the flag or castigating someone as a communist, on the other hand, focus more upon viewers (and the assumption that certain emotional responses are widely shared) than upon the subject or the source of the argument.

A nonfiction scriptwriter relies upon expository structures that help to organize information in a logical manner. Widely used expository structures include effects-to-causes, problem/solution, enumeration, classification into logical categories, and theme/countertheme. Many network television documentaries, for example, begin with scenes that dramatize the effects of a particular social problem. These highly charged, emotional scenes act as a hook to grab the audience's attention. A dispassionate narrator then begins to explore some of the causes that have produced these effects. In a classic documentary, such as *The River* (1936) or *Harvest of Shame* (1960), the film or television program ends with proposed solutions to the problem. Specific goals are cited and specific courses of action are recommended to viewers concerning flood control (the Tennessee Valley Authority) and migrant worker welfare (federal legislation), respectively. Each documentary is structured as an argument for the elimination of a pressing social problem, and the information is logically presented through a problem/solution and effects-to-causes organization (Figure 3.9).

Visual and audio information can also be edited to compare and contrast different opinions and points of view. This can take the form of a theme/countertheme structure, where one idea or point of view clashes repeatedly with another, much like a theme and countertheme in a piece of music. For example, the documentary film *Hearts and Minds* (1975) uses a theme/countertheme structure to alternate between antiVietnam War and proVietnam War interviews and statements.

Figure 3.9 A documentary, such as *The River*, not only needs to tell a coherent story, but must make a specific point or argument for or against a social issue.

Enumeration refers to a listing of various possibilities or realities, while logical categories might consist of different aspects or approaches to a subject. For example, an educational documentary about a Latin American country might examine political, social, economic, cultural, and artistic aspects of that country. These are logical categories by which nonfictional information and arguments can be organized.

A nonfiction scriptwriter uses dramatic as well as expository structure. Events in a documentary, for example, can be considered to be rising and falling actions. The overall structure of a documentary can obtain emotional power by building toward a climax where a central problem or conflict is resolved. The pace of a nonfiction work is extremely important in terms of maintaining audience interest. The pace should vary to provide an effective emotional (as well as a logical) flow of events. Pacing is difficult to control during the writing stage, because it depends on so many factors that are evident only when the actual sound and image recordings are available. While the writer must exhibit some concern for pacing during the scriptwriting phase, it is really the documentary director and editor who finally determine the pace of specific elements and of the documentary film or videotape as a whole. Pacing is affected by the editing together of long- and short-duration camera shots as well as the speed of actions within shots, dialogue, and narration.

The opening of a nonfiction film or video should define what the piece is about and where it is going. It should serve as a hook to grab the viewer's attention, peak his or her curiosity, and generate a sense of expectation. Presenting a problem or conflict in dramatic, human terms is one of the best ways of gaining immediate audience attention. Presenting a particularly exciting segment of scenes or vignettes, which will be shown in their entirety somewhat later, acts as a teaser that can stimulate interest. Short segments from longer interviews can be edited together to dramatize a conflict or to present alternative points of view at the start. The writer's job is to find a way in which the documentary's main idea, theme, point of view, or conflict can be concisely dramatized in human terms that the intended audience will immediately understand. Later, near the conclusion of the piece, a sense of completion and fulfillment can be achieved by providing a definitive ending that leaves few questions raised in the opening sequence unanswered.

Voice and Point of View

Many nonfiction and documentary scripts establish a particular point of view. A point of view is an important angle or perspective from which an issue or problem can be productively approached. Television documentaries and news magazines, such as "60 Minutes," for example, sometimes adopt the point of view of an individual person or underdog, such as an individual consumer, as opposed to a large anonymous corporation or bureaucracy. Establishing a specific point of view helps to dramatize and humanize the problem. The audience frequently identifies with the individual, underdog, or injured party, and this can be used to increase the audience's emotional involvement in the problem.

Nonfiction scriptwriters and directors often assert their own voices and opinions. The assertion of a voice can be direct and explicit, such as when a narrator states an opinion, belief, or argument. It can also be indirect and implicit in the expository structure and order in which information is presented. For example, the film *Hearts and Minds* shows a Vietnamese woman crying over a family member's grave immediately after General William Westmoreland states that Vietnamese people don't value life as dearly as Americans do. Here the expository structure and order of presentation undercuts General Westmoreland and asserts the filmmaker's editorial opinion.

Direct or indirect assertions of a voice are associated with a variety of nonfiction and documentary approaches. Classic rhetorical and expository documentaries, such as *The River* (1937) and *Harvest of Shame* (1960), for example, rely upon direct address through an authoritative narrator or reporter/anchor person. Observational approaches to nonfiction film and video, such as the so-called cinema verité approach, on the other hand, generally suppress the voice of the filmmaker, avoid using a narrator, and require little, if any, scriptwriting. Events are recorded as they happen in long, continuous camera and sound takes. Nonetheless, the order of presentation of these events, which is determined during editing and postproduction, can rely upon indirect means of asserting the filmmaker's opinion, such as those cited earlier regarding *Hearts and Minds.* An interactive approach encourages the subjects of a documentary to assert their own voices, often highlighting their interaction with the filmmaker. In this case the subjects directly assert their own voices, while the filmmaker relies upon both direct and indirect means of asserting his or her voice. Finally, a self-reflexive approach makes a filmmaker's implicit assertions explicit by self-consciously analyzing his or her own role in the filmmaking process. A self-reflexive approach turns the filmmaker's voice into the subject of the nonfiction film or video.

Narration and Interviews

A nonfiction scriptwriter needs to tell an interesting story in a gripping and imaginative way, using facts, anecdotes, and opinions collected during research. Sometimes narration facilities telling a story. At other times it gets in the way. If a nonfiction story unfolds through compelling sounds and images by themselves, leave it alone. There is no need to retell the story with narration. Narration should clarify images and provide important additional information rather than redundantly describe what sound and images themselves convey. Narration can also emphasize and explain important points and details.

Narration needs to be written so that it can be spoken by a narrator rather than read as text by the viewer. It should be colloquial and down to earth. It should also be personalized whenever possible. Narration written in the first person, which will be spoken by a participant in the events that sounds and images depict, for example, usually works much more effectively than narration written in the third person, which will be spoken by someone who has no connection to the events.

A nonfiction scriptwriter should use simple sentences and action verbs. Words should be particular rather than general, concrete and specific rather than abstract and indefinite. Narration should be factual and informative, directing the viewer's attention to specific details or enhancing the mood and atmosphere by using adjectives that create a more vivid and memorable experience. Using long lists of data, recitations of statistics, and difficult specialized terminology rarely provide narration that is sufficiently informal, subtle, and effective (Figure 3.10).

Interviews often add emotion and personalize events. They should be carefully planned by writing down questions on a piece of paper after carefully and thoroughly researching the subject, but the interviewer should memorize these questions and never simply read them during the interview. An interviewer needs to maintain eye contact with the interviewee and use questions to facilitate rather than disrupt a personal or emotional response to questions. Interview questions should not be able to be answered by a simple "yes" or "no" from the interviewee. They should be specific and directive rather than rambling or excessively general. They should encourage the interviewee to divulge information through personal anecdotes as well as through the expression of attitudes, feelings, and opinions that generate enthusiasm or emotional power. An interviewer should come prepared with a bevy of specific questions whose order of presentation will be determined in large part by the interviewee's responses.

Short Nonfiction Forms and Formats

Many scriptwriting principles used with longer nonfiction forms, such as documentaries, are also applicable to shorter forms, such as news stories, talk shows, instructional programs, and commercials, but each of these shorter forms of nonfiction writing has its own principles and practices as well.

Figure 3.10 The writer or producer must gather information before the script is written. Interviewing the sources of information provides basic and accurate information upon which to base the script.

News Stories

A television newswriter, for example, writes *copy* or narration to be spoken by on-camera or off-camera anchor people and reporters. Most reporters write their own stories. Only in larger markets do anchor people generally read copy written by a newswriting specialist. Network and most local station newscasters are generally involved in writing their own copy. Whether one is working as a news anchor, reporter, producer, or director, some knowledge of basic newswriting is essential.

Unlike print journalism, television newswriting does not begin with a who, what, when, where, and why approach. There isn't time to answer all of these questions immediately. Television *story leads* quickly identify the situation. Key information is usually delayed until the second sentence delivered by the newscaster. The first sentence orients the viewer to the general issue to be discussed. "Another accusation of voter fraud surfaced today," leads into a story about a close senatorial election. "Candidate Sherlock Holmes accused the committee to re-elect Senator Moriarity of foul play in Baskerville County," then provides the specific information. News copy generally plays a subservient role to accompanying sounds and pictures. Like good documentary narration, good newswriting doesn't try to compete with visual information, but rather sets a context for its interpretation (Figure 3.11).

Newswriting does not have to describe what happened, when news clips are available. The writer simply sets a context for the viewing experience, establishes links or transitions between different stories, and provides a limited summary or

Figure 3.11 Many television news stories are produced and shot in the field. A crew of a reporter, a producer, and a camera operator make up the basic electronic news gathering (ENG) crew. In some markets a crew as small as one person or as large as five persons may make up the ENG crew.

conclusions. When commentary accompanies images and sounds, it should identify key participants. Since the camera cannot jump from one participant to another as quickly as they can be verbally identified, a descriptive phrase about each person allows sufficient time for close-ups to be edited together. The alternative to this practice is to use a less dramatic long shot, which includes all participants at once and allows them to be quickly identified as a group or, in any case, by no more than three individual identifications.

Newswriting should be simple and conversational, so that a newscaster can clearly and concisely communicate the essential information as though he or she is talking to a friend. Remember that a newscaster is an invited guest in private homes. A writer must use discretion when discussing difficult issues. Shocking or disturbingly violent visuals should be clearly identified in advance, giving children and sensitive adults an opportunity to avoid them. Newswriters, like print reporters, must be careful to attribute information to specific sources and to protect themselves from charges of falsehood. All too often, careless TV news reporters present suppositions as facts. False broadcast news reports can have an immediate and profound effect on viewers.

The first component of a field-recorded news story to be written and recorded is usually the reporter's on-camera commentary. This commentary introduces the subject, provides bridges between various segments, and offers a summary at the end. It is used as voice-over narration to order dramatic visual images and sounds that illustrate what the reporter is talking about.

A newswriter must be concerned with pace. Numerous stories are presented during a half-hour (actually twenty-three minutes plus commercials) newscast. Each must be cut down to minimal length in a way that retains excitement and interest. While a newscaster often seems calm and in control, the delivery and pace of the entire newscast must be both rapid and smooth. A television newswriter emphasizes active rather than passive verbs to increase pace and viewer interest. The sources of information must be given at the beginning of a sentence rather than at the end of a sentence for better oral communication. The order of words should result in an unambiguous interpretation of events. The purpose of a television newscast is to describe events rather than to interpret them or editorialize about them.

Each story is written as a separate computer file so that the producer can assemble the show as she or he sees fit. When the producer determines the best order of the stories, the computer files can be arranged in that order. Stories must be accurately timed. A good average reading speed is about 150 words of copy per minute. The combination of written copy and edited visuals and sounds must be precisely timed so that the total program fits into the allotted time slot. The completed script indicates if and when commercials will be inserted, and functions as a timing and source guide to live production for the entire staff and crew. A copy of the script goes to the producer, the director, and all on-set newscasters, often called *talent.* The copy to be read should include phonetic spellings, so that pronunciation is understood. The script is automatically formatted in news script format and also is sent to the teleprompters on the cameras for the anchors to read. It is possible and often necessary to make last minute changes to the script while the newscast is on the air moments before the story being changed is seen by the anchors on the prompter.

The material a newswriter edits, rewrites, condenses, or originates comes from a variety of sources. Broadcast news often relies on wire services, such as Associated Press. Some stories are simply downloaded from computer files provided by wire services. However, using these stories verbatim fails to establish a unique news style. Although wire services usually offer different story renditions for print and broadcast news clients, it can be quite risky to present unedited copy written by print-oriented wire-service journalists. Relying on wire-service copy also fails to provide viewers with news of local or regional interest. Assigning print journalists who have no experience with broadcast journalism to write broadcast copy can also be disastrous. Network and the most comprehensive local news usually originates from experienced reporters in the field who are investigating specific events, issues, and topics, and who receive tips from interested participants. Local stations also keep a close eye on the print media and competing newscasts to catch up on stories they might otherwise miss. Follow-ups on major stories from preceding days are another important news source.

The news producer must determine the significance of each story and the viewer interest it is likely to arouse so that the lead story, or most important beginning segment, can be selected and the other stories coherently ordered. Which stories will actually be aired depends on a number of factors, including program length, the availability of accompanying still images or videotape, the number of major events that have occurred that day, and the producer's own preferences and priorities. A large number of stories will be written each day; some of those will actually be aired and others either presented later, if they have accompanying visuals of continuing interest, or abandoned entirely. The selected stories are usually presented in blocks that reflect geographical or topical relationships. Innate interest and importance to the audience are equally valid considerations. Many producers try to end a news program with a humorous or human interest story.

Many factors, including the quality of the news writing, affect the selection and placement of news stories for a particular broadcast. Ordering stories in a newscast can be somewhat subjective and quite complex. The trend in commercial television broadcasting is toward many short items, rather than a few long reports on selected topics, and a significant use of actual footage and flashy graphics. While a fast-paced structure and format for a news broadcast raises many questions about the quality of in-depth understanding available to the American public on any single topic through commercial television, this approach is obviously economically advantageous to commercial broadcasters since it attracts many viewers.

Talk Show

News and entertainment functions are combined on many talk shows. There are basically two types of interviews conducted on these shows: celebrity interviews and authority interviews. Celebrity interviews are frequently seen on afternoon and evening entertainment programs. Comedy or singing performances often accompany such interviews. Celebrity interviews generally try to explore the human side of guests and coax them into revealing more about themselves than they may have initially intended. The interview can be purely a performance to entertain the audience or an occasion for self-disclosure, depending on the interviewer's success in gaining the confidence of the celebrity. Celebrity interviews almost always have a commercial purpose. The guest is often promoting a recent book, film, or television program when they appear on the "Tonight Show" or on "The Letterman Show." Sometimes he or she simply wants to become better known to the general public. Authority interviews focus for the most part on issues, information, ideas, and attitudes rather than personalities. The interviewer's purpose is often to play devil's advocate and force the guest to clarify and substantiate a position and possibly to reveal some important detail that has been omitted in previous reports and interviews. It is not the authority's personality that is of primary interest, but his or her knowledge and/or opinion of some significant topic. The authority interview comes perilously close to the celebrity interview, however, when the primary objective is simply to find a political skeleton in the guest's closet.

Writers and researchers must carefully prepare the interviewer for his or her interaction with the guest. A good interviewer is at least as well informed as the audience, and has anticipated what questions audience members would ask if they could. Interviewers often write the questions they plan to ask on note cards. They then go over these cards, paring them down to a reasonable number of questions that they are confident will appeal to their audience. A good interviewer is less concerned with impressing the audience with brilliant questions than with functioning as an effective representative of the audience during the interview. Background information on the guest and topic must be thoroughly researched. But the interviewer must also be a glib respondent to unpredictable events, a careful and sensitive listener, at times a cajoler and at other times a provocateur or a catalyst.

While a tremendous amount of writing may be compiled prior to the interview, only a small fraction of it will actually be used during the interview. The interview must appear to be unrehearsed and spontaneous. Questions cannot be read from a sheet of paper. They must be presented as though they are spontaneous. A written script provides a general outline of guests to be interviewed and topics to be discussed. Introductions and background material can be written out and displayed at the appropriate time on a teleprompter, which projects copy on a see-through mirror in front of the camera lens. Cue cards are also created for the interviewer's use. A script also indicates when commercials will appear and the precise timing of segments of a show.

Talk-show writers and interviewers, like good documentarians and newswriters, are concerned about ethical issues, such as the potential conflict between the public's right to know and the citizen's right to privacy. When a sensitive topic or personal problem is to be discussed, the interviewer must satisfy the audience's curiosity without embarrassing the guest or placing him or her in an awkward position. A good interviewer knows how to phrase questions in a tactful manner so that the guest is not offended, although the audience's curiosity and expectations are fully satisfied. Indirect methods of questioning can be quite effective, and they raise fewer ethical dilemmas about pressuring a private citizen into revealing more personal details than he or she really cares to have the public know.

Discussing her celebrity-interviewing techniques, Barbara Walters has said that she often uses indirect methods of questioning. For example, she felt that it would be in bad taste to ask Mamie Eisenhower, the former President's widow, any direct question about a supposed problem with alcohol. Instead, she simply asked Mrs. Eisenhower if there was ever a time that she felt concerned about public impressions of her in the White House. Mrs. Eisenhower revealed that she had an inner ear problem that sometimes caused her to lose her balance, and that the press had misinterpreted this as a sign of alcoholism.

Commercials and Public Service Announcements

Commercials are brief messages that advertise products, company names, and services. Unlike many other types of nonfiction, commercials aim directly at modifying audience behavior and attitudes. The chief test of a commercial's success is not whether people watch and enjoy it. The true test is whether people buy a specific product or are positively predisposed toward a particular company. Commercials are primarily persuasive; they are informative only to the extent that audiences become aware of the existence of new products and services or corporate goodwill.

Commercials vary considerably in terms of their production values and formats. Network commercials and national spot commercials (network-level commercials aired on local stations in major markets) are generally written and controlled by major advertising companies, such as Leo Burnett, J. Walter Thompson, and McCann-Erickson, which oversee all aspects of the creation of a commercial from writing, through storyboarding, to actual production by an independent production company. They are often shot on 35mm film, and budgets can run as high as several hundred thousand dollars. On the local level, commercials are usually made on videotape by a television station or by a small production studio. The people who produce local commercials often write them as well. Many regional and local commercial producers use digital production effects and transitions as well as computer graphics whether the commercial was shot originally on film or videotape.

The first step in writing a commercial is to establish the main goal. In most cases the goal is to sell a specific product or service, but some commercials sell corporate goodwill. Public utilities do not always compete directly with other companies supplying the same type of power or service. They nonetheless need to maintain a positive public image, if only to obtain periodic rate increases. Targeting a goal in terms of products, services, or corporate goodwill, is helpful in terms of selecting a specific selling strategy.

Commercial scriptwriters rely quite heavily on advertising research to determine the best way to sell a product or service. The look and selling approach of a television commercial are often dictated by audience testing and positioning. *Positioning* refers to the most effective means of reaching prospective buyers for a product or service. Audience testing and positioning determine the overall approach that a writer should take, how a commercial will look, and how it will communicate to a selected target audience. Market research reveals the best selling strategy.

Writers of commercials try to define three things before they begin writing the script: the intended audience, the major selling points of the product, and the best strategy or format with which to sell the product. The audience can be defined generally or very specifically in demographic terms of sex, age, race, socioeconomic status, and so on. Air time for the presentation of the commercial can be selected on the basis of this well-defined target audience. The writer must be familiar with the types of expressions and selling techniques that will appeal to the intended audience. Advertising agencies conduct research before actual writing begins, trying to ascertain why a particular group of people likes or uses a product and why others do not. A commercial is usually designed to broaden the appeal of the product without alienating the current users or consumers. Writing a commercial requires a firm understanding of the specific product or service that is being sold. Listing the major selling points of the product will help the writer select those elements that appeal primarily to the main target audience and to determine the best selling format, whether it is a hard sell or a soft sell, a serious or a humorous tone, a testimonial, and/or a dramatization.

Both hard-sell and soft-sell commercials are used to promote specific products. They are usually based on a careful study of the nature of the product and its appeal. Consumer testing reveals that a hard sell works well with automobiles and soap products, for example. An aggressive pitch does not turn off potential customers. Many soap-product commercials present "real-life" dramatizations that end in a hard sell from a typical consumer who is satisfied with the product. Other products rely on a soft sell or a less direct appeal. They create a particular image that entices consumers to seek beauty aids or brand-name clothing in order to have a more satisfying social life. A commercial can create an attractive image that is associated with the product and that the customer aspires to emulate. This approach often reinforces social stereotypes, such as traditional or emerging trends in male and female roles. Commercials generally reinforce the status quo because advertisers are afraid of offending potential customers. Testimonials, which are endorsements of a product or service made by celebrities, often rely on hard-sell techniques. Dramatizations, except in the case of soap products, usually offer a more indirect approach. The viewer is left to draw his or her own conclusions about why someone is so attractive, successful, or satisfied.

Generally, humorous treatments work well in some cases but not others. Humorous treatments of products or services related to death, personal hygiene, or profound social problems are generally in poor taste and can be offensive to audiences and thus counterproductive. Humor can be used effectively to deflate the sophisticated image of a specialized foreign product, such as Grey Poupon Mustard, or to associate a product with fun and good times, as McDonald's commercials have done. Humor can create amusement and attention, but if poorly handled it can also distract attention from the product or company name. Appropriate use of humor generally requires talented performers. A variety of means can be used to help the audience remember the product or company name, such as simple name repetition or a song with a catchy phrase or slogan, called a *jingle.* Many commercials begin with the creation of a song to which the visual elements will be edited. The lyrics and music are frequently performed by top-name musicians and performers, and they often set the tone and pace for the entire commercial. The emphasis in jingles is on repeatable phrases that will help the consumer remember the product or company name.

Commercials are often extensively tested on audiences and potential consumers prior to purchasing expensive air time. The objective of most scientific tests is to determine the effect of the commercial on product recall or name retention. It is assumed that if viewers can recall the product or company name, they are likely to buy the product. Other tests examine actual or simulated purchasing behavior, such as the opportunity to select a soft drink from among several competing products after viewing commercials. Sometimes several versions of a commercial may be tested, only the most effective of which will actually be used.

Written or spoken advertising copy must be clear, succinct, concrete, and active. Clarity is of utmost importance. If the message is to be understood, it must be expressed in terms that the average viewer can easily comprehend. Time for commercials is both limited and expensive, so the message must be short and direct. There is no time for wasted words that distract attention from the central point. It is usually best to use very concrete nouns and adjectives, as well as active verbs. Passive verbs are too tentative and rarely help sell products. Writers of commercials try to use words that will be popular with the anticipated audience and consumer. Key words or *buzz words,* such as "natural" or "no artificial ingredients," can increase the appeal of a product for potential buyers, despite the fact that chemists often consider such words to be imprecisely applied to soft drinks and food, since very few edible substances are actually artificial.

A *storyboard* is a preproduction tool consisting of a series of drawings and accompanying written information. In some ways a storyboard is similar to a comic strip. The storyboard tells the commercial story or message in still pictures. Narration or dialogue, camera movements, sound effects, and music are usually specified under or next to each frame. An advertising agency usually creates a storyboard to show clients and producers what a commercial will look like. The storyboard suggests how images and sounds will be ordered, the placement of the camera, and the design of the set. Today computer storyboard programs or programs that combine both word processing and a storyboard segment provide a flexible and efficient method of creating and editing scoreboards.

Directors sometimes use storyboards along with the script as a guide to actual recording of the finished commercial on film or videotape, and its use is highly recommended for any type of production where step-by-step planning is possible. Many feature film directors compose their shots on storyboards prior to actual production. A television storyboard consists of four elements: hand-drawn sketches, camera positions and movements, dialogue or narration, and sound effects or music. Each hand-drawn sketch is composed within a frame that has the same proportions as a television screen (4 units wide by 3 units high, a ratio of 4:3). A frame is drawn for each shot. Camera positions and movements, lines of dialogue or narration, and sound effects (SFX) and music are specified under or next to each frame.

A public service announcement or PSA is produced much like a commercial. PSAs are usually aired free of charge by commercial broadcasting stations, and most noncommercial stations offer no other form of announcements. PSAs often promote nonprofit organizations. They can attempt to raise public awareness of specific social problems and social service agencies, and are usually persuasive in the sense that they have clear behavioral objectives, such as appeals for help or money. In the case of a social need or charity event, the emphasis is usually on developing audience empathy for people in need rather than on appealing to the audience's materialistic needs and drives.

The writing of a PSA is virtually identical to that of a commercial. The same steps and procedures can be followed, including researching the particular organization or cause, specifying the goal, matching the selling or promotional strategy to the intended audience, and creating a storyboard. PSAs offer an opportunity for students and beginning production people to obtain valuable experience in writing and production, because they are usually produced on very low budgets and incur few, if any, expensive airtime costs.

Instructional Films and Videos

Instructional films and videos often serve one of following purposes: to supplement lectures in the classroom; to inform the public and government employees about new government policies; or to inform employees and/or the public about corporate practices, policies, and points of view. These three purposes reflect the institutional needs of producers in educational, government, and corporate environments, respectively. Instructional programs are designed as either supplementary or primary materials. They may accompany an educational, government, or corporate speech, or they may have to stand on their own without the help of a person who can set a context for viewing or answer questions.

The most important factor in planning instructional programs is to understand the needs, expectations, and level of knowledge of the audience. Different demographic (age, socioeconomic status, and educational level) groups often require entirely different instructional strategies. A four-year-old child requires a different approach than a ten-year-old. While the overall objective of any instructional program is to impart knowledge, effective communication depends on the writer's awareness of the audience's sophistication, age, and educational level. A writer must use terms with which the audience is already familiar or define new terms in words the audience already understands.

Instructional information must be clear and well organized. Each step or concept must follow logically from preceding steps and concepts. Suppose, for example, that a program is designed to instruct beginning photography students about basic concepts of developing film. It is logical to begin with a description and graphic demonstration of a piece of film, showing the various light-sensitive layers and substances. The camera can be described next, along with the process of exposing the film to light. Finally, the stages of developing and printing the film, using different chemicals and pieces of equipment, can each be described sequentially. A short review of the fundamental steps then summarizes the overall process.

An instructional program must be more than clear and logical, however. It must graphically demonstrate concepts and ideas. Otherwise, what is the point of making a videotape or film? Cross sections of a piece of film and the working parts of a camera can be drawn. Actual scenes might be shot in a photographic darkroom under red lights, which give the impression of a darkroom setting but provide sufficient light for recording purposes. A photographer can actually demonstrate the various stages of developing and printing photographic images, so that students are brought out of the classroom into an actual work environment. Educational films and videotapes present materials that cannot be easily demonstrated through a lecture or the use of other less expensive media, such as slides, audiotapes, or graphic projections. Moving images should move. There is no justification for using film or videotape recording for something that can be done just as well and much less expensively with still pictures. Carl I. Hovland's experiment comparing slides/lectures with movies as teaching devices demonstrated that slides/lectures were better, not just less expensive. Of course, motion is an important component of many educational subjects. The narration that accompanies this graphic material must be concise, clear, and easily comprehended. A sense of drama, like a sense of humor, can add interest and excitement, but it can also be overdone. The main object is to show rather than tell. The narration should be authoritative, but not condescending. It must impart accurate information, link various parts of the demonstration, and establish a context within which the accompanying images can be clearly and completely understood.

Interactive Learning and Training

Writing for interactive multimedia educational applications is an important aspect of authoring. *Authoring* includes everything from designing a flow chart for the interactive learning or training process to writing actual text that will appear on a computer monitor when the application is run. Authoring begins with the development of an interactive training concept. An author clarifies the training concept and specifies the intended audience, the purpose of the application, and the basic subject matter by writing a treatment document, which provides a narrative description of the proposed project. The treatment may also indicate the anticipated platforms (Mac, PC, Amiga, etc.), operating systems (DOS, PowerPC, OS/2, Amiga DOS, etc.), style (command or object), and interface (text-based or graphical). Like a treatment for an interactive game, the latter information defines the authoring environment, that is, the computer hardware and software that will be used to design the application as well as the intended avenues of its distribution. This aspect of authoring is also similar to a producer's development of a proposal and treatment for a (noninteractive) film or video. The author defines the objec-

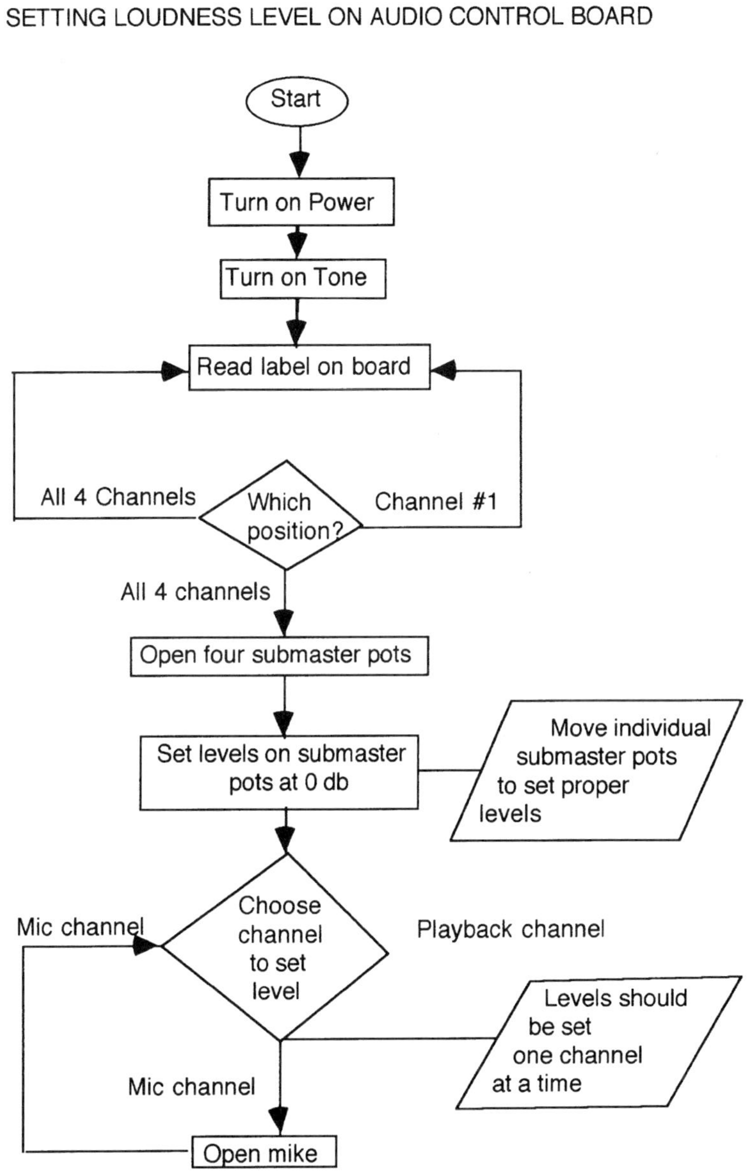

Figure 3.12 An interactive program diagram shows the various paths or choices the person using the program has to follow. Arrows indicate directions the paths may take in moving forward, retracing, or starting a new path.

tives for a project and the means by which those objectives will be accomplished (Figure 3.12).

Similar in many respects to authoring/writing computer games and other forms of interactive entertainment, which was discussed earlier, the scriptwriting phase of interactive educational multimedia production is sometimes referred to as the *design stage*. The purpose of the design stage is to provide an architectural blueprint for the overall project that will guide the selection and arrangement of content. Creating a design can take the form of flow charting, as well as actual scriptwriting. A flow chart indicates the possible avenues that a student can pursue to acquire information or be trained in the use of various hardware or software. A fixed flow chart on paper can become very complex and somewhat confusing when there are many different interactive choices and options that result in numerous intersecting lines, but using computer software for authoring that includes screen icons that move the flow chart to different levels when a mouse pointing to an icon is double-clicked can increase the clarity and flexibility of a flow chart.

The script for an interactive learning or training application indicates all the content that will appear in the completed project, including graphics, animation, video, and audio, as well as written text. The flow chart provides an overview of the program architecture and interactive training options, while script material added to the flow chart indicates in some detail all of the content that will appear at various points along the flow chart. Descriptions of visual images and sounds are generally kept to a minimum. Various icon symbols are often used to indicate repeated (as opposed to unique) sounds, graphic images, animation sequences, and live action video that will appear at different points along the flow chart. Text may appear as spoken narration or written text that accompanies visual images and sounds. For example, CD-ROMs and videodiscs of music videos or feature films can include written text that provides additional information about its production. An interactive CD-ROM or videodisc can also allow a student to manipulate various components, such as remixing the sound or altering special effects in the image. In this case a viewer/listener becomes an active participant in the creative process and learns how to control sounds and images through hands-on experience. Educational multimedia products can also provide written text in the form of specific questions and correct or incorrect answers to these questions, which test a student's knowledge, providing immediate feedback. Several incorrect responses might indicated to a student that he or she needs to repeat one section before going on to the next.

Interactive multimedia provides obvious educational advantages over published manuals and textbooks that an author or scriptwriter should utilize whenever possible. Since some students are primarily auditory learners, while others learn better through visual or tactile stimulation, authors should make some attempt to vary the form of media presentation. Sometimes media redundancy, that is, conveying similar information using audio, visual, and hands-on interaction, can be extremely effective for all types of learners. Authors should also allow for different learning rates or speeds of information acquisition. Flow charts should provide enough options to facilitate the learning process for students who learn relatively quickly or slowly.

Summary

Scriptwriting can be divided into two basic categories: fiction and nonfiction. Every scriptwriter should be familiar with basic elements of both fiction and nonfiction writing. Principles of dramatic and narrative structure used in fiction may also be applicable to nonfiction, and principles of rhetorical persuasion and expository structures used in nonfiction can be helpful in a dramatic production. Elements of dramatic, narrative, rhetorical, and expository structure are of practical value to scriptwriters working in a variety of areas and formats.

Scriptwriting demands visual thinking. Scriptwriters know how to use the full creative potential of moving images and sounds. Thinking visually demands that a scriptwriter think in practical terms of actual settings, concrete actions, and specific dialogue that will actually be performed or observed and recorded. Television, film, audio, and interactive multimedia are visual and acoustic media. A fiction scriptwriter establishes settings, describes actions, and defines characters through concrete sounds and visual images. In a dramatic production, for example, settings are established very economically as specific buildings, locations, and/or props, and characters are defined by their actions and reactions, as well as by what they say to other characters.

Preparation for scriptwriting includes performing research and writing a treatment. Research is a creative process of uncovering new sources of information. The more knowledgeable a writer or researcher becomes, the more information he or she will elicit from additional sources. Like a good detective, a writer learns that one piece of evidence leads to the discovery of another, and a project acquires depth and integrity through careful research. Using computers as a research tool aids writers as well as producers in the gathering of information for each type of production efficiently and accurately. In addition, the physical tedium of formatting scripts, budgets, schedules, storyboards, and other written materials has been greatly reduced through the use of computers and specifically written computer programs

A synopsis of the story or subject matter is called a treatment. A treatment provides a summary of the project in short story form. It provides an outline of the script that can serve as a guide for future writing.

There are three basic script formats: full-page master scene, split-page, and semi-scripted. The full-page master scene script is used more frequently for dramatic production. It is organized on the basis of scenes, that is, actions and events occurring at one time and place. Scene numbers, interior and exterior locations, and time of day-listed scene headings, followed by stage actions and then character dialogue, covering the full page. The split-page script places the visual elements on one side of the page and audio elements on the opposite side. It allows for a direct comparison and coordination of images and sound elements. Much informational and live television programming is semi-scripted.

Dramatic films and television programs can be plotted into a framework that consists of a basic three-act structure and a series of rising and falling actions, which culminate in a climax and resolution. Act One of a drama usually sets up the main plot by establishing the central characters, their goals and conflicts, as well as the basic time, place, and situation of the story. Act Two and Act Three each begin with a turning point, such as a major shift in the main plot. Secondary as well as primary characters and themes are usually more fully developed through both main plot and subplot actions in Act Two. Conflicts and problems eventually reach a climax and are resolved as the main plot and subplot are brought together near the end of Act Three. Dramatic structure includes rising actions and falling actions, text, and subtext.

Fictional stories are usually told or narrated by someone. Narrative structure has two basic elements: time and point of view. The historical time of a story can be manipulated or changed from present to past or future time. Time can also be compressed and expanded through editing. Point of view refers to the person or perspective from which a story is told. A narrator can be omniscient and effaced, or a narrator can be a character in the story, called a ***dramatized narrator.*** Point of view can be revealed through actual spoken narration or through what is shown and where a camera is placed.

Dramatic narratives develop characters and themes. Characters' values reveal themselves through actions and words. The writer's job is to externalize these values through speech, mannerisms, and actions, which reflect a more complex internal value system and give a character depth and significance. A theme is a significant statement made by a work of fiction or an important issue that is raises. The topicality of a theme generates audience interest, while the significance and universality of a theme in large part determines a work's lasting value.

Adaptation is a complex art, which requires that the writer be thoroughly familiar with the original work. Published works are copyrighted, and permission must be obtained from their authors or publishers before they can be adapted and recorded as films or television programs. Changes, additions, and deletions inevitably are made in the original piece of fiction to make it more compatible with other media.

There are a variety of specific formats within which writers of film and television must work. Short fiction includes half-hour series episodes and a variety of fictional film and video shorts. A writer must consider the lengths and structures that are conventionally practiced within each format. Writers of half-hour television series, for example, must work somewhat more formulaically than writers of feature films, who are freer to develop more complicated plot structures and characters. But creative writers can often turn limitations to artistic advantage.

Nonfiction scripts often convey information about actual events. Nonfiction scriptwriters work in a variety of formats, including documentary, news and talk shows, commercials, and educational programs, such as interactive multimedia applications. These nonfiction formats are often structured or organized to transmit information or to motivate people to change their attitudes or behavior. They make frequent use of expository and rhetorical structures to convey information and to make persuasive appeals to an audience.

Arguments are fashioned on the basis of rhetorical strategies. An argument can take the form of inartistic or artistic proof. Inartistic proofs are dependent upon factual material available to the writer, editor, or speaker. There are three main types of artistic proof: ethical, emotional, and demonstrative. Rhetorical strategies and approaches can also be distinguished on the basis of whether the argument focuses upon its source, its subject, or the viewer.

A nonfiction scriptwriter relies upon expository structures that help to organize information in a logical manner. Widely used expository structures include effects-to-causes, problem/solution, enumeration, classification into logical categories, and theme/countertheme.

Many nonfiction and documentary scripts establish a particular point of view. A point of view is an important angle or perspective from which an issue or problem can be productively approached. Nonfiction scriptwriters and directors often assert their own voices and opinions. The assertion of a voice can be direct and explicit, such as when a narrator states an opinion, belief, or argument. It can also be indirect and implicit in the expository structure and order in which information is presented.

Narration needs to be written so that it can be effectively spoken. It should be colloquial and down to earth. It should also be personalized whenever possible. Interviews often add emotion and personalize events. Interview questions should encourage the interviewee to divulge information through personal anecdotes as well as through the expression of attitudes, feelings, and opinions.

Short nonfiction formats include news stories, talk shows, and commercials. A newswriter's job is to organize a story and to describe events straightforwardly, clearly, and succinctly. The building blocks for most news segments are the picture and sound sequences that have been recorded. There are basically two types of talk show interviews: celebrity interviews and authority interviews. Celebrity interviews concentrate on the personality of the guest and are often intended to promote his or her latest work. Authority interviews usually focus on a specific topic or issue rather than the personality of the guest.

Commercials are brief messages that are broadcast as persuasive appeals. The main purpose of commercials is to sell products or services or to promote corporate goodwill. Writers use a variety of selling strategies, such as hard sells and soft sells, humorous and serious treatments, dramatizations and testimonials. Advertising copy must be clear, succinct, concrete, and active. It must be quickly comprehended by an average viewer. The script for a commercial is usually written after a visual storyboard, consisting of sequentially drawn images similar to a comic strip, is constructed. Commercials that are aired free of charge for nonprofit organizations and various causes are called public service announcements or PSAs.

Instructional films and videos often serve one of following purposes: to supplement lectures in the classroom; to inform the public and government employees about new government policies; or to inform employees and/or the public about corporate practices, policies, and points of view. They must be clear and well organized. Writers must rely on terms and concepts that will be easily comprehended by the appropriate educational level or demographic group to which the instructional material is directed.

The script for an interactive learning or training application indicates all the content that will appear in the completed project, including graphics, animation, video, and audio, as well as written text. A flow chart provides an overview of the program architecture and interactive training options, while script material added to the flow chart indicates in some detail all of the content that will appear at various points along the flow chart. Educational multimedia products can also provide written text in the form of specific questions and correct or incorrect answers to these questions, which test a student's knowledge, providing immediate feedback.

Interactive multimedia provides obvious educational advantages over published manuals and textbooks. Some students are primarily auditory learners, while others learn better through visual or tactile stimulation. Interactive multimedia authors should make some attempt to vary the form of media presentation for different types of learners. Authors should also allow for different rates of learning.

Additional Readings

De Abreu, Carlos and Howard Jay Smith. *Opening the Doors to Hollywood: How to Sell Your Idea/Story.* Beverly Hills, CA: Custos Morum, 1995.

Em, Michele. "The Ever Changing Story: Writing for the Interactive Market." *Journal of the Writers Guild of America West,* June 1994, pp. 16-21.

Luther, Arch C. *Designing Interactive Multimedia.* New York: Bantam Books, 1992.

Luther, Arch C. *Authoring Interactive Multimedia.* Cambridge, MA: AP Professional, 1994.

Rabiger, Michael. *Directing the Documentary,* 2nd ed. Boston: Focal Press, 1992.

Rosenthal, Alan. *Writing, Directing, and Producing Documentary Films.* Carbondale, IL: Southern Illinois University Press, 1990.

Rosenthal, Alan. *Writing Docudrama.* Boston: Focal Press, 1995.

Seger, Linda. *Making a Good Script Great,* 2nd ed. New York: Dodd, Mead & Company, 1994.

Whitcomb, Cynthia. *Selling Your Screenplay.* New York: Crown Publishers, 1988.

4

Directing: Aesthetic Principles and Production Coordination

Introduction

Video and film directors are artists who can take a completed script and imaginatively transform it into exciting sounds and images. Directors creatively organize many facets of production to produce works of art. They know how and when to use different types of camera shots and have mastered the use of composition, image qualities, transition devices, and relations of time and space. Directors know when and how to use different types of sound and how to control sound and image interaction. By using all of their creative powers, directors are able to produce films and video programs that have lasting value. Digital effects are often combined with miniatures (smaller copies of objects) and models (full-size mockups) to produce startlingly realistic special effects in Hollywood feature films, such as "Jurassic Park," for example (miniatures and models are discussed more fully in Chapter 13). Computer graphics hardware and software (discussed in Chapter 9) has played an important role in the creation of special effects as well.

Directors prepare a shooting script by indicating specific types of images and sounds to be recorded within each scene. Armed with a final shooting script, a director is ready to organize production. In order to record the different scenes and sequences described in the script, the director must organize the activities of many different people who are involved in production. The role of the director is quite different in multiple-camera versus single-camera productions. The director must be able to communicate precisely and quickly with cast and crew. A specific communication system and language must be understood and followed by each person as a command is directed at them. Each of these facets of the director's responsibility in the production process will be covered in this chapter. The director usually selects and organizes images and sounds according to one of the three basic aesthetic approaches introduced in Chapter 1.

Aesthetic Approaches

A convenient way to organize aesthetics, or approaches to the creative process, is to use three very general categories: realism, modernism, and postmodernism. Most artistic approaches reflect one or more of these three aesthetic tendencies, which differ in their emphases on function, form, and content. *Function* refers to why something is expressed, its goal or purpose. *Form* can be thought of as how something is expressed in a work of art. *Content* refers to what is expressed. Function, form, and content are closely connected aspects of any creative work.

Realism

Realism stresses content more than form. In realist works, artists use forms and techniques that do not call attention to themselves, a so-called transparent style. Realist artists depict a world of common experience as naturally as possible. Smooth, continuous camera movements and actions, continuity of time and place, and the use of actual locations and real people (i.e., nonactors) help to sustain a sense of reality. Realist art relies on conventions that some artists and viewers believe will preserve an illusion of reality. While realist techniques and conventions change, as in the shift from black-and-white to color images for added realism in photography, film, and television during the 1950s and 1960s, the mimetic tradition and the intention to preserve an illusion of reality in western art has persisted over time. A realist artist is a selector and organizer of common experience, rather than a self-conscious manipulator of abstract forms, principles, and ideas.

Many prime-time network television dramas, such as "ER" and "Chicago Hope," and nonfiction programs, such as "60 Minutes," "48 Hours," and "20/20," select and organize common experience as naturally as possible. Continuity of space and time is evident even in the titles of some of these programs, such as "48 Hours." Forms and techniques rarely call attention to themselves. Instead a transparent but very dramatic style helps to depict worlds of common experience and sustain an illusion of reality.

Modernism

Modernism stresses the idea that form is more important than function. Creators of avant-garde works of video and film art explore their medium beyond the usual restrictions and limitations without considering the illusion of reality. The works of modernist director's show less objectivity and tend to explore feelings of ambiguity and may lack continuity in space and time. Many music video productions and some science fiction programs may be classified as modernist.

Some European feature film directors, such as Ingmar Bergman in Sweden and Luis Buñuel in Spain and France, have used modernist aesthetics to guide their approaches to filmmaking. Bergman's film *Persona* (1966), for example, offers a collage of images that reflect the psychological states of mind of an actress, who refuses to speak, and a nurse, who is trying to take care of her both inside and outside a Swedish mental hospital. Their personalities and faces seem to merge during the course of the film. The editing of this film and the world that Bergman depicts often conform more closely to internal mental states than they do to an external illusion of physical reality. Space and time are often discontinuous. Like Luis Buñuel's early Surrealist avant-garde film, *Un Chien Andalou* (*An Andalusian Dog*, 1929), which he codirected with a surrealist painter, Salvador Dali, his later narrative feature films, such as *The Discreet Charm of the Bourgeoisie* (1973) and *Tristana* (1970) or *Viridiana* (1961), often defy logic and rational thought as well as continuity in space and time. The surrealist world that Bunuel depicts allows the irrational thoughts and unconscious feelings and desires of his characters to be freely exposed at the same time that it makes a satirical comment on social conventions and institutional religious practices. Ingmar Bergman and Luis Buñuel are strongly personal, modern artists who sometimes stress style more than content and explore feelings of ambiguity and interior states of mind in their films rather than present an external illusion of reality.

Postmodernism

Postmodernism stresses viewer participation within open-ended works with vaguely defined characteristics. A scattered blending or pastiche of new and old images, genres, and production techniques may intentionally confuse the audience, yet at the same time attempt to emotionally and sometimes interactively involve the viewer or listener in the creation of texts rather than treat them as passive consumers of entertainment. Film and video directing and production in the postmodernist mode continues to evolve, and its precise definition remains somewhat elusive.

An example of a postmodernist work is Peter Gabriel's CD-ROM entitled, *Explora 1 Peter Gabriel's Secret World* (1993), which was developed and directed by Peter Gabriel, Steve Nelson, Michael Coulson, Nichola Bruce, and Mike Large. This interactive CD-ROM contains Peter Gabriel's music and music videos as well as minidocumentaries about the artist and the production of his works, including information about performing artists with whom Gabriel has collaborated as well as other visual artists. Viewers/listeners control the sequence and duration in which the entertainment and information contained on this CD-ROM is presented in the "INTERACT" mode, while the "WATCH" mode takes them on a guided journey through the disk. Viewers/listeners have to correctly put together an image of Peter Gabriel to gain entry and to select different worlds to explore and different areas with which to interact. In one section viewers/listeners can even add or subtract different musicians and control the sound levels of the audio mix for a selection from Peter Gabriel's music during an interactive recording session. The ways in which this CD-ROM combines animation, live action, and documentary recordings, information and entertainment, and "INTERACT" and "WATCH" modes of presentation clearly offers a postmodernist approach to directing that directly involves the viewer/listener in the creative process.

Realism, modernism, and postmodernism are not mutually exclusive, nor do they exhaust all aesthetic possibilities, but they offer a convenient means of organizing the field of aesthetics from the standpoint of production. The relation of expressive forms and techniques to program content and purposes often reflects these three general tendencies. They are applicable to all the aspects of production that will be covered in this section, including visualization, lighting and set design, as well as postproduction editing.

Visualization

The director answers the questions concerning the types of pictures that should be created to tell the story of the script by considering the choices available. The process is reached by an analysis of the types of shots possible, composing those shots, and deciding how to combine the shots visually and with the proper sounds into a comprehensive whole.

Types of Shots

A director's ability to select and control visual images begins with an understanding of specific types of shots. The camera can be close to or far away from the subject. It can remain stationary or move during a shot. The shots commonly used in video and film production can be described in terms of camera-to-subject distance, camera angle, camera (or lens) movement, and shot duration.

Long Shot (LS)

The long shot orients the audience to subjects, objects, and settings by viewing them from a distance; this term is sometimes used synonymously with the terms *establishing shot, wide shot,* or *full shot.* An establishing shot (ES) generally locates the camera at a sufficient distance to establish the setting. Place and time are clearly depicted. A full shot (FS) provides a full frame (head-to-toe) view of a human subject or subjects (Figure 4.1).

Figure 4.1 A long shot (LS) may refer to the framing of a human from head to foot, or the longest shot in the sequence.

Medium Shot (MS)

A medium shot provides approximately a three-quarter (knee-to-head) view of the subject. The extremes in terms of camera-to-subject distance within this type of shot are sometimes referred to as a *medium long shot* (MLS) and a *medium close-up* (MCU) (Figure 4.2). The terms *two shot* and *three shot* define medium shots in which two or three subjects, respectively, appear in the same frame.

Close Shot (CS) or Close-Up (CU)

The terms *close shot* and *close-up* are often used synonymously. A close-up refers to the isolation of elements in the shot, and normally indicates the head and shoulders of a person. When someone is making an important or revealing statement or facial gesture, a close-up will draw the audience's attention to that event. Close-ups focus and direct attention and create dramatic emphasis. When they are overused, however, their dramatic impact is severely reduced. A very close camera position is sometimes called an *extreme close-up* (ECU). See Figures 4.1, 4.2, and 4.3 for illustrations of long, medium, and close-up shots.

There are times when the standard nomenclature of framing is not appropriate. If the widest shot in a program is from a blimp and the tightest shot is of one football player, then the blimp shot would be the LS and the player shot would be a CU. Conversely, if the entire commercial is shot in close-ups, the tightest shot would be an ECU, and the widest shot would be a LS, even if it was only a shot of a hand holding a product (Figure 4.3).

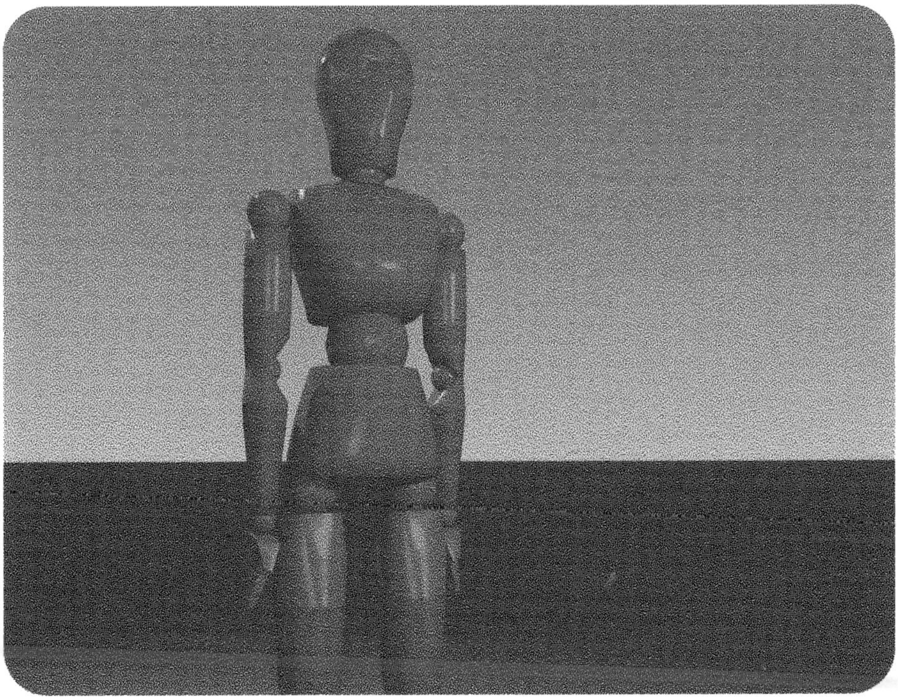

Figure 4.2 A medium shot (MS) may refer to the framing of a human from just head to just below the knees, or a shot framing two persons sometimes called a two-shot.

Figure 4.3 A close-up (CU) may refer to the framing of a person from the top of the head to just below the neck line, or if framing an object, filling the frame with the object.

Camera Angle

The camera angle is frequently used to establish a specific viewpoint, such as to involve the audience in sharing a particular character's perspective on the action. The goal may be to enhance identification with that person's psychological or philosophical point of view.

Point-of-View Shot (POV Shot)

A point-of-view shot places the camera in the approximate spatial positioning of a specific character. It is often preceded by a shot of a character looking in a particular direction, which establishes the character's spatial point of view within the setting, followed by a shot of that same character's reaction to what he or she has seen. The latter shot is sometimes called a *reaction shot.* A closely related shot is the *over-the-shoulder shot* (OS). The camera is positioned so that the shoulder of one subject appears in the foreground and the face or body of another in the background. Another variation on the point-of-view shot is the *subjective shot,* which shows us what the person is looking at or thinking about. Like point-of-view shots, subjective shots offer a nonobjective viewpoint on actions and events, and can enhance audience identification with more subjective points of view (Figures 4.4 and 4.5).

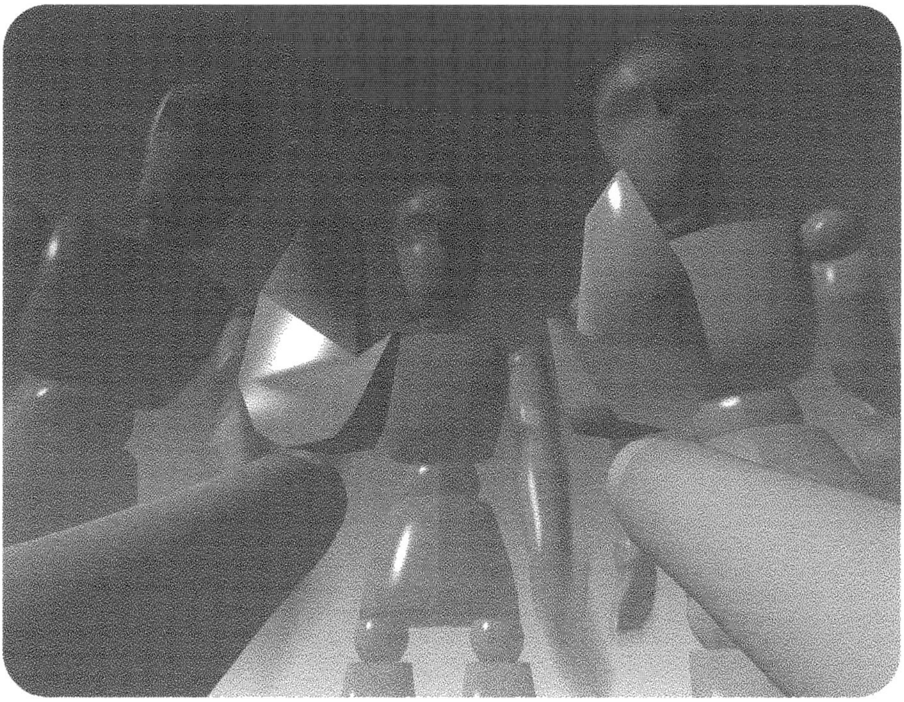

Figure 4.4 A point-of-view (POV) refers to framing as if the observer were viewing from inside the camera or if the camera lens represented what a character would be viewing from their position in the set.

Figure 4.5 An over-the-shoulder (OS) refers to a two shot from behind one of the subjects who is facing the other subject. Generally the framing is a medium shot.

Reverse-Angle Shot

A reverse-angle shot places the camera in exactly the opposite direction of the previous shot. The camera is moved in a 180-degree arc from the shot immediately preceding it.

Low-Angle Shot

A low-angle shot places the camera closer to the floor than the normal camera height, which is usually at eye level. A low angle tends to exaggerate the size and importance of the subject (Figure 4.6).

High-Angle Shot

The high-angle shot places the camera high above the subject and tends to reduce its size and importance (Figure 4.7).

Overhead Shot

An overhead shot places the camera directly overhead and creates a unique perspective on the action. This can sometimes be accomplished by a set of periscope mirrors, an overhead track, or by attaching the camera to an airplane, helicopter, or crane (Figure 4.8).

Figure 4.6 A low angle shot is the view from a camera positioned well below the eye level of the subject looking up at the subject.

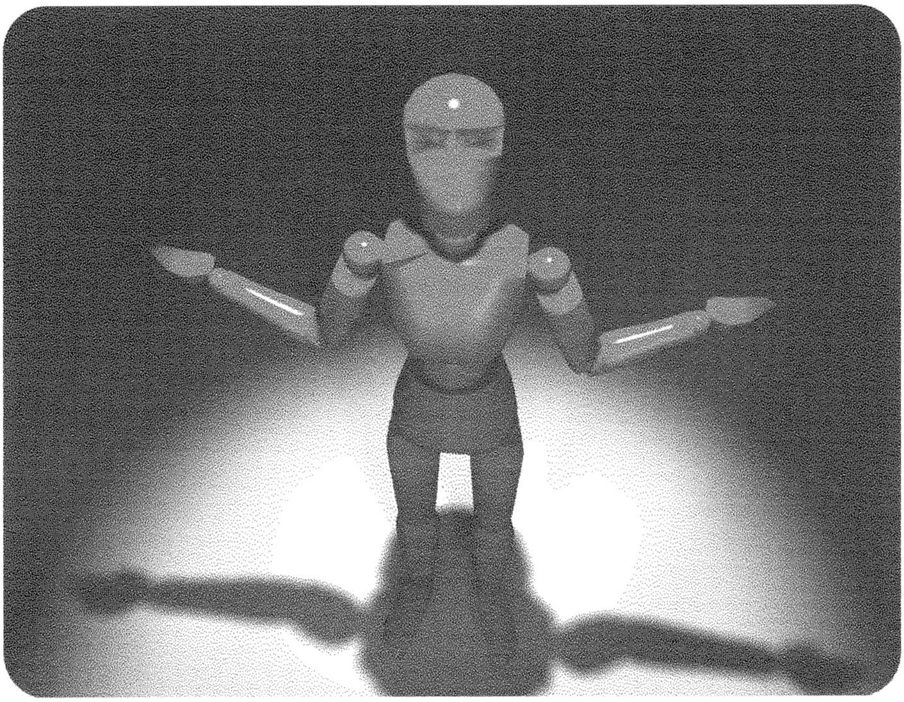

Figure 4.7 A high angle shot is the view from a camera positioned well above the eye level of the subject looking down on the subject.

Figure 4.8 Among many other means of mounting either film or video cameras is the gyroscope mount which can be mounted on an airplane, helicopter, or any moving vehicle. The stabilizing system provides a solid smooth picture which the operator inside the vehicle can pan, tilt, and/or zoom the camera as the shot requires.

Stationary versus Mobile Camera Shots

An objectively recorded scene in a drama establishes a point of view that conforms to the audience's main focus of interest in the unfolding events. This objective placement of cameras can still be quite varied. A director can use a continuously moving camera gliding through the scene to follow the key action. This approach establishes a point of view that is quite different from recording a scene from several stationary camera positions. Both approaches can be objective in the sense that neither attempts to present a specific person's point of view, although a moving camera creates a greater feeling of participation and involvement as the audience moves through the setting with the camera.

A moving camera adds new information to the frame and often alters spatial perspective. A moving camera shot can maintain viewer interest for a longer period of time than a stationary camera shot. But a moving camera shot can also create difficulties. It is often difficult to cut from a moving camera shot to a stationary camera shot. The camera should be held still for a moment at the beginning and end of a moving camera shot so that it can easily be intercut with other shots. One moving camera shot can follow another so long as the direction and speed of movement remain the same. Both moving the camera and cutting from one stationary camera shot to another can give us a spatial impression of the setting from a variety of perspectives, but the former generates feelings of smoothness and relaxation, while the latter creates an impression of roughness and tension, as used in *Natural Born Killers*. Many types of mobile camera shots can be recorded with the camera remaining in a relatively fixed position.

Pan Shot

A camera can be panned by simply pivoting it from side to side on a fixed tripod or panning device. This shot is often used to follow action without having to move the camera from its fixed floor position.

Tilt Shot

A camera tilt is accomplished by moving the camera up and down on a swivel or tilting device. This shot is also used to follow action, such as a person standing up or sitting down. It can also be used to follow and accentuate the apparent height of a building, object, or person.

Pedestal Shot

A camera can be physically moved up and down on a pedestal dolly. A hydraulic lift moves the camera vertically up and down within the shot, such as when a performer gets up from a chair or sits down. A pedestal shot allows the camera to remain consistently at the same height as the performer, unlike a tilt shot, where the camera height usually remains unchanged. Pedestal shots are rare, but a pedestal is often used to adjust the height of the camera between shots (Figure 4.9).

Zoom Shot

A zoom can be effected by changing the focal length of a variable focal length lens in midshot. A zoom shot differs from a dolly shot in that a dolly shot alters spatial

Figure 4.9
A studio pedestal is designed to allow the heavy weight of a studio camera, lens, and prompter to be moved about the studio with relative ease. The direction of the wheels under the skirt of the pedestal can be changed to allow the camera to be guided in any direction. The vertical pedestal column is counter weighted or controlled by compressed air to allow the operator to raise or lower the camera easily and smoothly. The pan head is mounted on the top of the pedestal column.

perspective by actually changing the spatial positioning of objects within the frame. During a zoom shot the apparent distance between objects appears to change because objects are enlarged or contracted in size at different rates. During a zoom-in objects appear to get closer together, while during a zoom-out they seem to get farther apart. Other types of mobile camera shots require camera supports that can be physically moved about the studio.

Dolly Shot

A dolly shot is a shot in which the camera moves toward or away from the subject while secured to a movable platform on wheels. It is often needed to follow long or complicated movements of performers or to bring us gradually closer to or farther away from a person or object.

Trucking Shot

In a trucking shot, the camera is moved laterally (from side to side) on a wheeled dolly. The camera may truck with a moving subject to keep it in frame. If the dolly moves in a semicircular direction, the shot is sometimes referred to as an *arc* or *camera arc*.

Crane or Boom Shot

The camera can be secured to a crane or boom so that it can be raised and lowered or moved from side to side on a pivoting arm. This type of shot can create a dramatic effect when it places the subject in the context of a large interior space or a broad exterior vista.

Composition

Composition is a term used by painters, graphic artists, and still photographers to define the way in which images can be effectively structured within a frame. Composition is affected by the frame dimensions or aspect ratio of the specific media format. Two basic principles of composition discussed later are symmetry and closure. Composition is complicated by the fact that video and film images move in time. Therefore, composition is constantly changing.

Aspect Ratio

A frame limits the outer borders of the image to specific dimensions. The ratio of these dimensions, that is, the ratio of a frame's width to its height, is called the *aspect ratio* of the frame. Composition is obviously slightly different for different aspect ratios. If you were to put identical paintings in frames with different dimensions and aspect ratios, for example, the paintings would look very different. The relations between shapes and objects or composition within the frames would not be the same. Video, Super-8mm, 16mm, and standard 35mm film all have the same aspect ratio: 4:3 or 1.33:1. But feature films in super 16mm, 35mm, and 65mm, which are made for wide-screen projection in theaters, have aspect ratios that vary from 1.85:1 to 2.35:1.

High-Definition TV (HDTV) may closely approximate the 1.85:1 academy aperture feature film format or aspect ratio. Wide-screen images can enhance an illusion of reality by involving more of our peripheral or edge vision, but they also alter the aesthetics of object placement and composition within the frame. Consider the different impressions created by a wide gulf between two characters on wide screen and a greater proximity of two characters in the same video frame. It is difficult to copy or transfer visuals from one aspect ratio to another intact, such as copying magazine photographs with a video camera or showing a widescreen film on television (Figure 4.10).

Essential Area

An important factor in terms of frame dimensions is the concept of essential area. The full video or film camera frame is rarely, if ever, viewed in its entirety. Part of the border or edge of the full frame is cut off during transmission and conversion in the home receiver. *Essential* or *critical area* refers to the portion of the full frame that will actually be viewed. All key information, actions, and movements must be safely kept within this essential area.

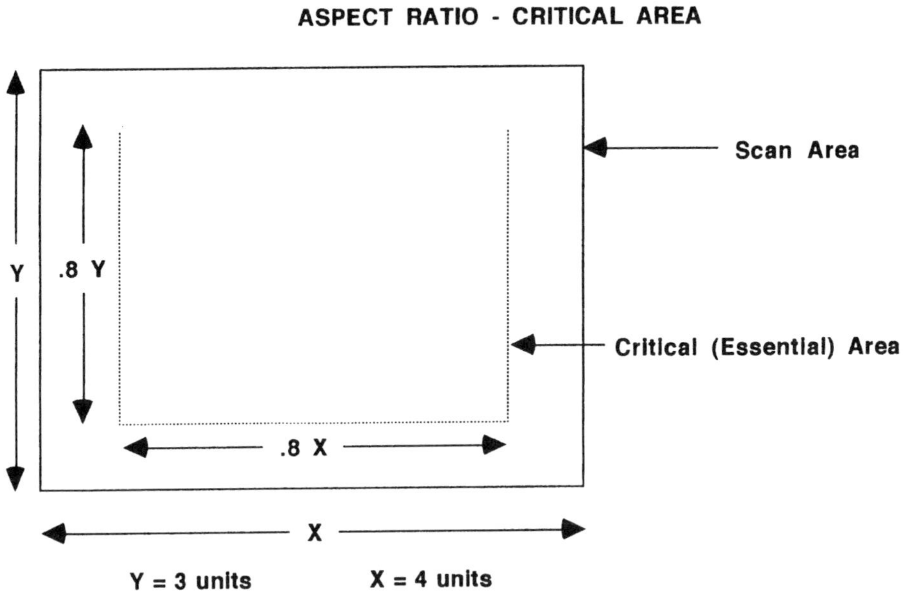

Figure 4.10 The aspect ratio is the ratio of the height (Y axis) of a frame by the width (X axis). The standard (except for wide screen film and ATV) is 3 x 4. Critical or essential area is considered to be the portion within the frame outlined by a 10 percent border of the full scanned area.

Rule of Thirds

One well-practiced theory of composition involves dividing the frame into thirds, both horizontally and vertically. If you mentally draw two vertical and two horizontal lines that divide the frame into thirds, objects can then be arranged along the lines. Important objects may be placed at the points where these lines intersect for added interest or emphasis. Following the rule of thirds allows a picture to be quickly comprehended in an aesthetically pleasing way. Placing subjects in this manner is more interesting than simply bisecting the frame. Other slightly more complicated forms of visual composition can also be used with success, but they are not always comprehended so quickly and easily (Figure 4.11).

Symmetry

Symmetry is an important aesthetic principle of composition in any two-dimensional, framed visual medium. A director can create a symmetrical or balanced spatial pattern by using objects in the frame. A symmetrical frame appears stable and solid, but eventually uninteresting and boring as well. An asymmetrically or unbalanced frame is more volatile and interesting but can also be extremely distracting. When properly used, both symmetrically and asymmetrically organized frames can be pleasing and effective.

The key is to know when it is appropriate to use one form of composition rather than the other. Framing the head of one person talking directly into the

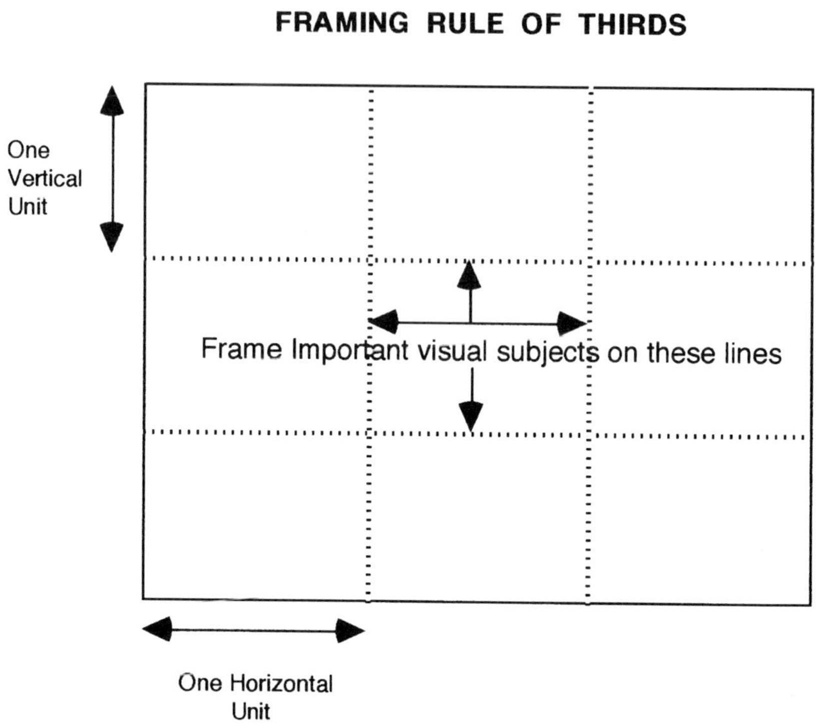

Figure 4.11 The rule of thirds divides the frame into nine areas by drawing two vertical lines one-third of the way in from each side and two horizontal lines drawn one-third of the way from the bottom and the top of the frame.

camera in an asymmetrical pattern can be distracting. The audience's attention is supposed to focus on the spokesperson, but it is distracted by the lack of balance in the frame. An asymmetrical image of one or more people in the frame can suggest that someone or something is missing. The entrance of another person or character then balances the frame (Figures 4.12 and 4.13).

An asymmetrical frame can suggest that something is wrong or that the world is out of balance. The concept of symmetry must be integrated with the rule of thirds and other concepts, such as lookspace, walkspace, and headroom. *Lookspace* refers to the additional space left in the frame in the direction of a performer's look or glance at something or someone outside the frame. *Walkspace* is the additional space in the frame left in front of a moving performer. Following the rule of thirds, the performer's face in the case of a look or glance, and the performer's body in the case of a walk or run, is placed on one of the trisecting vertical lines, leaving two thirds of the remaining space in the direction of the glance or movement. This asymmetrical composition is much better than having the performer in the exact center of the frame (Figure 4.14).

Headroom refers to the space left in the frame above the subject's head, which is most pleasing visually when there is a slight gap between the top of the head and the top of the frame.

SYMMETRICAL FRAMING

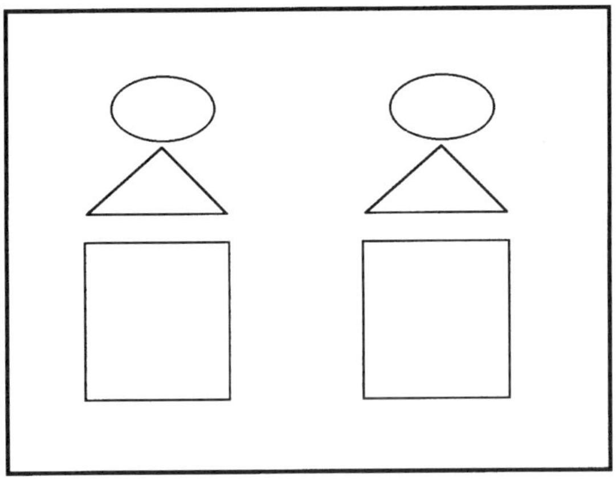

ASYMMETRICAL FRAMING

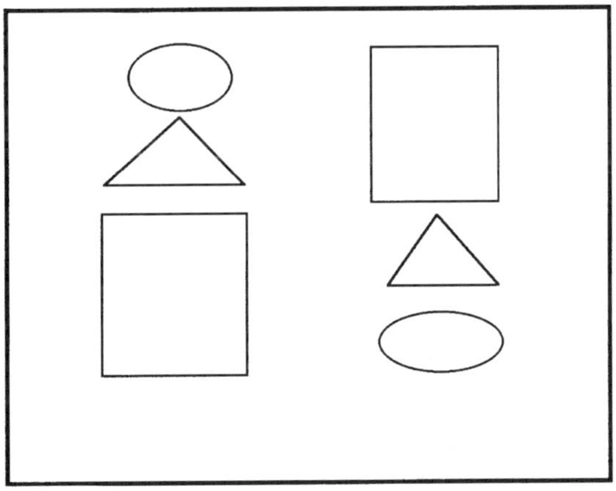

Figures 4.12 and 4.13 Symmetrical balance in composing the objects within a frame show exactly the same items on each side of a line drawn down the middle of the frame. Asymmetrical framing can vary from equal weight of objects on each side of the frame to totally unbalanced as well as asymmetrical groupings of objects.

Closure

The concept of lookspace is related to another aspect of visual composition, called *closure.* On-screen space, that is, space within the frame, often suggests continuity with off-screen space. An open frame suggests that on-screen space and objects continue into off-screen space. A completely closed frame, on the other hand, gives the illusion of being self-contained and complete in itself. The way in which an image is framed and objects are arranged can create a sense of closure or a sense of openness. Symmetrically framing a performer's head in the center of the frame creates a sense of closure. The composition does not allude to parts of the body that are missing off-screen. Framing body parts between normal joints of an arm, leg, or waist, on the other hand, suggests continuity in off-screen space. Something appears to be missing, although our memories readily fill in the missing parts (Figure 4.15).

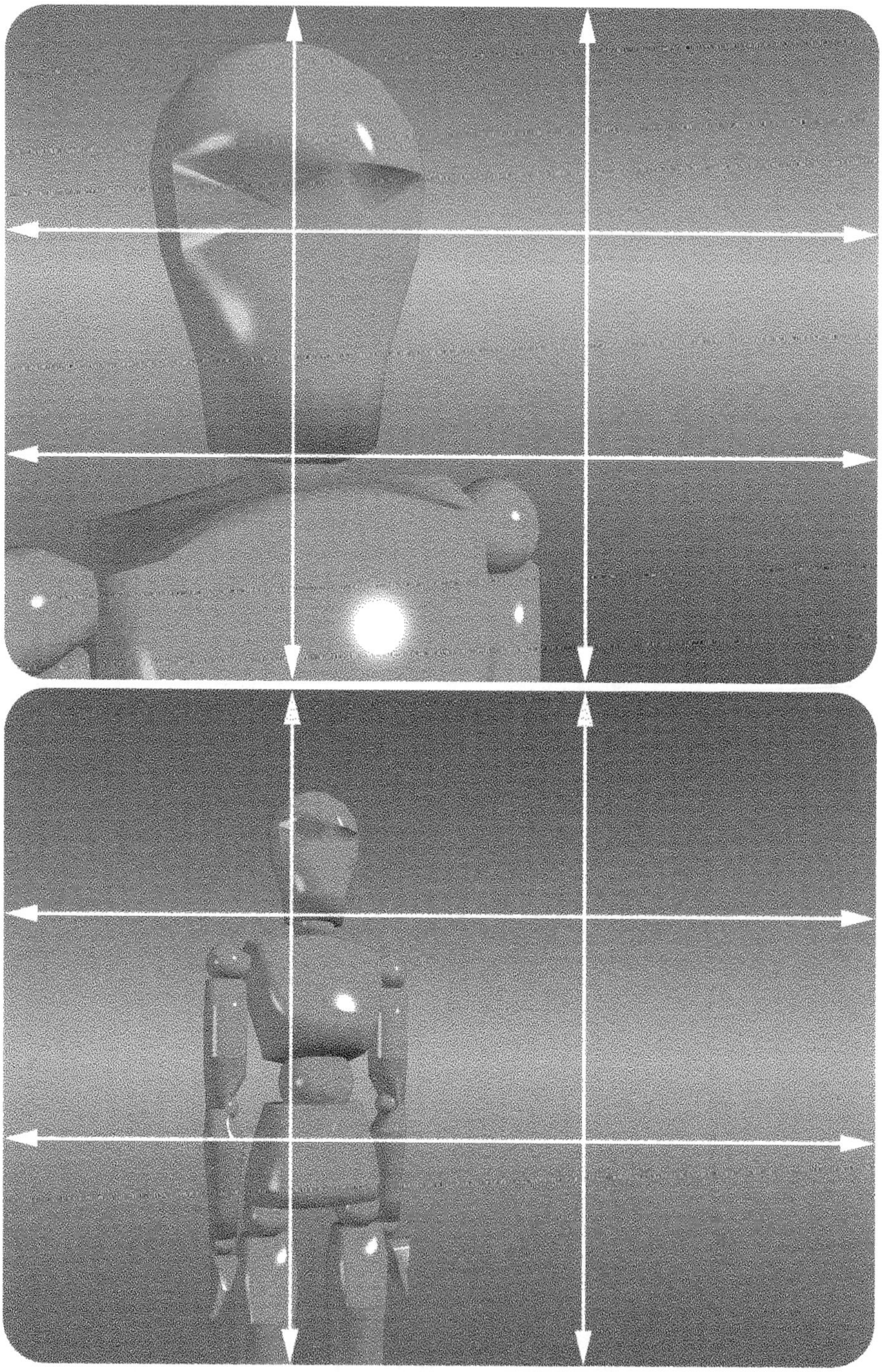

Figure 4.14 Any object either moving in the frame or facing in an obvious direction needs room to "move" and "look" within the frame. A common framing practice is to place such subjects on either of the lines splitting the frame into nine sections.

Depth and Perspective

Screen composition can enhance an illusion of depth and three dimensionality. Lighting can add depth to the image by helping to separate foreground objects from their backgrounds. Placing the camera at an angle so that two sides of an object are visible at the same time creates three dimensionality. Including foreground objects in a frame can enhance the illusion of depth by setting a yardstick by which the distance, size, and scale of the background can be determined. A person, tree branch, or object of known scale in the foreground can set a context for depth. Diagonal or parallel lines, such as those of a railroad track, can guide the eye to important objects in the frame and create a greater illusion of depth. Placing objects or people at several different planes of action within the frame and frames within frames, such as a person standing inside a doorway, increase the perception of depth within the frame.

Of course, a certain degree of care must be exercised when using multiple planes of action so that two planes do not unintentionally connect to create one confused plane, as when a plant in the background appears to be growing out of a person's head. *Image perspective* refers to the apparent depth of the image and the spatial positioning of objects in different planes. Perspective can be affected by the type of lens that is used. Telephoto or long focal-length lenses often seem to reduce apparent depth, while wide-angle or short focal-length lenses seem to expand space and apparent depth. Lenses help an image look deep or shallow. A moving camera, as in a dolly shot, can also affect the apparent depth and perspective by changing the relationship between objects in the frame. Cutting from one camera angle to another can help create an illusion of three dimensionality out of two-dimensional video and film images.

Frame Movement

A moving frame changes visual composition. In video and film, composition is constantly in flux due to camera or subject movement. In this respect, film and video are quite unlike photography and painting, which present motionless images. One type of composition can quickly change to its opposite. A symmetrical frame can quickly become asymmetrical or an open frame closed. The illusion of depth can be enhanced by the movement of a camera or of objects within the frame. Objects that move toward or away from the camera naturally create a greater sense of depth than those that move laterally with respect to the camera. Diagonal lines of movement, such as diagonal lines within a static frame, add dynamism and force to the composition. A canted frame can also add a sense of dynamic strength to an image, such as an exciting shot within a car chase, but a canted frame used in less intense action sequences often looks out of place.

Image Qualities

A director must be conscious of subtle differences in image tonality, especially when editing or combining images. *Image tonality* refers to the overall appearance of the image in terms of contrast (gradations of brightness from white to black) and color. Image contrast can be affected by lighting and recording materials. Combining two shots that have very different contrast levels can be disconcerting to the viewer, but it can also arouse attention. A high-contrast scene, that is, one

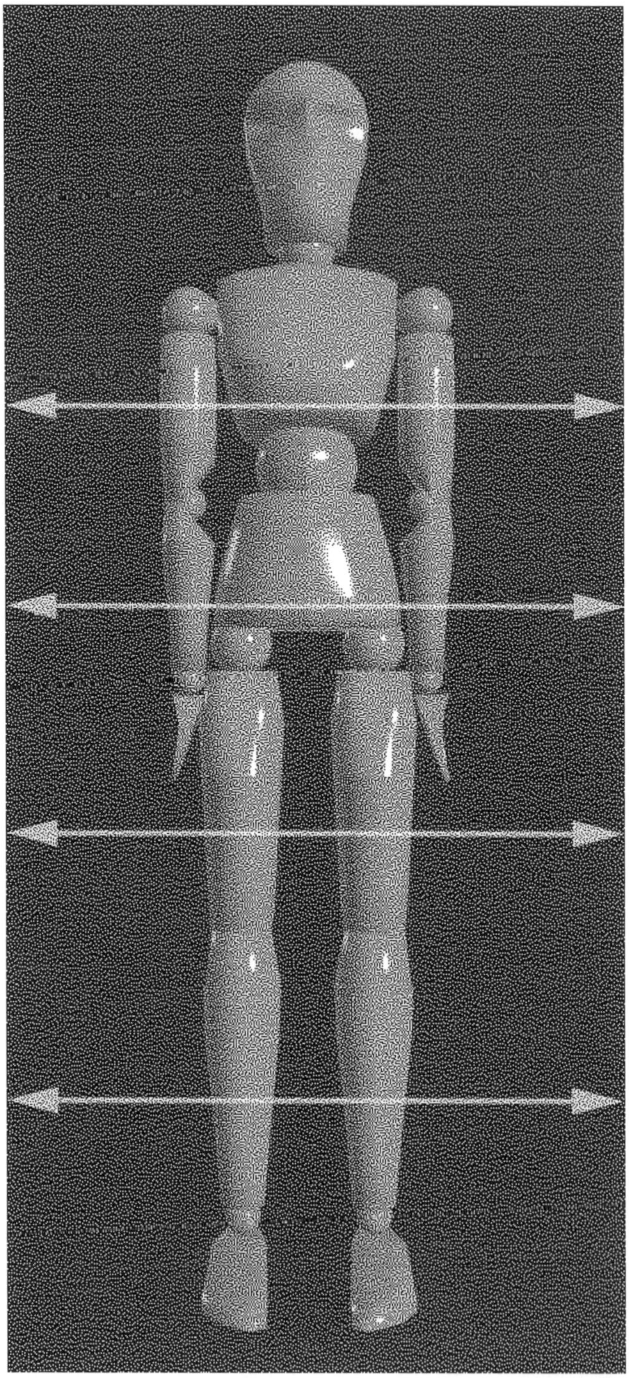

Figure 4.15
Logical cut-off points to keep in mind when framing subjects DO NOT fall at the joints of the body. To allow for closure and assumption the body continues beyond the cut-off point, camera operators must frame subject BETWEEN joints, that is between ankle and knee, or between waist and breast.

that has a limited range of gray tones with mostly dark black and bright whites, will look quite different from a low-contrast scene, which has a wide range of intermediate tones. Matching image tonalities in terms of contrast and color can help effect smooth transitions from shot to shot and scene to scene. Combining mismatched tones can have a shock or attention-getting value. Excessive contrast is a common problem in video production, especially field production, where outdoor lighting is difficult to control. High contrast is sometimes more of a problem in video than in film, due to the wider range of contrasting shades or tonalities the latter can record, but it is an important consideration in both media.

Scale and Shape

Scale refers to the apparent size of objects within the frame. Camera-to-subject distance, camera angle, and the type of lens used can affect the apparent size of objects. Lower camera positions and angles sometimes increase the apparent size of an object in the frame. The apparent size of an object can increase or decrease its importance.

Directors can create a balanced/symmetrical frame by arranging objects of equivalent size or similar shape in different parts of the same frame. Graphic similarities, such as similarities in the shape or color of objects, can create smooth transitions between shots. Graphic differences can be used to create an asymmetrical frame or to emphasize transitions from one shot to another.

Speed of Motion

Images can have different speeds of motion. *Speed of motion* refers to the speed at which objects appear to move within the frame. This speed can be changed by altering the film recording speed or the video playback speed to produce fast motion or slow motion. Editing many short-duration shots together can enhance the speed of motion, while using fewer shots of longer duration can help slow down actions and the speed of motion. The pace of editing is called *editing tempo*. The apparent motion of objects is also affected by camera placement, lenses, and the actual motion of the photographed objects. A long focal-length lens often slows down apparent motion by squashing space, while a wide-angle lens can speed up motion by expanding the apparent distance traveled in a given period of time.

Combining Shots

One of the director's key jobs, which is shared by the editor during postproduction, is to determine the precise duration of each shot. An exposition section may call for a number of long takes that slow down the action and allow the audience to contemplate character, situation, and setting. A dramatic climax, on the other hand, may call for many different short-duration shots, which help intensify the action. The famous three-minute shower scene murder in Alfred Hitchcock's *Psycho* (1960), for example, is made up of well over 100 separate pieces of film cut together to intensify the action. Modernist aestheticians, such as Sergei Eisenstein, have sometimes advocated the use of many short-duration shots, while realist aestheticians, such as André Bazin, have often recommended the use of longer duration shots.

A good director is usually a good editor; that is, directors know how and when to combine specific images. Editing begins with an understanding of composition, image qualities, and different types of shots. Shots can be combined using a variety of transition devices, including straight cuts, fades, dissolves, wipes, and digital transitions.

Straight Cut or Take

A straight cut or take is a direct, instantaneous change from one camera shot to another, say from a long shot of a scene to a close-up of a performer's face. Time is assumed to be continuous over a straight cut, except in the case of jump cuts, where actions are discontinuous and do not match from one shot to the next, suggesting a gap in time. If a cut is made from a shot of a person talking to someone on one side of a room to a second shot showing the same person talking to someone else on the opposite side, the result is a jump cut. Jump cuts are widely used in commercials, in which stories are condensed to thirty seconds by using rapid editing tempos, and in documentary and news interviews, where this procedure is sometimes considered more honest than using cutaways to mask deletions. It is becoming more and more common to use jump cuts to compress time in fiction as well.

Fade

The picture of a video program or film can fade in from blackness to image or fade out from image to blackness. A fade-out followed by a fade-in usually indicates a significant passage of time. A fade, like a curtain on the stage, can be used to mark the beginning and the end of a performance and to separate acts or scenes (Figure 4.16).

Dissolve

A dissolve is actually a simultaneous fade-out and fade-in. One scene or shot fades out at the same time that another shot fades in to replace it. For a very short duration, the two shots are superimposed on one another. Dissolves are frequently used to conceal or smooth over gaps in time rather than emphasizing them as in a fade-out and fade-in. A very rapid dissolve is sometimes called a *soft cut* or *lap dissolve.*

Wipe

A wipe is a transition device created on a switcher, special effects generator, or an optical film bench whereby one image or shot is gradually replaced on the screen by another. A wipe may begin on one side of the screen and move across to engulf the opposite side. It can also begin in the middle of the frame and move outward. Ending one shot by dollying or zooming in to a black object that fills the frame and beginning the next shot by dollying or zooming out from a black object is sometimes called a *natural wipe* (Figure 4.17).

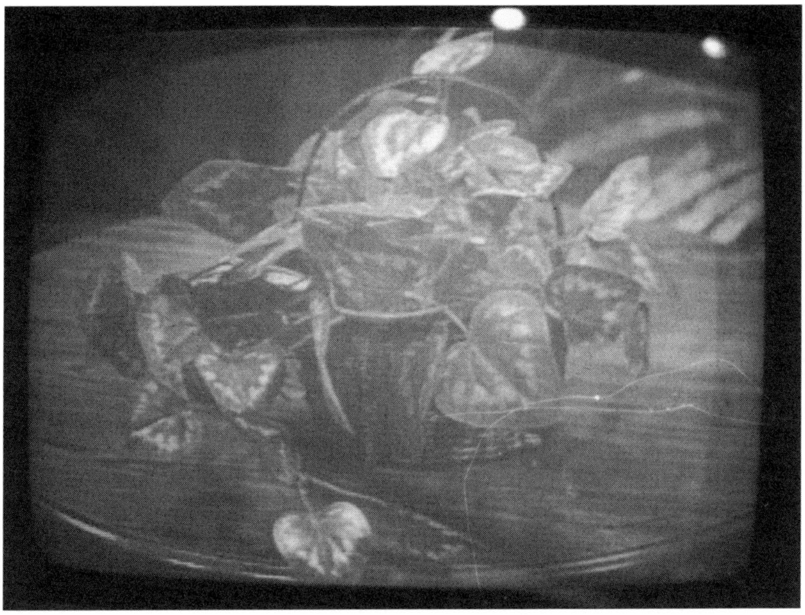

Figure 4.16 A fade to black shows the image slowly darkening until it disappears. A fade in from black starts with a totally blank frame and then the first image slowly appears.

Figure 4.17 A wipe appears as one image is replaced by another with a line or one of a wide number of different patterns separating the two images. A wipe stopped at a mid-point creates a split screen.

Digital Transitions

A wide variety of effects now can be created with a digital effects generator. Page turns, shots on each side of rotating blocks, a subject morphing into another subject, shots disintegrating into another shot, plus virtually any transition imaginable are all possible through the use of digital switchers (Figure 4.18).

Defocus

Placing one image out of focus and gradually bringing a replacement image into focus is a defocus transition.

Swish Pan

A rapid movement of the camera on the tripod swivel or panning head causes a blurring of the image, which can be used as a swish pan transition from one scene to another. This transition is frequently accompanied by up-tempo music, which accelerates the sense of action and movement rather than creating a pause.

Special Effects

Split Screen or Shared Screen Having one image occupy a portion of the same frame with another image is called a *shared screen.* When the frame is split into two equal parts by the two images, it is called a *split screen.* Sometimes these techniques make it possible to show two different but simultaneous actions on the same screen.

Figure 4.18 A digital effect is any one of a number of transitions such as page turns, unique patterns, or three-dimensional transitions.

Superimposition Having two different shots occupy the same complete frame simultaneously is called a *superimposition.* One shot is usually dominant over the other to avoid visual confusion. The superimposed images should not be excessively detailed or busy. In effect, a superimposition looks like a dissolve that has been stopped while in progress. Combining a long shot and close-up of the same person from different angles sometimes creates an effective superimposition (Figure 4.19).

Keying and Chroma Key A specific portion of a video image can be completely replaced with a second image using keying or chroma key techniques. Titles and graphics can be inserted into a portion of another image. A scene from a still photograph or slide can be inserted into a blue- or green-colored area (a green or blue screen on the set, for example) in another shot using video chroma key. The monochrome blue or green portion of the latter shot is replaced with the former shot.

Matte and Blue Screen A matte is used in film to black out an area in one image that will then be filled in with a second image. Matting is to film what keying is to video. Blue screening in film is equivalent to chroma key in video, since the blue screen area in one image is replaced by a second image.

Negative Image A normal visual image is positive. A negative image reverses the brightnesses and darknesses of the original image. Blacks become whites and whites become blacks. Colors turn into their complements. In television this can be

Figure 4.19 A superimposition is a combination of two images created by stopping a dissolve at a mid-point. Depending on the intensity of each image part of one will bleed through the other images.

done by simply reversing the polarity of the electrical picture signal. In a film a negative print can be made from a positive image.

Freeze Frame A freeze frame is a continuing still image from one frame of a video or film shot created during postproduction. Usually the action stops by freezing the last frame of a shot, such as at the conclusion of a film or video program.

Scene Construction

A scene is a series of shots of action occurring in continuous time at one place. It is important to ensure that significant changes in camera angle and/or camera-to-subject distance occur between two successive shots within a scene. The camera angle should change at least forty-five degrees with respect to the subject from one shot to the next, unless there is a significant change in camera-to-subject distance. A few aesthetic reasons for making a cut that involves a change of camera-to-subject distance are (1) to depict an action that was omitted in the previous shot, (2) to provide a closer look at an event or object, (3) to emphasize an object or action, and (4) to draw back and establish the setting. A cut from a medium shot to a close-up provides a closer look at an object or event, while a cut from a long shot to a close-up emphasizes an object or action. Cutting from a medium shot to a long shot helps to reestablish the setting and place the action in context or in broader spatial perspective.

A conventionally constructed scene might begin with a long shot or establishing shot to place the subjects within a specific setting. Then the camera gets progressively closer to the subject as the action intensifies, and finally the camera pulls back to reestablish the setting at the conclusion of the scene. An alternative approach is to begin a scene with a close-up and gradually pull back from shot to shot to reveal more and more of the setting as the action progresses. The latter approach is initially somewhat confusing and spatially disorienting, but it also arouses viewer curiosity.

Certain types of cuts involve quite severe changes in camera-to-subject distance, such as those from long shot to close-up or vice versa. In realist situations, these dramatic changes of scale should be used sparingly and primarily for emphasis, because they often have a distracting effect on the audience. More gradual changes of scale are less disruptive and provide a smoother transition. A new shot or image should serve a purpose different from that of the previous shot. It can anticipate the audience's next point of interest, that is, it can be psychologically motivated on the basis of viewer expectations. It can present additional or contrasting information by revealing actions that were hidden from a previous angle. In general, every shot should be cut as short as it can be without inhibiting its function. A good director separates essential from nonessential information to determine how long a specific shot will maintain viewer interest.

Continuity Editing

Continuity editing usually means creating a smooth flow from one shot to the next. Actions that begin in one shot are completed in the following shot with no apparent gaps in time. There is continuity in the spatial placement and the screen direction of moving and stationary objects from shot to shot. Conventional continuity can, of course, be disrupted in time and space. Gaps or jump cuts in the action can be consciously edited into a scene. Actions can be repeated over and over again, slowed down, and speeded up. But it is important to learn the basics of continuity editing before attempting to disrupt it. Beginning video and film directors need to first acquire some appreciation of the difficulty inherent in trying to maintain continuity and in meeting conventional viewer expectations.

Pace and Rhythm

The selection of long- and short-duration shots affects the pace or rhythm of a scene. A director must be very sensitive to changes in pace and rhythm. To build a scene out of different shots, a director must match the tempo or rhythm of the editing to the subject matter and the audience's expectations. Rapidly cutting together many short-duration shots for a how-to film about woodworking, for example, distracts the audience's attention from the primary subject matter. Slow-paced editing for a soft drink commercial may be extremely boring and an ineffective persuasion technique. A fast-paced exposition and a slow-paced climax in a dramatic production usually fail to achieve the desired emotional effect and dramatic structure.

Compression and Expansion of Time

Directors can compress and expand time through editing, even while preserving the illusion of temporal continuity. For example, suppose that you wish to record the action of someone getting dressed and ready for work in the morning. A single shot of this activity that preserved exact temporal continuity might last ten minutes or more in actual duration. But by recording different segments of action and editing them together, the essential elements of the activity can be preserved without creating any readily apparent gaps in time. How can this be done? Simply by cutting from a long shot of the action to a close-up of a hand or an object in the room, and then cutting back to a long shot in which the person is more completely dressed than could actually have occurred in the duration of the close-up.

A director can speed up an action by eliminating unimportant or repetitious actions between cuts. The action and time are condensed and compressed. The same technique can be used for someone crossing a street. For instance, we begin with a full shot or long shot of the person starting to step off one curb, then cut to a medium shot and then a close-up of his or her feet or face. Finally, we present a long shot of the person reaching the other side of the street. This edited version of the street crossing might last just five seconds, while actually walking across the street takes more than twenty seconds. Condensing or compressing action can increase the pace and interest of actions. Actions can also be expanded through editing. An action can be shown, followed by the thoughts of one or more of the characters as the action occurs. In reality the action and the thinking would have occurred simultaneously, but in a media production each must be shown separately, lengthening the time it takes to depict the actual time of the incident.

Screen Directionality

Depicting a three-dimensional world in a two-dimensional medium presents the director with special problems of screen directionality. *Screen directionality* refers to the consistent direction of movements and object placement from one shot to the next. Inconsistent screen direction causes spatial confusion. What viewers actually see seems to contradict their expectations. This type of confusion can be effective in music videos and formative works of art. But, in general, maintaining directional consistency of looks and glances, object placements, and subject movements within the frame reduces viewer confusion by increasing spatial clarity in realist and functionalist works.

Directional Glances

It is important to record a consistent pattern of performers' spatial looks and glances within the frame to preserve an illusion of reality. The improper placement of a camera can result in confusing inconsistencies (which again can be useful in a modernist approach). A close-up of one character looking screen left at a second character is usually followed by a shot of the other character looking screen right to suggest that he is looking back at the first character. When one person looks down at another person, the other should look up within the frame of the second shot, and so on. The camera must be placed and the image framed so that there is directional consistency from one shot to the next.

The 180-Degree Axis of Action Rule

The 180-degree rule of camera placement ensures directional consistency from shot to shot. An imaginary line can be drawn to connect stationary subjects. Once the camera is placed on one side or the other of this axis of action, all subsequent camera placement must occur on the same side of the line to prevent a reversal in the placement of objects in the frame (Figure 4.20).

A moving subject establishes a vector line, and all camera placements are made on one side of this line or the other to maintain consistent screen direction of movement. If the camera crossed this line, a subject going from left to right in one shot would appear to be going in the opposite direction in the next shot. There are ways to break the 180-degree rule without creating spatial confusion or disrupting an illusion of reality. First, the camera can move across the line during a single shot, establishing a new rule on the opposite side of the line to which all subsequent shots must conform. A director can also cut directly to the line itself by placing the camera along the line and then cross over the line in the next shot to establish a new rule. Finally, the subject can change direction with respect to the camera during a shot and thus establish a new line.

Sound and Image Interaction

An overvaluation of visual images can lead directors to neglect accompanying sounds, but sound is an extremely important aspect of video and film production. Sound can complement and fill out the image. It can also conflict with corresponding images or produce an independent experience. Sound can shape the way in which images are interpreted. It can direct our attention to a specific part of the image or to things not included in the image. Some sounds and music have the ability to stimulate feelings directly. Sounds can create a realistic background or a unique, abstract, impressionistic world.

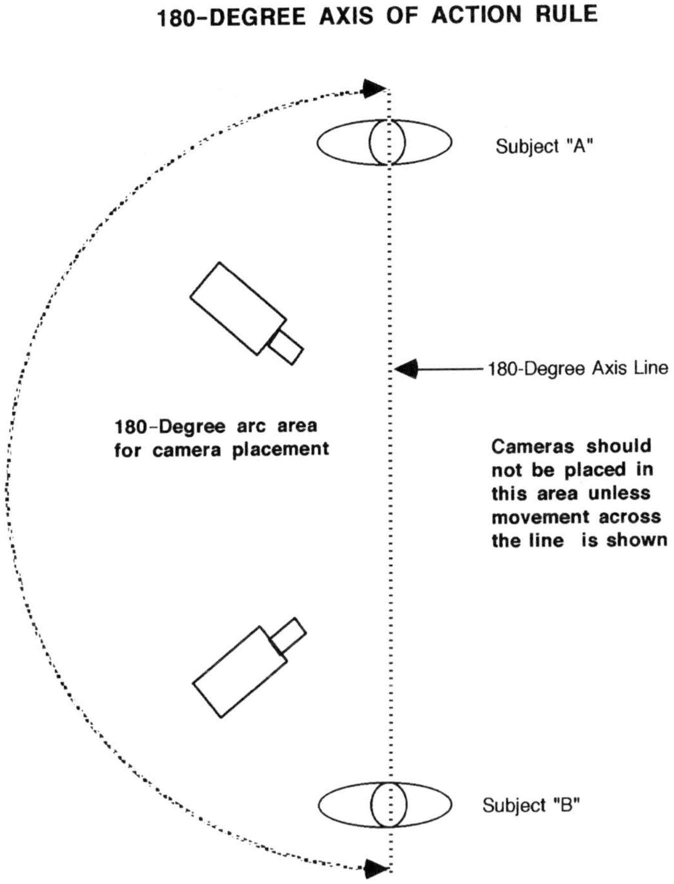

Figure 4.20 A line drawn through the two main subjects in a scene divides the plot into two areas, one on each side of that line. Once shooting in that scene has started on one side of the line, the rest of the scene must be shot from that same side unless a shot moves from one side to the other while recording.

Sound and image relations can be divided into four oppositional categories: (1) on-screen versus off-screen sounds, (2) commentative versus actual sounds, (3) synchronous versus asynchronous sounds, and (4) parallel versus contrapuntal sounds. Understanding each of these categories opens up a broad range of aesthetic possibilities. This section concludes with a separate consideration of combining music and visual images from two different standpoints: editing images to prerecorded music and composing original music for video and film.

On-Screen versus Off-Screen Sound

A sound coming from a source that is visible within the frame is called an *on-screen sound. Off-screen sounds* come from sources assumed to be just outside the frame. The use of off-screen sounds can enhance spatial depth. Noel Burch, a media theorist, has pointed out that an off-screen sound can seem to come from six possible positions outside the frame: from the left, from the right, from above, from below, from behind the wall at the back of the frame, and from behind the camera. The precise spatial placement of an off-screen sound is not always discernible. Stereophonic or multichannel sound obviously helps us to determine the position of an off-screen sound, but the effect is the same. Our attention is directed off-screen to the source of the sound, particularly if on-screen performers are looking in the appropriate direction. By arousing our curiosity, off-screen sound can set up an expectation of the visual presentation of its source. It can also break down some of the limitations of a visual frame, opening it up as a realistic window on the world, as opposed to a more abstract, self-contained, modernist aesthetic world.

Commentative versus Actual Sound

Sound and image relations can also be classified on the basis of the supposed actuality or artificiality of their sound sources. Commentative sound has no known source, while actual sound is presumed to come from some actual or real sound source either inside or just outside the frame. Spoken dialogue is usually actual sound. Narration is commentative sound, unless the narrator appears on-screen. Music can be either commentative or actual sound. Scoring is commentative sound, and source music is actual sound. Commentative sound effects, such as shrill metallic sounds that have no readily apparent source, can help to create a impressionistic emotionally charged atmosphere. Commentative music, narration, and sound effects can be effectively used to reinforce specific feelings. Lush, romantic music, for example, might complement a romantic scene, such as the reunion of long-separated lovers, although such conventions easily become musical clichés.

Synchronous versus Asynchronous Sound

Synchronous sounds match their on-screen sources. Lip-sync sounds synchronize with the lip movements of the on-screen speaker. Sound effects match their on-screen sound sources. For example, the sounds of a runner's feet striking the pavement should be synchronized with the corresponding visual images. Music can also be said to be synchronous with visual actions or cuts that precisely follow the beat or rhythm. Asynchronous sound does not match its sound source. Poor quality lip-sync is asynchronous sound, such as a film dubbed into a foreign language that fails to match the lip movements of the speaker. But asynchronous sound is not always poor quality sound. In fact, asynchronous sound offers many exciting aesthetic possibilities, such as providing a basis for contrapuntal sound. Commentative sound effects can be used asynchronously to contrast with their corresponding visuals. One example is the substitution of a train whistle for a woman's scream in Alfred Hitchcock's *The Thirty-Nine Steps* (1935). Commentative, asynchronous sound effects can produce emotional effects or meanings that counterpoint rather than parallel their accompanying visual images.

Parallel versus Contrapuntal Sound

The emotional effect or conceptual meaning of sounds and images can be virtually the same or completely different. Speech, sound effects, and music can parallel the meaning or emotions of the visuals, or they can counterpoint them. The term *counterpoint* in music refers to two separate and distinguishable melodies that are played simultaneously, as discussed earlier. The same term has been applied to image and sound interaction in video and film. Contrapuntal sound has an emotional effect or conceptual meaning that is separate from its corresponding visuals. Sounds and images are aesthetically separate and often contrast with one another.

Parallel sound, like musical harmony, blends together with its corresponding visuals. Like musical notes played simultaneously and in harmony, sounds and images can have parallel meanings or emotions that are mutually supportive. Suppose that the visually depicted events are sad or tragic but the accompanying music is upbeat and in a major key, so that it communicates a bright, happy, strong feeling. In this case the music counterpoints the corresponding visuals. The same thing happens when sad music accompanies a happy event. But when sad, minor key music accompanies a tragic scene, the sounds and images parallel one another in emotional tone.

Speech sounds and sound effects can parallel or counterpoint their corresponding images. For example, the film musical *Singin' in the Rain* (1952) begins with the main character, Don Lockwood, describing his path to Hollywood stardom. Lockwood gives a short autobiography to his fans in which he claims to have received his training and background at elite, high-class schools and cultural institutions. But what we see contradicts his voice-over narration. We see that he actually began his performance career in pool halls and bars, and gradually worked his way into the movies as a stuntman. His elitist posturing provides a pseudosophisticated, tongue-in-cheek commentary on Hollywood. The meaning of what we see contradicts the meaning of what we hear, producing a powerfully humorous effect.

Composing Images for Prerecorded Music

The use of music in video and film is a rather complex art. It is important for directors to understand some of the basic aesthetic possibilities inherent in two approaches to combining images and music: (1) editing visual images to preselected, prerecorded music and (2) composing original music for video and film, even if the responsibility for music is in the hands of a specialist, such as a music director, composer, or performer.

Visual images can be selected and ordered into a pattern that is prescribed by prerecorded music. For example, fast-paced music might be accompanied by rapid cutting of visual images and rapid action within the frame, while slow-paced music might call for less frequent cutting and slower movements. The visual action might reach its climax at the same time as a musical crescendo or swelling in the volume and intensity of the music. The timing of the visuals can be made to coincide with the timing of the music so that both begin and end at the same points and achieve a parallel structure throughout. Dancing and singing sequences require a high degree of synchronization and parallelism between the music and visuals. The music can be recorded in advance and used as a basis for the choreography. Prerecorded music establishes a basic structure and timing to which the performance and editing of visual images must conform, unless conscious asynchronization or contrapuntal relations between the sounds and images is desired.

Composing Music for Prerecorded Images

Another approach to music and image interaction is to compose original music for specific film or video sequences. Music composed for video or film usually serves one or more of the following functions: (1) intensifying the action or dramatic tension, (2) establishing the period or place, (3) setting the atmosphere or mood, (4) stimulating a specific emotion in conjunction with a character or theme, and (5) avoiding screen silence. Music rhythm can intensify action and create dramatic tension. The pace of music can increase with the speed of the action, such as a crescendo that accompanies a dramatic climax or crisis. Music can communicate time and place by virtue of its source, period, and style. Selecting a specific mode of music affects the overall mood or atmosphere. A specific melody can develop an emotion in conjunction with an important character or theme. Leitmotifs can intensify audience identification with specific people or characters and stimulate emotions. Finally, music can be used simply as a filler to cover silence or to attempt to create viewer interest during slow-paced visual action sequences.

Background music is all too frequently used to fill a void rather than to create a specific effect in conjunction with visual images. Careful selection and design of music is a much better approach to the problem. Original music for television and film can consist of sounds from a single instrument, such as a solo guitar or flute, or a fully orchestrated symphonic score. The number of musicians required and the complexity of the music can vary considerably depending on the specific needs and requirements of the project and the available budget. Sometimes a scarcity of materials and resources can be an advantage. Simple music and solo performers can be easier for beginning producers to obtain and control. New computer music programs and synthesizers make it easier to have original music composed, played, and recorded by one person. Regardless of the sophistication of the music, video and film directors should make every attempt to collaborate with composers and musicians so that the music can be designed and performed for their specific needs. Original music can be tailored to a video or film production much better than prerecorded library music.

Preparing the Shooting Script

Directors begin to apply aesthetic principles to concrete production problems when they plan a production. Production planning is usually done on paper. Directors specify shots and sound effects for each scene in the script as they prepare a final shooting script. (Figure 4.21).

After the shooting script is completed, shot lists are often written up for camera operators. Sometimes a storyboard consisting of still-frame drawings of every shot in the final shooting script is drawn up as a visual guide to production.

After carefully analyzing the script, a director begins to prepare a final shooting script by indicating specific types of shots, transition devices, and sound effects.

Directorial terms for specific types of visual images and sounds must be thoroughly learned before a shooting script can be created. Shots are continuous recordings of actions within a scene made by a single camera. Abbreviations are used to specify camera placements and movements, such as ECU (extreme close-up) or MS (medium shot), which specify the desired distance of the camera from the sub-

SHOOTING SCRIPT

1. INT WS UNIVERSITY CLASSROOM DAY 1.

Classroom is full of students, some wide awake, gossiping, others sleeping or nodding off as they wait for the professor to arrive.

2-Shot of Jane and Jack, Jane turns around in her seat to whisper to Jack.

JANE
(Quietly so only Jack can hear her.)
Are you sure there isn't going to be an exam
during tomorrow's class?

CU Jack, he leans forward toward Jane.

JACK
(With a bravado, all-knowing tone)
Of course not, have I ever lied to you?

The professor enters the room, downstage right, walks to the lectern and the room becomes quiet.

MWS from back of classroom, students in foreground, Professor in background.

PROFESSOR
(Emphatically as a reminder)
If I am forced to repeat myself again, I WILL
be forced to give you your first examination in
tomorrow's class.

MS Students as they react to Professor, groans, turning to each other in sympathy.

(DISSOLVE TO)

2. EXT WS CAMPUS DAY 2.

The clouds suddenly darken the sky as rain, thunder and lightning start and the lights go out plunging the room into darkness.

Figure 4.21 A shooting script should provide the director with enough information to shoot the scene as closely as possible to the vision the writer had when writing the script. If the script is not clear, then the director must make decisions on how specifically to shoot the scene.

ject. Where the camera is placed can have a considerable impact on what action is viewed or how a subject appears. Camera movements, such as CAMERA PANS RIGHT or CAMERA DOLLIES IN, are also specified in a shooting script, as are transitions between one shot and another, such as CUT TO, FADE OUT, FADE IN, and DISSOLVE. Camera movements add motion to the recording of a scene and can also change the perspective or point of view on a subject or action. Various transition devices are used to communicate changes of time and/or place to the audience. Sound effect designations, such as SFX (sound effect): PLANE LANDING, specify concrete sounds that should accompany specific images.

Preparing a final shooting script allows a director an opportunity to shoot and reshoot a video or film production on paper at minimal expense before actual recording begins. To compose a final shooting script, a director must understand a full range of aesthetic possibilities. There are many different ways to record a specific scene in any script. A director interprets the action and decides on the best shots, transition devices, and sound effects for each scene. Directors select specific recording techniques, such as different types of shots, for each scene on the basis of the aesthetic approach they have chosen. A director's overall aesthetic approach in large part determines the meaning of images and sounds by setting a context for interpretation. A realist approach often involves the use of techniques that help to preserve an illusion of reality through a transparent or unnoticed style. Modernist and postmodernist approaches call attention to techniques and highlights a director's manipulation and control over the recording medium and subject matter.

Some types and combinations of visual images and sounds can be realist in one context but modernist postmodernist in another. For example, jump cuts are discontinuities in human actions or movements from one shot to the next. Since they disrupt the continuous flow of realist time and space, jump cuts are often considered a modernist technique, but they are also used in news and documentary interviews. A jump cut indicates that something has been removed and is often considered more honest than using techniques which disguise the fact that editing has been done. From a modernist perspective, jump cuts, such as those in Jean-Luc Godard's *Breathless* (1959), call attention to directional control by breaking down the illusion of temporal continuity or the smooth, continuous flow of time from shot to shot, but from a realist perspective in news and documentary productions, they make it clear that the recording of an event has been edited.

Production Coordination

Video and film directors are personnel managers as well as artists with moving images and sounds. Directors coordinate production by working with their staff, crew, and performers. Frequent production meetings facilitate coordination. A cooperative, collective effort has to be carefully orchestrated and managed by the director if a quality product is to be achieved. The director must be a good judge of character.

Production Meetings

Frequent production meetings provide the director and the production staff with an opportunity to work out important details and problems collectively. Prior to actual production, the director usually meets with key staff members, such as the producer, the art director or scenic designer, and the lighting director. The overall goals and objectives of the film or video project are clarified during these meetings. Everyone must understand the overall purpose and design of the production to prevent members of the production team from working at cross purposes. Everything must be worked out and all problems solved prior to actual live video production, since live production means that there is no postproduction and therefore little or no room for mistakes during production.

The director must be able to communicate effectively with the staff if these problems are to be quickly and efficiently resolved. The more talented, independent, and opinionated the staff, crew, and performers are, the more likely it is that problems and disputes will arise, unless a common purpose has been collectively determined or hierarchically imposed at the beginning. The director's authority may be questioned, and his or her status with the staff, crew, and other performers jeopardized, if an unruly participant is allowed to dominate the proceedings. The director must be explicit and authoritative about commands. The director must also listen to the needs, desires, and problems of the staff, crew, and talent. Production meetings provide the director with an opportunity to exercise authority and give commands, but also to listen to the ideas, needs, and problems of others. Effective managers are often good listeners.

Casting

To cast a specific performance effectively, the director must have a firmly established interpretation of each character or role. Each role, however small, is important in terms of the quality of the final product, and a video or film program is often only as good as its worst performer. It is often said that almost any director can evoke an excellent performance from an experienced, talented performer but that good direction is most evident in the quality of smaller roles and bit parts. Good casting depends on a director's understanding of at least three factors: the audience, the character or role, and the physical appearance of specific performers. The natural look and feel of a performer is probably the most important factor in terms of his or her appropriateness for a specific role, although skilled actors can drastically change their appearance and still appear naturally suited to a role, for example, Robin Williams in *Mrs. Doubtfire* (1993).

Casting sessions often consist of actors reading a short scene from the script so that the director and producer can evaluate their suitability for a role. Sometimes several actors will be auditioned before a part is cast. Directors often have to deal with performers who have different levels and types of acting experience. Inexperienced actors need to be explicitly told what is wanted. Most fail to understand or prepare themselves for the rigors of video and film acting. Inexperienced performers have difficulty relating to an awkward, unfeeling camera. Constant feedback and praise from a director can greatly improve the quality of a performance. Experienced professionals, on the other hand, may require more freedom in some situations and a firmer hand in others. Most directors work somewhere in between two extremes of management styles: Either a director allows the actor to find his or her role, or the director takes an authoritative approach in order to develop a consistent interpretation (Figure 4.22).

Rehearsals

Once the performers have been selected, a director can begin a preliminary run-through of the production by helping the actors to develop their specific characters. Preliminary practices of a performance are called *rehearsals.* Rehearsals

Figure 4.22 The range an actor can portray stands them well especially if they are asked to take the part of someone as different from their own persona as Robin Williams was able to do in 20th Century Fox's production of *Mrs. Doubtfire.* (Courtesy of 20th Century Fox.)

sometimes begin with reading sessions, in which actors sit around a table and read their respective parts prior to actually performing them. Many rehearsals may be necessary before the actors are fully prepared to perform unerringly before the camera(s). All the bugs have to be worked out before a performance can proceed without problems or disruptions. The final rehearsal, which usually takes place with the sets fully dressed and the performers in costume, is called a *dress rehearsal.* It simulates the actual recording session in virtually every respect.

Multi-camera and live productions usually demand more rehearsal time than single-camera productions, because entire scenes or programs are recorded at one time rather than broken up into segments for a single camera. The entire performance must be worked out to perfection so that even minor mistakes are avoided during actual recording. Actors in single-camera productions do not always know how one shot relates to another. Single shots are often recorded in isolation, and performers cannot build a performance in perfect continuity as they would on the stage or for multiple-camera production. Close-ups are often recorded out of sequence, for example. The director must be able to provide the performer with a context that will achieve a proper performance level so that shots can be combined during postproduction editing. One of the director's primary responsibilities during rehearsal and production is to ensure that the actors maintain continuity in the dramatic levels of their performances from one shot to the next. Many directors prefer to have a complete rehearsal in advance.

Performer and Camera Blocking

The director usually stages and plots the action in two distinct stages, performer blocking and camera blocking. Prior to selecting final camera placements, angles, lenses, and so on, the director will frequently run through the basic actions to be performed by the talent. This is called *performer blocking*. A director must carefully preplan the entire performance in advance. Only rarely are the performer's movements precisely set during performer blocking alone. Instead, a general sense of the action is determined, which facilitates camera blocking and prepares the performers for actual recording.

Camera blocking refers to the placement of cameras so that they can follow the movements of the talent. Whether several cameras or a single camera will actually record the action, the director must be able to anticipate the types of shots that will provide adequate coverage, dramatic emphasis, and directional continuity from shot to shot. Shot lists can be drawn up and supplied to the camera operator(s). These lists are a helpful guide to camera operation during blocking sessions and actual production. Every consecutive shot in each scene for each camera is written on a piece of paper that the camera operator can tape to the back of the camera for easy reference. Shot lists indicate types of shots and camera movements called for in the final shooting script. In some recording situations, there is minimal time to block the cameras and the performers separately, and the two stages are combined. During camera blocking the performers, the director, and the camera operator(s) exchange ideas and discuss problems as the action is blocked or charted on the floor or on location. The director refines his or her conception and interpretation of the script, making notations of any deviations from previous shot selections. Performers not only learn and remember their lines, they must also remember their marks, that is, the precise points where they must position themselves during actual recordings (Figure 4.23).

Multiple-Camera Directing

Directing several cameras simultaneously requires a different approach from that of single-camera recording. The preproduction planning stages are always very extensive, because major changes are more difficult to make once recording has begun. Performers must learn the lines of dialogue for several scenes since more script material will be recorded in a single session. Camera operators must anticipate what camera positions, lens types and positions, and framing they are to adopt for upcoming segments. Ample time and space must be provided for the cameras to be

CAMERA BLOCKING FOR SINGLE CAMERA

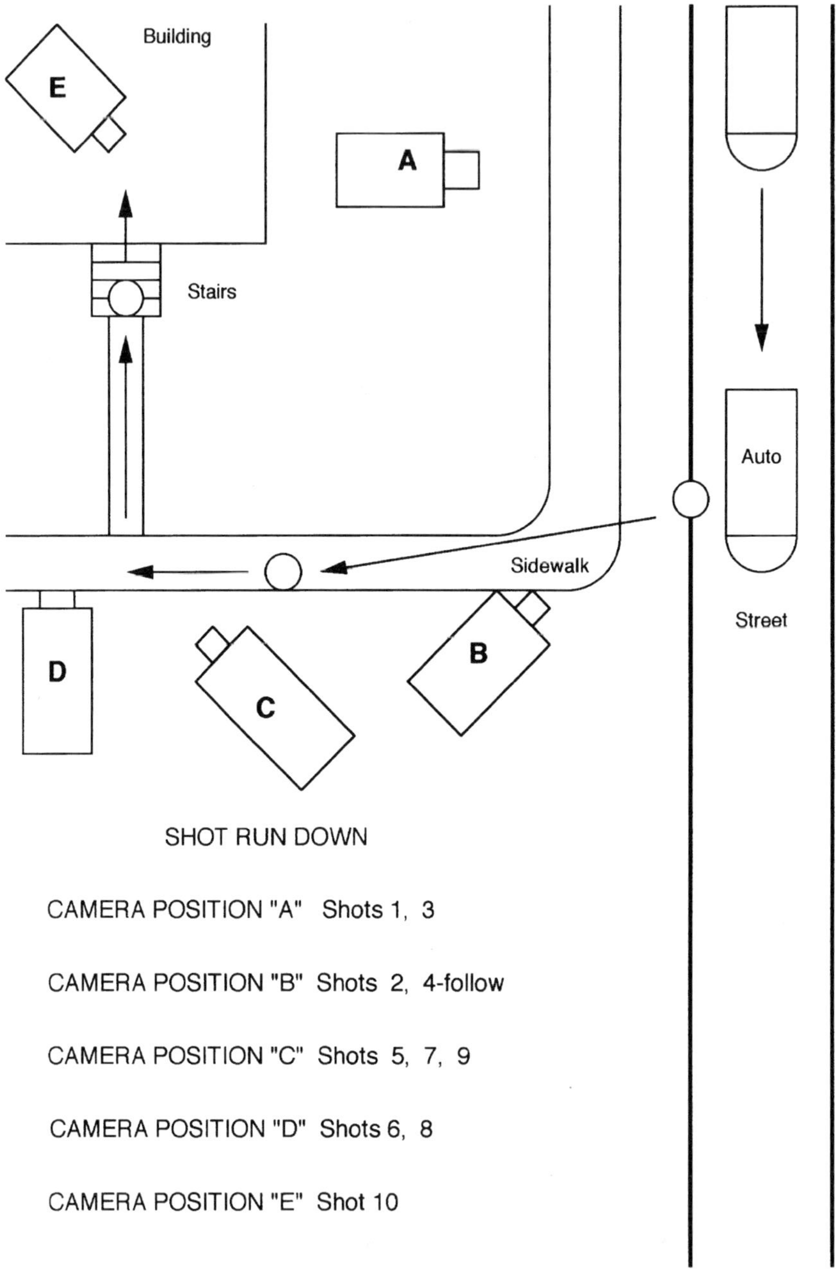

Figure 4.23 A director blocks performers and cameras before and during rehearsal in order to determine the best placement of each to provide the framing and movement intended for each shot. A plot drawn as if looking straight down on the scene is helpful in visualizing where cameras and performers need to be blocked.

moved during recording. Every detail must be worked out in advance, and a detailed shooting script or camera shot sequence must be provided to each key member of the production team.

Tremendous economies in the time and expense can be accomplished by using multiple-camera recording, when the recording session has been properly planned and practiced. But a multiple-camera situation can also be extremely frustrating if a key individual is improperly prepared or the director has failed to anticipate all the problems that can arise. Murphy's law—**if anything can go wrong, it will**—is an optimistic expectation in multiple-camera and live television recording situations where directors, crews, and talents are insufficiently prepared.

For multiple-camera recordings of uncontrolled events, such as sporting events, cameras are often placed in fixed positions. Each camera operator is responsible for covering a specific part of the action from one position. The director of a live production, such as coverage of a sporting event, may have to watch and control as many as ten cameras, some of which are connected to slow-motion recorders. The director must be able to respond instantaneously to any action that occurs, rapidly cutting from one camera to another. The director selects from among the images displayed on a bank of television screens. Since only minimal scripting is possible, the action and atmosphere within the director's control room itself often becomes very intense during a sporting event or similar production. Accurate decisions must be made very quickly. To anticipate actions and cuts, directors must be intimately familiar with the particular sport.

Timing

An important function performed by the director is timing. The control of program pace in terms of the speed of dialogue, actions, and editing is one form of timing. As discussed in Chapter 3, dramatic pacing is a subjective impression of time in video, film, and sound productions. Through effective editing, a sequence of action can be made to seem longer or shorter in duration to the audience. Other types of timing are equally important in the production process.

Running Time

A director is responsible for ensuring that the program length or actual running time of a completed program conforms to the required length. In video production, running time should be distinguished from clock time. The latter refers to the actual time of day on the studio clock. Each video or film program or program segment has its own running time, which is the exact duration of the program, regardless of what time of day it is actually shown. During live productions, a timer is used to calculate the running time of each program segment so that the total running time will conform to the scheduled overall length of the program.

Timing During Production

Television commercials, public service announcements, and broadcast or cablecast programming must be accurately timed during production. When recording a commercial, for example, a director must obtain shots that will add up to exactly ten, thirty, or sixty seconds. The screen time of the various shots and vignettes must add up to the exact screen time of the commercial format that has been chosen. Live video production demands precise screen timing with a timer as well as a studio clock, since the show cannot be re-edited, lengthened, or shortened.

Backtiming is the process of figuring the amount of time remaining in a program or program segment by subtracting the present time from the predetermined end time. Music is sometimes backtimed so that it will end at the conclusion of a live production. This means that if the music should last three minutes, you backtime three minutes from its end and start playing it three minutes before the end of the program, gradually fading it up. In other words, if you want it to end at 6:59, you backtime it three minutes and start it at 6:56. In multiple-camera video production, the talent is often told how much time remains by means of hand signals. Five fingers, followed by four, three, two, and one, indicate how many minutes of running time remain for that segment. Rotating the index finger in a circle indicates that it is time to wind up a performance, since the time is almost up. A cutoff signal (the hand cuts across the neck, as though the stage or floor manager's own head is coming off) indicates the actual end of a segment or show.

On-the-Air Timing

Prerecorded videotapes such as commercials, which will be inserted into a program as it is being broadcast or cablecast, must be accurately backtimed or cued and set up on a playback machine. A countdown leader displaying consecutive numbers from 10 down to 0 is placed just ahead of the prerecorded pictures and sound. The numbers indicate how many seconds are left before the start of the prerecorded material. The playback can then be prerolled; that is, begun the appropriate number of seconds before the commercial is due to start.

Production Switching

In multiple-camera video production, the director supervises virtually all of the editing in the control room during actual production. Production editing is done by means of a switcher, a device that allows shots to be selected from among several different cameras instantaneously. The director usually commands the technical director (TD) to change the transmitted image from one camera to another. (In many local stations, the director actually operates the switcher.) The TD then pushes the correct buttons on the switcher. Each button on the switcher is connected to a different camera or image source. When the TD pushes a button, the switcher automatically substitutes one picture for another.

The TD and the director view these changes on television monitors as they are taking place. The images sent out of the switcher can either be directly transmitted and broadcast during live production or recorded on videotape. A videotape recording can be used for subsequent postproduction editing and/or delayed broadcast, cablecast, or closed-circuit showing. A switcher is both an electronic editing device and a special effects machine. The TD can not only cut from one image or camera to another, but also fade in, fade out, dissolve, wipe, key, chroma key, and superimpose images. Various transition devices can be used in changing from one image or camera to another.

A switcher consists of a series of buttons organized into units called *buses* (Figure 4.24). There are three types of buses: preview, program, and special effects or

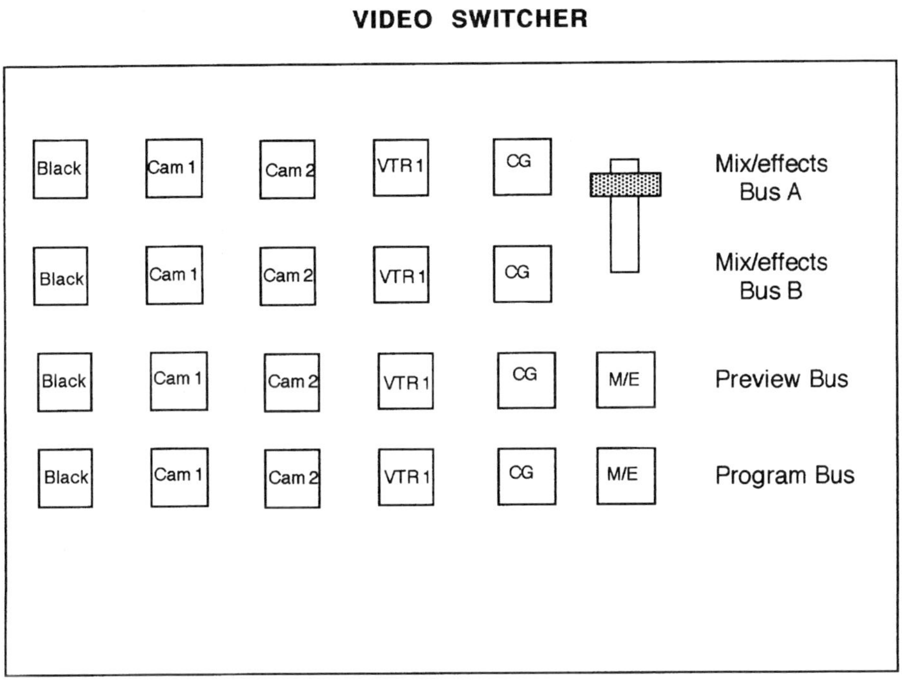

Figure 4.24 The simplest switcher would contain at least four buses. One for on-air (program), one to check shots ahead of time (preview), and two buses for mixing or wiping shots (mix/effect). In addition to all other inputs to the switcher, the program bus must also contain a button for switching to the M/E bus.

mix. Individual buttons within each bus are linked to specific sources, such as camera 1, camera 2, camera 3, a videotape player, a remote source, still store, character generator, digital generator, and a constant black image.

Each bus has one button assigned to each of these image sources. Thus a bus allocated to previewing images prior to sending them out of the board, called a *preview bus,* would have at least nine individual buttons connected to the nine image sources listed earlier. When one of these buttons is pressed, the image from that source appears on the preview monitor. A second bus having the same number of buttons is assigned to the actual program feed; on a simple switcher, this is the signal that will actually be transmitted or recorded.

A switcher having just two buses would only allow the TD to preview images and to cut directly from one image to another. If any special effects are to be created, the switcher must have special effects or mix buses. These two effects or mix buses are usually designated "A" and "B." In order to send any visual signal on the effects buses out of the switcher, a button designating the effects buses must be activated on a secondary program bus called the *master program bus.* The master program bus acts as a final selection switch, determining what will be transmitted by the switcher. The TD can select the program bus (which contains one of the nine visual sources) or the effects bus by depressing one of these two buttons on the master program bus. A *master preview bus* is also available on more sophisticated switchers, so that an effect, such as a split-screen or digital effect, can be previewed prior to recording or transmission via the master program bus.

Director's Commands

A director must communicate accurately with the entire crew in order to effectively coordinate a production, but communication with the TD is critical since the TD's response and action determines what pictures will be seen on air or fed to the tape. Operating the switcher during production requires careful preparation and infallible communication between the director and operator of the switcher. The TD must know in advance exactly what switcher operations will be called for by the director and the order in which they will be called for. It is very easy to become confused and push the wrong button or misunderstand the director's commands. It is the director's responsibility to convey clear and distinct commands to the TD and to provide adequate time between the preparatory command and command of execution.

Video and film directors have developed relatively precise terminology and methods with which to communicate with their cast and crew. The method is based on a two-step system of first warning of an impending command with a preparatory (prep) command, followed by a command of execution at the precise timing moment. A preparatory command always begins with either the word "stand-by" or "ready." This tells everyone that a new command is about to be announced—pay attention. The prep command needs to be detailed and precise and clearly stated so that the crew and cast directly involved know what to prepare themselves for when the command of execution arrives a few seconds later. The command of execution needs to be as short and as precise as possible, since that command determines the precise moment when an action is to take place.

A typical command series if the director wanted camera 3 to zoom in to a two-shot is as follows: Prep command: "Camera 3, stand-by to zoom in to a two-shot." Command of execution: "Three-zoom." More often a single command series is directed at more than one crew or cast member. The beginning command of a newscast might be directed at the TD (the switcher transition), the audio operator (to open a mic), the camera operator (who gets the opening shot), and the floor manager to give the anchor a stand-by and a cue to start talking. Prep command: "Stand-by to anchor, ready mic, ready to fade in camera 2 on the anchor." Command of execution: "Mic, fade in 2, cue anchor." The order of the commands and the precise nature of their execution is critical. Sloppy or inaccurate calls by a director will guarantee a sloppy production. Commands to the TD and camera operators are especially important because in both cases some preoperation activities may need to be carried out before the command can be followed. The switcher may need to have a complex set of buttons aligned or set up, or a camera or lens may need to be moved or adjusted before the shot is ready.

Live-on-Tape Recording

A live-on-tape (multiple-camera) director can use the techniques of live multiple-camera video to record events quickly and efficiently but also has the option to change the shot sequence during postproduction. This is accomplished by recording the images from several cameras simultaneously while at the same time making some editing decisions on the switcher that are recorded on a separate recorder. Editing decisions made during production can then be changed during postproduction by inserting different camera shots. This method gives the director maximum flexibility to produce a program economically in the shortest possible time without jeopardizing the quality of the final product, since changes can always be made later. In this way multiple-camera recording techniques can be combined with the techniques discussed next, allowing the director to benefit from the advantages of both methods.

Single-Camera Directing

The number of cameras used and the order and time frame of recording/filming shots constitute the major differences between multiple and single camera directing. The types of shots are the same, but the physical arrangement and order of shooting those shots differ between the two production modes. Recording with a single camera usually takes longer than multiple-camera recording. The lighting, camera, and set are sometimes moved and readjusted for each shot. Better quality images are often obtained using this method, since fewer compromises have to be made in terms of recording logistics. Each shot is composed and the action repeated so that an optimal recording is made. But potential problems can arise in terms of discontinuity or mismatched action from one shot to the next. The director and the script continuity person must observe and duplicate every detail recorded or filmed in the master shot during the shooting of the inserts.

Both film and video use three different types of setups for one camera: (1) master shots, (2) inserts, and (3) cutaways. Single-camera recording normally begins with a shot of the entire action in a scene, or as much of the complete scene as it is possible to record in a single shot. This is often called a *master shot.* Master shots are usually, but not always, long shots. Specific actions occurring within the master shot are then repeated after the camera has been placed closer to the subject for shots known as *inserts.* Inserts are usually the medium shots and close-ups indicated in a script. Master shots and inserts may be re-recorded several times before an acceptable recording has been made. Specific recordings are called *different takes* of the same shot. The shooting script is then marked (as shown in Figure 4.25) by a script continuity person with the number of the exact shot specified in the script, and each take is circled at the beginning point of actual recording.

A line is drawn vertically through the script to the point where actual recording of that take ends. Inserts are normally extended before and after the exact edit points in the script to allow for overlapping action and a range of editing choices. A marked shooting script provides a complete record of actual recording in terms of master shots and inserts. Cutaways are additional close-ups and medium shots of objects or events that are not central parts of the action and are often not specified in the script. They can be inserted into a scene to bridge mismatched actions or to hide mistakes within or between a master shot and an insert. The master shot or long shot can act as a safety net in the event that matching medium shots or close-ups specified in the script do not prove satisfactory. A continuously running long shot or master shot can be quite boring in comparison with using several different long shots, medium shots, and close-ups for emphasis and variety. But the knowledge that the master shot covers the entire action and can be used at any point can be of some comfort to the editor (see Figure 4.25).

Inserts shots, which record some of the same actions as the master shot, but from a closer camera position or a different angle of view, are called *inserts* or *cut-ins*, since they will be cut into the master shot. The director and the script continuity person must observe and duplicate every detail recorded in the master shot

SHOOTING SCRIPT WITH CONTINUITY MARKS

1. INT WS UNIVERSITY CLASSROOM DAY 1.

Classroom is full of students, some wide awake, gossiping, others sleeping or nodding off as they wait for the professor to arrive.

2-Shot of Jane and Jack, Jane turns around in her seat to whisper to Jack.

JANE
(Quietly so only Jack can hear her.)
Are you sure there isn't going to be an exam
during tomorrow's class?

CU Jack, he leans forward toward Jane.

JACK
(With a bravado, all-knowing tone)
Of course not, have I ever lied to you?

The professor enters the room, downstage right, walks to the lectern and the room becomes quiet.

MWS from back of classroom, students in foreground, Professor in background.

PROFESSOR
(Emphatically as a reminder)
If I am forced to repeat myself again, I WILL
be forced to give you your first examination in
tomorrow's class.

MS Students as they react to Professor, groans, turning to each other in sympathy

(DISSOLVE TO)

2. EXT WS CAMPUS DAY 2.

The clouds suddenly darken the sky as rain, thunder and lightning start and the lights go out plunging the room into darkness.

Figure 4.25 Continuity marks on a script are made as the scene is shot. The continuity clerk indicates with codes agreed upon by the editor when a shot starts and ends. Often the codes will indicate the framing of a shot as well as its length and the number of takes. These kinds of markings are invaluable to the editor during post production.

during the recording of the inserts. The actors must perform the same gestures, wear the same clothing, and repeat the same actions and lines of dialogue if actions are to overlap and match from one shot to the next. In extremely low-budget situations, where it is impossible to record several takes of each insert, a director is well advised to record a few cutaways for use in bridging mismatched actions between shots that are discovered during postproduction editing. It is the director's responsibility to provide adequate coverage of events and actions so that a program can be edited with minimal difficulty. Good coverage provides insurance against costly reshooting.

Cutaways

Cutaways are shots of secondary objects and actions that can be used to hide mismatched action and to preserve continuity, or simply to add depth and interest to the primary action of a film or television program. Cut-ins depict actions that appear within the frame of master shots, while cutaways depict actions and objects outside the master shot frame. In single-camera news recording, a reaction shot of the reporter or interviewer is sometimes used to bridge gaps or to avoid jump cuts in a condensed version of an interview or simply to use facial expressions to comment on what is being said. Close-ups of hands gesturing and relevant props can be also used as cutaways. They can be inserted at almost any point to bridge mismatched action in master shots and inserts, or simply to add more detail to the spatial environment. Cutaways provide an editor with something to cut away to when editing problems are discovered.

Shooting Ratios

While every single-camera director tries to get an acceptable shot in as few takes as possible, nonetheless there can be considerable variation in shooting ratios from one production to another. Shooting ratios, which refer to the ratio of visual material shot to visual material actually used, can range from about 5:1 to 100:1 in different types of production situations. Obviously, more takes of each shot translate into higher shooting ratios. Network commercials often have the highest shooting ratios. At the other end of the spectrum, student productions often have shooting ratios as low as 5:1 or even 3:1, due to limited production funds. Low budget situations call for highly efficient production methods.

Director's Terminology

Since a single-camera director is normally present on the set with the camera operator rather than isolated in a control room, as in multiple-camera production, he or she can communicate directly with the crew and talent. Directorial terminology for camera placements and movements is generally the same as that for multiple-camera recording, but a few commands are quite different. When the crew and the talent are ready to record a single shot, the director says "roll tape" to the videotape or audiotape (in film) recordist and "roll film" to the film camera operator. When the tape or film is up to speed, the operator says "speed" or "camera rolling." The director then calls, "slate," and a grip or camera assistant slates the shot by calling out the scene, shot, and take numbers, which are also written on a board called a *slate*. In film the slate has electronic or physical clapsticks that are brought together so that separate sounds and pictures can be synchronized later. The scene, shot, and take numbers displayed on the slate are used as a reference during postproduction editing. They are usually written down on a camera report sheet, which is sent to the film laboratory or used by the videotape editor (see Figure 4.26).

When the talent is ready and the slate has been removed from the shot, the director says "action," and the performance begins. When a shot is over or a problem develops in midshot, the director says "cut." If the director wants a scene printed for later viewing, the command "print" will be given. This type of command is noted on the camera report. Since editing can be done during postproduction, there is no need for the director to communicate with a technical director (switcher operator) during actual production. Editing decisions will be made later.

Summary

Video and film directors are artists who can turn a completed script into a shooting script and produce works of art from recorded visual images and sounds. They understand basic realist, modernist, and postmodernist aesthetics. Realist aesthetics stresses content more than form, and modernist and postmodernist aesthetics stresses form over content. These aesthetic approaches can be applied to the use of specific visuals and sounds. To prepare a shooting script, a director must know when to use different types of shots. Shots can be categorized by camera-to-subject distance, camera angle, camera (or lens) movement, and shot duration.

Figure 4.26 The director on a single camera shoot stands next to the camera to give directions to both the camera operator and the talent. An accurate record of each shot is kept on a camera log by either the director or a production assistant.

Directors know how to control various aspects of visual composition, such as frame dimensions, symmetry, closure, perspective, and frame movement. They must also understand image qualities, such as tone, scale and shape, depth, and speed of motion, and the use of various transition devices and special effects. A director can create smoother transitions between different spaces through graphic similarities of shape and color between shots, or can create more emphatic or shocking transitions through dramatic differences in shapes, sizes, and colors.

In scene construction, shots of varying camera-to-subject distance may be combined for one of the following aesthetic reasons: to include an action that could not be shown in a prior shot, to render a closer look at an action or subject, or to draw back and establish the setting. Conventional continuity often begins with a long shot and gradually moves closer to the subject as the action intensifies. Often the shot length is shorter during crises and climaxes. Continuity suggests an uninterrupted flow of time, with no apparent gaps or mismatched actions from shot to shot. Shot changes may be psychologically motivated to anticipate the audience's next point of interest or may be based on a specific point of view or approach adopted by the director.

Video and film are temporal and spatial arts. The perception of time can be controlled. Time can be condensed or expanded through editing. The perception of space can also be manipulated. Classical continuity implies respect for rules of screen direction, such as the 180-degree action axis rule, and the maintenance of spatial clarity.

The aesthetic use of sound is an extremely important, if often neglected, aspect of film and television production. While sound can be used simply to accompany and complement the visuals, it can also be treated as an independent aesthetic element. There are four basic categories of sound: speech, music, sound effects, and ambient noise. Speech usually consists of dialogue or narration. A director must be sensitive to speech intonation and levels of performance to be able to select and order different recordings of dialogue or narration.

Music will either be selected from prerecorded tapes and records, or composed and recorded for a specific project. A director must be familiar with the basic elements of music, such as rhythm, melody, harmony, counterpoint, and tonality or timbre, as well as different types of music. Sound effects are sometimes used to enhance an illusion or reality, or to create imaginative sound impressions.

Background sounds are present in any location. Background sounds can be used to preserve temporal continuity and to create an illusion of spatial depth. A director should be familiar with different sound qualities, such as loudness and pitch, reverberation and tone, pace and rhythm, and fidelity and distortion, and the various means of controlling these qualities. Temporal relations between sounds include continuity versus discontinuity, repetition of specific motifs, and audio transition devices. A director can affect the perception of temporal continuity through the selection and ordering of sounds. Mismatched levels and gaps in the presentation of sounds can create discontinuity, thus disrupting the flow of time.

It is possible to condense and expand time without disrupting the illusion of continuity, however. Certain sounds, such as musical themes, can also be presented repeatedly in conjunction with specific characters or settings. All of these relations and qualities of sound can be used to complement or fill out the image. They can also be used independent of the image to create a unique aesthetic experience. Sound and image interaction can be divided into four basic oppositional categories:

(1) on-screen versus off-screen sounds, (2) commentative versus actual sounds, (3) synchronous versus asynchronous sounds, and (4) parallel versus contrapuntal sounds.

Visual images can be edited to prerecorded music, or music can be originally composed for video and film. Music composed for television or film often performs one of the following functions: intensifying the drama, establishing the period or place, setting the mood or atmosphere, stimulating a specific emotion in conjunction with a character or theme, or simply filling in and avoiding silence. The director and the composer should collaborate with one another, fully and creatively exploring the artistic potential of visual image and music interaction.

The director supervises the creative aspects of television and film production by coordinating the production team, initiating and chairing preproduction and production meetings, casting the film or television program with the producer and casting director, and organizing production rehearsals. Working with the talent is one of the director's most important responsibilities. Excellent performances must be obtained with extreme efficiency, but a director must also be sensitive to the emotional needs of performers. Working with the talent and crew during rehearsal is so essential to the quality of the final product that it is sometimes considered a separate stage of production. The director plots and stages the action by determining the positioning and movement of talent and camera, plans the composition of the images within the camera frame, and establishes and maintains continuity of action and screen direction.

In live and multiple-camera production, directors are usually directly involved in the selection of specific types of shots, and the creation of transition devices and special effects. In live, multiple-camera, and live-on-tape productions, directors employ a technical director (TD) to operate a video switcher and to take or dissolve from one camera or shot to another. The director also controls the timing of a television program or film. Timing can refer to the subjective pace of the action or the objective running time and clock time. Backtiming is frequently used in live television production to cue the talent or to preset closing music or a videotape or film segment.

A video switcher consists of several sets of switches, called buses, such as preview, program, and effects or mix buses. The switches on each bus allow an operator (usually the technical director) to select a specific visual input, such as one of several different camera inputs, VTR playbacks, remote feeds, digital sources, and visual black. Operating a switcher requires careful preparation. The director must give the TD explicit commands and sufficient warning prior to complicated effects to ensure effective production editing. The director's function can vary considerably between multiple-camera and single-camera recording situations. The multiple-camera video director frequently sits in a control room isolated from the talent and crew during actual recording. The single-camera director, on the other hand, is usually present on the set during the shooting. The multiple-camera director supervises the movement of several cameras, using an intercom, and controls the editing by having the TD punch buttons on the switcher, changing the main signal from one camera or source to another.

The single-camera director often works directly with the talent and crew during the period of time between shots, when the camera is being moved and the lighting and sound recording devices reset. The editing of single-camera production is usually left to a specialist who cuts the film or electronically edits together videotape during postproduction.

Exercises

1. Repeatedly view a scene or sequence from a completed production and write a (postproduction) shooting script or shot analysis for it based on actual shots in the finished product. Compare your shooting script or shot analysis for this segment to a published version to determine if you have made proper use of shooting script terms and concepts.
2. Take a segment from a completed script and attempt to transform it into a shooting script by adding specific shots, sound effects, and so on. Use techniques that are consistent with a realist, modernist, or postmodernist approach when creating your shooting script. Do this exercise for both a multiple camera production and a single camera production.

Additional Readings

Andrew, J. Dudley. *Major Film Theories.* New York: Oxford University Press, 1976.

Armer, Alan A. *Directing Television and Film,* 2nd ed. Belmont, CA: Wadsworth, 1990.

Bare, Richard L. *The Film Director, a Practical Guide to Motion Picture and Television Techniques.* New York: Collier Books, 1971.

Bernstein, Steven. *Film Production,* 2nd ed. Boston: Focal Press, 1994.

Bordwell David, and Kristin Thompson. *Film Art: An Introduction,* 2nd ed. New York: Alfred A. Knopf, 1986.

Burch, Noel. *Theory of Film Practice.* Trans., Helen R. Lane. New York: Praeger, 1973.

D'Agostino, Peter, ed. *Transmission: Theory and Practice for a New Television Aesthetics.* New York: Tanam Press, 1985.

DiZazzo, Ray. *Directing Corporate Video.* Boston: Focal Press, 1993.

Hickman, Harold R. *Television Directing.* Santa Rosa, CA: Cole Publishing Co., 1991

Kindem, Gorham. *The Live Television Generation of Hollywood Film Directors.* Jefferson, NC: McFarland, 1994.

Kingson, Walter K., and Rome Cowgill. *Television Acting and Directing.* New York: Holt, Rinehart and Winston, 1965.

Lukas, Christopher. *Directing for Film and Television.* New York: Anchor Press/Doubleday, 1985.

Millerson, Gerald. *Effective TV Production,* 3rd ed. Boston: Focal Press, 1993.

Rabiger, Michael. *Directing the Documentary,* 2nd ed. Boston: Focal Press, 1992.

Rabiger, Michael. *Directing: Film Techniques and Aesthetics,* 2nd ed. Boston: Focal Press, 1996.

Richards, Ron. *A Director's Method for Film and Television.* Boston: Focal Press, 1992.

Rowland, Avril. *Continuity Handbook for Single Camera Shooting,* 3rd ed. Boston: Focal Press, 1994.

Verna, Tony. *Live TV: An Inside Look at Directing and Producing.* Boston: Focal Press, 1987.

Watkinson, John. *An Introduction to Digital Video.* Boston: Focal Press, 1994.

Weis, Elizabeth and John Belton. *Film Sound: Theory and Practice.* New York: Columbia University Press, 1985.

Zettl, Herbert. *Sight, Sound, and Motion: Applied Media Aesthetics,* 2nd ed. Belmont, CA: Wadsworth Publishing Co., 1993.

5

Audio/Sound

Introduction

Commonly used audio production techniques and equipment used to control sound and sound perspectives are explored in this chapter. Quality audio is extremely important in media production as poor quality sound can destroy the impact of high quality visuals. Some directors feel that sounds and visual images should be almost completely independent of one another so that each component could stand entirely on its own, while others feel that sounds should reinforce accompanying visual images. The former approach is consistent with modernist aesthetics, while the latter reflects a realist approach to production. Some directors combine these approaches and suggest that high quality sound should function well on its own as well as in combination with visual images.

Aesthetics of Audio/Sound

Audio/sound can be approached from the three aesthetic perspectives of realism, modernism, and postmodernism. A realist approach uses sound to stimulate an illusion of reality, reinforcing the temporal and spatial continuity of visual images. Modernist audio develops sound independently of accompanying visual images, breaking down realist conventions and stimulating more abstract impressions and visceral feelings. Postmodernist audio emphasizes listener participation within productions in order to emotionally involve the audience as much as possible.

Types of Microphones

The ability to duplicate quality audio in film, video, and audio-only situations depends on careful mic selection and placement. This means choosing a mic designed for the specific purpose at hand and positioning it properly. A microphone is a type of transducer. Transducers are devices that change one form of energy to another form of energy. mics convert sound wave action into fluctuations in electrical voltage. Sound is created by the very rapid vibration of objects, and sound waves consist of rapidly contracting and expanding particles of air. A tuning fork, for example, causes air molecules to compress and expand as it vibrates, creating a sound pressure wave. As one arm moves forward, it pushes the air molecules, and as it moves backward, the air molecules, which are elastic or resistant to being pushed, expand again to fill the partial vacuum or void. Rapid vibration creates a pressure wave of alternately compressed and expanded air molecules.

This pressure or sound wave moves in a relatively straight line and strikes other objects, such as the human ear or a microphone element. The eardrum vibrates in response to the sound wave and produces an auditory impression in the mind. A mic has an element that is sensitive to these air waves and converts the wave action into corresponding fluctuations in electrical current. The electrical signal thus becomes an analog, or copy, of the sound wave. Once an electronic equivalent of the audio signal has been created, that signal may be converted into a digital signal for processing and maintenance of the highest quality.

mics can be classified on the basis of the type of transducer element they use into three basic categories: dynamic, ribbon, and condenser. One type of mic element may be better suited to a specific audio situation than another.

Transducer Elements

A dynamic mic consists of a moving coil attached to a vibrating diaphragm or disc suspended between two magnetic poles. As the diaphragm vibrates with the sound wave, the coil moves up and down within a magnetic field and changes the voltage of the electrical current flowing through the coil. In general, dynamic mics are very durable, not extremely susceptible to wind noise, and relatively inexpensive.

A ribbon mic contains a narrow strip of corrugated foil suspended in a magnetic field. This ribbon vibrates in response to the difference in air pressure in front and in back of it, and produces an alternating current along the length of a coil. The ribbon itself is quite fragile and can easily be damaged by simply blowing into the mic, although newer ribbon mics have been designed to be more durable but still are best confined to studio use. A ribbon mic usually produces a smooth, bass-accentuated sound, is preferred by many radio and television announcers for that reason, and is ideal for digital recording since their warm sound accentuates high frequencies. Most ribbon mics are priced at the top of the range of professional microphones.

Condenser mics are relatively complex in comparison with dynamic or ribbon mics. The element is a capacitor that requires two charged plates: a diaphragm and a fixed backplate. As the diaphragm vibrates, the space between it and the fixed plate changes in capacitance, that is, in its ability to pass an electrical current or signal. The strength of the electrical sound signal increases or decreases accordingly. The signal is very weak, however, and a preamplifier is required to boost the signal to a usable level. Additional current may be supplied to the preamplifier by a battery in the mic handle or by a power supply located in the mixer called a *phantom supply*. An electret condenser mic is constructed with permanently charged plates, reducing the power needed to operate the mic. Condenser mics vary in price from relatively inexpensive to quite expensive, and some inexpensive cameras and cassette recorders have built-in condenser mics of lesser quality. Condenser mics generally reproduce high-quality sound, and with their built-in pre-amp can be considered quite sensitive.

Pickup Patterns

Mics can be classified according to their directional sensitivity or pickup patterns, as well as their transducer elements. Different recording situations require the use of mics that pick up sounds from a very narrow or very wide area. Some mics pick up sounds coming from every direction, while others are sensitive to a very restricted area. The three basic categories of pickup patterns are as follows: omnidirectional, bidirectional, and unidirectional or cardioid.

An omnidirectional mic is equally sensitive to sounds from all directions, that is, from the entire 360-degree area surrounding it. A bidirectional mic is sensitive to sounds coming from two opposite directions.

Its sensitivity drops off rapidly at sixty degrees on either side of these two opposite directional points. At ninety degrees (perpendicular to the two optimal sound source directions), it is almost totally insensitive to sound. Unidirectional mics are sensitive to sounds from one direction only.

A cardioid mic is a type of unidirectional mic so named because its pickup pattern is heart shaped.

A cardioid mic is somewhat more sensitive to sound emanating from directly behind it, but it is very sensitive to sound coming from directly in front of it. A supercardioid mic is somewhat more sensitive to sound coming from the rear of the mic but has an even narrower optimal response area (about 60 degrees as opposed to 120 degrees for a cardioid mic). Shot-gun mics are long narrow tubes; they frequently have a supercardioid pickup pattern.

Impedance

A third characteristic of microphones that determines their use and placement is impedance. Impedance is a complex measurement of the property of wires and equipment that determines the ability of a signal to pass through that piece of equipment. It is critical that all audio equipment be designed to match input and output impedances. For microphones there are two basic impedance choices, high or low. High-impedance mics are low cost amateur mics, whereas all professional mics are low impedance. High-impedance mics may be connected with wires that contain one conductor and a shield, which does not provide the maximum protection for the signal from outside interference. Low-impedance mics normally are connected with wires that contain two conductors and a shield, providing maximum protection for the signal.

Mic Placement and Selection

Mic placement during recording can be either on-camera or off-camera. On-camera mics, such as a reporter's handheld mic, are visible to the viewer. Off-camera mics are not visible to the viewer. An off-camera mic can be hidden somewhere on the set or under a speaker's clothing, or it can be situated just outside the camera frame.

On-Camera Mics

Hand mics are the most common on-camera mics. Mics that are to be hand held should be shock mounted; that is, they should be well insulated so that noise is not created as the performer moves the mic. Since a hand mic can be moved and controlled by the performer, it does not always stay in a fixed position, and it generally has a relatively wide pickup pattern, such as omnidirectional or cardioid. It is wise to use a mic with a durable element, such as a dynamic or an electret condenser mic, in a handheld situation. An inexperienced performer should be instructed in how to keep the hand mic at a relatively constant distance from his or her mouth in order to keep the loudness relatively constant. A problem that frequently arises with the use of a hand mic is controlling the mic cable. Performers must learn to move the mic around without stretching the cable or tangling it (Figure 5.1).

Desk mics often have less durable elements than hand mics. If a desk mic is placed in a relatively permanent position, it does not have to be shock mounted. If a desk mic is to be removed from its mount and also function as a hand mic, as frequently occurs, it must have some of the same qualities as a hand mic. Most desk mics have cardioid pickup patterns and are placed one to two feet from the speaker.

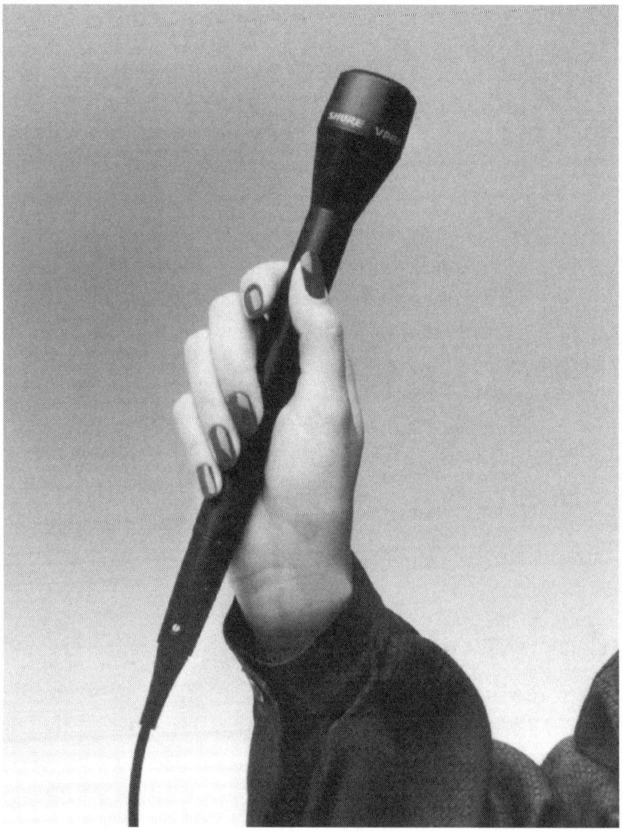

Figure 5.1
Hand microphones also may be mounted on a desk stand, floor stand, or boom, but must be designed to fit comfortably in the hand with reasonable sensitivity. (Courtesy of Shure.)

Sometimes a single bidirectional or omnidirectional desk mic can be used for two speakers to limit the number of mics needed (Figure 5.2).

A stand mic is supported on an adjustable pole in front of the performer; thus it offers a distinct advantage to a person who has his or her hands occupied with a musical instrument. The stand mic can usually be tilted and adjusted to a comfortable height for different performers. In general, more sensitive ribbon and condenser mics are used on a stand to record relatively soft sound sources such as stringed instruments, while dynamic mics with omnidirectional or cardioid reception patterns are often used for singers and amplified instruments. Sometimes more than one mic may be attached to a single stand, perhaps a condenser mic positioned from below to pick up the sounds of a guitar and a dynamic mic above to pick up the singer's voice (Figure 5.3).

Lavalier mics also leave a performer's hands free and do not require a stand that restricts his or her mobility. This type of mic, which is either hung around the performer's neck with a strap or clipped to a tie or outer garment, is relatively unobtrusive compared with a desk mic or a stand mic. Care should be taken in the placement of a lavalier mic to ensure that it will not create noise by rubbing against rough clothing or jewelry. Lavalier mics are often susceptible to cable problems because their cables are relatively thin and fragile. To guard against this on live broadcasts, performers such as newscasters often wear two lavaliers clipped together to create a dual-redundancy system, where one mic serves as a backup for another. Only one mic at a time is live to prevent phasing problems, which are discussed later in this chapter. A lavalier microphone can be hidden or concealed behind clothing, although this can lead to added rubbing noise (Figure 5.4).

Some handheld and lavalier mics have battery-powered FM transmitters, which allow the speaker using the mic to move around quite freely without a re-

Figure 5.2 A desk stand is designed to hold a microphone in position to pickup persons seated at the desk. Usually works best for one person, but can be placed between two people if their audio levels are nearly the same.

Figure 5.3
A stand mic is designed to allow one or more persons to stand on each side of the microphone depending upon whether the microphone is a bidirectional, unidirectional, or omnidirectional microphone. (Courtesy of Sony Corporation.)

Figure 5.4 A lavaliere microphone is designed to be clipped to the clothing of the person speaking. The design of a lavaliere compensates for the microphone resting against the chest of the speaker and located below the speaker's mouth. A lavaliere should not be used as a hand-held microphone away from the body.

strictive mic cable. Wireless lavalier mics can also be used as hidden mics by concealing the mic and its transmitter under clothing. An FM receiver at the audio input of the recording machine receives the transmitted signal. While wireless mics can be extremely helpful in many difficult recording situations, they also have a number of pitfalls. Like any FM radio, the wireless receiver can pick up interfering signals, such as noise from CB radios. Batteries can expire in the middle of a recording, especially when performers forget to turn them off. Finally, wireless mics are more expensive to rent or purchase than wired mics (Figure 5.5).

Off-Camera Mics

Off-camera mics may be attached to a mic boom. A *mic boom* is a long pole that can be placed (usually above the heads of the talent) just outside the camera frame. It can also be hidden on the set. There are three different types of mic booms: fishpole, giraffe, and perambulator booms. A *fishpole boom* is an aluminum pole with a mic mounting device at one end. Some fishpoles can be telescoped to allow for maximum extension during shooting and contracted for compact storage. The fishpole's greatest asset is its portability. A fishpole and the attached mic are usually lightweight enough to be hand held for a relatively long period of time without excessively tiring the operator. One disadvantage of the fishpole boom is that the length generally cannot be changed during recording. The boom operator must move as the talent moves. Also, the entire pole must be twisted to change the positioning of the microphone, making it somewhat difficult to alternate the placement

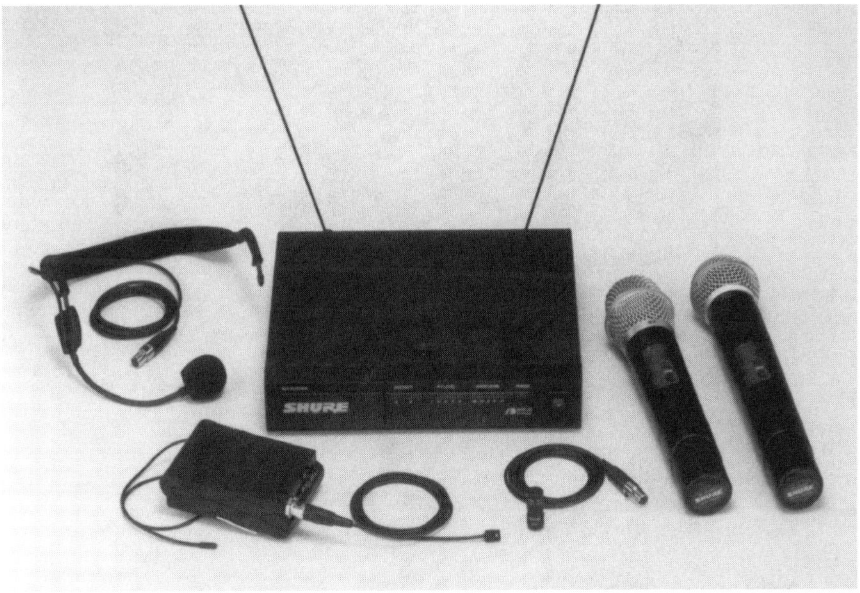

Figure 5.5 Wireless microphones may be designed as either hand-held, as a lavaliere, or on a head-mount. The transmitter may be built-in to the base of the hand-held microphone or the lavaliere and head-mount may be connected to a small transmitter fastened to the body of the performer. (Courtesy of Shure.)

of a directional mic between two different performers. The portability and flexibility of a fishpole may be increased by using an FM mic instead of a wired mic.

A *giraffe boom* is somewhat more bulky and less portable than the fishpole, but it allows for greater mobility and flexibility during recording. The giraffe is basically a fishpole attached to a three-wheeled dolly. It can be quickly and easily moved around the studio. It also has the advantage of allowing the operator to rotate the mic on a swivel to which the pole is attached. It requires only one operator and can be extended to different lengths during camera setups (Figure 5.6).

The *perambulator boom* is the heaviest type of boom. It has a large pole, which can be telescoped during a camera take; a swivel mechanism for rotating the mic; an operator platform, which can be raised and lowered; heavy-duty rubber tires; a guide pole, which requires the presence of a second operator to push or pull the boom around the studio; and a boom pan and tilt control. The perambulator boom is designed primarily for studio use. It is not very portable. It is counterweighted so that it can support a heavy microphone and a mounting device. Some perambulator booms allow an attached microphone to be panned or moved a full

Figure 5.6
A giraffe microphone boom is a small boom generally used to pick up the voice of one or two persons in fixed locations.

180 degrees, so that a highly directional mic can be used to pick up a moving performer or to switch from one speaker to another.

Boom Operation

Operating a boom demands great care and manual dexterity. Movements of the mic and the boom must be smooth, precise, and carefully planned. Excessively rapid movements of the boom or mic will create objectionable noise. The movement of the talent must be fully anticipated by the boom operator. If the boom operator has not preplanned the movements of the boom so that it can follow the talent, it will be difficult to maintain a constant sound level or to avoid crashing into other equipment on the set. The boom operator's job is to keep a moving sound source within the mic's primary pickup pattern. The operator listens to the sounds on headphones, which serve the same function as a viewfinder for a camera operator.

Omnidirectional mics are rarely used on a boom, even though they might make it easier to follow the movements of the talent, they simply pick up too much unwanted additional noise. Unidirectional mics seem to work best on a boom. They cut down on unwanted sounds by focusing on the sound source, and they provide good reception at a greater distance from the subject than mics with wider pickup patterns. This can be especially helpful when recording long camera shots with an off-camera mic.

Boom Placement

The optimum placement of a cardioid mic on a boom is one to four feet in front of and one to three feet above the speaking subject. In general, the boom operator should keep a uniform distance between the subject and the mic. Sometimes it may be necessary to vary this distance, however. To achieve proper sound perspective in single-camera recording, the mic may have to be slightly closer to the subject for close-ups and farther away for long shots (Figures 5.7A and B).

An overhead boom can create harsh shadows that disrupt the image. The placement and movement of a boom must be carefully preplanned to prevent objectionable shadows on the set. Sometimes it is simply impossible to place the microphone directly overhead on a boom without noticeably affecting the lighting or camera and performer movements. In these situations, a fishpole boom may be placed at the bottom or side of the frame, or a hidden mic may be used.

Boom operators who are attempting to record the best quality sound often place the mic as close to the subject as possible without entering the camera frame. In multiple-camera production, the audio operator informs the boom operator when the mic has entered an underscanned TV monitor. In single-camera productions, the camera operator carefully monitors the frame area. One strategy boom operators sometimes use to obtain good quality sound is to place the mic within the camera frame during a rehearsal or blocking session. This forces the director, audio operator, or camera operator to ask for the mic to be raised out of the frame. This strategy ensures that the mic will always be as close as possible to the subject and forces the director to consider whether the camera placement is compromising the quality of the sound. While directors usually are well aware of these limitations,

Figures 5.7A and B A hand-held microphone boom may be placed above the speaker's head or below, depending on the noise at the location or the type of shot. The mic may be placed closer to the speaker's mouth if the shot is a close-up rather than a wide shot.

a periodic reminder can go a long way toward preventing subsequent objections to the quality of the sound recording.

Hidden Mics

There are three different types of hidden or concealed mics: the hanging mic, the prop mic, and the concealed lavalier mic. Hanging and prop mics are stationary, while the concealed lavalier moves with the talent to whom it is attached. A stationary hanging mic can be attached to an overhead grid. It is usually an omnidirectional mic capable of covering a wide area of action. Its chief advantage is that it does not require a boom operator. Its obvious disadvantages are that it cannot be moved to vary or improve the audio during visual recording, and it often picks up ambient noises below it, such as footsteps and equipment being moved. Prop mics are microphones that are concealed on the set. A telephone at the center of a table around which several performers are seated can conceal a mic. Since a prop mic is stationary, it often has a relatively wide pickup pattern so that the talent does not have to stand immediately in front of the prop, calling attention to the presence of the mic or making it the focal point of a scene (Figures 5.8A and B).

A prop mic can be extremely useful in situations in which it is difficult to use a boom, such as when the camera is shooting an extreme long shot or when the space is so confining that a boom necessarily affects the lighting. A concealed lavalier mic is frequently used as a hidden mic for extreme long shots and complicated movements of the camera or talent. The concealed lavalier mic may be wrapped in foam rubber and taped to the subject underneath his or her clothing. It should not be free to rub against garments or jewelry and create noise, and care must be taken to ensure that the sound reaching it is not muffled by heavy clothing.

Selecting the Best Mic

Selecting the best mic for a specific recording situation depends on an understanding of sound aesthetics and different mic characteristics. The more versatile and widely used mics are the dynamic and electret condenser cardioids. They have extremely durable elements and a pickup pattern about halfway between a full-range omnidirectional and a narrow unidirectional mic. As on-camera mics they can be hand held (in this case they should be shock mounted) or mounted on a floor or desk stand. As an off-camera mic they can be suspended overhead on a mic boom just outside the frame.

A cardioid mic works best when it is relatively close to the speaker or sound source; thus it is not always the best mic to use for long distance pickup. Suppose an off-camera mic at some distance from the speaker must be used during the recording of an extreme long shot. A unidirectional condenser mic, such as a supercardioid shot-gun mic, may be the best choice. The narrow pickup pattern isolates the primary signal from the surrounding space. The condenser element provides a stronger signal because of its built-in preamplifier. Care must be exercised when using a shot-gun mic, however, so that noise coming from directly behind the speaker is not amplified along with the primary voice signal.

A second concern with the dynamic cardioid mic is that it is difficult to make inconspicuous on camera. A lavalier condenser mic can be the size of a tie tack. It can be placed very close to the speaker without dominating the frame. It can also

Figures 5.8A and B
In an emergency a microphone can be hung from a light batten over sound sources, but it works best if the person speaking stands in one position and should be a cardiod microphone. A microphone may be concealed in a set-piece or hand prop on a set near where people will be talking if the production requires off-camera microphones.

be completely hidden in a person's clothing. When connected to a tiny FM transmitter, it can even allow for freedom of movement without mic cables or extremely long-range camera shots with extremely high quality voice sounds. This can be an advantage when recording functional sound, but realistic sound perspective is better achieved by using a shot-gun mic. The ribbon mic is best left to completely stationary performance situations, such as talk shows, interviews, or dramatic radio productions. The ribbon mic can be quite versatile in such a situation, since it is capable of producing a very resonant sound. It can be set for an omnidirectional, bidirectional, or unidirectional pickup pattern so that it can be used by several speakers, a single speaker, or two performers facing each other. An omnidirectional dynamic or condenser mic is often used to record several speakers simultaneously. It can be suspended overhead in a fixed position or permanently positioned at a central location on the set.

Using Multiple Mics

Using a single omnidirectional mic is not necessarily the best way to record several different sound sources, such as several talk show performers. For one thing, even if the mic is centrally located, it will probably pick up a good deal of unwanted background sound along with the primary signals or voices. Using a different mic for each sound source provides better control and higher quality sound recording, provided each mic can be placed close to its sound source. One advantage is that each mic can be selected for the particular characteristics of its sound source. For example, suppose that you are recording a singer on camera, while a band is playing off camera. If the singer moves with a handheld mic, the loudness of the band music will vary with the mic direction, unless one or more stationary mics are set up specifically for the band.

These two sound sources should be separately controlled and combined (or mixed) together, using two mic inputs on a recorder or a device called a *mixer*. The music now maintains a constant loudness. The singer can use a dynamic cardioid, while an omnidirectional dynamic or ribbon mic is set up for the band. Better yet, several different mics can be set up for different instruments in the band.

Separate mics can be set up for several different speakers at a table. Each mic must be carefully placed, however, so that different mics do not pick up the same signals. This can lead to multiple-microphone interference, in which some of the sounds picked up simultaneously by two different mics cancel each other out. Such cancellation is a phasing problem that occurs when similar sound waves passing through the same medium are 180 degrees out of phase with respect to each other. Phasing is sometimes used deliberately, to create special audio effects such as the noise of a robot, or to disguise a speaker's identity.

The best way to find out if multiple-microphone interference exists is to set one mic at its proper level and then turn on the other mic. If the volume goes down rather than up when both mics are on, there is interference, which must be corrected by changing the distance between the two mics and/or their directional placement. Some sophisticated audio consoles allow the audio engineer to eliminate phasing problems electronically. Multiple-microphone interference can be prevented by keeping live mics well separated, using directional mics, and having them directed at different sound sources. If two subjects are seated quite close together, a single mic should be used for both, either by swiveling an overhead mic or a boom, or by placing a stand mic or a desk mic with a relatively wide pickup pattern between them. When more than two people are involved, two or more mics should be set up so that they are at least three times as far apart as their subject-to-mic distances. This three-to-one rule ensures that there will be no phasing problems with multiple mics (Figure 5.9).

Another solution is multichannel recording, where each mic is fed to a separate recording channel on an audiotape recorder. Using multiple mics can also cause problems with excessive ambient noise. Each mic picks up the same ambient noise, and when more than one mic is used the ambient noise adds up and can become disturbingly loud. Placing mics as close as possible to their sound sources so that loudness levels can be turned down helps reduce ambient noise in some instances. At other times different speakers can simply share the same mic.

Stereo Mic Placement

Stereo provides an additional spatial dimension by giving sound a directional placement from left to right. This is accomplished by recording sounds with at least two mics. Two cardioid mics can be arranged so that they crisscross one another, forming a forty-five to ninety degree angle.

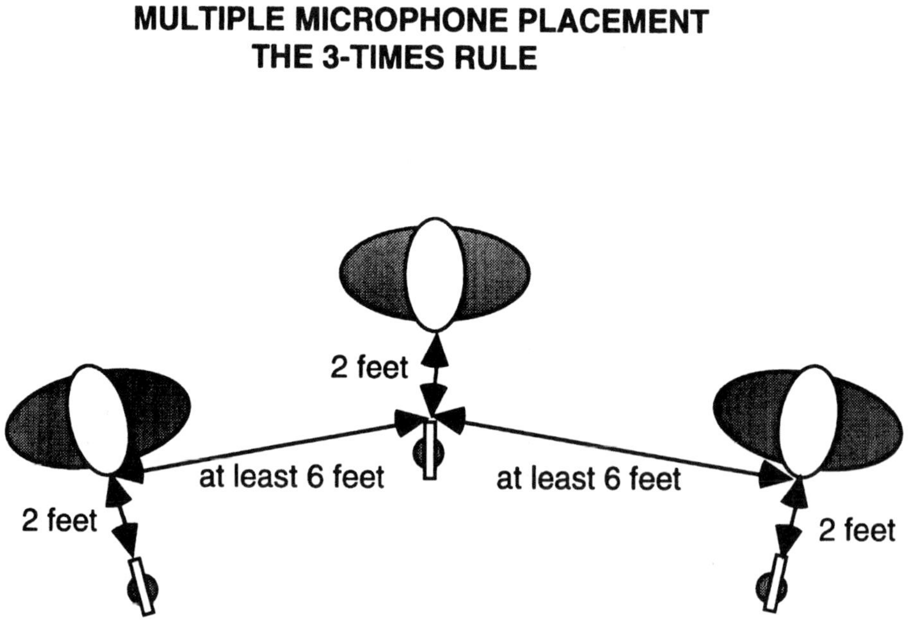

Figure 5.9 When using multiple microphones, the 3-times rule should be followed. The rule indicates each sound source must be three times the distance from any other microphone as they are from their own microphone. Any closer and audio phasing may occur causing distortion in the sound.

Each mic picks up sounds from a different direction. This setup works quite well for speech. Using two parallel cardioid mics separated by ten to fifteen feet and well in front of an orchestra or band works well for music. The sounds picked up by each mic are kept separate and recorded on different audio channels, which can then be played back through speakers that are spatially separated from one another. For proper balance, the mics must be adjusted so that a sound coming from a source directly between them creates a signal that is equally strong on both channels.

Cardioid mics are well adapted to stereophonic use because they are slightly more receptive to sounds directly in front of them than to sounds coming from the right or left. Stereophonic sound can be used to bring added realism or simply more spectacular audio effects to a film or television program. But stereo can also bring added production problems. In terms of production logistics, it is often difficult to record stereophonic sound on location. Handling additional mics and audio equipment inevitably leads to greater risks and problems. Stereophonic recording also complicates the postproduction process, since many additional sound elements must be smoothly combined and balanced during final mixing.

Digital Mic Placement

Most equipment, including microphones, originally designed for analog sound systems emphasize high frequencies to compensate for losses. Digital systems do not suffer the same problem so that mics designed for analog systems used on digital systems tend to sound strident and shrill. Noises created in preamplifiers or other sources of noise unnoticed in analog systems may become obvious in digital systems. Therefore mics must be positioned to avoid emphasizing high frequencies by placing them off-center rather than straight out from a sound source.

Close miking also may cause distortions or noise that would not be obvious in analog systems but would be heard in digital.

Sound-Signal Control

Audio Problems: Distortion and Noise

Distortion and noise are two different unwanted changes in an audio or video signal. *Distortion* is an unwanted change in a signal; *noise* is an unwanted addition to the signal. In both cases audio may be distortion or noise in a specific production, or simply an additional audio element. Rock musicians often add distortion for an effect to their music. Someone trying to listen to a country and western recording would consider a classical music recording played simultaneously as noise. But, of course, to a classical music fan, classical music is not noise (Figure 5.10).

One of the most common problems encountered in audio recording is distortion. The most common type of distortion encountered by beginning media production students is loudness distortion, which occurs when a sound is recorded at a level that exceeds the limitations of the electronic system. The peaks or high points of the sound wave are flattened, and new, unwanted frequencies of sound are produced. The end result is a reproduction that sounds like there is some kind of variable interference or garble on the line. Loudness distortion is controlled by setting the volume so that it does not exceed the limits of the system. A volume

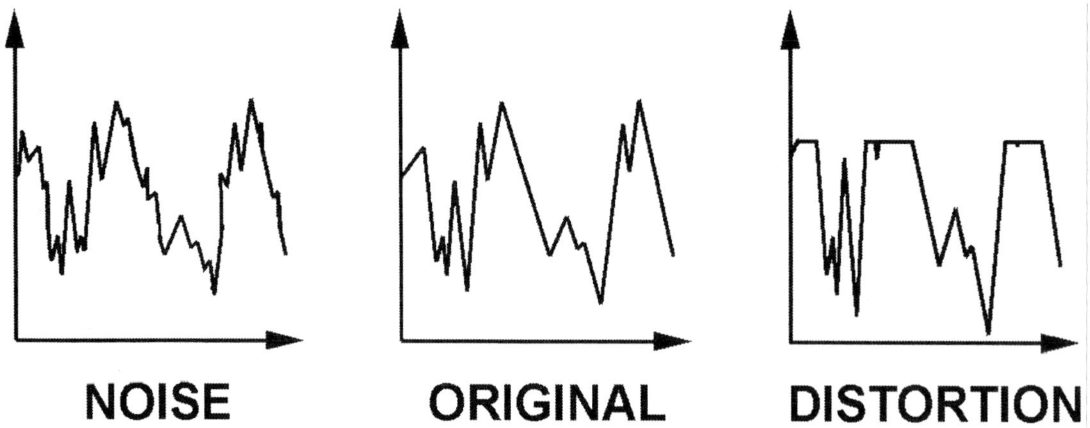

Figure 5.10 There are two types of destruction to sound, either noise or distortion. Noise is unwanted sound added to the original sound and distortion is an unwanted modification of the original sound.

unit or VU meter allows the recordist to set the volume controls as high as needed for a good quality recording without distorting the sound.

There are basically two types of noise, ambient noise, discussed earlier, and system noise. *Ambient noise* comes from open mics fed into an audio console or tape recorder which pick up the sound of air ventilators, lights, cameras, or other devices. (Fluorescent lights frequently cause a hum or buzzing sound, for example.) A second type of noise is called *system noise,* which can come from the electrical recording system and equipment. Microphone lines placed too close to lights and electrical cables often create system noise. So do worn volume controls or bad circuit boards and cable connections. Most ambient noise and some system noise can be controlled, but most system noise is simply inherent in the recording equipment. Digital audio systems cannot control ambient noise any differently than an analog system, but a digital system does reduce system noise to a minimum level. Therefore, signal-to-noise ratios are less important in digital systems (Figure 5.11).

An important determinant of sound quality is a system's signal-to-noise ratio. This is the ratio of desired sounds to unwanted system noise. Many professional audio systems have signal-to-noise ratios of 55:1 or above; that is, the main signal is fifty-five times as loud as the system noise level. Quality audio production requires the maintenance of high signal-to-noise ratios throughout all stages of the process.

Sound Intensity Measurement

There are many different devices for indicating the volume intensity or loudness of a sound signal. Less expensive tape recorders often have a red light that flickers with volume peaks. Overmodulation or loudness distortion is indicated when the light stays brightly lit for a continuous period rather than flickering intermittently. Other recorders employ a needle device that indicates loudness distortion when the needle enters a red zone. These less expensive meters are quite small and do not

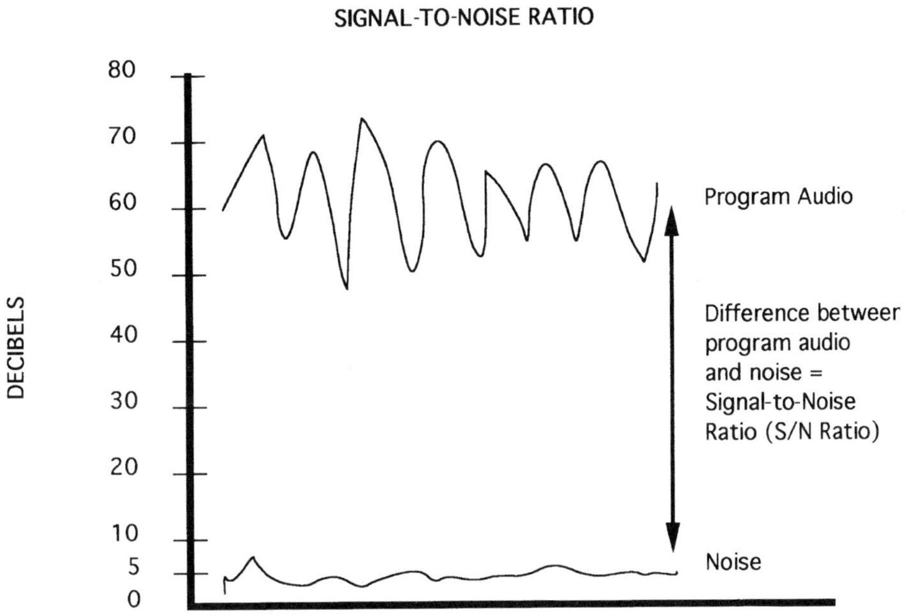

Figure 5.11 The ability to minimize the signal-to-noise ration is one of the critical measures used to determine the quality of an electronic system. Noise inherent in magnetic tape systems and noise picked up by cables are the leading creators of poor signal-to-noise ratios.

have precise volume scales. More expensive meters are calibrated in specific units of sound intensity, such as volume units or percentages of modulation. There are basically two types of professional sound intensity meters: volume unit (VU) meters and peak program meters (PPMs). The VU meter is the American standard. It is a special type of electrical voltmeter, which reads voltage shifts in electrical current as changes in sound intensity.

Needle readings are calibrated in both percentages of modulation and volume units or decibels (dBs). Approximately every 3 dB increase indicates a doubling of sound intensity. (A decibel is a logarithmic unit of sound intensity.) The modulation percentages are usually indicated on the lower scale of a VU meter. They range from 9 percent to 100 percent, the thresholds of signal detection and distortion, respectively. The upper scale indicates volume units or decibels. A reading of 0 dB usually corresponds to 100 percent modulation or peak loudness before distortion occurs, and the scale reads down on the left side and up on the right side (+1, +2, +3, and so on) of 0 dB.

A VU meter provides an electrical analog to human hearing. It does not show instantaneous peaks and immediate distortion, but indicates the average sound intensity over a very short period of time. This average reading closely approximates the response of the human ear to peak sound intensities. In general, signals on a VU meter should register between 50 percent and 100 percent modulation or between -6 dB and 0 dB. Below 50 percent modulation or -6 dB, the signal-to-noise ratio becomes relatively low. Above 100 percent modulation or 0 dB loudness, distortion occurs. Sounds that intermittently peak above 100 percent modulation, or 0 dB, for very short periods of time rarely cause noticeable distortion, but sounds that continuously pin the needle to its maximum above 100 percent modulation, or 0 dB, not only cause distortion but frequently cause meter damage as well. The audio operator continually watches the VU meter and makes minor adjustments in the sound level throughout a recording, using a volume control mechanism such as a potentiometer (pot) or a sliding fader bar. Volume level adjustments should be made smoothly and slowly. Major shifts in volume level affect the noise levels and background sounds as well as the primary signal and change the sound perspective and dynamics of the recorded sounds.

The PPM (sometimes called a *modulometer*) is another type of loudness or voltmeter and is the European standard. Rather than averaging sound intensities, a PPM responds immediately to peak sounds. The human ear cannot perceive extremely rapid loudness distortion, but many PPM users believe that such distortion nonetheless affects a sound recording. Obviously an operator using a PPM or modulometer must respond to needle readings on the devices somewhat differently, probably more reservedly and slowly, than one would respond to a VU meter reading. Both types of meters facilitate sound signal control, however. Some recorders have automatic gain controls (AGC) or automatic level controls (ALC) for a mic input. An AGC prevents loudness distortion automatically. However, it also boosts the ambient noise level when primary sounds are at low levels, such as at pauses in dialogue. To avoid this problem, levels should be set manually using a VU meter and the AGC turned off, if possible. Peak limiters are sometimes more useful than AGCs, as these simply limit the upper level of loudness without automatically setting the basic recording level and running the risk of increasing ambient noise levels. But most professionals prefer to control recording levels manually. Volume levels on a digital recording must also be carefully set. Although digital signals are either off or on, they do vary in intensity. An overmodulated digital recording will suffer uncorrectable distortion or total loss of the recording (Figures 5.12A and B).

Cables and Connectors

Professional mic cables have two conductor wire lines, a ground and a grounded shield. These balanced lines are less susceptible to cable noise than unbalanced lines, which have a single conductor wire and a grounded shield. The two conductor lines are usually well insulated from each other, the ground wire, and the cable exterior in balanced lines. Poorly insulated cables are much more susceptible to interference from other electrical cables and devices. Mic cables should never be placed near lighting instruments or electrical power cables, which can cause interference. Nor should they be wound tightly together or twisted in any manner that will reduce their life expectancy and damage the wire conductors. Less expensive recorders sometimes have mics attached by an unbalanced line cable with a single-prong miniplug at one end that is inserted into the front or side of the recorder. Balanced line cables are attached to three-prong XLR connectors, which can be plugged into mics, audio consoles, or tape recorders. These connectors have separate prongs for the two conductors and the ground. Male and female connector

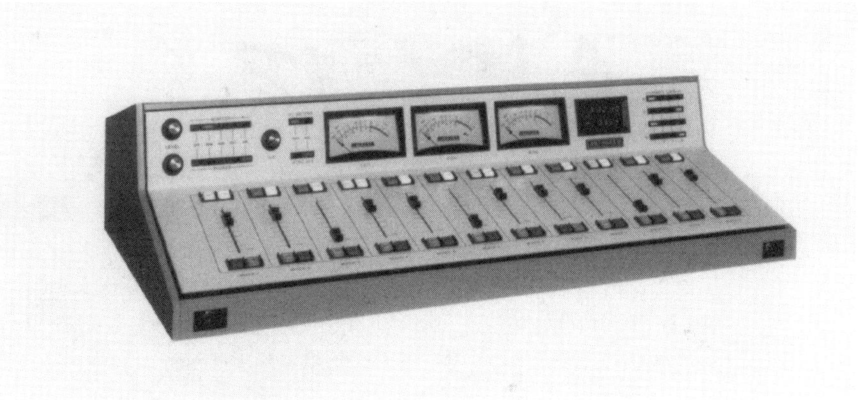

Figures 5.12A and B Audio control boards vary from small portable boards for field and post production facilities to large multi-input and multi-output boards for motion picture mixing theaters and music recording studios. (Courtesy of Autogram and Studer.)

ends lock into each other so that they do not easily become disconnected (Figure 5.13A).

It is probably a good idea to wrap two cables together in a very loose knot around the connectors, so that any pulling on the cables will pull the connectors together, rather than apart. Even though this procedure may place considerable stress on the cables in the case of an accident, such as someone tripping over a cable, it would undoubtedly be more expensive to reshoot the entire sequence in the event of a complete disconnection. Care should be taken, of course, to minimize the amount of twisting and stress that occurs at the juncture of the cable and con-

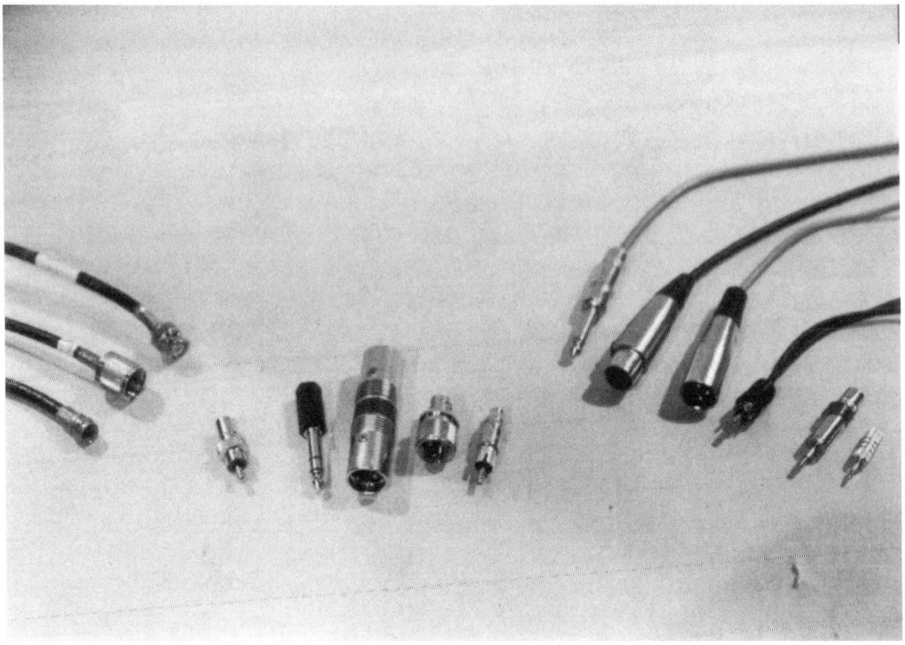

Figure 5.13A Audio and video signals are carried through different cable types and connected by a variety of connectors. On the left: three video cables, RF of "F," UHF, and BNC. In the center: adapters, RCA to BNC, ¼″ stereo to mini-plug, an XLR male to male barrel, UHF to BNC, and an RCA to mini-plug. On the right: ¼″, XLR female, XLR male, RCA to ¼″ adapter, and a micro-plug to mini-plug adapter.

nector, since this part of the cable is extremely vulnerable to damage and wear. Also cables should be coiled carefully before storing. Two methods of coiling cables are the over-under method and the figure eight method. Each system, when properly carried out, prevents internal twisting and damage to conductors inside the cable (Figure 5.13B).

Mixing

An audio console or mixer is designed to combine sounds from several different sound sources, such as mics, tape recorders, and playback units. These devices can vary from an elaborate studio audio console to a simple multiple-input mixer, which allows for separate volume control over each input. Basically the audio console routes signals from sound sources or playback units to a control device or recording unit. It can send a signal from a particular mic or a playback unit to a recorder, so that a duplicate copy or dub can be made, for example. It can combine or mix together several sound sources into one (monophonic) or onto two or more (multitrack) sound tracks or channels, which are recorded as a final or master audiotape.

An audio console consists of a series of faders, each of which controls the volume level of a single input. The inputs can come from microphones, turntables, analog and digital audiotape recorders, compact disc (CD) players, or audio play-

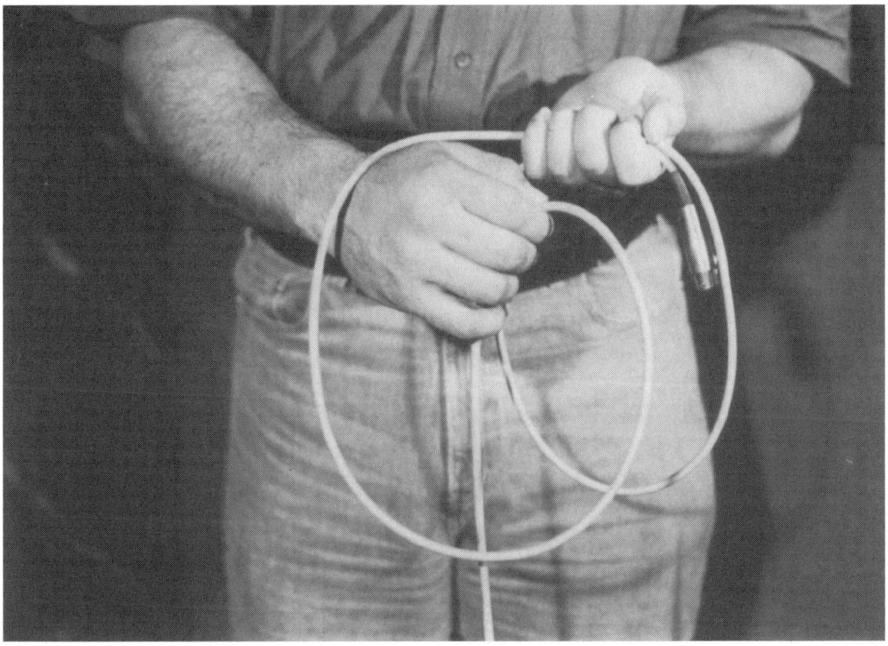

Figure 5.13B In order to properly coil cables, an "over and under" method may be used. This system protects the cable from twisting and provides a clean straight unwinding when uncoiled for use.

backs from videotape recorders. The output is controlled by a single (or dual) master pot(s). Each pot or fader often has its own equalization controls for increasing or decreasing bass and treble (low frequencies and high frequencies) directly above or below it. Most television studio audio consoles also have a talk-back system that allows a director or assistant director to communicate with the crew and thus does not affect the program signal (Figure 5.14).

Most audio consoles and mixers have two types of audio inputs: high impedance and low impedance. Impedance cuts down on the flow of alternating current; it is analogous to resistance in devices operated on direct current (batteries). Impedance and resistance are measured in ohms. High-impedance signals come from some nonprofessional mics, from playback machines, and from some signal-processing equipment. Low-impedance signals usually come from professional quality microphones and other equipment. Professional mics usually have an impedance of about 50 ohms, while playback units and other high-impedance sources are about 600 ohms.

An impedance imbalance or mismatch between the sound source and the mixer or console input will result in a signal that is either too loud and distorted, or too soft and weak to be useful for recording purposes. Different sound sources can have different levels of sound intensity or signal strength (volts), as well as different impedances (ohms). These also require separate inputs on an audio console. Mic levels are usually lower than line levels from playback units. Preamplifiers in the audio console can boost a low-level signal to a higher level so that it equals that of

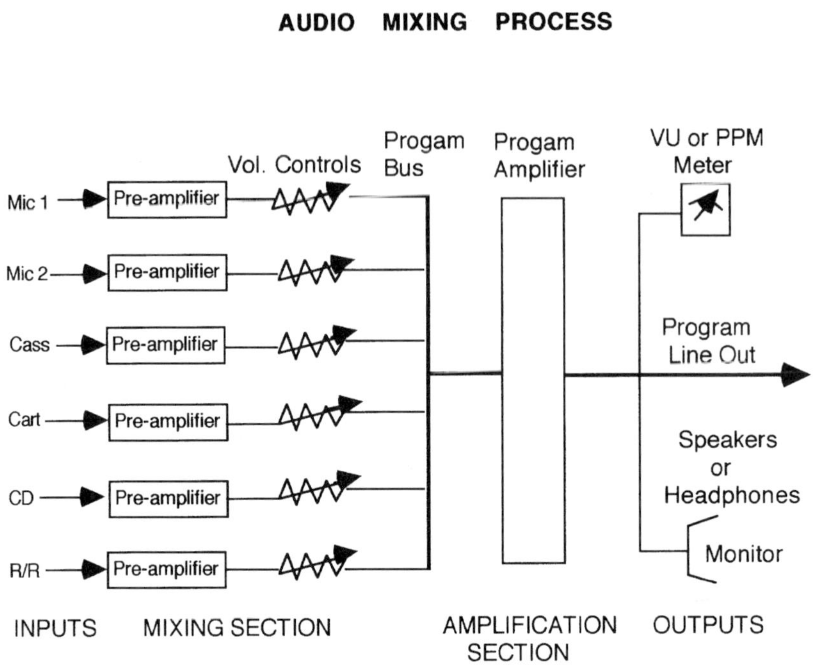

Figure 5.14 Audio mixing board circuits follow the basic pattern of pre-amplifying low level inputs, mixing all inputs through a program bus, and monitoring the program output signals by viewing a metering system and listening on headphones or through loud speakers.

other sound sources. When a high-level signal enters the console through a low-level input, distortion occurs. The level out of a mixer can be either high or mic (low) level, or if amplified, speaker level which is generally the highest level (Figure 5.15).

Any computer equipped with sufficient memory, a sound processing board and audio editing program can function as an audio postproduction board. The functions of mixing, equalizing, setting and varying levels, editing, and adding special effects are performed quickly with such a computer system.

Console Operation

Once the impedance and line levels of source and input match, the console operator can set the proper loudness levels for recording each sound source. To accomplish this on an audio console or mixer with only a single VU meter, all of the faders should be closed, except the one being set. If each input has its own VU meter, then it can be set independently of the others. The level for each input should be set between 80 percent and 100 percent modulation for an optimal signal-to-noise ratio. In some instances, such as background music and sounds, the level may be set somewhat lower for a proper overall balance between sounds. Balance is an aesthetic concept that refers to the best proportion of sound intensities from different elements, such as speech and music. Generally speaking, music must be toned

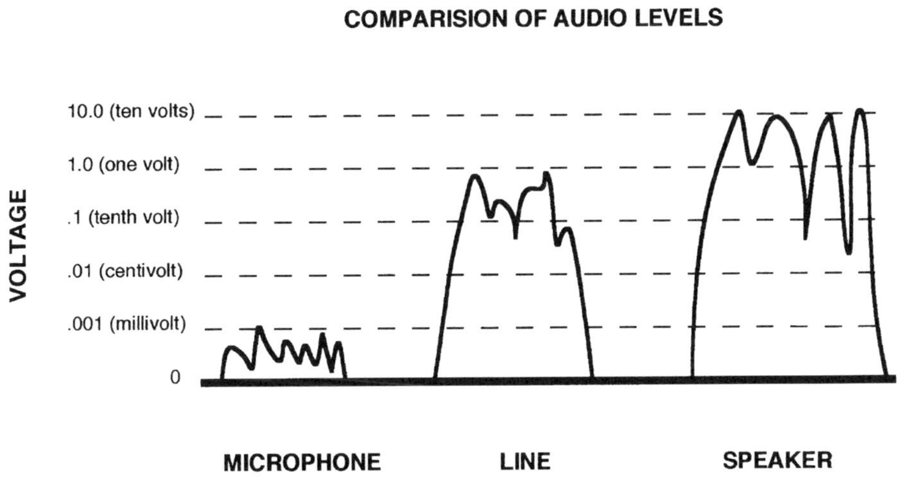

Figure 5.15 The three primary audio levels vary in voltage from the very weak signal directly from a microphone, turntable pickup arm, and magnetic recorder playback head, to a middle level of a preamplified signal (called line level), to the high level of the output of an amplifier intended to power a speaker or speaker system.

or faded down to achieve a proper balance with accompanying dialogue or narration. In addition to balancing sounds, an audio operator should check for multiple-microphone interference by determining if the volume levels of specific sources increase as others are shut off. It is generally a good idea to label each fader with the number or name of the mic or sound source it carries for each sound source and fader to eliminate any confusion when adjustments have to be made during actual recording.

Recording and Mixing Commands

To perform well at the audio console or mixer, the audio recordist should be familiar with each of the following audio terms, cues, and commands:

Fade-in audio. The sound intensity is gradually raised to an audible level and its proper volume setting from an inaudible or nonexistent level.

Fade-out audio. The sound intensity is gradually lowered to an inaudible level.

Segue. One sound source is faded out while another is immediately faded in without any overlap or dead air in between the two sounds.

Cross-fade. One sound source is faded out while another is faded in over it. The sum of the two sounds should remain at a peak level.

Open mic. The fader or pot for a specific mic is raised immediately to its proper level or is simply switched on.

Cut sound or kill sound. The fader or pot is abruptly closed or the channel switch is cut off.

Sound up and under. The sound is faded up promptly to its proper level and then is faded down to a lower level, at which level it is still audible but less prominent to allow for a voice to be balanced over the original background sound, usually music (Figure 5.16).

Backtime. Prepare a prerecorded sound or music track so that it will end at a specified time. This requires a calculation by subtracting the length of the track from the end time of the production. The playback machine must begin at the exact backtime in order for the track to end correctly. The pot or fader assigned to is not turned up until required, so that the sounds or music can be gradually faded in at the appropriate point.

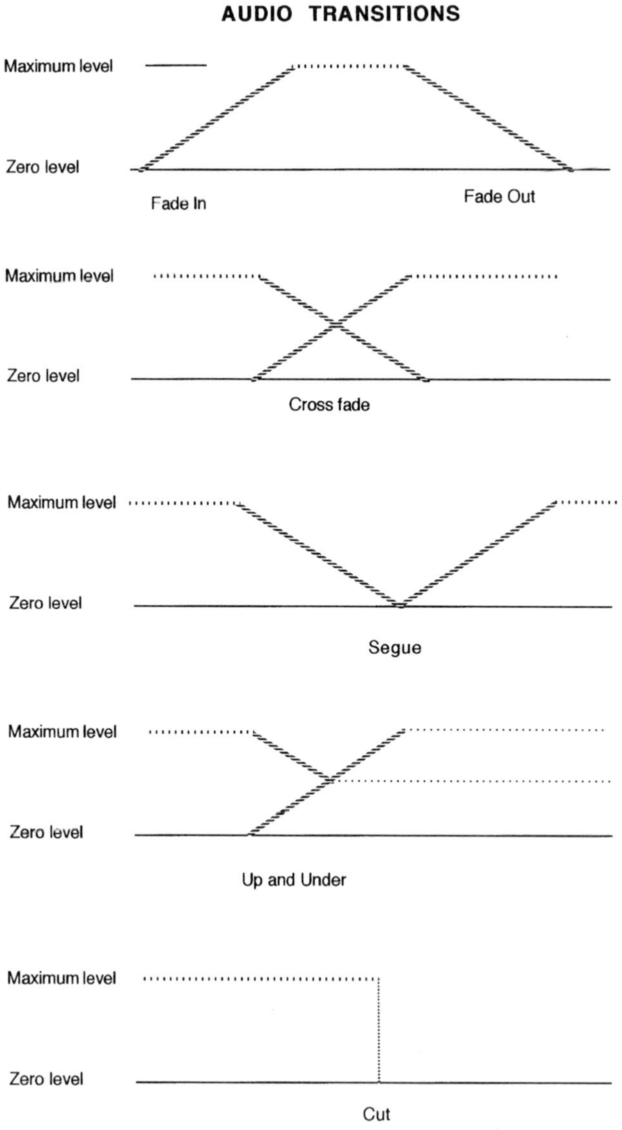

Figure 5.16
Audio transitions provide a means of mixing audio from two or more sources, or providing a means of switching from one audio source to another.

Sound Perspectives

The relationship of sound to space parallels that of the picture with three dimensions: left-right, up-down, and in front or behind the listener. In order to duplicate audio realistically, the perception of these dimensions must be duplicated. The characteristics to be duplicated are distance and directionality. Sound that appears to be originating close or far away may be recorded by placing the mic(s) close or at a distance from the sound source. The sound indicating the size of the environment will be determined by the reflective or absorption values of the walls, furniture, or other objects in the space, and the size of the room. The direction of the sound can only be determined through the use of one of several multichannel systems to give the audience the sense that the sound is to the left, right, in front of, or behind them.

Stereo Sound

Both stereo and surround-sound systems and modifications are attempts to duplicate the three-dimensional aspects of a sound environment. Stereo offers two or three channels of sound; left, right, and, depending on the size of the audience (as in a motion picture theater), a center channel. Reproduction of sound through the left or right channel to match the objects originating the sound on the screen may add to the realistic effect, but also may become confusing if overdone. Now that stereo television receivers are available, the impulse to split sound into left and right must be weighed against the realization that television is a close-up medium that requires audio to be concentrated in the center of the screen or balanced between the left and right channels.

Wide-screen films, on the other hand, offer much greater opportunities to utilize sound originating from the side of the screen matching the source of the sound. Care must be taken not to overbalance sound to one side or another, or else the audience seated on the opposite side of the theater may miss some critical sounds. In the recording industry, music is recorded either to duplicate the physical arrangement of the group (symphonic orchestras) or to enhance the vocals or a solo instrument (rock groups). Today music is recorded with the assumption that it will be reproduced on a stereo rather than monaural system.

Surround Sound

Surround sound was the next logical step from stereo in creating the realistic three-dimensional sound environment. Mixing the sound into at least four channels to be reproduced through speakers located in the four corners of the listening space enhances the sense of the original recording, but such a process increases the complexity of mic placement, mixing, and speaker location. Surround sound in the past has not proved practical for the average home or video production. Modification of the theory has opened new avenues for film sound. Most theaters today are capable of reproducing sound recorded on as many as ten channels using three to four speakers lining the side walls of the theater to supplement the normal stereo and center speakers located behind the screen. Multichannel sound increases the illusion of both the width and depth of the picture.

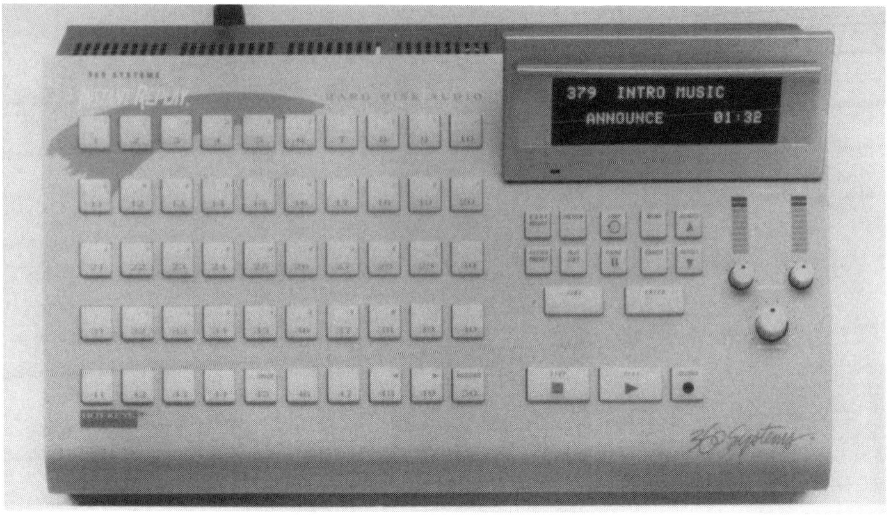

Figure 5.17 A hard disk audio player/recorder providing instant access to 1,000 individual digitized audio cuts of any length. The operator can quickly call up any of the recordings in any order instantaneously. (Courtesy of 360 Systems.)

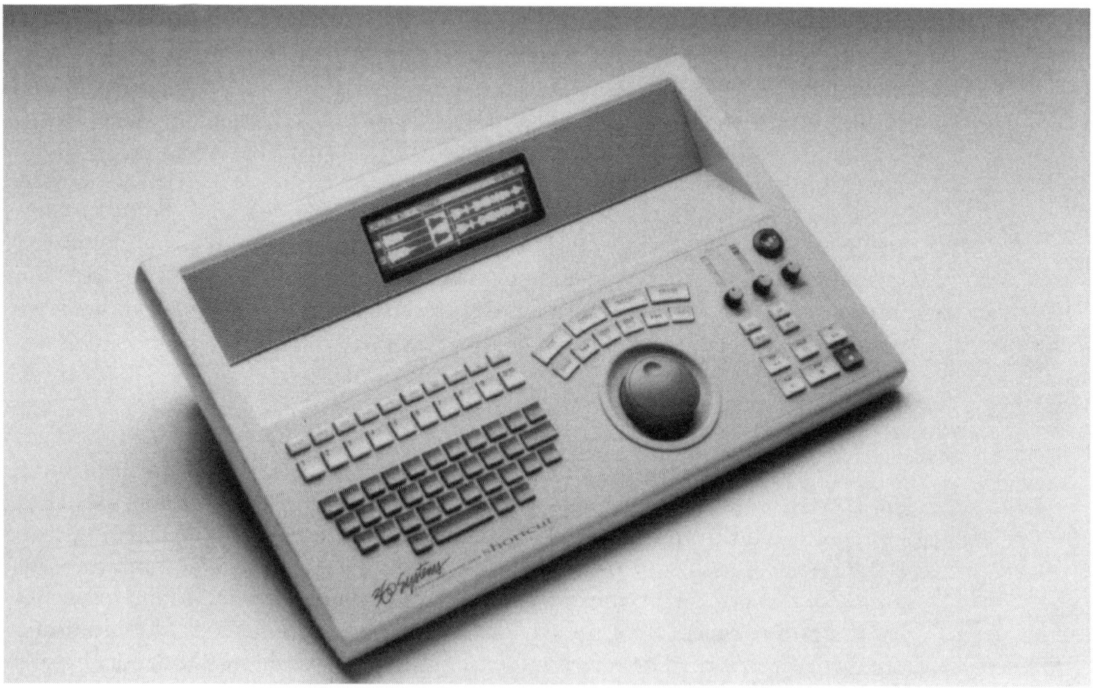

Figure 5.18 A digital stereo audio editor designed for quick editing for talk radio, call-in clips, news actualities, promotional announcements, and commercials. Designed to edit like a word processor with cut/copy/paste and precision scrubbing functions. (Courtesy of 360 Systems.)

Summary

Sound recording can be approached from three aesthetic perspectives: realism, modernism, and postmodernism. Realist sound appears to be transmitted naturally, as though there were no recording device mediating between the speaker and the listener. Modernist sounds fail to meet our realist expectations and can be effective devices for attracting attention, arousing emotions, and stimulating innovative ideas.

The aesthetic use of recorded sounds demands an understanding of recording devices and their selection, placement, and control. A mic or microphone is a transducer that converts sound wave energy into electrical energy. Mics can be classified into three different categories on the basis of their transducer elements: dynamic, ribbon, and condenser. Dynamic mics are very durable and not extremely susceptible to wind noise. They make good handheld mics and are frequently used outdoors. A ribbon mic is fragile and susceptible to wind noise. But it is also quite versatile and is frequently used as a stationary mic in a studio, and is ideal for digital recording. Condenser mics do an excellent job of boosting weaker sounds. They are often used for distant mic placements and wireless FM mics.

Mics can also be classified on the basis of pickup patterns. Omnidirectional mics are sensitive to sounds coming from all directions and are used when these sounds are equally important. Bidirectional mics are sensitive to sounds coming from two directions, such as from two speakers on opposite sides of the mic. Unidirectional mics, such as the cardioid mic, are sensitive to sounds from one direction. Highly directional mics, such as a supercardioid or shot-gun mic, can be used to exclude all sounds except those from a distant speaker, although they also pick up sounds from directly behind the speaker. Mics can be placed in on-camera and off-camera positions. Hand mics, desk mics, stand mics, and lavalier mics are examples of on-camera mic positions. Mics on booms, such as fishpole, giraffe, and perambulator booms, as well as various hidden mics, such as the hanging mic, prop mic, and concealed lavalier mic, are off-camera mics.

Selecting the best mic and mic position depends on an understanding of what mic characteristics and placements are best suited to a specific situation. When there are several sound sources or speakers, it is often advisable to use several mics, each positioned to isolate specific sounds. When two mics pick up the same sounds and some are cancelled out, multiple-microphone interference occurs. Multiple-microphone interference can be controlled through proper mic placement or multitrack recording. Multiple mics are also used to record stereophonic sounds on separate sound tracks. These separate but simultaneously recorded sounds are then played back through speakers separated by some distance to allow for a perception of the directional placement of sounds.

Digital recording of audio requires greater care in mic selection and placement as well as noise reduction. Sound signal control helps a sound recordist achieve the best quality recorded sound by eliminating specific audio problems. Loudness distortion can be eliminated by setting volume controls so that the volume never exceeds the limits of the electronic system. Ambient noise and system noise can be reduced with respect to the primary signal, such as a speaker's voice, by moving a mic closer to the subject, thus making the primary signal stronger. A sound measuring device, such as a VU (volume unit) meter, can be used to set the sound level as high as possible for optimal signal-to-noise ratio, while avoiding loudness distortion. Signals on a VU meter should register between 50 percent and 100 percent modulation. Balanced mic cables should be used to minimize noise and electrical interference.

Audio mixing is done on an audio console or mixer. Mixing refers to combining several different inputs, such as different mics or playback machines, into a single (monophonic) or dual (stereophonic) output, which is directed to a tape recorder. Faders on the audio console or mixer are used to adjust the volume very gradually. They should be clearly marked for the sound source designated for them. Audio operators using a console or mixer must be familiar with basic audio terms, cues, and commands, so that they can effectively communicate with the rest of the staff and crew. Sound perspectives should match the perspectives of the matching visual as well as the requirements of the drama or music. Perspectives include both distance and dimensionality.

Exercises

1. Practice following a moving speaker with a cardioid mic on a mic boom as he or she walks around a studio on a precise, preplanned route. Try to keep the mic one to four feet in front of and one to three feet above the speaker. Record the sounds on audiotape or videotape without changing the pot or fader setting on the recorder so that the initial volume setting is used constantly. Change the mic to a supercardioid or shot-gun mic, and perform the same exercise. Did you keep a constant distance between the mic and the speaker? Was the mic always in the best position to pick up the speaker's voice? Listen to your recording critically for fluctuations in the loudness of the speaker's voice. Discuss what you could have done to improve recording consistency. Did the shot-gun mic increase overall sound quality while making it more difficult to maintain a constant recording level?
2. Set up an on-camera narration videotape recording outdoors. Select a location that is relatively quiet. Bring along three mics: a cardioid hand mic, a small lavalier mic, and a supercardioid or shot-gun mic. Record the same on-camera narration with the speaker looking directly into the camera three times, once with each type of mic. Make sure that each mic has a windscreen and position the speaker with his or her back to the wind, if possible.

   When using the shot-gun mic, make sure that there are no loud sounds coming from directly behind the speaker. Position the shot-gun mic as close to the edge of the camera frame as you can without entering the frame. Have the speaker hold the cardioid mic about six to nine inches from his or her mouth. Attach the lavalier so that no clothing or jewelry rubs against it and the mic cable is well hidden. Compare the three recordings. Which mic gave the best quality recording with the least amount of noise?

Additional Readings

Alkin, Glyn. *Sound Techniques for Video and TV,* 2nd ed. Boston: Focal Press, 1989.
Alten, Stanley. *Audio in Media,* 4th ed. Belmont, CA: Wadsworth, 1994.

Bartlett, Bruce. *Stereo Microphone Techniques.* Boston: Focal Press, 1991.
Borwick, John. *Microphones: Technology and Technique.* Boston: Focal Press, 1990.
Borwick, John. *Sound Recording Practice.* New York: Oxford University Press, 1976.
Frater, Charles. *Sound Recording for Motion Pictures.* New York: A.S. Barnes, 1979.
Gayford, Michael. *Microphone Engineering Handbook.* Boston: Focal Press, 1994.
Gross, Lynne S. and David E. Reese. *Radio Production Worktext,* 2nd ed. Boston: Focal Press, 1993.
Rumsey, Francis. *Digital Audio Operations.* Boston: Focal Press, 1991.
Watkinson, John. *An Introduction to Digital Audio.* Boston: Focal Press, 1994.
Weis, Elisabeth. *The Silent Scream. Alfred Hitchcock's Sound Track.* Rutherford, NJ: Farleigh Dickinson University Press, 1982.
Weis, Elisabeth and John Belton. *Film Sound: Theory and Practice.* New York: Columbia University Press, 1985.
Yale French Studies. Special issue on Sound in Film. 60 (1980).

6

Lighting

Introduction

One of the most creative and visually exciting tasks in video and film production is lighting. Visual artists refer to lighting as painting with light. A lighting director or director of photography can use lights just as effectively and expressively as any painter uses color pigments to evoke a specific mood or visual impression. Lighting can be used to emphasize and dramatize a subject by bringing objects into sharp relief or contrast, or it can be used to soften and to harmonize. Lighting directly affects the overall impressions and feelings generated by recorded visual images. It is a complex art, but basic video and film lighting can be reduced to a limited number of concepts and techniques. This chapter provides an introduction to the basic aesthetic approaches, techniques, and equipment needed to design and control the lighting of moving images.

Lighting Aesthetics

The expressive design and effect of a lighting setup can be described as realist, modernist, or postmodernist.

Realist Lighting

Realist lighting appears to come from actual light sources in a setting or location. It enhances an illusion of reality. Realist lighting conforms to the audience's expectations of how a scene should normally or naturalistically appear in real life. In conventional popular dramas, the lighting is usually realistic. The major problem for the lighting director is to determine the actual light source in the scene. The brightest lights are positioned according to the direction and intensity of the central or main source of light. Directional lighting continuity is maintained from one shot to the next in the same scene. If the main source of light is a window, the direction of the lights basically preserves the spatial positioning of the window on the set. The same holds true for firelight or candlelight. The lighting director tries to match the natural scene under normal vision using artificial lights. Multiple shadows should be minimized, if not eliminated, so that the lighting rarely calls attention to itself. There is a logical consistency to the direction and intensity of the lighting, which has a presumed cause or real source.

Few productions are completely realist. Some degree of modernist stylization is often needed to stimulate dramatic interest. Lighting directors use lighting to bring out and emphasize specific aspects of a personality or setting. They highlight details that add depth to performers and actions. Strict authenticity often fails to stimulate emotions and viewer interest, and a purely realist lighting setup often seems flat and boring.

Modernist Lighting

Modernist lighting has no real-life referent. The lighting director is much freer to design a lighting setup according to purely abstract or subjective emotional criteria, that is, to stylize the use of light. The lighting director literally paints with light to create emphasis and spatial impressions. Modernist lighting tries to achieve a specific emotional effect or abstract design through non-naturalistic patterns of light. The actual sources of light are often of little interest.

Modernist lighting stimulates emotions and creates a dynamic visual impression. For example, the lighting setup for a musical variety program may light an empty stage with pools of colored light, creating abstract patterns. The mood or atmosphere can coincide with the central theme or emotion expressed by a song or dance. Even in a realist drama, a dream sequence might call for highly stylized lighting that mirrors the internal state of mind of the central character. These are often highly abstract and unrealistic visual sequences, but they effectively convey the character's feelings, emotions, and state of mind. Excessive or inappropriate stylization calls attention to the lighting and distracts viewer attention from the central message or information of a nonfiction program. It can also destroy the illusion of reality in a realistic drama, but the absence of any stylization at all leads to viewer disinterest.

Postmodernist Lighting

Postmodernist lighting often mixes a variety of different lighting styles drawn from different genres. For example, highly stylized Hollywood studio lighting is used to record interviews in Errol Morris' *Thin Blue Line* (1987), a documentary. Postmodernist lighting often appeals to the emotions on a different level from modernist or realist lighting. At first glance postmodernist lighting may not make any sense on a practical level, but by mixing concrete realism with abstract modernism, it can evoke an emotional response in the viewer. Some music videos and rock concerts use postmodernist lighting effects and styles, bombarding the viewer with powerful sensations unrelated to any realist action in the film or video or any specific thoughts or feelings inside the mind of a character. These lighting effects and styles reflect the complexity and diversity of contemporary life, art, and culture.

Postmodernist lighting in *Batman Forever* (1995) relies on computerized lighting effects similar to those used at rock concerts to create a feeling of disorientation at a circus, and by controlling the projection of Chinese symbols and motifs in exterior settings of Gotham City, the film combines different cultures, times, and places through lighting in distinctly postmodernist ways.

Light and Color

There are a variety of light sources that can be used for television and film recording. Each of these can be distinguished in terms of the color temperature of the light it emits. Color temperature is usually defined in technical terms of degrees Kelvin. *Degrees Kelvin* is a unit of measurement that refers to the type of light that would theoretically be given off by a perfect light radiator (what physicists call a black-box radiator) when it is heated to a specific temperature. White light, as noted in Chapter 5, is actually composed of relatively equal amounts of all the colors in the visible spectrum, but light sources with different color temperatures emit slightly different amounts of the various color wavelengths (red, green, blue light), which together make up white light and the visible spectrum. Sunlight has a relatively high color temperature, about 5400 or 5600 degrees Kelvin, while tungsten or incandescent light, such as that given off by many living room lamps and much professional lighting equipment, has a much lower color temperature, about 3200 degrees Kelvin.

Sunlight has somewhat more blue light (short wavelengths) than does tungsten light, which has slightly more red light (long wavelengths.) As a result, a film stock or video camera designed or preset for tungsten light will record bluish images when it is exposed under sunlight, and a film stock or video camera rated or adjusted for daylight (sunlight) will record reddish images under tungsten light. Because video and film recording devices are often more sensitive to these differences in color temperature than our eyes, specific light sources must be carefully selected and controlled (Figure 6.1).

Sunlight

Sunlight is a natural light source. Burning gases on the sun's surface emit light that has a relatively high color temperature when it reaches the earth's surface, 5400 degrees K. Sunlight contains approximately equal proportions of all color wavelengths in the visible spectrum. Unless it is broken up and diffused by clouds, direct sunlight produces intense, harsh, contrasty light. This kind of light quality is called *hard,* as opposed to *soft,* light. It creates harsh shadows. Diffusion screens and reflectors can be used on location to reduce the intensity and contrast of direct sunlight and to create soft light. Indirect sunlight, often called *skylight,* has a higher color temperature than direct sunlight: from 6000 degrees K to 20,000 degrees K. Indirectly lit shadow areas also contain a higher proportion of ultraviolet light than areas lit by direct sunlight. To reduce the bluish cast that is often produced by this ultraviolet light, an ultraviolet (UV) or skylight filter can be placed over the camera lens.

Tungsten Light

One of the earliest sources of electrical lighting was Thomas Edison's incandescent bulb. An incandescent bulb consists of a tungsten filament in a glass-enclosed vacuum. A strong electrical current encounters considerable resistance at the filament, generating both heat and light. In general, a tungsten light source produces somewhat more light of longer wavelengths, such as red and orange, than of shorter wavelengths, such as blue and violet. Professional tungsten light has a color tem-

COLOR TEMPERATURES OF LIGHT SOURCES

SOURCE	DEGREES KELVIN	MIREDS
Match flame	1700K	588
Candle flame	1850K	541
Sunrise or sunset	2000K	500
Consumer lamps	2650K-2990K	317-345
Standard Tungsten/Halogen	3200K	313
Photoflood	3400K	294
Early morning, late afternoon	4300K	233
Daylight photoflood	4800K	208
HMI	5600K	179
Typical noon	5400K-5800K	185
Carbon arc	5800K	172
Overcast sky	6000K	167
Summer shade	8000K	125
Full summer sun	10,000K-30,000K	100
	Comparable Degrees Kelvin for Fluorescent Sources	
Warm white	3050	
White	3500	
Natural white	3700	
Cool white	4300	
Daylight	6500	

Figure 6.1 The differences in the actual color of light sources range from full summer sun to a candle flame. Fluorescent light sources also vary over a range, but not as varied as incandescent and natural light sources.

perature of 3200 degrees K. Incandescent lamps in the home and office may emit a much lower color temperature.

The color temperature of all tungsten lamps decreases with age. Tungsten-halogen-quartz bulbs (usually called *quartz lights*) have become an important source of 3200 degree K indoor lighting. Caution needs to be exercised in the handling of quartz bulbs, however. They should never be touched, since the oil in your skin breaks down the quartz-like glass and reduces the life of a bulb. Quartz lights are usually rated in terms of the watts of electrical energy they consume: The most common sizes are 650 and 1000 watts.

Carbon Arc Light

Carbon arc lights produce intense light, which has very high color temperature. Light is produced by passing a spark between two carbon poles. Carbon arcs generally require vast amounts of DC electrical current and produce intense heat and noxious vapors and exhaust, which must be ventilated. The high intensity and high color temperature of arc lights make them useful for location production in combination with sunlight. However, they are extremely bulky and require special electrical generators on location.

Metal Halide Light

A relatively recent development in location lighting is the metal halide light, three of which are in use today: HMI, CID, and CSI. HMI and CID lamps provide light at approximately 5400 degrees Kelvin and now are replacing carbon arc lamps. HMI lamps, the most popular of the three, give almost four times the amount of light for the same electrical input as tungsten-quartz-halogen lamps. This light source produces high intensity, high color-temperature light (similar to daylight) with great efficiency. It generates little heat and operates on standard 120-volt, 60Hz AC current (although a few use 220-volt current). HMI lights are frequently used to raise the lighting level at outdoor locations, which may be partially lit by indirect sunlight. HMI lights are fully glass-enclosed arc lamps that require separate start and ballast mechanisms to control electrical current. HMI lights can also be filtered so that they duplicate 3200 degree K tungsten light sources.

Fluorescent Light

Unlike all the other types of light sources discussed thus far, fluorescent light is discontinuous throughout the visible spectrum. Certain bands of colored light, such as bands of red, yellow, green, or blue light, are strong, while others are almost nonexistent in a fluorescent light source. Light is produced through phosphorescence rather than incandescence, and different phosphors produce different wavelengths of light. In film recording, color filters placed over the light source or camera lens can compensate for some of this spectral discontinuity, but there are so many differences between most fluorescent bulb types and brands that no simple filter or combination of filters will properly remedy every situation. Video recording devices can be at least partially adjusted for fluorescent light sources by white balancing the camera under fluorescent lighting. Professional fluorescent lighting instruments have been developed that produce highly intense but diffuse light of

3200 degree K color temperature using minimal electricity. While these instruments are expensive, they are also highly efficient sources of fill light.

Conventional fluorescent lighting often produces humming and flickering. The alternating current mechanisms used to create fluorescent light can cause flicker in a recorded image and produce an audio hum, which is easily picked up by even distant microphones and affects the recorded sound track, but professional fluorescent systems are designed to avoid hum and flicker. Because of negative audio and visual effects, it is often advisable to shut off conventional fluorescent lights, if possible, and to use tungsten or HMI lighting instead. In some situations, such as certain industrial locations, it is virtually impossible to replace all the pre-existing fluorescent lights with other artificial lighting. In this case, one type of light source is selected as primary and all other light sources are reduced as much as possible in intensity. Light sources having different color temperatures should not be used simultaneously unless filters can be placed in front of light sources, including windows, to change and equalize different color temperatures.

White Balance

In order to adjust either video or film systems to various Kelvin temperatures, compensation must be provided. Video cameras can be adjusted to the degree Kelvin of the light source through the process of white balancing. Once the lighting has be determined and set, the camera(s) are pointed at the subject area focused on a white card. A switch is thrown on the camera or camera control unit and held until an indicator shows that the camera has adjusted its electronic circuits to that lighting temperature. A video camera must be rewhite balanced each time the location or light source has been modified. Video cameras are designed to operate under 3200 degree Kelvin tungsten lighting without filters. If operated under daylight or other 5400 degree light sources, a filter must be inserted to compensate for the difference in light temperature. Normally an 85 (yellow-orange) filter is used (Figure 6.2).

Film systems, on the other hand, must match the film stock to the lighting temperature. If shooting under tungsten, a film balanced for 3200 degree Kelvin must be used, or daylight film with an 80 blue filter. If shooting under daylight conditions, a film balanced for 5400 degrees Kelvin or tungsten film with an 85 filter must be used to compensate for the difference in Kelvin temperature (Figure 6.3).

Lighting Instruments

The housing within which a light source or lamp is encased is called a *lighting instrument* or *luminaire*. Lighting instruments can be generally classified according to the directness or indirectness, and hardness or softness, of the light they emit. Sharply focused and concentrated light produces harsh shadows and high contrast. Diffused or softened light minimizes shadows and reduces contrast. Lighting instruments with lenses that sharply focus light are referred to as *spotlights*. Lighting instruments without lenses that have reflectors that spread and soften light are called *floodlights*.

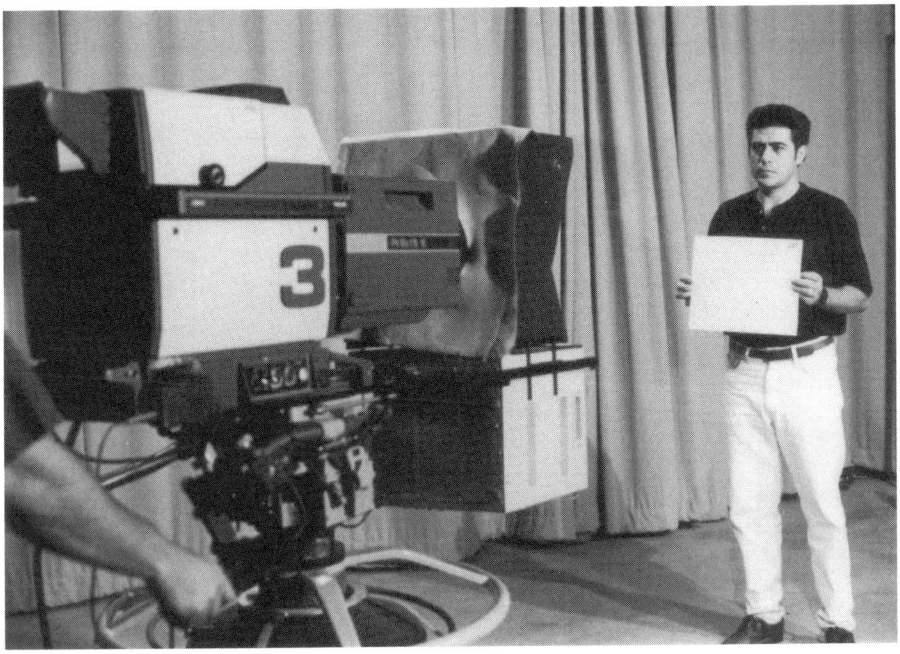

Figure 6.2 With the proper filter placed between the video camera lens and pick chips or tubes, the camera's internal circuits will automatically white balance when focused on a pure white card and the white balance switch is thrown. Film camera white balance is dependent upon the type of film stock and filter arrangement, not the camera or the camera's internal operation.

Spotlights

Fresnel and ellipsoidal lighting instruments are two different types of spotlights. *Fresnel* refers to a specific type of lens, which bends the light so that it travels in a relatively narrow path. The term *ellipsoidal* refers to the shape of a mirror or reflector at the back of the instrument that concentrates the light rays focused by a lens. Both types of spotlights concentrate the light emitted by a lamp or bulb into a narrow, intense band of light (Figures 6.4A and B).

Floodlights

The most commonly used types of floodlights are scoops, broads, soft lights, and strip lights. These open lights lack lenses and mirrors that focus light into a narrow beam. Instead, they diffuse or spread light, decreasing both its intensity and harshness. Scoops, broads, and soft lights usually consist of one, two, or three lamps, and have somewhat larger and more diffuse reflectors than spotlights. Strip lights have several bulbs, each with its own built-in reflector, placed in close proximity to one another so that they diffuse and soften the light in combination. Strip lights may be equipped with colored lenses to throw a "colorized" wash on to cyk or other neutral background. Floodlights are frequently used to light wide areas. They are also used to fill in the shadows created by spotlights and thereby reduce contrast within a scene (Figures 6.5A and B).

MOTION PICTURE FILM EXPOSURE CHARACTERISTICS

NAME	LIGHT BALANCE	EI	FILTER
Color Negative			
Agfa XT 100	Tungsten	100/80	85
Agfa XT 320	Tungsten	320/200	85
Agfa XTS 400	Tungsten	400/250	85
Eastman EXR 50D	Daylight	12/50	80A
Eastman EXR 100T	Tungsten	100/64	85
Eastman EXR 200T	Tungsten	200/125	85
Eastman EXR 500T	Tungsten	500/320	85
Eastman HS Day	Daylight	80/250	80B
Fujicolor F-64	Tungsten	64/40	85
Fujicolor F-64D	Daylight	64	
Fujicolor F-125	Tungsten	125/80	85
Fujicolor F-250	Tungsten	250/160	85
Fujicolor F-500D	Daylight	64/250	80A
Fujicolor F-500	Tungsten	500/320	85
COLOR REVERSAL			
Eastman Ekta-day	Daylight	40/160	80A
Eastman Ekta-tung	Tungsten	125/80	85B
Eastman Ekta-HS-D	Daylight	100/400	80A
Eastman Ekta-HS-T	Tungsten	400/250	85B
Kodachrome 25	Daylight	6/25	80A
Kodachrome 40	Tungsten	40/25	85
BLACK & WHITE NEGATIVE			
Agfa Pan 250		200/250	
Eastman Plus-X		64/80	
Eastman Double-X		200/250	
Fuji FG		64/80	
Fuji RP		64/80	
BLACK & WHITE REVERSAL			
Eastman Plus-X Reversal		40/50	
Eastman Tri-X Reversal		100-125	

Figure 6.3 The design and manufacture of motion picture film stock determines whether the film is designed to be shot under daylight or tungsten light sources. The speed of film stock also is determined by the manufacturing process. Each of these characteristics can be modified with filters and processing modifications. (Courtesy of Eastman Kodak, Fuji Films, and Afga Films.)

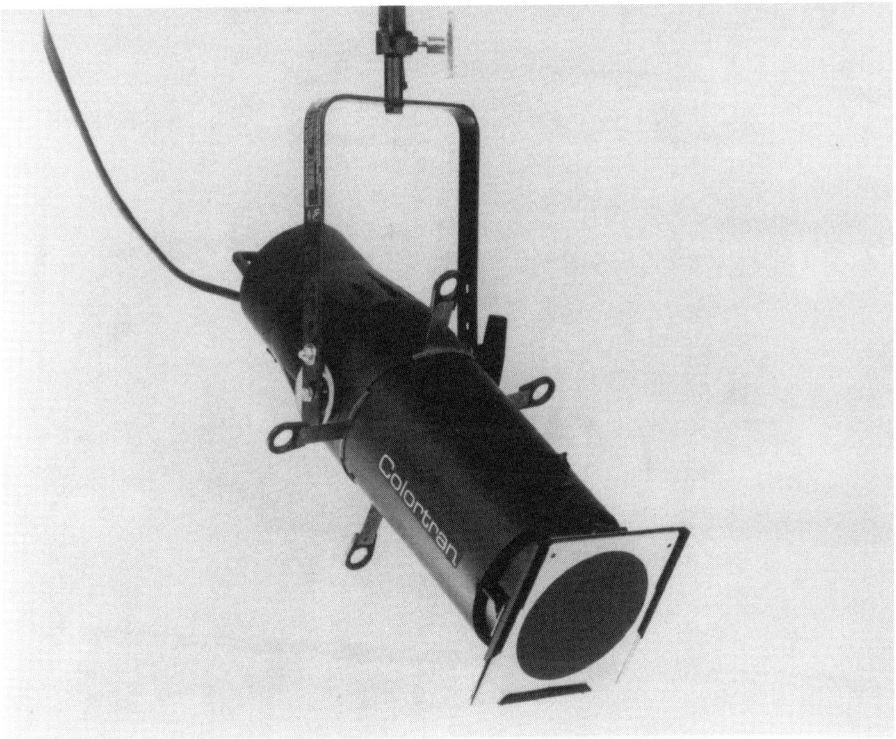

Figures 6.4A and B The light pattern from a Fresnel lighting instrument is controlled by moving the lamp inside the fixture closer or farther away from the stepped lens in the front of the instrument and by adjusting the barn doors mounted on the outside front of the lamp. The light pattern from an ellipsoidal lamp is controlled by adjusting shutters mounted inside the case of the lamp between the lamp and the front lens. Barn doors also may be mounted on ellipsoidal lamps. (Courtesy of Colortran.)

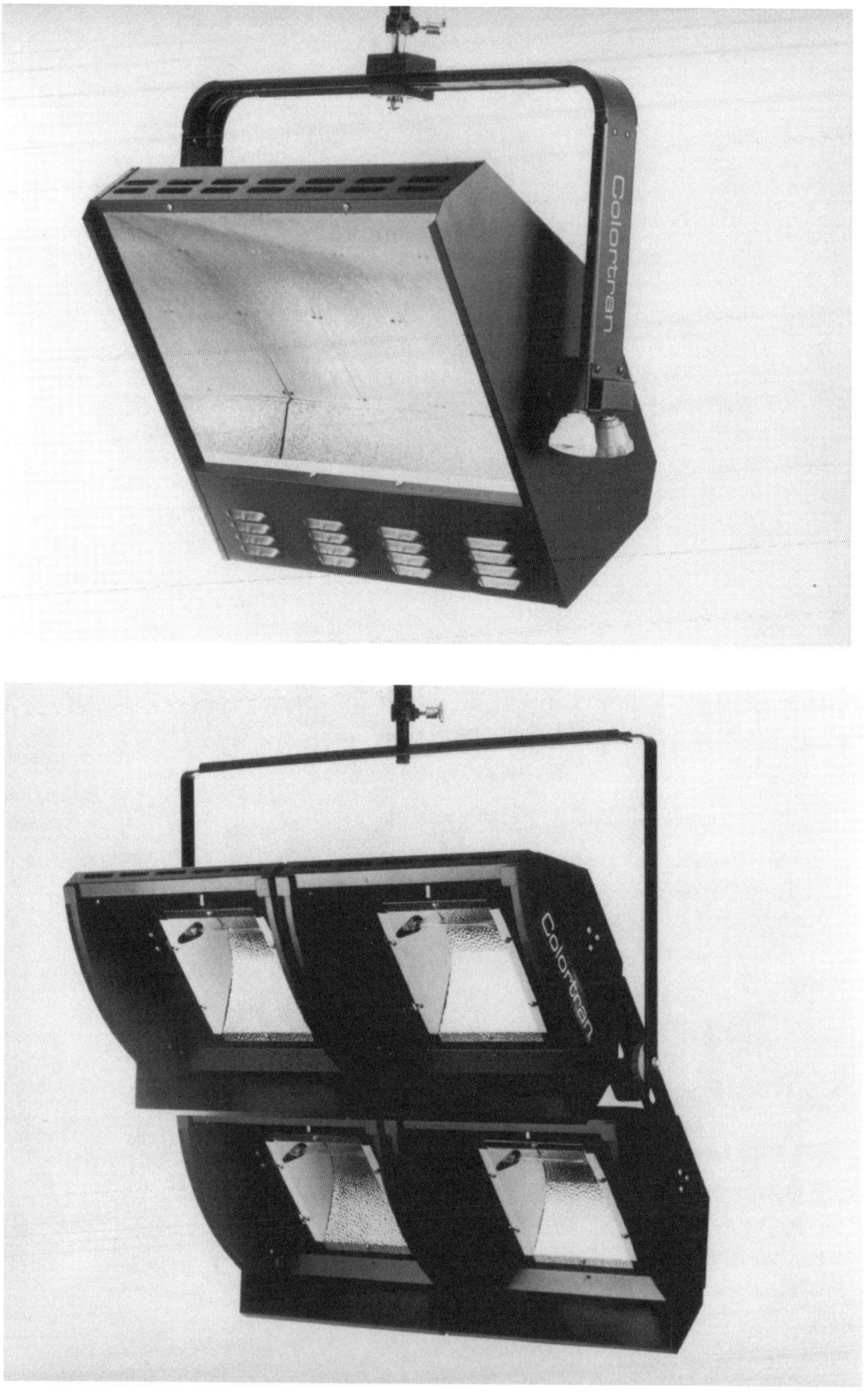

Figures 6.5A and B Flood lamps are manufactured in a variety of shapes and sizes, but the purpose is to provide a soft, diffused light. Control of light from flood lamps is more difficult due to its diffused nature. (Courtesy of Colortran.)

Portable Lights

A wide variety of lighting kits are available for use on location. Portable lighting kits usually have open, nonlensed lighting instruments and quartz lamps rated from 500 to 2000 watts. These instruments lack some of the controls of studio spotlights. Lighting kits contain several open reflector quartz lights and collapsible light mounting equipment, power cords, and other lighting accessories. Photofloods, such as lowell-light units, are highly portable lamps with self-contained reflectors inside the bulb (see Figures 6.6B, C, D). Some lightweight lighting instruments have their own portable power supply or rechargeable battery pack. Battery-powered lights, such as the Sylvania Sun Gun, can be used in moving vehicles or on remote locations, where a standard power supply is not available. The batteries should be fully charged, since the color temperature gradually decreases as the battery weakens and the voltage drops (Figure 6.6A).

With the increase of available power in newer battery designs, more efficient luminaires, and cameras and films that are more sensitive, battery-powered lighting has become more practical. Standard alternating current power sources are still preferable to batteries for lights, where possible.

Mounting Devices

Studio lighting is done with overhead lighting instruments, which are attached to a grid. This makes it easier for cameras and performers to move about the studio floor without running into lights. The pipe grid, which consists of a series of pipes suspended in parallel rows above the studio floor to which instruments are attached with C-clamps, is probably the most common type of grid. Safety chains or heavy-gauge wire loops ensure that no accident will occur if the C-clamp slips on the pipe. Another type of grid has a sliding track to which instruments can be attached and along which they can be moved (Figure 6.7).

A collapsible floor stand is one of the most frequently used light mounting devices on location. The seven- or eight-foot stand telescopes for portability. Sandbags can be placed over the three legs of the stand for added stability. Lights can also be mounted on special clips and clamps, such as a spring-tension alligator clip, or simply taped to a wall with a strong adhesive gaffer's tape. The latter must be used with care as it sometimes damages paint or wallpaper on removal (Figures 6.8A and B).

Shaping Devices

Light can be shaped, manipulated, and controlled by a variety of devices, such as barn doors, scrims, diffusers, flags, gels, cookies, and reflectors. These are often attached to a lighting instrument. *Barn doors* are black metal flaps that can be attached to the top, bottom, and sides of a lighting instrument. When properly positioned, they prevent light from spilling into areas of the set where it is not wanted. *Screens* are pieces of wire mesh that can be placed over the front of a lighting instrument to cut down the amount of light transmitted. *Scrims* and *diffusers* are pieces of translucent material, such as spun glass, that break up direct light and spread it out in all directions. *Flags* are opaque pieces of metal, plastic, or cardboard that prevent light from spilling into an undesired area.

Gels are flexible sheets of transparent colored plastic that can act as color filters when they are placed in front of light sources, such as windows or lamps. A gel can

Figures 6.6A, B, C, D Portable light kits are designed to provide the maximum amount of light output in small easily moved and controlled lighting fixtures also drawing a minimum amount of amperage. The kits are designed to provide both spot light and flood light with a variety of designs or adjustments of the lamp fixtures. (Courtesy of Lowell Light.)

Figure 6.7 The lighting grid in a studio is constructed to support both the batten, which carries the power to the pigtails, and the lighting instruments. The grid must be high enough to allow wide angle shots but also must allow for space above the grid for the heat generated by the lighting instruments to dissipate.

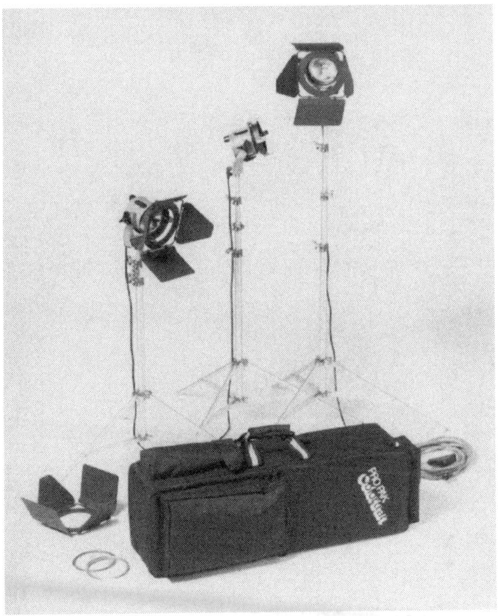

Figures 6.8A and B The design of portable light fixtures allows them to be mounted on floor stands, anchored by sand bags, hung from doorways, or clipped to other handy positions on the set. (Courtesy of Lowell Light and Colortran.)

be used to convert 5400 degree K light coming through a window to 3200 degree K light, which is the same color temperature as interior room lighting. A *cookie* or *cucaloris* is a piece of opaque material with holes in it, which patterns the light into shadowed and brightly lit areas. Cookies are built to be slipped into a slot between

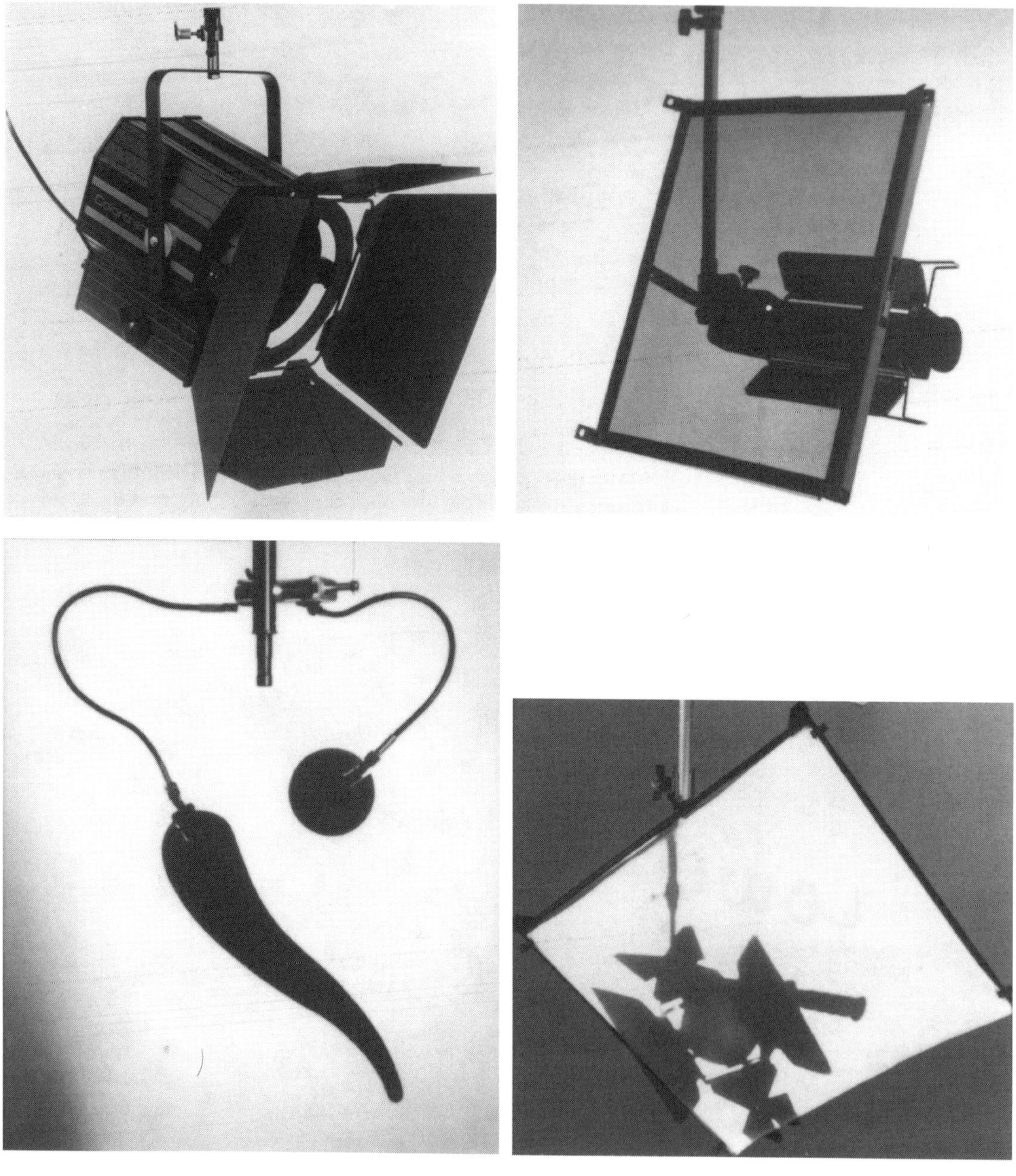

Figure 6.9 The control and shape of light as it falls on the set may be controlled by barn doors mounted on the front of the instrument, by reflecting light from a light surface such as an umbrella, or by placing scrims, flags, and diffusers between the lamp and the subjects. (Courtesy of Colortran and Lowell Light.)

the lamp and lens of the body of an ellipsoidal spotlight. *Reflectors* provide indirect, reflected light, which is usually less harsh than the primary direct light. Sunlight, for example, can be reflected to function as fill light outdoors, while direct, unreflected sunlight functions as a key light (Figure 6.9).

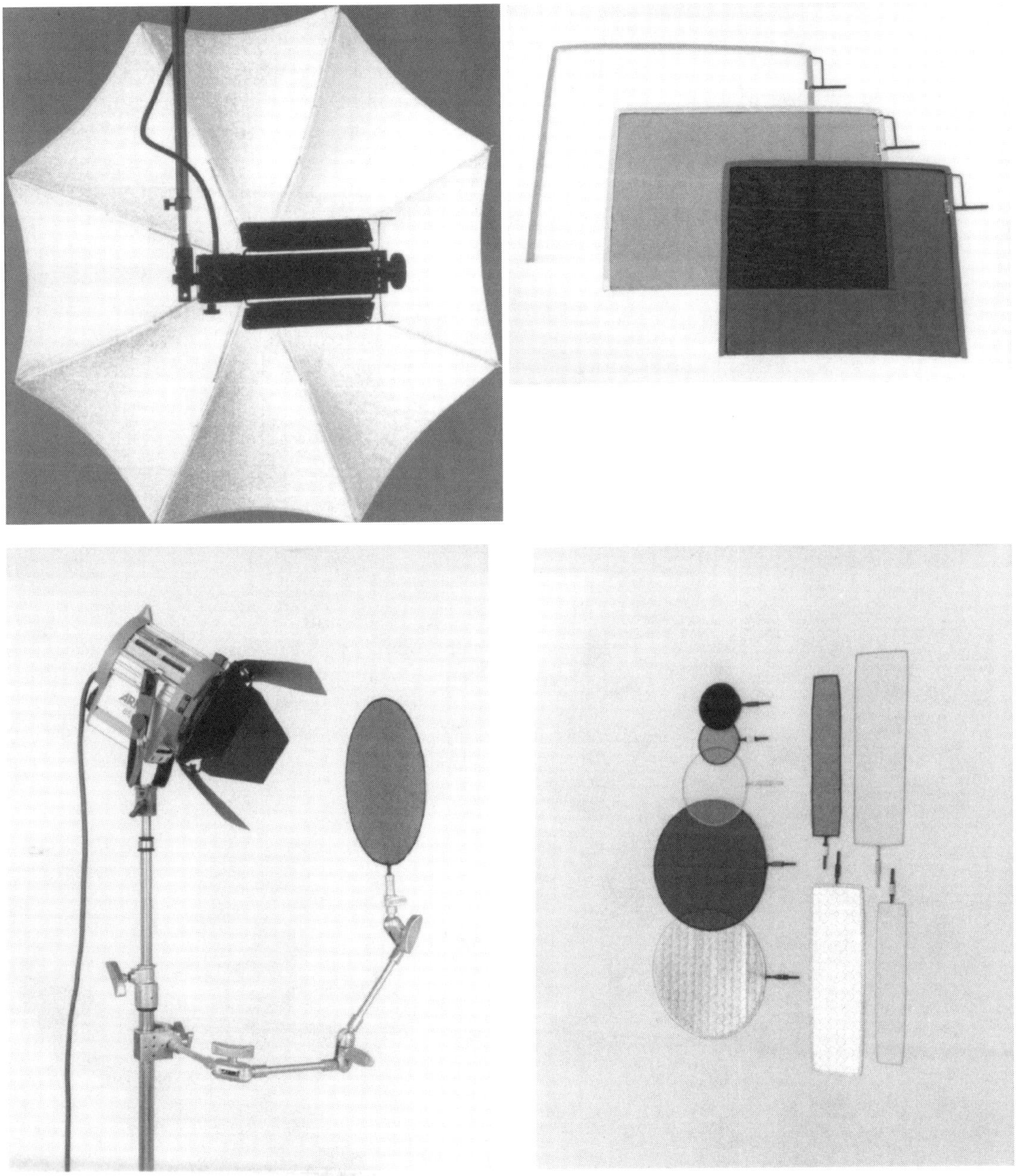

Figure 6.9 (*Continued*)
(Courtesy of Lowell Light.)

Light Control

Lighting Control in the Studio

Electrical lighting in a studio can be controlled by means of patch panels and dimmer boards operated either electronically or digitally. A patch panel or electrical distribution center consists of a series of plugs for specific electrical circuits to which lighting instruments can be connected. The voltage carried by each circuit can be controlled by a dimmer board. Each circuit has a limited electrical capacity, varying from about 20 to >50 amps (Figures 6.10A and B). Using the formula watts = amps × volts (W = A × V), you can determine the maximum number of lamps that can be safely attached to each circuit without blowing a fuse or tripping a circuit breaker. For example, five 1000-watt, 110-volt lamps can be safely plugged into a 50-amp circuit, since each lamp will draw slightly more than 9 amps (watts/volts = amps; 1000/110 = 9.1 amps per lamp; 5 × 9.1 = 45.5 total amps) (Figure 6.11).

For quick reference for calculating wattage and amperage in your head, use 100 volts instead of 110 or 120. This allows approximately a 10 percent safety factor. In the examples above: 1000/100 = 10 amps; 10 × 5 = 50 amps.

Figures 6.10A and B
Light control patch bays may be designed to require physically placing patch cords into patch panels or all connections are performed through a computer program and computer controlled distributor systems. (Courtesy of Colortran.)

OHMS LAW AS APPLIED TO LIGHTING SITUATIONS

The Wattage portion of Ohms Law is stated:

WATTAGE EQUALS VOLTAGE TIMES AMPERAGE
or
POWER = ELECTRICAL PRESSURE X ELECTRICAL FLOW

or stated as a formula:

$$W = V \times A$$

a converse of the law is stated:

$$A = \frac{W}{V}$$

Either formula is simplified by using 100 V for Voltage although the normal Voltage in the U.S. is between 110 and 120 V, the difference provides a margin of protection.

The Wattage formula is used to determine how many Watts of lamps may be hooked to any one circuit once the Amperage of that circuit is known.

For example: typical electrical household or business building circuits provide 20 Amps of current, therefore:

$$W = V \times A \qquad W = 100 \times 20 \qquad W = 2000 \text{ Watts}$$

That means a total of 2000 watts of lamps and equipment could be connected to that one circuit.

If the total Wattage is known (total the wattage required to power all lamps & equipment) and then using the Amperage formula. If your location requires 2450 Watts of power then:

$$A = \frac{W}{V} \qquad A = \frac{2450}{100} \qquad A = 24.5 \text{ Amps}$$

That means a circuit that provided at least 24.5 Amperage of current would be required. Neither a 15 Amp nor 20 Amp circuit would work, so either a 25 Amp circuit would need to be located, or the lamps would have to be split between a 15 Amp and a 10 Amp circuit or more likely two 15 amp circuits in order to provide enough current without blowing a fuse or breaker.

Using 100 for Voltage means that in most cases these calculations can be completed mentally, since it is easy to remember to multiple by 100 to obtain Wattage or divide by 100 to obtain Amperage.

Figure 6.11 As complicated as it may seem, calculating the amount of power required to power equipment and lighting instruments can be accomplished with simple formulas dividing or multiplying by 100.

The dimmer board is a useful means of reducing or adjusting light intensity for black-and-white production, but it is not very useful in this respect for color recording. A dimmer board reduces the light intensity by dropping the voltage, and dropping the voltage below 120 volts causes a consequent drop in color temperature, which is not acceptable in color production. In color production, lighting intensity is reduced by moving a lighting instrument or using a screen. To determine the result of moving a lighting instrument, the inverse square law may be used. This law of physics states the amount of light change caused by increasing the distance between the light source and the subject will decrease by the square of the inverse of the change in distance.

Conversely, the amount of light change caused by decreasing the distance between the light source and subject will increase by the square of the inverse of the change. For example, if the incident light from a lamp 8 feet from the subject measures 100 foot-candles and then the lamp is moved to 16 feet away (doubling the distance), then the light will decrease by the square of the inverse of the change: $\frac{1}{2}$ squared is $\frac{1}{4}$, and $\frac{1}{4}$ of 100 foot candles is 25 foot-candles. On the other hand, if the lamp's distance is cut in half to 4 feet, then the amount of light would increase by the square of the inverse of the change. $\frac{2}{1}$ squared is $\frac{4}{1}$ or 4. 100×4 is 400 foot-candles. It is obvious that it takes very small changes in the distance between the lamp and subject to make a major change in the amount of light reaching the subject (Figure 6.12).

Dimmer boards are useful for controlling entire banks of instruments simultaneously and for presetting a series of lamps for the next scene. Modern dimmer boards are computer controlled and allow an infinite number of instrument series to be preset and changed at the press of a button (Figure 6.13).

Lighting Control on Location

Securing adequate electrical current for lighting on location presents more problems and hazards than does studio production. The most pressing problem is how and where to secure adequate power. If sufficient electricity is not available, portable gasoline generators are sometimes brought in. When using a private home or office, a lighting director and electrician may decide to tap the main power supply or to use the existing circuits. If the former course is taken, a qualified electrician must perform the operation of tapping into the 100 amp (or more) main supply, which can then be channeled to a portable circuit board for distribution to individual instruments. If you decide to use existing circuits in the home or office, you can determine which outlets are on the same circuits and how many amps each circuit can carry by simply checking and closing a circuit at the main circuit box or fuse box, and then testing outlets in the rooms where filming is to take place. Load demands should never exceed those specified at the circuit or fuse box, because excess power traveling along a line can melt the wires and start a fire. Any situation in which an extensive amount of lighting and electrical energy is required demands the expertise of a qualified electrician.

Light Measurement

The basic unit of light intensity measure is the foot-candle. One foot-candle is an agreed-upon standard that represents the approximate light intensity produced by a candle one foot away. The normal measurement range of a light meter is from 1 to about 250 foot-candles. A light meter is extremely useful in both video and film production for determining lighting levels and contrast within a scene, as well as

INVERSE SQUARE LAW AS APPLIED TO LIGHTING SITUATIONS

The Inverse Square Law states that the light intensity falling on a subject will vary inversely by the square of the variation in the distance between the light source and the subject.

A simpler variation is that changing the distance between a source of light and the subject will result in a major change in the amount of light falling on the subject.

Stated as a formula:

$$I = \frac{1}{D^2} \text{ fc}$$

When **I** is the change in light intensity and
D is the change in distance between the light source and subject

An example:

If the measured light at the subject is 100 foot-candles (fc) when D = 10 feet, and the D changes from 10 to 20 feet which is double the distance then:

$$I = \frac{1}{2^2}\ 100$$

(the distance doubled and the inverse of 2 is 1/2)

$$I = \frac{1}{4}\ 100 \text{ fc}$$

$$I = 25 \text{ fc}$$

Or, if D changes from 10 to 5 feet, which is 1/2 the distance then:

$I = 2^2$ (The distance is 1/2 inverse of 1/2 is 2) **x 100 fc**

I = 4 x 100 or 400 fc.

Just remember moving a luminaire or the subject in relation to each other will modify the light measurement on the subject radically. A small movement will result in a great change in the light on the subject.

Figure 6.12 Calculating the amount of light falling on a subject as the lamps are moved back and forth is accomplished with a simple formula based on dividing by the square of the light source if the change in distance is increased or multiplying by the square of the light source if the distance is decreased.

for properly positioning and setting individual lights. In film recording, a light meter must be adjusted to the proper sensitivity scale or EI number (DIN in Europe) so that it provides the correct f-stop readings for the specific sensitivity of the film stock (Figure 6.14).

The three major light sources are key light, fill light, and separation light. The *key light* is the brightest, hardest light. It provides modeling or texture. Modeling

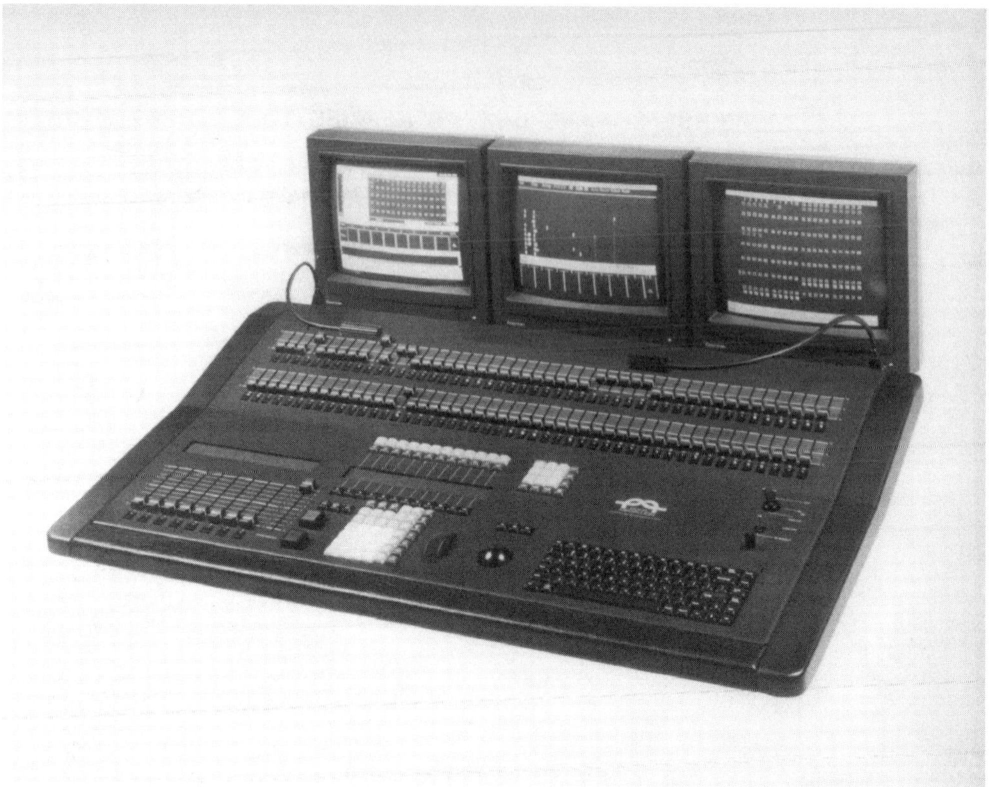

Figure 6.13 A modern computer operated lighting control dimmer board allows all of the adjustment functions of lighting instruments (except for moving the lamps) from the control board. (Courtesy of Colortran.)

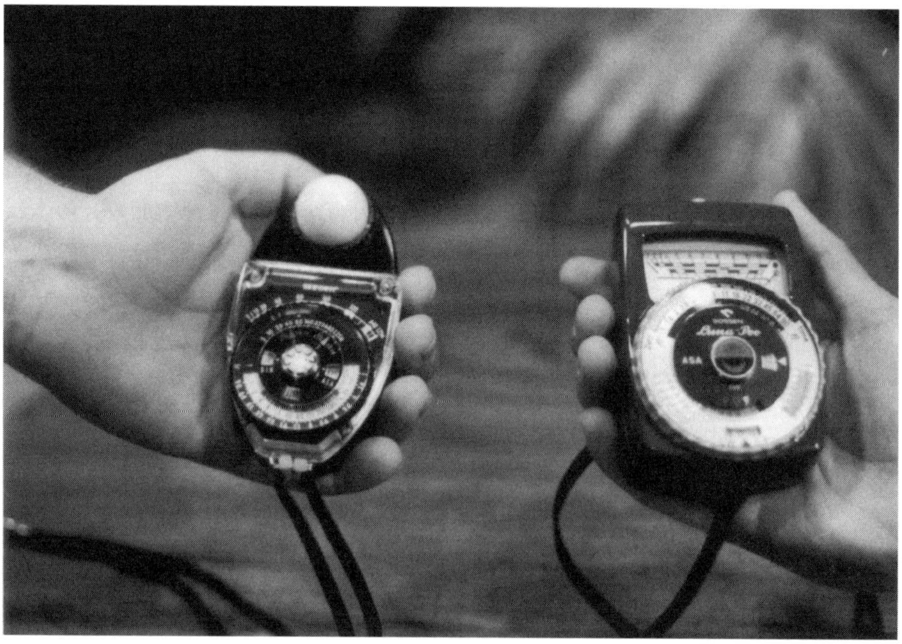

Figure 6.14 Hand-held light meters may be designed for different functions. The one on the left is designed primarily to read incident light, the one on the right, reflected light, although both meters will read either incident or reflected light.

refers to the appearance of a textured surface that has shadows where there are indentations in the surface. A surface with good modeling looks three dimensional. *Fill light* is softened, lower intensity light that helps to fill in some of the shadows created by the key light and to reduce the contrast between light and shadow areas. *Separation light* comes from behind the subject. It creates a halo effect, which outlines the subject and helps to separate it from the background.

Types of Light Meter Readings

There are two basic types of meter readings: incident and reflected. *Spot meters* are a specialized type of reflected meter. Another type of reflected reading may be gained through a meter built into the film camera on electronic circuits built into a video camera. This type of metering is called *through the lens* (TTL). Some light meters are capable of producing only one type of reading. Others can be used for several different types of readings. Each reading has a specific purpose in terms of lighting control. On some light meters a white hemisphere or flat circle is placed over the photoelectric cell so that the meter can measure the intensity of the light falling on the subject, the incident light. This white surface gathers and diffuses light falling on the meter from several directions. For a reading of direct light falling on the subject, the meter is pointed at the camera from the position of the subject (Figure 6.16).

A reading of incident or direct light is called an *incident reading*. Because such a reading measures the light falling on the subject, it is not affected by the reflectance of the objects to be recorded (Figure 6.15).

Figure 6.15 To take a reflected light reading, the meter is held close to the camera and pointed at the major subject. A narrow angle light meter provides the most accurate reflected meter reading.

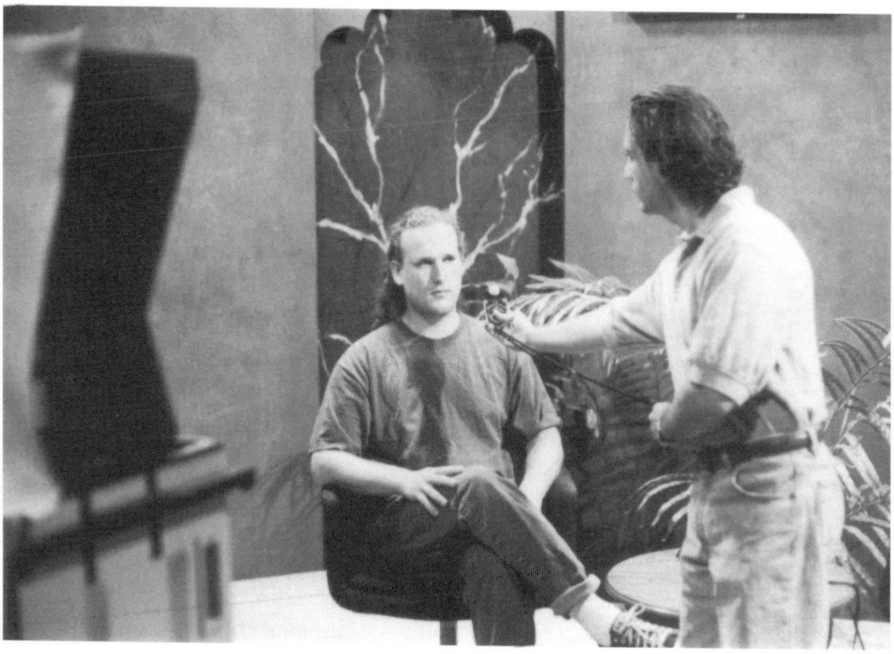

Figure 6.16 To take an incident light reading, the meter should be held close to the subject pointing toward the light source(s). A wide angle light meter with a diffusion cap provides the most accurate incident meter reading.

A measurement of indirect light, that is, light reflected by the subject, is called a *reflected reading*. The white covering is removed from the photocell for a reflected reading, and the meter is pointed at the subject from the camera. A reflected reading of the subject or whole scene averages the amount of light reflected by objects in the scene to determine the best overall exposure or base light level. A *spot meter reading* is the reflected light from a small isolated area within the frame. Spot meter readings are often used to take light readings of objects that are too far away to make an incident reading practical or from subjects that reflect far more or less light than the average subject in the area.

A *TTL* or *through the lens reading* provides a reflected reading of the exact image framed within the camera and can be used to adjust the lens automatically. Some TTL systems do not respond instantaneously to light changes, and the proper exposure lags slightly behind actual changes in light intensity. In essence, a video camera is a TTL meter. The operator can determine the proper exposure by reading an oscilloscope attached to the camera output, or by gauging the contrast and exposure through the camera viewfinder, assuming the viewfinder is properly adjusted. The operator actually is viewing the reflected light in the viewfinder.

Determining Contrast Ratios

A light meter can be used in both video and film production to determine contrast within a scene. Apparent contrast within the image area can affect image clarity as well as the overall emotional mood. There are two important contrast ratios in any lighting setup: lighting ratio and contrast ratio. The mathematical relationship between light intensity in foot-candles or between f-stops on a light meter can be used to determine these specific ratios. (Foot-candles can be directly compared, whereas each higher f-stop number indicates a doubling and each lower f-stop a halving of the light intensity.)

Lighting Ratios

Key-to-Fill Ratio Key-to-fill ratio indicates the proportion of key light to fill light in any lighting setup. This is called the *lighting ratio,* but should not be confused with the inherent contrast ratio of a video camera or film stock, discussed in Chapter 7. Lighting contrast is caused exclusively by lights. It is actually a comparison of key plus fill light to fill light alone.

Some fill light always spills over into the key light area and increases its intensity. An incident reading is taken of the key and fill lights together. Then the key light is shut off and a fill light reading is taken. A comparison of the two readings in terms of foot-candles or recommended f-stop readings indicates the key-to-fill light ratio. A key plus fill light reading of 250 foot-candles compared with a fill light reading of 125 foot-candles equals a 2:1 lighting ratio. One f-stop difference between the two indicates a 2:1 ratio, two f-stops a 4:1 ratio, three f-stops an 8:1 ratio, and so on. In most situations, video and film recording is done under a key-to-fill light ratio of 4:1 or less, unless a highly dramatic effect with high contrast is desired. Since video has less tolerance for contrast than film, it generally is advisable to use a 2:1 or lower key-to-fill light ratio in video recordings or film recordings that will be transferred to video. The key-to-fill ratio determines whether a high-key or low-key aesthetic of lighting is in effect. Low-key lighting has a high key-to-fill ratio, while high-key lighting has a low key-to-fill light ratio.

Key-to-Back Ratio The relative proportion of key light to back light is called the key-to-back ratio. In most instances back lights and key lights should have approximately the same intensity. This ratio is usually kept at about 1:1 or 1:1.5. A weak back light does little to separate the subject from the background or to create a halo effect. An extremely strong back light, on the other hand, can cause an excessively bright halo to form around the subject's head and back.

Contrast Ratios

Contrast ratios can be determined by taking reflected light meter readings of the brightest and darkest reflecting objects in the scene. A spot meter is a great help in isolating a specific object, although moving a standard reflected light meter closer to an object without interrupting the light falling on it accomplishes the same goal. Again, a comparison of light meter foot-candle or f-stop readings indicates the contrast ratio between the brightest and darkest reflecting areas in the scene. Video cameras cannot record a reflectance contrast ratio greater than 30:1 or at most 40:1 (approximately five f-stops). Some standard film stocks, such as color negative, can often record reflectance contrast ranges as high as 100:1 (six or seven f-stops).

Adjusting Contrast

There are several ways of altering a scene's contrast to make it more acceptable for visual recording. Specific lights that are too strong or too weak can be moved farther from or closer to the subject. Scrims and diffusion materials can be used to cut down on the light intensity. Additional instruments can be focused on the subject, although care must be taken to keep these multiple keys and fills close together so that objectionable multiple shadows are not created. Altering the lighting contrast ratio can affect the reflectance contrast ratio since the two are interdependent: Objects reflect key and fill light. In some cases, a change in the color or brightness of props, sets, or costumes may be required to increase or decrease light reflectance.

Three- and Four-Point Lighting

Three-point and four-point lighting are realist techniques that help create an illusion of three dimensionality and depth in two-dimensional media such as video and film (Figure 6.17). Three-point and four-point lighting setups use three specific types of light, which have different directional placements, degrees of softness and hardness, and intensities.

Key Light

The key lights are the brightest and, in some ways, the most important lights on the set. The key light determines the overall recording or exposure level. The placement of a key light suggests the direction of the primary source of light within a scene, such as a window, an overhead light, the sun or moon, or even a candle or fireplace. When the key light strikes a subject directly from the front or camera side of the subject, few shadows or variations in surface texture are created and the result is a flat, uninteresting image. For optimal modeling and aesthetic effect, the key light should be thirty to forty degrees away from the camera-subject axis, and it should light the short or narrow side of a face, that is, the side of the face that is least exposed to the camera. Moving the key light up and down, and from side to side, affects the direction and length of facial shadows and increases or decreases facial modeling.

Key light usually has a hard quality. The beam of light is narrowly focused and rarely if ever diffused or softened, except perhaps in a situation where softness is needed to create a romantic or light mood. The height of the key light affects the length of shadows falling on the set. Key lights should be placed high enough that long shadows do not spill onto the background from foreground subjects. The key light is usually placed much higher than the camera, unless a special effect is desired, such as the presentation of a flat, untextured image (in which case, the key light is at camera height) or a mysterious and horrifying face (in which case the key light is placed lower than camera height). In multiple-subject setups, the same light that functions as a key light for one subject can also function as the fill or back light for another. The term *key light* simply refers to the brightest light source striking a subject from the camera's viewpoint. The specific instrument designated as the key light can change as the camera or subject moves.

Fill Light

Fill light is used to provide general illumination on the set and to fill in the shadows created by the key lights. Fill light is usually softer than key light. It is frequently diffused by reflectors or translucent materials placed in front of the lighting instrument. The fill light is often placed at approximately camera height or just slightly

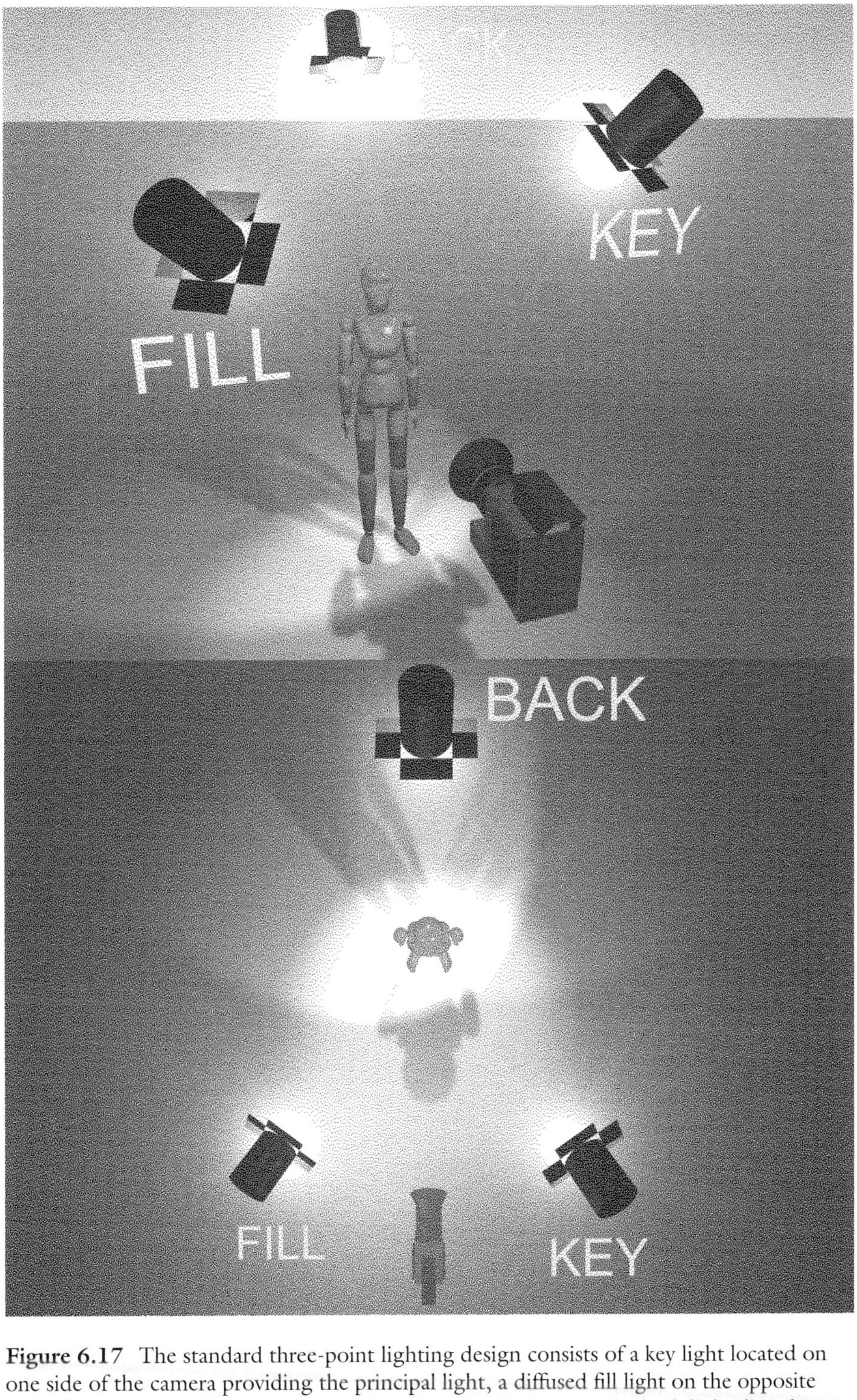

Figure 6.17 The standard three-point lighting design consists of a key light located on one side of the camera providing the principal light, a diffused fill light on the opposite side of the camera to lower contrast and erase some shadows, and a back light directly opposite the camera to provide a rim of light on the head and shoulders of the subject to pull them away from the background.

above so that shadows created by overhead key lights can be properly filled in. It is usually on the opposite side of the camera from the key light. The intensities and physical placement of the key and fill lights will determine to a significant extent the emotional mood and lighting atmosphere within the scene.

Separation Light

One or two separation lights complete the three-point lighting triangle or four-point rectangle. A back light is usually placed above and behind the subject to create a halo effect that outlines the subject, separating it from the background. The back light completes the three-point lighting setup, but it is not the only light that can be used to separate the subject from the background. In a four-point lighting setup, another separation light, called a *kicker,* may be placed exactly opposite the key light on the set. A kicker functions similarly to a back light, but it is directed from the back and the side of the subject (usually opposite or facing the key light), rather than from directly behind and above the subject's back and head. Separation of subject and background through back lights and kickers is extremely important in black-and-white recording. The height of the back light or kicker and its intensity in comparison with the key light affect the amount of separation that takes place.

The use of different colors for the subject and background can effect much the same separation in color production, but separation lights have not been entirely abandoned in color production because they add so much texture, dimension, and depth to the visual image. In an optimal three-point lighting setup, the key, fill, and back lights form the points of a triangle or a Y. When a kicker and a back light are used together, the four lighting points form a rectangle or an "X." Such ideal placements are rarely, if ever, consistently maintained. Only static artificial, intensely boring still scenes with subjects and cameras that never move would allow for a permanent, perfectly triangular three-point or rectangular four-point lighting setup. A more typical situation is characterized by constant movement of the subject(s) and cameras, and a complex, constantly varying relationship between keys, fills, and back lights or kickers. The three-point and four-point lighting procedures outlined earlier simply provide a starting point and an idealized model that is necessarily and continually manipulated in complex recording situations (Figure 6.18).

Background Light

Background light illuminates the background or set. It affects every lighting setup and is extremely important in the overall aesthetic appearance of a scene. While fill lights and key lights frequently spill over onto the background and partially illuminate it, it is important to light the background separately so that its appearance can be more carefully controlled. The amount of light cast on the background obviously affects subject/background separation. It can also affect visual emphasis within a scene. If the background is brighter than the subject, the viewer's attention will be distracted from the primary focus of interest. If the background is too dark, the set may look unnatural or the scene too contrasty. To add interest and texture to an otherwise flat, monochromatic background, patterns can be cast on the background to break it up and give it some modeling and texture. While too

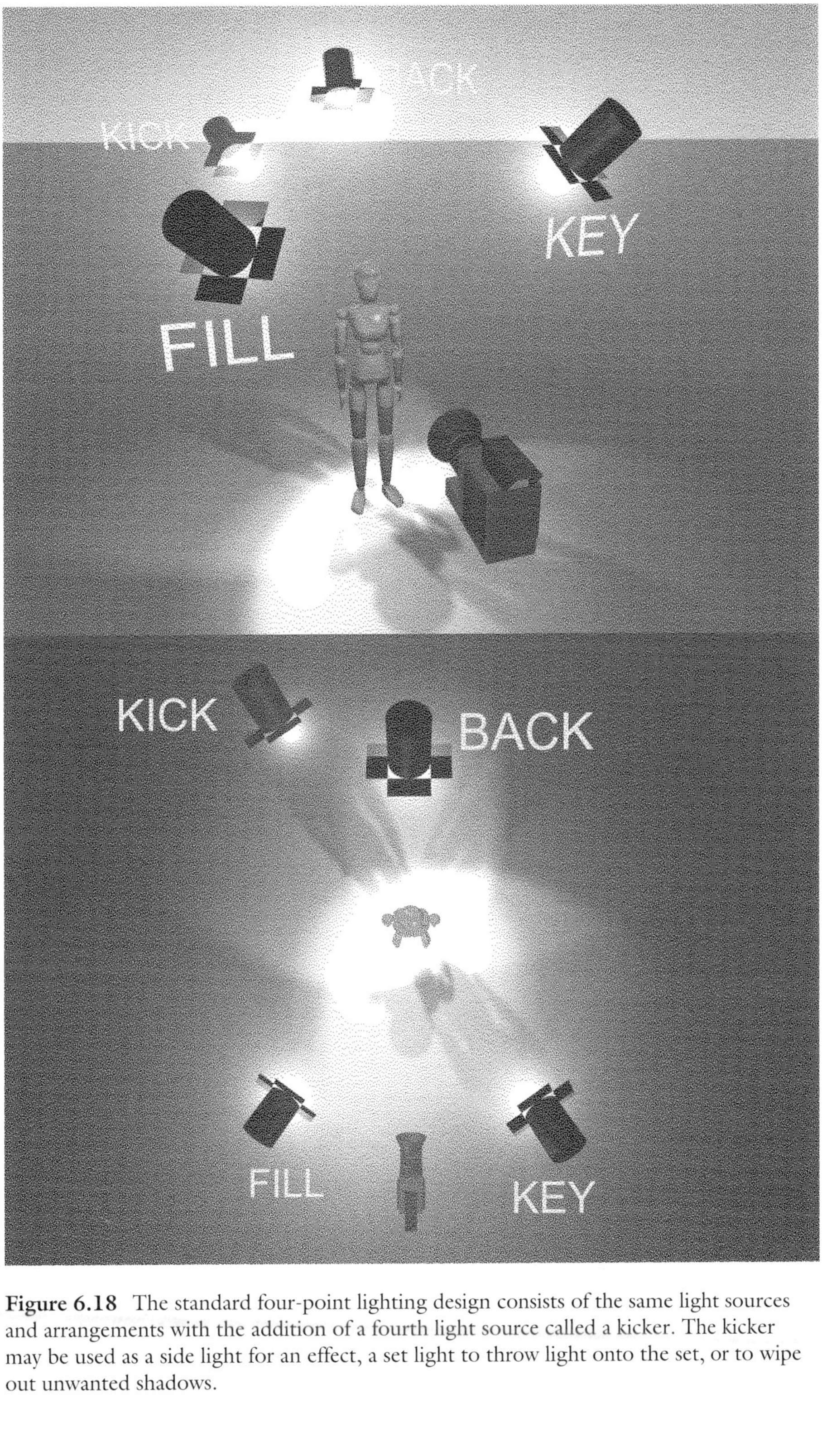

Figure 6.18 The standard four-point lighting design consists of the same light sources and arrangements with the addition of a fourth light source called a kicker. The kicker may be used as a side light for an effect, a set light to throw light onto the set, or to wipe out unwanted shadows.

much patterning can be distracting, a flat, monochrome, evenly lit background looks dull and unimaginative.

Controlling Shadows

Background light should not be used to try to burn out shadows from foreground performers that fall on the background. The most effective means of eliminating bad shadows is proper placement of the key lights. Key lights should be placed high enough above the performers that prominent shadows are not cast on background walls as they move around the set. Performers should also be kept at a safe distance from the back wall whenever possible. Another complicating factor in three- and four-point television and film lighting is the creation of objectional shadows by microphone booms. Since the key light creates the most noticeable shadows, microphone-boom placement and movement must be arranged to minimize interference with the key lights. Sometimes this can be accomplished by adjusting the barn doors of the key lights so that light does not spill into the microphone-boom area. In other cases, the key lights may have to be placed higher overhead than normal, so that boom shadows fall on the floor, rather than on more noticeable parts of the set. A microphone-boom shadow can often be hidden in a part of the set that is already riddled with a shadow pattern. Obviously, the planning of the lighting setup must include consideration of the placement and movement of the microphone boom, before the key and fill lights are firmly positioned.

Lighting Moving Subjects

The discussion of lighting to this point has assumed that the subject to be recorded is relatively stationary. A moving subject significantly complicates a lighting setup. The major problem inherent in lighting a moving subject is how to maintain relatively consistent light levels as the subject moves about the set. A moving subject in the studio must be lit by multiple key lights.

If a subject were to walk too close or too far away from a single key light, he or she would become too light or too dark, and realist continuity in lighting would be lost. Multiple key lights are hung at constant distances from the moving subject so that the subject can move from one key light to another without a noticeable change in lighting. Problems arise when key light beams overlap or when there are gaps of darkness between key lights. To prevent these problems, the barn doors or shutters on the key lights are adjusted so that key light beams are exactly adjacent to each other along the performer blocking line (where a subject will move on the set). As long as the talent follows this prearranged line of action and hits his or her marks, no gaps or overlaps of lighting will occur.

Low-Key versus High-Key Lighting

The terms *low-key* and *high-key* lighting originated in the studio eras of feature film production in Hollywood. They seem counterintuitive, that is, the terms mean the opposite of what we think they should mean. Low-key lighting refers to the minimal use of fill light, that is, a relatively high key-to-fill ratio. This kind of lighting creates pools of light and rather harsh shadows. Many Warner Bros. gangster films and detective films produced in the 1930s and 1940s used low-key lighting for aesthetic effect. However, a whole genre of Hollywood films, called *film noir* (literally French for "black film"), relied on low-key lighting in the 1940s. Low-key lighting evokes a rather heavy and serious mood or feeling that enhances the emotional atmosphere of certain types of films. Low-key lighting is similar to an effect in painting known as *chiaroscuro.*

This technique is evident in the paintings of Rembrandt, for example, where shafts of light illuminate central figures in the painting, while the remaining parts of the scene are dimly lit and heavily shadowed. Low-key lighting can have a similar effect in video and film, although contrast ratio differences between video and film call for different lighting techniques to create the same effect in the two media.

High-key lighting presents a brightly lit scene with few shadow areas. It has been suggested that during the 1930s and 1940s, MGM (Metro-Goldwyn-Mayer) studios used high-key lighting for its lavish musicals so that no detail in its elaborate and expensive sets would be hidden in shadows.

In any case, the use of high-key lighting in musical comedies is another example of form following function. The term *notan* is often applied to high-key lighting. The word *notan* refers to the bright, low-contrast paintings of the Japanese master painters. The light, happy atmosphere stimulated by high-key lighting contrasts with the somber, mysterious, or threatening atmosphere of low-key lighting. Thus, an important consideration in selecting either high- or low-key lighting styles is attempting to match the form of the lighting to the specific function it is intended to serve.

Lighting Plots

A specific lighting setup can be outlined or diagrammed on a gridded piece of paper that represents an overhead scale diagram of the studio. This outline is called a *lighting plot.* The overhead lighting grid to which specific instruments can be attached is drawn onto the studio diagram. The basic elements of the set are added to this overhead view. The placements and movements of the talent and camera(s) can be added to the diagram after preliminary performer and camera blocking, so that the lights can be positioned accordingly. Lighting plots also may be created using specifically written computer programs that allow for manipulation of diagrams of sets, instruments, and performers. Such programs also allow for the printing of hard copies of the diagrams as well as storage of the files on discs for recall at a later time. The lighting director equipped with such computer programs uses the computer graphics to create these plots quickly and efficiently without tediously hand drawing each instrument and connection.

The program also will create lists of instruments required and indicate patchboard connections. Several key lights may have to be arranged so that they maintain an even or balanced brightness on the moving performer throughout the set. Only when the exact blocking line of the talent is known can these lights be properly placed. The distance of the key lights from the talent can be determined by relying on the inverse square law (light intensity changes according to the square of the distance of the light source from the object) and the scale dimensions of the gridded paper. One-quarter inch on paper may equal one foot of actual studio floor space, for example (Figure 6.19).

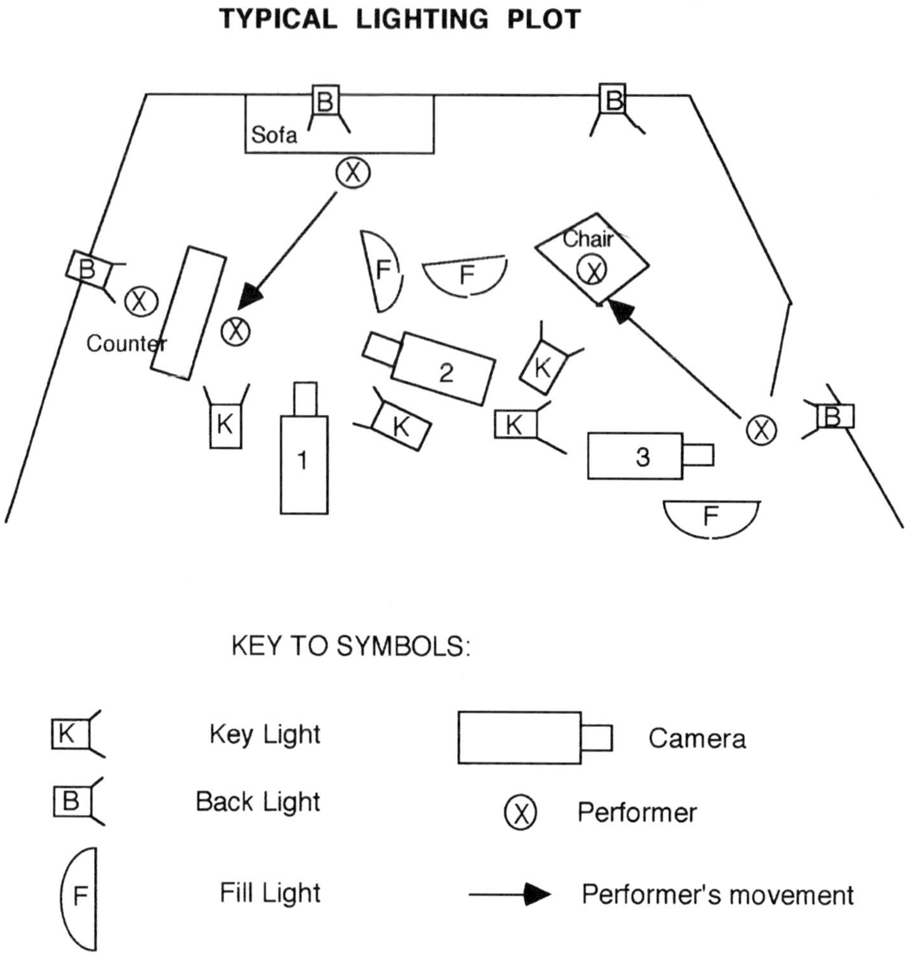

Figure 6.19 Lighting plots provide a means of carefully planning ahead of time for the placement of lighting instruments to avoid unnecessarily physically moving fixtures after the sets and blocking has been completed. The plot must be drawn to scale or it is of little value for accurate planning.

Composing a lighting plot allows the lighting director to consider all relevant factors that can affect the selection and placement of lighting instruments prior to actual production. He or she must consider placement and movement of the talent, cameras, and microphone booms, as well as the electrical and spatial capabilities and limitations of the studio or location environment. The lighting plot must also incorporate many aesthetic or stylistic variables. It can be low key or high key; realist, modernist, or postmodernist. The lighting director must develop a lighting setup that is both aesthetically satisfying and practical from an engineering standpoint.

Single-Camera versus Multiple-Camera Situations

In single-camera recording situations, the lighting is sometimes changed for each shot or each major change in camera position. Of course, changing the lighting slightly for each separate shot can be extremely laborious and time consuming. Subtle changes in lighting are made in realist productions, not drastic changes that call attention to the lighting. Lighting continuity from shot to shot and scene to scene will break down with too much shifting of lighting instruments. Feature films and network television commercials, which have big budgets, long shooting schedules, and large production crews, can better afford the luxury of lighting each separate shot perfectly than can lower level productions.

The aesthetic expectations of audiences and the demands of clients make lighting a high priority in some single-camera productions. Still, the lighting for any single-camera production can benefit from the added time and care this production method affords. Since recording is continuous in multiple-camera production, the lights cannot be reset for different shots. Lighting decisions and compromises must be fully worked out prior to actual recording. The same lighting setup is used for long shots, medium shots, and close-ups. The lighting director must be able to anticipate every camera angle and placement that will be needed before arranging and setting up the lights on the set.

Summary

Aesthetic lighting setups can be divided into three categories: realist, modernist, and postmodernist lighting. Realist lighting attempts to recreate the presumed natural sources of lighting within a specific location. Key lights are used to maintain the consistent directional placement of the presumed central light source in a room, while fill lights reduce contrast to a normal or acceptable level. Lighting can also be used in a modernist or stylized manner to achieve a particular atmospheric effect, psychological mood, or abstract design.

Light sources, such as the sun and incandescent, carbon arc, HMI, and fluorescent lamps, emit light of a specific color temperature. Color temperature ratings in degrees Kelvin indicate the proportion of short wavelength (blue violet) and long wavelength (red) light and so on, emitted by a specific white light source. Daylight, carbon arc, and HMI light have higher color temperatures and a greater proportion of blue in comparison with red light than incandescent or tungsten light. Fluorescent light is discontinuous throughout the visible spectrum. Color film stocks must be selected and video cameras balanced for the color temperature of the primary light source if a normal color rendition is to be recorded.

Spotlights and floodlights are two different types of lighting instruments. Spotlights produce bright, narrow beams of light, while floodlights provide softer, more diffused lighting for wider areas. A Fresnel lens on the front of a spotlight focuses the light rays into a narrow beam. An ellipsoidal instrument uses an ellipsoidal mirror and a lens to focus the light rays. Scoops, broads, soft lights, strip lights, and clusters provide general floodlight illumination by spreading the rays of light in many directions. Portable lights are somewhat smaller, open lighting instruments, which can sometimes be flooded or spotted without lenses, and a portable lighting kit usually contains portable light stands and various light-shaping devices. Lighting instruments can be secured to a variety of mounting devices, including overhead studio grids and lightweight portable light stands. Light-shaping devices, such as barn doors, scrims, flags, and cookies, help direct and control lighting and create shadow patterns.

Artificial lighting consumes significant amounts of electricity. Load limits for specific electrical circuits must be carefully observed to avoid dangerous overloading, and the help of a qualified electrician should be obtained if the electrical requirements for a specific production situation are at all unusual. A patch panel and a dimmer board help to route and control electrical supply and light intensities by varying the voltage of the current. However, in color production, the drop in color temperature that results from a drop in voltage affects the color quality of the recorded image. In color production, light intensity can be reduced by moving lighting instruments or using screens.

Light meters measure light intensity. An incident light meter reading measures the intensity of the light falling on a scene, while a reflected reading measures the intensity of the light reflected by objects in the scene. These readings help to determine image contrast, as well as the proper exposure level. Lighting ratios can be determined by using incident light meter readings to compare specific lights in terms of their intensity. A contrast ratio is indicated by comparing the intensity of light reflected off the darkest object in a scene with that of the brightest reflecting object. Reflectance contrast in video is usually restricted to 30:1 or 20:1, while it can be as high as 100:1 for certain film stocks. Key-to-fill contrast ratios rarely exceed 2:1 in video, while key-to-back light ratios are normally 1:1 or 1:1.5. Contrast ratios in a scene affect visual aesthetics and techniques such as low-key and high-key lighting.

Three-point and four-point lighting consist of a triangular or rectangular arrangement of three types of light: key light, fill light, and separation light. The key light is the brightest, most direct light source on the set. It is usually produced by a spotlight. Fill light fills in the shadows created by the key light, reducing the contrast and providing general illumination. Back lights and kickers create a halo that outlines the subject and helps to separate it from the background. A background light is often used to illuminate the set separately. Basic three- or four-point lighting in television and film production is complicated by movement of subjects and cameras, which gives a dynamic, constantly changing character to a lighting situation. Multiple key lights can be used to maintain consistent light levels as a subject moves through a scene.

A lighting setup should be carefully planned to avoid problems on the set, such as blocking difficulties, unbalanced light intensities, and microphone-boom shadows. A lighting plot, which presents an overhead view of the studio floor or actual location drawn to scale, can help a lighting director to organize and plan a lighting setup. Lighting instruments can be positioned and repositioned on paper, so that logistical problems are solved and aesthetic decisions are made prior to actual production.

Low-key lighting refers to a relatively high key-to-fill light ratio that creates pools of bright light surrounded by dark shadow areas. It is frequently used to effect an atmosphere suitable for horror and gangster films and television programs, although it can be an effective dramatic device in many productions. High-key lighting, which has a low key-to-fill light ratio, presents few shadows and is frequently used in comedies and musicals.

Exercises

1. Design two sets of lighting plots for a specific dramatic scene: one for single-camera recording and another for multiple-camera recording. Make subtle changes of light placements for close-ups in the single-camera production that will enhance the view of the subject without disrupting the overall appearance of the lighting when the camera is moved to another perspective. Find the best (compromise) position for lights used in multiple-camera production so that the subject looks reasonably good from many different camera perspectives at the same time.
2. Light a stationary, two-person interview, using cross-key lights and fill lights, creating a 2:1 key-to-fill ratio and a 1:1.5 key-to-back light ratio.
3. Set up multiple key, fill, and separation lights, which will keep a moving subject lit by relatively constant light intensity, while maintaining a 2:1 key-to-fill ratio and a 1:1 key-to-back light (or kicker) ratio.

Additional Readings

Beacham, Frank. *American Cinematographer Video Manual.* Hollywood, CA: The ASC Press, 1992.

Box, Harry. *Set Lighting Technicians Handbook,* 2nd ed. Boston: Focal Press, 1996.

Brown, Bain. *Motion Picture and Video Lighting.* Boston: Focal Press, 1992.

Carlson, Verne, and Sylvia E. Carlson. *Professional Lighting Handbook,* 2nd ed. Boston: Focal Press, 1991.

Clark, Charles G. *American Cinematographers Manual,* 7th ed. Hollywood, CA: The ASC Press, 1993.

Ferncase, Richard K. *Basic Lighting Worktext for Film and Video.* Boston: Focal Press, 1992.

Ferncase, Richard K. *Film and Video Lighting Terms and Concepts.* Boston: Focal Press, 1994.

Fitt, Brian, and Joe Thornley. *Lighting by Design: A Technical Guide.* Boston: Focal Press, 1993.

GTE/Sylvania Lighting Handbook, 8th ed. Danvers, MA: GTE/Sylvania, 1989.

Malkiewicz, J. Kris. *Cinematography.* New York: Van Nostrand Reinhold, 1973.

Mathias, Harry, and Richard Patterson. *Electronic Cinematography.* Belmont, CA: Wadsworth, 1985.

Millerson, Gerald. *The Techniques of Lighting for Television and Motion Pictures,* 3rd ed. Boston: Focal Press, 1991.

North American Philips Lighting Handbook. Bloomfield, NJ: North American Philips Corp., 1984.

Risko, Alan J. *Lighting for Location Motion Pictures.* New York: Van Nostrand Reinhold, 1979.

Wilson, Anton. *Cinema Workshop.* Hollywood, CA: The ASC Press, 1983.

7

Camera

Introduction

Camera operators try to provide directors with the best possible pictures that will enhance a particular aesthetic approach. To accomplish this they must know how to use basic framing, composition, and camera movements, and how to control numerous technical camera and lens devices. To record clear, functionalist images, for example, camera operators must understand how lenses work and then place key information in sharp focus. Significant image depth, that is, having a wide range of distances from the camera in sharp focus, can be an effective realist approach to camera operation. Limiting or restricting image depth can help to create a modernist perspective on everyday objects.

Some aesthetic aspects of camera use, such as composition and camera movement, were considered in terms of directing in Chapter 4, but they bear repeating here from the standpoint of camera placement and control. After reading this chapter and before attempting to use any camera, you should read the instruction manual carefully for the specific camera you wish to operate. Continual practice with the camera is necessary to make it an extension of your eyes and body. Basic camera exercises, such as those recommended at the end of this chapter, can significantly improve your skills as a camera operator.

Potential camera operators should be aware of the capability of studio systems to include remote controls for all of the camera operations: panning, tilting, zooming, and even dollying and trucking across the studio floor. The cameras used on major network newscasts now are all remote controlled from the control room. One of the functions of a camera operator may be to operate several cameras simultaneously with remote controls while seated in the control room. The traditional setting of the electronic controls of cameras by a camera control operator before each production also has been replaced by a computer built into the camera control unit. With a single press of a button, the computer runs a complete check of all electronic circuits and sets the camera controls for that particular production.

Camera Placement

Placing a camera in the best position for recording realist or modernist images consists of three camera operations: framing, positioning, and movement. *Framing* refers to the arrangement of actions and objects within the camera frame. *Positioning* includes the selection of camera-to-subject distance and angle, while *movement* of the camera is accomplished by means of various camera mounting devices.

Framing

Four key concepts help camera operators frame visual images: essential area, lookspace, walkspace, and headroom. *Essential area* refers to the safe recording area within the camera frame. All key information should be placed within the essential area of the frame so that it is not cut off by mistake. Objects and actions can be placed within the essential area by moving the camera closer to or farther away from the subject or by altering the focal length of a zoom lens. *Lookspace* is the frame area in front of an on-screen performer who is looking at an off-screen object or person. Leaving some space in the frame for the performer's look or glance creates the best spatial composition. Lookspace can be increased by panning the camera. *Walkspace* refers to the additional space left in the frame into which a performer can walk or run. When following a performer with a camera, as during a panning or trucking shot, walkspace should be placed in front of the subject within the frame. Otherwise, the edge of the frame acts as a restrictive border and the visual composition seems awkward.

Another important aspect of composition is providing an appropriate amount of headroom, that is, space above the performer's head within the frame. Too little headroom creates a sense of confinement, while too much gives an impression of limitless space that sometimes dwarfs the performer. Of course, tight close-ups often have little or no headroom. Changes in headroom result from tilting the camera, moving the camera closer or farther away, or zooming the lens (Figure 7.1).

Camera operators also need to be familiar with the basic rules of camera placement and composition. For example, the 180-degree action-axis rule should be followed in camera placement, if the directional relationship of objects in the frame and subject movements is to remain spatially consistent from shot to shot. Crossing the line with the camera can reverse screen direction. In terms of composition, the rule of thirds, that is, dividing the frame into three parts both vertically and horizontally, allows the camera operator to place objects along the lines and at the intersection points to help achieve a satisfying frame composition. Additional compositional factors from the standpoint of aesthetics, such as symmetry or balance and closure, should also be considered (see Chapter 4).

Positioning

Camera operators and directors control the placement and movement of cameras and put aesthetic principles into actual practice. A specific terminology is often used to refer to common types of camera placements and movements. Terms such as *medium shot, dolly, pan, pedestal,* and *crane shot* have specific meanings when

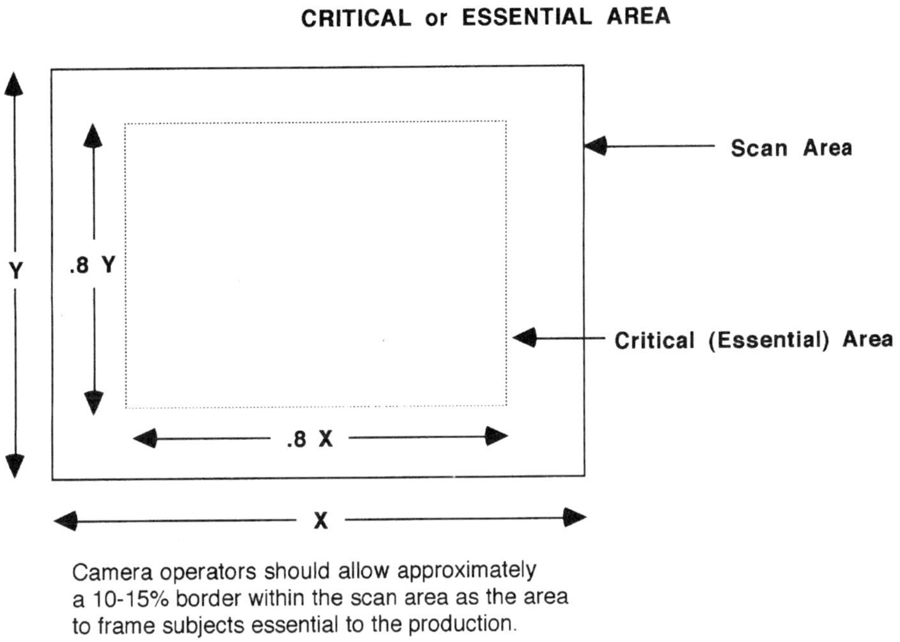

Figure 7.1 Camera operators need to be aware that all viewers at home will not be able to see in their receivers the subjects exactly the same as they see in their viewfinder. There is a certain amount of loss of the picture around the edges through the conversion and transmission process and most home receivers sweeps slowly increase as the receiver ages. This trims off a border around the picture that could amount to as much as 20 percent of the total picture. To be safe a camera operator should include within the central 80 percent all subjects that are critical to the shot, but with the reminder that some people may see virtually everything the operator is viewing.

they appear in a final shooting script and/or shot lists supplied to camera operators by the director.

A *close-up* is basically a head-and-shoulders shot of a person. An *extreme close-up* fills the frame of the camera with a character's face, a part of the face, or some specific object. Close-ups are used for emphasis, to achieve a degree of intimacy or involvement, or to focus the audience's attention on a particular detail. Used sparingly, close-ups can be an effective way of achieving dramatic emphasis. Close-ups are created by moving the camera closer to the subject or by zooming in.

A *medium shot* includes one half to three quarters of a character's body. The camera is placed farther away from the subject or the lens is zoomed out from a close-up. This type of shot is a compromise between the long shot and the close-up. Some details and facial gestures are readily apparent, but many broad actions of several characters can sometimes be included within the frame as well. A *two-shot* is generally a medium shot that presents two people or characters within the same frame. Television and film directors frequently frame the image as a two-shot so that the audience can see the actions and reactions of two characters simultaneously.

A *long shot* gives a full-body image of a character or characters. An *extreme long shot* might include a broad exterior vista. Long shots allow audiences to see broad action but do not provide emphasis or subtle details. The long shot is often called an *establishing shot* when it sets the character(s) in the context of the setting or location. Many standard scenes begin with an establishing shot to set the context or physical location, and then cut to combinations of closer shots of specific actions and characters. A camera is normally placed at the subject's eye height in video and film production, but some shots call for a higher camera angle, while others call for a much lower camera position. These high- and low-camera angles can be used to simulate the spatial positioning and points of view of specific characters, or simply to provide perspectives that will exaggerate or reduce the apparent size of the object(s) in the frame.

Movement

Camera movements in midshot should be made only when they significantly improve our understanding of what is being presented. When overused, they can be visually distracting. Moving camera shots should begin and end with the camera stationary so that they can be intercut or combined with stationary camera shots.

When a camera is placed on a moving tripod or dolly, it can be moved toward or away from the subject. These camera movements are called *dolly shots.* They differ from *zoom shots,* which result from changing the focal length of a zoom lens. Dolly shots alter perspective, that is, they change the apparent spatial positioning of objects in a scene. They give the audience the feeling that they are actually moving through the scene, as well as shifting their perspective and focus of attention.

Physically moving the camera horizontally or laterally with respect to the subject is called a *trucking shot.* Trucking shots can be used to keep a moving subject in frame. A lateral movement of the camera in a semicircular path is called an *arc.* To perform a trucking shot or arc, the camera must be mounted on a wheeled dolly. Sometimes tracks are laid on the floor or ground so that the wheels of the dolly will follow a prearranged path. If the tracks are laid properly, minimal bounce of the camera will occur, even over rough terrain. During trucking and dolly shots, it is often advisable to use a wide angle lens to minimize the bouncing of the image. Telephoto lenses accentuate camera bounce.

A stationary tripod usually has a panning and a tilting device. A *pan action* slowly and smoothly rotates the camera from side to side on a tripod pivot, while a *tilt action* moves it up and down. These movements can be used to change the angle of view or to follow action. Panning too quickly can cause vertical lines or objects to strobe or flicker. Pans and tilts can also be used to follow performer movements. Tilts are often used to follow a performer sitting down or standing up. Like all camera movements, they usually begin and end with a well-composed stationary frame. A camera can be physically moved up and down on a pedestal dolly. A hydraulic lift pushes the camera straight up or brings it straight down. This technique is called a *pedestal movement* and is used to adjust the camera for a high- or low-angle shot rather than to move the camera in midshot. A crane shot uses a long pivoting arm to move the camera up and down, or from side to side, in the studio or on location. It is usually reserved for wide establishing shots and is often used to move the camera in midshot.

Mounting Devices

Camera placements and movements usually require the use of specific camera mounting devices in order to record steady images. Mounting devices for video cameras range from pistol grips to cranes. A *pistol grip* is used to hand hold a lightweight portable small-format camera. This device is rarely used for professional recording. The *crane* is a relatively large mounting device, which consists of a long counterweighted arm on a four-wheeled dolly or truck. It allows a camera to be raised to extreme heights in a studio or field situation, and usually requires several technicians to assist the camera operator in actually moving the camera. In between these two extremes we find the body mount, tripod dolly, and pedestal dolly (Figure 7.2).

Body Mount

A shoulder harness can be anything from a built-in camera mold or special body brace that fits perfectly over the operator's shoulder to a more elaborate servo stabilizer, such as a *Steadicam,* which minimizes vibration of the camera and allows the camera operator to move around freely. A Steadicam uses a complex system of springs and counterweights to smooth out the jerky movements of the operator and to simulate dolly or crane movements of the camera. The Steadicam can be

Figure 7.2 The smallest and most flexible camera mount is a pistol grip mounted on either the camera body or the lens. Using such a mount requires upper body strength since all of the weight of the camera and lens rests on the operator's shoulder and right hand. Much practice is necessary to learn to hand-hold a camera in order to provide a steady unwavering shot.

used with a film camera as well as a video camera. (A Steadicam Jr. can be hand held with a lightweight video camera.) However, a Steadicam positions the camera in such a way that the normal film camera viewfinder cannot be used. The camera is usually at the operator's waist and is detached from his or her body. A video pickup is fitted into the camera viewfinder, and a video signal is fed to a small black-and-white monitor on the top of the camera, where it can be viewed by the operator. The video signal can also be fed to a recorder, so that immediately viewable television images are recorded at the same time as the film. Film, of course, cannot be screened until it is developed (Figures 7.3A and B).

Tripods

A *tripod* is a three-legged device upon which a stationary camera can be secured. The legs of the tripod can be extended to raise or lower the camera. Tripods are one of the most frequently used single-camera supports. They usually consist of three extendible legs, with pointed spurs on the tripod shoes, a cradle and ball joint for leveling, a fluid head or other form of panning and tilting device, and a camera locking bolt. A *fluid head* allows the camera to be smoothly panned or tilted on the tripod. When used outdoors, the spurs of the tripod can frequently be secured in soft ground, but on hard surfaces and indoors, the spur must be secured in a *spider*

Figures 7.3A and B Body mounts are manufactured to carry either film or video cameras of all sizes. They are designed with a built-in spring and gyro system to maintain positioning on a level and even keel as the operator moves about the set. (Courtesy of Cinema Products.)

(sometimes called a *triangle* or *spreader*), which provides a device for locking down the shoes of a tripod to prevent them from slipping. Tripods for small-format video cameras often have flat rubber shoes rather than pointed spurs and are intended for both indoor and outdoor use without a spider (Figures 7.4A, B, C, D,).

Figures 7.4A, B, C, D Tripods vary in size to match the size and weight of the cameras to be mounted on them. Specialized accessories such as spiders to hold the tripod feet, quick release mounts to allow the camera to be quickly placed on or off the tripod as necessary to move to the next set-up, and a high hat which allows the camera to be mounted close to the ground or on the side or top of a vehicle. (Courtesy of Matthews Studio Equipment.)

The head of a tripod frequently has a bubble device for proper leveling of the tripod. *Leveling* a tripod refers to making the camera horizontally level, so that the horizontal frames of the image are parallel with the horizon outdoors or the lines formed by the floor and the back wall, or the ceiling and back wall in an interior setting. The nut that secures the head to the tripod cradle can frequently be removed to allow the tripod head to be secured to another support device, such as a high hat. The *high hat* places a camera just a few feet above the ground, but well below the lowest tripod height. When it is equipped with suction cups, a high hat can be secured to almost any flat surface, such as the hood of an automobile or the top of a boat. A tripod can also be secured to a *hitchhiker,* which is a spider with wheels on it. The hitchhiker allows a tripod and attached camera to move around the studio and transforms a stationary tripod into a moveable dolly.

Dollies

A *dolly* is a camera platform or support device on wheels, which allows the camera to move smoothly about a studio. A *pedestal dolly* can be vertically moved up and down to raise or lower the camera in midshot. A tripod can be attached to a hitchhiker to create a dolly. The wheels of a hitchhiker, like those of a pedestal dolly, can usually be locked to prevent movement of the camera. Three wheels give the hitchhiker or pedestal dolly ample stability and ease of movement, although care must be taken to plan the movement of a camera so that the bulky coaxial cables connecting the camera to the camera control unit do not get in the way. A dolly should never roll over audio or video cables on the studio floor (Figures 7.5A and B).

Various types of dollies and other mobile mounts can be used with film and video cameras. A *crab dolly* allows up-and-down pedestal movements. Some dollies, like the Elemac spider dolly, are collapsible yet extremely versatile and stable. Sometimes a wheelchair or moving vehicle, such as a car or van, can serve as an excellent dolly. A special mount, such as the *Tyler mount,* can be used to record vibra-

Figures 7.5A and B Dollies are constructed in a variety of shapes and sizes. These two are designed to be operated by hand, rather than motorized. One is designed for the camera operator to ride seated, while the second is designed with the camera mounted on a tripod and the operator rides standing behind the camera.

tionless images from a helicopter or an airplane in combination with a special fluid-filled lens called a *dyna lens*. Finally, a *crane* can be used in studio or field productions to raise even the heaviest film camera to tremendous heights.

Lens Control

Another way in which camera operators control the presentation of visual images is by using various camera lenses. A *camera lens* consists of one or more pieces of glass that focus and frame an image within the camera. Lens control begins with an understanding of basic optics.

Basic Optics

A *lens* is a curved piece of glass that causes light rays to bend. Because glass is denser than air, light slows down at the point where it enters the lens. Lenses bend light so that it can be controlled and projected in proper focus and size at a specific point behind the lens, where a light-sensitive material can record or transmit the image. The curvature of the lens, as well as the type of glass from which it is made, affect how much the light bends and, to a certain extent, determine the classification and function of a specific lens. Simple, single lenses fall into two basic categories: concave and convex (Figure 7.6).

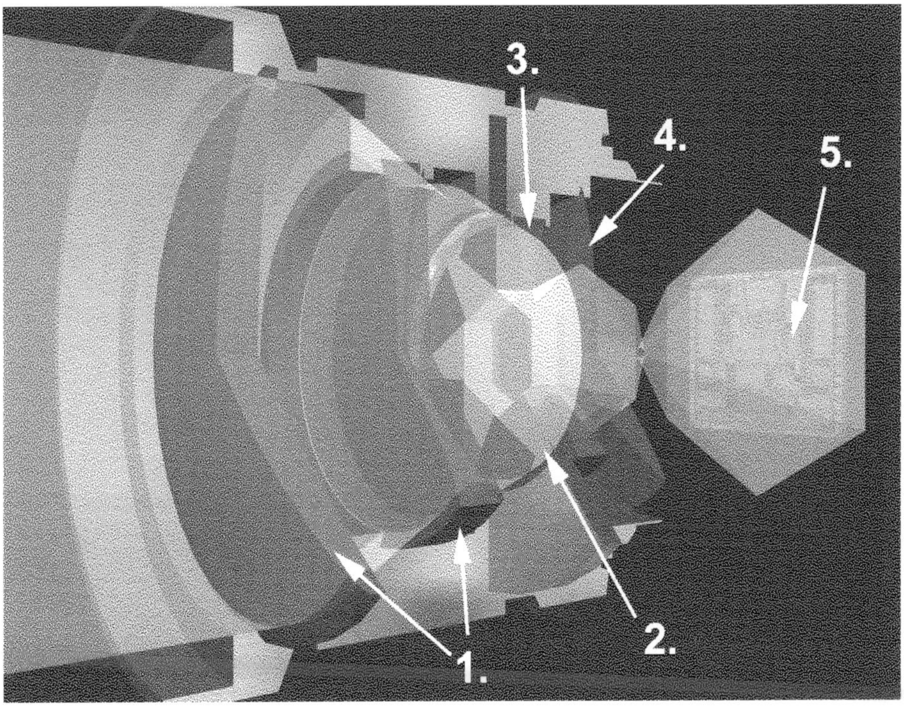

Figure 7.6 Typical parts of a lens are: 1. Lens front surface, 2. Iris, 3. Concave element, 4. Convex element, and 5. Focal point.

Concave lenses, which are thinner at the center than at the edges, bend light rays away from the center of the lens, causing them to diverge from each other. *Convex lenses,* on the other hand, are thickest at the center and bend light toward the center so that the light rays converge or intersect at a specific point behind the lens, known as the *focal point.* The distance from the optical center of a lens to its focal point is known as a lens's *focal length.* The curvature of a lens affects its focal length (Figures 7.7A and B).

Lenses can be classified according to their focal lengths. For example, film and video lenses with short focal lengths are sometimes called *wide-angle lenses.* Beyond the focal point the light rays diverge from each other, and at some area behind the lens, known as the *focal plane,* they form an inverted, reversed image of the objects reflecting light in front of the lens. Images at the focal plane are in acceptable focus, that is, the objects are clear and sharp. A piece of light-sensitive material, such as the front surface of a film or an electronic pickup chip, placed at the focal plane will record an inverted and reversed image of the original scene. Modern film and video lenses are composed of more than one piece of glass and are called *compound lenses.*

Aberrations

Compound lenses combine several concave and convex lenses in various configurations to cut down on disruptions of, or imperfections in, light transmission, which are called *aberrations*. A simple convex lens, such as a magnifying glass, creates several types of aberration, including field curvature, distortion, and chromatic aberration. *Field curvature* refers to the fact that the image projected by a simple convex lens falls into best overall focus on a curved, rather than a flat, plane or image surface. Motion picture film and front surfaces of video pickup chips are flat, not

Figures 7.7A and B Lenses for video and film cameras come in a wide variety of sizes and purposes. Pictures are various variable focal length studio and field lenses. (Courtesy of Fujinon Corporation.)

curved. *Distortion* is caused by changes in magnification that occur in different parts of the image projected by a simple, convex lens. *Chromatic aberration* refers to the fact that various color wavelengths bend at different angles when they enter a piece of glass, such as a prism or a simple lens.

A modern lens combines several concave and convex lenses to reduce these types of aberration. Modern lenses are also coated with substances such as magnesium fluoride that reduce the reflection of light entering the lens and therefore increase light transmission. The lens coating is usually placed on the outside element of a lens. Never touch the front surface of a lens with your finger. Body oils can etch the lens coating if they are not removed immediately with lens cleaning paper and proper cleaning solutions. Clean the lens with fluids infrequently since repeated cleanings can wear down the lens coating. An air blower or camel-hair brush usually does a good job of cleaning loose dirt off a lens. Lenses must be handled carefully, and cleanliness is essential.

Lens Perspective

Focal Length and Angle of Acceptance

Lens perspective, or the way in which a lens presents the spatial relations between the objects it records or transmits, varies with a lens's focal length and angle of light acceptance. The *angle of acceptance,* or the angle at which a lens gathers light in front of a camera, is determined by the focal length of the lens and the format (size) of the recording medium. Shorter focal-length lenses generally have wider angles of acceptance than long focal-length lenses. Focal lengths usually range from 10mm (about ½-inch) or less to 200mm (about 8 inches) or more. Short focal-length lenses are usually called *wide-angle lenses,* while long focal-length lenses are frequently referred to as *telephoto lenses. Normal lenses* are so called because they present an image perspective that seems to approximate that of normal monocular (single-eye) human vision (Figure 7.8).

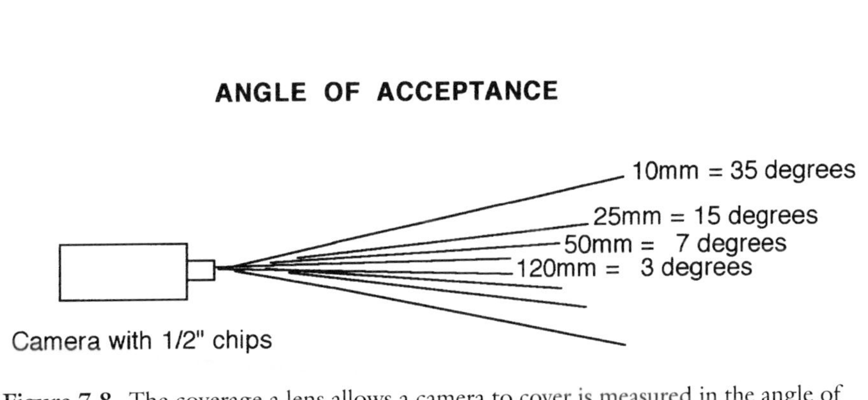

Figure 7.8 The coverage a lens allows a camera to cover is measured in the angle of acceptance. The shorter the focal length, the wider the angle of acceptance, and conversely, the longer the focal length, the narrower the angle of acceptance.

Variable Focal Length Lens

A variable focal length lens (zoom) allows a camera operator to change the focal length of a lens from wide angle through normal to telephoto and vice versa by manually turning the zoom barrel (or by pushing the button for an electric zoom motor). Zoom-ins and zoom-outs in midshot are easily misused and overused by beginning students. A zoom-in should direct our attention to something within the frame, while a zoom-out presents new information, often clarifying the setting. A zoom-in or zoom-out during a shot should be made smoothly and precisely.

A zoom lens also makes it easier to change focal length between shots, since one lens does not have to be physically replaced by another on the camera. Changing the focal length magnifies and demagnifies the image. At a long focal length the objects in the frame seem to be closer together, and at a short focal length they seem to be farther apart. A zoom lens should first be focused at its maximum focal length (telephoto). This ensures proper focus at all other focal lengths, assuming the subject to camera distance does not vary, including the end point of a zoom-in. Zoom lenses are available in a variety of focal length ranges, with minimum focal lengths as short as 10mm and maximum focal lengths as long as 200mm.

Field of View

Field of view refers to the exact dimensions of the image framed by the camera. The field of view of an image captured by a specific film or video camera is largely determined by the focal length of the lens and the video or film format. Shorter focal-length lenses present a wider field of view than longer focal-length lenses when used in the same film or video format. But the field of view provided by any lens changes when the format of the recording medium changes. A 25mm or 1-inch lens provides a narrower field of view in 16mm film or ⅔-inch video camera pickup chips than it does in 35mm film, or the same lens provides a wider field of view for ½-inch or smaller chips. In short, lens classifications, such as wide angle, normal, or telephoto, and fields of view for specific focal length lenses vary from one format to another. Whether a specific lens is wide angle, normal, or telephoto, and whether it has a wide or a narrow angle acceptance and field of view, depends on both its focal length and the dimensions of the film or video format (Figure 7.9).

Image Depth

Image depth is a general term describing the overall range of distances and objects that appear to be in sharp focus within the frame. It can be affected by a variety of specific factors, including the type of lens used, various lens adjustments, the placement of the objects within the set, and the lighting; the latter two are discussed more fully in subsequent chapters. In this chapter, depth is considered from the standpoint of specific lens factors that affect one aspect of image depth, called *depth of field*. The primary factors creating depth of field are focus distance, lens aperture, and focal length. It is easier to understand the concept of depth of field by first explaining the primary factors that can be used to control it on a lens.

Focus Distance

Focus distance refers to the distance of the subject from the focal plane of a camera. On film cameras, the focal plane is indicated on the outside of the camera by a line drawn through the center of a circle. Focus distance can be accurately measured

ANGLE OF VIEW

FOCAL LENGTH	1/2" CCD/S-8Film	1" Tube/ 16mm Film	35mm film
10mm	35 degrees	50 degrees	95 degrees
25mm	15 degrees	30 degrees	45 degrees
50mm	7 degrees	15 degrees	25 degrees
80mm	4.5 degrees	7 degrees	15 degrees
120mm	3 degrees	4.5 degrees	10 degrees
200mm	1.75 degrees	3 degrees	6 degrees

Note: a 25mm lens for a small format (1/2" CCD or S-8 film) is a telephoto lens while the same focal length in a medium format (1" tube or 16mm film) is a normal lens. In a large format (35mm film) the 25 mm lens is a wide angle lens.

Figure 7.9 The field of view of a camera varies with the size of the camera tube or chip or the aperture opening of the film, and the focal length of the lens. A 50mm lens on a small format medium would provide a narrow angle shot, for a medium format a standard shot, and for a large format medium a wide angle shot.

with a tape measure stretched from the focal plane to the subject. The focus ring on the lens barrel is adjusted according to the exact distance in feet or meters. On a reflex camera or video camera, focus distances can be set by simply turning the focus ring, while viewing the subject through a properly adjusted viewfinder.

The *viewfinder diopter* on the reflex film camera is a device that adjusts the focus of a lens to the eyesight of a particular camera operator. This can be done by setting the lens focus ring on infinity and then looking through the viewfinder at an object that is at least fifty feet away. Turn the diopter focus ring until the object appears in proper focus and then lock down the diopter. Now the focus ring on the lens can be turned to set the focus on any subject regardless of its distance from the camera. A video camera does not have a viewfinder diopter or focus adjustment, since the viewfinder is usually a small black-and-white monitor, but for accurate focusing, the contrast and brightness of the monitor must be set properly.

Lens Aperture

An *aperture* is an opening through which light is allowed to pass. A camera has a fixed rectangular aperture or frame with a specific aspect ratio, where the film or pickup chip actually is exposed to light. A lens has a variable, circular-shaped aperture or iris, which allows the amount of the light passing through the lens to be increased or decreased. The amount of light a lens transmits to a recording device can be controlled by varying the diameter of the lens aperture (Figure 7.10A).

Lens aperture settings are calibrated in sequential f-stops or T-stops. *f-stops,* which are the most commonly used measure of light transmission, have been mathematically calculated from a lens's physical characteristics. Some lenses have both T-stops and f-stops. *T-stops* provide an accurate index of actual light transmission by a specific lens. They are often used with zoom lenses, because the complex elements within the lens and the many air-to-glass surfaces can absorb a great deal of the light before it finally reaches the film or pickup tube. The most commonly

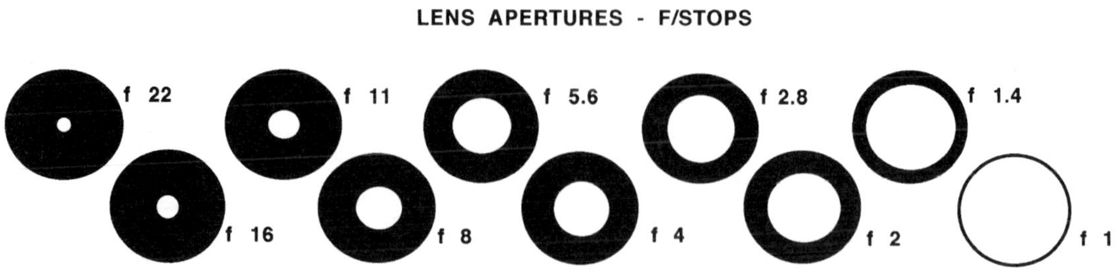

Figure 7.10A The numbers designating f-stops seem to act in reverse to their actual function. A small number such as f 1.4 actually is a relatively large opening in the aperture, but an f 22 is a relatively small opening allowing very little light to enter the camera.

labeled f- and T-stops on an aperture setting ring are 1, 1.4, 2, 2.8, 4, 5.6, 8, 11, 16, and 22. The higher the number, the narrower the opening in the lens and thus less light is actually transmitted through the lens. It is sometimes helpful to conceive of the increasing numbers as reciprocals or fractions, that is, 1.4 = $1/1.4$ and 16 = $1/16$. Each higher f-stop represents a 50 percent decrease in light transmission from the f-stop immediately below it in numerical scale and two times the f-stop above it. Thus, an f-stop of 2 transmits half as much light through a given lens as an f-stop of 1.4, and twice as much as an f-stop of 2.8.

Deciding exactly which f-stop to use is complicated by the many other variables that can affect exposure, such as the sensitivity of film stocks and pickup chips, as well as the amount of available light. In the 1930s many Hollywood cameramen always tried to light a scene for an f-stop of 5.6. There were several reasons for this beyond mere habit. First, and most important in terms of image quality, every lens has an optimum aperture, which is usually two to three full stops down from wide open. At an optimum aperture, such as a midrange f-stop of 5.6, the objects in focus are at their maximum sharpness. When the iris is closed down to a tiny hole, diffraction occurs around the blades of the iris, causing the sharpness of the image to be reduced. Such diffraction is more severe with wide-angle than with telephoto lenses. Studio cameramen selected 5.6 because even with poorer quality lenses, it consistently produced sharp images. Second, certain studios simply wanted to preserve a theoretical normal depth of field. A great deal of studio video recording today follows the same practice of using an f-stop of 5.6 for similar reasons.

Depth of Field

Depth of field refers to the range of distances in front of the lens that are in acceptable focus at the focal plane. Depth of field depends on the lens factors described earlier: (1) focus distance (which is usually the same as camera-to-subject distance), (2) lens focal length, and (3) the lens aperture or f-stop number. It also varies with the size of the recording format. Depth of field increases as the camera-to-subject distance increases, the focal length of the lens decreases, and the lens aperture narrows within a single format. Moving to a larger recording format increases the depth of field of a particular lens. For example, a 25mm lens offers a greater depth of field when used with ⅔-inch diameter video camera pickup chips than when used with ½-inch pickup chips (Figure 7.10B).

DEPTH OF FIELD RANGES
16mm FILM - 25mm LENS

Hyper-focal distance	134.6'	96.1'	62.3'	48.0'	33.6'	24.0'	16.8'	12.2'	8.4'	6.1'
f-stop	1	1.4	2	2.8	4	5.6	8	11	16	22
Lens Focus	Near Far	Near Far	Near Far	Near Far	Near Far	Near Far	Near Far	Near Far	Near Far	Near Far
50'	36' 80'	33' 104'	29' 195'	25' Inf.	20' Inf.	16' Inf.	13' Inf.	10' Inf.	7' Inf.	5' Inf.
10'	9'3.5" 10'9.5"	9' .5" 11'2"	8'9" 11'9"	8'3" 12'7"	7'9" 14'3"	7'1" 17'2"	6'3" 25'	5'6" 55'	4'7" Inf.	3'10" Inf.
3'	2'11.25" 3' 3/4"	2'11" 3'1.25"	2'10.5" 3'1.75"	2'9.75" 3'2.5"	2'9" 3'3.5	2'8" 3'5.25"	2'6.5 3'8"	2'5" 3.11.5"	2'2.5" 4'8"	2' 5'11"

Figure 7.10B The depth of field of a lens is determined by three factors: the f-stop, the focal length, and the hyper-focal distance, that is the point of best focus. Each of these three can be manipulated to increase or decrease the depth of field, depending on the desires of the camera operator.

Depth of field charts for different focal-length lenses and film or video formats indicate the range of distances in front of a lens where objects will appear to be in focus at different lens settings. The range of distances are mathematically calculated from f-stop settings, focal lengths, and camera-to-subject distances. Obviously focus does not immediately drop off beyond the nearest and farthest distances listed for each combination of focal length, camera-to-subject distance, and lens aperture setting. But the chart recommendations provide a relative standard for gauging depth of field and acceptable focus range.

Changing the focal length, either by changing lenses or by zooming out or in, obviously changes the depth of field. So does moving the camera closer to or farther away from the subject and changing the focus distance setting of the lens. The same holds true if the subject moves and the focus setting is changed. If a subject begins to exceed the depth of field range, the camera operator may have to adjust the focus distance setting, which is known as *pulling focus.* Sometimes a camera operator may intentionally try to limit the depth of field, either to isolate the subject from the background by putting the background out of focus or to shift the viewer's focus of attention by pulling focus from an object or face in the background to another in the foreground or vice versa. Depth of field limitations are extremely important in terms of the placement and movements of the talent, who must be accurately informed about the range of distances within which they can safely walk and still hit their marks during a shot. Controlling depth of field affects the perception and aesthetics of image depth within the frame, which was discussed more fully in Chapter 6. A camera operator who learns the basic principles of depth of field can fully exploit the creative and aesthetic potential of film and television images.

Video Cameras

Video and film cameras are sophisticated pieces of electronic and mechanical equipment. There are many different types of video and film cameras, which must be fully understood before they can be artistically controlled. This section considers basic camera design, function, operation, and artistic control.

Basic Video Camera

A basic video camera consists of pickup chip(s), a black-and-white viewfinder, a tally light, a lens, and all the electronic and mechanical controls needed to operate each of these devices.

Color cameras have one or more light-sensitive pickup chips, while black-and-white cameras have only one pickup chip. Even on color cameras, most viewfinders present black-and-white images, which show the camera operator what is being recorded by the camera. The lens focuses light rays on the video camera pickup tube. Most modern cameras have a single zoom lens, which allows for power or manual control of the image size. Telephoto lenses magnify the image, while wide-angle lenses present a wide field of view and demagnify the image. The *tally light* is usually positioned on the top of the camera. It lights up to inform the talent and crew which of several cameras in multiple-camera production is actually being used for recording or transmission.

The Camera Chain

A basic video camera chain consists of five separate parts: (1) a camera, (2) a power supply, (3) a sync generator, (4) a camera control unit, and (5) an encoder, which combines the luminance (brightness or amount of light) and chrominance (saturation or amount of color and hue, or shade of color) channels of visual information into a single video signal. The power supply for American television systems consists of either 120-volt AC current for a studio camera or a 12-volt DC battery (usually) for a field camera (Figure 7.11).

A separate *sync generator* (which is housed inside a field camera) supplies the signal that ensures proper synchronization between the scanning of the camera pickup tube and the scanning of a videotape or a monitor or receiving picture tube, such as a video camera viewfinder. A *camera control unit* for a studio camera allows the video engineer to shade the camera, that is, to control the levels and color values in the video camera signal. This is done by adjusting the pickup chips' output levels and color. Multiple cameras must be shaded and white balanced so that all shots will be comparable in brightness and color. Field cameras have built-in controls, which also allow the color signal to be properly set for white balance and brightness.

Video Camera Filters

There are two types of filter controls used on video cameras: a filter wheel or a filter switch. A *filter wheel* consists of several different filters arranged around the perimeter of the wheel so that each filter can be positioned between the lens and the camera pickup tube(s). One of the wheel settings has no filter for normal studio

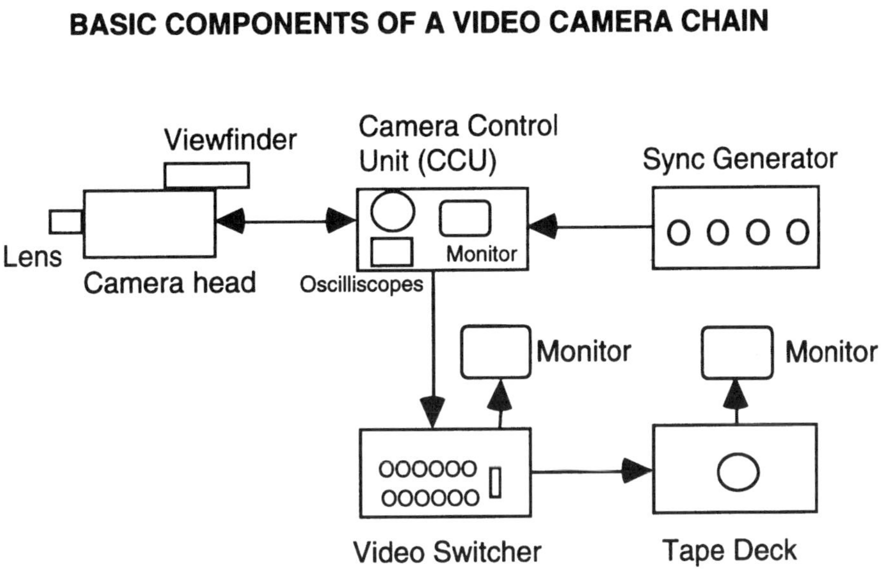

Figure 7.11 A basic camera chain consists of the following parts: the camera, its head, lens, and viewfinder. A camera control unit (CCU) with a vector scope, oscilloscope, and monitor. A sync generator provides synchronizing signals. If the camera is used in a studio setting then the signal is fed to a switcher with monitors, and to a recording medium with its monitor. A portable camera will have the CCU and sync generator built into the camera body so that it may operate independently of any other equipment.

operation. A *cap filter* on the wheel is opaque. It is used to protect the pickup tube when the camera is not actually recording. *Color correction filters* on the wheel alter the color temperature of daylight so that it corresponds with the preset color sensitivity of the video camera. *Neutral density filters* reduce the intensity of excessively bright light. The amount of light or brightness in a signal can also be controlled by adjusting the lens aperture and/or the brightness control on a field camera. A *filter switch* is commonly used on a portable video camera in place of a filter wheel. This switch allows a color correction filter to be positioned between the lens and the pickup tube(s) when recording under sunlight.

Types of Video Cameras

The most basic distinction between video cameras was that of color versus black and white, but the standardization of color for most video situations suggests that the most important distinctions today are those of field cameras, studio cameras, and convertible cameras, which can be converted for either field or studio use. Within each of these categories there is a variation in terms of image quality, and a distinction is often made between professional and consumer quality cameras. Recorded images must be of high quality to be edited and duplicated for broadcast, and this usually requires more sophisticated and expensive equipment. The most sophisticated and highest quality cameras are those that maintain the video signal in the digital domain from the pickup chips to the built-in digital recorder. The recorder could be either a ¼-inch or ½-inch digital videocassette recorder, a built-in computer with either a removable hard drive or RAM memory package.

The image quality of a video camera should be matched with the format and quality of the videotape recorder being used. It is as pointless to use an expensive, three-chip, studio camera to make a ½-inch VHS original videotape recording as it is to use 1-inch helical, ½-inch Betacam SP or M-II VTR with an inexpensive single-chip consumer video camera. The characteristics and image quality of both the video camera and recorder must be compatible with the production expectations and standards of the specific task at hand (Figure 7.12).

Field Cameras

Field cameras vary from lightweight, 8mm or ½-inch consumer cameras that can be hand held with a hand or pistol grip, to expensive ¼-inch digital, Betacam SP, or M-II machines. Many of the least expensive, consumer model cameras are primarily intended for personal home video use and come with a ½-inch S-VHS or 8mm Hi8 built-in recorder, or camcorder. Hi8 and S-VHS camcorders are sometimes used in educational, corporate, and government video production situations as well. Digital, Betacam SP, and M-II machines employ more sophisticated electronics, such as three pickup chips instead of one, and have built-in high speed video recorders. They produce images of high quality and are often used for professional recording.

The newest camcorders record a digital signal directly from the camera chips to a built-in minicomputer that records the video and audio signals onto a floppy disc. After recording, the disc can be inserted directly into a digital nonlinear video edi-

Figure 7.12 A professional video camera is a self-contained unit consisting of the camera head, lens, viewfinder, microphone, and built-in CCU and sync generator. The camera may be powered either by batteries or an adapter pack from 100 volt power. (Courtesy of Sony Corporation.)

tor without having to download the signals. Such a design allows for an editing system the size of a briefcase with two built-in monitors, a disc player, and a second disc recorder and edit controller to edit discs while seated in an automobile or even an airplane. The acceptance of such miniaturized equipment for full broadcast use is dependent upon development of efficient and cost-effective digital storage systems and video compression circuits capable of maintaining broadcast quality signals (Figure 7.13).

It is rarely possible to record images and sounds of sufficient quality for television broadcasting using low-end consumer video cameras. These cameras allow insufficient control over the quality of recorded images and sounds. Some field cameras designed for use with ¾-inch U-matic videotape recorders are still used in documentary and news situations, where an image quality slightly less than M-II or Betacam SP will suffice for television broadcast. A major limitation of M-II and Betacam SP is the twenty minute recording capacity of the videocassettes.

Convertible Video Cameras

Many video cameras offer a compromise in size (portability) and electronic hardware (control) between studio and field cameras. So-called convertible cameras can be used both in the studio and in the field. They are relatively expensive because they are nearly equivalent (in terms of the attachments that control electronic image quality) to the best studio cameras, and yet they quickly convert to more portable field operation. Several convertible video cameras have been developed for electronic field production (EFP) in the digital videotape recording format. They often weigh less than twenty pounds and use multiple, high quality pickup chips. At the top end of the convertible cameras in terms of price are portable studio cam-

Figure 7.13 Field cameras generally are designed to be hand held or mounted on lightweight tripods for easy movement and setting up. They are designed to be a stand-alone camera to be connected to a switcher or to an independent tape deck, or as a camcorder with a built-in tape deck. (Courtesy of JVC.)

eras that use sophisticated camera pickup chips to record high quality images, but they are much more bulky and unwieldy in the field than standard field cameras. Recordings from convertible cameras are usually made on digital, or in some cases, Betacam SP or M-II tape recorders.

Studio Cameras

Studio cameras must be mounted in a relatively fixed position, as they are usually too large to be shoulder mounted or hand held. Such cameras frequently feature a large viewfinder, high quality lenses, and sophisticated camera pickup chips. The quality of the optics, the number of attachments, the size and configuration of the pickup chips, and the sophistication of the electronics can vary considerably among studio cameras. The highest level studio cameras, such as those used in network broadcasting situations, are capable of reproducing high quality images under a full range of lighting situations. Many newer studio cameras are digitally controlled by microprocessors or electronic chips. Recordings from studio cameras are usually made on 1-inch, Betacam SP, M-II, or in some cases, digital VCRs.

Film Cameras

Film cameras can be categorized in terms of their film formats (the width of the film in millimeters), viewing systems, and sound recording capabilities. The most basic distinction between film cameras is that of film format. *Film format* is a major determinant of image quality. As the width of the film increases, so does the quality of the recorded image. Small-format cameras, such as Super-8mm cameras, are much smaller and more portable than 16mm, 35mm, or 65mm cameras. The latter are manufactured primarily for professional use, while the former are made primarily as consumer (home movie) products.

Film cameras have one of two types of operator viewing systems. *Reflex viewing* is a system whereby the operator's eye sees exactly what is coming through the camera's eye, or objective lens. Older cameras sometimes have nonreflex viewfinders. When the camera operator looks into the viewfinder, he or she does not look directly through the objective camera lens, but sees an entirely separate image of the same scene. The discrepancy between what the viewfinder sees and what the objective lens sees is called *parallax.* Parallax can usually be corrected by changing the angle of the viewfinder so that its image or field of view is the same as that which the camera actually records.

Film cameras can also be differentiated on the basis of sound-recording capabilities. Mechanical or spring-wound cameras cannot run the film at a consistent speed and therefore cannot record synchronous or matching sounds. There are two basic systems by which electronic film cameras can record synchronous sounds: single system and double system. *Single-system* or *sound-on-film* (SOF) recording refers to the recording of synchronous sounds on the edge of the film as it runs through the camera. The camera records images and sounds at the same time. The sounds are recorded by a magnetic sound head, which is 18 (Super-8mm) or 26 (16mm) film frames ahead of the picture aperture, on magnetic tape striping on the edge of the film. During *double-system recording,* a separate high quality audiotape recorder records sounds, which can be played back in perfect synchronization with the recorded film images. The camera and sound recording motors for double-system recording are usually crystal controlled for extremely accurate and precise recording and playback.

Types of Film Cameras

8mm Cameras

Most Super-8mm cameras have reflex viewfinders and are used for recording home movies, but a few professionals prefer to work in this small format as well. The Super-8mm home movie format is being rapidly replaced by Hi8, and S-VHS camcorders. Most Super-8mm cameras are battery powered and automatic. Super-8mm cameras can usually be run at 16 frames per second (fps; fast motion) in silent (nonsynchronous sound) mode. Synchronous sound on some Super-8mm cameras can only be recorded at 24 fps, while others use a speed of 18 fps. Some sophisticated Super-8mm cameras can be used with separate synchronous sound tape recorders. Super-8mm cameras use single and double Super-8mm film cassettes, which contain 50 to 100 feet of unexposed film.

16mm Cameras

There are many different types of 16mm cameras. Some lack the ability to record synchronous sound, such as spring-wound mainspring-driven cameras, which create considerable camera noise and run at imprecise speeds. Cameras that have quiet running, battery-powered electric motors and film advance mechanisms are called *self-blimped* film cameras. Single-system sound-on-film cameras were once widely used for recording news footage; they are now being replaced by ENG video camcorders. A few film cameras are capable of both single-system and double-system film recording. Many self-blimped, double-system cameras are driven by crystal-sync electric motors that allow the camera to be used without any cable connection between it and a separate synchronous sound recorder. The absence of a cable connection allows for more freedom of movement and is particularly helpful in documentary situations. The camera operator can move about independently of the sound recordist (Figure 7.14).

Unlike video cameras, whose viewing systems can be electronically controlled, the viewing system of a reflex film camera is often quite dim during actual recording. Film cameras are often focused with the aperture wide open (lowest f-stop) prior to actual recording; when the aperture is closed down to the proper f-stop for recording, less light is transmitted to the viewfinder. Some viewing systems reflect only 18 percent of the light to the viewfinder, and a camera operator must become used to recording under difficult conditions. Sometimes a videotape is attached to a film camera to monitor the image and to provide immediately viewable results.

35mm Cameras

It is important to note that 35mm motion picture cameras differ quite dramatically from 35mm still cameras. The latter run 35mm width film horizontally through the camera, while 35mm motion picture cameras run the film vertically through the camera, recording film frames that are not as wide as still-frame slides. The aspect ratio and image size of a 35mm motion picture frame are thus quite different

Figure 7.14 16mm film cameras vary from light weight spring wound non-sync sound cameras to heavier cameras with built-in video tapes, crystal sync systems, and sound deadening blimp cases. They may be stripped down with few accessories, or fully equipped with the accessories found on 35mm feature film cameras. (Courtesy of Arri Corp.)

from a still-camera frame. A 35mm still-camera frame has a much higher aspect ratio (2.35:1) than video or 35mm motion picture film (1.33:1 or 4:3); thus it is difficult to record complete slides on a motion picture or video camera (Figure 7.15).

Some smaller 35mm motion picture cameras, such as the Arriflex II-C, are used exclusively for MOS (mitt out or without sound) nonsynchronous sound recording. Other, very bulky cameras, such as the Mitchell BNC and Panavision, are used almost exclusively for studio synchronous sound recording situations. A Panavision camera is frequently used for wide-screen feature film recording in the studio. The latter has an extremely lightweight and portable stepchild, called the Panaflex camera, which is frequently used for feature film work on location. Only extremely high budget feature films use 65mm cameras for original recording. Most 70mm feature film prints are not made from 65mm camera originals but rather from 35mm original recordings that have been blown up to this larger format. Professional motion picture camera recording in 16mm, 35mm, and 65mm sets a very high standard in image quality, which is gradually being rivaled by Betacam, EC-35, and HDTV (high definition television).

Camera Accessories

Many cameras have attachable matte boxes or lens hoods that shade the lens from direct sunlight and allow filters to be attached to the lens for color correction or special effects. A frequently used film camera accessory is the *cable release,* which

Figure 7.15 35mm film cameras may vary in size from simple hand-held to large mult-format with a variety of accessories mounted to facilitate the best possible production. (Courtesy of Arri Corp.)

minimizes the vibration to the camera when single frame images are exposed individually. Another important film camera accessory is a *changing bag*, which is a black, light-tight bag that can serve as a portable darkroom for loading and unloading longer rolls of film wound on open cores.

Camera Care

Cameras are extremely delicate instruments. They must be handled with great care because they can be damaged very easily. Cameras should be kept clean and dry. Never leave a camera unprotected and exposed to elements, such as rain, sleet, snow, or sand. Never leave a camera unattended or in a hazardous position, where it is likely to fall or be stolen. Always make sure that you have sufficient battery power by charging batteries well before actual recording begins. Nothing is more frustrating than having a group of people waiting around for the batteries to be recharged (Figure 7.16).

Video cameras with tubes can be permanently damaged by exposing the camera pickup tubes to direct sunlight or allowing the camera to focus on a bright light or reflecting surface for an extended period of time. Never, never, never point a video camera directly at the sun; a permanent spot on the pickup tube may result! If the video camera has a built-in recorder, use the same operating procedures you

CAMERA CARE

DO'S

Keep clean and dry
Carefully clean the film gate with each film load
Clean lenses properly and periodically
Clean filters before each use
Check for proper filter before each take
Protect from elements such as snow, rain, dust, sand, dirt
Check for properly charged batteries
Allow time for adjustment to changes in temperature and/or humidity
Insulate from extremes in temperature
Check for proper film threading by visually watching with an open cover and then again by listening with the camera closed

DON'TS

Bump, drop, or shake violently
Point a tube camera at a bright light, especially the sun
Leave unattended at ANY time
Leave exposed to public view in a vehicle
Leave tripod or pedestal head with pan or tilt controls unlocked
Expose to high heat, humidity, rain, or salt water
Ignore changes in sound when running
Assume anything

Figure 7.16 All cameras, whether video or film must be treated as fine sensitive pieces of expensive equipment. Careful handling requires a knowledge of what can harm the camera and how to avoid damaging the camera either inadvertently or through ignorance.

would for a separate VCR (discussed in the next chapter) to avoid having the tape jam within the recorder. Video cameras are even more sensitive to high heat and humidity than film cameras, and therefore require shading under intense sunlight, insulation from the cold, and careful use of videotape in high humidity.

Operating a film camera requires extreme care and sensitivity to every possible malfunction of the equipment. Since film is quite expensive to record, minor mistakes can translate into significant financial losses as well as reshooting time. Videotape, on the other hand, is immediately viewable and can be reused.

It is important to develop a checklist of camera operating procedures and to make sure that every item on the list is checked off before recording. First, make sure that the lens is clean and that there are no hairs or pieces of film stuck in the film gate of the camera where it is exposed to light. On professional film shoots for commercials, the camera lens is usually removed from the camera periodically to check the film gate for hairs or debris, since the image must be perfectly clean. If a filter must be placed in the camera or on the lens, make sure that it is completely clean so that there will be no spots or marks on the film and no loss of light.

Carefully load the film into the camera and its magazine, and then run the film with the camera and magazine cover open to make sure that it is running properly and not tugging at the film gate, which will cause jittery images. (If you are shooting 8mm film in a cartridge, there is no way to check this, since loading is automatic.) Finally, close the camera and the magazine where the film is exposed and stored, and listen to a properly running and loaded camera. It has a characteristic sound. If this sound changes during actual recording, stop shooting immediately! Something is wrong. The camera should be opened and the aperture area inspected for problems. The film will probably need to be reloaded. Potential problems with a videotape deck also maybe determined quickly by listening carefully to the sound of the tape motor and drive movements.

Summary

Camera operators must be thoroughly familiar with camera techniques and equipment to provide directors with the best possible visual images from the standpoint of a particular aesthetic approach. A camera operator controls image composition and camera placement by employing four key concepts: essential area, lookspace, walkspace, and headroom. Key information must be placed within the essential area of the screen. Some space must be left within the frame in the direction a person is looking or walking and above a person's head. Camera operators also employ the rule of thirds and realist conceptions, such as the 180-degree action-axis rule.

Camera operators understand the best position and angle at which to place the camera. Long shots, medium shots, and close-ups describe camera placement in terms of camera-to-subject distance. High-angle and low-angle camera positions alter the perception of people and actions. Camera movements alter spatial perspective and are often used to follow performer movements. Pans, tilts, and pedestals and crane movements can be made with a stationary tripod or camera mounting device. Dollies, trucking shots, and arcs are accomplished using movable camera mounting devices. Moving camera shots are used primarily to keep moving subjects within the camera frame or to reveal new information by altering spatial perspective.

Camera operators must understand how lenses function in order to control them. Lenses are curved pieces of glass that bend light in a predictable manner. Lenses help a camera operator control an image's field of view, brightness, focus, perspective, and depth of field. Lenses can be categorized by their focal lengths within a specific video or film format into wide-angle, normal, and telephoto lenses. Wide-angle lenses have a wide field of view, while telephoto lenses have a narrow field of view and magnify an image. Zoom lenses allow an operator to manipulate field of view by varying the focal length of the lens. A zoom lens should usually be focused at its longest focal length (telephoto). Varying the aperture, or iris, of a lens changes the amount of light transmitted through the lens. Adjusting the focus setting of a lens puts some objects into focus and others out of focus. The depth of field of an image, that is, the range of distances in front of the lens that remain in focus, will vary with changes in focal length, aperture, and camera-to-subject distance or focus distance within a specific film or video format. Changing the format changes the depth of field as well. Depth of field is an important determinant of image depth, along with the placement of objects or scenic design and lighting.

A video camera contains one or more light-sensitive pickup chips. The camera chain consists of a camera, power supply, sync generator, and a camera control unit. Power can be supplied by line current or a battery. A sync generator and control of image brightness and color can be built into a camera or housed in a separate camera control unit. A color video camera must be white balanced for a proper balance of red, green, and blue colors in the video signal. Video cameras can be divided into three basic categories: field cameras, convertible cameras, and studio cameras. Field cameras are lightweight and portable. They can range from consumer cameras to sophisticated and expensive M-II and Betacam SP high-speed ½-inch or digital videotape recording equipment, which records the highest quality images. Convertible cameras can be used in the studio with more cumbersome studio attachments, or they can be stripped down for use in the field. Convertible cameras often use a ½-inch or digital videotape recording format. Studio cameras are usually much heavier and more cumbersome then portable units. They afford a camera operator maximum control of high quality images, usually recorded in 1-inch, high quality ½-inch or digital videotape formats.

Film cameras can be divided into different levels of image quality on the basis of film formats, such as Super-8mm, 16mm, 35mm, and 65mm, which refer to the width of the film in millimeters. Super-8mm film cameras are often used for home movies, although they are rapidly being replaced by consumer video cameras. Some film cameras have quiet and precise (often crystal-controlled) electric motors, which allow synchronous sounds to be recorded, either single system (sound-on-film) or double system, with a separate high quality sound recorder. Single-system film cameras were once used to record news footage, but they have been virtually replaced by ENG video cameras. Professional film camera recording still sets a high standard of image quality, which is gradually being rivaled by digital video technology.

Exercises

1. Use a handheld or shoulder-mounted video camera to follow a person moving around in a random fashion outdoors. Maintain good framing and focus while following this unpredictable action. Move your body and the camera as slowly, smoothly, and deliberately as you can without missing any key action. View the recorded videotape to determine why problems occurred at certain points.
2. Use a dolly-mounted video camera to follow a person moving around in a random fashion within a studio. Maintain good framing and focus while following this unpredictable action. Move the dolly as slowly, smoothly, and deliberately as you can without missing any key action. View the recorded videotape to determine why problems occurred at certain points.
3. Select the best lens settings for each shot designated in a shooting script scene by determining the depth of field that will be necessary to keep the performers safely in focus throughout each shot. Remember that depth of field depends on the camera-to-subject distance, the focal length of the lens, and the aperture of f-stop opening of the lens.

Additional Readings

Beacham, Frank. *American Cinematographer Video Manual.* Hollywood, CA: The ASC Press, 1992

Bernard, Rob. *Practical Videography: Field Systems and Troubleshooting.* Boston: Focal Press, 1990.

Clark, Charles G., ed. *American Cinematographer Manual,* 7th ed. Hollywood, CA: The ASC Press, 1993.

Elkins, David E. *Camera Terms and Concepts.* Boston: Focal Press, 1993.

Hodges, Peter. *The Video Camera Operator's Handbook.* Boston: Focal Press, 1995.

Mathias, Harry, and Richard Patterson. *Electronic Cinematography.* Belmont, CA: Wadsworth, 1985.

Millerson, Gerald. *The Technique of Television Production,* 12th ed. Boston: Focal Press, 1990.

Millerson, Gerald. *Video Camera Techniques.* Boston: Focal Press, 1994.

Pincus, Edward, and Steven Ascher. *The Filmmaker's Handbook.* New York: Plume, 1984.

Samuelson, David. *David Samuelson's "Hands On" Manual for Cinematographers.* Boston: Focal Press, 1994.

Samuelson, David. *Motion Picture Camera and Lighting Equipment.* Boston: Focal Press, 1986.

Wilson, Anton. *Cinema Workshop.* Hollywood, CA: The ASC Press, 1983.

Wurtzel, Alan, and John Rosenbaum. *Television Production,* 4th ed. New York: McGraw-Hill, 1994.

Zettl, Herbert. *Television Production Handbook,* 5th ed. Belmont, CA: Wadsworth, 1992.

8

Recording

Introduction

Recording good quality sound and images is extremely important as poor quality recordings can destroy the impact of a high quality production. Some directors feel that sounds and visual images should be almost completely independent of one another so that each component could stand entirely on its own, while others feel that sounds should reinforce accompanying visual images.

Acquiring a basic understanding of media technology increases your ability to control aesthetic variables, whether they are realist, modernist or postmodernist. If you understand the means by which images and sound are recorded, you can consistently obtain high quality recordings of the intended production. Visual and aural media are based on digital and analog electronic, magnetic, and photochemical recording processes. This chapter provides an introduction to audio and video electronics, and film photochemistry.

Analog Audio

The most common form of audiotape recording, called *analog recording*, produces a continuously varying magnetic copy of the electrical fluctuations stimulated by the original sound waves. The original sinewave variations of the audio signal are duplicated in sinewave magnetic variations, matching as closely as possible the original signal. Magnetic tape passes over a magnetic sound record head, consisting of a magnet with a coil wrapped around it, which carries the electrical sound signal. As the voltage in the electric sound signal fluctuates, the magnetic field through which the tape is passing changes, and the sound signal is recorded on tape. A bias signal (30,000 Hz or above, which is outside the range of human hearing) produced by a bias head aligns the signal to record on the linear portion of the magnetization curve. In the playback mode, the tape is passed over a playback head (in some recorders the same head is used for both record and playback), which picks up the prerecorded tape's magnetic variations and causes a weak electrical current passing through the magnetic head to fluctuate accordingly. This signal is then amplified; that is, it is increased in strength and intensity, so that it can be sent to a loudspeaker, headphones, or another tape recorder.

Audiotape Formats

Audiotape is made up of particles of iron oxide or other metallic substances attached to a flexible support base. Tape formats can be categorized on the basis of two factors: the dimensions of the tape and the form in which it is packaged. Audiotape dimensions differ in terms of thickness and width. Audio quality generally increases with increasing tape thickness and width, and relative speed of the head to tape. The thickness of audiotape is measured in mils (thousandths of an inch). The most common tape thicknesses are 1½, 1, ½, and ¼ mil. The most durable tape is 1½ mil; it is less likely to print through from one layer to the next. This has become the professional standard. Audiotape also comes in a variety of widths, such as ⅛-inch, ¼-inch, ½-inch, 1-inch, and 2-inch. Multitrack analog tape recorders (each track is a separate tape path) require wider audiotape. As many as sixty-four separate tracks can be recorded on some multitrack machines using 2-inch-wide audiotape (Figure 8.1).

Audio signals in video recording are usually recorded directly on videotape in a variety of formats, which are discussed later in this chapter. Film audio may be recorded on a separate ¼-inch audiotape, full-coat film stock, or directly onto the film itself. In the latter case, the edge of Super-8mm or 16mm film is coated with magnetic material; this is called *magnetically-striped film* (Figure 8.2).

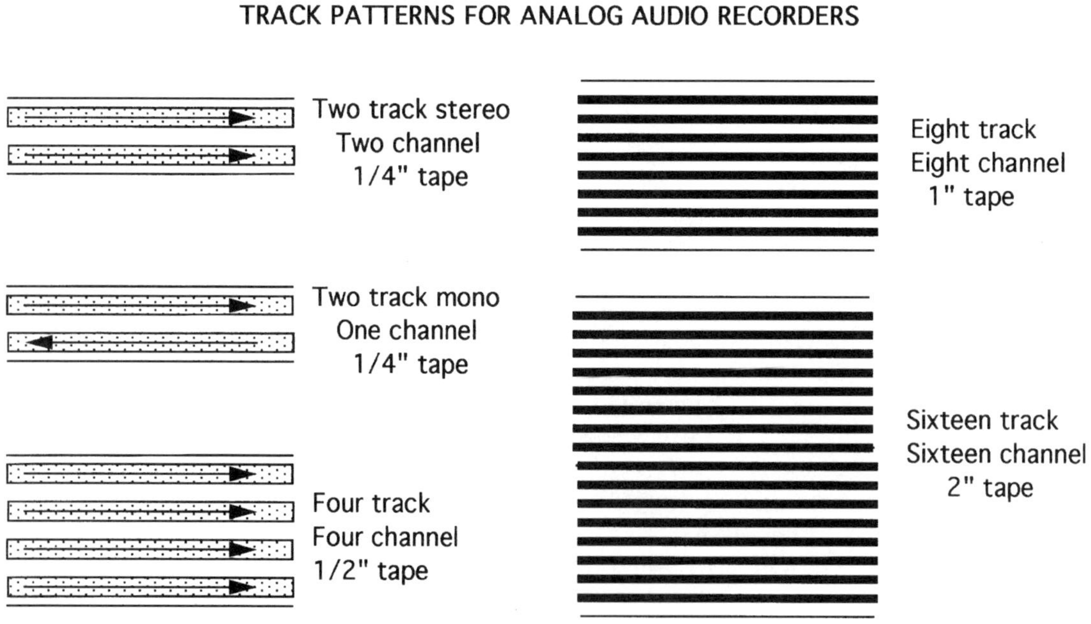

Figure 8.1 Analog audio tracks are arranged in a linear pattern down the length of the tape stock. In some cases the tracks may be laid down in opposite directions to conserve tape. There must be some space between each track to avoid cross-talk between tracks. Tape stock varies from ⅛″ to 2″.

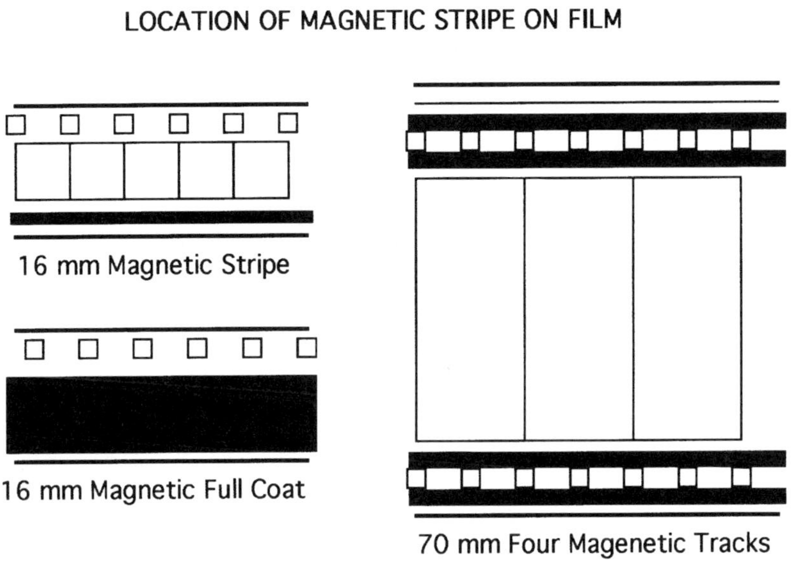

Figure 8.2 Magnetic film tracks are laid down on the edge of the film if a picture also is recorded on the same stock. If the film is to be used for sound only, the track can be laid down in one or more paths down the middle of film as magnetic full coat film.

Analog Audio Recorders

The enclosures in which tape is packaged and the type of machines on which the recordings are made provide another means of differentiating recording formats. Analog tape can be obtained in the form of cartridges and cassettes, as well as in open reels. Cartridges consist of continuous loops of $1\frac{1}{2}$-mil, $\frac{1}{4}$-inch audiotape, ranging from a few feet to several hundred feet in length and from a few seconds to several minutes in duration. Cassettes are pairs of small reels encased in a plastic housing. Thirty to sixty minute cassette tapes are usually $\frac{1}{2}$-mil thick, while longer playing ones are only $\frac{1}{4}$-mil thick and are decidedly inferior in terms of their potential recording quality. The standard width of cassette tape is $\frac{1}{8}$-inch, and the normal cassette tape recorder speed is relatively slow: $1\frac{7}{8}$ inches per second. As a result, the potential quality of a cassette recording cannot equal that of many other formats although improvements in motor design, tape oxides, noise reduction circuits, and head designs now allow four-track music recordings to be made on $\frac{1}{8}$-inch cassettes. Open reel tape has the advantage that it can be edited (see Chapter 11), runs at higher speeds, and is available in a variety of tape sizes. Cartridges are quicker and easier to set up and recue, that is, to find the specified starting point. Cassettes are inexpensive, but are difficult to cue and are only available in smaller tape sizes and slower recording speeds (Figure 8.3).

Audiotape Speeds

The speed at which an audiotape is driven directly affects the amount of tape that is used and, more importantly, the quality of the tape recording. In general, faster re-

Figure 8.3 The common analog audio tape decks are: on the a $\frac{1}{4}''$ reel-to-reel, on top on the right, a broadcast cartridge, and under the cart, a standard $\frac{1}{8}''$ cassette deck.

cording speeds produce better quality recordings. Some analog tape recorders have a speed control setting that can be adjusted to two or more of the following standard tape speeds: $\frac{15}{16}$, $1\frac{7}{8}$, $3\frac{3}{4}$, $7\frac{1}{2}$, 15, and 30 inches per second (ips). Professional recordings of live music, if recorded on analog equipment, are usually made at tape speeds of 15 ips or above. Most multitrack sound analog recording is done at a speed of 30 ips. Simple voice recordings are frequently made at $7\frac{1}{2}$ ips or even $3\frac{3}{4}$ ips for reasons of economy, but only rarely is a tape-to-head speed of $3\frac{3}{4}$ ips or $1\frac{7}{8}$ ips used in professional recording situations, except perhaps with a high quality cassette recorder. LP (long play) analog audiocassette machines have a tape speed of $\frac{15}{16}$ ips (Figure 8.4).

Digital Audio

A digital audio recorder samples or evaluates the electrical sound wave thousands of times every second and gives an exact numerical value to the electrical sound signal for each specific instant of time. The numerical values are coded into a series of on and off electrical pulses, known as *binary code.* These are the same types of signals used by computer systems. These electrical pulses are not an electrical copy or analog of the sound wave. The only signal that is recorded is electricity that is either entirely on or entirely off, rather than different gradations of electrical current, as is the case in analog recording.

The values of the recorded digital signal are determined by two factors: sampling and quantization. The analog signal is analyzed by periodically sampling its frequency. The more often the signal is sampled, the higher the quality of the digi-

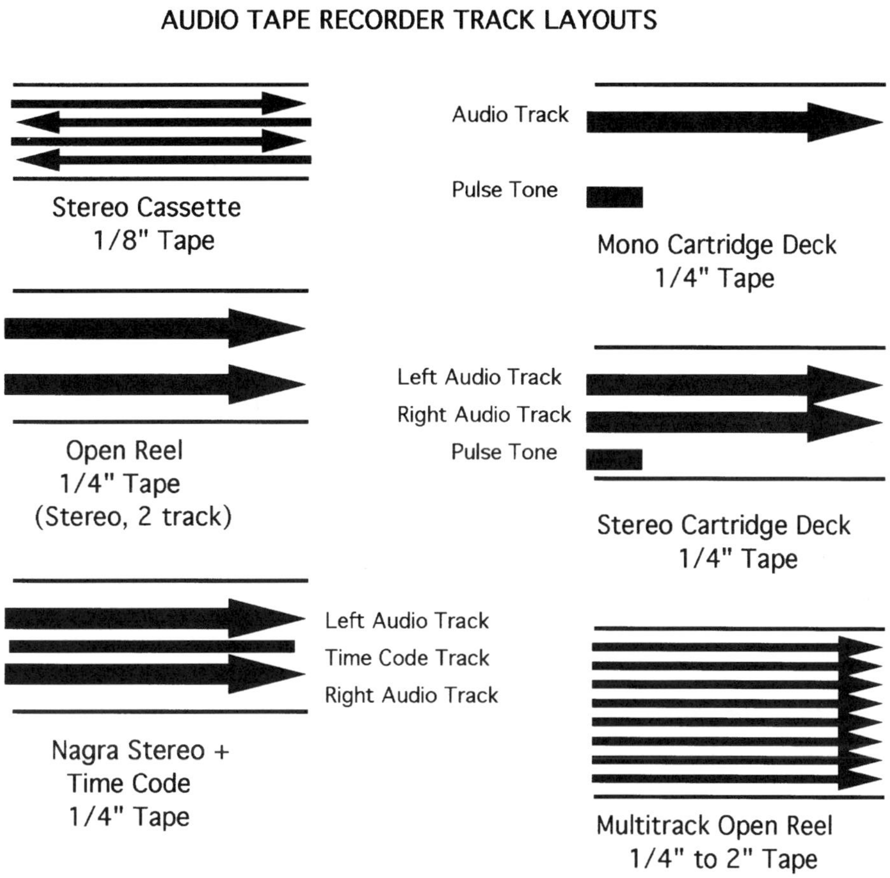

Figure 8.4 The arrangement of audio tracks vary with the type of tape deck and the number of audio tracks, sync, pulse, or time code tracks that need to be recorded.

tal signal. The rate must be at least twice the highest frequency to be reproduced. Today the standard sampling rates are 32 kHz, 44.1 kHz, and 48 kHz. In order to determine dynamic or loudness range, assigned binary bits determine how many different discrete audio levels can be recorded. Standards vary from a low of 8 bits to a high of 32 bits. In both sampling and quantization, the higher the rates, the better quality, but at the same time the cost and amount of memory required increase (Figure 8.5).

Digital recording extends the recordable range of intensities and frequencies, and virtually eliminates many other problems inherent in analog recording, such as tape noise, crosstalk (two recorded tracks on the same tape interfering with each other), and print through (one layer of recorded tape bleeding through and interfering with another). Flutter (an unwanted fluctuation in pitch) is another common analog recording problem. Digital recordings can be duplicated without degradation of the signal and can produce a much more permanent record than analog recording. Fine gradations of analog signals can completely fade away and be lost forever, while a magnetic signal that is completely on or off can easily be re-

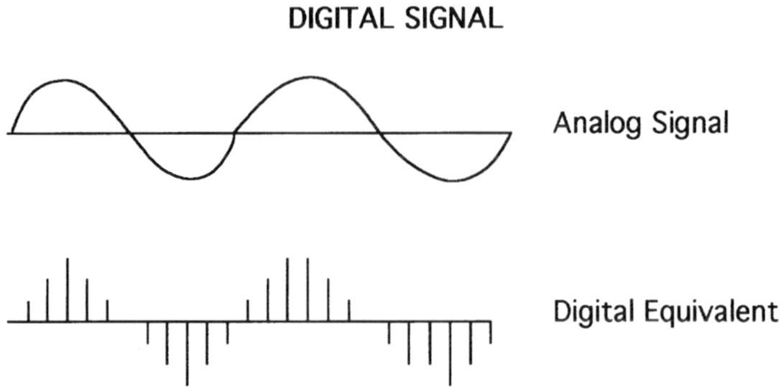

Figure 8.5 An analog signal is a continuous signal equivalent to the frequency and level of the comparable audio signal. On the other hand, a digital signal is a series of pulses that "sample" the original sound at frequent intervals and then convert those samples to on-off digital signals that can be converted back to the original sound.

stored to its original state as the on's begin to fade. For these reasons, digital recording is gradually replacing analog recording as the professional audio standard.

Digital Recorders

Today there are three types of digital audio recording media: Digital Audio Tape (DAT), Digital Compact Cassette (DCC), and tapeless systems. DAT recorders operate in two different methods: stationary head (S-DAT) and revolving head (R-DAT) (Figures 8.6A, B, C).

The design and operation of the stationary head DAT recorders are much like analog decks in that a tape is drawn across a head or series of heads, depending upon number of tracks to be recorded at a set speed. A ¼-inch S-DAT recorder can record up to 8 tracks plus sync tracks, and a 1-inch deck can handle up to 32 tracks. The R-DAT machines borrow from helical videotape technology by mounting the record heads in a revolving drum and wrapping the tape part way around the drum. The heads in the drum rotate in the opposite direction of the tape movement and, as in VCR technology, this movement increases the tape-to-head relative speed, increasing the quality of the recording. There are several different noncompatible S-DAT standards, but most R-DAT recorders are compatible, and because they can be manufactured in relatively small packages, make ideal field recorders for video, film, and concert recording.

The format DCC was designed by Philips of Europe to take advantage of the already popular analog cassette. The DCC uses a cassette the same size as the analog cassette and will play back both analog and digital cassettes, but records only in the digital mode through compressing the audio. The DCC is intended as a consumer recorder, and its success may depend on the quantity of prerecorded tapes of popular music available for that format (see Figure 8.7). DAT was designed as a professional recording medium, and the two forms have found their niches in the recording industry.

Tapeless audio recording is still in the experimental stages, but with the rapid increase in computer memory and lowering of costs, the technology will develop

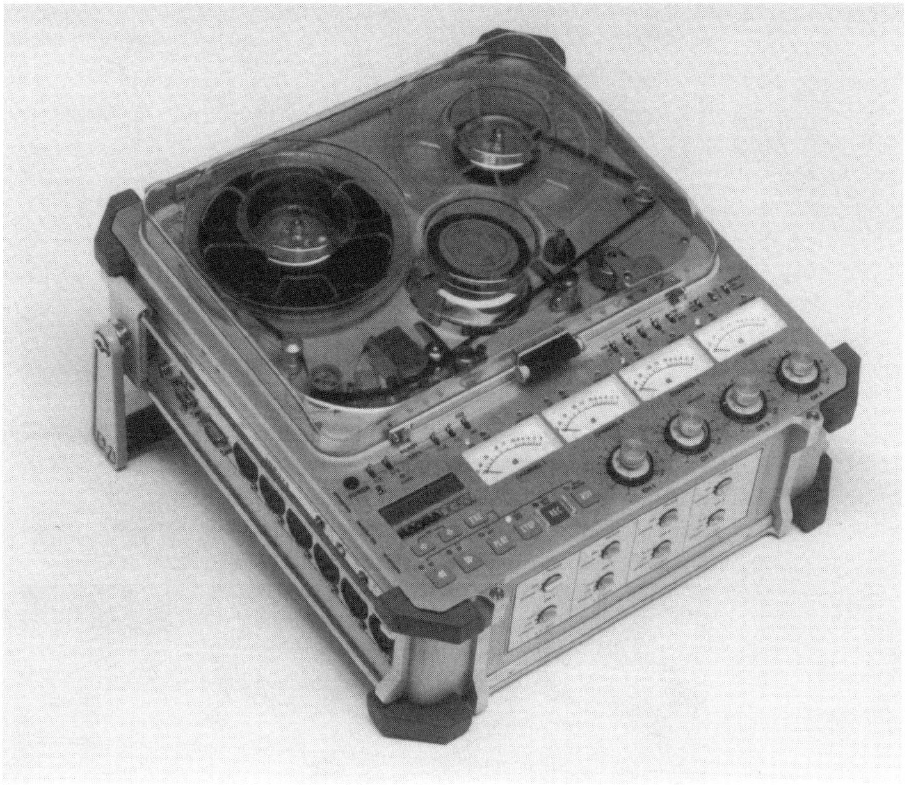

Figure 8.6A Digital tape decks operate in either R-DAT, S-DAT, or DCC format. Digital decks, like analog can record several tracks simultaneously in any of the formats. (Courtesy of Nagra.)

and find a place in the industry. Audio is simply fed into a computer and the digitized signal is recorded on one of three recording media: one or more computer hard drives or floppy drives, solid state random access memory (RAM), or some form of optical disc. The most common form of the latter is write-once-read-many (WORM) drive, which has a high memory capacity, or a recordable compact disc (CD-R).

It is possible today to fed a signal directly from a microphone into a computer, add any number of tracks, manipulate the signals in any manner desired, and output the finished signal to a digital format for distribution or playback without ever leaving the digital domain. Once the audio has been digitized, it may be edited as if the audio was a series of symbols in a word processor. The audio can be cut, rearranged, equalized, and mixed in any combination, depending on the complexity of the computer program. Once entered into the computer, the editing process is much more efficient than any other form of audio editing, but all of the audio must be entered into the computer in real time, which may be time consuming if there is much original material.

How soon digital audio processes will totally replace analog processes is uncertain, but just as magnetic recording replaced electronic disc recording, and electronic disc recording replaced acoustical recording, the day will come when the majority of audio recording and processing will be through a digital means.

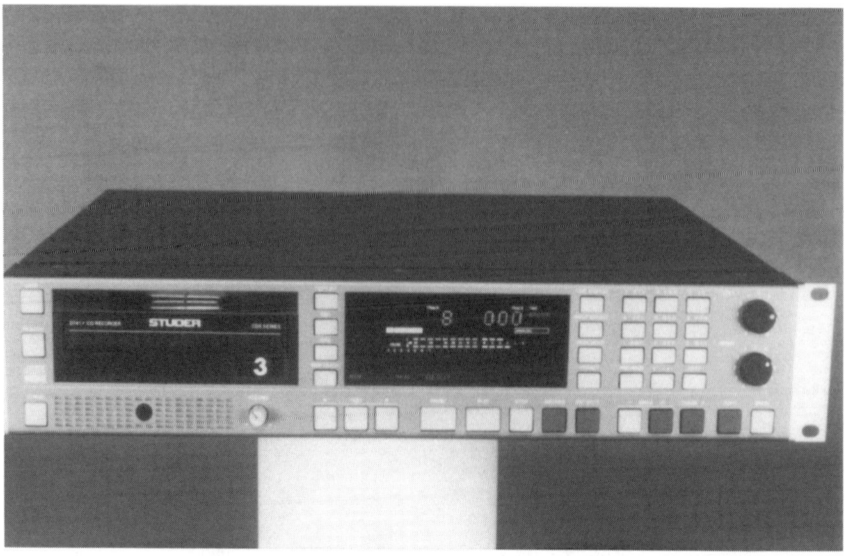

Figures 8.6B and C Audio may be recorded without using tape by recording directly onto computer floppy discs, hard disc, or into RAM to be converted to another format. Audio also may be recorded directly or as a final format on CD discs. (Courtesy of Studer.)

Analog Video

Composite Video Signal

Video cameras transform and transmit visual images by converting light energy into electrical energy. The composite video signal of a visual image can be transmitted along an electrical conduit or wire in a closed-circuit system to a video monitor or a video recorder. The composite (or complete) video signal must be made up of three major components in order to be accurately recorded. The three components are the video signal, synchronization pulses (sync), and control track (CT) pulses.

Video Signal

The portion of the composite video signal that actually carries the voltages that are transformed into picture elements in a monitor and are recorded on a tape deck is called the *video signal.* That signal varies in voltage in direct proportion to the intensity of the light striking the camera tube or chip. In the analog system, it is a constantly changing signal, varying from a fraction of a volt to a maximum of one volt (assuming proper levels are being maintained). In a composite color system, the video is more complex because there are three separate color signals combined out of phase, but the basic concept of an analog signal is the same.

Synchronization Signal

In order for a video recorder or monitor to use the electronic signal transmitted from a camera, it must have some reference for the scan and the field rates of the picture. A synchronizing or sync signal, which functions like electronic sprocket holes, is fed either to the camera or generated internally in the camera during recording. The sync signal is necessary for stable reproduction of the original signal. There are actually two sync signals: horizontal sync and vertical sync. The horizontal sync signal controls horizontal scanning and blanking, while the vertical sync signal controls the rate of the vertical scanning and blanking. These sync signals are passed along within the composite video signal so that all recipients of the whole signal will reproduce the picture at the same rate and direction as the camera originating the signal.

Control Track Pulse

A video recorder records a pulse signal, called a *control track (CT) signal,* that guides the playback video heads into position to accurately follow or track the signal laid down by the record head at the time of recording. A servo capstan, that is, a rotating tape drive cylinder with an accurate motor, varies the speed of the playback so that proper synchronization is maintained and moves the videotape through the recorder at the correct speed, and is aligned properly by the CT (Figure 8.7).

Monochrome and Color Video

Thus far our description of the video process has only described the transmission of black-and-white images. A black-and-white system transmits only the brightness values of light, not hue or saturation. There are several different camera pickup sys-

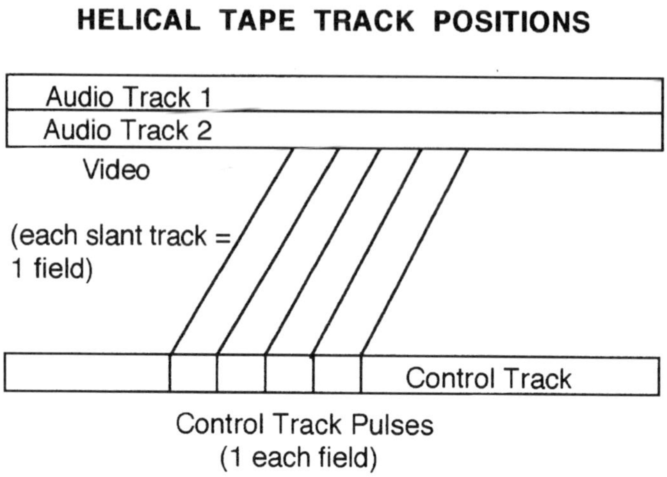

Figure 8.7 Helical videotape tracks follow a general pattern of several linear audio tracks, a linear control track, a linear time code track, and video recorded at a steep angle in slashes across the tape by a video head rotating at a high speed in the opposite direction of tape travel. This method of recording video is necessary for the high head to tape speed necessary to record the high frequencies of video.

tems for creating color video images. Some use only one pickup tube or chip, while others use two or three. Light entering a video camera is divided into its red, green, and blue components by using color filters. The three-color information picked up by color tubes or chips is then encoded as two chrominance or color signals, which are called the *I and Q signals,* and one luminance or brightness signal, which is called *Y signal.*

This chrominance and luminance information is then transmitted to the tape deck, where it is recorded. Light, as explained in Chapter 6, can be analyzed and manipulated on the basis of its three characteristics: hue, saturation, and brightness. Different wavelengths of light are perceived as different colors, or *color hues,* such as red, green, and blue. Color video and film systems are capable of recording and projecting a wide range of color hues. Like our eyes, these systems depend on three basic hues: red, green, and blue, called the *additive color system.* Light can be described in terms of its color saturation and brightness as well as its hue. The *saturation* of a specific hue indicates its color purity, that is, the amount of grayness the color contains. A vibrant but pure color of red, such as on a stop sign, is heavily saturated. In video, saturation is translated in to a chroma or chrominance signal. *Brightness* refers to a light's intensity, its lightness or darkness. Bright lights have strong intensities.

In video, brightness is reproduced in the luminance signal. Black-and-white video and film recording devices are only sensitive to the brightness or luminance of a light, not its hue or saturation. Two distinctly different colors may contrast with each other to the naked eye, but if they are equal in brightness, a black-and-white recording depicts them as virtually identical. When recording in black and white, hue and saturation can generally be ignored, since brightness values are paramount. Hue, saturation, and brightness play key roles in video and film color recording processes. The basic principles of colored light, covered in Chapter 6 provide the basis for the recording processes of both video and film. An NTSC video signal reproduces color by keeping the three signals (I, Q, and Y), separate either by combining them in one signal with each of the components out of phase with each other (the composite system) or by actually using three circuits to keep the signals separate (the component system).

Analog Video Recorders

There are two basic methods of recording a video signal. These distinguish the two general categories of videotape recorders: helical scan and quadruplex.

Quadruplex Recording

Quadruplex, or simply quad, videotape recorders no longer are manufactured or in general use but provided the first practical professional means of recording video, first in black and white and later in full color. The term *quad,* meaning four, describes the four vertically rotating heads on these machines. The four heads rotate diagonally across the tape while the tape is driven longitudinally across the heads. The passage of one head across the tape in a quad machine records several scan lines of actual television picture information. Since the quad machine divides up complete television fields among several tape scanning lines and does not record a single field for each transverse pass of a record head, the speed of playback could not be varied to produce fast/slow motion or freeze frames, or to provide an easy method of editing (Figure 8.8).

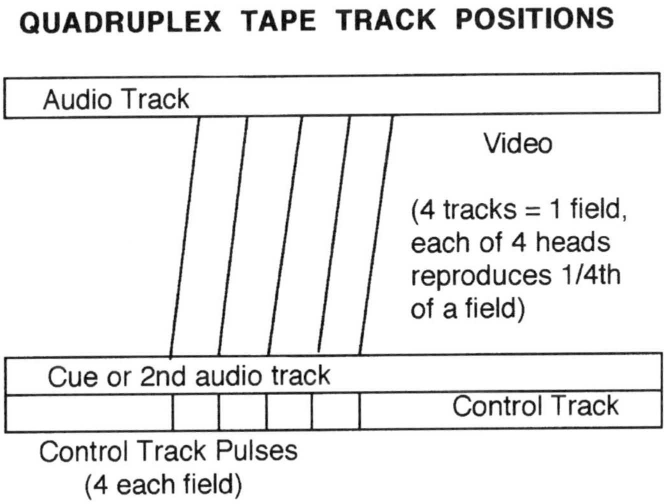

Figure 8.8 The original quadruplex videotape recorder used four heads that each recorded a portion of the video frame at near a vertical angle to tape movement. Audio and control signals were recorded on linear tracks on the edges of the tape stock. Although relatively high in quality, the tape was difficult to edit since it could not be paused for precise selection of an edit point.

Helical Scan Recording

All videotape recorders, either analog or digital, now use the helical scan method of recording. Helical scan recorders use two or more video heads, which continuously record electrical video signals. As magnetic tape travels from left to right across the recording heads, the heads rotate in a clockwise direction, opposite to the movement of the tape. On a two-head recorder, each time a single head passes over the tape it records a complete field of 262½ lines of video. At the exact instant that the first rotating head disengages from the tape, the second head engages it, so that a continuous recording of the television signal is made along the tape by consecutive heads. The passage from one head to the next corresponds to the vertical blanking period and is a crucial part of maintaining synchronization. The combined passage of the two heads records a complete frame of 525 lines (Figures 8.9 and 8.10).

The videotape is wrapped around a semicircular drum, and the heads maintain continuous contact with a semicircular wrap of tape around the drum, moving in a downward diagonal direction as they rotate past the tape. Because the recording is made in a slanting movement of the head across the tape, a helical scan recorder is sometimes called a *slant-track recorder*. A ¾-inch tape runs through a helical machine at about 3¾ inches per second, and the heads rotate counterclockwise at slightly less than 200 inches per second, producing a combined tape-to-head speed of about 700 inches per second (3¾ × 200 = 700 ips). While the speed of initial recording cannot be varied, a helical scan recorder can be slowed down or speeded up in playback to create slow or fast motion action. During slow motion, scan lines are repeated, while during fast motion, some are skipped. The image can also be

Figure 8.9 The video head of a helical recorder contains from two to eight different recording or erasing heads depending on the complexity of the format.

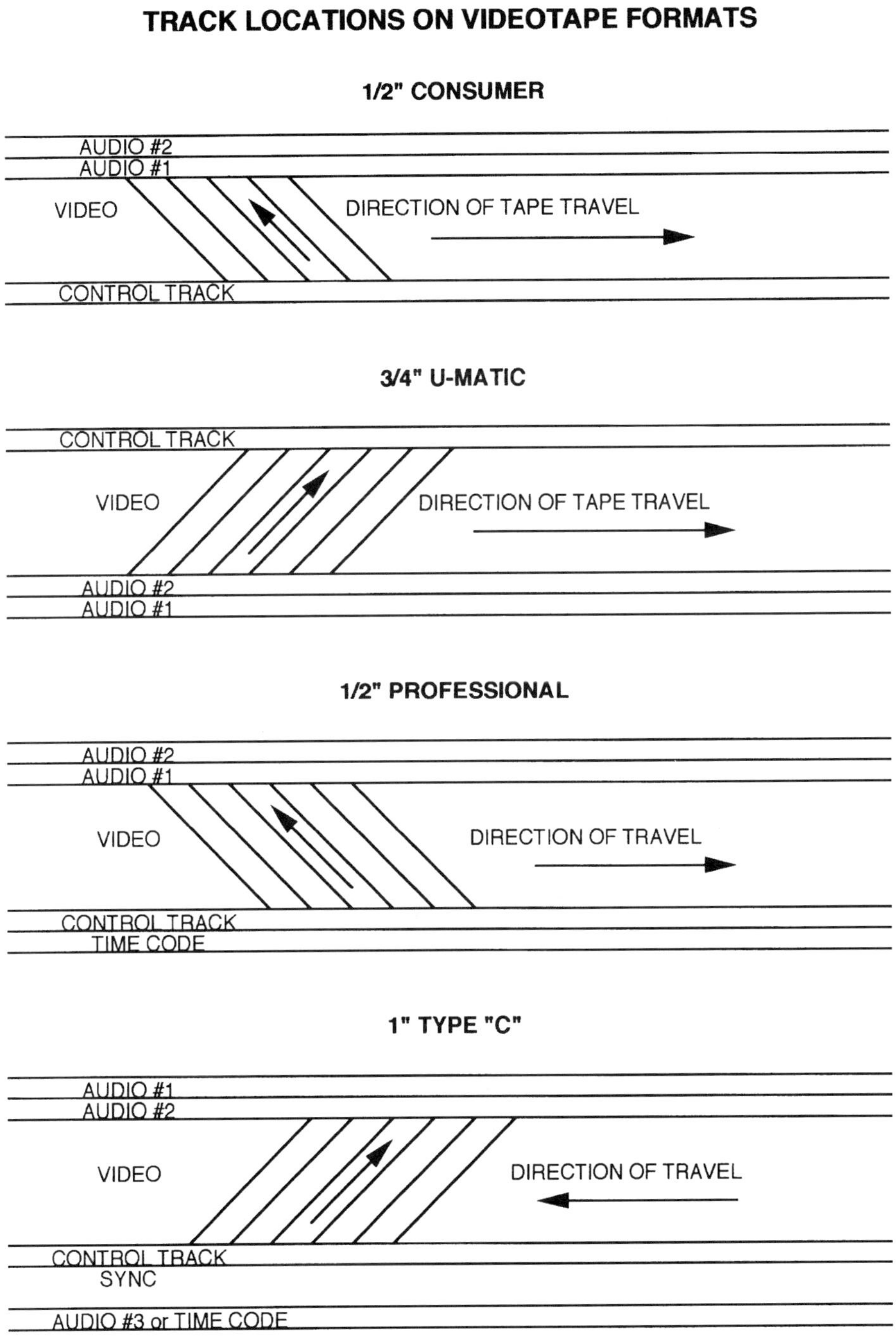

Figure 8.10 Each of the helical videotape formats records their signals in different paths, at different angles, and at different speeds. Each format historically was developed to provide a higher quality at lower cost. As time passes, the newer digital formats will replace the present analog formats.

stopped and the action frozen by repeating one recording line or complete field of the video image, called a *freeze frame*, which is often designated as the pause mode during playback. High quality 1-inch helical scan recorders and digital recorders allow for special effects creation without sacrificing image quality.

Analog Videotape Formats

Videotape contains iron oxide or other metallic particles that store electrical information in magnetic form. These microscopic particles are attached to a flexible support base, such as cellulose acetate or polyester (mylar). Videotape recorders (VTR) or video cassette recorders (VCR) are capable of both recording and playing back video information on reels or cassettes of videotape. The signals may be either analog or digitized video or audio signals (Figure 8.11).

The actual recording of video and audio signals is done by video and audio record heads, which also function as playback heads. The *audio and video heads* are usually separated from one another because the recording of a video signal requires a complex movement of the head with respect to the videotape, while an audio head remains stationary. Hi-fi recording in ½-inch S-VHS and digital recording in Hi8 videocassette recordings and some professional formats are important exceptions. They both record audio signals using rotating audio heads parallel to the video heads or record the audio imbedded within the video signal. An *erase head* erases previous information stored on the videotape prior to recording new images.

The format, or width, of videotape ranges from 8mm to 2 inches. Quad recorders used 2-inch-wide videotape. Helical scan recorders use one of the follow-

Figure 8.11 Audio and video tape stock is manufactured in a great variety of widths, thicknesses, and magnetic coatings depending upon the purpose for which the tape is intended. (Courtesy of BASF.)

ing formats: 8mm (⅓-inch), 12.5mm (½-inch), 19mm (¾-inch), or 25mm (1-inch) wide videotape. Small-format helical scan recorders use 8mm or ½-inch videotape, while 1-inch videotape is used in state-of-the-art or highest quality large-format helical scan analog recorders. Digital recorders use tape from 8mm to 19mm. A variety of different helical scan systems have been developed for recording on ½-inch video cassettes: VHS, S-VHS, M-II, DCT, Betacam SP, Digital Betacam, D-3, and D-5. These systems all use ½-inch videotape in closed cassettes and helical or slant tracking techniques, but the actual scanning of the videotape is sufficiently different so that they are noncompatible systems. As an example, an M-II recording, which uses a slightly larger videocassette and a different loading mechanism, cannot be played on a Betacam SP machine and vice versa.

The digital systems are all high quality recording systems, but they are also incompatible with each other (except for D-3 and D-5; and Beta, Betacam SP, and Digital BetaSX) or with any other ½-inch system. Some consumer ½-inch videocassette recorders are capable of running at a variety of speeds, so that anywhere from one to six hours of recording can be made on the same videocassette. The ¾-inch analog system is called *U-matic* and is slowly being replaced by other newer higher quality recording systems. Some videocassette recorders are capable of recording and playing back several different types of television signals, such as NTSC, PAL, and SECAM, using different types of electrical current (Figure 8.12).

The 1-inch and digital tapes used for professional recordings allow sufficient space for a control track, up to four sound tracks, a time code track, and one video

Figure 8.12 A video server designed to record and playback digital video/audio cuts on a nonlinear basis. Emulates videotape recorders, cart machines, and video storage systems. (Courtesy of Philips Broadcast Television Systems Company.)

track. One inch, once the professional broadcast standard, has been replaced by digital and ½-inch formats. Smaller consumer format videotapes can be broadcast when they have been channeled through an image stabilizer, known as a *digital time base corrector* or *TBC*, which accurately synchronizes the scanning process by changing a conventional analog signal into a more easily controlled digital one and provides high quality video sync signals (see Chapter 10). Minor variations in synchronization that cause a picture to jitter are eliminated using a TBC, which makes it possible for smaller format recordings, such as ENG news or documentary recordings on ¾-inch, Hi8, or even S-VHS, to be broadcast directly or dubbed up to better quality videotape formats.

Videotape Sound Synchronization

Synchronization between sounds and images is very simple to maintain in videotape recording. A single videotape recording machine may be used to record picture and sound elements simultaneously on the same tape. In most videotape recording, on-set or synchronous sounds are recorded on the track located away from the edge of the tape. There is a slight distance separating the points at which the sounds and the picture are recorded on the videotape, due to the fact that on most types of videotape recorders the video record and playback heads rotate while sound heads remain stationary. During electronic editing, then, the corresponding sound and images must be picked up from slightly different points on the tape. However, since videotape is always played back on a machine that has the same gap between images and sounds, this distance creates no real problem in terms of synchronizing sounds and images. Control track recording is an important reference for postproduction editing, although some machines provide another type of reference, called SMPTE time code, which is discussed in Chapter 11.

Digital Video

Digital video technology is the same as digital audio, except that much higher frequencies and a greater quantity of recorded material must be handled. The original analog video signal is sampled and quantitized, requiring up to 200 Mbytes per second of recorded program, as compared with less than 100 kBytes per second for digital audio. Higher tape speeds and/or compression of the signal before recording allow sufficient video to be recorded without consuming an impractical amount of tape stock (Figure 8.13).

Signal Compression

The compression process removes redundant or repeated portions of the picture, such as the blue sky or white clouds. As long as there is no change in the hue, saturation, or luminance value, the digital program will "remember" the removed portions and decompresses and restores them on playback of the tape. This process saves space on the tape, disc, or chip, depending on the recording method. Compression allows a reasonable amount of programming material to be recorded, but the price is a degradation of picture quality (Figure 8.14).

DIGITAL VIDEOTAPE FORMATS

DESIGNATOR	DATE INTRODUCED	WIDTH	TAPE SPEED	COMPONENT/ COMPOSITE	TRACKS/SECTORS
D-1	1986	19mm 3/4"	286.588mps 12.74 ips	Component	V,CT,TC,Cue, 4 audio
D-2	1988	19mm 3/4"	131.7 mps 5.85 ips	Composite	V,CT,TC,Cue, 4 audio
D-3	1990	12.7mm 1/2"	83.2 mps 3.7 ips	Composite	V,CT,TC,Cue, 4 audio
DCT	1992	19mm 3/4"	131.7 mps 5.85 ips	Component	V,CT,TC,Cue, 4 audio
Digital Beta	1993	12.7mm 1/2"	96.6 mps 4.29 ips	Component	V,CT,TC, Cue, 4 audio
D-5	1993	12.7mm 1/2"	167.2 mps 7.43 ips	Component or Composite	V,CT,TC,Cue, 4 audio
DVC	1994	6.35mm 1/4"	33 mps 1.33 ips 18.3 mps .753 ips	Component	V, 2 audio No CT or TC or Cue
D-6	1996	19mm 3/4"	497.4mps 19.9 ips	Composite	V,CT,TC,Cue, 10-12 audio

Figure 8.13 As of the printing of this text the formats listed above are in use. Each year new formats are developed and perfected, in some cases replacing earlier formats. Compatibility between formats ended with Analog U-matic and Type "C1."

The greater the compression, the greater the loss of quality. There are two basic systems now in use: JPEG, developed by the Joint Photographic Experts Group and originally intended for compression of still images, and MPEG, developed by the Motion Picture Experts Group and intended for compression of moving images. Each system offers advantages and disadvantages, and the possibility exists that new and better systems will be developed.

Component versus Composite Recording Systems

When a standard NTSC video signal is recorded, that is, the entire video signal made up of the three (red, green, and blue) color signals, blanking and sync signals

VIDEO COMPRESSION STANDARDS

LABEL	FUNCTION	ORIGINATING ORGANIZATION
H.261 or P64	Compressed video over telephone wires	Int'l Tele/Tele Consultative Comm.
JPEG	Compressed still images	Joint Photo Experts Group & ISO
Motion-JPEG	Edit moving video	Joint Photo Experts Group & ISO
MPEG-1	Compressed moving images, VHS quality	Moving Pictures Experts Group & ISO
MPEG-2	Compressed moving images, B-cast quality	Moving Pictures Experts Group &ISO
MPEG-2+	Edit moving video, Broadcast quality	Moving Pictures Experts Group & ISO
MPEG-3	Undeveloped	
MPEG-4	Video telephony	Moving Pictures Experts Group & ISO

Figure 8.14 In order to record and manipulate high frequency video signals within a digital format, some method of compressing the signals needed to be developed to avoid requiring tremendous amounts of computer memory. Two basic systems and variations on those systems have been developed, JPEG and MPEG. Researchers constantly work at developing newer systems that require less memory yet maintain the highest quality possible.

are combined into one signal called the *composite system*. This system allows the video and audio to be recorded, transmitted, and processed as a single signal. All analog NTSC, D-2, and analog formats (except S-VHS) are composite signals. Such a system has built-in negative factors that cannot be removed and become obvious in multigeneration editing and recording.

A system that delivers a higher quality signal has been developed, called the *component system*. In this system the video signal is kept in its original three parts: the luminance signal and two chrominance signals. This maintains the highest quality possible in a 525 line system. The negative factor is that a component system requires three of everything: wiring, special switching equipment, and more complex recording technology. Most digital recorders, except for D-2 and D-3, are component recorders. Despite the incompatibility between all of the digital recording formats, the number and layout of tracks is similar. They each record four digital audio tracks, a control track, a time code track, a cue track, and, of course, a video track.

Digital Videotape Formats

D-1 was the first industry accepted digital format. The Society of Motion Picture and Television Engineers (SMPTE), the organization that sets standards in the visual fields, agreed upon the D-1 standards in 1986. It has become the universal component digital standard. The signal is recorded on a 19mm oxide tape, offering the highest quality and most flexible recording system, but also the most expensive. It is capable of recording compressed HDTV signals but does not compress standard signals. It is especially useful for multilayering of graphics and animation.

D-2 was the second SMPTE standardized digital system, but it is a composite system. It also records on 19mm tape but requires special metal tape. D-2 is less expensive than D-1, can be modified to record in the component mode, and is very commonly used by broadcasters. Neither D-1 nor D-2 are practical for use in a camcorder due to the physical size of the tape transport system.

D-3 and D-5 are compatible systems, despite D-3 being designed as a composite system and D-5 as a component system. Neither system compresses the video, both use 12.5mm (½-inch) metal tape. D-3 has a four-hour capacity on one reel, D-5 two hours. D-5 is designed to record HDTV signals when the standards for that format are agreed upon.

Two systems created by competing videotape companies have not received standardization from SMPTE as of this writing. Both are being manufactured and finding their individual markets. DCT is an Ampex format recording a compressed component signal on 19mm metal tape. The longest tape has a three-hour capacity and is popular for recording long format programming such as feature films. Sony developed Digital Betacam, BetacamSX, to record on the same 12.5mm metal tape stock as the Betacam SP recorder. It also is downward compatible with Betacam tapes. Digital Betacam also is a compressed component system compatible with the D-2 signal, but not the D-2 tape.

Tapeless Video Recording

Video and audio signals may be recorded in digital form without using magnetic tape. Digital pulses may be recorded on Random Access Memory (RAM) chips within a computer. RAM chips are capable of recording as much as 16 Mbytes per chip. With compression, over an hour of video material can be recorded on one chip. The advantages of impressing production information on computer chips are instant access, no moving parts, no maintenance, no need to shuttle through other information and there are no physical aberrations, such as dropouts, tracking, or skewing, in digital pulses. There are no problems of compatibility, only possible differences in compression standards between computer programs. Expensive digital tape decks can be replaced by relatively inexpensive personal computers.

Many of the same advantages exist if the digital pulses are recorded on computer hard drives or floppy discs. Hard drives now are designed to hold multiple gigabytes (1000 Mbytes) and can be disengaged from the computer, stored, and moved to another computer. The removable feature provides an advantage if more than one project is assigned to the same computer and for archiving the material. Write-Once-Read-Many (WORM) optical discs also offer the same advantages, except once recorded they are not erasable. Erasable and reusable optical discs called

Direct-Read-After-Write (DRAW) exist, but both optical disc systems are expensive and are still in development stages.

Individual single frames of video are recorded on an Electronic Still Store (ESS) digital recorder designed to provide instant access to any one of over a thousand images entered into its files. Such a machine easily replaces individual 35mm slides and background graphics.

Film Recording

Basic Photochemistry

Photography uses light energy to transform the chemical properties of light-sensitive substances. Photographic film consists of light-sensitive materials, such as silver halide crystals or grains, attached to a flexible support base, such as cellulose acetate. Silver halide forms an invisible latent image when it is exposed to light in a camera. Light stimulates a chemical change in silver halide crystals, which can only be made visible and permanent by developing the image in certain chemical solutions. The film image appears dark or opaque where it was struck by light and clear where the light energy was not strong enough to stimulate the silver halide crystals. The resulting image is called a *negative image*. It inverts the whites and the blacks of the original scene. A white wall appears black and a black curtain appears white (Figure 8.15).

In order to get a positive image, which reproduces the whites and blacks of the original scene, the negative film must be printed or copied onto another piece of film on a device called a *contact printer*. When the copy is chemically developed in the same manner as the negative film from which it was printed, it reproduces the correct whites and blacks. The bright areas in the original scene are now white and the black areas are black. This method, in which a negative is copied to produce a positive image, is called the *negative/positive process*.

An alternative approach to this two-stage, negative/positive process is known as the *reversal process*. The difference between negative/positive and reversal film is similar to the difference between snapshots and slides in still photography. Reversal recording is a single-stage process that produces a positive image after one development of the originally exposed film. The negative image resulting from initial exposure is converted to a positive image during several stages of development (Figure 8.16).

Reversal film produces a positive image immediately. It does not have to be printed to view the original scene, as does negative film. The size and composition of the silver halide crystals in large part determine the overall light sensitivity and graininess of the film stock.

Light sensitivity or film speed is rated in EI, which stands for exposure index. The American Standards Association rating, called ASA (or EI), or a German standard, called DIN, is often printed on the film package. These indices of a film's overall sensitivity to light provide a relative indication of how much light will be required to properly expose a specific film. Slower films, with lower numbers, require more light than those with higher numbers. The term *graininess* refers to the size and visibility of particles in the film. A grainy image is one in which these particles are readily visible, and a fine-grain image is one in which they are not. Faster film

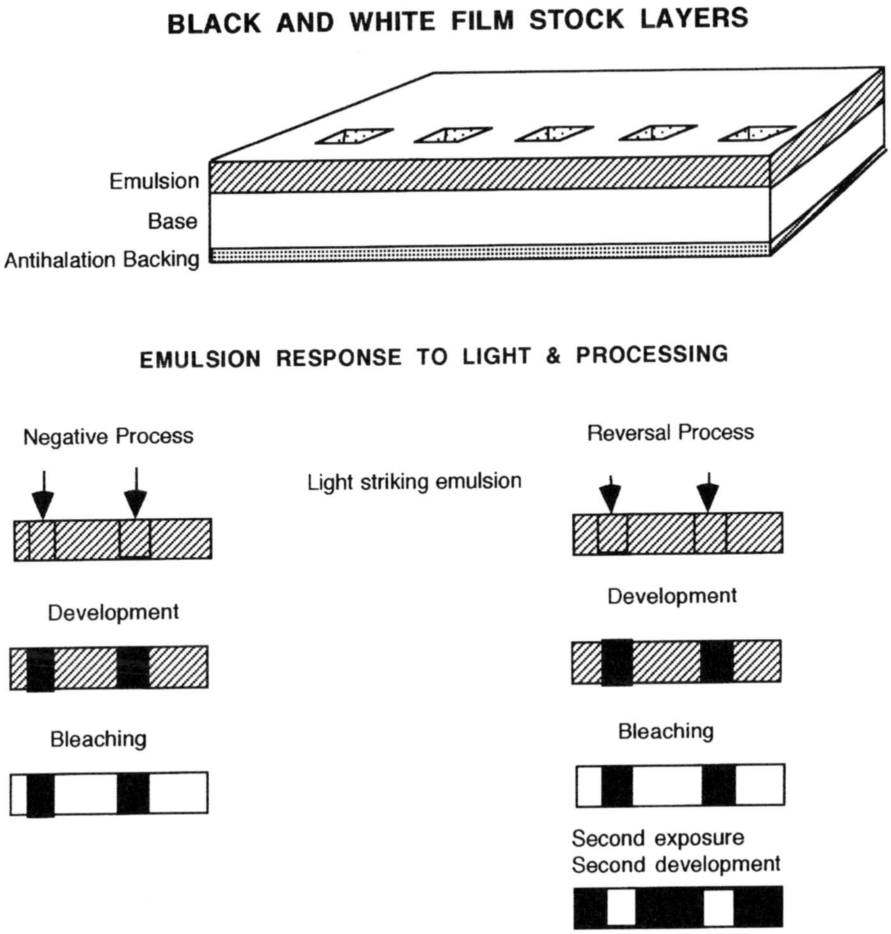

Figure 8.15 Black and white film consists of a layer of light sensitive material, a flexible base, and an antihalation backing layer to prevent light reflecting back through the base to the emulsion. Reversal film requires additional processing to create a positive image rather than a negative image.

stocks, which are more sensitive to light and therefore have higher EI numbers, generally have more visible grain structures than slower films, producing grainier images.

The size of the grain in the image can affect its resolution and sharpness, which refer to image clarity. Slower film tends to have higher resolution and sharpness than faster film. The size of the film grain also will determine the film's latitude, or the ability to reproduce a wide range of reflected light. Better films are able to reproduce an image in lighting with a 100:1 contrast range, while a standard video camera pickup tube has an effective contrast ratio of 30:1 and a video camera chip has a ratio of 50:1. If there is a wide range of dark to light reflecting objects in a scene, a video camera will not record as wide a range of grey scale as film. Many neutral tones will be recorded as completely black or completely white, rather than

Figure 8.16 The label on a film canister provides all of the information the camera operator or director of cinematography needs to adjust the camera and make exposure decisions. The I.E. numbers indicate the film speeds for daylight or tungsten lighting, the other numbers indicate the type of film (the top can is 7278, a high speed black and white reversal film sock), batch numbers, inventory, and order numbers.

some shade between them. In film a full range of tones may be recorded. The effect of contrast ratio on lighting and scene design is discussed more fully in Chapter 6, and the difference between lighting for film and video is important (Figure 8.17).

Color Film

We have so far considered only the recording of different brightness of light on black-and-white film. Color film responds to different hues and saturations of light, as well as different levels of brightness. A color-film emulsion consists of a multilayered suspension of light-sensitive particles and color dyes attached to a flexible support base, such as cellulose acetate. When light enters a camera, it strikes three different layers of color dyes and light-sensitive particles. These layers are sensitive to blue, green, and red light, respectively. Light first strikes the blue-sensitive layer, where only the blue light affects the particles and dyes. The other colors of light then pass through this layer and a yellow filter, which removes excess blue light, before striking the green- and red-sensitive layers. These layers are sensitive to blue light, as well as their own wavelength bands. The blue-sensitive layer thus records the blue component, the green-sensitive layer the green component, and the red-sensitive layer the red component of white light (Figure 8.18).

Like black-and-white film, color-film stocks come in negative or reversal processes, and a variety of light sensitivities and contrast ranges.

LUMINANCE CONTRAST RATIOS

The difference between the brightest subject and the darkest subject for which detail can be seen is the contrast ratio. Different media are able to reproduce detail under different maximum contrast ratios.

Television camera tube	**20:1**
Television camera CCD	**30:1 - 50:1**
Average film	**250:1**
Human eye	**1000:1**

Different lighting situations provide a variety of contrast ratios.

Foggy day	**10:1**
Average daylight	**130:1**
Bright day	**800:1**
White object next to black velvet lit by bright direct sun	**2000:1**

Figure 8.17 The contrast ratio of a medium determines how wide a variation in light reflectance values that medium can reproduce without losing either the brightest or the darkest values. Any attempt to reproduce a subject or frame containing a higher contrast range than the medium is capable of reproducing will result in either muddy dark areas or flared out white areas.

Film Exposure

Film is exposed inside a lightproof mechanism called a *camera*.

A basic film camera consists of a *lens*, which focuses an image on the film; a *viewfinder*, which allows the camera operator to see the image that is being recorded; a *film feed and takeup mechanism*, which supplies film to the exposure area and rolls it up after it has been exposed; a *motor*, which drives the film through the camera; a *rotating opaque shutter*, which rapidly opens and closes to expose each frame of film; an *aperture*, which determines the dimensions of the frame that is exposed; a *pressure plate*, which holds the film flat against the aperture to ensure good focus; a *pulldown claw*, which intermittently grabs film sprocket holes or perforations to advance the film for each single frame or still photograph at the aperture; a *speed control*, which determines how many individual frames will be exposed each second; and a *run/stop button*, which turns the camera on and off.

Motion-picture film is perforated at regular intervals so that it can be driven intermittently by a camera and a projector. This intermittent movement allows a single frame of film to be held stationary while a rotating shutter opens up and allows light passing through the lens to expose the film. A projector uses the same mechanism to project recorded images through the lens onto a screen. The feed and

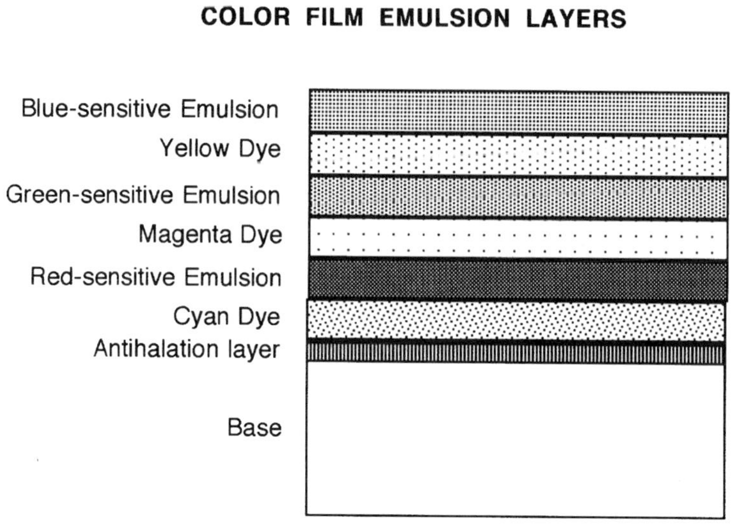

Figure 8.18 Color emulsion film layers alternate between specific color sensitive layers with opposite color dye layers. This produces a negative reproduction of the image exposed to the camera. Color reversal film, like black and white reversal film requires additional layers and processing.

takeup mechanisms push the film continually through the camera, while the claw pulls the film at the aperture. Film is constantly pushed and pulled through a 16mm camera at a rate of thirty-six feet per minute or ninety feet per minute in 35mm. Normal sound speed exposes 24 frames per second (fps) in 35mm, 16mm, and Super-8mm.

The camera shutter and claw must be synchronized so that the shutter stays open when the claw disengages the film and retracts behind the aperture plate. At this point the film is stationary in the aperture. Sometimes it is held stationary by a device known as a *registration pin,* which holds the film in firm registration, that is, it holds it very steady when it is not being pulled by the claw. The shutter must be closed when the registration pin retracts and the claw engages the film to advance it, or the film images will blur as they pass the light in the aperture.

The speed control allows the camera operator to alter the frame per second speed of the camera. Film recorded at speeds above 24 fps will reproduce images in slow motion when it is projected or played back at normal sound speed (24 fps). Camera images recorded at fewer than 24 fps will produce fast motion. Thus slow and fast motion are produced during actual recording in film, unlike video recording, which always occurs at 30 fps. Increasing the film recording speed also changes the synchronized shutter speed and affects the amount of light exposing the film. Faster recording speeds produce more rapid shutter speeds and less light reaches each frame during exposure, since the duration of each exposure is reduced. To compensate for these changes in exposure, the lens must be adjusted so that more light passes through it and strikes the film when the camera speed is increased.

Motion Picture Formats

Motion picture film, which is exposed to light inside a camera, is available in a variety of formats or film widths, including 8mm, 16mm, 35mm, and 65mm. These distinctions between various formats refer to the width of the film in millimeters. The width of the film affects image size and quality, as well as the cost of supplies and equipment. There used to be two 8mm formats: standard 8mm and Super-8mm. Super-8mm cameras record images that are 50 percent larger than those of standard 8mm cameras. Standard 8mm is now virtually obsolete. All subsequent references in this book are to Super-8mm, which is sometimes used for home movies, as well as for some independently produced, low-budget films.

The 16mm format has been widely used for professional recording of industrial, educational, governmental, and documentary films, as well as some commercials and low-budget feature films, but now videotape productions are competing for the same markets. Network-level commercials and television programs are recorded in 35mm, as are most feature films. Some feature films are recorded on 65mm film, which is then printed onto 70mm film, with the added 5mm being the width of the sound track area, for projection in large, specially outfitted theaters. Other 70mm film prints for projection are enlargements or blowups from original 35mm recordings (Figure 8.19).

Film stocks are available in different film lengths and loading arrangements or configurations. Super-8mm film usually comes in a lightproof cartridge and is exactly 8mm wide. It is normally packaged in fifty-foot lengths, which lasts for 2 minutes and 46 seconds. Sixteen millimeter film is available on daylight spools, which contain 100, 200, or 360 feet of film. It is also available on plastic cores, which simply provide a firm center on which the film is wound and do not protect the edges of the film from light. Film that comes on a core must be loaded in complete darkness. The standard length of 16mm film cores is 400 or 1200 feet. One hundred feet of 16mm film, when exposed at 24 fps, runs for 2 minutes and 46 seconds. Thirty-five millimeter film comes on cores in standard lengths of 100, 200, 400, and 1100 feet. Ninety feet of 35mm film runs for 1 minute at 24 fps.

Film stocks differ in terms of their perforation or sprocket hole sizes and placements. Super-8mm film has sprocket holes on only one side of the film, while 16mm films are available with single-sided or double-sided perforations, which are called *single perf* and *double perf* film, respectively. Magnetically striped 16mm film

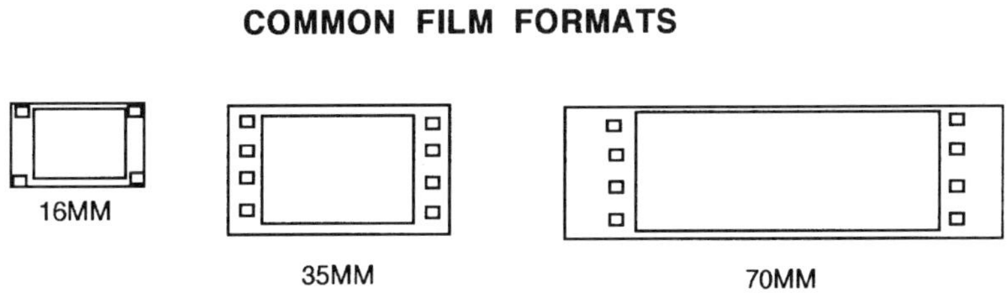

Figure 8.19 Virtually all professional film now is exposed on one of the three formats: 16mm, 35mm, or 70mm. Super-8 film is still available for consumer use, and special larger feature film formats also are in use along with I-MAX film for specific purposes.

has audio track in place of one row of sprocket holes. Thirty-five millimeter film is always double perf.

Film Sound Synchronization

Synchronous sounds match their visual sound sources and are usually recorded at the same time as the corresponding visual images. Many different systems have been developed to synchronize recorded visual images with recorded sounds. Early portable ¼-inch reel-to-reel tape recorders had the capacity to record a sync signal that allowed them to be used in conjunction with a motion picture camera. Today separate digital recorders are used since they run to absolute speed and do not have to be connected to the either the video or film camera to maintain sync as long as the film camera receives a sync signal from a crystal control or the video camera is locked to its sync signal. This allows the separate recording of sounds that are synchronous with their corresponding pictures.

Single-System Film Recording

There are basically two different systems of synchronous sound film recording in common use today: single system and double system. Single-system recording, as shown in Figure 8.20, puts sounds and images on the same piece of film; usually, the sound is recorded on the edge of original motion picture film (Figure 8.20).

This technique is called *sound-on-film* (SOF). As a general rule, 35mm film is not used for sound-on-film or single-system original recording. Sixteen millimeter magnetic sound-on-film is recorded 28 frames ahead of the picture gate or film aperture. (Sixteen millimeter optical sound-on-film is 26 frames ahead of the picture. Optical sound is created by exposing the edge of the film to light.) Super-8mm sound-on-film is recorded 18 frames ahead of its corresponding pictures. These standard spacings allow the film driven through a camera to change from an intermittent movement at the film aperture, where a rapid series of still frames are re-

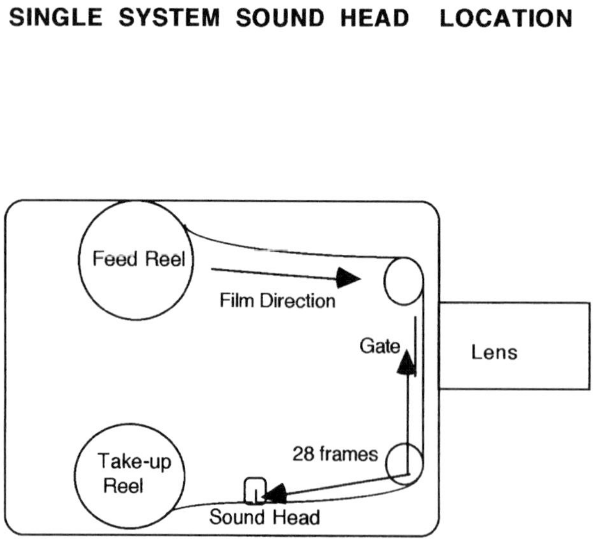

Figure 8.20
On those cameras that record sound simultaneously with exposing the film are called single system cameras. Of necessity the sound recording head must be located apart from the aperture since physically the two could not be located at the same place within the body of the camera. The sound head on 16mm single system is located 28 frames ahead of the aperture. This separation must be taken into consideration when shooting to edit original film without transferring the sound to another medium.

corded, to a continuous movement over the sound recording head. The same 28, 26, or 18 frame advance of sound ahead of the picture is standard in most 16mm or Super-8mm film sound projectors. Single-system sound is commonly used for exhibition purposes. The final film prints marry an optical or magnetic sound track with their corresponding pictures on the same piece of film.

Single-system recording is extensively used in small formats, such as Super-8mm film recording. Editing problems arise from the fact that the sounds are always a specific number of frames ahead of the corresponding pictures. Sound-on-film yields an initial sound recording that is decidedly inferior in audio quality to a double-system film sound recording. If SOF is to be edited, either it must be shot with pauses in the voice track, so that edits can be made without losing portions of the sound, or the sound track must be dubbed to a separate piece of film for double-system editing.

Double-System Film Recording

In double-system synchronous sound recording, the sounds and images are recorded on separate materials. (This approach is normally used for production and editing but not for final projection.) Rather than recording sounds directly on the edge of the film during production, an independent tape recorder is used, which can record and play back sound in exact synchronization with the corresponding images. There are two basic systems for synchronizing the recording of the separate sounds and pictures: cable sync and crystal sync (Figure 8.21).

Figure 8.21 The camera and sound recorder stay in synchronization because they are both running with internal crystal sync or they are connected by a synchronizing cable.

Cable sync refers to the use of an electrical cable, which connects the camera to the tape recorder like an umbilical cord. The cable carries a 60 cycle per second sync signal, called *Pilotone,* which is generated by the camera. The Pilotone is recorded on the audiotape by a special sync head on the audiotape recorder. *Crystal sync* allows the camera and the tape recorder to be physically separated. This can be a distinct advantage because it increases the flexibility, mobility, and independence of sound and picture recording machines and operators, who are otherwise linked by an umbilical cable. For crystal sync, the speed of the camera is controlled by a crystal oscillator so that the film is driven at a precise speed of 24 fps. The analog audiotape recorder uses a separate crystal oscillator to place a sync signal on the audiotape, so that its original recording speed can be duplicated during playback and a digital recorder runs true to speed.

Slating

Creating a common point where separately recorded elements of sound and picture match is called *slating.* In video recording this generally is not necessary since the audio is recorded directly onto the same tape as the picture but does provide a means of accurately logging scenes as they are shot. Normally a slate, sometimes called a *clapstick* or *clapboard,* is used for this purpose in motion picture production. The clapboard consists of a piece of wood with a hinged arm that makes a clapping sound when it strikes the bottom portion of the clapboard. This device produces a loud recorded sound that can be matched to the corresponding visual image of the closing arm (Figure 8.22).

In the absence of a clapboard, a person can call out "Slate!" followed by a sharp handclap. If the separate sound and picture tracks are perfectly matched at the beginning of a shot, the editor can be reasonably sure that the entire cable or crystal sync recorded shot will maintain synchronization. Slating is also used to identify the project title, director, and shot and take numbers during single-camera film or videotape recording. This information is written on the chalkboard surface of the slate or clapstick, and read aloud at the beginning of each camera shot. Thus each take is fully identified on both film, videotape and audiotape.

Some film cameras are designed for documentary shooting in situations where the use of a clapboard is impractical. They have an electronic means of providing a reference synchronization point for editing, called an *automatic slate.* At the beginning of each camera take, the first few frames (usually the first eight) of picture are flashed or fogged with a small light inside the camera and a signal that is separate from the Pilotone is sent to the tape recorder either by cable, if cable sync is being used, or by radio transmitter, if crystal sync is being used. This signal triggers a clap alarm, which creates an audible tone, known as the *bloop.* The proper flash frame of picture can then be matched to the bloop at the beginning of the shot for editing synchronization.

Another development in slating is the electronic clapboard, which generates a tone fed to the camera and recorder and illuminating a continuously running SMPTE time code visible to the camera and recorded on the edge of the film or on the videotape.

Figure 8.22 After both the camera and recorder have reached speed, a production assistant holds the clapboard in front of the camera. The board contains information indicating shot and take numbers, director and camera operator's names, and other information critical to the shot. Once speed has been reached, the assistant snaps the clapper shut smartly, creating a sharp intensive sound and visual record that will be used to sync the film and sound track later during the editing process.

Summary

Understanding the technology that makes audio, video, and film recording possible helps us to obtain better quality images. Recording media are based on digital, optical, electronic, and photochemical recording processes. Film uses a subtractive mixing process, with cyan, magenta, and yellow filters embedded in different layers of the film to subtract different color wavelengths from a white light source to produce a variety of colors on a screen. A video camera records and transmits visual images electronically using an additive color process of mixing red, green, and blue light to produce color video.

Film contains silver halide crystals, which form a latent image when they are exposed to light. These latent images become visible through chemical processing. There are two basic film development processes, negative and reversal, which are analogous to color prints and slides in still photography. Film generally has a wider contrast ratio than video. Some film stocks, such as Eastman Color Negative, can record and differentiate brightness levels that are 100 times as bright as the darkest object in a scene, yielding a contrast ratio of 100:1. The maximum contrast ratio in video is usually 30:1 or 50:1.

Videotape and film recording materials are available in a variety of formats. Helical scan recorders use 1-inch, ¾-inch, or ½-inch (8mm) videotape. Super-8mm, 16mm, 35mm, and 65mm film require different cameras and recording equipment. Wider or large-format recording materials generally reproduce higher quality images than smaller formats. However, some smaller ½-inch formats, such as M-II and Betacam SP, reproduce extremely high quality images. A series of digital videotape recorders, from D-1 through D-5 and newer formats, provide even higher quality than the older analog videotape formats

The aesthetic use of recorded sounds demands an understanding of recording devices and their selection. Audiotape is available in a variety of formats in terms of tape sizes (widths and thicknesses) and tape enclosures, such as cassettes and cartridges. An analog audiotape recorder converts the electrical audio signal to magnetic pulses stored on magnetic recording material. Digital recordings consist of a series of on and off pulses, and are less susceptible to recording problems, such as crosstalk, print through, and fading, than are analog signals, which record the entire electrical signal. Tape speed directly affects the amount of tape consumed, and higher speeds generally produce higher quality recordings. In general, the larger the tape size and faster the speed, the better the quality of the recorded sound.

There are several ways to obtain sounds and images that synchronize with each other. In videotape recording, sounds and images are recorded on the same piece of videotape. A control track, which is a recording of the sync signal, allows the videotape to be played back at the same speed at which it was recorded and synchronizes the playback head with the recording on the videotape. Film sound and images can be recorded on the same piece of film, which is called single-system sound-on-film (SOF) recording, or they can be recorded on separate sound and picture mechanisms, which is called double-system film sound recording. Double-system recording allows for more editing flexibility than single system. Slating refers to the placement of a common starting point on the picture and sound recordings. It is also used to identify the project title, director, and shot and take numbers during single-camera recording.

Exercises

1. Find a CD recording and a vinyl disc recording of the same music. Transfer both to audiotape and compare the frequency response and dynamic range. Then compare the two to the original CD recording for the same characteristics.
2. Record the same scene on videotape and film. Then transfer the film to a videotape that has the same format as the originally recorded videotape. Compare the two videotape images in terms of image contrast, hardness and softness, and resolution.
3. Record and view several network television commercials. Try to determine which ones were originally recorded on videotape and which ones were recorded on film and then transferred to videotape. Do some commercials use the apparent contrast and hardness or softness of videotape and film to good effect? When might you prefer to use videotape or film for original recording?

Additional Readings

Alten, Stanley. *Audio in Media,* 4th ed. Belmont, CA: Wadsworth, 1994.

Amyes, Tim. *Audio Post-Production in Video and Film.* Boston: Focal Press, 1990.

Borwick, John. *Sound Recording Practice.* New York: Oxford University Press, 1976.

Frater, Charles. *Sound Recording for Motion Pictures.* New York: A.S. Barnes, 1979.

Happe, Bernard. *Basic Motion Picture Technology.* Boston: Focal Press, 1974.

Hartwig, Robert L. *Basic TV Technology,* 2nd ed. Boston: Focal Press, 1995.

Lipton, Lenny. *Independent Filmmaking.* New York: Fireside/Simon & Schuster, 1972.

Mathias, Harry, and Richard Patterson. *Electronic Cinematography.* Belmont, CA: Wadsworth, 1985.

Millerson, Gerald. *The Technique of Television Production,* 12th ed. Boston: Focal Press, 1990.

Nisbett, Alec. *The Sound Studio,* 6th ed. Boston: Focal Press, 1995.

Pincus, Edward, and Steven Ascher. *The Filmmaker's Handbook.* New York: Plume, 1984.

Rumsey, Francis. *Tapeless Sound Recording.* Boston: Focal Press, 1990.

Watkinson, John. *An Introduction to Digital Audio.* Boston: Focal Press, 1994.

Watkinson, John. *Digital Compression in Video and Audio.* Boston: Focal Press, 1995.

Watkinson, John. *The Digital Videotape Recorder.* Boston: Focal Press, 1994.

Weis, Elizabeth, and John Belton. *Film Sound: Theory and Practice.* New York: Columbia University Press, 1985.

Wilson, Anton. Cinema Workshop. Hollywood, CA: American Society of Cinematographers Holding Corporation, 1983.

Wurtzel, Alan, and John Rosenbaum. *Television Production,* 4th ed. New York: McGraw-Hill, 1995.

Yale French Studies. Special issue on Sound in Film. 1980.

Zettl, Herbert. *Television Production Handbook,* 5th ed. Belmont, CA: Wadsworth, 1991.

9

Design and Graphics

Introduction

Almost every object that human beings create is the product of a conscious design that organizes spatial forms. Graphic design involves the creation and coordination of many different production elements, including sets, properties, costumes, titles, and performer makeup. Graphic designers rely on basic design principles, such as design elements, color, and composition. These basic design elements fulfill the requirements of a design, whether the designer uses a pen, pencil, paint brush, or a computer graphics paint box. Computer graphics programs have been written specifically for newscasts, election returns, costume and scene design, and animated sequences. Designers put these principles into practice when they approach specific production problems from the following aesthetic perspectives: realism, modernism, or postmodernism. This chapter examines aesthetic approaches to graphic design, principles, and applications. The chapter concludes with a consideration of the overall integration of graphic design with other production components, such as lighting, performance, and visual and sound recording.

Aesthetic Approaches

Realist Design

A realist design simulates an existing setting, location, or graphic format. While a realistic set, for example, can be filled with objects and furnishings that one would expect to find in such a place, emphasis is placed on the illusion of reality, not necessarily the depiction of reality itself. Maintaining basic principles of spatial perspective and proportional size are extremely important in realist design, since they help to sustain an illusion of reality. Sets are often constructed out of lightweight materials that give the impression of being real and are much easier to construct and move around than actual objects. Realist designs are rarely defined by their supposed fidelity to nature or reality alone. Almost every realist design that has emotional impact has some degree of subjective stylization. A realistic setting, title, or illustration should convey a psychological impression that reinforces the central theme of a drama or the central message of an informational program. It can reflect warmth or coldness, tension or relaxation, simply by virtue of the colors, lines, and shapes it presents. It is even possible for a realistic setting to reveal a specific character's emotional state through the feelings that the design conveys.

Modernist Design

Modernist designs are much more abstract than realist designs. The subjective feelings they arouse and the subjective impressions they convey are rarely tied to actual experience or production efficiency alone. Modernist artists usually have much freer rein to explore specific design elements or subjective impressions for their own sake. A designer may decide to call attention to textures, shapes, lines, and colors themselves. Visual innovations often stem from such formative experiments, which can be incorporated into more conventional narrative, documentary, or instructional programs. Innovative television programs and films by many experimental artists have shown how a formative approach to scenic design can break down conventional illusions of reality by ignoring spatial perspective and using highly artificial, stylized sets, backdrops, and lighting.

Postmodernist Design

Postmodernist designs leave much of the visual perception to the imagination of the viewer. Graphics, color, and movement can be juxtaposed in a series of apparently unrelated images. Postmodernist designs often mix a variety of design styles drawn from different genres and historical periods. For example, the settings in the film *Who Framed Roger Rabbit* (1988) suggested 1940s Los Angeles in a semirealist way until the timeless, garish cartoon world of Toontown collided with the live action world. The production design in *Chinatown* (1974) limited the color blue to appearances of the main theme, water, in 1930s Los Angeles, while pastel colors and art nouveau designs were reminiscent of the 1930s in the contemporary (1980s) urban setting of the television series "Miami Vice." Postmodernist designs sometimes appeal to the emotions and often are difficult to analyze or categorize, just as postmodernist paintings and writings are difficult to place in traditional categories. A blend of classical and modern, traditional and contemporary, elite and popular patterns and combinations of colors and textures can serve as the basis for postmodernist designs.

Principles of Design

A designer works with three basic principles of design: design elements, color, and composition. The ways in which these elements are selected and combined determines the nature and success of the design. The selection of design elements must support the themes, plots, and characterizations of a drama or the central message of a nonfiction production. Their use conforms to one of the three aesthetic approaches discussed earlier as well as the basic design elements to be discussed next.

Design Elements

The artist's design elements are line, shape, texture, and movement.

Line

Line defines the form of a design. An independent line can be straight, curved, or spiral. Edges are lines formed by shapes or objects that overlap each other, such as a foreground door and background wall. Lines can be repeated to create parallel lines or concentric circles. They create a path or direction of movement for the eye. Converging parallel lines create an illusion of depth or spatial perspective, for example. Straight lines are more dynamic than curved lines and circles. They create a strong sense of directional movement. Smooth curves and circles communicate a smoother, softer feeling of more gradual movement. Sergei Eisenstein's famous "Odessa Steps" sequence in *Potemkin* (1925), for example, associates straight-line diagonals with the merciless, advancing Cossack soldiers, and curved lines or circles with defenseless women, children, and students, who are attacked on the steps.

Shape

Shapes are composed of combinations of lines. There are an infinite number of different shapes reflected by specific objects, but some common, recurring shapes with which all designers work are circles, squares, rectangles, triangles, ellipses, trapezoids, octagons, and hexagons. Shapes can carry symbolic meaning. They can be repeatedly used in conjunction with specific people or settings to evoke specific themes. In the film *Ivan the Terrible* (1942), Eisenstein used circular shapes surrounding Ivan to connect the circular shape of the sun to the symbolic meaning of Ivan as the "Russian sun king." Basic design elements often reinforce specific themes.

Texture

Texture provides a tactile impression of form. Texture can be real or represented. Real textures are revealed by directional light, which creates shadows and modeling on a nonsmooth surface. Represented textures, such as granite, marble, or wood grains, have smooth surfaces that create a tactile impression. The texture of a surface affects our perception of depth. A rough texture with heavy shadows provides a greater sensation of depth than a smooth, flat surface. A heavily textured material used in drapes or costumes can create a richness that relates to a theme of opulence, splendor, or decadence, for example. Texture, like shapes, can create a sense of space that affects our emotions and relates symbolically to the major themes of a story.

Movement

Movement can be real or imaginary. The movement of performers on a set is real movement, while the illusion of movement stimulated by a series of still drawings or stationary backgrounds is imaginary. In design, imaginary movement is just as important as real movement. The illusion of movement can be enhanced by the use of parallel diagonals in a design, for example. It can also be limited or reduced by the use of verticals and horizontals. Specific shapes and lines, such as spirals, concentric circles, and radial designs, can generate significant movement in a static frame. Transference can take place between real or imagined movement and otherwise stationary objects. A simple figure placed against a pulsating background will appear to dance or vibrate itself. A moving background can transfer the illusion of movement to a stationary figure placed in front of it. Movement throughout a stationary image is carefully controlled through changes in color, shape, space, and direction that guide the eye through a design.

Color

Three aspects of color are of primary importance to a designer: color harmony, color contrast, and the emotional or symbolic effect of color.

Color Harmony

Various relationships between color pigments on a two-dimensional color wheel in large part determine the degree to which specific colors will harmonize with each other. A two-dimensional color wheel is a series of different colored chips or samples arranged in a circle from cool (short wavelengths of light) colors, such as violet, blue, and green, to warm (long wavelengths of light) colors, such as yellow, red, and orange. Traditional color judgments indicate that colors distant from each other on the wheel harmonize better than close colors, which tend to clash with each other. Several harmonious colors for sets and costumes can be selected by lay-

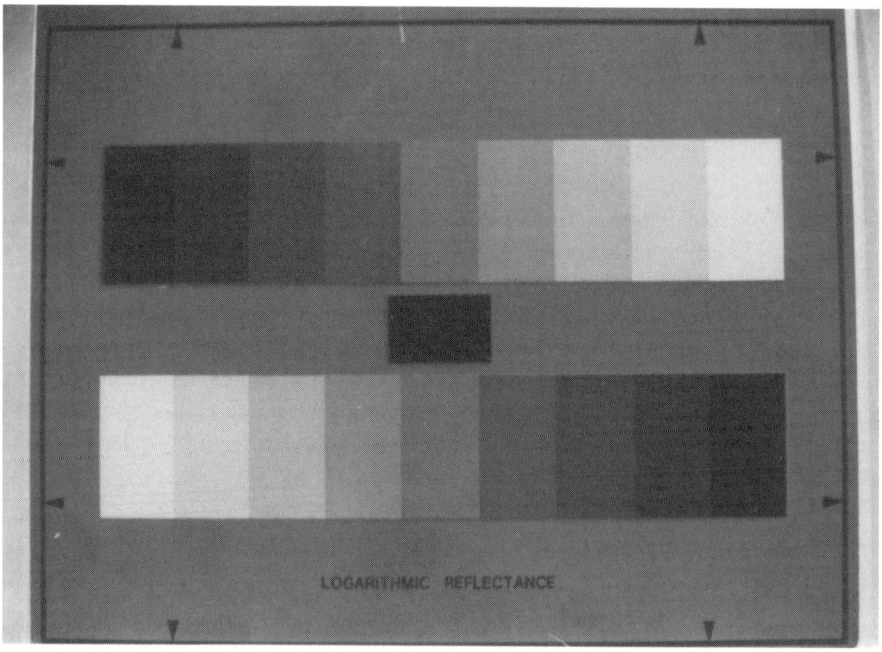

Figure 9.1 A gray scale chart contains 19 specifically designed chips ranging from TV white to TV black on two strips. The center chip is pure black. This chart provides a standard against which a technician may adjust a video camera for maximum quality under the lighting conditions present.

ing an equilateral triangle or square on top of a color wheel and using the colors at the points. As the triangle or square is rotated, the group of harmonious colors changes.

Color Contrast

Different colors help separate objects in a scene through their mutual contrast. If two objects or shapes did not contrast with one another, they would appear as one object or shape. Contrast can help us perceive spatial depth. If specific colors of foreground and background are different, we will perceive their separation and hence spatial depth. Adjacent colors tend to interact. If you place a gray object against different colored backgrounds, it will appear darker or lighter depending on the color and brightness of the background. A particular hue takes on a completely different feeling depending on the hues adjacent to it. Complementary colors of the same intensity should not be placed next to each other, unless the intense contrast is intentional.

Maintaining brightness and contrast between different lines, shapes, and masses is extremely important when designing graphic images for television and film. A television graphic designer cannot rely exclusively on color contrast, since a television program may be received in either color or black-and-white. Adjacent colors should have gray value brightness contrast of at least 30 percent, that is, each object or shape should be 30 percent brighter or darker than the one next to it. Brightness contrast between different shapes and objects can be determined by using a gray scale (see Figure 9.1). A gray scale consists of a sequential series of gray tones from white to mid-gray to black. Pure white has virtually 100 percent reflectance; video white, approximately 90 percent; while pure black has 0 percent and video black approximately 3 percent. The midpoint on the gray scale is about 18 percent reflectance, that is, about 18 percent of the light falling on this shade of gray is actually reflected back to the eye. In order to maintain adequate brightness contrast, dark letters and shapes should be placed on light backgrounds and vice versa.

Emotional Response to Color

Most designers believe that a general distinction can be made between warm colors and cool colors in terms of their emotional effect on an audience. Colors such as reds, oranges, and yellows create a sense of warmth in a scene. A romantic scene lit by firelight and surrounded by red, orange, and yellow objects on the set uses these warm colors to enhance a romantic mood. Caution should be used with reds and yellows in video recording, because video noise can occur in these colors on repeated generations of a videotape. Colors such as blue and green, on the other hand, are often considered to be cool colors. They are sometimes used to enhance a sense of loneliness or aloofness in a character, or a general mood that is related to a lack of human as well as physical warmth.

Cool colors tend to recede, while warm colors tend to advance. For example, pure hues of greenish yellow, yellow, yellowish orange, orange, and orangish red tend to advance and call attention to themselves, while pure hues of violet, red violet, blue, and blue-green tend to recede. Warm colors can convey a mood of passion or action, while cool colors tend to reinforce a sense of passivity and tranquillity. The colors of sets, costumes, and graphic images must be selected with an eye toward their visual prominence, whether they recede or advance, as well as the degree to which they contrast with other colors. Colors that are repeatedly associated with specific objects, people, and settings can take on symbolic or thematic meaning. The red dress of a character in a drama can be used to signify sensuous passion. This color might contrast with the cool green or blue colors associated with a competitor for the affections of a male character.

Cultural Response to Color

Color symbolism also varies with different cultures. For example, the color white (or lack of color) to Japanese signifies mourning, but for western culture white signifies purity and hope. The same color may have different connotations depending on its use. The color yellow may mean cowardice, sinfulness, or decay, yet it also can carry the meaning of spring, youthfulness, and happiness. Both blue and green also carry various meanings depending on their cultural background. The use of color must be carefully considered based on the expected or targeted audience and their cultural background and traditions.

Composition

A designer organizes basic design elements by using principles of balance and perspective within the limitations of the video or film frame. These principles can be applied to any visual design problem, including the arrangement and selection of sets, props, furniture, and costumes. They are concepts employed by designers in many other fields as well.

Balance

A design is balanced when there is an equal distribution of visual weight on each side of an imaginary center line bisecting the image. Balance or equilibrium enhances unity and order. There are at least four different types of balance: symmetrical, asymmetrical, radial, and occult. Symmetrical balance consists of a mirror image of one half of a design in the other half. Identical but reversed elements are arranged on either side of the axis line, which seems to cut the design in two. Asymmetrical balance does not have completely identical elements or mirror reflections on either side of the axis line, but the weight or size of the elements on both sides is nonetheless equivalent. Asymmetrical balance permits a higher degree of variation and viewer interest than symmetrical balance. In radial balance, two or more similar elements are placed like the spokes of a wheel about a central point. This creates a strong sense of motion or movement around this point, while preserving balance. Occult balance is a sense of equilibrium achieved through the placement of unlike elements. Balance is intuited without reliance on conventions or rules. There is usually a strong sense of movement and a dynamic quality to the design (Figure 9.2A).

Perspective

Perspective refers to the arrangement of various elements to draw attention to the most important aspect of the image, which is called the *focal center*. A common focal center is the performer, but more abstract aspects of a frame can also function as a focal center. Designers rely on a number of basic principles of perspective, such as

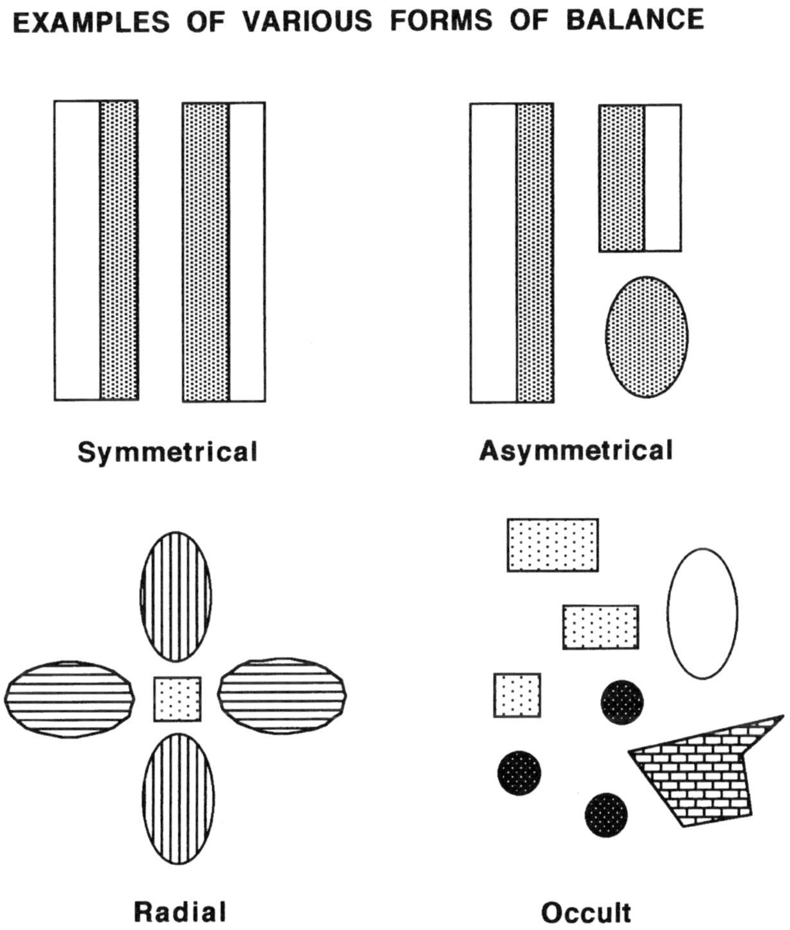

Figure 9.2A Graphic designs may be laid out in a variety of patterns. They may be symmetrical (exactly balanced on each side of the frame), asymmetrical (balanced visually on each side of the frame, but not exactly matched), radial (a pattern balanced around a central figure), or occult (without any obvious balance or symmetry).

proximity, similarity, figure/ground, equilibrium, closure, and correspondence. All of these principles are based on the common ways in which our eyes and minds attempt to organize visual images (Figure 9.2B).

Proximity

Objects placed in close proximity to each other form common groupings. Conventional wisdom has it that graphic information should be grouped into common topics within the frame for greater intelligibility. It is unwise to try to pack too much information into a single graphic image. A second graphic frame is usually required when another topic is introduced or there is a great deal of information to convey about a single topic (Figure 9.2C).

PERSPECTIVE

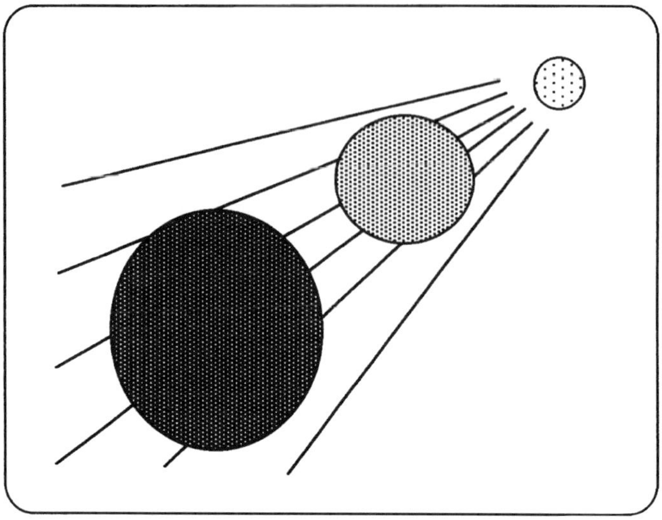

Figure 9.2B Forcing perspective in a graphic design develops a feeling of depth along the Z axis which does not actually exist in a two-dimensional medium. A design appears to have a three-dimensional look by making some objects larger with others appearing smaller, or by creating graphic lines that appear to converge toward the background.

PROXIMITY

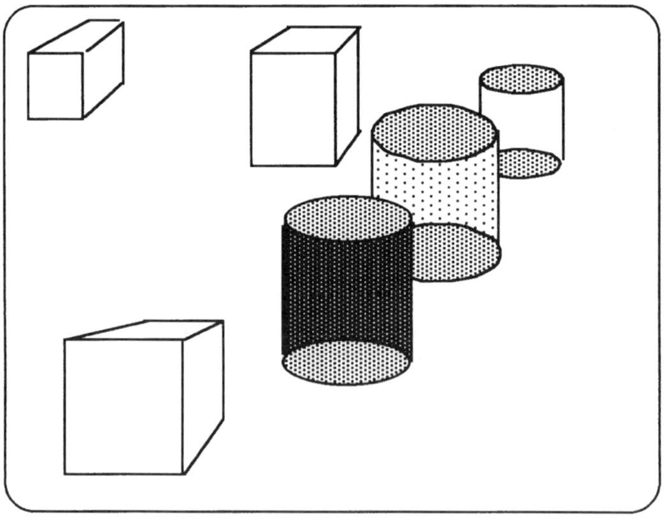

Figure 9.2C One way of graphically indicating a group of objects belong together is to group them close together in an obvious pattern. The cylinders appear to belong together, the boxes do not.

Similarity

The perception of similarity between shapes and objects in a frame provides another means by which graphic images can be organized. Objects with similar shapes, sizes, colors, and directions of movement are united into common groups. Any deviation from this similarity, such as a runner moving in the opposite direction from the pack or a red object in the midst of green objects, draws immediate attention on the basis of its lack of similarity (Figure 9.2D).

Figure/Ground

Figure/ground refers to the relationship between backgrounds and foregrounds. Our eyes try to organize visual images into background fields and foreground objects. Some visual illusions are ambiguous, and we can alternate the foreground and background to create different shapes and objects from the same picture. A corporate logo or graphic marks that consist of letters and words, such as Eaton Corporation or Playmakers Repertory Company, combines white and black letters that reverse figure and ground. The reversal in the Playmakers' logo suggests a rising curtain that is consistent with its theatrical subject matter. Symbols and signs that use figure/ground relationships can be effective means of gaining audience attention and communicating ideas (Figure 9.3A).

SIMILARITY

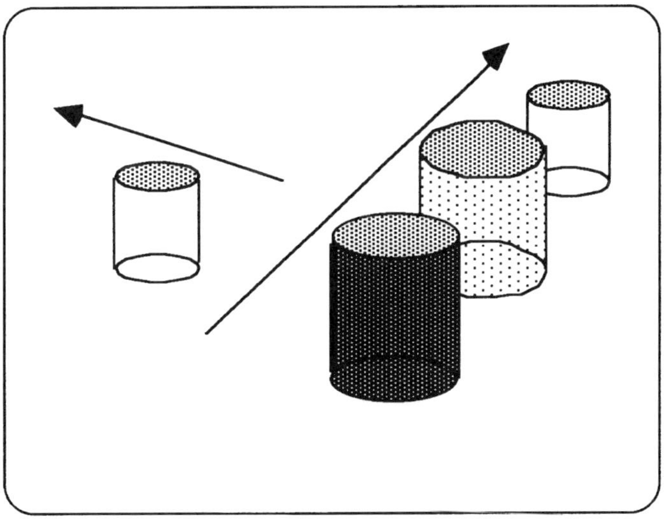

Figure 9.2D By grouping similar objects together in an obvious pattern, any other object, even if similar, but not in the pattern will appear to move away from, or at least not belong to the similar grouping.

Figure 9.3A A figure-ground illustration. The design conceals which part is the background and which is the foreground by alternating black and white within the type and the background. (Courtesy of the Repertory Company.)

Equilibrium

Another way in which our eyes try to organize graphic images is through a principle of equilibrium. An image in equilibrium is logically balanced and ordered. Equilibrium can be based on natural scientific laws, such as gravity or magnetic attraction, as well as a balancing of object weights and sizes on either side of a center line in a frame. This organizing principle reflects a well-ordered, logical universe. When images defy a sense of balance or accepted physical or scientific laws, they are in disequilibrium, which can arouse interest, but also cause distracting confusion (Figure 9.3B).

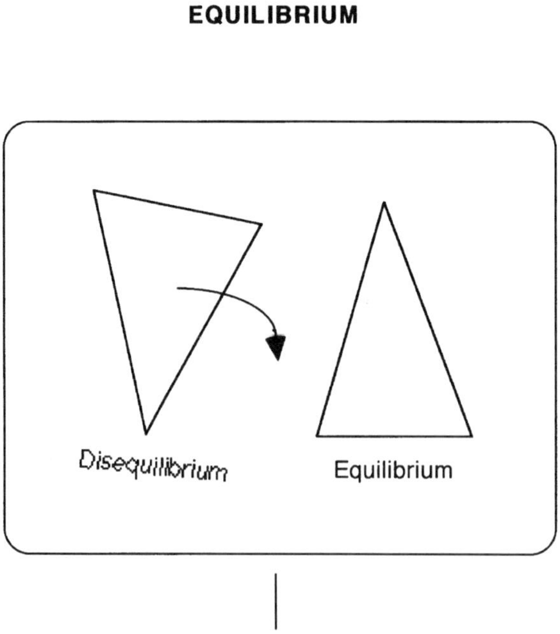

Figure 9.3B
A triangle or other object with a broad base indicates a graphic arrangement of equilibrium giving the arrangement a stable, firm graphic appearance. An arrangement with a smaller bottom or an object leaning without any visible support gives the audience a feeling of being off-balance or very unstable.

Closure

Viewers have a natural tendency to try to complete an unfinished form, a principle which is called *closure*. An open form is ambiguous and leaves some questions unanswered. A partially hidden form can still be identified because we expect good continuation of a form off-screen or behind another object, but this is a projection onto the image of our need for closure. A designer can frustrate or fulfill our desire for closure by completing graphic forms or leaving them partially incomplete. The former seem stable and resolved, while the latter seem unstable, although they sometimes stimulate creative and imaginative impressions (Figure 9.3C).

Correspondence

Correspondence is a principle by which viewers extend graphic images into analogous human experiences. The ability of a graphic image of food to stimulate hunger, a smoking gun to arouse fear, or an attractive figure to arouse desire is based on their correspondence with socially learned or acquired experiences. Viewers often organize and comprehend images by projecting them into a world of common human experience.

Emphasis

Brightness and contrast, size and placement, and directionality are devices that help create emphasis. Generally, a bright object attracts attention more readily than a dark object. Our eyes are drawn immediately to the brightest part of a design. However, if the image is almost completely white, emphasis can be achieved by using contrasting image darkness for an object. Objects in contrasting colors can create emphasis. Since warm colors advance and cool colors recede, emphasis can be created by using contrasting reds, oranges, or yellows for important objects.

CLOSURE

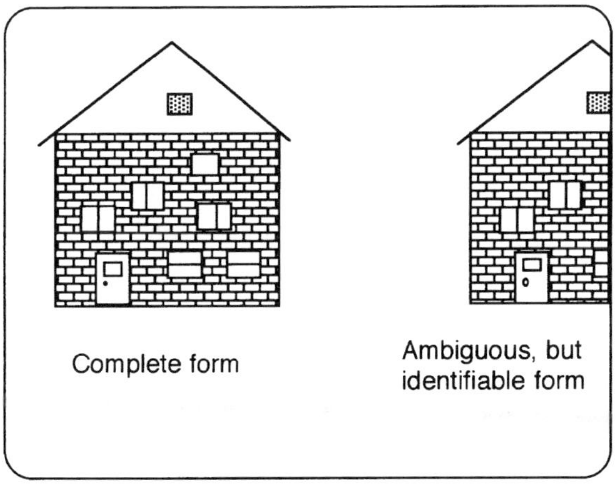

Figure 9.3C
The psychological condition of closure actually arises from an ambiguous or incomplete graphic that is designed to allow the viewer to fill in the rest of the picture through prior or common knowledge. A single house by itself will appear to be just that, a single house, but a row of houses may be depicted by only two houses, one on each side of the frame only partly visible. The viewer will fill in the rest of the houses and assume there are more houses out of sight on each side of the frame.

The size or dimension of an object and its placement within the frame can also create emphasis. In general large objects attract more attention than small objects. However, if most of the objects in an image are large, then a single small object is emphasized by virtue of its deviation from the norm. The placement of objects in a frame can also create emphasis. Closer objects are usually more prominent than distant objects. If several objects are grouped together, the one that is set apart acquires emphasis through variation and contrast. An isolated, individual object can be singled out from a group and thus be emphasized. If the single object outside the group is also different in size, brightness, or color from the members of the group, emphasis is reinforced. One of the most common forms of directional emphasis is created by the use of converging parallel lines that direct the eye to a specific object. These lines enhance the illusion of perspective and depth at the same time that they add emphasis. The lines can be formed by natural objects, such as a row of trees or a road leading to a house, for example. Many different lines and shapes can direct the eye to various parts of the image, focusing attention in the desired direction.

X-Y-Z Axis

The three dimensionality of reality is created in either a video or film frame with a two-dimensional reproduction. In order to give the impression that the picture represents the 3-D world, an understanding of how the three dimensions relate to the frame is necessary. The movement or composition along a line running from left to right or vice versa is considered the X axis. Any movement or composition running from the bottom to top, or vice versa, is considered the Y axis. The Z axis does not actually exist, but can be depicted or created through the use of compositional arrangements within the frame. If objects are arranged at an angle, instead of straight across the frame, or a series of objects diminish in size as they rise in the frame, a false Z axis is created. To avoid boring or static pictures, efforts should always be made to create a Z axis in each sequence.

Readability

The size and amount of detail in an image affects readability, which refers to the ease of deciphering and comprehending graphic images (Figure 9.4).

The size of a typeface or style of lettering, for example, is an important determinant of how easy it is to read a graphic image. Type of extremely small point size is usually avoided in video production because small titles are difficult to read on a film or television screen. *Point size* refers to the height of letters; the higher the point size, the larger the letter. (The text you are reading is in 10 point type.) Lettering sizes smaller than $\frac{1}{10}$ to $\frac{1}{20}$ of the full picture height should be avoided in television graphics.

Graphic artists also avoid finely drawn lettering and serifs, which are delicate decorative lines that are often difficult to reproduce. Because of the limited size, resolution, and sharpness of television images, boldface type is recommended for titles and subtitles. Plain backgrounds give prominence to foreground titles and lettering. A highly detailed or multitoned background is distracting. Good contrast between foreground and background tones and colors is essential for legibility. When titles are keyed over live-action images, bright lettering should be used, preferably with some kind of border, drop shadow, or edge outline, which gives greater legibility and three dimensionality (Figure 9.5).

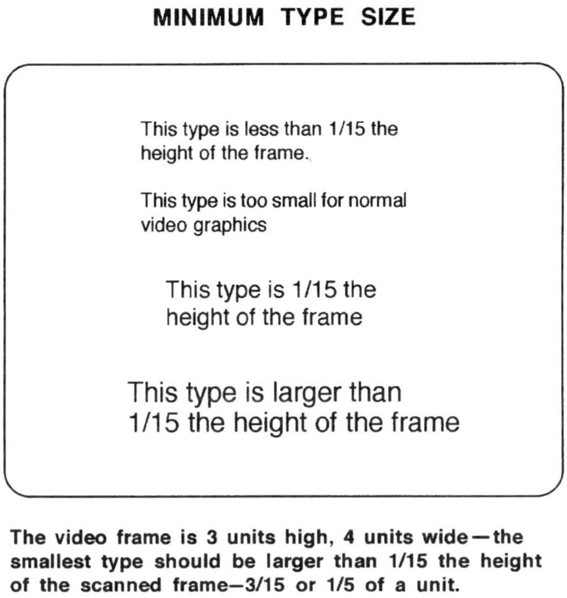

Figure 9.4
Partly due to the relatively low resolution of a home television receiver, and partly because some of the audience may be watching on a small screen receiver, graphic material in type form should not be smaller than 1/15th of the scanned height of the graphic.

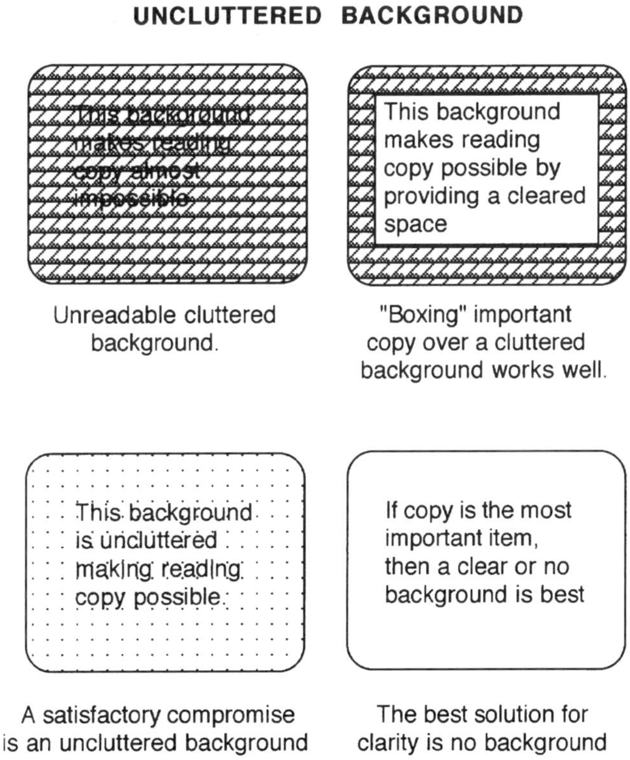

Figure 9.5
Any type or important graphic should not be framed in front of a busy background or a background with many small elements. If such a background must be used, the graphic can be framed within a plain box, by defocusing the background, or increasing the lighting contrast so that the important graphic will stand out and be clearly visible.

Image Area

An important determinant of composition in television and film graphics is the aspect ratio or frame dimensions of the recorded and displayed image. As noted earlier, frame dimensions vary in television and film. The aspect ratio, or proportion of height to width, of standard television images is 4:3 or 1.33:1, and depending on the final specifications of HDTV, the television aspect ratio may be 16:9 or 1.85:1, while projected film images vary somewhat in terms of their aspect ratios from 1.33:1 to 2:1 (Figure 9.6).

A standard 35mm still camera film frame has an aspect ratio of 5:3 or 1.66:1. Graphic images must be composed for specific formats and aspects ratios. If an illustration is produced in an aspect ratio other than 3:4, as shown in Figure 9.6, some of the information recorded on the sides of the frame will be cut off by the narrower aspect ratio of the video camera or additional background material will need to be added to fill the frame.

Scanning or Full-Aperture Area

The *scanning area* is the full field of view picked up by the video camera. The *full-aperture area* is the equivalent in film of this area. It refers to the entire field of view recorded on an individual frame of film (Figure 9.7).

Any graphic illustration or title card must be framed in the camera so that it is slightly larger than the actual scanning or full-aperture area so that the edges of the card do not appear in the frame. The scanning area should be about 1½ inches inside the outer edge of a 14 foot × 11 inch or 11 foot × 8 inch illustration or title card.

Essential Area

The essential area of the frame is the safe recording portion of the frame. Graphic information is placed within the essential area, so that it will not be cut off by somewhat overscanned TV receivers (home TVs usually reproduce less than the full camera frame because the horizontal scanning is expanded) or film projector apertures. The essential area of the video camera should allow at least a 10% border within the scanning area so that there is no possibility of eliminating essential information. If a graphic image falls within the essential area, an artist can be confident that all key information will be safely recorded and projected.

Graphic Applications

Graphic applications can be divided into at least three categories: sets and properties, costume and makeup design, and graphics and illustrations. Set design includes the creation of scenery, props, and backgrounds. Costume design focuses on the creation of costumes for performers, while makeup enhances or changes the facial features and physical appearances of performers. Graphics and illustrations focus on the arrangement of letters, symbols, and visuals within the frame. All three of these aspects of graphic design must be coordinated with one another to effect a consistent and unified approach to all elements that appear within the frame.

Graphic design has three basic functions in a dramatic production: to establish the time, place, and mood; to reflect character; and to reinforce specific themes. A historical time period and setting must be easily identifiable. Costumes, sets, props,

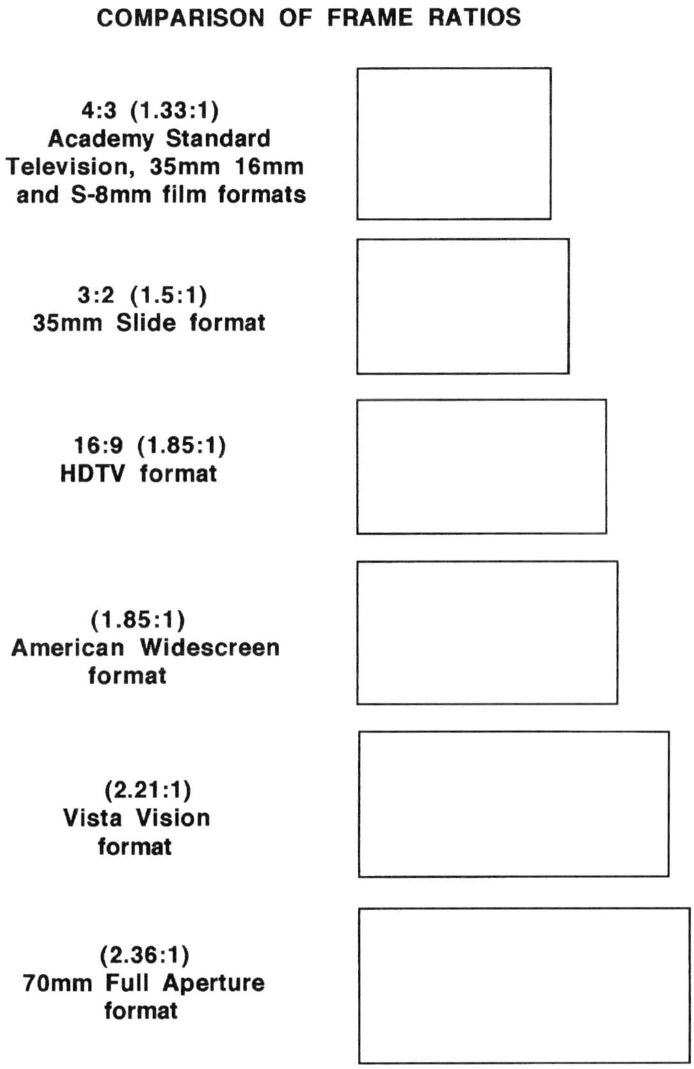

Figure 9.6 If 35mm photographic slides are converted to standard video or used on a television program produced in the NTSC standard, the photographer must remember that not all of the slide will be visible on the video screen. The 35mm slide is wider than either a 35mm film frame or the video frame and a small border top and bottom of the slide also will be lost from scanning and reproduction. Motion pictures shot in any but the Academy Standard 3 × 4 ratio will have to be reproduced by leaving a black stripe across the bottom and top of the frame, or by losing portions of the film frame on each side of the video frame.

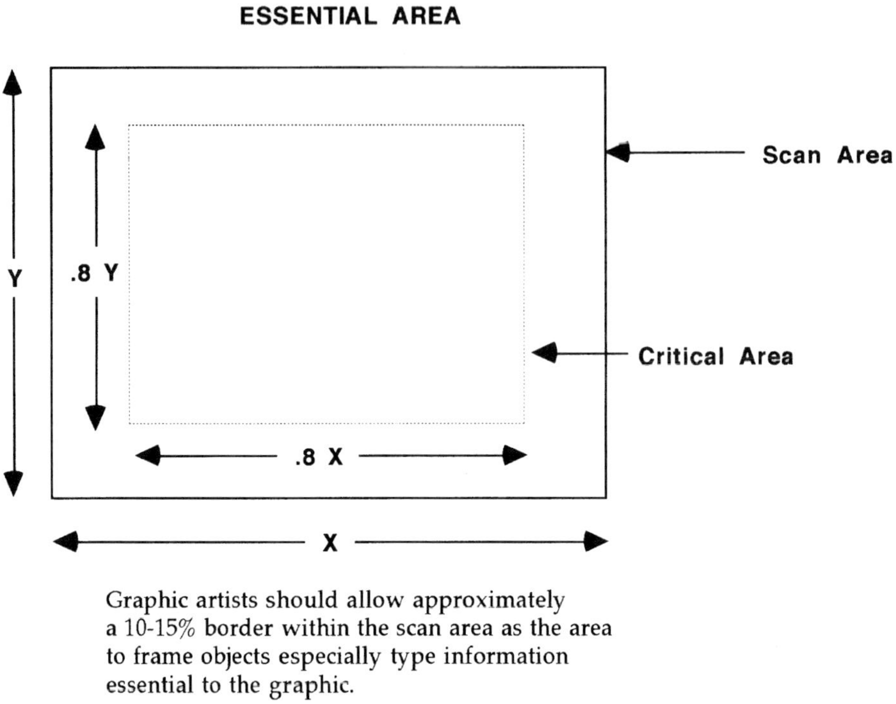

Figure 9.7 In order to make certain all essential or critical graphic subjects will be visible on a home television receiver, all such material should be framed within the central 80 percent of the frame, leaving a 10 percent border on all sides of the frame.

and titles denote a specific time and place at the same time that they reflect a specific style or mood. The mood or atmosphere results primarily from the abstract, emotional aspects of design elements and principles. Specific colors and shapes create an emotional mood that can reveal character and reinforce themes. The idea that you can tell a great deal about people from where they live and what they wear can be applied to scenic design. A cold, formal setting or costume reveals a great deal about a character, as does as a warm, relaxed setting or costume. The opening titles warn the audience of the mood, genre, and often the time and location of the production.

Scenic Design

Scenic design is an important contributor to overall characterization and thematic meaning. The first stage of scenic design is analyzing the script to determine what kinds of sets, costumes, and makeup will be required. A script usually provides a clear indication of general time and place, even if it does not describe settings and costumes in detail. Judgments concerning time, place, mood, character, and theme can only be made after the script has been carefully and thoroughly analyzed. The script itself can be broken down into a list of specific times and places, in much the same way as a breakdown is done for production scheduling and budgeting. A designer can then note the specific psychological mood of the action and characters for each time and place. Finally, more abstract concepts, ideas, and themes that result from in-depth analysis can be integrated into and reinforced by the selection of specific settings, costumes, and makeup (Figure 9.8).

The design of specific sets can be conveniently divided into two stages: layouts/floor plans and actual set construction. Design research, layouts, floor plans, and costume sketches are considered above-the-line expenses. They are created prior to actual production and before a commitment is made to actual construction, so that changes can be made before more sizable below-the-line construction expenses have been incurred. Each stage of design from planning to execution results in a specific two-dimensional or three-dimensional product. By following these stages, a designer refines rough ideas into workable sets that can be efficiently and economically constructed, significantly contributing to overall program effectiveness. Before undertaking the work and expense of set design and construction, some designers may consider the use of a neutral background, called a *cyclorama* or *cyc*. A cyc is a heavy, monochrome curtain that provides a neutral set backdrop. It is convenient to set up in a studio and can be used for many production settings. A cyc will often suffice in many modernist and postmodernist situations (Figure 9.9).

During preproduction a designer first draws a rough layout sketch for each set. These preliminary drawings are extremely important preproduction elements. They provide a focus for discussions at preproduction meetings, facilitate the estimation of set construction costs, and serve as a preliminary guide for the actual construction sets.

Figure 9.8 Costumes and settings are crucial in the staging of historical films such as Paramount Pictures' production of *Braveheart* with Mel Gibson and fellow actors wearing the traditional clothing and face painting of a Scottish warrior. (Courtesy of Paramount Pictures.)

Figure 9.9 A sky cyclorama (skycyk) is a plain off-white curtain which may be lit with a variety of different colors or patterns depending on the lighting instruments used. It also represents an infinite or non-descript background if that is called for in the set design.

A fully scaled floor plan translates actual set dimensions into a proportional ¼-inch or other convenient scale on a piece of gridded paper. The designer creates a bird's-eye view of the proposed set in reduced dimensions that are proportional to the actual size of objects on the set. If a wall is to be 8 feet long, it will be 2 inches long on the scaled floor plan (eight ¼-inches = 2 inches). Using a fully scaled floor plan, a director can determine if there is sufficient room to move the cameras or talent from one position to another in the set. A fully scaled floor plan can also be used by the lighting director to prepare the studio lighting. The final floor plan layout will include such things as scenery, set pieces such as furniture and props, and set dressings such as curtains. Skilled carpenters and painters translate the drawings into set materials that conform in every possible respect to the designer's original intentions.

Set Construction

Sets can be constructed out of new materials, or they can be constructed out of reusable flats and risers. The choice between new and reusable materials is usually made on the basis of budget size and available resources. Obviously, a high-budget production can better afford to create and discard new materials than a low-budget production. However, reusable set materials must be stored and maintained. Film and video studios, television stations, and networks often store and maintain such materials. Flats and risers can be simply redecorated or repainted to depict new locations.

Flats are relatively lightweight rectangular boards that are braced and supported by 2 × 3 inch or 2 × 4 inch boards on the back so that they are quite sturdy and durable. A variety of devices are used to connect flats together: rope tied over pegs, fastened with metal hinges, or secured with C-clamps. To keep them upright, flats are usually supported by angle braces. *Risers* are hollow rectangular boxes that can be placed on the floor to raise a portion of a set. Risers might be used in a news set, for example, to raise the news desk and seated performers to camera height.

Permanent sets are sometimes constructed out of more durable materials. A set that is going to be used day after day, such as for an evening news program, may be permanently secured to the studio floor for added stability. Since set materials are rarely viewed from behind, carpenters can cut costs by finishing only one side of a set piece and using inexpensive support materials.

Properties

The designer of a more realistic set must also select the necessary furniture and dressings, which fill in the set with objects and materials that add interest, realism, or atmosphere. Considerable searching may be required to locate unusual items, such as period furniture, drapes, or antiques that are needed to authentically recreate a specific setting or atmosphere. Props or properties are functional furnishings that are integrated into the program. Hand props are actually handled by performers, while set pieces are simply interesting, perhaps symbolic details on the set. Hand props are often used for bits of stage business or action, such as a gun kept hidden from the view of other characters. During camera and performer blocking, the set crew often helps arrange and rearrange the props on the set, so that they work well compositionally, are readily accessible to specific performers, and do not obstruct the movement or placement of cameras and other talent (Figure 9.10).

Costume Design

Most television and film productions require costumes and clothing that are selected and designed specifically for that show. For the majority of such productions, the wardrobe person procures costumes from rental houses that specialize in supplying costumes to theater, film, and video productions. In some cases, the clothing will be supplied by clothing manufacturers who want to advertise their products. Higher budgeted productions employ costume designers who create original costumes. Regardless of whether the costumes and clothing will be originally designed, rented, or supplied by a manufacturer, the person in charge of their selection must understand the basic principles of costume design. The garments worn by performers must be consistent with the overall production design. Costume designers must carefully consider color harmony and contrast between costumes and sets.

Purple sets and chartreuse costumes, for example, are disturbing when they appear together in a realistic setting, although in a modernist or postmodernist setting, that combination of colors might be appropriate.

Figure 9.10 Hand props are objects decorating the set that are small enough to be picked up and used by the performers.

A two-dimensional color wheel, discussed earlier, helps a designer select colors for costumes and sets that will both harmonize and contrast with each other. Using a three-dimensional color wheel, such as a Munsell 3-D color spindle, costume and set designers can select costume colors that will contrast with sets in terms of both color (different hues) and brightness (different light reflectances) and saturation (different hue intensities). Different colors that also differ in brightness will contrast with each other when projected as black-and-white as well as color television or film images.

In terms of texture, designers know that shiny, highly reflectant materials appear much brighter than thickly or coarsely textured materials. Bold plaids and stripes call too much attention to themselves. Certain fabric shapes and designs should be consciously avoided by the designer of video costumes and sets because they cause problems during recording. For example, parallel lines that are quite close together, as in herringbone cloth, can cause a moiré effect on a video screen. A moiré effect is a distracting vibration of visual images caused by the interaction of close-set lines in the materials being recorded and the video scanning lines. In television, the color blue or green, when used for chroma key, is usually avoided in costumes and sets.

Makeup

Video and film performer makeup can be divided into two types: cosmetic and prosthetic. *Cosmetic makeup* enhances the appearance of performers by hiding imperfections, adding needed color, and accentuating their better features, while *prosthetic makeup* transforms the appearance of a performer's face through temporary plastic surgery and other corrective means. Prosthetic makeup can add years to a performer's appearance or entirely transform his or her physical appearance. Cosmetic makeup enhances the beauty of a performer. It compensates for the heightened awareness of imperfections caused by film and video recording equipment and weak features in a performer's face. It also brings out the best features of a performer's face. Cosmetic makeup hides reddish cheeks and noses, beard lines, freckles, and blemishes. Eyes and lips are the most important aspects of a female performer's face. Makeup can hide or compensate for defects in these facial structures. If a female performer's eyes are too close together, for example, eyeliner can be placed on the outside edges of her lids to make them look farther apart.

Male performers often require makeup to cover beard lines, although many newscasters shave just before they appear on the evening news to avoid whisker stubble. Bright shades of cheek and lip color are generally avoided with males to prevent the appearance of a heavily made-up look. A weak chin can be made more prominent with a subtle accentuation of jaw lines and cheek color. Female performers are usually less concerned or embarrassed about applying makeup than men, but properly explaining the technical need for makeup can help to assuage the timidity of inexperienced performers. Men who are unaccustomed to wearing makeup often need to be convinced of its utility. Makeup and lighting can improve or eliminate such facial defects as the baggy eyes and pasty complexions often displayed by political candidates at the end of an exhausting campaign. Makeup on a bald head makes a person look better and cuts down on lighting problems, such as backlights reflecting off the top of a head.

It is possible to hide blemishes and create a consistent overall facial color and texture by simply applying a base or foundation makeup to a performer's face. Gently rubbing with cold cream and numerous tissues will remove makeup. Remember that the purpose of cosmetic makeup is usually to enhance the appearance of a performer, not to call attention to itself unless, or course, a modernist approach is employed. The best way to check a performer's makeup is to test it with a live video camera or an instant film camera. If it does not hide blemishes and improve the appearance of the talent, it should be removed and redone. The performer should look natural, except, of course, in postmodernist, avant-garde works.

Prosthetic makeup gives mobility to the expressive features of an actor and allows him or her some facial versatility in terms of playing many different roles. Prosthetic appliances can be used to make changes in the apparent age, race, nationality, and even sex of an actor. Prosthetic appliances are usually made of foam latex, which can be applied to the performer's face and hands. Prosthetic appliances can also be used to create specific facial effects, such as sagging folds and a double chin or heavy bags under the eyes. Prosthetic appliances can entirely restructure a performer's face so that a Caucasian performer can portray an Asian or African-American character or vice versa. Foam latex can be used by makeup artists to create purely imaginary facial structures, such as that of a prehistoric or futuristic creature, as well as life masks of living persons.

Graphic Design

Graphic design, like scenic design, is concerned with structuring pictorial content. Graphic images should be closely tied to overall scenic design, including sets and costumes. For example, the red titles and sepia-toned still photographs (black-and-white pictures with an overall reddish-brown color tone) at the beginning of *Bonnie and Clyde* (1967) foreshadow the violence and bloodshed to come and establish the 1930s setting of the film through costuming and props in each photograph. A good graphic design organizes visual information so that it can be efficiently communicated to viewers. Graphic designs organize many different types of information, including lettering and illustrations. Titles are often the first images presented on a videotape or film, and they must set a context for what is to follow. Graphic titles and illustrations answer questions about who, what, when, where, why, and how or how much. Graphic images often convey information more directly than speech and live-action images. They can boil down complex ideas into simple concepts, which are represented by shapes, words, or numbers. Titles and illustrations can clarify the ideas inherent in more complex, live-action images and speech.

Principles of Graphic Design

The best titles often are very simple. Trying to convey too much information at one time produces ineffective or unintelligible messages. Each image should convey one general thought or idea. Everything presented within that image must contribute to a central theme. A complex array of statistics can often be boiled down to a simple graph or chart. An arithmetic line or curve chart, a bar or column chart, a pie chart, or simply an array of appropriate symbols can graphically portray information much more effectively than an oral presentation alone. Titles and subtitles that clarify visual information or give credit to contributors must be clear and concise. Good titles and subtitles do not crowd the image, yet title size is often used to convey their relative importance. Illustrations should not be filled with complex, busy images. It is much more effective to present a simplified outline, a caricature or a symbolic illustration, than a highly detailed drawing or photograph to illustrate a particular idea. Everything extraneous should be removed. Simple images are generally more intelligible images. They eliminate confusion and frequently have great aesthetic and emotional impact.

Types of Graphics

Graphics can be divided into two different categories on the basis of the placement and use of graphic images during production: on-set and off-set graphics.

Off-Set Graphics

Off-set graphics are generated somewhere besides a live studio camera in the same studio as the production. They may come from a title card, computer-generated image, videotape, or a still-store recording fed directly into the switcher.

On-Set Graphics

The most commonly used types of on-set graphics are handheld cards, photographic blowups, and three-dimensional graphic set pieces. Handheld cards are images that a performer holds up to the camera during a scene. The talent controls the timing and placement of this type of graphic illustration. It is frequently used for informational or educational programs. The card must be held very steady, while a camera zooms or dollies in on the graphic image (Figure 9.11).

Still photographs can be blown up or enlarged so that they provide a convenient background or backdrop on the set. The photographs are usually poster size or larger, and are often mounted on stiff cardboard or plywood. These photographic enlargements can add depth and dimension to a scene or simply place an on-screen narrator in the proper context. Such photographs should have a matte, rather than a shiny or glossy surface, so that they do not reflect a great deal of light, and they should be positioned so that no glare or reflection is directed to the camera lens. Three-dimensional structures placed on the set for illustration purposes are called

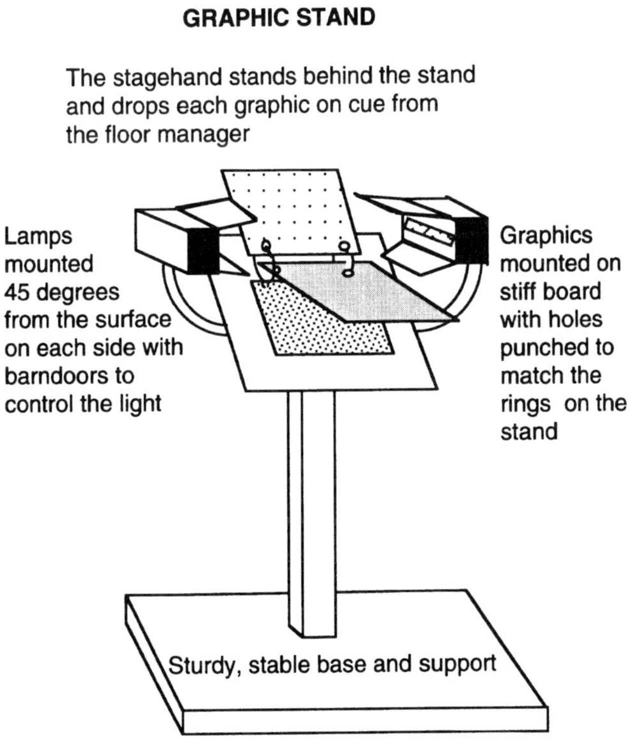

Figure 9.11 A graphics stand is a handy tool to use in the studio to shoot graphics mounted on stiff board. The lamps should be adjustable to prevent unwanted reflections and the graphics should be stacked with the first on the bottom and the last on top. All of the boards are held at the top and they are dropped to the stand one at a time on cue from the floor manager.

graphic set pieces. A graphic set piece could be an item to be demonstrated, such as a piece of machinery, or an art object.

Camera cards are usually placed on an easel, which is an adjustable display platform or graphic support. The lights on the easel, which illuminate the card, are normally placed at a 45-degree angle from the card surface to minimize light reflection in the camera lens. When the cards are attached to the easel by rings, they can easily be flipped, while maintaining perfect registration for the camera. It is also possible to zoom in to different elements in a card or photograph. This adds dynamic movement to static images. Dissolving from one card illustration to another is another common technique. The camera should record a card or illustration directly head-on to avoid keystone distortion. *Keystone distortion* exaggerates the size of the top, bottom, left, or right side of a card when the camera positioning is slightly off dead center (Figure 9.12).

A section of the studio wall painted blue or green as the background for weather is commonly used as a graphic set piece in television news production. The weather board allows various weather maps and figures to be chroma keyed behind the weather reporter. A chalkboard on which the talent can write or draw with chalk is also a graphic set piece. During elections, tally boards are sometimes used to present updated voting returns. Today tally boards are entirely electronic in operation.

Figure 9.12 Keystoning is the effect created by shooting a graphic at an angle rather than straight on. The closer edge of the graphic will appear to be larger and the farther will appear smaller when in reality they are the same size.

Lettering and Titles

Graphic images can be divided into two additional categories, titles and illustrations, on the basis of the nature of the images themselves. *Titles* are various forms of lettering that either accompany illustrations and live-action images or are presented as written text. The lettering for titles can be drawn by hand, produced mechanically, reproduced photographically, or created electronically on a device called a *character generator. Illustrations* are visual images, such as charts, graphs, and pictures. They can be hand drawn, photographed, or produced with the aid of computer graphics equipment.

Lettering and titles are used for a variety of purposes in video and film production. One of their most common uses is to introduce the name of a film and television program and to list the credits or names of people who have contributed in some way to the production. The opening titles of a program are called a *title* or *credit sequence* (Figure 9.13).

Another common use of titles is to clarify live-action images. Subtitles or name keys are titles keyed in the bottom third of the video or film frame, indicating the person or place being shown. Lettering and titles can also be used to accompany and clarify graphic illustrations, indicating the basic factors depicted in a chart or table, for example. Finally, lettering and titles can be presented as pure text, that is, without any other visual accompaniment.

Textual materials are used to convey written information in the form of electronic newspapers, advertising, or financial statements.

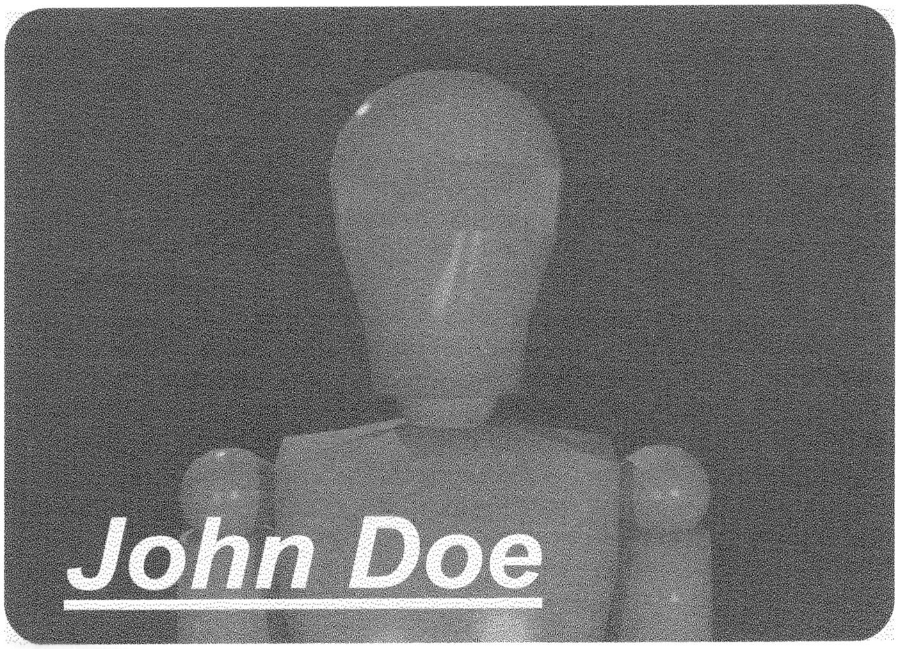

Figure 9.13 To identify key performers the name is typed on the character generator and then keyed over the MCU of the performer below their face but high enough in the frame to be visible by all viewers.

Types of Lettering

It is important to understand some basic methods and principles of lettering before trying to apply specific techniques to different title uses, purposes, and situations. Experienced artists and calligraphers sometimes draw letters for film and television titles by hand, but a more common technique is to produce them mechanically, photographically, or digitally.

Mechanical Lettering

Mechanical lettering can be created for television and film by using rub-on lettering. Rub-on lettering consists of multiple copies of each letter in the alphabet attached to a clear plastic sheet. The letters can be applied to virtually any surface, such as a paper title card, by simply rubbing the back of the plastic over the letter to be transferred. Rub-on lettering will adhere to almost any surface, including clear acetate, paper, cardboard, and photographs (Figure 9.14).

Photographic Lettering

Lettering can be produced photographically by machines such as a VariTyper Headliner. This machine allows an operator to select different letters by turning a wheel. Each letter is then photographed on internally processed 35mm film. Different typefaces and sizes can be obtained by replacing one wheel with another. White letters can be produced on a black background or black letters on a white background.

Figure 9.14 Rub-on lettering is an easy and fast way of creating lettered graphics to be shot on camera. A wide variety of type styles make the layout of the graphic flexible in size and composition.

Digital Lettering

The easiest and most efficient way to produce lettering for video is to use a digital character generator. A *character generator* or CG functions like a computer word processor in that it produces words directly on a television screen. It consists of a typewriter keyboard, a small computer, and a video monitor. Letters are positioned on the screen by means of a cursor, a blinking light on the video screen that is manipulated from the keyboard. Different typefaces or fonts, such as roman and italic letters, different type sizes, and letter borders, edge outlines, and drop shadows can be selected at the touch of a button.

A CG is more than a word processor. Logos or special graphic identifiers, such as product logos in advertising, and symbols can also be stored. Some CGs can use computer graphics and provide multicolored lettering. A full frame of information can be stored on floppy or hard disks and accessed later by referring to its designated page or frame number. Several frames of written material can be stored and immediately retrieved during a news, weather, or sports broadcast, for example. The output of a CG or disk storage can be keyed into any video switcher. Electronic keying and matting allow the lettering from a CG to be combined with different backgrounds and live-action images (Figure 9.15).

Credit or Titles

Credit and title sequences present an opportunity for creative, abstract expression on the part of a graphic artist. They are carefully designed to communicate the central message and feelings of a film or television program. The opening credits or ti-

Figure 9.15 A character generator (CG) is a relatively simple computer graphics machine designed to create lines of type, including numbers, simple color graphics backgrounds, or lines of type to be keyed over other video frames. (Courtesy of Scitex Digital Video.)

tle sequence offer the audience an introduction to the basic subject matter of the program. It must arouse the audience's interest, excitement, and curiosity. Titles should integrate well with overall scenic design. Graphic design and lettering styles should be appropriate to the overall subject matter. Sloppy lettering and graphic design provide a poor introduction and arouse a low level of expectation. Uneven, poorly spaced or off-centered mechanical lettering looks amateurish. Opening and closing credits should be well integrated with other sequences. Above all, imagination and creativity should be exercised.

Illustrations

Illustrations are drawings, photographs, graphs, charts, diagrams, and maps that provide visualizations of abstract concepts. Illustrations are usually intended to simplify information and to make it more accessible and understandable. Charts, graphs, diagrams, and maps are often used to display trends or to unravel complicated ideas or relationships inherent in statistical data. Illustrations can be used redundantly as an accompaniment to verbal descriptions or independently to add additional information that cannot be as effectively presented through the written or spoken word.

Photographic Illustrations

Still photographic illustrations, such as slides and prints, should be clear and unambiguous. They should be in sharp focus, have a range of tones from white to black, be of medium contrast, be immediately recognizable subjects, have no extraneous details, and be known objects for scale and size comparison. Busy photographs distract attention from the main point they are supposed to communicate. A copy stand can be used to photograph art work or other photographic and printed illustrations.

Photographic prints can be mounted so that they can be recorded by a film or television camera. Positive prints made from 35mm negative film are normally used. Photographic prints can be blown up to 8 × 10 inches or 11 × 14 inches from 35mm negatives. The prints can then be mounted on a rigid piece of cardboard in one of two ways: (1) rubber cement can be applied to the back of the photograph, which is then pressed onto the mounting board with a book or heavy object until the cement dries and the excess is wiped off; or (2) a dry mounting press can be used. A mounting press consists of a heated set of pressure plates. Mounting tissue is placed between the back of the photograph and the mounting board; this sandwiched material is then secured inside the mounting press, where heat and pressure are applied. A piece of plain paper is often placed over the face of the photograph to protect it during the twenty or thirty seconds that it remains within the heated press. A dry mounting press usually provides a more permanent mount than rubber cement, but it requires additional materials and expense (Figure 9.16).

Computer Graphics

One of the most promising applications of computer technology to film and television production is computer graphics. The advantage of computer graphics sys-

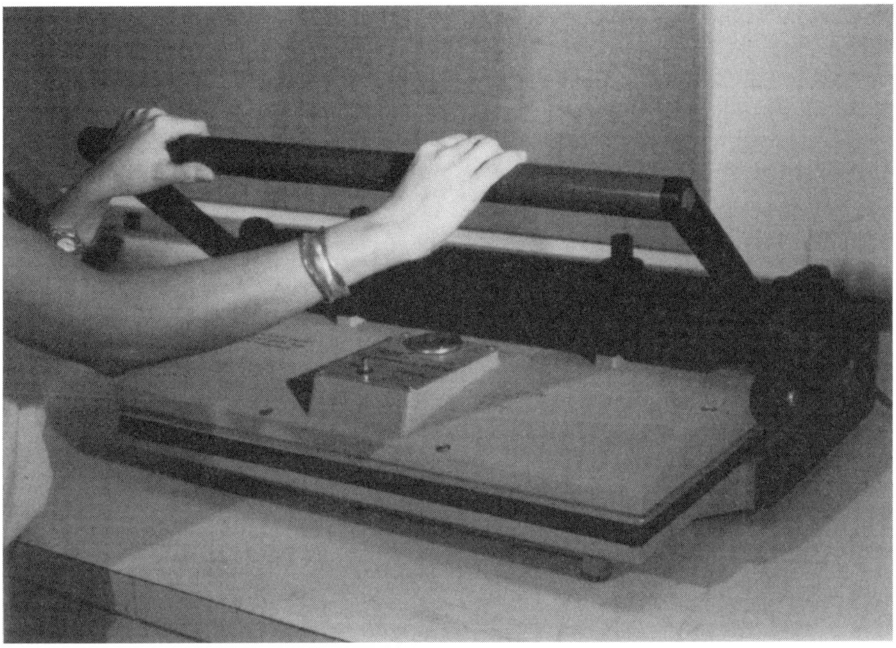

Figure 9.16 When using photographs and other two-dimensional graphics, it is critical that they be mounted on a sturdy and flat surface. A dry mounting press performs that service quickly and efficiently.

tems, like that of the character generator, is that the images do not have to be recorded by a camera and individual frames can be digitally stored.

A variety of hardware and software systems are currently available for use in video and film production. Most systems allow the operator or artist to control all of the elements of graphic design, including line, shape, and color. Images can be created directly on the screen, using a light pencil, stylus, mouse, or keyboard. The artist can select and control various lines and shapes, as well as image size, color, and placement on the screen. It is also possible to use a stylus to trace a hand-drawn sketch or outline so that it can be computer manipulated and stored in disk form. Some computers have *frame-grabbers,* which allow a single video frame from a camera or VCR to be manipulated by the computer. Some computer software allows graphics programs to be integrated with animation programs to create apparent motion. Images can be placed in disk storage and accessed at any time. A graphics computer that has a standard NTSC video signal output can be fed directly to a VCR or a switcher.

The primary advantages of computer graphics systems are savings in time and convenience. In preproduction use, storyboards can be quickly and efficiently generated, and then modified immediately prior to actual production to mirror changes. Hard copies can then be printed for camera operators and other members of the production team. During production, illustrations such as charts, graphs, and drawings can be generated quickly and used immediately. Computer-generated graphics provide the background information for weather forecasts. Titles and lettering can be corrected immediately and then added to images to clarify the information they contain. All of this information can then be conveniently stored and accessed during production without using a camera. Images can also be modified efficiently and easily during production. While sophisticated computer graphics systems are still very expensive, low-cost systems, such as those available with many home computer systems, can be inexpensively purchased and integrated into a television production facility.

Integration of Design

Set furnishings, props, costumes, and performer makeup are not completely independent elements in the production process. Elements of scenic design interact with each other and many other areas of production to create an overall visual impression. The most important interactions are those between scenic design and each of the following: lighting, performer movement, and camera and microphone placement. Important set elements, such as key props, can be emphasized by lighting them more brightly than other elements. The texture of a rough surface can be accentuated with side lighting, which creates textural shadows in the surface indentations. The color of set elements can be drastically altered by using colored lighting. A colored surface can only reflect wavelengths of light that are present in the light that illuminates it. Different lighting contrast ratios and lighting styles can enhance a specific mood or atmosphere inherent in the setting.

Camera and Mic Placement

Sets are usually designed to facilitate the placement and movement of the cameras and microphones, as well as the talent. One of the main advantages of constructing sets in the studio is that there is always an open wall on the set, where the cameras can be placed. A location interior always has four walls. When shooting with a single camera in the studio, the fourth wall can be put up or taken down between shots or camera takes. Single-camera productions can create the illusion of a fourth wall in the final edited product, but during production they maintain the flexibility of the open wall. During multiple-camera studio production, using only two walls provides a great deal of space within which the cameras are free to move. In a confined setting, transmitter microphones are invaluable.

Summary

Graphic design can be approached from three aesthetic perspectives: realism, modernism, and postmodernism. Realist sets and design formats depict an actual or general type of place or experience; it is important to efficiently create an illusion of reality. Realistic sets are often constructed out of lightweight materials that give the impression of being real and are much easier to construct and move around than actual objects. Realist designs are rarely defined by their supposed fidelity to nature or reality alone. Almost every realist design that has emotional impact has some degree of subjective stylization. A realistic setting, title, or illustration should convey a psychological image format with which the audience is already familiar. A realist setting can provide an atmosphere that reflects the subjective state of mind or perceptions of a specific character. Modernist designs are relatively abstract. They reflect an artist's abstract conception of space, a subjective feeling, or a state of mind. Postmodernist designs combine a variety of design styles and patterns and emphasize emotional responses and an intentional distortion of realistic visuals.

Scenic design involves three basic design principles: design elements, color, and composition. Design elements include lines, shapes, textures, and movement. Intersecting or parallel lines create different spatial impressions than curved or circular shapes. A designer can create spatial perspective and control image size by manipulating various shapes. The texture of a surface can be defined in terms of its tactile roughness or smoothness. Color and contrast are interrelated aspects of design, as are color and shape. Contrasting colors can be used to separate foregrounds and backgrounds, and to create various shapes. Using different colors in costumes and sets will prevent characters from blending into sets. Finally, colors, like shapes, can be used symbolically, or they can be used repeatedly in conjunction with specific characters, settings, and themes.

Graphic artists design images that convey information. They use basic principles of design, such as simplicity, proximity, similarity, figure/ground, correspondence, equilibrium, and closure as part of the art of composition to stimulate viewer interest. Graphic artists work within the constraints and limitations of visual media. They select lettering that is highly readable and clearly visible. They compose images designed for different aspect ratios and film and video formats that are pleasing to the eye. They avoid designs and colors that are difficult to record or are visually distracting. Titles and illustrations are designed and selected on the basis of their appropriateness for specific topics.

Sets are designed to provide an environment for a production. The setting and properties must be practical and utilitarian for both the performers to be able to move and interact, and for the director to be able to place cameras and microphones where they are needed. Set design and construction starts early in the preproduction phase and continues throughout production.

The design of makeup makes it possible to hide blemishes and to create a consistent overall facial color and texture by simply applying a base or foundation makeup to a performer's face. Prosthetic makeup gives mobility to the expressive features of an actor and allows him or her some facial versatility in terms of playing many different roles. Prosthetic appliances can be used to make changes in the apparent age, race, nationality, and even sex of an actor. Prosthetic appliances are usually made of foam latex, which can be applied to the performer's face and hands.

Graphic design is an integral part of the overall production process, and like scenic design, is concerned with pictorial content. One purpose of graphic design is to organize and simplify visual material and information so that it can be efficiently recorded and communicated to viewers. Graphics can be divided into two categories on the basis of use or placement: on-set and off-set. The most commonly used on-set graphics are handheld cards, photographic enlargements, and graphic set pieces. The most commonly used off-set graphics are camera cards and photographic slides, as well as graphics created on character generators or computers.

Graphic images can be divided into two additional categories on the basis of their nature as images: titles and illustrations. Titles are forms of graphic lettering. Letters for titles can be created mechanically, photographically, or electronically. A person with minimal design and lettering skills can operate an electronic character generator, or CG, and immediately produce viewable and recordable results. A CG allows letters to be created, arranged, and manipulated at the touch of a button. Boldface, relatively large-size type is normally used for television. Lettering should contrast with background illustrations in order to be clearly legible. Subtitles and credit sequences usually combine lettering with live-action images or illustrations. A credit or title sequence names the production contributors. It is usually designed to communicate the flavor of a film or television program and to generate audience interest and excitement. Illustrations are drawings, photographs, graphs, charts, diagrams, and maps that visualize abstract concepts and ideas. They can be produced by a variety of techniques: drawn by hand, photographed, or produced electronically with the help of a computer graphics system.

Sets, set furnishings, props, costumes, and performer makeup are not completely independent elements in the production process. Elements of scenic design interact with each other and many other areas of production to create an overall visual impression. The most important interactions are those between scenic design and each of the following: lighting, performer movement, and camera and microphone placement. Sets are usually designed to facilitate the placement and movement of the cameras and microphones, as well as the talent.

Exercises

1. Design a realistic room interior on the basis of the description of this setting in a script, short story, or novel. Carefully select and coordinate furniture, props, sets, and costumes so that all of these elements create a realistic impression of time and place. Color and brightness levels of foreground and background elements, sets, and costumes should contrast but not clash with each other. Provide detailed layouts drawn to scale so that the set can be efficiently and accurately constructed. Incorporate elements into the set that are economical to obtain or already on hand, such as specific flats, props, set dressings, and pieces of furniture.
2. Use a cyclorama to create a setting that has no borders where walls and/or ceilings meet so that space appears infinite. Use lighting techniques discussed in Chapter 6 to create abstract shapes, colors, and patterns that create a dramatic and unusual sense of space. Discover ways of manipulating the viewer's sense of spatial perspective by simply altering the lighting.
3. Using the description of a specific setting in a dramatic script, short story, or novel, find an existing building that meets the essential criteria needed to represent this place. Assess the difficulties inherent in using this facility from the standpoint of recording and determine what elements will have to be removed or added to make this an ideal setting.
4. Design a credit or title sequence for a specific production project. Determine how you can best use abstract graphic images and titles to introduce a production or select live-action images on which titles can be keyed. Select a letter style or font that is consistent with the overall theme, message, and style of your project which creates an impression that reinforces the central theme of a drama or the central message of an informational program. It can reflect warmth or cold-

ness, tension or relaxation, simply by virtue of the colors, lines, and shapes it presents. Your project will eventually be shown on a video screen, be sure to use type sizes that are large enough for titles to be clearly legible. Allow sufficient time for each title to be read twice before another title appears on the screen, unless there are too many credits that must be presented within a relatively short period of time. Remember that a title sequence must effectively introduce viewers to the topic.

Additional Readings

Arntson, Amy E. *Graphic Design Basics.* New York: Holt, Rinehart and Winston, Inc., 1988.

Ayers, Ralph. *Graphics of Television.* Englewood Cliffs, NJ: Prentice-Hall, Inc., 1984.

Baker, Georgia O'Daniel, and Helen Redel Pullen. *A Handbook of Costume Drawing.* Boston: Focal Press, 1992.

Barsacq, Leon. *Caligari's Cabinet and Other Grand Illusions: A History of Film Design.* New York: The New American Library, 1978.

Baygan, Lee. *Techniques of Three-Dimensional Makeup.* New York: Watson-Guptill, 1982.

Blank, Ben, and Mario R. Garcia. *Professional Video Graphic Design: The Art and Technology.* Englewood Cliffs, NJ: Prentice-Hall Press, 1986.

Buchman, Herman. *Film and Television Makeup.* New York: Watson-Guptill, 1973.

Byrne, Terry. *Production Design for Television.* Boston: Focal Press, 1993.

Hurrell, Ron. *Television Graphics.* New York: Van Nostrand Reinhold, 1977.

Kehoe, Vincent J.R. *Special Make-Up Effects.* Boston: Focal Press, 1991.

Kehoe, Vincent J.R. *The Technique of Film and Television Make-Up Artists for Film, Television and Stage.* Boston: Focal Press, 1985.

Levitan, Eli L. *Electronic Imaging Techniques.* New York: Van Nostrand Reinhold, 1977.

MacGregor, A.J. *Graphics Simplified.* Toronto: University of Toronto Press, 1979.

Merritt, Douglas. *Graphic Design in Television.* Boston: Focal Press, 1993.

Millerson, Gerald. *TV Scenic Design Handbook.* Boston: Focal Press, 1989.

Olson, Robert. *Art Direction for Film and Video.* Boston: Focal Press, 1993.

Wade, Robert J. *Designing for TV: The Arts and Crafts in Television Production.* New York: Pelligrini and Cudahy, 1952.

Whyte, Ron, Jim Minton, and Bob Regliev. *Designing for Television: News Sets.* Lincoln, Nebraska: Boomer's Printing Co./Broadcast Designers Assoc., 1980.

10

The Editing Process

Introduction

Selecting, combining, and trimming sounds and visual images after they have been recorded constitute the craft of editing. For example, a film or video editor can trim a continuous recording of visual images, usually called a *shot,* by removing unwanted portions at the beginning or end of the shot. Trimmed shots can then be combined with other shots using various transition devices, such as cuts, fade-out/fade-ins, or dissolves. A *cut* is a direct, instantaneous transition from one shot to the next. During a *fade-out/fade-in,* the first shot gradually disappears and is replaced by blackness. This is called a *fade-out.* It is followed by the gradual appearance of the second shot from blackness, which is called a *fade-in.* A *dissolve* consists of a simultaneous or overlapping fade-out of the first shot and a fade-in of the second shot. Unlike a fade-out/fade-in, the image never becomes entirely black during a dissolve. Transitions generally imply a change of time and/or place from one shot to the next. For example, a cut usually implies a very short, if any, temporal change from one shot to the next, while a dissolve suggests that some time has elapsed. However, a dissolve generally suggests a shorter passage of time than does a fade-out/fade-in.

A similar procedure is followed when editing sounds. A continuous sound recording is trimmed by removing unwanted portions at its beginning and/or end. Sounds can be combined using various transition devices, such as a segue, a fade-out/fade-in, or a cross-fade. A *segue* is a virtually instantaneous transition from one sound to the next, while a fade-out to silence followed by a fade-in from silence suggests a greater passage of time than a cross fade, which consists of a simultaneous or overlapping fade-out and fade-in of one sound recording to the next.

Trimming and combining visual images and sounds define the craft or mechanics of editing, which is extensively examined in two subsequent chapters (11 and 12), but any discussion of the overall process and art of editing must begin with a consideration of editing stages, systems, modes, and aesthetic approaches. The editing process consists of at least two stages: preliminary and final editing. During preliminary editing, images and sounds are repeatedly viewed before they are selected, trimmed, and combined, usually using a copy of the original recordings to create a rough cut or off-line edited version. During final editing, the original recordings are themselves edited into a polished, on-line edited version that will actually be released to viewers and listeners.

While editors use many different types of equipment, most editing systems fall into two categories: linear and nonlinear. Linear systems require sounds and images to be edited in sequential order (imagine a straight, uninterrupted line) from beginning to end, and they do not allow the editor to subsequently change the overall length or duration of the program. A nonlinear system allows an editor to subsequently add or subtract sounds and images, which change the overall length or duration of a program, and therefore editing does not need to proceed in a straightforward fashion from beginning to end. The editing process usually proceeds somewhat differently in fictional than in nonfictional modes due to the fact that fiction is often more tightly scripted than nonfiction, and dramatic and narrative structures sometimes require different editing techniques and strategies than rhetorical and expository structures. The choice of an overall aesthetic approach, such as realism, modernism, or postmodernism, significantly affects the editing process as well.

EDITING PROCESSES

STAGES OF EDITING	MOTION PICTURES	VIDEO or TELEVISION	AUDIO or SOUND
PRELIMINARY	Rough cut and final cut of work print	Off-line non-linear of lower quality tape stock or in a computer	Record each source on separate track of multi-track recorder or physically cut the original tape or enter each track into a multi-track computer program for non-linear editing
FINAL	Conform original film to edited workprint or to digitally edited timecode & KeyKode	On-line linear of original tape controlled by computer following the EDL or on-line nonlinear of original tape	From multi-track recorder or computer dub to stereo tracks in computer to final mix for reproduction

Figure 10.1 The two stages of editing media programs, whether audio, video, or film follow the same basic pattern. A preliminary stage assembles the material into a tentative order and pattern, and then the final stage completes the editing by trimming and molding the produciton into its final form.

Editing Stages

Postproduction editing can be divided into two stages: preliminary editing and final editing. The difference between these two stages is most clear in larger scale or more expensive video and film productions, where final editing is subsequently performed on the original recordings, such as BetaSP, BetaSX, D-2, and 1-inch videotape or 16mm and 35mm negative film, after copies of the originals have been preliminary edited. The original recordings are usually dubbed, digitized, or copied to another (sometimes a smaller) format for preliminary editing. This preserves the quality and safety of original recordings while allowing an editor some flexibility to edit and re-edit materials in a preliminary way. The editing decisions made during the preliminary stage are then used to guide final editing.

In traditional videotape editing, preliminary and final editing are sometimes referred to as *off-line* and *on-line* editing, while in traditional film editing the two stages are often called *rough cutting* and *conforming*, and in traditional audiotape editing and postproduction, they are referred to as *editing* and *mixing*, respectively (Figure 10.1).

Off-line videotape editing sometimes involves the use of a smaller format than the original recordings. An on-line editing facility is much more expensive than an off-line editing facility, and initially editing off-line can be very economical, since preliminary editing is usually quite time consuming. The purpose of off-line editing is to produce an *edit decision list* or EDL, which is a list of the time code numbers at the beginning and end of each consecutive shot in the edited videotape. The EDL numbers can then be fed into a computer, which is used to control the playback and recording of higher format videotapes during on-line editing, when cuts, fade-out/fade-ins, dissolves, and other transition devices are created from multiple videotapes playing simultaneously (Figure 10.2).

The rough cutting of film usually involves cutting and tape splicing together various shots in a workprint or copy of the original film. The splices or cut points, which are very noticeable in an edited workprint, are made virtually invisible during final editing. The purpose of rough cutting is to produce a list of latent edge num-

EDIT DECISION LIST (EDL)

EDIT#	REEL	DESCRIPTION	VIDEO IN/OUT	AUDIO IN/OUT	TRANSITION
001	3	WS-Ext	00:06:00:20 00:06:02:16	00:06:01:10 00:06:15:04	FI
002	3	MS-Ext	00:00:03:16 00:00:11:04		C
003	5	CU	00:10:02:15 00:11:29:05	00:10:02:15 00:11:29:05	D
004	2	CU	00:19:03:10 00:20:10:28	00:19:03:10 00:20:10:28	D

Figure 10.2 An Edit Decision List (EDL) is a precise listing (usually assembled on a computer) of each edit; its start and end point, transition, and any special effects or differences in audio and video edit points.

Figure 10.3
An off-line editor assembles either a film or video production in either its rough-cut form or in its final form using a lower quality video or computer format to save money. The EDL created by such an edit session is then used for the on-line edit using the highest quality format required for the project. (Courtesy of Scitex Digital Video.)

bers at the beginning and end of each consecutive shot that can be used to match or conform the original film to the edited workprint. The original film is *hot spliced,* that is, it is physically cemented to black or opaque film in two parallel rolls of film, called *A and B rolls,* so that the splices will not be visible for cuts and fade-outs/fade-ins, and dissolves can be seen after the two rolls have been printed to the final copy or *answer print.* The original film is preserved and protected during rough cutting, which often permanently mars the workprint and is quite time consuming (Figure 10.4).

Traditional audiotape editing usually involves cutting and splicing separate reels of ¼-inch audiotape or 16mm magnetic film, which will run on synchronized playback machines during the mixing stage. An alternative approach involves recording separate sounds on different tracks of multitrack audiotape. Each track is recorded at its optimum level during preliminary editing, and then the recording levels are adjusted as the different tracks (or tapes) are mixed together and segues, fade-outs/fade-ins, and cross-fades are created during final editing. A list of time code numbers or film footage and frame numbers that indicate when specific level changes and transitions will take place during an audio mix, which is called a *cue sheet,* is created during preliminary editing.

Figure 10.4 The synchronizers on an editing bench are set up with the "A" and "B" rolls threaded along with the workprint as the third roll of film. All are locked in sync by the synchronizer. The shots alternate on the "A" and "B" rolls with black leader spliced between shots in a checkerboard pattern.

Preliminary Editing

One of the editor's first tasks is to organize and catalogue all the material the director has provided. The original recorded images and sounds are usually dubbed or copied before they are seen and heard by the editor. Little, if any, material that has been rejected during actual production will be copied for viewing or listening purposes. Using a copy protects the original recording, which can be safely stored away. Copies or dubs made for viewing or audition purposes are sometimes made on a smaller format.

They can also be digitized for nonlinear digital editing, that is, the original videotape images and sounds can be captured in digital form, such as on a computer hard drive, by running them through a digitizing board, which is often mounted in the computer. The digitizing board usually compresses the video and audio somewhat to reduce the amount of memory on the hard drive that is required for storage. Generally hardware compression, which is built into the board itself, produces higher quality digital images and sounds than software compression, which compresses the video images and sounds within the editing program or software. Regardless of the analog or digital format to which the original recordings are dubbed or copied, the recorded images and sounds are repeatedly played back and listened to or viewed by the editor.

In fully scripted video and film productions, the individual shot and take numbers recorded from the slate at the beginning of each camera take are catalogued

EDIT LOG

PRODUCTION ____________________ PAGE ________ DATE__________

PRODUCER____________ EDITOR______________

EDIT #	REEL	DESCRIPTION	VIDEO IN/OUT	AUDIO IN/OUT	TRANSITION Audio	TRANSITION Video

Figure 10.5 A manually created edit log form may be assembled by viewing a videotape copy of the production that has a time code window visible in the frame. The frame accurate time code location for each anticipated edit is written (logged) on the form to be used as a guide when the editor actually assembles the production in the edit suite. This process saves time and the expense of tying up an edit suite while decisions are being made about the location of edits.

on paper. Videotape or audiotape time code numbers, or the film keycode numbers, are usually catalogued as well. When time code is recorded in original videotape and audiotape, each consecutive frame of videotape or audiotape can be numbered from 00:00:00:00 to 23:59:59:29 (zero to twenty-three hours, fifty-nine minutes, fifty-nine seconds, and twenty-nine frames). Each separate original tape usually begins with a different hour, such as 01:00:00:00, 02:00:00:00, etc. Original film can have Keykode, a bar code system developed by Eastman Kodak similar to systems used by retail stores, which can be subsequently converted to time code, when the film is transferred to video for electronic editing and converted back to Keykode later to cut the original negative (Figure 10.5).

As mentioned earlier, film also has latent edge numbers, which are placed along one edge of the original film by the manufacturer. They can be photographically copied to a workprint for preliminary film editing so that matching frames from the original can be obtained during final editing. Matching yellow ink edge numbers can also be printed onto preliminary editing materials, such as workprint and synchronized magnetic film sound.

Editing decisions can be gradually refined and tightened up as the preliminary stage of editing progresses. An editor should not limit her or his choices too early in the editing process but rather try out various alternatives before deciding on the final form. Careful cataloguing of all the shots or sound takes on each roll, reel, or cassette of videotape, film, or audiotape helps an editor to find the precise shot or sound that he or she needs. If an alternative approach to editing a specific sequence is being considered, it is advantageous for the editor to be able to find different shots, takes, or segments of the existing shots and takes, which were removed during trimming, very quickly. After all the edit decisions have been made, the editor creates a list of the time code numbers or latent film edge numbers and footage and frames for anticipated effects and transitions, such as fades, dissolves, segues, cross-fades, and sound level changes, which will be needed for final editing. This list will then be supplied to the on-line videotape editor, film conformer, or audio mixer.

Final Editing

Once all the editing decisions have been completed, the originally recorded videotape, film, or audiotape is edited or mixed so that it conforms to the preliminary edit decision list, film workprint edge numbers or Keykode, or the audio cue sheets. Few creative decisions are made during final editing. In videotape editing, for example, using an on-line editing system is often too expensive to creatively experiment with alternative versions of specific sequences. In film editing, the original film must be physically cut with great care and precision according to a predetermined order and duration, since it is virtually impossible to experiment with different versions during final editing without permanently altering or marring the original film. In audio editing, the various tracks are synchronized in a fixed order and duration, which facilitates blending or mixing them together in predetermined ways during final editing, but which makes it difficult to alter the order or duration of each separate track during the mixing stage.

In final videotape editing, the EDL is programmed into a computer edit controller, after inputting the edit decision list as a computer file that is readable by that particular edit controller. The EDL indicates where specific shots begin and end, as well as transition devices between shots. Separate original videotapes are loaded onto different playback machines, and the computer determines the order and duration of the playback for each videotape, while a switcher is used to create transitions between different sources. The video signal output by the switcher is fed to a videotape recorder. Audio mixing can be accomplished at this stage as well by sending various audio signals through a mixing console.

During final film editing, a conformer uses the list of latent edge numbers from the edited workprint or the Keykode converted from the EDL to pull each shot from the original film. Using a cement splicer, the conformer attaches each consecutive shot alternately to the A or the B roll, placing black leader on the corresponding portion of the opposite roll. Conforming is usually accomplished under extremely clean conditions and with great care to avoid damaging the original film. The conformed A and B rolls are then sent to a film laboratory, where they are sequentially printed to create a composite answer print and a release print. Sound tracks are also transferred to these prints after they have been final mixed.

Audio mixing requires several edited sound tracks to be played simultaneously and their signals run through a mixing board, where levels can be adjusted and transitions created as the separate tracks are combined. Using the cue sheets, the mixer knows when to raise or lower the sound levels; to create a segue, cross-fade, or other transitions; and to adjust the sound frequencies or equalization (EQ). When the audio will accompany video or film images, an edited version of the videotape or film is usually played in synchronization with the sound tracks during the

Figure 10.6
A CCD telecine film-to-video converter. Each film frame is scanned individually allowing for color correction and filtering in real time as the film is converted to a video signal. (Courtesy of Philips Broadcast Television Systems Company.)

mix so that visual cues can be observed and the compatibility of the sounds and visual images can be assessed.

Editing Systems

Linear

Linear editing systems require an editor to add visual images and sounds in consecutive order from the beginning to the end of a piece. Once an edit is made, its duration is fixed with respect to the sounds or images that come before and after it. An editor cannot remove a sound or image and directly connect those that come before and after it, although an editor can usually replace a shot or sequence with other sounds or images that have the same duration. Most analog videotape and audiotape editing systems are basically linear editing systems.

Linear editing requires careful preplanning. An editor should be quite confident about the order and duration of each shot or sequence before he or she edits it into the project, since it is often difficult to remove or replace it later. If an editor subsequently decides that an earlier shot or sequence needs to be removed, he or she generally needs to return to the beginning of the shot or sequence to be removed and begin editing in a linear fashion with other material from that point on. The only other option that is sometimes available to the editor is to skip a generation, that is, to edit the master tape itself by using it as a playback source for a new edit master, which then becomes a copy of a copy, or one generation removed from the master tape. Since most linear systems are analog rather than digital and the quality of the sounds and images is reduced in each succeeding generation, skipping a generation is not always an acceptable or preferred option.

Linear editing is often facilitated by first performing a paper edit. Each trimmed shot is described in terms of its duration and time code or control track location in sequential order on the original videotape. This shot list can then be rearranged into the anticipated order of the edited videotape. Performing a paper edit allows an editor to make changes in the order of the shots prior to actually editing the videotape. The order of the shots can be rearranged much more efficiently on paper (or as written text using a computer program) than it can during linear videotape editing.

Nonlinear

While traditional film rough cutting and audiotape splicing constitute nonlinear editing, new digital technologies have created much more efficient nonlinear editing systems for audio, video, and film. Traditional film cutting and tape splicing allow an editor to remove unwanted shots and sequences without requiring all the subsequent shots and sequences to be re-edited, but this method of editing is somewhat slow and laborious. Digital nonlinear editing systems allow digitized recordings of images and sounds to be removed or replaced, and the overall duration of a project to be changed very efficiently. Digital nonlinear editing systems treat sounds and images in much the same way that computer word processing programs treat text. Just as text can be highlighted and moved or removed using computer word processing software, so can specific files or clips of images and sounds be moved or removed using digital nonlinear editing software. In addition, digitized images and sounds can be shaped and filtered during the nonlinear editing process.

Sounds or video images are digitized by turning them into computer files using an audio or video computer capturing board. The digital computer files can then be manipulated by an editor using a computer equipped with substantial memory and processing speed. Editing software programs allow the editor to place sounds and images sequentially along a time line. Images usually appear as series of still frames or written description along the time line, while sounds are often depicted visually as continuous sound waves. An editor can trim specific image and sound clips, removing portions at the beginning and/or end of the clip, and then combine them with other images and sounds along the time line. Several separate sound tracks can be independently or jointly edited, as well as several visual tracks, including various transitions between clips. Removing a sound or image clip is usually as simple as highlighting it and pressing a delete button. The adjacent clips can then be attached to each other, changing the overall duration of the piece without requiring any re-editing of subsequent images and sounds.

Editing Modes

Fiction

Classical Hollywood conventions for shooting and editing fiction films and videos include master scene shooting and continuity editing. A *master shot* consists of a relatively long duration shot that includes most of the action in a specific scene, usually recorded from a medium to long range camera distance. Shooting a master shot allows the actors to achieve some degree of continuity in their performance before the action is broken up into shorter duration shots with the camera in closer proximity to the actors. A master shot provides an editor with continuous coverage of the action. Closer shots can then be inserted into the master shot to intensify the action by revealing a character's facial expressions and gestures. For example, when two characters are talking to one another in a scene, alternating over-the-shoulder, shot/reverse shot close-ups of the two characters are often inserted into the master shot so that their actions and reactions can be seen more clearly (Figures 10.7A, B, C).

Continuity editing refers to an editing system that developed in Hollywood and elsewhere beginning about 1910. It consists of a number of shooting and editing conventions that sustain an illusion of continuous time and place within a scene. For example, maintaining the 180-degree action axis or consistent screen direction from one shot to the next sustains the illusion of spatial and temporal continuity. If a character moves from left to right in shot A but from right to left in shot B, he or she will appear to have dramatically changed direction without any passage of time. This may be perceived as a *jump cut,* that is, a mismatch in spatial continuity suggesting that a gap in time has occurred. When no mismatch in action or gap in time is apparent over a cut from one shot to the next, this is called a *match cut.*

An editor must also be conscious of *eyeline matches,* that is, maintaining directional continuity in terms of characters' looks and glances within a scene. If one character looks screen left in shot A followed by another character looking screen

Figures 10.7A, B, C The standard shot series in a scene starts with a LS establishing relationships and positioning in the environment. A tighter MS brings the performers closer. A CU will concentrate the audience's attention on the specific performer.

right in shot B, they will appear to be looking at (and perhaps talking to) one another. A common variation on the eyeline match is called a *point-of-view shot.* Here the editor cuts from one character looking in a particular direction to a shot of what they are looking at from their approximate (usually over-the-shoulder) spatial position in the scene. Cutting back to a close-up of a character who has been looking at something in order to see his or her facial expression is sometimes called a *reaction shot.* Point of view and reaction shots not only maintain directional continuity, they can also enhance viewer identification with specific character's points of view.

Nonfiction

Partially or completely staged scenes in nonfiction productions sometimes rely upon master scene and continuity techniques used in fiction. Variations upon these techniques have also been developed that take into account the difficulties of scripting and staging nonfiction events as well as the use of expository and rhetorical structures that can disrupt spatial and temporal continuity. A variation upon master scene shooting and editing commonly used in news and documentary production, for example, is called *A and B roll editing.* "Talking head" interviews constitute the A roll (equivalent to the master shot), while additional recordings of various activities and events that illustrate what the interviewee is talking about constitute the B roll (equivalent to the inserts). The editor inserts B-roll material into the A roll, as the interviewee continues to be heard on one of the audio tracks. A and B roll editing adds viewer interest by interspersing rather static shots of a talking head with a wide variety of visual illustrations.

Master scene techniques can also be simulated during the editing of the interview itself. If the camera-to-subject distance or type of shot (long shot, close-up, etc.) varies through the manipulation of a dolly or zoom lens during the recording of the interview, an editor can sometimes change the order in which the interview statements were made by cutting directly from long shot to close-up, such as when a particularly revealing statement is about to be made, to intensify the impact. In this way the basic effect of master scene shooting can be simulated during the editing process by cutting and reorganizing continuously recorded interviews. Viewer interest can be intensified further by then adding illustration materials. Similar techniques are often used with voice-over narration. Either the narration audio is edited first and then images illustrating the narrator's statements are added later, or the visuals are edited first and narration, which explains or complements the visuals, is edited and inserted later.

Aesthetics

The director's aesthetic intentions regarding combinations of images are fully realized during editing. A good editor is both a practical problem solver, who comes to grips with the limitations of the visual material that the director has provided, and a creative artist, who sometimes reshapes and improves this material through the use of imaginative editing techniques. Visual images can be combined using principles of editing derived from each of the three aesthetic orientations: realism, modernism, and postmodernism. Few editing situations are guided by one perspective alone. It is often effective to combine different approaches.

Realism

Many techniques used in classical fiction and nonfiction editing that preserve an illusion of reality are basically realist in aesthetic approach. Realist editing preserves spatial and temporal continuity from shot to shot. A smooth, unbroken flow of actions and events from one shot to the next maintains an illusion of continuity in time and space. A movement begun in one shot is completed in the next. A realist approach maintains the consistent directional placement of objects and movements in the scene by following a 180-degree axis, as discussed earlier. Directional glances must be consistent from one shot to the next. If one person is looking up at another person in a close-up, then a close-up of the latter should show him or her looking down. Point-of-view shots can be an effective means of enhancing realism and intensifying viewer involvement and identification with specific participants in a scene. Even in a documentary, point-of-view shots can create a "You are there!" feeling which adds to the illusion of reality.

Realist editing also involves eliminating mistakes and clarifying and simplifying the message content. Flubbed lines of dialogue or narration are removed and replaced. Gaps and omissions in coverage are concealed whenever possible. Some mistakes simply cannot be corrected with the material provided. An editor may need to salvage an acceptable combination of images out of bad material, but sometimes bad material simply has to be reshot by the director or eliminated entirely from the final edited version.

Cutting from a moving camera shot to a stationary shot sometimes causes editing problems. If the camera is simply tracking along with a moving subject, cutting directly from a moving camera shot to a stationary one rarely causes problems for the viewer. Cutting from one moving camera shot to another, or from one zoom shot to another moving in the same direction, is usually not a problem either, provided the speed of movement is approximately the same from shot to shot. But cutting from camera movements that are independent of subject movements to stationary camera shots often causes problems. The editor should wait until the camera movement has stopped within the shot before cutting to a stationary camera shot. Also, the use of moving camera shots tends to slow down the action in comparison with stationary camera cuts, such as from a stationary long shot to a medium shot to a close-up. Using stationary camera shots gives the editor more flexibility in terms of editing possibilities. However, moving camera shots can enhance spatial and temporal realism and provide a somewhat smoother, slower, and more deliberate pace.

Realist editing often follows basic patterns of scene construction. A scene or sequence often begins with an establishing long shot and gradually moves closer to the subject as the action intensifies to reveal more intimate details of character and setting. The overall scene and setting can be re-established with another long shot at the end of the sequence. A variation on this approach is to begin in close-up to arouse interest and attention, and then gradually use more distant shots to establish the setting and orient the viewer. Initial viewer disorientation is gradually overcome and message clarity is eventually reestablished, while interest is added to the scene.

An effective means of enhancing message clarity is to follow a logical cause-and-effect structure when combining images. In a documentary, an editor can begin with the effect or result of certain actions and then present the causes of this event. For example, an instructional sports program about how to perform a specific gymnastic routine can begin with a presentation of the completed routine and then show the type of preparation and practice that goes into perfecting it. Such a sequence can then conclude with a second version of the completed routine, highlighting the various components.

Modernism

A modernist approach to editing often deliberately disrupts spatial and temporal continuity between shots and calls attention to the editing process. Jump cuts, radical shifts in time and place, a rejection of conventional rules of scene construction, directionality, and continuity all focus the viewer's attention on the manipulative powers of the artist and his or her control of the visual medium. A modernist artist is free to experiment with unusual combinations of shots without the constraints of logical clarity or realism. But an artist is not totally free of all constraints and structure. Both aesthetic unity and patterned disruptions of unity are achieved through a conscious and precise manipulation of aesthetic forms.

Modernist approaches to editing often focus on abstract qualities and elements of design within and between shots, such as similarities and differences in shape, color, movement, and texture. Sharp diagonal lines can be juxtaposed with smooth curves and circular shapes. Visual rhythms can be established between shots that are related to audio rhythms in music and sound effects, for example. Modernist approaches to editing are often incorporated into specific sequences within more conventionally realist programming. A dream sequence in a classical Hollywood drama and a poetic sequence of natural beauty in a documentary about the environment incorporate modernist techniques into a more conventional format. Transition devices, such as a dissolve from one scene to the next, can rely on similarities in shape and color between the last shot of one scene and the first shot of the next. Deliberate breaks in temporal and spatial continuity can generate visual interest through temporary viewer disorientation in a more conventional work of fiction or nonfiction.

Postmodernism

A postmodernist approach to editing can take the form of a collage or pastiche that combines diverse images and sounds and modes of production. For example, documentary and fiction approaches to editing can be combined within a single scene. A dramatic enactment can be staged as a direct cinema interview, as in Mitch Block's *No Lies* (1974), or as a cinema verité documentary about past or even future events, as in Peter Watkins' *Culloden* (1965) and *The War Game* (1966). A documentary, such as Errol Morris' *Thin Blue Line* (1987), can edit together re-enactments of events that occurred in different interviewees'/witnesses' imaginations. Hollywood feature films, such as *JFK* (1991) and *Forrest Gump* (1994), can edit historical documents, such as the Zapruder film of John F. Kennedy's actual assassination, together with an imaginatively staged fictional drama, or in the case of the latter film, can digitally manipulate the image to place a fictional character within the frame of documentary images.

In addition to mixing modes and editing techniques, a postmodernist approach to editing can actively engage the viewer/listener in the process of constructing the art work. For example, an interactive multimedia production, such as Peter Gabriel's *Xplore* (1993), can allow the spectator to control the audio mixing or editing of various channels of his music within certain parameters determined by the project designer and computer programmers. A postmodernist approach to editing can highlight the impermanent performance aspects of a media production rather the completion of permanent perfected texts and works of art. It also encourages the participation of the spectator in the artistic process, rather than reinforcing the controlling presence of the individual artist (modernism) or the artist's transmission and preservation of the natural world or an illusion of a continuous reality (realism).

Summary

Trimming and combining visual images and sounds define the craft or mechanics of editing, but any discussion of the overall process and art of editing must begin with a consideration of editing stages, systems, modes, and aesthetic approaches. The editing process consists of at least two stages: preliminary and final editing. During preliminary editing, images and sounds are repeatedly viewed before they are trimmed and combined, usually using a copy of the original recordings to create a rough cut or off-line edited version. During final editing, the original recordings are on-line edited (video) or conformed (film) into a polished version that will actually be released to viewers and listeners.

Linear editing systems require an editor to add visual images and sounds in consecutive order from the beginning to the end of a piece. Most analog videotape and audiotape editing systems are basically linear editing systems. While traditional film rough cutting and audiotape splicing constitute nonlinear editing, new digital technologies have created much more efficient nonlinear editing systems for audio, video, and film. Nonlinear editing systems treat sounds and images in much the same way that computer word processing programs treat text. Just as written text can be highlighted and moved or removed from a document using computer word processing software, so can specific files or clips of images and sounds be moved or removed using digital nonlinear editing software. In nonlinear editing the overall duration of a production can be lengthen or shortened at any time, and images and sounds do not have to be edited in consecutive order from beginning to end.

Classical Hollywood conventions for shooting and editing fiction films and videos include master scene shooting and continuity editing. A master shot consists of a relatively long-duration shot that includes most of the action in a specific scene. Matching close-ups can be inserted into the master shot during editing. Continuity editing refers to an editing system that developed in Hollywood and elsewhere beginning about 1910. It consists of a number of shooting and editing conventions that sustain an illusion of continuous time and place within a scene.

Variations upon master scene and continuity editing techniques have also been developed that take into account the difficulties of scripting and staging nonfiction events, as well as the use of expository and rhetorical structures that can disrupt spatial and temporal continuity. A variation upon master scene shooting and editing commonly used in news and documentary production, for example, is called A and B roll editing. A and B roll editing adds viewer interest by interspersing rather static shots of a talking head with a wide variety of visual illustrations.

Visual images can be combined using principles of editing derived from each of the three aesthetic orientations: realism, modernism, and postmodernism. Many techniques used in classical fiction and nonfiction editing that preserve an illusion of reality are basically realist in aesthetic approach. Realist editing preserves spatial and temporal continuity from shot to shot. A modernist approach to editing often deliberately disrupts spatial and temporal continuity between shots and calls attention to the editing process. A postmodernist approach to editing can take the form of a collage or pastiche that combines diverse images and sounds and modes of production. In addition to mixing modes and editing techniques, a postmodernist approach actively engages the viewer/listener in the process of constructing the art work.

Additional Readings

Anderson, Gary. *Video Editing and Postproduction: A Professional Guide*. Boston: Focal Press, 1986.

Browne, Steven. *Video Editing: A Postproduction Primer*, 3rd ed. Boston: Focal Press, 1996.

Dancyger, Ken. *The Technique of Film and Video Editing*, 2nd ed. Boston: Focal Press, 1996.

Dmytryk, Edward. *On Film Editing*. Boston: Focal Press, 1985.

Ohanian, Thomas A. *Digital Nonlinear Editing: New Approaches to Editing Film and Video*. Boston: Focal Press, 1993.

Rabiger, Michael. *Directing the Documentary*, 2nd ed. Boston: Focal Press, 1992.

Reisz, Karel, and Gavin Millar. *The Technique of Film Editing*, 2nd ed. Boston: Focal Press, 1968.

Schneider, Arthur. *Electronic Post-Production Terms and Concepts*. Boston: Focal Press, 1990.

11

Visual Editing

Introduction

This chapter explores one of the most creative stages of the entire production process: the editing of prerecorded visual images. Single-camera recordings are combined and edited during postproduction. Multiple-camera visual images are often edited during actual production by routing them through a video switcher, as discussed in Chapter 6. While many of the aesthetic principles presented in Chapters 4 and 10 apply to editing during both production and postproduction, this chapter develops additional principles and techniques that are applicable to postproduction editing.

The director's aesthetic intentions regarding the succession of visual images are fully realized during editing. A good editor is both a practical problem solver who comes to grips with the limitations of the visual material that the director and cinematographer or camera operator have provided and a creative artist who sometimes reshapes and improves this material through the use of imaginative editing techniques. Visual images can be combined using principles of editing derived from each of the three aesthetic approaches discussed in the previous chapter: realism, modernism, and postmodernism. Editing decisions, of course, can be guided by more that one perspective, and it is sometimes effective to combine different aesthetic approaches. One of the editor's first tasks is to organize and catalogue all the single-camera recordings that the director has provided. The original recorded images are usually dubbed or copied before they are viewed by the editor. Using a copy protects the original recording, which can be safely stored away. Little if any material that has been rejected during actual production will be copied for viewing purposes. The copy or dub of the originally recorded images is repeatedly played back and viewed by the editor. The individual shot and take numbers recorded from the slate at the beginning of each camera take are catalogued or "logged." Time code or control track numbers are often logged at this time as well. The editor makes notations to the log, indicating particularly useful or problematic shots and camera takes. These notations are often extremely useful regardless of what technology and techniques are used to perform visual editing (Figure 11.1).

EDITING LOG

EDITING LOG DATE ________

LOCATION ________ PRODUCTION ________

CAMERA ________ REEL ________

PRODUCER ________ DIRECTOR ________ OPERATOR ________

COUNTER	TAKE	DESCRIPTION	REMARKS
00:00:30:00	1	WS-Establishing	Poor pan
00:01:20:13	2	"	Car in BG
00:02:40:28	3	"	Good take
00:04:20:10	1	2-Shot	Bad sound
00:04:50:10	2	"	Good take
00:05:20:15	1	CU-Sam	Framing
00:06:20:15	2	"	Tilt,poor
00:07:20:15	3	"	Delivery
00:08:20:15	4	"	Pix -OK, PoorSound
00:09:20:15	5	"	Good take

Figure 11.1 An editing log can be kept by either the director or production continuity clerk of a production. The log indicates precise location of takes, the description of the shot, and a judgment or notation of the take so that the editor will have some guidance as to which takes to consider during the editing process.

One of the best uses of a catalogued list of the individual shots and camera takes that were recorded during production is for the editor to perform a paper edit. During a paper edit an editor simulates the editing process on paper by cutting out each individual shot in a log and placing these shots in the anticipated sequential order of the completed project. Performing a paper edit is an effective method of determining whether or not there is sufficient coverage to complete the editing process. It is also an efficient and economical means of manipulating the overall structure of a media production on paper without incurring the expense and labor of actually editing the recorded images themselves. Documentary editors, who rarely have access to an extremely detailed script as a guide to postproduction, often rely upon a paper edit to help them organize the editing process.

Editing Technology and Techniques

Three different types of editing technology and techniques are discussed in this chapter: digital nonlinear editing and conventional videotape and film editing. Although digital nonlinear technology offers certain advantages in terms of editing flexibility and efficiency, all three editing technologies continue to be widely used in media postproduction.

Digital Nonlinear Editing

Digitizing or Capturing Video

Digital nonlinear editing begins with the digitization of the original videotape recordings. Because digitizing video requires tremendous information storage capacity, only those shots and takes that are very likely to be used during editing are likely to be digitized using a computer board or card. A digitizing or capture card or board consists of hardware that rapidly samples electrical signals during videotape playback. These signals carry analog video and audio information, and the capture board converts them to digital information. Capturing video and audio signals requires fairly sophisticated hardware and considerable information storage capacity, especially when high quality images and sounds must be digitized (Figure 11.2).

Computer storage units range from bits to gigabytes. A bit is the smallest amount of information a computer can handle. Eight bits make up a byte, 1000 bytes equal a kilobyte (kB), 1,000,000 bytes equal a megabyte (MB), and 1,000,000,000 bytes equal a gigabyte (GB). It takes slightly less than 1 MB to store just one full frame of video information. A full frame of digital video consists

Figure 11.2
A non-linear editing station consists of a series of monitors for viewing and hearing the material being edited and a computer to store and manipulate the footage. The footage is not actually cut and spliced, but stored in the computer memory in the order determined by the editor. Changes may be made quickly, easily, and many times over without damaging the original footage. Once the final edits are satisfactory, the final production can be fed out to either film or videotape for distribution.

of 640 pixels horizontal by 480 pixels vertical, or a total of 307,200 pixels (640 × 480) multiplied by 24 bits of color (307,200 × 24 = 7,372,800 bits/8 bits per byte = 921,600 bytes or approximately 1 MB per frame).

During digitization each NTSC analog video frame, which consists of two interlaced scanning fields that add up to 525 scan lines, is converted to a frame of 640 × 480 pixels that can be displayed in a non-interlaced mode on a computer monitor. As mentioned earlier in Chapter 6, there are almost 30 (actually 29.97) video frames in each second of NTSC video, so it requires almost 28 MB to store just one second of full frame (640 × 480 pixels at 24 bit color), full motion (30 frames per second) video. Consequently, just one minute of full frame, full motion video would require a storage capacity of 60 (seconds) × 28 MB, or about 1680 MB (or 1.68 GB), which is a significant amount of storage space. Sixty minutes of full frame, full motion video would require a whopping 100 GBs of storage space. Most home computers have internal hard disk drives that provide 2 GB or less of storage space, and some professional editing systems use a 9+ GB hard disk drive. Obviously some way to reduce the amount of storage space is usually required, especially for editing longer duration projects (Figure 11.3).

DIGITAL MEASUREMENTS

Bit = 1/8 Byte	8 Bits = 1 Byte
Byte = 1/1,000 Kilobyte (KB)	1,000 Bytes = 1 KB
KB= 1/1,000,000 Megabyte (MB)	1,000,000 KB= 1 MB
MB= 1/1,000,000,000 Gigabyte (GB)	1,000,000,000 MB= 1 GB

Video frame requires nearly 1 MB

Pixel = smallest element of a picture

Video frame = 640 horizontal pixels x 480 vertical pixels = 307,200 pixels

Color video frame =307,200 pixels x 24 bits of color =7,372,800 bites or 921,600 bytes

1 Second of video = 30 frames = 28 MB of memory

1 Minute of video = 1680 MB or 1.68 GB of memory

60 minutes of video = 100 GB of memory

Most consumer computer hard drives are limited to less than 1 GB of memory

Professional computers require increased amounts of memory for non-linear editing

Figure 11.3 The relationships between the measurements of the digital world are all based on the metric system. The amount of memory required for a specific amount of video or film depends on the compression system used. The amount of memory available in computers increases continually as the price continues to drop.

The most common forms of storage space reduction used in digital nonlinear editing are compression, frame size reduction, and frame rate reduction. *Compression* refers to a reduction of the volume of information in order to force it into less storage space. Basically compression reduces the amount of information that must be stored in an individual frame or still image by ignoring some pixel and color information during storage and then duplicating adjacent pixels and colors when the image is displayed during playback. Compression can also be achieved in motion video by storing only the pixels and colors that change from one frame to the next, and then duplicating stationary pixels and colors in subsequent frames during playback.

The volume of information can be reduced in still or motion images by using hardware and software compression, such as Digital Video Interactive (DVI), Joint Photographic Experts Group (JPEG), and Moving Picture Experts Group (MPEG). DVI is sometimes used for interactive multimedia, since it supports both still images and motion video, and it can be operated in two modes: presentation-level video (PLV) and real-time video (RTV). PLV is widely distributed on CD-ROM, while RTV is used in digital nonlinear editing. JPEG uses intraframe (within a single frame) compression to reduce the volume of information for each frame of video independently of every other frame and is frequently used for still photographs, but it can also be used for motion. MPEG is used exclusively for motion images since it involves both intraframe and interframe (between successive frames) compression. RTV, JPEG, and MPEG compression are all applicable to digital nonlinear editing.

Compression is usually indicated in terms of ratios, such as 2:1, 10:1, or 15:1. If it requires 1680 MBs of space to store a minute of full frame, full motion video, then a 2:1 compression ratio would require 840 MBs of storage space, a 10:1 compression ratio would require 168 MBs, and a 15:1 compression ratio would need only 112 MB of storage space. Why not use a 15:1 compression ratio all the time? The answer, of course, is that the quality of the images usually deteriorates as the compression ratio increases. The best compression, that is, the least reduction in the quality of images, is usually achieved through a combination of hardware and software compression, rather than through software compression alone.

Storage space can also be reduced by reducing the frame size and frame rates of digitized images. For example, instead of editing full frame video (640 × 480 pixels), an editor can work with quarter-frame images (160 × 120 pixels). At some point reductions in frame size begin to affect image clarity and visibility. For example, it may be difficult for an editor to see clearly when the frame size of video images has been reduced from 640 × 480 to 160 × 120 pixels, or when images have been compressed by a 15:1 ratio. By the same token, a frame rate of 15 frames per second requires half the storage space as a frame rate of 30 frames per second, but again, the images may seem to flicker or strobe at reduced frame rates, such as when motion video is digitized at 10 or 15 frames per second rates. So an editor must decide what compression ratio, frame size, and frame rate she or he finds most comfortable and effective while working within the storage capacity limitations of a particular nonlinear editing system. An editor should also allow considerable time to digitize images, since images are frequently digitized in real time, that is, it takes as much time to digitize images as the duration of the original recordings, and in some cases, more time.

Digital Nonlinear Editing Hardware

Most digital nonlinear editing systems employ computer hardware that is capable of processing and storing vast amounts of visual and audio information. In addition to a video and audio capture card, discussed earlier, a nonlinear editing system usually includes a computer processing unit (CPU) with a 60+ megahertz (MHz) processing system, 30+ MB of random access memory (RAM), a keyboard, a mouse, one or two computer monitors, an NTSC television monitor, a videotape recorder, an amplifier and loudspeakers, and a 2+ GB hard disk drive designed for audio visual (AV) use. Many professional nonlinear editing systems include a 100+ MHz processing system, 50+ MB of RAM, a 9+ GB hard disk drive, and a high quality videotape recorder featuring SMPTE time code. Some professional editing systems can be used for on-line editing, that is, they can be used to complete the entire postproduction process, including video and audio editing, as well as adding graphics and special effects. These top-of-the-line systems employ a video capture card that is capable of digitizing and then "printing to video" on-line or broadcast quality NTSC video (Figure 11.4).

Digital Nonlinear Editing Software

Digital nonlinear editing software offers several advantages over conventional means of editing film, audiotape, and videotape, including increased flexibility or creativity, as well as potential time and cost savings. A common cliché is that digital nonlinear editing is the equivalent of word processing and desktop publishing for

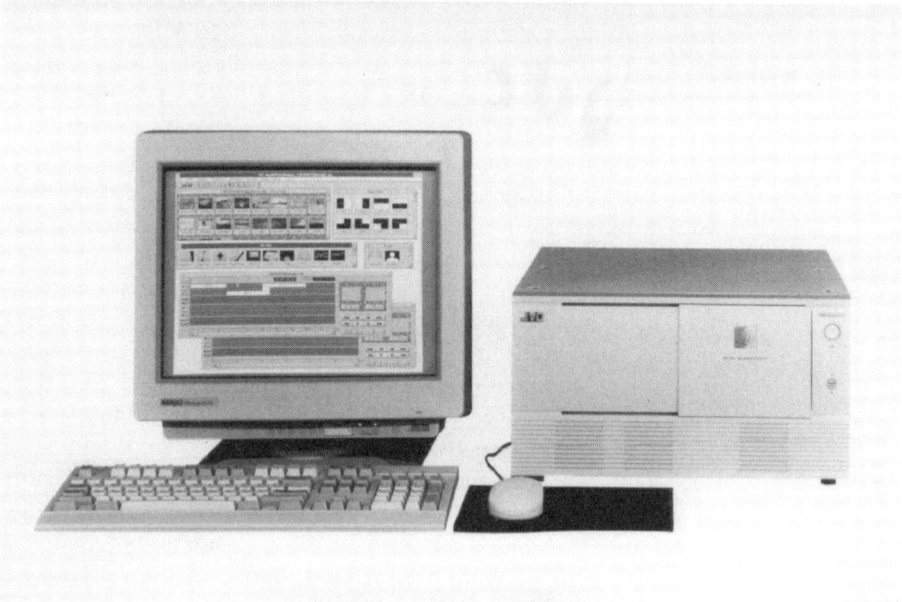

Figure 11.4 The screen of a non-linear editor reveals the types of transitions available, the segments available to edit, the sound in visual form, time code information, and running times of the production. Depending on the brand and model of editor other characterstics of controls also may be visible on the screen. (Courtesy of Scitex Digital Video.)

audio, film, and video postproduction. The analogy holds for many aspects of editing that are shared by word processing and various digital nonlinear editing software programs. For example, most word processing software allows a writer to cut, copy, paste, and delete words, paragraphs, and pages of text. Digital nonlinear editing affords an editor similar flexibility in terms of instantaneously changing the order and duration of sounds and images. For example, clips of video or audio information can be cut, trimmed, copied, pasted, inserted, and deleted along a timeline.

A *clip* is usually the smallest unit of digital video (or audio) information that can be stored and manipulated during editing. It can range from just one frame to an entire movie in duration, but it often consists of a single shot, that is, a continuous camera recording or take. Digitized clips are usually imported (or copied) into a particular editing project file, where they are edited along a timeline with other images and sounds. Most editing software provides several windows or screens, including a project window, a timeline (or construction) window, a trimming window, a transition window, and a locking window. Different windows can usually be displayed simultaneously on one or more computer monitors. A project window usually contains the individual clips in alphabetical order based on the first letters of their written descriptions.

The timeline or construction window, displays a timeline that contains several video, audio, transition, and superimposition or special effects tracks and indicates the overall duration and order of the edited project. The trimming window is used for cutting directly (e.g., a straight cut) from one clip to the next. It usually displays the adjoining frames at the cut point between the two clips, allowing the editor to trim off video frames and/or add additional video frames from one or both clips on the timeline. A transition window displays dissolves and wipes that can be dragged or copied into the transition track of the timeline window wherever two separate video tracks overlap and a transition (other than a straight cut) from the first to the second clip is needed. Finally, a locking window allows the editor to lock together or unlock various visual and audio tracks in the timeline window, so that they can be cut and trimmed collectively or individually.

Images from each motion video clip are often displayed as a series of representative still frames along the timeline, while audio is often displayed visually as a continuous, variable area sound track, where high peaks represent loud sounds and rapid fluctuations indicate high frequency sounds. Clips can be copied and inserted at various points along the timeline, and they can also be deleted from the timeline and the remaining images and sounds attached to one another. Motion video and still frame clips can also be placed in preliminary order using a storyboard display that presents one frame from each clip. A storyboard allows an editor to place the clips in rough sequential order prior to trimming precise cut points and adding various transition devices in the timeline window.

Every edit made using a digital nonlinear software program is usually a virtual edit. No digitized material is discarded when clips are trimmed, cut, or deleted along an editing timeline, since each clip is usually stored separately outside the timeline window. Every clip stored on a disk drive is instantaneously accessible in its entirety and can be grabbed in the project or clip window and reinserted at any point along the timeline. Many alternative versions of a scene or sequence can thus be quickly edited and examined without prematurely eliminating material that may be needed later. Transitions from one shot to another can be previewed, as can the superimposition of titles and various digital video effects without ever actually cutting, discarding, eliminating, or deleting any originally digitized video or audio.

The ability to manipulate clips of video and sound along a timeline not only adds flexibility to the editing process, it can also make editing more efficient and cost effective. Clips can be very rapidly trimmed, cut, inserted, and deleted. Digital nonlinear editing is extremely fast compared to physically cutting and splicing a conventional feature film, for example, and the time it takes to find and insert videotape images and sounds from a source onto a master videotape can be dramatically reduced by using instantaneously accessible digital clips along a timeline. The amount of time scheduled for postproduction editing can be significantly diminished, facilitating the editing of projects that require a short turnaround time, such as topical newsmagazine segments and mini-documentaries. Increased editing efficiency can also translate into cost savings that affect the overall budget of longer term projects, when an editor's time and salary can be reduced. Clearly, digital nonlinear editing offers a number of advantages in terms of flexibility and efficiency over conventional videotape and film editing.

Videotape Editing

Videotape editing is usually divided into two stages: off-line editing and on-line editing. The difference between these two stages is most clear in large-scale productions, where final editing is eventually performed using a broadcast quality format, such as D-1, D-2, D-3, D-5, BetaSP, or 1-inch videotape. These original recordings are often dubbed or transferred to a smaller format for off-line editing. This preserves the original recordings while allowing an editor some flexibility to edit and re-edit materials without jeopardizing the quality of the final product. Each duplication of a videotape diminishes the quality of the recorded images and sounds. This is why off-line editing is often done in a smaller format, and off-line editing decisions are later performed on an originally recorded larger format videotape. Off-line editing decisions can be used to guide on-line editing of the larger format videotape. Digital nonlinear editing can also be used for off-line editing. In either case, SMPTE time code numbers at the beginning and end of each shot form an edit decision list or EDL that can be fed into a computer to guide the on-line editing of original videotapes that have the same time code numbers.

Assemble Editing

After cataloguing all the shots that have been recorded, the editor organizes the shots she or he is likely to use into the rough order of the sequence specified in the final shooting script. The editor basically follows the script and selects the best takes of each shot, leaving a five second preroll at the beginning of each camera take, which will allow the videotape to be "up to speed" (precise edits cannot be made from a stationary videotape) when subsequent frame accurate edits will be made.

Assemble editing is only used to place the shots in rough sequential order, since it does not provide sufficient editing control to edit exactly from one shot to the next. During assemble editing, both the control track and the visual images from the original recording are transferred to the new assemble-edited version (Figure 11.5).

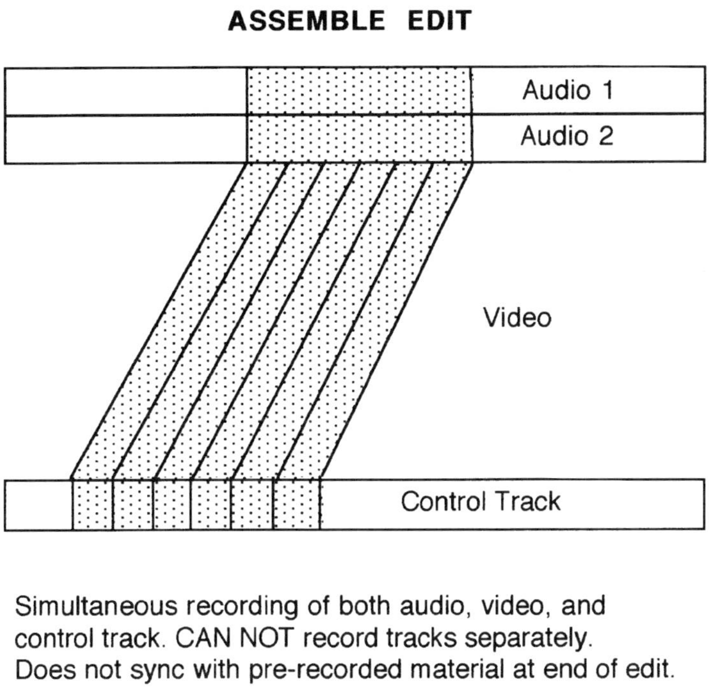

Figure 11.5 A video assemble edit involves editing all of the tracks simultaneously: control track, all audio tracks, and the video track. An assemble edit may be made on videotape stock that has not had a signal recorded on it previously, but at the end of the edit, the control track stops requiring another assemble edit to be added, not an insert edit.

Any discontinuities in the control track over instantaneous cuts (e.g., no five second preroll) from one shot to the next could cause problems in synchronization and tracking during the playback of an assemble-edited videotape. High quality, instantaneous cuts from one shot to the next are simply not possible. Inconsistencies in the control track may cause the picture to roll or jump at edit points. Assemble-edited rough cuts cannot be tightened up later in spots without possibly going through the entire editing process a second time, but the main advantage of assemble editing is that it allows an editor to efficiently organize vast amounts of material into a very rough sequential order. Editing decisions can be gradually refined and tightened up during insert editing. An editor should not limit choices too early in the editing process, but rather leave room for various alternative possibilities before deciding on the final form.

Insert Editing

Insert editing (Figure 11.6) allows for precise, instantaneous cutting from one videotape shot to the next.

During insert editing the control track from the original recording is not transferred to the edited videotape. Instead, the entire edited videotape is prerecorded with a continuous black signal and constant control track. Specific shots and visual images can then be inserted into the black signal, and playback rate and synchroni-

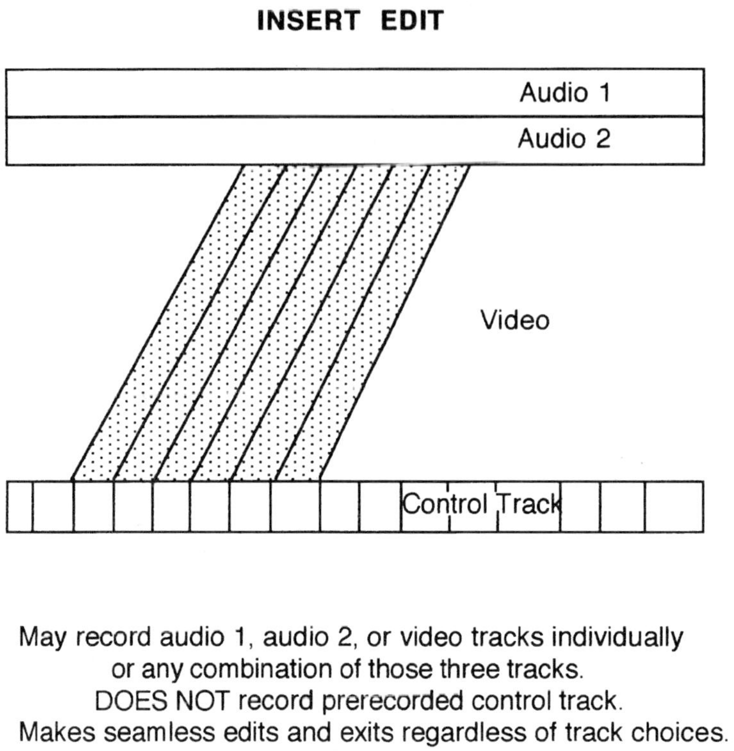

Figure 11.6 A video insert edit provides the editor with the flexibility to add or change either audio track or the video track independently or simultaneously. A continuous control track must have been recorded before attempting an insert edit by laying down continuous color bars, a black sync signal, or previously recorded video. (Courtesy of JVC.)

zation is governed by this constant control track. Thus there will be no gap or mismatch in control tracks from one shot to the next during insert editing. In addition to the prerecorded black signal and control track, insert editing usually begins with the prerecording of such information as the tape title; color bars, which are reference bands of colors, including black and white; and a timing or countdown leader, which is a sequential series of numbers of time in seconds used for prerolling the videotape. The first shot is inserted after two seconds of black following the number two on the timing leader.

Insert editing allows for considerable editing flexibility compared with assemble editing. A major advantage of insert editing over assemble editing is that a portion of one shot can be replaced by another shot. For example, a complete master shot can be recorded first, and then matching close-ups and cutaways can be inserted within it later. A talking head, for example, can be replaced with images showing what that person is talking about. During insert editing, video-only and audio-only edits can be made, as well as video-plus-audio edits. A portion of the video image can be removed and replaced, while leaving the accompanying audio intact. In the example cited earlier, the speaker's voice continues and the picture is simply replaced with visuals depicting what is being described. If replacement images require additional sound, a separate track will have to be used on the edited videotape. Audio-only inserts, such as specific sound effects, music, or narration, can be inserted where they are needed to accompany the visuals.

Off-Line Videotape Editing Systems

An editing system designed for off-line or preliminary editing usually allows an editor to perform both assemble and insert edits, video-only or audio-only edits, and video-and-audio edits. Off-line editing systems rarely allow for special effects and transitions other than straight cuts from shot to shot. An off-line editing system has three basic components: two VCRs and an edit control unit. One VCR, called a *source,* is used to play a prerecorded videotape; the second, called a *record,* is used to record an edited version of the prerecorded material. The edit control unit is an electronic device that allows the operator to select edit points and to transfer images and sounds from the source VCR to the record VCR. The edit control unit locks the two VCRs together, relying on the videotape control tracks and the servomechanisms in each machine to synchronize the playback and record movements of the two videotapes. If the two videotapes are not synchronized, there will be a gap or mismatch in the video tracking of the recording between two successive shots. One shot might begin somewhere in midframe, such as halfway down the scanning of the image, and the next might begin somewhere else in the scanning of the screen. If two successive shots are not in phase with one another, the image will temporarily flip or break up on the screen when the recording is played back. This problem is similar to that encountered in assemble editing when there is a discontinuity in the control track from shot to shot.

The edit control unit has jog and shuttle controls linked to the source and record VCRs. A *jog control* allows the editor to move a videotape one frame at a time, while a *shuttle control* allows a number of frames of videotape to be moved while the editor searches for the best edit point. Using these controls, the editor locates and still-frames the edit points on the two videotapes. The edit *in-point* on the source videotape is the first frame of the shot following the cut, while the edit in-point on the record videotape is the last frame in the shot preceding the cut. An *out-point,* where the shot to be inserted will end, is usually set by the editor from either the source videotape or the record videotape, but not both, since the edit controller automatically determines the out-point of the other. The edit controller will also automatically preroll the two videotapes the same number of frames in front of the two edit points (usually five seconds), so that they will reach the two edit points simultaneously when the two machines are started at the same time. Most edit controllers allow the editor to preview the cut before it is actually made so that essential material on the record videotape is not accidentally erased and replaced by the material on the source videotape. Once the cut has been previewed, it is a simple matter to actually record the new shot by depressing the edit button. When the precise out-point cannot be known until a subsequent shot will be edited to it, the editor can simply select an out-point that is a safe distance beyond where the next edit point is likely to occur (Figure 11.7).

When making a videotape edit, it is usually wise to examine the audio and video meters on the record machine during the edit preview to make sure that

Figure 11.7 An off-line editor controller controls tape decks of quality lower than the original or final format. In many cases it is a cuts-only editor rather than an editor that allows dissolves or other effects. An off-line editor may become an on-line editor if it is used to control the highest quality level desired by the producer.

maximum video and audio levels and signal-to-noise ratios have been achieved during the video or audio dubbing. Weak video or audio signals will produce poor quality recordings. Some VCRs have automatic gain controls (AGC), which keep the video and audio signals at constant levels, but it is usually preferable to set and adjust these levels manually. A *peak audio limiter* prevents extremely loud sounds from distorting without boosting background sounds. In addition to the audio and video signal meters and controls, the VCR's tracking meter should also be monitored and adjusted for peak reading for every dub to ensure that proper synchronization and speed is being maintained throughout the dubbing process.

On-Line Editing

Once all the editing decisions have been finalized, the original videotapes are edited in conformity to the off-line edited version, using the Edit Decision List or EDL. On-line editing is usually performed using D-1, D-2, D-3, D-5, BetaSP, or 1-inch videotape. On-line editing often involves special editing devices, such as time-base correctors, SMPTE time code, and computerized editing controls, as well as a digital effects generator, which is discussed in Chapter 4.

Time-Base Corrector

The time-base corrector (TBC) is a device that stabilizes pictures from a videotape recorder. Extremely accurate digital TBCs modify the video signal so that is can be significantly corrected and stabilized. A TBC improves and stabilizes the tracking of a videotape with mediocre sync, replacing it with entirely new and improved sync when the composite video signal (sync plus picture information) passes through it, but it cannot improve a videotape that refuses to track properly on a playback VCR. A TBC can also be used to prepare a small-format videotape for broadcast.

Time Code

A time code is a series of digits that provides an exact reference for each frame. One of the most widely used time codes has been standardized as the SMPTE (Society of Motion Pictures and Television Engineers) time code. It is sometimes added to one of the tracks of the originally recorded videotape, or it is recorded during the vertical intervals between video fields. It consists of an eight-digit series of numbers beginning with either zero (called *zero start*) or with actual clock time in hours, minutes, seconds, and fields (sixty per second). Thus, 01:00:00:01 indicates a point one hour and one field into the recording. Separate cassettes or reels of videotape can be differentiated by hours: 01, 02, and so on. The SMPTE time-code system requires a special generator and reader. The time code can actually be viewed in the video image as "burn-in" time code, which can be helpful during off-line editing, especially when using machines that cannot otherwise read time code, to make editing notations, because the code is actually recorded in the picture area of the videotape.

Many off-line editing systems use an alternative form of editing reference, known as *control track*. During control track editing, a counter displays each frame by simply counting the sync pulses in the control track of the original videotape, beginning at whatever point the counter is zeroed. The frame count is not recorded on the videotape but is calculated by the editing control unit from a specific point where the counter is zeroed. Control track numbers are not as useful in terms of translating preliminary editing to final editing as SMPTE time code because they are not recorded on the videotape. Both types of notation can be addressed for electronic editing purposes, but SMPTE time code is much more reliable and accurate because it does not depend on monitoring control track pulses, which can themselves be somewhat irregular. Most control track editing systems are not frame accurate, that is, they are only accurate to 2 frames before or after the edit point.

Computer-Assisted Time Code Editing

Videotapes can be on-line edited using a computer after the SMPTE time code reference numbers for each shot or effect have been determined and fed into the computer. The computer will assemble the entire videotape, when it is properly programmed with the time code reference numbers for the ending and beginning points of each shot in its proper sequence. During on-line editing, several playback machines are connected to the computer control unit so that they can be fed to the master record tape. The computer efficiently records each shot in its proper sequence in the videotape in one of two ways: either by assembling shots from each different recorder in sequence, or by dubbing shots in the sequence in which they were originally recorded to their designated spots on the master record tape. The EDL (as shown in Figure 10.2), which was created by off-line editing, can be used on-line to guide the editing process. While minor adjustments may be needed during on-line editing, the creative part of the editing process is usually accomplished off-line, since on-line editing time is often very expensive. A fully outfitted computerized videotape editing and special effects facility, which can cost over $1 million, is too expensive for many producers to purchase for their own exclusive use. Many producers rent a computerized editing facility by the hour, often paying more than $500 per hour for equipment and personnel time. Obviously these cost levels usually prohibit the use of such facilities for creative experimentation.

Computerized Videotape Editing System

There are many different brands and types of computerized editing systems, including Sony BVE and CMX (Consolidated Film Industries and Memorex). Both systems use SMPTE time code numbers for reference and allow all of the edit points to be programmed into a computer, which automatically drives several VTRs. When creating a series of special effect transitions, such as a succession of dissolves, using a computerized editing facility, the edit controller starts several (at least two) tapes simultaneously, so that they are synchronized as they enter the special effects generator or switcher. A minimum of three VCRs or VTRs are required, since at least two source machines and one record machine are involved, although more source machines can be added.

An electronic special effects switcher, an analog special effects generator (SEG), or a digital video effects generator (DVE) is often used in postproduction editing to generate special effects, such as dissolves, wipes, fades, split screens, and graphics and titles from a character generator or computer animation machine (the latter two can be added with a downstream keyer, that is, to a keying device that changes the video signal after it has left the switcher). In order to produce dissolves, wipes, and split screens, two videotapes must be played back simultaneously using an editing control unit. The two VCRs must be connected to TBCs for accurate synchronization. All of these special effects can then be produced on the effects buses in the same manner that they are created during live or live-on-tape production switching. The output of the switcher is then fed to a master videotape recorder. Fade-outs and fade-ins require that constant black be fed to the switcher, as is the case in a live or live-on-tape production. Graphics can be keyed into the image using various types of keys or a downstream keyer into which a character-generated or computer-animated image can be fed. The presence of the switcher, a video synthesizer, an SEG, and/or a DVE in a computerized editing system allows many different special effects to be created. A variety of wipes, fades, dissolves, and key effects can be accomplished automatically on a postproduction switcher.

A video synthesizer can manipulate an analog video in ways that are similar to digital effects generated by a DVE. That is, it can convert the component parts of a video signal, such as each color, into separate electrical signals that can be modified by a computer programmer. The height, width, depth, shape, clarity, or position of an image can be changed by turning a dial or flipping a switch. *Solarization* is a technique that relies on a separation between luminance and chrominance information in a video signal. The color can be drained out of the image to produce a high contrast black-and-white image, which can then be synthetically colored by assigning different colors to different shades of gray.

Digital video signal processing devices convert the analog video signal into a digital one by using a numerical code and rapid sampling techniques. The digitally coded signal is easier to store and manipulate than an analog one, and image quality is not lost in dubbing. It is possible to create a wide variety of special effects using digital devices, such as a digital video effects (DVE) or a digital video manipulator (DVM). An image or full frame can be continuously compressed to a point of light. It can be expanded, stretched, freeze-framed, pushed-off or on, made into an abstract paintinglike image, and replicated as multiple images on a screen. The DVE or DVM can also be connected to the video switcher to create automatic chroma key tracking in which the size of the chroma key window can be automatically shaped and positioned. The inserted picture can be proportionately compressed and expanded to fill the window more efficiently and realistically than can conventional chroma key, especially when the main signal camera is tracking or moving, and thereby changing chroma key perspective. These kinds of digital effects can provide an editor with tremendous flexibility in terms of image manipulation during on-line editing (Figure 11.8).

Figure 11.8 A digital effects generator creates a variety of effects not possible with an analog switcher or effects generator. Visible on the screen are a few of the effects possible. (Courtesy of Sony Corporation.)

Film Editing

Film editing follows a series of stages similar to videotape editing, from rough cutting, the equivalent of off-line videotape editing that includes viewing a copy of the originally recorded images, called the *workprint, rushes,* or *dailies,* and selecting and ordering specific shots and scenes, to conforming the original film to the edited workprint and answer printing, which are equivalent in some ways to on-line videotape editing. Unlike videotape editing, however, traditional film editing usually involves mechanical processes, such as physically cutting and splicing the film. Film images can also be transferred to videotape and digitized so that they can be off-line edited electronically, but at some point the original film must be cut if a film prints are going to be made in a film laboratory and projected in a movie theater.

Electronic versus Mechanical Editing

The choice between electronic and mechanical film editing can be a complex one. It is important for film producers who want to be broadly based to acquire electronic and mechanical editing skills, since both technologies are widely used in production. Each technology has inherent advantages and disadvantages, which must be recognized before an intelligent choice between them or a decision to combine them can be made. In comparison with electronic videotape editing, mechanical film editing can seem quite laborious and time consuming, but this is not always the case. For example, it is much simpler to shorten or lengthen an entire film by a few frames during preliminary editing than it is to shorten or lengthen a videotape. An edited videotape cannot be shortened or lengthened without re-editing the entire recording from that point on. Of course, this problem does not affect digital nonlinear editing, which is very similar to, although also much more efficient than, traditional film editing. As a result, digital nonlinear editing is rapidly becoming the preferred method of off-line film editing or rough cutting. Whether he or she uses traditional mechanical techniques of rough cutting or digital nonlinear editing techniques, a film editor has a great deal of freedom to experiment with a variety of different takes and shot sequences and durations at all stages of the editing process until the conforming stage.

Screening the Workprint

A film copy made from the originally recorded film is called a *workprint.* During production the film director usually specifies which camera takes should be printed, and these selections are noted on the camera report that is sent to the film laboratory (Figure 11.9).

This information is the transferred to a lab report sheet. Because workprinting is expensive, only takes that are likely to be used during editing will actually be workprinted. The editor, director, and producer view each day's workprint, called the *dailies,* in order to evaluate how well things are going. After viewing and approving the footage, the editor catalogues it before beginning a rough cut. An editor will often view the dailies over and over again to get a feel for the production and to stimulate ideas about how images can and should be combined. Sometimes the original film is immediately transferred to videotape and digitized for viewing and editing purposes.

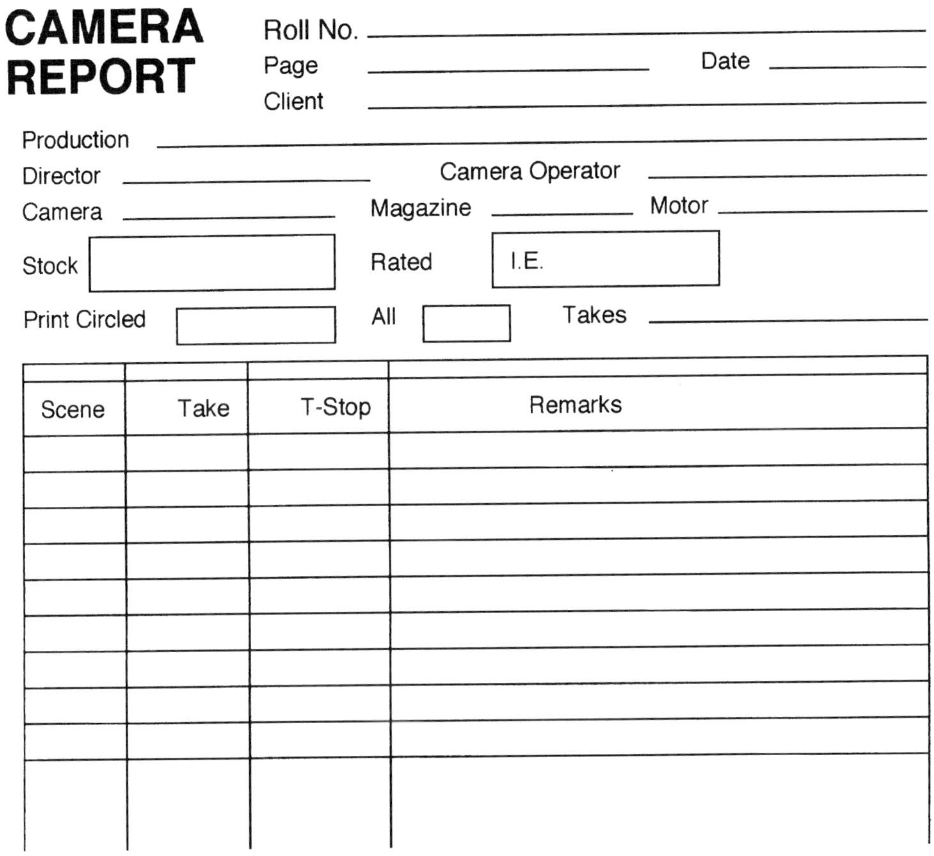

CAMERA REPORT

Roll No. ______
Page ______ Date ______
Client ______

Production ______
Director ______ Camera Operator ______
Camera ______ Magazine ______ Motor ______
Stock [ ] Rated [I.E.]
Print Circled [ ] All [ ] Takes ______

Scene	Take	T-Stop	Remarks

Figure 11.9 A camera report form lists all of the pertinent information that the laboratory needs to know to properly process the film that it describes. The form indicates which takes are to be printed and comments the editor may need to have while editing the work print.

Assemble Editing

The next stage of preliminary editing is to assemble the individual shots into sequential order. Since films are often shot out of continuity, that is, all shots from one location are recorded at the same time, regardless of when they occur in the script, the editor must assemble the shots into the order specified by the script. During the assemble stage of editing, the entire shot is left intact. As the rough cut progresses and each shot is placed in its proper sequential order, the editor gradually refines the cuts, cutting out all extraneous or unnecessary material. Unused shots are called *out-takes.* They are often left on the original camera rolls. The pieces removed from the shots that are actually used are called *trims.* They are frequently stored on the pegs of a trim bin, which is placed near the editing bench. Trims are sometimes spliced back into the film after an editor has tried a specific cut, usually because the cut does not work quite as well as was anticipated. It is therefore unwise to dispose of trims too soon.

Synchronizing the Dailies

The recording and editing of film sound is usually kept physically separate from the recording of film images. Film sound is normally recorded on DAT audiotape, which can be synchronized with the film recorded in a camera, as was described earlier in Chapter 8. The audiotape is transferred to magnetic film so that it can be edited in synchronization with the accompanying pictures. One of the first tasks of film editing is to sync up the film visuals with their corresponding sounds so that the workprint can be screened. This is accomplished by finding a common starting point, such as the visual and audio marker at the beginning of each shot provided by a clapstick. Once the visual image of the closing clapstick or slate is linked up with the "clap" sound, the entire shot will be in proper synchronization. The editor cuts together all of the shots in this manner so that they can be screened by the director, producer, and cinematographer while production is still in progress. The editor screens and carefully catalogues this material while preparing for the rough cut (Figure 11.10).

Rough Cutting

Rough cutting usually begins with the selection of a master shot containing virtually all the action occurring in one scene. The editor then attempts to insert various matching medium shots and close-ups into the master shot, and he or she gradually trims the shots and refines the edit points throughout the rough cutting process. An editor must be careful to remove equivalent amounts of picture and sound

Figure 11.10 A flat bed film editor allows the operator to work with two sound tracks and the picture track simultaneously viewing the picture on the screen in front of him. The tracks can be adjusted to sync with the picture while editing.

when trimming a shot, or the film and sound will no longer be in perfect synchronization. If four frames of picture are removed, four frames of sound must be removed. However, an editor can also manipulate the sound track to advantage without completely losing sync. For example, the sound from one shot can be overlapped with the picture of a subsequent shot. The sound accompanying the subsequent shot is spliced into the sound track in midshot after trimming off a portion of its beginning equivalent in length to the overlap from the previous shot. Synchronous sound effects can be spliced into an existing synchronous sound track or added to a second sound track, and later mixed with the primary synchronous sound track. When additional sound tracks have been added, the editor must then cut out or add in equivalent amounts on all the tracks wherever a general change is made.

Tape Splicing

A tape splicer allows the editor to cut photographic and magnetic film and splice the pieces together with tape. The teeth in the splicer hold the film in precise registration so that accurate, frame-line cuts can be made. The tape is placed on both sides of motion picture film, but only on one side (the base or shiny side) of magnetic film, so that it does not affect the sound track. If film images are taped on

Figure 11.11 After each roll of sound track has been edited together, they are threaded onto individual fullcoat players. All players are locked together with the picture threaded onto a synchronized projector. All of the sound is fed through a mixing board and the operator combines the tracks into one or more final sound tracks on a fullcoat recorder. The conformed film and mixed tracks are sent to the lab where they are combined into a release print for the clients approval.

both sides, they will form a proper loop as they run through the projector gate and thus avoid jamming or breaking. There are a variety of tape splicers and types of splicing tape available. Some are called *guillotine splicers,* because they cut the tape and punch out the sprocket holes when the editor depresses the handle. Other tape splicers use preperforated splicing tape, which must be carefully aligned with the sprocket holes. Regardless of which type of splicer is used, it is important to make sure that all of the sprocket holes are clear of tape, so that the film can be driven properly by the sprocket teeth in a projector. Straight frame-line cuts are usually made on the picture film, while a diagonal splice or cut line is often used with magnetic film to suppress popping sounds when the magnetic film passes over a head and to reduce head wear.

Head Leaders

Film editing begins with the construction of picture and sound head leaders, which are needed to thread up the film on a projector (Figure 11.12).

The leaders identify the film by title and provide a common start (X) mark for picture and sound. A timing countdown, such as a standard academy leader, normally begins with the number 10 at ten seconds prior to the film's beginning and ends on the number 2, with an accompanying beep on the sound track, indicating 2 seconds to the start of the film. An opaque black leader appears after the last number of the academy leader, and the film screen is then black for two seconds

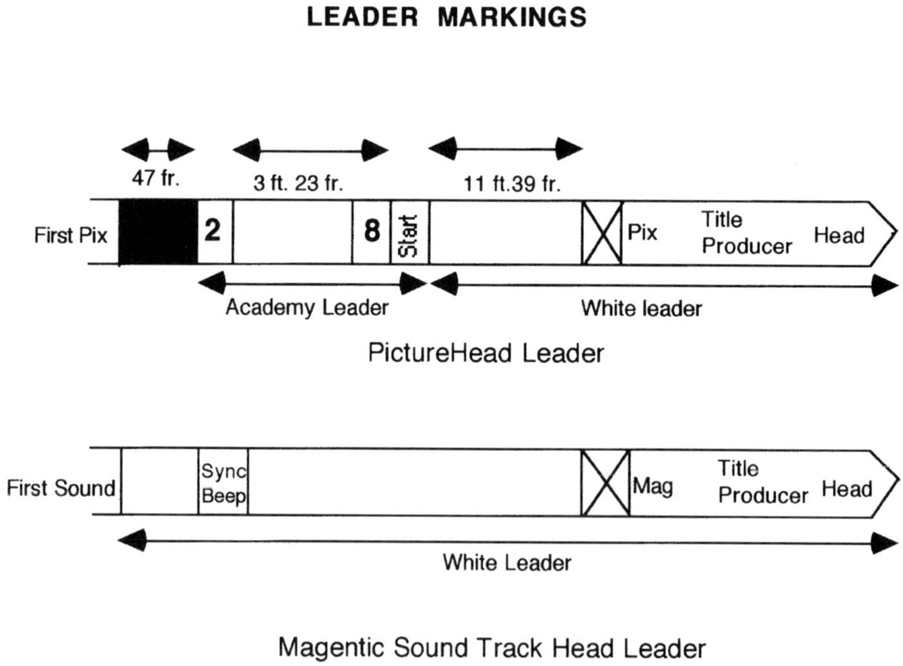

Figure 11.12 Leader markings are standardized by the film processing industry, but each lab may vary the markings for their own purposes. The magnetic full coat and all picture rolls must have leaders spliced to exactly the same length to maintain sound synchronization during the printing process.

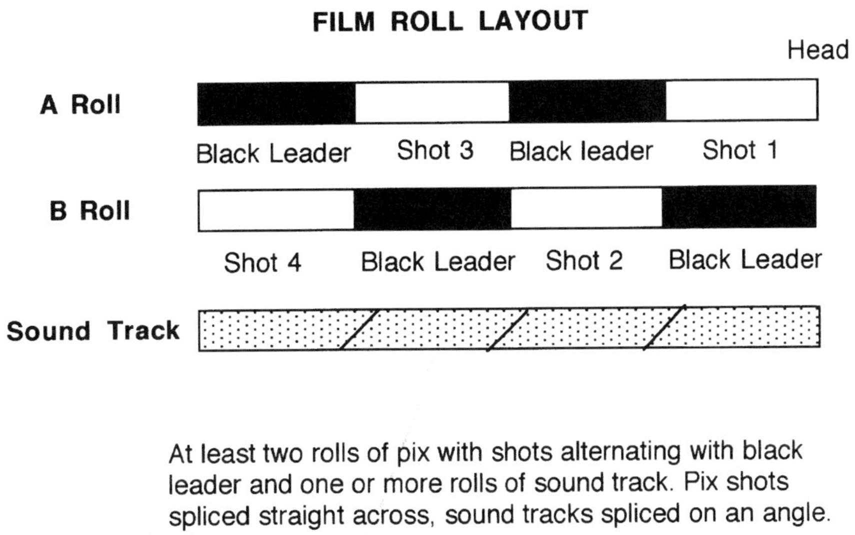

Figure 11.13 Original film edited to be printed is conformed into at least two rolls: "A" and "B." This gives the editor the opportunity to splice alternate shots on each roll so that the printer can perform dissolves, supers, or other effects during the final printing stages. Black leader is spliced opposite the film to be printed unless there is a super or effect. The film splices are made on the frame line, full coat sound tracks are spliced at an angle to avoid "pops" at the edit points.

until the actual film begins. Having established a common synchronization point at the beginning of the film, the editor assembles shots in the order called for in the script (Figure 11.13).

Basic Film Editing Bench

A basic film editing bench consists of a variety of mechanical and electronic devices that make it possible to view the film and listen to the sound track simultaneously. They also allow an editor to maintain perfect synchronization between the visual and audio tracks, to move the film and sound backward and forward, and to physically cut and splice the film images and accompanying sound tracks. A film viewer projects film frames passing through it on a small screen so that they can be inspected by the editor. The sound tracks run over sound heads and are made audible by accompanying amplifiers and speakers. A gang synchronizer locks the film and sound tracks in synchronization with each other. The gang synchronizer consists of several sprocketed wheels or hubs on a common drive shaft. A footage and frame counter on the drive shaft keeps an accurate record of the footage and frames of the picture and sound tracks (Figure 11.14).

A set of rewinds are hand rotated to move the film and sound tracks through the gang synchronizer, movie viewer, and over the sound heads. The take-up reels placed on the rewinds should be equal in diameter so that the picture and sound tracks are driven at the same rate. Spacers are needed to separate both the take-up and the feed reels in conformity with the distance between hubs on the gang synchronizer. Clamps are needed to secure the reels to each other so that they can be

Figure 11.14 The basic film editing bench consists of a pair of rewinds, a viewer, and a synchronizer and a supply of reels and spacers for the rewind shafts.

driven by the common drive or rewind shaft, which is hand operated. Bench editing is a mechanical process. While mechanical editing puts everything under the editor's direct manual control, it also suffers from a number of disadvantages, such as difficulty in maintaining a constant speed when driving the film and sound by hand. Manually driven edit benches do not reproduce high quality pictures and sounds, making evaluation difficult. To overcome some of these problems, a variety of film editing machines have been developed, such as the Moviola Jr., which uses an electric motor to drive the film on an edit bench.

Editing Machines

The *Moviola Jr.* is a relatively inexpensive editing machine, which can be added to an edit bench to provide brighter, clearer pictures and better quality sounds. A motor drives the gang synchronizer, and a viewer and sound playback system are incorporated into the synchronizer. Instead of driving the film and sound tracks by turning the rewinds, an electric motor drives the hubs itself at a constant speed. The bench rewinds simply feed and take up the film and sound tracks as they are moved by the gang synchronizer hubs.

An *upright film editing machine,* such as a Moviola Sr., interconnects the sound and picture drive mechanism through a common drive shaft. They can also be disconnected so that the sound and film tracks can be driven independently by separate motors. The built-in take-up mechanism is directly above the feed mechanism, thus the name *upright* editor. The picture and sound playback quality are excellent. There is a variable-speed motor on the picture side and a constant-speed motor on the sound side, used for driving both tracks simultaneously. Additional

Figure 11.15 The upright Moviola editor has been the standard professional editing tool for many years. It has become less popular as the use of flatbed editors and posting film on video has increased.

sound track or picture elements can often be added to an upright machine (Figure 11.15).

Undoubtedly the most convenient film editing machine that has been developed to facilitate film viewing and mechanical film splicing is the *flatbed editor*, which moves the film horizontally on a table. There are many different types and models of flatbed editors. Some, such as a Steenbeck horizontal editor, advance the picture and sound tracks by a mechanical interlock between sprocket drive mechanisms connected to a common motor, while others, such as the Moviola horizontal editor, rely on electronic synchronization of separate motors connected to a common electrical distributor. Some flatbed editors can drive only one picture and one sound track at a time. They are called *four-plate flatbed editors*, because they have four take-up and feed dishes or plates. More sophisticated flatbeds have six or eight plates, and can run one or two picture tracks and several sound tracks simultaneously in perfect synchronization. The flatbed offers an editor convenient access to all sound and picture tracks, because of its horizontal configuration. It often provides a digital counter display of time or footage, a large viewing screen, and a good quality sound playback and amplification system. Some models allow the sound tracks to be advanced and retarded in relation to the picture, providing added flexibility in finding or manipulating sound/image sync.

A flatbed editor can save a great deal of time in comparison with conventional bench editing. It also allows for more accurate editing by virtue of providing higher quality picture and sound playback, and better means of manipulating the sound and pictures independently or together. Splices can be made on a flatbed editor by simply pulling the marked film out to a splicer at the front of the machine. The open projection gate and sound heads on the flatbed allow the splice points to be easily seen and marked with a grease pencil.

Electronic Film Editing

If the final distribution medium for a film project is exclusively videotape, original film recordings are often immediately transferred to videotape and sometimes digitized for electronic editing. When both film and videotape final copies are needed for different distribution and exhibition outlets, there are several options in terms of postproduction editing. One option is simply to transfer the on-line edited videotape back to film. However, recent developments in electronic editing have made it possible to edit film electronically in videotape or digital nonlinear form and then use the time code (videotape) and Keykode (film) numbers generated by the EDL for final film editing or conforming. A project can be shot as film, edited as videotape or digital images, and then conformed as film for both videotape and film distribution. This allows a producer to combine the image qualities and characteristics of film with the editing speed and convenience of electronic editing.

Conforming

Once the film editing decisions have been finalized, the original film is conformed to the edited workprint. Conforming is a professional skill that is often performed by a person called a *conformer,* particularly when a negative original must be cut together without error or getting the film dirty. All of the shots from the originally recorded film are permanently spliced into two or more rolls, called *A* and *B* (and C, and so on) rolls, using a cement splicer that physically welds two overlapping pieces of film together. During conforming, the individual shots must be divided into two rolls of alternating shots. One difference between 16mm and 35mm conforming is that there is sufficient space between frames in 35mm to be able to make overlapping cement splices on a single roll, although a B roll is required for dissolves, fades, and superimpositions. Individual shots on an A or B roll of 16mm film must alternate with black leader so that overlap splices always overlap into the black leader and are thus invisible when the film is printed. The completed A and B rolls are printed to a single piece of film, called an *answer print,* at a film laboratory, before a final viewable image is obtained. A film on which picture and sound tracks are "married" together is called a *composite print.*

Marking the Workprint

Because the edited workprint serves as a guide for subsequent editing stages, it must be properly marked with appropriate symbols and designations. A grease pencil should be used to mark the film, since these markings can easily be rubbed off the film if changes are needed. The most commonly used symbols indicate the location of fades, dissolves, superimpositions, extended scenes, and unintended splices. To mark a fade-in, simply separate two lines from a point where the shot is to begin fading. The lines reach the outer edges of the frame where the shot is fully lit. The number of frames covered by the lines should equal the length or duration of the effect. A fade-out is marked by connecting two lines from the outer edges of the frame, where the fade-out begins to the precise point where the scene is supposed to be completely faded out. Again, the number of marked frames corresponds to the length of the effect. At 24 frames per second, a 24 frame fade-out will, of course, last exactly one second.

A dissolve is indicated by placing a fade-out marking on top of a fade-in mark. In this case one shot fades out, while another fades in. For a superimposition or double exposure, the basic shot or dominant scene is spliced into the workprint at the beginning and ending points of the effect, but the recessive, superimposed shot is cut into the middle section. A wavy line drawn through the entire sequence indicates a double exposure or superimposition. An extended scene is one that continues despite the fact that the actual footage for this scene is missing in the workprint. A straight horizontal line shaped like an arrow indicates how far the prior shot extends. Finally, unintended splices in the workprint are clearly marked with two short horizontal lines drawn through the splice so that there is no confusion about shot changes at this point in later editing stages (Figure 11.16).

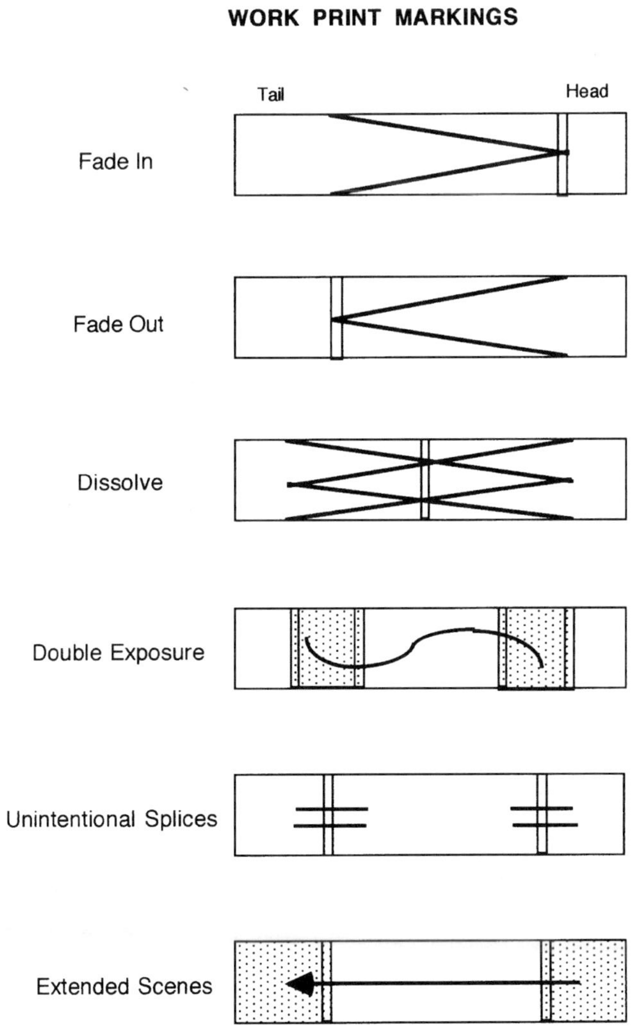

Figure 11.16
Since the workprint film rolls cannot actually have dissolves or effects cut into them, then industry uses standard markings on the workprint to notify the printer at the lab how to place transitions, place supers or double exposures, or correct errors that may have been made in the rough cut of the film.

Edge Numbers

Edge numbers are consecutive reference numbers printed onto the edge of original film, either by the manufacturer of the film or by the film laboratory after processing. The latter are usually referred to as *yellow ink edge numbers.* Edge numbers corresponding to those of the camera original film from which the workprint has been copied can be printed onto the edges of the workprint. After the workprint has been edited, the edge numbers at the beginning and end of each shot are used, much like SMPTE time code in off-line videotape editing, to select the correct shots from the original film for conforming to the edited workprint. The beginning and ending edge numbers of each shot in the edited workprint are written down so that the corresponding shots in the original film can be pulled and spliced together in their correct order.

Splicing the A and B Rolls

Once the workprint has been edited and marked, the original film from which the workprint was copied must be conformed to the workprint. Instead of editing shots together into a single roll as in workprint rough cutting, the camera original is conformed into two rolls, an A roll and a B roll. This is done to make the splices between different shots invisible and to allow for special effects, such as fades, dissolves, and superimpositions. The splices are made invisible by using black leader between successive shots on a single roll of film. Thus, where there is a shot on the A roll, there is black leader on the B roll. The only exception to this rule occurs in conforming fades for negative film, which require clear leader opposite a fade-out. In negative film, black is created by fading light in, not fading it out.

In either case, the two rolls of film are edited in a checkerboard fashion, except for dissolves and superimpositions, where shots are completely or partially overlapped. The individual shots are cement spliced to the black leader. Splices require a slight overlap, so that the two pieces of film can be welded together. To make the splices invisible, the overlap always occurs in the leader area. The emulsion must be scraped off the picture film where it will be bonded to the black leader, so that the two bases come into contact. Film emulsion inhibits the action of the cement. The cement splice provides a permanent bond, and it leaves no unsightly marks.

A conformer prepares the original for splicing by pulling all the shots from the camera original and placing them on individual plastic cores, which are labeled and arranged in sequential order. An alternative approach is to simply pull each shot from its respective camera original roll as it is needed. The conformer makes a complete list of the edge number markings of the edited workprint, and the original camera shots are pulled on the basis of the edge numbers. The film is usually cut with a frame and a half extra at both the head and tail ends of an individual shot, so that there is ample room for overlap.

Conformers usually adopt a standard set of procedures with no variations to avoid mistakes while cutting and splicing original film. Cleanliness is extremely important, because dirt and scratches will show up in the final prints. This problem is aggravated when using negative film, because the scratches and dirt then show up as white marks on the final prints. When all the shots have been prepared for splicing, the conformer places the A and B rolls and the workprint in the gang synchronizer on the editing bench, and proceeds to splice the shots alternately into one of the two rolls, leaving overlaps of specified lengths for dissolves and superimpositions.

Cement Splicing

Cement splicing requires the use of a properly adjusted cement splicer. The proper adjustment and alignment of the cutting blade and arms is crucial to the quality of the splice. They should only be adjusted by a trained professional. Cement splicers can be either hot or cold: Hot splicers have a heating element that was once needed to speed the drying process; cold splicers do not have any heating element. Today, cement has very little water that must evaporate, so heating is rarely necessary. It is important to use fresh cement, however, since the welding capacity of cement deteriorates with exposure to air.

To make a 16mm splice, the black leader is positioned with the emulsion side up in the right-hand side of the splicer, by placing the teeth of the splicer in the correct sprocket holes of the leader and then locking down the top portion of the arm. Generally this should leave about 1½ frames of excess leader beyond the cutting edge or blade of the splicer. Raising the blade and then bringing it down over the left-hand arm severs the leader at the proper point. Now the adjacent shot is positioned in the left-hand arm so that the frame line where the splice will occur is placed close to the end of the blade or on the cut line. The emulsion is firmly and evenly scraped off the overlapping portion of the excess 1½ frames of the film so that only the clear base remains. Cement is applied to the scraped portion of the left-hand piece of film, and the right-hand arm is brought down quickly and locked into its welding position. This both cuts off the excess portion of the shot and brings it into contact with the black leader. In five to ten seconds the cement is completely dried and the spliced film can be removed and inspected. A splice should be able to withstand considerable gentle pulling and twisting. This will ensure that it will not break on the printer. Black leader is never scraped in the cement splicer, unless you are splicing black leader to black leader, as this will cause the splice line to be visible in a frame of picture.

Combining the A and B Rolls

Once the A and B rolls are conformed to the workprint, they are sent to the laboratory so that they can each be printed in succession to a single roll of film, called an *answer print.* The answer print is a test printing of the A and B rolls, after they have been properly timed, that is, after the color and density of each shot has been adjusted by a laboratory professional, called a *color timer.* A composite print marries the A and B rolls together with a sound track so that it can be run in a conventional projector. The composite print usually has an optical soundtrack, which is advanced twenty-six frames in 16 mm or twenty frames in 35mm ahead of the corresponding pictures.

Summary

The director's aesthetic intentions regarding the succession of visual images are fully realized during editing. Visual images can be combined using principles of editing derived from each of the three following aesthetic approaches: realism, modernism, and postmodernism. One of the editor's first tasks is to organize and catalogue all the single-camera recordings that the director has provided. In documentary productions that lack a detailed script, performing a paper edit from a catalogue of shots and camera takes can help an editor efficiently and economically organize the editing process.

Three different types of editing technology and techniques are discussed in this chapter: digital nonlinear editing and conventional videotape and film editing. Digital nonlinear editing software offers several advantages over conventional means of editing film, audiotape, and videotape, including increased flexibility or creativity, as well as potential time and cost savings. The amount of time scheduled for postproduction editing can be significantly diminished, and increased editing efficiency can also translate into cost savings that affect the overall budget.

Digitizing video and audio signals requires fairly sophisticated hardware and considerable information storage capacity, especially when high quality images and sounds must be digitized. During digitization each NTSC analog video frame, which consists of two interlaced scanning fields that add up to 525 scan lines, is converted to a frame of 640 × 480 pixels that can be displayed in a non-interlaced mode on a computer monitor. Digitized movies can require several gigabytes of information storage capacity. The most common forms of storage space reduction used in digital nonlinear editing, especially for editing longer duration projects, are compression, frame size reduction, and frame rate reduction. Basically compression reduces the amount of information that must be stored in an individual frame or still image by ignoring some pixel and color information. Compression is usually indicated in terms of ratios, such as 2:1, 10:1, or 15:1. Storage space can also be reduced by reducing the frame size and frame rates of digitized images. For example, instead of editing full frame video (640 × 480 pixels), an editor can work with quarter-frame images (160 × 120 pixels). A frame rate of 15 frames per second requires half the storage space as a frame rate of 30 frames per second.

A clip is usually the smallest unit of digital video (or audio) information that can be stored and manipulated during editing. It can range from just one frame to an entire movie in duration, but it often consists of a single shot, that is, a continuous camera recording or take. Digitized clips are usually imported (or copied) into a particular editing project file, where they are edited along a timeline with other images and sounds. Clips of video or audio information can be cut, trimmed, copied, pasted, inserted, and deleted along a timeline.

Videotape editing is usually divided into two stages: off-line editing and on-line editing. Off-line editing is often done in a smaller format, and off-line editing decisions are later performed on an originally recorded larger format videotape. Off-line editing decisions can be used to guide on-line editing of the larger format videotape. Assemble editing is only used to place the shots in rough sequential order, since it does not provide sufficient editing control to edit exactly from one shot to the next. During assemble editing, both the control track and the visual images from the original recording are transferred to the new assemble-edited version. Assemble editing is that it allows an editor to efficiently organize vast amounts of material into a very rough sequential order. Editing decisions can be gradually refined and tightened up during insert editing. Insert editing allows for considerable editing flexibility compared with assemble editing. A major advantage of insert editing over assemble editing is that a portion of one shot can be replaced by another shot. During insert editing, video-only and audio-only edits can be made, as well as video-plus-audio edits.

Once all the editing decisions have been finalized, the original videotapes are on-line edited in conformity with the off-line edited version, using the Edit Decision List or EDL. On-line editing often involves special editing devices such as time-base correctors, SMPTE time code, and computerized editing controls, as well as a digital effects generator. Videotapes can be on-line edited using a computer after the SMPTE time code reference numbers for each shot or effect have been determined and fed into the computer. The computer will assemble the entire videotape using the ending and beginning time code numbers for each shot, transition, and effect in its proper sequence. During on-line editing, several playback machines are connected to the computer control unit so that they can be fed to the master record tape.

Film editing follows a series of stages similar to videotape editing, from rough cutting, the equivalent of off-line videotape editing that includes viewing a copy of the originally recorded images, called the workprint, rushes, or dailies, and selecting and ordering specific shots and scenes, to conforming the original film to the edited workprint and answer printing, which are equivalent in some ways to on-line videotape editing. Unlike videotape editing, however, traditional film editing usually involves mechanical processes, such as physically cutting and splicing the film.

A film copy made from the originally recorded film is called a workprint. The editor, director, and producer view each day's workprint, called the dailies, in order to evaluate how well things are going. Since films are often shot out of continuity, that is, all shots from one location are recorded at the same time, regardless of when they occur in the script, the editor must assemble the shots into the order specified by the script. Rough cutting usually begins with the selection of a master shot containing virtually all the action occurring in one scene. The editor then attempts to insert various matching medium shots and close-ups into the master shot, and he or she gradually trims the shots and refines the edit points throughout the rough cutting process. The editor gradually refines the cuts, cutting out all extraneous or unnecessary material. Unused shots are called out-takes. The pieces removed from the shots that are actually used are called trims.

Manually driven edit benches do not reproduce high quality pictures and sounds, making evaluation difficult. To overcome some of these problems, a variety of film editing machines have been developed, such as the Moviola Jr., the upright Moviola, and various horizontal or flatbed film editing machines. Recent developments in electronic editing have made it possible to edit film electronically in videotape or digital nonlinear form and then use the time code (videotape) and Keykode (film) numbers generated by the EDL for final film editing or conforming. A project can be shot as film, edited as videotape or digital images, and then conformed as film for both videotape and film distribution.

Once the film editing decisions have been finalized, the original film is conformed to the edited workprint. All of the shots from the originally recorded film are permanently spliced, using a cement splicer, which physically welds two overlapping pieces of film together. The corresponding edge numbers at the beginning and end of each shot in the original and the workprint are used, much like SMPTE time code in off-line videotape editing, to select the correct shots from the original film, which are conformed to the edited workprint. The camera original is conformed into two or more rolls, A, B, C rolls, etc. This is done to make the splices between different shots invisible and to allow for special effects, such as fades, dissolves, and superimpositions. Once the A and B rolls are conformed to the workprint, they are sent to the laboratory so that they can each be printed in succession on a continuous contact printer to a single roll of film, called an answer print. A composite print marries the A and B rolls together with a sound track so that it can be run in a conventional projector.

Exercises

1. Edit together a short movie trailer or television promotion for a documentary or dramatic feature film, using an exiting videotape that is in public domain and not copy protected. View the videotape at least twice, writing down the control track numbers for each shot or sequence that you think you might use in your trailer or promo. Then, using these notes, perform a paper edit of the sequence so that the edited promos, at least on paper, approximates a specific duration, such as one minute or three minutes. Using the paper edit, then actually edit the sequence on videotape or digitize the clips that you have selected and edit them using a digital nonlinear editing system. Remember that you are trying to promote the film. Therefore you will want to select sequences that will attract viewers but not disappoint them by setting up false expectations that the films themselves cannot fulfill. Basically you want to capture the essence of the film and promote it.
2. Edit your own version of a professionally recorded scene or sequence. Obtain a copy of the original, unedited recordings of a professional quality production. The American Cinema Editor's or ACE's annual student editing contest is a potential source of professional recordings or film rushes. After you have edited these shots in film, videotape, or digital form, compare your version with the version actually produced by a professional editor and determine what you could do to improve your own editing.

Additional Readings

Anderson, Gary H. *Video Editing and Post Production,* 2nd ed. Boston: Focal Press, 1988.

Brown, Steven E. *Video Editing: A Post Production Primer,* 3rd ed. Boston: Focal Press, 1996.

Burder, John. *The Technique of Editing 16mm Films.* Boston: Focal Press, 1979.

Happe, L. Bernard. *Your Film & the Lab.* Boston: Focal Press, 1974.

Ohanian, Thomas A. *Digital Nonlinear Editing, New Approaches to Editing Film and Video.* Boston: Focal Press, 1993.

Pincus, Edward, and Steven Ascher. *The Filmmaker's Handbook.* New York: Plume, 1984.

Rabiger, Michael. *Directing the Documentary,* 2nd ed. Boston: Focal Press, 1992.

12

Sound Editing

Introduction

Sound editing is an extremely important stage of postproduction. Sounds can breathe life, realism, emotion, and power into visual images. Sounds can also develop their own form of expression apart from visual images, and they can be edited before, during, or after visual editing. The fact that sounds and images can be edited in tandem or independently of each other allows for considerable flexibility in terms of editing different types of sound and different combinations of sounds and visual images.

Each different type of sound, such as speech, sound effects, and music, can be edited in conjunction with visual images. As noted in Chapter 5, sounds can be synchronous or asynchronous, on-screen or off-screen, and parallel or contrapuntal in meaning with respect to accompanying visual images. Separately edited speech, sound effects, and music tracks can be blended or mixed together to form one monaural sound track or several stereophonic tracks.

Sound editing can be a complex process. It involves combining many different types of sound using various forms and stages of both editing and mixing. From the standpoint of aesthetics, the complexities of sound editing can be approached from three different perspectives: realism, modernism, and postmodernism. Realist sound recording, as discussed in Chapter 5, preserves a feeling of authenticity and accuracy of specific sounds, while realist sound editing preserves a continuity of sounds in time and space. Generally speaking, time flows continuously and sequentially from one sound to the next. There are no apparent gaps or breaks in the audio action.

Realist sound editing often reinforces realist visual editing. Sounds can follow the lead set by visual images, enhancing, filling out, and reinforcing the images they accompany. Realist sounds are usually synchronous, on-screen, and parallel in meaning with the accompanying images. They rarely develop an independent meaning that competes with the accompanying visual images. Speech, sound effects, and music are basically conformed to the requirements of specific visuals throughout the editing process. In some situations, such as news and documentary editing, a sound track composed of voice-over narration and interviews may be edited prior to the selection and editing of illustrative images. Nevertheless, sounds and images remain parallel in meaning and complement one another.

Like realist visual editing, realist sound editing emphasizes message clarity. The editor removes mistakes, such as flubbed lines of dialogue or disruptive background sounds, and tries to achieve a proper balance between speech, sound effects, and music. Primacy is usually given to one of these elements at a time, so that the main message is clear and distinct. By simplifying and ordering sounds, an editor avoids listener disorientation and confusion. The space between lines of dialogue or narration is made long enough to allow for a smooth, clear, and natural delivery, but short enough to maintain interest and excitement.

News stories and prerecorded interviews in documentaries are examples of situations that often call for a realist approach to editing. A reporter's or filmmaker's voice-over narration or the responses of an interviewee are often edited to maintain better message clarity and flow. In editing narrative fiction, the editor's choices are often restricted by the script, which indicates what lines of dialogue must be used as well as which visual shots must be used at a specific time. But the editor must deviate from the script slightly when problems arise in the original recordings and neither the sounds nor the images can be re-recorded.

Modernist sound editing often develops sound as an independent aesthetic element. Continuity of time and space are sometimes disrupted. Sounds may be asynchronous and/or contrapuntal with respect to accompanying visual images, and the audience frequently experiences the thoughts and feelings of the film/video artist, a fictional character in the story, or a social actor within a nonfictional work. In short, modernist techniques develop subjective impressions. Sound effects, for example, can create imaginative impressions of what a character is feeling, thinking, or experiencing rather than an illusion of objective reality or authenticity. The pace and meaning of music can contrast with or counterpoint the accompanying visuals, such as when slow-paced music accompanies rapidly paced visual action. The editor freely develops abstract audio relations and qualities. Modernist sound editing techniques, of course, can be incorporated into realist films and videos to add a degree of unpredictability, generating viewer interest and emotional excitement. The sound films of Alfred Hitchcock were good examples of modernist sound editing within generally realist films.

Postmodernist sound editing offers a pastiche of audio impressions, often mixing documentary, narrative fiction, and experimental modes. Rather than promoting subjective psychological impressions or a realist sense of objectivity, authenticity, and continuity, postmodernist sound editing plunders a variety of genres, historical periods, and previously distinct styles, often generating a feeling of nostalgia for bygone eras and breaking down distinctions between popular and elite cultural forms. Postmodernist editing gives spectators more freedom to explore, respond to, and play with recorded speech, sound effects, and music. It does not reinforce an illusion of reality or the artist's subjective impressions, but instead evokes a sense of free play with sounds and encourages audience participation in the creative process. This chapter explores a variety of audio editing techniques, some of which reflect postmodernist, modernist, or realist aesthetics that are applicable to digital nonlinear, videotape, magnetic film, and audiotape editing technologies.

Digital Nonlinear Editing

Digital nonlinear audio editing offers a number of advantages over analog editing. First, the quality of digital audio does not significantly diminish from one generation to the next, since the binary encoding of audio signals generally allows an editor to maintain a consistent signal-to-noise ratio throughout the editing process. Second, multiple audio tracks can be edited independently or in conjunction with one another. Third, most nonlinear editing programs provide a visual image of a sound track, which indicates fluctuations in loudness and pitch and allows the editor to quickly and easily find and mark precise edit points, such as the beginning or end of specific sounds. Fourth, digital audio can be initially edited in conjunction with visual images, using a relatively simple editing program, (simple in terms of limited audio editing capabilities), such as Adobe Premiere, and then the same audio can be fine-tuned independently using a more sophisticated audio editing program (sophisticated in terms of the number of editing options), such as Pro Tools, before it is recombined with the visuals again. The fact that digital audio can be used in different programs without degrading its quality and a digital nonlinear edited sound track can maintain exact synchronization with accompanying videotape or film images by using SMPTE time code and/or film KeyKode as common reference points provides considerable editing flexibility.

Digitizing audio, like digitizing video, requires considerable time and disk space. Audio can be digitized at the time of its original recording, using a separate digital audiotape (DAT) or disc recorder, or an analog recording can be rapidly sampled and digitized during postproduction, either in conjunction with or separately from visual images. Unless the original recording has been digitized in a format that is computer readable, placing the audio information on a hard disk will generally take as long as the real time duration of the original recording. The sampling rate and bandwidth of an audio signal can be varied during digitization to reduce the amount of storage space that is required. There are two steps to digitizing audio: setting the audio level controls and setting the audio resolution or quality. Setting the audio level controls avoids distortion and ensures a high signal-to-noise ratio in digital audio, just as it does in analog audio.

The quality of digitized audio and the size of the audio file also depend on the sampling rate and bit depth of the audio. The sampling rate for audio is similar to the frame rate for digitizing video. It measures the number of frequencies into which the sound is broken. The bit depth, which is similar to color depth in visuals, measures the number of tones per sample. A high sampling rate stores and reproduces very high quality sound. The higher the sampling rate and bit depth, the better the sound quality. Audio sampled at 22 kHz (kiloHerz), that is, at 22,000 cycles per second, and 8-bit resolution (8 bits equal 1 byte of computer information and storage) may be sufficient for monophonic speech and sound effects, but a sampling rate of 22 kHz and 16-bit resolution is probably the minimum required for stereo sound and music, which will require about twice the disk storage space.

Compact Disc (CD) audio is normally digitized at 44 kHz and 16-bit resolution. A bit is the smallest amount of information a computer can handle. Eight bits make up a byte, 1000 bytes equal a kilobyte (kB), 1,000,000 equal a megabyte (MB), and 1,000,000,000 bytes equal a gigabyte (GB). Thus it takes slightly more than 2.6 MBs to store one minute of audio information at 22 kHz and 16-bit resolution (22,000 cycles per second × 60 seconds × 2 bytes = 2,640,000 bytes or 2.64 MB). This is considerably less than uncompressed video information, as discussed in Chapter 11. Remember that one full frame of picture requires slightly less than 1 MB. There are 30 frames per second, and thus one minute of uncompressed full-frame video requires 1680 MBs or about 1.7 GB per minute.

Digital audio, unlike digital video, is not usually compressed when it is digitized, since digitized audio already requires considerably less storage space than digitized video, and audio compression could significantly reduce the quality of the audio signal. *Compression* refers to a reduction of the volume of information in order to force it into less storage space. In audio production, compression is frequently used during recording to prevent distortion by, for example, compressing the loudness range of a singer, who alternately sings very loudly and very softly. Compression is rarely used while digitizing audio that was originally recorded as an analog signal, however. Basically compression during digitization of an analog signal would reduce the amount of information by ignoring some loudness and/or pitch information during storage and then duplicating adjacent loudness and/or pitch information when the sounds are emitted during playback.

Digital Nonlinear Editing Hardware

Most digital nonlinear editing systems employ computer hardware that is capable of processing and storing vast amounts of visual and audio information. In addition to a video and audio capture card, a nonlinear editing system usually includes a computer processing unit (CPU) with a 60+ megahertz (MHz) processing system, 30+ MB of random access memory (RAM), a keyboard, a mouse, one or two computer monitors, an NTSC television monitor, a videotape recorder, an amplifier and loudspeakers, and a 2+ GB hard disk drive designed for audio visual (AV) use, as discussed earlier in Chapter 11.

Digital Nonlinear Editing Software

Digital nonlinear editing software offers several advantages over conventional means of editing magnetic film, audiotape, and videotape, including increased flexibility or creativity, as well as potential time and cost savings. Digital nonlinear editing affords an editor flexibility in terms of instantaneously changing the order and duration of sounds and images. For example, clips of audio information can be cut, trimmed, copied, pasted, inserted, and deleted along a timeline.

A *clip* is usually the smallest unit of digital audio information that can be stored and manipulated during editing. It can range from a fraction of a second to an entire movie in duration, but it often consists of a continuous audio recording or take. Digitized clips are usually imported (or copied) into a particular editing project file, where they are edited along a timeline with other sounds and images. Most editing software provides several windows or screens, including a project window, a timeline (or construction) window, and a locking window. Different windows can usually be displayed simultaneously on one or more computer monitors. A project window usually contains the individual clips in alphabetical order based on the first letters of their written descriptions. The timeline or construction window displays a timeline that contains several audio tracks and indicates the overall duration and order of the edited project. A locking window allows the editor to lock together or unlock various audio and visual tracks in the timeline window so that they can be cut and trimmed collectively or individually.

Audio is often displayed visually as a continuous, variable area sound track, where high peaks represent loud sounds and rapid fluctuations indicate high frequency sounds. Clips can be copied and inserted at various points along the timeline, and they can be cut, trimmed, and split into several clips as well as deleted from the timeline and the remaining sounds attached to one another. The overall volume of a clip can usually be increased or decreased by adjusting an accompanying volume control band. Fade-outs, fade-ins, and cross-fades can be created by adjusting the volume band, and sounds can be increased or decreased at will throughout the clip, such as to bring a music track down and under a voice track. Rapid fade-ins and fade-outs of audio clips at cut points from one audio track to another often help to hide digital "popping" sounds, or digital noise, which is sometimes audible at cut points. (Some digital editing systems, such as Avid, have programs that facilitate the elimination of digital "popping" sounds in this manner.) Clips can also be filtered, that is, the entire clip can have its frequency response altered. The high frequency sounds can be reduced and the low frequency sounds increased in intensity, for example. The reverberation or attack and decay of a sound clip can also be altered to enhance or diminish echo.

Every edit made using a digital nonlinear software program is usually a virtual edit. No digitized material need be discarded when clips are trimmed, cut, or deleted along an editing timeline, since each clip is usually stored separately outside the timeline window. Every clip stored on a disk drive is instantaneously accessible in its entirety and can be grabbed in the project or clip window and reinserted at any point along the timeline. Many alternative versions of a scene or sequence can thus be quickly edited and examined without prematurely eliminating material that may be needed later. Transitions from one sound track to another can be previewed, as can the filtering of specific tracks without ever actually cutting, discarding, eliminating, or deleting any originally digitized video or audio.

The ability to manipulate clips of sound along a timeline not only adds flexibility to the editing process, it can also make editing more efficient and cost effective. Clips can be very rapidly trimmed, cut, inserted, and deleted. Digital nonlinear editing is extremely fast compared with physically cutting and splicing a conventional magnetic film sound, for example, and the time it takes to find and insert videotape sounds from a source onto a master videotape can be dramatically reduced by using instantaneously accessible digital clips along a timeline. The amount of time scheduled for postproduction editing can be significantly diminished, facilitating the editing of projects that require a short turnaround time. Clearly, digital nonlinear editing offers a number of advantages in terms of flexibility and efficiency over conventional videotape, magnetic film, and audiotape editing.

Videotape Editing

Videotape sound is edited electronically. Electronic editing of videotape can be divided into two categories: control track editing and time code editing. Control track editing is somewhat less precise than time code editing. In *control track edit-*

ing each frame of video and audio is counted in terms of pulses in the control track, while in *time code editing* a sequential numerical code is recorded on the videotape and each frame of video and audio has a permanently coded number that does not change. In control track editing the frame numbers are sequentially counted from the point at which the VTR counter is zeroed. Most control track editors slip a bit or skip frames when the videotape is repeatedly stopped and started. Edits are usually accurate to plus or minus two frames in control track editing, while time code editing is usually frame accurate.

Control track videotape editing usually allows for video-only, audio channel one-only, audio channel two-only, audio channels one and two-only, and audio channels one and/or two-plus-video editing in the insert mode, as discussed in Chapter 14. To insert edit sound onto prerecorded images without erasing those images, the sound must first be recorded on a separate videotape along with a control track. Sound can then be dubbed onto one of the audio tracks or channels of a prerecorded videotape without disturbing the picture or separate audio information on another sound channel. Video can also be added to a videotape without disturbing the prerecorded audio signal. Using synchronized sounds and images originally recorded on videotape, an editor can edit the audio simultaneously with the video, maintaining precise synchronization. Audio editing on videotape can involve a single synchronous sound track on the original videotape or the building of complex dialogue, narration, sound effects, and music tracks (Figure 12.1).

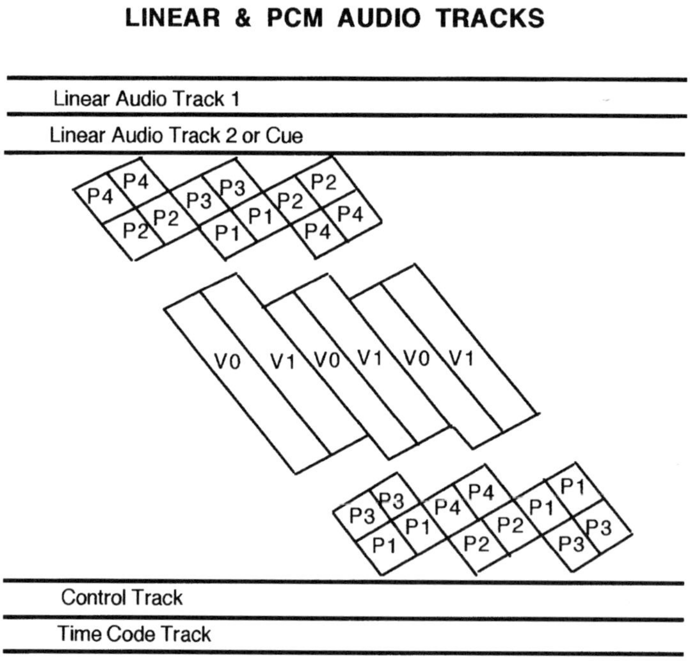

Figure 12.1 PCM audio tracks are recorded along with the video in the same slant track. PCM is a digital audio format and may be recorded in short bursts located at the ends of the video tracks. The linear audio tracks can be either analog or digital.

Control track videotape editing usually allows sounds to be inserted at any point in a videotape. To insert audio into a prerecorded video segment, the audio can be dubbed from any sound source to a blank videotape by using the assemble mode on the source VCR. Control track must be recorded on the videotape at the same time so that the sound will play back at a constant speed. The source videotape, which now contains recorded sound effects, speech, or music, is then played back in conjunction with a record videotape containing prerecorded images so that the source sound can be inserted into the record images. A common insert edit point is found and, using the insert mode of electronic editing, the sound on the source videotape is inserted into an audio track on the record videotape so that it accompanies corresponding images. The editor usually sets the edit in-point and out-point for the record videotape and the in-point only for the source videotape, which will be inserted into an audio channel of the record videotape. If the on-set sound already occupies channel number two on the record videotape, additional sound effects, narration, or music from the source videotape can be insert edited onto channel number one of the record videotape without erasing the on-set sounds.

Simple videotape mixing is done by combining two separate audio tracks on a single prerecorded videotape. The two tracks are recorded separately and then played back on a source VCR through a mixer or audio console so that they can be combined onto one track on the record videotape. Mixing videotape audio is limited only by the number of audio tracks and playback machines available. If only one audio track is available, a separate source VCR or an audio playback machine must be used. When synchronization is not crucial, an audiotape recorder can be connected to the record VCR through a mixer several times before a final sound mix is achieved.

A more expensive alternative to using the control track of a videotape is to use a computerized videotape editor with addressable time codes. The computerized editor can control several video and/or audio sources simultaneously. Sound editing and mixing decisions can be programmed into the computer, which will control the playback and adjust the volume of each different sound source. Any audio or video machine capable of reading the SMPTE time code can be used for computerized editing and mixing. With computer assistance, a complex sound track can be designed, programmed, and mixed automatically on the basis of a mix log that is programmed into the computer along with all editing decisions (Figure 12.2).

Time code editing allows an editor to perform more complex mixing of separate audio tracks. Time code can also be used to mix or combine separate sound tracks, such as those that are recorded on a multitrack audiotape recorder (ATR) that is capable of reading time code. One of the tracks, usually track #8 on an eight track ATR or track #16 on a sixteen track ATR, is designated for recording time code, while the track immediately adjacent to it, track #7 or #15, respectively, is left blank to prevent cross-talk or bleeding between the time code and the recorded audio. Sounds can then be added to different tracks of the multitrack audiotape. For example, the dialogue that is originally recorded and edited on videotape in synchronization with the video images can be dubbed to an audiotape along with other sound elements, such as several music and sound effects tracks. All of the tracks can be mixed down to one track (mono) or two tracks (stereo) on the same

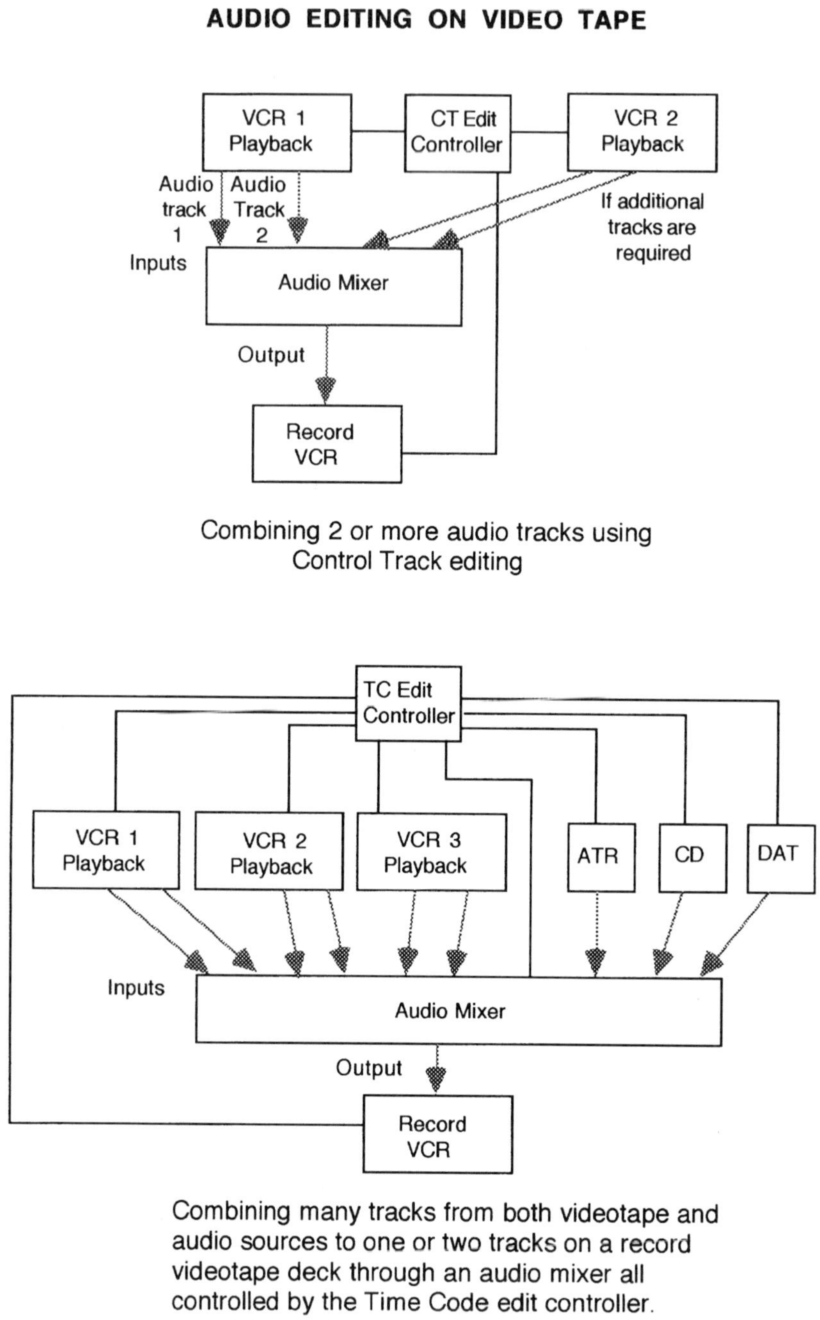

Figure 12.2 The process of editing audio on videotape provides a very precise means of assembling a variety of different audio sources onto either one or both of the audio tracks on the final edited videotape. The simplest method is to use tracks from two play decks and mix the audio through an audio mixer. More complex editing can be accomplished by using non-videotape sources mixed with audio from more than one videotape play deck.

multitrack audiotape before the mix down is transferred back to videotape. Music and sound effects can be combined with the dialogue and then dubbed back to an audio channel of the original videotape in perfect synchronization with the images. A potential problem with multigeneration dubbing and mixing with analog audiotape, however, is that the music or sound effects may be severely degraded in quality by virtue of having been dubbed.

Magnetic Film Editing

This section is concerned solely with conventional double-system film editing of magnetic film sound. Synchronous film sound is often recorded on ¼-inch audiotape, using a separate synchronous sound recorder. The originally recorded sounds are accompanied by Pilotone. This sync signal or Pilotone track, which is recorded on the audiotape along with the primary sync sounds, is used to maintain precise synchronization with the separately recorded visuals. It determines the playback speed of the tape recorder when the film sound is transferred from audiotape to 16mm or 35mm magnetic film. Magnetic film can be physically cut and spliced in conjunction with motion picture film. Splicing allows an editor to combine sounds in sequential order and to synchronize them with accompanying images. This can be accomplished through physical cutting of magnetic film. If synchronization is not crucial, it may be advantageous to edit sounds initially on conventional ¼-inch tape (to be discussed later in this chapter) since a common film format is not required. Any sounds that are to be synchronized with visual images during editing must first be dubbed to magnetic film (Figure 12.3).

Physically splicing magnetic film requires several pieces of equipment, including a splicing block and cutting blade, mylar splicing tape, and some means of locking pictures and sounds in synchronization, such as a gang synchronizer or a flatbed editor. The first step in splicing magnetic film is locating the precise edit points on the two pieces of tape that are to be joined. These points are marked on the base (shiny) sides of the magnetic film with a permanent felt-tip pen. The magnetic film can then be placed in the splicing block so that the proper edit points line up with the diagonal splice edge of the cutting block. Using a diagonal splice line minimizes the chance of creating a "popping" sound when the splice passes over a playback head. A film splicing block normally has pegs on which the sprocket holes of the film are placed to ensure proper alignment for exact cutting and joining (Figure 12.4).

There are basically two types of film splicers: those that use preperforated mylar tape laid horizontally across the splice and those that use unperforated tape laid vertically across the splice. In the latter case, the sprocket holes are punched out as the tape is cut. Both types of tape splicers are available with diagonal splicing blocks for audio cutting and joining, allowing the two diagonally cut pieces of magnetic recording film to be held together with pegs in adjacent sprocket holes so that mylar tape can be applied to the base side to make a secure splice. The excess tape is cut off by a blade and the tape joint is smoothed out by rubbing across the top of the splice. The splice should be inspected to see if the sprocket holes are clear and to make sure there are no gaps between the two pieces of audiotape. A tape splice can easily be redone by simply removing the mylar tape and putting the two pieces

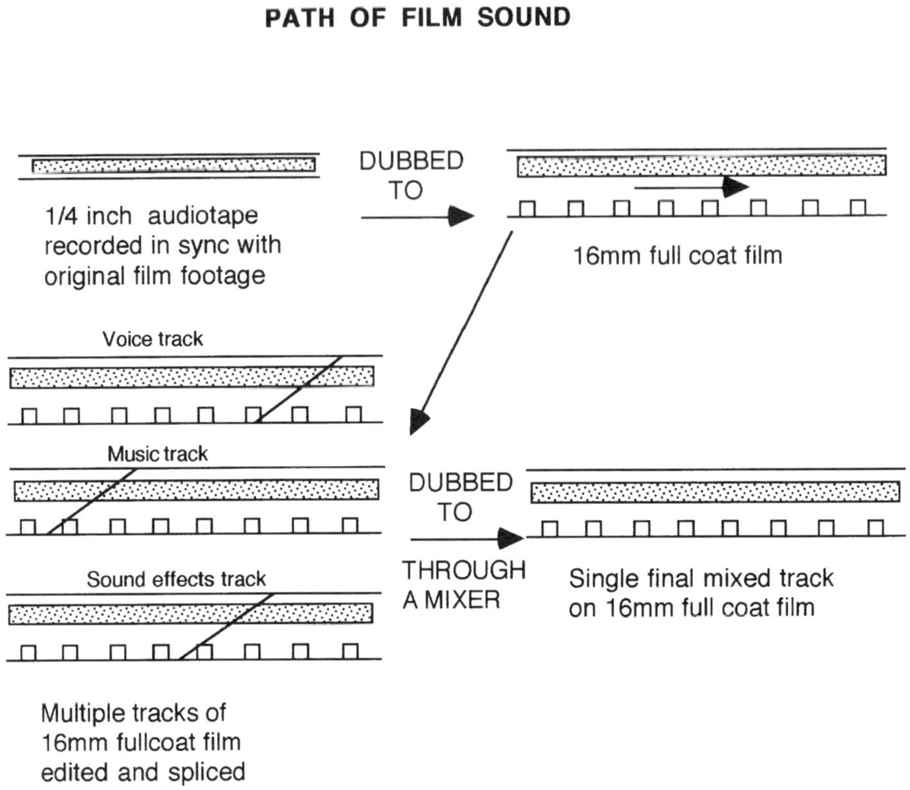

Figure 12.3 Most film sound tracks are recorded on either a ¼″ reel-to-reel or digital tape deck on location or in the studio. That tape is then dubbed to either 16mm or 35mm magnetic full coat film. Several tracks of full coat are threaded on individual full-coat players and then dubbed through a sound mixing board to create the final sound mix.

of audiotape back in the splicing block. Note that mylar splicing tape should never be placed on the oxide side (usually, but not always, the dull side) of the audiotape, where it will interfere with the playback of the recorded sound. Magnetic film is synchronized with accompanying images by finding the precise frames where the sound of the clapstick is heard on the sound track and seen on the image track for each shot. Once synchronized, magnetic film can be edited frame by frame with the accompanying images. Prerecorded sound effects can be added at the precise points where they mirror the visual action. A crescendo or musical beat can be aligned with a specific action or cutline through physical splicing. To maintain synchronization between the sound and picture once it has been achieved, an editor must add or subtract the same number of frames in both the picture and the sound tracks when any change is required (Figure 12.5).

Separate magnetic film tracks are sometimes slugged or interspersed with clear leader, which is completely transparent film with no oxide coating. Using clear leader between recorded sounds is less expensive than using magnetic film, and it also clearly identifies where recorded audio occurs on the roll. Slugging with clear leader simultaneously on all edited sound tracks prevents any continuation of am-

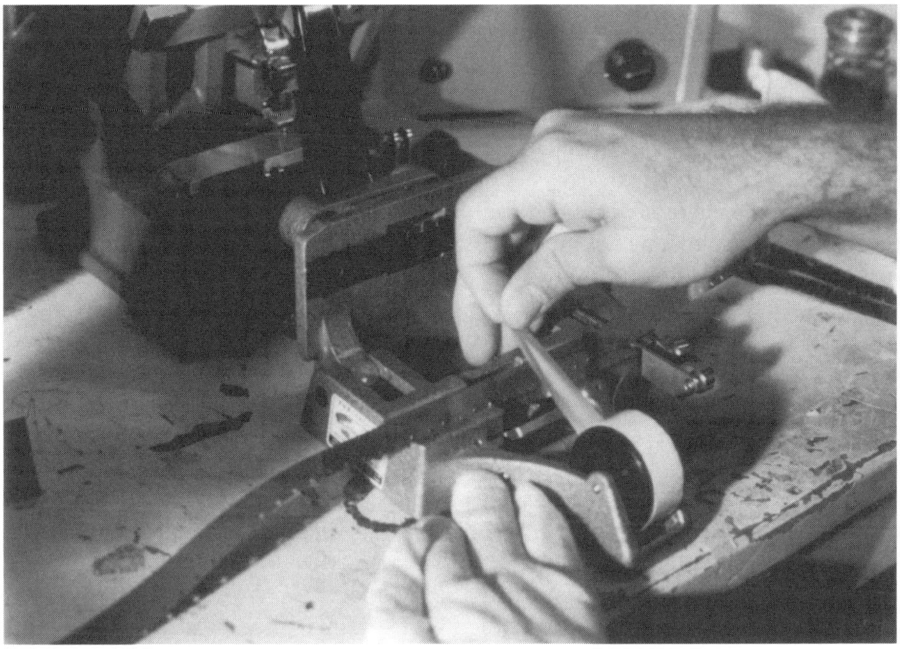

Figure 12.4 A splicer used to edit sound full-coat film and workprint film uses a wide clear or opaque tape stretched across the film. The handle is brought down sealing the tape and punching holes in the tape lined up with the sprocket holes in the film.

Figure 12.5 A splicer used to edit film to be projected or to assemble "A" and "B" rolls is called a hot splicer. A heating element built into the metal base of the splicer warms the deck of the splicer so that as soon as the acetone is applied to the joint between the film segments, the splice will quickly and permanently bond to create a secure splice.

bient noise or "room tone" and results in patches of completely silent or dead audio. Thus clear leader should only be used with tracks that will eventually be mixed with others.

Synchronizing sounds with film images requires that the sounds be transferred to magnetic film of the same format as the recorded film images. When the sounds and images are in a common format, they can be spliced in complete synchronization. After several different sound tracks, such as separate music, dialogue, and sound effects tracks, have each been independently synchronized with the edited film images, they can be mixed together onto a single master sound track. Each separate synchronized sound track is played back on its own magnetic film playback unit or *dubber*. Dubbers can be synchronized by means of a physical or electronic interlock between drive mechanisms or motors. The dubbers and the magnetic film recorder that will be used to record the master sound track must be driven at exactly the same speed. Each separate dubber can then be fed to a different fader at an audio console or mixer so that they can all be combined. The output signal of the audio console is fed to a single magnetic film recorder. A synchronous film sound mix is often accompanied by a synchronous playback of the filmed images using an interlocked projector, which is connected to the same electrical signal as the sound playback and record machines. Mixing magnetic film provides precise synchronization between sound tracks as well as between all sounds and the film images.

Audiotape Editing

When synchronization between sounds and images is not crucial, it is often convenient to edit and mix sounds in an audiotape format, such as ¼-inch audiotape. Audiotape editing can then be done using physical splicing techniques. A variety of different audiotape formats can be used for nonsynchronous sound mixing. The resulting mix can be dubbed to the same format as the visual images.

Splicing Audiotape

Splicing ¼-inch audiotape requires several pieces of equipment, including a splicing block, a single-edge razor blade, a permanent felt-tip pen, a set of rewinds with a playback head, an amplifier, and a speaker. Sometimes ¼-inch tape is edited while it is played back on a ¼-inch tape recorder with a built-in splicer. The original audiotape recording should be safely stored away after a dub has been made for splicing.

The best procedure for editing ¼-inch audiotape is to find the edit point on one piece of tape by running it over the playback head. This point is then marked on the base side (usually the shiny side) of the audiotape with a permanent felt-tip pen. The tape is then placed securely and flatly in the splicing block with the precise edit point over the diagonal cut-line indentation on the block. The tape is severed with a single stroke of a sharp razor blade (razor blades should be replaced before they get dull). The audiotape is then advanced and the second edit point is marked. The second cut is made in the same manner as the first. After the excess tape has been removed from the splicing block, the two pieces of tape can be butted together and joined by placing a piece of adhesive ¼-inch splicing tape on the base side of the audiotape.

The spliced tape should be removed from the splicing block and played back at normal speed to ensure that a correct splice has been made. If a pop is heard while the splice passes over the playback head, the splice should be inspected to see if the two pieces of tape are slightly separated. If they are, the splicing tape can be removed and the splice reattached in the splicing block. If there is no gap between the two pieces of tape, two other possible sources of the popping sound should be investigated. First, the pop could be caused by a magnetized razor blade. It is possible for a steel blade to become magnetized and alter a recording. If a magnetized razor blade is responsible, cut off the affected portion of the tape and demagnetize or throw the razor blade away. A second common cause of popping is the improper selection of an edit point on one or both tapes. Cutting in the middle of a sound or failing to eliminate a prior or subsequent sound at the edit point can create a perceptible pop at the splice point. In this case the audiotape may have to be recut so that the pop is eliminated.

When audiotape will be spliced it is best to maintain as high a tape-to-head speed as possible during initial recording. For music the best editing speed is 15 inches per second, but for voice a tape-to-head speed of 7½ inches per second is usually sufficient to separate most words. It is never advisable to use speeds below 7½ inches per second, since this will make it difficult to separate sounds or produce high quality recordings (Figure 12.6).

One advantage of editing of ¼-inch audiotape prior to transferring onto magnetic film or videotape is that this format is quite inexpensive. Sound effects, music, and narration, can often be edited very efficiently in the ¼-inch tape format prior to transferring them to magnetic film or videotape. When synchronization between images and sounds is necessary, sounds must be transferred to magnetic film or videotape so that they can be edited in conjunction with their corresponding visual images. When precise synchronization between sounds or between sounds and images is not crucial, an editor has tremendous flexibility in terms of selecting playback devices. Sounds can be played back on many different machines, such as a

Spatial Differences in Audiotape Recording Speed

T h i s i s o n e s e c o n d w o r t h o f c o p y a t 1 5 I P S

This is one second worth of copy at 7.5 IPS

The faster the recording speed, the higher the quality of the recording, and for editing purposes, the faster the speed, the greater the distance between words and sounds for easier editing.

Figure 12.6 Physically editing audio tape is a matter of finding a space between words or sounds. The more wide-spread the sounds, the easier to and more accurate the editing can be.

¼-inch reel-to-reel, a cartridge, a cassette tape recorder, or even a record player, without the necessity of dubbing them to a common format. Each of these playback units can then be fed into an audio console or mixing board, where their individual volumes can be controlled as they are mixed together and sent out of the console to an audio recorder.

A mix log or cue sheet indicates when each playback machine should be started. Normally this involves prerolling the playback source in advance of the point where it will be blended into the master sound mix. Different machines are often started at different times. Combining sounds in this way eliminates the added step of dubbing sounds to a common format, such as magnetic film or videotape. When synchronization is not crucial and the production budget is too small to accommodate computerized editing, working in smaller audiotape formats can greatly increase the speed and efficiency of audio mixing.

Multitrack audiotape recorders that cannot read time code provide one means of maintaining synchronization between different sound sources that do not need to be synchronized with visual images. Most multitrack audiotape recorders allow the sounds recorded on one track to be played at the precise speed at which the original recording was made, while additional sounds are added on a parallel track. For example, music might be prerecorded on one track. This music could be played back while a singer's voice is recorded on a parallel track. Using this technique several musicians and singers, for example, can each be recorded at different times and places. Multitrack recorders allow many different sound tracks to be combined, such as those for narration, music, and sound effects. Synchronization between the separate tracks is inherent in the tape since each track is recorded and played back on the tape parallel with the others. Narration can be recorded while the sound effects and music are played back, for example. When each of the different tracks has been properly recorded, they can all be mixed onto a single track. It is important to note that time code readable multitrack recorders can also be used to maintain synchronization between different tracks, as noted earlier. To initially synchronize sounds with visual images, they are usually edited and mixed in the same format as the accompanying visual images.

Mixing Sound

Mixing Techniques

Sound mixing combines several different sounds or sound tracks that are running simultaneously. Editing, on the other hand, pieces sounds together in sequence, usually on one sound track at a time. Mixing is a process by which various sound tracks are blended together or combined with each other. Individual sound tracks for speech, sound effects, and music, for example, are first edited into sequential order, often in conjunction with visual images, prior to mixing them together to form one sound track. The volume and equalization or EQ (the attenuation or amplification of specific frequencies) of each different audio channel or track is separately controlled using a fader and EQ controls on an audio console or mixer (Figure 12.7).

It is extremely important to maintain a high signal-to-noise ratio in each separate sound track prior to the mix. During the mix, the audio level of one sound

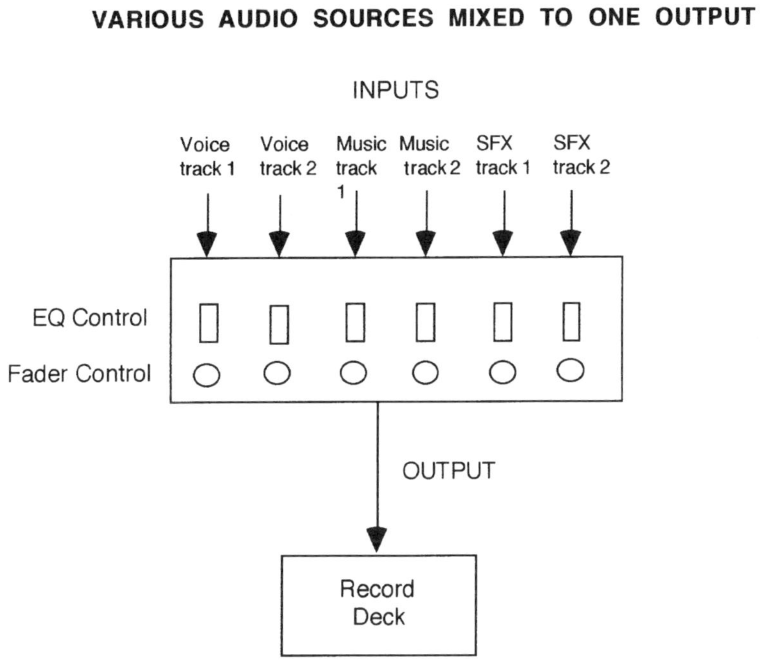

Figure 12.7 To combine several audio sources simultaneously, all of the individual sounds are fed through an audio mixer where the individual sounds can be equalized and levels can be properly set in relationship to each other.

track can always be reduced. But speech, sound effects, or music that were initially recorded or dubbed at a low sound level cannot be increased in volume during the mix without simultaneously increasing the accompanying noise level, and thereby reducing the quality of the audio. Whenever possible, sounds should be kept at their maximal level until the mix and then adjusted to accommodate other sounds.

AGCs (automatic gain controls) are sometimes used to maintain consistent audio levels during audio recording and dubbing. This method too often boosts background noise to unpleasant levels during nonspeaking passages. A *peak limiter* reduces excessively loud sounds without boosting background sounds. Both of these devices can affect the setting of maximal mixing levels.

During a mix, the sound editor adjusts the volume of one sound element with respect to another. Sounds can be superimposed on one another, and transitions between sounds such as fades, cross-fades, and segues, can be created. During an audio *fade,* the *pot* (short for *potentiometer,* a type of volume control) or fader for a sound is gradually turned up or down. A *cross-fade* combines a fade-out on one track with a simultaneous fade-in on another track. A *segue* is an instantaneous change from one track to another. Sound mixes usually involve several playback units channeled through an audio console to a single (monophonic) or dual (stereophonic) track master tape. The editor or mixer operator must set the proper volume for each playback source and control all special effects and transitions (Figure 12.8).

AUDIO MIXING CUE SHEET

Production ______________________ Date ________

Producer __________ Director __________ Mixer __________

Track A *Dialogue 1*		Track B *Dialogue 2*		Track C *SFX*		Track D *Music*	
Reel #1		Reel #2		Reel #3		Reel #4	
000	Dead Sync	000	Dead Sync	000	Dead Sync	000	Dead Sync
00:15	Sync pop	00:15	Sync pop	00:15	Sync pop	00:15	Sync pop
00:30		00:30		00:30	Crickets	00:30	FI Theme
				00:45	Slow fade		
					Hold under		
	Sam:						
01:10	(1stword)		Harold:				
	Hi, what's	01:20	Hi back to ya			01:20	FO
02:00	(Last word)						
	Thanks, see ya						
	FI=Fade In		FO=Fade Out				

Figure 12.8 The audio mixing log provides the mixing operator a guide as to when to use sound from different tracks. The verbal and timing cues give precise locations for making transitions or adding effects.

A mix is carefully preplanned on a mix log or audio cue sheet. A *mix log* or *audio cue sheet* indicates all the volume and EQ changes and transitions for every sound source the sound mixer must control. It is organized sequentially according to the overall time of the program. Changes in any sound source or the fader assigned to it are then listed under the column devoted to that source, indicating the precise time the change is to occur. The mixer operator consults the cue sheet as a guide to the adjustment of each individual sound source. For example, the opening music may have to be faded in at the beginning of the program and a narrator's voice may then be faded in over the music a few seconds later. The music may have to be decreased in volume at this point, so that it does not drown out the narration. Forty seconds later, the music may segue to another musical composition, which conveys a different mood or pace. Sound effects may have to be combined with this music, and at certain points, speech, sound effects, and music will probably occur simultaneously. Without a cue sheet, the editor or mixer could easily become confused during a sound mix (Figure 12.9).

Synchronous dialogue is generally recorded simultaneously with accompanying visual images. The sounds and images are then edited at the same time in the same format. When editing synchronous dialogue, an editor must be sensitive to the performance level, intonation, and accuracy of the speaker. Speech sounds that are radically different in intensity or intonation should not be edited together, even though their visual images match. Mistakes in the delivery of lines of dialogue should be removed. Compromises in editing synchronous speech sounds are inevitable, since editing together the best quality images does not always result in the best quality synchronous sounds.

The editor is sometimes forced to compromise between image quality and sound quality. An editor must be flexible and creative. For example, it may be necessary to use cutaways, such as a character's reaction to the speech of another character, to cover over mistakes in synchronous dialogue. Two or more portions of the same on-camera speech can be combined to remove missed lines or poor inflection, but unless there are cutaways, visual jump cuts will result. An editor must constantly make decisions on the basis of what is least objectionable, poor quality sounds or poor quality images, when editing synchronous dialogue and visuals.

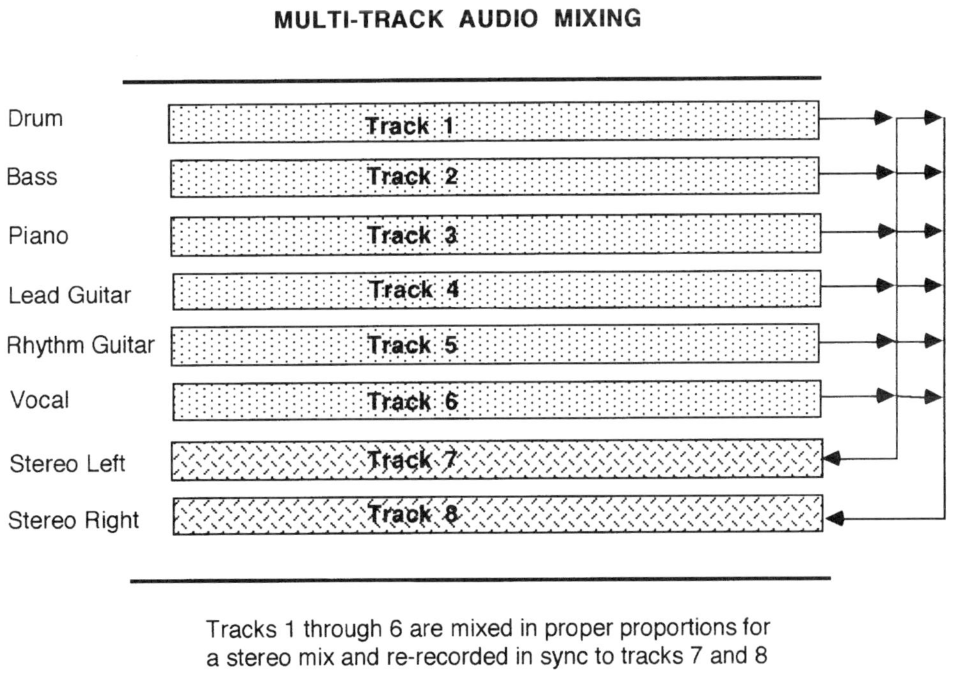

Figure 12.9 Several individual audio tracks on a multi-track audio tape can be combined into a single or stereo set of tracks through the process of "ping-ponging." A multi-track recorder can be adjusted so some heads are play-back heads while others are set to record. Since they are aligned on one head stack all of the tracks will be kept in sync.

Looping (which gets its name from loops of film that repeat the same shots over and over) or *Automatic Dialogue Replacement (ADR)* refer to the creation and replacement of lip-sync dialogue in the sound studio during postproduction. The visual images are repeatedly projected onto a sound studio screen, while the talent attempts to repeat the lines of dialogue exactly in sync with the lip movements of the on-screen speaker. These newly recorded speech sounds can be used to replace poor quality original recordings. ADR is often done with the performer trying to speak in unison with the playback (via headphones) of the original, on-set speech, which is used as an audio reference. It is usually less expensive to replace defective dialogue than to reshoot the whole sequence. However, sound studio speech often seems dead and lifeless in comparison with the original recordings with which it must be intercut, unless the sound signal is properly processed. An editor must pay particular attention to the pace, intonation, and vocal quality of the specific lines of dialogue that are to be inserted within an originally recorded scene.

Nonsynchronous or voice-over narration is frequently used to provide a commentary on visual actions. Voice-over narration can be edited together from audio interviews conducted in the field or it can be recorded after visual editing in real time with the narrator watching a preliminary edit of the film or videotape and pacing his or her speech to the changing shots and speed of the action. In the former case, the visuals are edited to the narration. In the latter case, the editor's job is to touch up various narration segments so that they coincide with specific visuals and mistakes are removed. The pace of the narration may need to be speeded up or

Figure 12.10 Sound effects libraries may be recorded on vinyl discs, audio tape, audio cassettes, CDs, or computer floppies.

slowed down during recording or editing to accommodate specific visual sequences. Errors in delivery can sometimes be removed through judicious editing

There are basically three kinds of sound effects: prerecorded library effects, spot recorded effects, and actuality recorded effects. *Library effects* are catalogued and maintained on phonograph records, audiotapes, or CDs for storage convenience and accessibility. *Spot effects* are created in a sound studio to duplicate the supposed off-screen or on-screen source. *Actuality effects* are recorded outside the sound studio. They either accurately reproduce a particular sound or create a vivid sound impression. Synchronous sound effects are immediately dubbed to the videotape or film format of the visuals so that they can be edited in synchronization with corresponding visual images. Library, spot, and actuality sound effects can all be placed in synchronization with visual images. Once the sound effect is dubbed to the proper format, it is edited into the videotape or film sound track accompanying the visual image. The sound of a door closing or a fist striking a face can be synchronized with the visual image of the action. In videotape editing, the sound effect is usually dubbed to a separate videotape along with a control track or time code so that it can be inserted into the proper videotape frame. In film editing, the sound effect is dubbed to magnetic film, which will correspond frame by frame with the accompanying visual images. In both cases the sound effect is precisely synchronized with its on-screen sound source (Figure 12.10).

A computer can be used to find and edit a collection of effects tracks on CD for either videotape or film. Computer storage, retrieval, and control allow a specific sound effect to be quickly accessed and its loudness, pitch, and duration to be altered and used in a variety of ways. For example, a single digitized sound of an airplane can be quickly found on a CD and then manipulated to create the complete illusion of an airplane circling an airport. Using this technique, a collection of basic sound effects can be used to provide an infinite variety of sounds. Each basic sound effect is catalogued and described as a computer file for easy selection and retrieval. It can also be stored digitally on a disk so that dubbing and signal processing does not result in any degradation of quality. Using the SMPTE time code of an edited videotape for reference, a sound effects editor can select, order, and manipulate all the sound effects that will be needed. Once the computer program is created, the sound effects are automatically dubbed, ordered, and processed to the editor's precise specifications.

Music for a film or television program can come from a variety of sources. Library music, which has been prerecorded on a CD, audiotape, or phonograph record, is often used to accompany visual images and other sounds. For public exhibition, the rights to prerecorded music must be secured, as discussed in Chapter 2 on producing and production management. Original music can be recorded in a sound studio for a specific project. It can either be recorded in advance of editing, so that visuals can be edited to the music, or it can be recorded after the visual editing has been completed, so that the performance of the music can be matched to the visuals.

After dubbing prerecorded music to the proper visual format, the editor carefully analyzes it by finding the precise frames where specific musical effects, such as rhythmic beats, crescendos, and changes in pace or tonality, occur. Visual images can then be added to the hard disk, videotape, or film and edited so that shot changes and changes in the intensity of the visual action and pace correspond with the music. Visual images can also be edited in counterpoint to the music, through the use of shot changes and visual tonalities and pacing that contradicts rather than complements the music. Synchronizing music to pre-edited visuals can be quite complicated. Music is usually composed with specific visuals in mind. The tempo of the music may need to be adjusted so that specific effects coincide with the visuals they are intended to accompany. The edited visuals are normally played back while the music is being recorded and are used as visual cues to guide the pace and tempo at which the music is performed.

There are two basic approaches to the problem of mixing music and speech sounds. One approach is to lower the level of the music "down and under" immediately prior to the delivery of a line of dialogue or narration, and then return the music to a normal level after the speech has concluded. A second approach is to keep the music at a consistently low level. If music is mixed at its full value, the speech sounds that accompany it will be difficult to understand. Even when the music is kept at a consistently low level, it is important to have clear and distinct dialogue and narration. An underlying assumption of both of these approaches to mixing music and speech is that the speech must be clearly understood. But it is sometimes necessary to hear the music at its full value, particularly when its pace, intensity, and mood are essential to the establishment of a particular feeling.

Mixing music requires the smooth operation of faders on an audio console. The music must have a relatively consistent pace and original recording level at points where it is to be effectively faded in or out or cross-faded with other music, speech, and sound effects. Music that varies in intensity or seems erratic is difficult to fade in and fade out smoothly. Faders should normally be moved very slowly so that one piece of music gradually blends into another piece of music or another type of sound. Sometimes popping on a sudden burst of music can be an effective transition device, a sort of musical punctuation. *Stingers* are short phrases of music, usually characterized by a rapidly descending scale or series of notes, which can also act as punctuation devices. In functionalist and realist situations, music is usually mixed smoothly and gradually with other types of sounds.

Summary

Sound editing can reflect realist, modernist, or postmodernist aesthetics. Realist sound editing preserves continuity in space and time. There are no apparent gaps or breaks in audio action. Sound and image combinations are usually synchronous, on-screen, and parallel in meaning. Modernist sound editing often develops sound as an independent aesthetic element. Vivid sound impressions and abstract audio qualities are often highlighted. Modernist sound editing can promote a more subjective world than realist sound editing by using a particular character's audio impressions to develop their point of view, just as modernist editing of visual images can create more subjective impressions and specific characters' spatial perspectives through point-of-view shots and other editing techniques. Postmodernist sound editing often bring together a pastiche of sounds and audio impressions, borrowing from previous texts; plundering sounds and music from older films and television programs; mixing dramatic, documentary, and avant-garde modes, classic art and popular culture; while encouraging spectator involvement and textual play.

Sounds can be edited using a digital nonlinear editing system, an analog videotape or audiotape electronic editing system, or by physically splicing analog magnetic film or audiotape. Digital nonlinear audio editing requires considerable disk space or storage, but it can offer a number of advantages over analog editing. The quality of digital audio does not significantly diminish from one generation to the next. Multiple audio tracks can be edited independently or in conjunction with one another. Finally, most nonlinear editing programs are very flexible. They often provide a visual image of a sound track, which allows the editor to quickly and easily find and mark precise edit points. A digital nonlinear edited sound track can maintain exact synchronization with accompanying videotape or film images, using SMPTE time code and/or film KeyKode as common reference.

There are two steps to digitizing audio: setting the audio level controls and setting the audio resolution or quality. The sampling rate and bandwidth of an audio signal can be varied during digitization to reduce the amount of storage space that is required. The quality of digitized audio and the size of the audio file also depend on the sampling rate and bit depth of the audio. The higher the sampling rate and bit depth, the better the sound quality. Digital audio, unlike digital video, is not usually compressed when it is digitized, since digitized audio already requires considerably less storage space than digitized video, and audio compression could significantly reduce the quality of the audio signal.

Digital nonlinear editing affords an editor flexibility in terms of instantaneously changing the order and duration of sounds and images. For example, clips of audio information can be cut, trimmed, copied, pasted, inserted, and deleted along a timeline.

Every edit made using a digital nonlinear software program is usually a virtual edit. No digitized material need be discarded when clips are trimmed, cut, or deleted along an editing timeline, since each clip is usually stored separately outside the timeline window. Many alternative versions of a scene or sequence can thus be quickly edited and examined without prematurely eliminating material that may be needed later. The ability to manipulate clips of sound along a timeline not only adds flexibility to the editing process, it can also make editing more efficient and cost effective. Clips can be very rapidly trimmed, cut, inserted, and deleted. Digital nonlinear editing can be much faster and easier than cutting and splicing conventional magnetic film or audiotape sound. Digital nonlinear editing offers a number of advantages in terms of flexibility and efficiency as well over other forms of sound editing, such as electronic videotape editing.

Videotape audio can be edited electronically by using either a control track or a time code readable editing unit. Control track editing is somewhat less precise than time code editing. Most control track editors slip a bit or skip frames when the videotape is repeatedly stopped and started. Control track videotape editing usually allows for video-only, audio-only, and audio-plus-video insert editing. To insert edit sound onto prerecorded images without erasing those images, the sound must first be recorded onto a separate videotape along with a control track. Sound can then be dubbed onto one of the audio tracks or channels of a prerecorded videotape without disturbing the picture or separate audio information on another sound channel. Video can also be added to a videotape without disturbing the prerecorded audio signal. Audio editing on videotape can involve a single synchronous sound track on the original videotape or the building of complex dialogue, narration, sound effects, and music tracks.

A more expensive alternative to using the control track of a videotape is to use a computerized videotape editor with addressable time code. The computerized editor can control several source VCRs or VTRs simultaneously. Sound editing and mixing decisions can be programmed into the computer, which will control the playback and adjust the volume of each different sound source. With computer assistance, a complex sound track can be designed, programmed, and mixed automatically on the basis of a mix log or audio cue sheet that is programmed into the computer along with all editing decisions. Time code editing allows an editor to perform more complex mixing of separate audio tracks. A potential problem with multigeneration dubbing and mixing with analog audiotape, however, is that the music or sound effects may be severely degraded in quality by virtue of having been dubbed.

Conventional film sound editing involves physically splicing magnetic film. Synchronous lip-sync dialogue for film is normally recorded during production using an audiotape recorder, which records both the sounds and a Pilotone track. The sound track is then dubbed to magnetic film so that it can be edited synchronously with the image. Exactly the same number of magnetic film frames will be obtained during the dubbing process as there are corresponding visual frames. Clapstick sound and corresponding images are recorded at the beginning of each shot, so that the separate sound and image tracks can be properly synchronized with each other during editing. Magnetic film can be physically spliced in conjunction with visual images, and thus synchronization between them is maintained.

Audiotape can be physically spliced in several different formats. Nonsynchronous splicing can be done with ¼-inch audiotape. The tape is cut diagonally with a razor blade and spliced together with mylar tape. The mylar tape should be placed only on the base side of the audiotape, so that it does not interfere with the audio recording and playback. Nonsynchronous audio mixing can be done using a variety of audio formats, such as cassettes, cartridges, reel-to-reels, and even turntables. Each different source is played back and sounds are blended together through an audio console or mixer. Multitrack sound recorders allow several different tracks to be recorded in synchronization with each other. A background music track can be recorded and then played back as an accompaniment to a singer whose voice is recorded independently on a separate track. In this way several different types of sounds can be combined on a single reel of audiotape in synchronization with each other.

Sound mixing is a process of blending together simultaneous sounds or sound tracks. This includes such transition devices as fades, cross-fades, and segues. Blending together different types of sounds, such as speech, sound effects, and music, demands smooth and precise operation of the faders on an audio console or mixer. It also requires careful preparation of a mix log, which specifies different audio levels and transitions from one sound track to another. Specific principles of editing and mixing apply to different types of sound, such as speech, sound effects, and music.

When editing speech sounds, an editor must be sensitive to the speaker's performance level, intonation, and accuracy. Mistakes and pauses must be eliminated. An editor who is editing synchronous sounds and images may have to make editing decisions on the basis of the least objectionable way to combine these sounds and images. Sometimes cutaways must be inserted into the visuals to hide audio or visual problems. Through a technique known as looping or automatic dialogue replacement (ADR), speech sounds can be added to and perfectly synchronized with pre-edited prerecorded visual images. Voice-over interviews and narration are often edited prior to the selection of illustrative visuals.

There are three basic kinds of sound effects: library effects, spot effects, and actuality effects. Library effects are prerecorded on CDs, phonograph records, and audiotapes. Spot effects are specially recorded in the sound studio, and actuality effects are recorded in the field. Synchronous sound effects must be immediately dubbed to magnetic film or videotape, so that they can be edited in conjunction with corresponding visual images. Spot effects are sometimes recorded in the sound studio in synchronization with specific visual images after the visuals have already been edited. Sound effects that function primarily as background sounds are often mixed at sound levels well below primary speech or music sounds. Sometimes it is necessary to raise the level of sound effects during a mix so that they can be used to stimulate startlingly vivid sound impressions.

Music can be analyzed and used as a basis for editing visual images. In this case, the two are synchronized by editing the images to the music. Actions within the visual frame and cuts from one shot to another are frequently synchronized with the beat or rhythm of the music. Music can be synchronized to pre-edited visual images by composing the music specifically for these images. The music is then performed while the images are simultaneously projected onto a screen or monitor for the conductor or musicians. When mixing music and speech sounds, it is essential that the speech be audible and intelligible. Music that overlaps speech is normally faded down to a lower volume level. The music can be placed at a consistently low level, or it can be faded down and under speech and faded back up to its full value during longer gaps in the recorded speech. When music is presented by itself without other sounds, it is normally recorded at its full value. Mixing music through fade-ins, cross-fades, and segues requires a smooth and consistent operation of faders or pots on an audio console, but loud sounds are sometimes "popped on" for emphasis and punctuation.

Videotape sound mixing requires several audio channels on the source videotape or several source VCRs running simultaneously, which are computer controlled. An edited audio track on videotape is sometimes dubbed to a multitrack audio recorder so that it can be combined with other sounds before the combined master mix is transferred back to the original videotape. If synchronization is crucial, the control track from the videotape must be dubbed to the audiotape as well. When precise synchronization between sounds and images is required, the audio must be immediately dubbed to a specific film or videotape format so that it can be edited in conjunction with the visual images. Synchronous film sound mixing requires several interlocked magnetic film source machines, called dubbers. Several audio tracks can then be combined through an audio console or mixer into a single master sound mix on a magnetic film recorder.

Exercises

1. Using a shooting script as your guide, prepare a mix log or audio cue sheet for combining all of the various sound elements that will be used in postproduction editing. While precise volume control settings cannot be known until actual materials are prepared for a mix, virtually all other factors can be anticipated in advance. Try to compose separate and continuous sound tracks or channels on paper for each different type of sound, such as synchronous dialogue, narration, sound effects or background sound, and music. Indicate where one piece of music will cross-fade or segue to another, requiring separate tracks or channels, or where several different sound effects or background sounds must be combined.

   A mix log or audio cue sheet will graphically depict the depth and texture of sound by indicating when several types of sounds or sound tracks coexist, such as narration, sound effects, and music. Indicate which type of sound will be dominant if they will not all be of equal intensity. Determine the series of stages sound-track preparation must go through if some types of sound must be premixed prior to the final master mix.
2. Replace some original sound (sound originally recorded with corresponding visuals) with library or spot effects. Grab an audio clip off a CD or digitize an analog audiotape recording of the sound effect. If you are using a digital nonlinear system, use the insert mode; if you are using electronic videotape editing, physically splice the new sounds into the existing magnetic film or audiotape sound track. Compare the edited sound track with the original for sound clarity and consistency.
3. Mix a voice-over narration track with music. Try to make the edits as smooth and indistinguishable as possible. Be careful to maintain consistency in terms of pace and timing in the delivery of narration. Find similar phrases of music on which to make an instantaneous transition from one piece of music to another. Pay careful attention to any discrepancy in terms of audio levels and background sounds when editing together speech, sound effects, or music recorded outside the studio. Fade the music down and under when the narrator is speaking, and fade the music up to its full volume when the narrator is silent for a reasonable period of time.

Additional Readings

Alten, Stanley. *Audio in Media,* 4th ed. Belmont, CA: Wadsworth Publishing Co., 1994.

Amyes, Tim. *The Technique of Audio Post Production in Video and Film.* Boston: Focal Press, 1990.

Mantell, Harold, ed. *The Complete Guide to the Creation and Use of Sound Effects for Films, T.V. and Dramatic Productions.* Princeton, NJ: Films for the Humanities, Inc., 1978.

Nisbett, Alec. *The Sound Studio.* Boston: Focal Press, 1995.

Roberts, Kenneth H., and Win Sharples, Jr. A *Primer for Film-Making.* New York: Bobbs-Merrill, 1971.

Watkinson, John. *An Introduction to Digital Audio.* Boston: Focal Press, 1994.

13

Animation and Special Effects

Introduction

Animation and special effects generate visual interest and can be used to create imaginative worlds that defy the physical laws of space and time. Animation simulates movement, allowing cartoon characters to inhabit a unique world and to perform unbelievable actions that would be impossible if not often fatal for humans. Special effects generate interest and excitement, often allowing futuristic or historical worlds to come to life, dangerous actions and events to be simulated, and live-action characters to accomplish superhuman feats.

Animation develops imaginative worlds by using single-frame recording techniques to make static images and objects appear to move. By breaking the motion of an object down into its component parts, an animator can control the movements of otherwise lifeless figures and images. Single-frame recordings of static images can create apparent motion when small changes in the positioning of objects occurs between successive frames. Thus animation creates apparent change in position. Only twelve different images may be required for each second's duration of the final sequence, although single-frame versus double-frame animation is always a trade-off between smoothness and cost. The animator's job is to create the desired illusion of movement. Slower movements will require the preparation of more individual frames and smaller changes of position between each frame than faster movements. Time and distance are interrelated. An object that moves a distance of two feet in twenty-four frames obviously moves more quickly in the final sequence than an object that moves only one foot in twenty-four frames.

Special effects used to be and still is in many ways a highly specialized area of media production. Producing most realistic effects was usually quite laborious and expensive in the past. Today, the widespread use of complex and convincing special effects in low-budget productions has been encouraged and simplified by the availability of relatively inexpensive digital image processing programs that are built into many video cameras as well as much digital nonlinear editing and special effects computer software. This chapter provides a broad survey of both traditional and contemporary special effects that are widely used in film, video, and multimedia production.

Animation

Animation is based on an animator's knowledge of time and motion. An animator must be able to break down motion into its component parts so that it can be artificially constructed out of static images. One of the best means of analyzing motion is to examine the individual frames of a live-action film. A live-action motion picture camera, for example, records twenty-four (twenty-five in Europe) frames every second at standard speed. Each frame represents 1/24th of the change in the subject's spatial positioning during one second. By looking at the amount of change that occurs between the successive frames of a live-action sequence, an animator can begin to determine how much change there should be in the position and movement of objects between successive animated frames.

It is not always necessary to record a different image for each film frame, however. A smooth illusion of continuous motion can often be obtained by recording two identical frames of each image or drawing position. Thus only twelve different images will be required for each second's duration of the final sequence, rather than twenty-four images.

Storyboards and Animation Preproduction

An animated sequence often begins with the construction of a storyboard. In this case, the storyboard is a series of sequential sketches that depict the composition and content of each shot or key action in an animated sequence. A storyboard is very similar to a newspaper comic strip. It helps a graphic artist or animator to visualize the entire sequence on paper prior to preparing the final images. The storyboard can be used to communicate the animator's basic idea and strategy to a producer. It can also serve as a blueprint or guide to the actual creation and recording of images. Storyboard images are not as detailed as the actual film or television images will be. They usually consist of simple sketches, line drawings, or photographs. A storyboard simply and clearly communicates the basic idea of a sequence.

Many animators design their storyboards in conjunction with prerecorded music, sound effects, and/or voice tracks. Because timing or synchronization between sound and images is often crucial to the success of an animated sequence, music and sound are initially recorded and analyzed. A log or audio cue sheet is often kept of the frame numbers of images where specific sounds occur so that the corresponding images can be perfectly synchronized. A log or audio cue sheet can be combined with the frames of a storyboard. A designer can then tell exactly how many seconds, and therefore how many film or video frames, are required for each storyboard frame. Frames for each point of synchronization between sounds and images can be included in the storyboard so that there is no confusion about precisely where a specific action is to occur. Once the storyboard has been constructed in conjunction with the recorded music and sounds, the actual production phase of animation begins (Figure 13.1).

EXPOSURE (Dope) SHEET

TITLE__________ SCENE____ ANIMATOR______ SHEET # ___

FRAME	ACTION	SETTING	LAYERS					CAMERA
			4	3	2	1	BG	

Figure 13.1 An animation exposure sheet, sometimes called a "dope" sheet, includes all of the information the camera operator needs to make the exposures and movements of the cels and which cels to stack in the layer.

Types of Animation

Many different types of images and objects can be animated, including hand-drawn illustrations, paper cutouts, puppets, clay figures, still photographs of live actions, and computer graphic images. All of these different forms of animation are based on single-frame recording techniques. It is often helpful to distinguish between flat and plastic animation, as well as between film and electronic animation. *Flat animation* includes such techniques as cel animation, in which individual illustrations are drawn for almost every frame of picture. Plastic animation encompasses the use of three-dimensional figures, such as puppets or clay figures. Single-frame recording of people and three-dimensional objects is sometimes called *pixillation.* In a sense, all of these techniques or types of animation elevate the animator to the status of director, editor, and scenic designer.

Flat animation refers to the recording of two-dimensional images using single-frame recording techniques. One of the most common forms of flat animation is cel animation. *Cels* are individual sheets of clear acetate on which images can be drawn or painted, usually with ink and opaque watercolors. An ink outline is traced onto each cel from an outline sketch. An outline sketch is made on paper for each cel, and a film or video recording of these sketches, known as a *pencil test,* is often made so that corrections can be made prior to the creation of actual acetate cels. The cel is painted on the opposite side so that the ink lines do not run and so that the rough surface texture of the paint is not apparent. Cels are preperforated with holes at one end so they can be inserted over the pegs of a movable table, called an *animation rostrum,* for precise registration and framing. An animation stand consists of a rostrum, lights, and a movable camera platform.

Cel animation gives the animator or graphic artist complete control over the design of the image. However, drawing each frame individually on a cel can be quite time consuming and expensive, so many shortcuts are used to conserve time. Because cels are transparent, they can be sandwiched together to combine images drawn on different cels. A background cel can be used over and over again while changes are made in the placement of foreground objects, eliminating the need to redraw the background for each frame. Individual movements of characters' feet, hands, and mouths can be repeated or recycled with different bodies and backgrounds. A series of lip movements synchronized to various consonant or vowel sounds can be used repeatedly rather than drawn individually for each occurrence. To cut costs more drastically, some animators draw only every fourth or fifth frame of recorded film or videotape. This can, of course, lead to rougher and therefore less pleasing animation.

Another commonly used technique for cutting costs and increasing cel-animation efficiency is called *rotoscoping.* In rotoscoping, a sequence is first filmed in live action; the individual frames of the motion picture are then projected on a cel and an outline of the objects in the frame is drawn and hand colored.

Subjects are normally photographed against a contrasting background so that outlines are clearly visible. The drawn outlines are then colored like standard hand-drawn animation cels.

While rotoscoping makes the production of cels more efficient, it often produces images that are less aesthetically pleasing than hand-drawn animation. The difference between rotoscoped and hand-drawn animation is similar to the difference between naturalistic painting and caricature. A caricature of a person emphasizes or exaggerates characteristic features. In a like manner, hand-drawn cel animation often uses nonrepresentational figures and techniques such as image squashing and stretching to exaggerate motion. An animator can sometimes create a more vivid impression of motion by exaggerating the compression of objects as gravity pulls them to the ground and then stretching or expanding their shape as they jump or run, temporarily escaping the pull of gravity. Stretching exaggerates acceleration, while squashing exaggerates deceleration. Animated motion is not always a direct copy of live action. These subtle differences in apparent motion become obvious when rotoscoped images are compared with original hand-drawn images.

The illusion of movement in cel animation can be achieved in one of two ways: by drawing a different cel for each change of position of objects within the frame or by moving the cel itself on the rostrum of the animation stand between recordings. If movement is to be achieved through differences between cels, each cel in the sequence must be placed in exactly the same position within the camera frame by using the registration pegs. On the other hand, if motion is to be achieved by moving the cel, this can be done by using the horizontal and vertical controls of the rostrum.

One problem that sometimes stands in the way of physically moving a cel is that the background movement within the two-dimensional image may seem unnatural when it moves at the same rate as the foreground. In live-action photography, the background and foreground seem to move at different rates, providing an illusion of depth and three dimensionality. This problem is sometimes solved by placing the background cels on a separate peg bar, or set of registration pegs, on the same rostrum or table so that they can be moved at a slower speed than the foreground. Virtually all animation stands are equipped with double peg bars so that backgrounds and foregrounds can be moved independently of one another.

Hand-drawn illustrations are not the only flat images that can be animated. Paper or fabric cutouts and still photographs can also be set into motion. A paper cutout of a person or animal can be constructed so that it has moving body parts. It can then be placed over a variety of backgrounds so that it seems to come alive and move on the screen. A flicker effect can also be achieved by recording frames of colored paper in between frames of specific photographs or illustrations. The change in photographs can be timed to the beat of music. In this way what might otherwise be a boring presentation of static images acquires kinetic energy. Still photographs and printed illustrations, such as magazine images, can be animated through single frame techniques, such as those used by Frank Mouris in his famous *Frank Film* (1978). Mouris' film is as much a feat of optical printing, discussed later in this chapter, as of animation (Figure 13.2).

Plastic animation refers to the animation of many different types of three-dimensional figures and objects using single-frame recording techniques. Puppets, clay figures, miniature vehicles, and even still frames of live action can be animated.

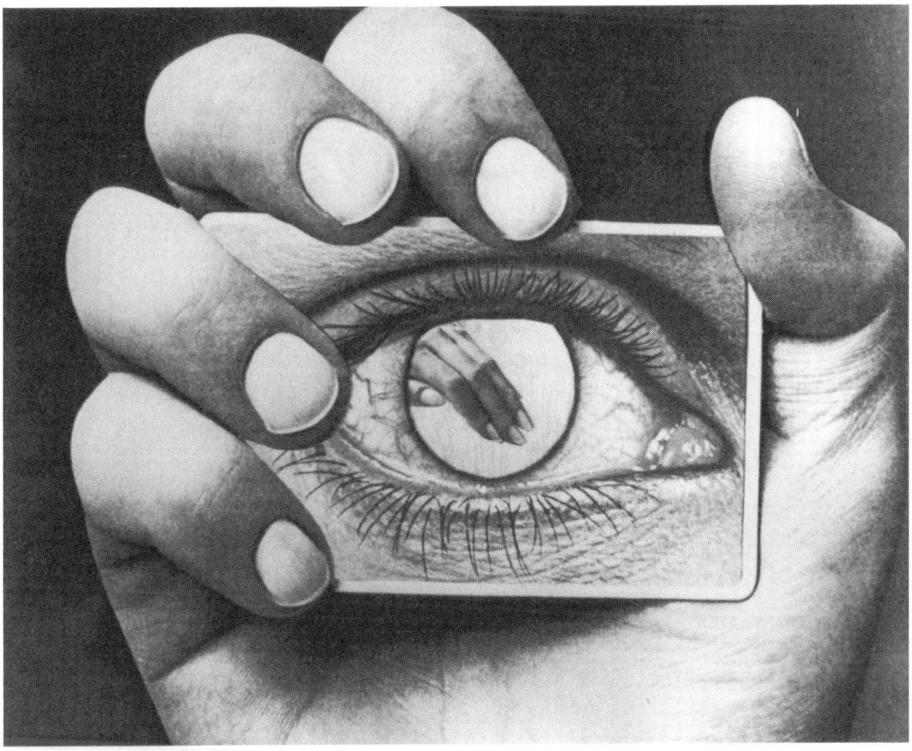

Figure 13.2 Frank Mouris specialized in producing films shot single frame, often using collages of unrelated images shot in sequences as short as two to three frames for a rapid, eye teasing format.

While hand puppets and marionettes are usually recorded in live action so that the mouth and body movements can be synchronized to speech or music, it is possible to animate more rigid puppets and clay figures by moving them slightly between frames.

Unlike the animator of flat, two-dimensional characters, however, the plastic animator must create a miniature three-dimensional world of sets and props within which puppets and figures will move. Careful attention must be paid to minute details. Backgrounds must be painted to scale, and everything must be proportional to the size of the figures. The camera is usually placed in a horizontal position with respect to the scene rather than above it, as with an animation stand. Miniature vehicles, such as cars and trucks, can also be animated through single-frame techniques. Sometimes these animated miniatures are used as a substitute for more costly and dangerous stunts and special effects in live-action films.

An animated three-dimensional figure sequence is shot much like a live-action scene, except that the pictures are recorded frame by frame. More than one camera is frequently used so that action does not have to be repeated for different shots, as in single-camera live action recording. The animation of three-dimensional objects sacrifices the artist's ability to simulate the blurring effect of photographing live-action figures in rapid movement, and mechanical, non-lifelike movement sometimes results.

Clay or malleable plastic material is often animated so that unique shapes and actions can be recorded. A technique known as *metamorphosis,* in which one figure gradually changes into a totally different form, can be accomplished with clay as well as with images drawn on cels. A famous animated film, called *Clay,* shows the evolution of one life form from another using clay metamorphosis. Virtually any shape and type of movement can be constructed using clay or malleable plastic materials.

Human figures can also be animated by a technique known as *pixillation.* Images of human beings can be pixillated by recording one frame, moving the image and then recording another frame. Pixillation has been used in many films to animate images of human beings so that they seem to perform extraordinary feats. In Norman McLaren's famous film *Neighbors* (1955), two neighbors fight over their adjoining territory. This clever film offers a symbolic treatment of war by presenting a unique abstract image of human behavior and actions. In one scene the human figures hover across the ground with no apparent movement of their limbs. McLaren achieved this image by photographing single frames of his subjects leaping into the air. Only the apex of each jump was recorded, making the people seem to hover over the ground.

Film Animation

Film animation requires the use of a camera that records single frames of motion-picture film. The camera is normally suspended above the artwork by mounting it on an animation stand. An animation stand consists of a camera platform attached to vertical poles or columns, so that it can be raised and lowered over the artwork. The camera platform is suspended above a large horizontal table, called a *rostrum,* which can be moved east, west, north, and south. The artwork is secured to this horizontal table by placing the hole perforations in proper registration over peg bars on the table.

The vertical columns and horizontal table of an animation stand allow for a variety of camera movements, such as dollies, zooms, pans, and tilts. During a dolly shot the camera is gradually moved toward or away from the artwork between exposures. For a zoom shot, the focal length of the lens is changed between one exposure and the next. Pan and tilt shots are made by simply moving the rostrum from side to side or from top to bottom between successive frames. A *pantograph* is often attached to one side of the stand so that precise movements can be charted on special graph paper by the pantograph pointer (Figure 13.3).

A *field guide*, which is a transparent sheet that has spacing and framing information etched on it, can be placed over the artwork to adjust the camera frame. The field guide is proportional to the aspect ratio of the film format, such as 1.33:1 or 4:3 for standard 16mm. It provides spacing and framing information for different field sizes. A field size of 11, for example, indicates a field 11 inches wide by 8¼ inches high, while a field size of 4 is 4 inches wide by 3 inches high. A reflex viewfinder is usually required to frame the image precisely for the camera lens.

The artwork can be evenly lit from above with little glare reflected into the camera by using two lights that are suspended at 45-degree angles to the horizontal table. Backlighting can be provided by a diffused lighting source, such as a light box, placed underneath the artwork on the table. A glass platen is often used over the artwork to keep it flat and in sharp focus. There are often exposure differences between live-action recording and single-frame animation with a film camera. The equivalent shutter speed for single-frame exposure often differs from that used when exposing frames at 24 fps, for example.

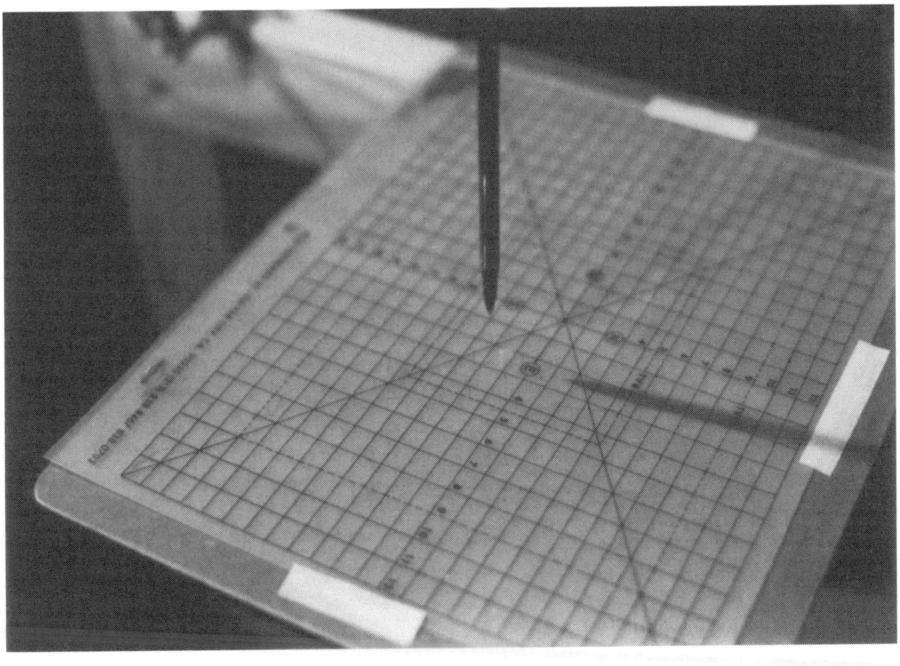

Figure 13.3 A pantograph pointer follows the movement of the animation table on the field. Each movement of the table may be accurately calibrated between exposures.

A *film animation camera* is normally equipped with special controls for specific animation effects. A variable shutter, for example, can be used to fade out from or fade in to a specific piece of artwork. By rewinding the film to the beginning of a fade-out as indicated by the frame counter on the camera and then fading in on another piece of artwork, a dissolve can be created. Superimpositions can be made by backwinding and double-exposing individual frames.

The efficiency and accuracy of film animation has been greatly increased by the development of computer-controlled animation stands. All of the complex camera movements, such as dollies, fades, focus changes, and movements of the table, such as east/west and north/south pans, can be preprogrammed and computer controlled. As many as fifty different pieces of artwork can be automatically placed in proper registration in sequential order on some computer film animation stands. Computer control dramatically decreases the setup time. Each repetition of a specific piece of artwork is recorded at different points on the film. The shutter is simply closed while the frames between them are passed. Thus frames 1, 9, 17, and 25 of an eight-frame cycle or repeated action are recorded consecutively before the artwork for frames 2, 10, 18, and 26 is recorded, until all the frames and artwork have been used. Setup time and operator errors are substantially reduced by having the computer control these operations automatically (Figure 13.4).

Images can be electronically animated by placing a video camera on an animation stand and record single video frames of the artwork on the table using the same techniques as film animation. An important difference between video and film animation is that the video camera records 30 fps, instead of 24 fps. Single-

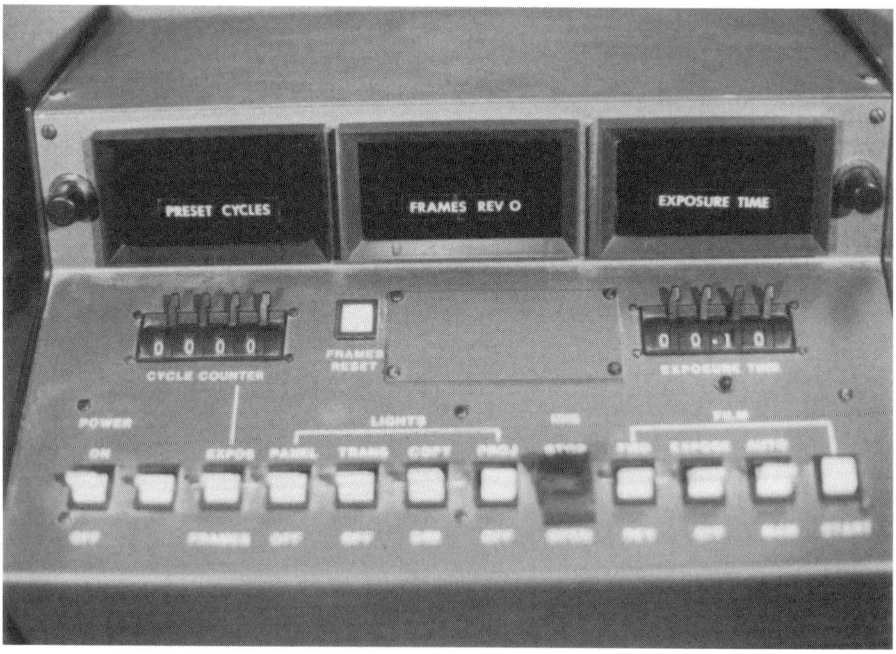

Figure 13.4 The control box for an animation stand provides the operator with the means of presetting the number of frames to be exposed on each cel, the exposure time, and all of the other camera controls such as iris setting.

frame video animation requires the use of a slo-mo (slow motion) recorder or a disc frame storage unit, rather than a conventional VCR. A *slo-mo recorder* or *video animator* can be used to record individual frames for a thirty-second animation sequence. The sequence can then be transferred to conventional videotape. A disk frame storage or memory unit, such as that which is used to store pages of text and titles composed on a character generator, can also be used to record individual animation frames. Some memory units have a limited storage capacity, however, while others are capable of storing and immediately accessing hundreds of figures or pages.

One advantage of recording animation electronically is that the results can be viewed immediately. Film animators frequently have to wait several days or longer to see the results of their work. Video animation and film animation can be combined by recording a pencil test with a video camera using disk storage of single frames and instantly viewing the results on a monitor so that problems can immediately be uncovered and corrections made. The final cels are recorded with a film camera for optimum quality and maximum storage capacity.

Computer Animation

Computer animation programs can be used for video production. Some animation programs fully integrate graphics programs and animation programs so that still-frame graphic images can be used to create apparent motion. Graphic images can be originally designed on a computer monitor by using various computer commands and devices, such as a light pencil or stylus to draw on a television screen, or an electronic tablet or a mouse to compose images on a computer screen. They can then be colored and manipulated by computer.

Live-action frames can also be grabbed or digitized by some computers for further graphic manipulation and/or combined with computer graphic images. Single-frame graphic images can be stored on disk. These images can be expanded in size for detailed work and then shrunk to a smaller size for actual presentation. The animator can manipulate the colors, lines, shapes, and size of the image. Motion can be created by cycling different movements and using the computer to interpolate intermediate frames of motion between two static frames. An NTSC standard video output can then be fed to a switcher or VCR.

Computer animation programs allow for interpolation in which the animator composes the first and last frames of a sequence, referred to as the *keyframes* (another form of animation interpolation uses paths and involves the drawing of lines through 3-D space), and the computer software then creates or interpolates the in-between frames. Even some of the least expensive computers programs can interpolate a number of frames. Computer animation allows an almost infinite number of repetitions of the same image. Image cycling is facilitated by simply drawing the first and last frame of a sequence, interpolating the rest, and then recycling this sequence wherever it is needed. It is also possible to make many duplicates of the same image within a single frame.

Rendering is the final step in both two-dimensional (2-D) and three-dimensional (3-D) animation. It is often the most time-consuming and memory-intensive stage of computer animation. The end product of rendering is the creation of a graphics file that can be combined with other graphics files to collectively produce the completed animation sequence. While the time and memory required for rendering is often extensive, it can sometimes be reduced by using shortcuts for color, procedural (mathematical approximations of "natural" patterns, such as marble or clouds), and texture (a graphic drawn on an object, such as a soft drink label drawn on a can) maps applied to images during the rendering process.

The greatest advantages of computer animation are speed and accuracy. Results are immediately viewable. An animator need not wait a day or a week for the film animation to be processed and printed at a laboratory. Images and frames can be quickly designed and accurately copied. They can be stored on disk for long periods of time and used again or redesigned for another animation sequence.

A sophisticated computer animation program can interpolate the three dimensions of a design from a two-dimensional image in much the same way that an engineering or architectural design computer program, such as a CAD program, does. A completely computer-controlled illusion of three dimensionality can also be obtained in films that combine live-action characters with computer-generated objects and backgrounds, such as *Tron* (1983) and *Who Framed Roger Rabbit* (1988). The live-action subject is usually recorded against a blue screen or a monochromatic background, so that it can be keyed or matted into a computer-generated scene. The availability of these combined animation and special effects techniques has allowed graphic artists to save time and experiment creatively with abstract visual images for film and video (Figure 13.5).

Figure 13.5 The Touchstone production of *Roger Rabbit* combined live action, cel drawn animation and computer animation sequences in a startling yet realistic manner. (Courtesy of Touchstone Pictures and Amblin Entertainment, Inc.)

Special Effects

Special effects can be divided into six basic categories: camera effects, optical effects, digital effects, models and miniatures, and physical effects. Camera effects include such features as fast and slow motion as well as single-frame (animation) recording. Optical and digital effects run the gamut of image processing techniques from *matting* and *keying* (where a portion of one image is replace by another) to *morphing* (transforming one object into another, which is also called *metamorphosis*) and *compositing* (placing different layers of images on top of another). Models and miniatures, when combined with single-frame animation as well as matting and keying effects, can be used to put an object, such as a spacecraft, in motion or to create the illusion of a 21st century city by placing futuristic buildings into an existing location. Makeup can transform an actor into an android, a zombie, or a werewolf, while physical effects, such as fog, rain, and explosions, can contribute to the emotional mood of a sequence and generate viewer interest and excitement. Each of these different types of special effects is discussed in this chapter, but the actual creation of specific effects may require considerable hands-on experience and, in some cases, such as the use of explosive devices, they should only be attempted by highly trained specialists.

Camera Effects

A significant number and range of special effects can be created within a film camera during initial recording. Some film cameras, for example, allow the frames-per-second speed to be altered from the normal sound speed of 24 fps. Recording rates in excess of 24 fps, such as 32, 48, and 64 fps, create slow motion when the processed film is projected at the standard projection speed of 24 fps. Recording rates less than 24 fps, such as 18 and 12 fps, create fast motion. Attaching an *intervalometer* to a film camera allows the frames per second to be significant reduced to one frame every 1, 2, or 20 seconds, or even every few minutes or hours, to create time-lapse recordings, such as images of clouds rolling overhead or flower petals opening and closing throughout the day. Single-frame control of a live-action film camera allows for pixillation effects, which are described earlier in this chapter (Figure 13.6).

In addition to varying the speed of the images, some film cameras allow fade-outs, fade-ins, superimpositions, and reverse motion to be created during initial recording. The fader control is closed down or opened up at the proper rate, such as one second for a twenty-four frame duration effect at standard speed, to create an in-camera fade-out or fade-in. The film inside the camera can be rewound with the fader closed and then the fader is opened up again to superimpose another shot on top of the first one, usually with the lens closed down slightly to prevent overexposure and to make one shot dominant and the other recessive. Reverse motion can be created by turning the camera upside down during initial recording and then reversing the shot end for end, that is, using the beginning of the shot as the end of the shot during editing, which turns the picture right side up and reverses the motion. While more control over these types of effects can be maintained through the use of optical effects during postproduction, some experimental filmmakers prefer to exercise control over these effect during initial recording.

Figure 13.6 The frame rate control on the side of this camera permits exposures from single frame to 64 frames per second.

In-camera matte effects can be created by blocking off a portion of the frame during the first exposure, rewinding the film, and then exposing the previously blocked portion of the frame. Matte boxes can have half of the frame filled with an opaque black filter, which is then reversed to the cover the opposite half of the frame to create a split-screen image. First one side of the frame is exposed, and then the film is rewound and the opposite side of the film is exposed. In-camera mattes, which are finely cut out of metal, can also be inserted behind the lens closer to the focal plane. An actor can then play two different roles within the same camera frame by first filming the actor on one side of the screen, rewinding the film, and then filming the same actor on the opposite side of the screen. Painted skylines and other scenic additions can be made using the same in-camera matte process by dividing the frame horizontally rather than vertically. Filters can also be placed over a lens, such as a gauze or haze filter, to create a softer image. Cinematographers often carry a variety of transparent materials with them on location that can be used to diffuse the image during recording.

Video cameras can also provide built-in special effects controls. Many of these effects are similar to some of the in-camera film effects described earlier. For example, fade-ins and fade-outs can often be created automatically at the beginning or end of a shot by depressing a fader control. Some cameras allow the speed of motion to be varied to create slow motion, fast motion, and time-lapse recordings. Other in-camera special effects include various forms of digital image processing, such as image patterning, blurring, solarization, and other visual image manipulations and distortions. Again, many of these in-camera effects can also be created during postproduction, such as digital nonlinear editing, although some experimental videographers prefer to create these effects during initial recording.

Optical Effects

One of the advantages of creating special effects during postproduction is that they can often be more carefully controlled at this stage than during the production stage. Mistakes made during production are often very costly if a scene must be reconstructed and actors re-engaged. Postproduction special effects are often "added on" to the initial recordings and rarely require the initial scene to be reshot. In the past, in-camera film and video effects were often undertaken to prevent generational loss in terms of reductions in the quality of the image during postproduction, but the advent of digital technologies has virtually eliminated generational loss in the creation of electronic special effects during the postproduction stage.

A variety of optical film effects are still widely used today, including step printing, traveling mattes, and aerial image printing. An *optical printer* is needed to create many special effects on film. A basic optical printer consists of a camera and a projector. The two machines face each other, and the lens of the camera is focused on the image from the projector. The camera and projector can be moved toward or away from each other to increase the size of the image. An optical blowup can be created by using a larger format and a smaller format projector. Using a smaller format camera and a larger format projector creates an optical reduction. The camera and the projector must be precisely positioned so that the full frame of picture in the projector fills the full frame of picture in the camera.

Many effects, such as dissolves, fades, and superimpositions, can be made more easily and less expensively on a conventional contact printer, which brings the original film and the copy into physical contact (emulsion to emulsion) as they pass over a light. A and B roll printing is conventionally done on a contact printer.

More sophisticated optical effects require the use of additional techniques and equipment. *Optical fades* can be made by gradually covering or uncovering the lamp in the projector with a fader bar. Optical fades are usually made with a *taper*, that is, with a logarithmic increase or decrease in light intensity. A taper assures that the light changes intensity gradually during a fade-out or fade-in. A strictly linear curve, as opposed to a taper, is used for *dissolves*, so that scene A fades out at exactly the same rate as scene B fades in. *Optical flips* can be achieved by simply rotating elements within special optical printer lenses. *Freeze frames* are made by exposing many frames in the camera, while holding the same frame in the projector. *Stretch printing* slows down or retards the perceived action by printing each frame more than once. *Skip printing* is often used to speed up a slow-moving sequence by recording every other frame of the original film.

Wipes, split screens, and optical combinations of animation and live action involve the creation of special *traveling mattes. Mattes* consist of special high contrast, black-and-white images that are made from normal film images or from artwork. For example, suppose a color title must be inserted into a background scene. The two images cannot simply be superimposed on one another, since the colors will bleed together rather than producing solid lettering. A black-and-white high-contrast copy of the titles can be made, so that the black letters will block out the portion of the background image where the colored letters are to be inserted.

The optical printer must have three projectors to do this: one for the background scene, one for the matte (unless the matte and the background scene are bi-packed or run physically in contact with each other in one projector), and one for the color titles. The combination of the three images is then recorded by the camera.

Wipes and split screens can be made from similar traveling mattes, which block out a portion of the screen into which a second image is then inserted. It is possible to combine live action and animation by using traveling mattes in this manner. One sequence can also be recorded against a blue or black screen so that another sequence can be inserted into the blue screen area. Many special effects in science fiction and horror films are achieved by using a blue-screen process. Spaceships are often recorded as they move in front of a blue screen. This blue screen portion of the frame is then used to create a matte that blocks out the area of the frame where the spaceship should appear in a highly detailed background scene with stars in outer space. The spaceship is then inserted as a foreground object into this area.

Aerial image photography combines optical printing and animation by using a film projector with an animation stand. Live-action images can be projected from beneath predrawn cels, so that color titles or animated figures can be combined with live action. The opaque portions of the cel block out the background scene, which is projected underneath it so that the titles are superimposed over the background scene. The combined image is recorded by the film camera suspended overhead. Aerial image photography eliminates the need for special intermediate mattes, such as those that are used during film printing to block out or blacken areas of the frame into which titles and other images are to be inserted. However, aerial imaging requires bright projection illumination.

The choice between doing special effects on film versus videotape is often a difficult one to make unless it has already been decided to use film or videotape for an entire production. The obvious advantage of video is the savings in overall production time. Effects can be set up and viewed immediately, without waiting for laboratory processing. Electronic effects facilities normally have sophisticated computerized editing and switching equipment, so that several images can be run simultaneously. Keys and mattes can be created instantaneously. The purchase or rental cost of these facilities can be staggering, however. Careful preplanning must go into the creation of a special electronic effect prior to entering the studio. Optical film effects are time consuming to produce, but a very high degree of control and precision can be achieved through multiple passes of the same artwork with film. It is also possible to make sophisticated special effects in film with very low cost equipment. A basic optical printer, consisting of a simple projector and camera on adjustable platforms, can be purchased for a modest sum, allowing freeze-frames, step printing, superimpositions, dissolves, and many other optical effects to be created.

Digital Effects

Digital image processing has greatly reduced the amount of generational loss in image quality that has traditionally accompanied the creation of conventional film and video special effects. Digital effects can be divided into three areas: transitions, filters, and superimpositions/keys/mattes; compositing; and morphing. *Transitions* are means of replacing one digital clip, which is usually a single image or shot, with another. *Filters* are means of altering a clip. *Superimpositions/keys/mattes* are combinations of more than one clip that appear simultaneously within the same frame. *Compositing* involves combining different layers of visual information, which can each be separately edited and animated using a digital nonlinear editing and an animation program, respectively. *Morphing* or *morphogenesis* refers to various techniques of transforming one shape or figure into another.

The types of transitions that can be created between one visual clip and another are virtually limitless. Most digital nonlinear editing and special effects programs offer a wide variety of transition devices as well as the capability of modifying the devices and creating custom transitions. Two of the most commonly used transitions are various dissolves and wipes.

During a *dissolve* one clip gradually increases in intensity and visibility throughout the fame while another clip simultaneously decreases in intensity and visibility. In *lap* or *cross dissolves,* one clip fades out at exactly the same rate that another fades in. In an *additive dissolve,* the two clips are combined or added together during the transition. In a *non-additive dissolve,* the luminance of one clip is mapped onto the luminance of the other. Digital control of a dissolves makes it possible to create interesting special effects by allowing the chrominance (color) and/or luminance (brightness) of the clips to be adjusted during the transition.

During a *wipe* one clip is entirely replaced by another clip, beginning in a specific area or several areas of the frame and gradually spreading throughout the frame. One clip can rise like a curtain, while the next is revealed behind it, or one clip can appear to push another off the screen. A wide variety of patterns, from pinwheels to clock hands, can be used to wipe from one clip to the next, and the movements of these wipe patterns or shapes throughout the frame can usually be adjusted.

A variety of digital filters allow a clip to be distorted, blurred, sharpened, smoothed, textured, and tinted or colored. Filters can also be used to pan, zoom, reverse motion, slow down, speed up, and flip a clip. The ability to alter the brightness, contrast, and color balance of individual clips allows an operator to function as a timer by smoothing out and eliminating subtle differences in color, brightness, and contrast between successive clips or shots, or to function as a special effects artist by radically altering the original image and generating unusual and interesting effects. For example, all colors except the color red can be removed from a clip so that the entire frame is black and white except those portions of the image that are red in color. A clip can be blurred to simulate the point of view of a character whose vision has been altered. Various mosaic grids of squares or other shapes can be used to create interesting patterns, and an image can be posterized by limiting the color spectrum to just a few colors or can be solarized by blending negative and positive images to create a halo effect. By resizing clips, unwanted areas within the frame can often be eliminated, and zooms and pans can be created on stationary or moving images within a clip.

Two clips can be combined within the same frame by superimposing them upon one another or by using various keys and mattes. Different keys and mattes process visual images differently in order to remove a portion from one clip and replace it with another clip. A *white alpha matte,* for example, removes a portion of a background scene, into which a foreground image, such as a title, which comprises a second clip, can be inserted. The area surrounding the titles is made transparent in the title clip so that the background image fills the nontitle areas.

Compositing refers to combining different layers of visual images. One layer might be a model of a rocket ship moving against a neutral background as though it is taking off. Another might consist of an actual launch side recorded at Cape Canaveral. A third layer might consist of digitally animated images of ice particles falling through space. Each of these layers can be separated, edited, and combined into a composite image using a special effects program. This type of special effect was used to create composite images that simulated an Apollo spacecraft taking off in *Apollo 13* (1995).

Using these same techniques, motion clips, such as moving or talking lips, can be inserted in place of stationary images, such as the stationary lips of a character in the background scene, in order to animate a live-action image. Similar types of digital effects have been used in Hollywood feature films, such as *Forrest Gump,* to allow prerecorded documentary images to be combined with studio recordings and to have historical figures appear to interact with and talk to fictional characters. Various compositing techniques can be used to combine several layers of images, just as superimposition, matting, and keying devices utilize different aspects of the image layer, such as the chroma or luminance portions of a video signal, or invisible gray-scale channels, such as alpha channels, black alpha mattes, and white alpha mattes, to eliminate a portion of one clip and replace it with another clip, combining the two within a single frame.

Morphing or *morphogenesis* refers to various techniques of transforming one shape or figure into another. Morphing can be accomplished in film animation by drawing individual cels that gradually change from one shape or form into another. Digital image processing and animation programs have facilitated the transformation process by allowing the computer to generate the gradual transformation from one figure, such as an automobile, into another, such as a tiger. Digital morphing is accomplished by placing corresponding dots at key points of comparison between two figures and then drawing vectors from the dot on one figure to the corresponding dot on the second figure into which it is being morphed. For example, to morph from one person's face to another's, which occupies the same general size and area of the frame, a series of dots are made by clicking the mouse at primary points of correspondence and transformation from one face to the next, such as around the eyes, ears, mouth, and the outline of their heads. Morphing is an effective technique for creating transitions from one image to another, or for altering shapes, forms, and figures and creating imaginative worlds through the use of special digital effects (Figure 13.7).

Models and Miniatures

Full-scale models and reduced-scale miniatures are used whenever a three-dimensional object or setting is needed that either does not exist or when it would be too expensive and/or dangerous to use an actual object. A miniature may be required for a historical setting that no longer exists, or a full-scale model may be needed for a spaceship that hasn't yet been constructed. In some situations, such as when the camera must move within the shot, which requires a three-dimensional set to maintain realistic perspective, a painted two-dimensional background cannot be used to

Figure 13.7 One of the methods of converting a solid object to a digital form is by tracing that form using a 3-D digitizer. The operator traces the object with a stylus over all key surfaces until a full 3-D object has been transferred to a digital file. (Courtesy of Immersion Corporation.)

create the illusion of a specific location. In this case, a three-dimensional miniature of that location can be constructed to allow for camera moves. Usually when actions occur with a miniature, the camera records the action in slow motion to adjust for the difference in time-scale relations between full-scale and miniature environments. Motion must be reduced proportionately to the reduced scale of the miniature. When complicated miniatures and movements are required, it is often prudent to shoot test recordings at a variety of speeds before recording final takes or disposing of the miniature.

Effective use of miniatures and models requires careful preplanning, since these types of special effects are often extremely expensive. Similar types of coordination and planning are required as those that are demanded of an art director, director, producer, and cinematographer during full-scale, live-action production. Drawings are usually prepared and approved before miniatures and models are actually constructed. Problems of linear perspective and scale between live-action, full-scale images with which miniatures may be intercut or combined will need to be worked out during preplanning sessions. Perspective projections and blueprints for miniatures are usually prepared prior to actual construction.

Miniatures are difficult to record not only because of potential problems in perspective, scale, and speed of motion, but also because audience disbelief is often difficult to overcome. Larger scale, highly detailed miniatures are usually required for longer shot durations, where the audience will have an opportunity to carefully scrutinize them. When smaller, less detailed miniatures are used, the editor often must keep the shot duration very short to reduce audience scrutiny and to maintain a willing suspension of disbelief. When miniatures are combined with live action, their believability is generally enhanced, provided that there are few if any discrepancies in perspective, scale, and speed of motion.

Miniatures can take advantage of single-frame recording and matting or keying techniques to create apparent motion from stationary objects. A miniature spaceship or airplane, for example, can be recorded against a blue screen background while it is moved slightly along a suspended, invisible wire between each frame. Later a composite of the background scene and the moving aircraft can be made using photographic or electronic matting and keying techniques. Another advantage of miniatures and models is that they can be used to create inexpensive physical effects, such as various explosions, which would otherwise be too expensive to accomplish using actual objects and locations.

Physical Effects

Physical effects include wind, fog, smoke, rain, snow, fires, explosions, and gunshots. They require the guiding hand of a highly trained professional, especially when their use can endanger the safety of the cast and crew. Wind is usually generated by very large fans or aircraft engines and propellers whose speed and direction can be carefully controlled. Fog is often produced by combining smoke, such as from slow-burning naphtha or bitumen mixtures, and dry ice, which produces carbon dioxide. Most smoke-producing devices use either oil or water-based smoke fluid, which is heated above the boiling point to produce a gas that looks like smoke. Since all smoke is toxic to some degree, it should only be used in well-ventilated areas.

Rain, like wind and fog, is often used to accentuate a mood and atmosphere. Ground-level rainstands and overhead rainheads can be used to produce rain in limited areas, and the surrounding areas can be wetted down prior to shooting to sustain an illusion of a general rainshower. Pumps, valves, hoses, and manifolds (feeding several hoses), and spray heads are used to control the flow of water. When rain effects are produced in a sound stage, it is extremely important to waterproof the floor, to have a means of drainage and/or water collection, and to avoid any contact between water and electrical equipment, such as lights, which could cause severe injury or even kill cast and crew members (Figure 13.8).

Snow can be created indoors or outdoors using a large, almost silent, wooden bladed fan, which can also be used for rain effects, called a Ritter fan. Plastic snow can be dropped in front of the fan, usually from the top of left side but never from behind (which would foul the blades and mechanism), by hand or a snow delivery machine. Polystyrene granules can be added to create a blizzard effect. Outdoors a variety of materials, in addition to plastic flakes, can and have been used to create snow, including shaved ice, foam machines, gypsum, salt (on windows and windowsills), and aerosol shaving cream on slippery surfaces.

While fire effects can add excitement and visual interest to a scene, they are also extremely dangerous and should only be created by skilled professionals who know

Figure 13.8 Most physical effects are the result of special effects crews using machines and chemicals to produce atmospheres and environments critical to the production such as the Paramount crew on this western set preparing to create wind. (Courtesy of Paramount Pictures.)

how to contain them. Torches, such as propane torches, are often used to project flames from outside the frame, while fire bars using LPG gas are often used to create and control flames in front of the camera. It is extremely important to have fire extinguishers on hand that can control all three classes of fire: Class A fires, which burn solid combustibles, such as cloth, rubber, wood, paper, and many plastics; Class B fires, which burn flammable liquids and gases; and Class C fires, which involve electrical or electronic equipment.

Explosions and pyrotechnics are the most difficult special effects to perform safely. They need to be set up and supervised by experts who are thoroughly familiar with the setting, detonation, and control of explosions and fires, since they are potentially dangerous to cast and crew members. Explosives and pyrotechnics are controlled by the U.S. Bureau of Alcohol, Tobacco, and Firearms. A federal license is needed to use explosives, and information concerning their use can be obtained from the bureau upon request. Building explosions usually require prebuilt structures constructed of light materials, such as balsa wood or cardboard. Blowing up a vehicle usually requires removing the carburetor and gas tank, while the engine, hood, trunk, and car doors are attached to the car by steel cables to prevent them from flying uncontrolled distances. Most explosions and pyrotechnics require remote detonation.

Bullet hits are created by remote detonation of small explosive devices, called *squibs,* which are positioned over body armor or a hit plate that protects the actor or stuntman. Blood packs, consisting of plastic bags containing corn syrup and red food coloring to simulate blood, and squibs are glued onto the back of the actor's or stuntman's shirt. Wires running down the pants leg are attached to the squibs at one end and to the firing box for remote detonation at the other end. Sometimes the wires have breakaway connectors at the ankles so that the actor or stuntman can break free of the wires just after the bullet hits have been detonated.

Summary

Animation and special effects generate visual interest and can be used to create imaginative worlds. Animation develops imaginative worlds by using single-frame recording techniques to make static images and objects appear to move. Special effects allow futuristic or historical worlds to come to life and dangerous actions and events to be simulated.

Animation uses single-frame recording techniques to make static images and objects move. By breaking the motion of an object down into its component parts, an animator can control the movements of otherwise lifeless figures and images. Single-frame recordings of static images can create apparent motion when small changes in the positioning of objects occur between successive frames. Animation begins with the construction of a storyboard. A chart or breakdown of the music and/or lip sync voice is combined with the storyboard so that the animator can calculate the precise order and number of frames that will be needed.

Flat animation is accomplished with two-dimensional drawings and illustrations. One of the most common flat animation techniques is cel animation, in which an individual clear acetate cel is used for each frame. Techniques that can be used to make cel animation more efficient include cycling recurring lip and body movements, drawing a new image for only every third or fourth frame, and tracing the outlines of live-action filmed images, a technique known as rotoscoping. There is a noticeable difference in animation style and effectiveness between rotoscoped animation and hand-drawn cel animation, however.

Plastic animation refers to the single-frame recording of three-dimensional figures and objects. Puppets, clay figures, miniature objects and vehicles, and even still frames of live action (a technique known as pixillation) can be animated. Three-dimensional figures are recorded using techniques that combine animation and live-action recording. The camera is usually placed horizontally rather than vertically with respect to the subject, and a three-dimensional miniature world of sets, props, and backgrounds must be constructed. Single-frame recording allows these inanimate objects to simulate motion and to accomplish seemingly impossible feats.

Film animation requires a single-frame camera and an animation stand. The animation stand consists of a camera platform that can be raised and lowered and an artwork table or rostrum, which can be moved east and west, north and south. A dolly shot can be created by raising or lowering the camera, and a pan can be achieved by moving the table. A variable shutter on the camera allows fades, dissolves, and other special effects to be accomplished. On the most sophisticated animation stands, a computer controls a complex set of camera and table movements, as well as changes of art. A technique known as aerial image photography combines a projector with the animation stand and camera, so that artwork titles or illustrations on cels can be combined with live-action film images projected from below without requiring more laborious matte printing techniques. A video camera can also be attached to an animation stand, and single frames can be recorded on a slo-mo disk recorder or a disk frame storage unit.

Computer animation generates images that can be recorded and stored as single frames on disc. The greatest advantages of computer animation are speed and accuracy. Images can be immediately viewed as well as accurately recorded and re-recorded. Some computers interpolate the in-between frames if the animator simply composes the first and last frames of a sequence. A computer can also be used to interpolate the changes in two-dimensional or three-dimensional objects. Three-dimensional computer animation can be combined with live-action photography, opening up a whole new world of illusion and abstract art to film and television audiences.

Special effects can be divided into five basic categories: camera effects, optical and digital effects, models and miniatures, and physical effects. Camera effects include such features as fast and slow motion as well as single-frame (animation) recording. Film recording rates in excess of 24 fps, such as 32, 48, and 64 fps, create slow motion when the processed film is projected at the standard projection speed of 24 fps, and film recording rates less than 24 fps, such as 18 and 12 fps, create fast motion. In addition to varying the speed of the images, some film cameras allow fade-outs, fade-ins, superimpositions, and reverse motion to be created during initial recording. Video cameras can also provide built-in special effects controls, some of which produce effects that are similar to in-camera film effects, such as fades and slow motion.

Optical film effects include step printing, traveling mattes, and aerial image printing. A basic optical printer consists of a camera and a projector. The two machines face each other, and the lens of the camera is focused on the image from the projector. Step printing is often used to speed up a slow-moving sequence by recording every other frame of the original film. Aerial image photography combines optical printing and animation, using a film projector with an animation stand. Live action images are projected from beneath predrawn cels, so that color titles or animated figures can be combined with live action.

Digital effects can be divided into five areas: transitions, filters, and superimpositions/keys/mattes; compositing; and morphing. Transitions are means of replacing one digital clip, which is usually a single image or shot, with another. Filters are means of altering a clip, and superimpositions/keys/mattes are combinations of more than one clip that appear simultaneously within the same frame. Different layers of images can be digitally combined to create a composite image. Morphing is an effective technique for altering shapes, forms, and figures and creating imaginative worlds through the use of special digital effects.

A miniature may be required for a historic or futuristic setting that no longer exists or has yet to appear. Usually, when actions occur with a miniature the camera records the action in slow motion to adjust for the difference in time-scale relations between full-scale and miniature environments. Motion must be reduced proportionately to the reduced scale of the miniature. Models and miniatures, when combined with single-frame animation as well as matting and keying effects, can be used to put an object, such as a spacecraft, in motion or to create the illusion of a 21st century city by placing futuristic buildings into an existing location.

Physical effects include wind, fog, smoke, rain, snow, fires, explosions, and gunshots. They require the guiding hand of a highly trained professional when their use can endanger the safety of the cast and crew. Physical effects, like other kinds of special effects, can significantly contribute to the emotional mood of a sequence and generate viewer interest and excitement.

Exercises

1. Construct a storyboard for an animation project. Create frames for each shot that will appear in the completed sequence. Either draw each frame by hand or use a computer graphics program to compose them. Make sure that all camera and figure movements are relatively simple to reproduce using an animation stand or a computer animation program. Determine how many individual frames or changes of figure pot movement and motion from still-frame images will be required. A series of single film or video frames in which recorded objects or materials gradually change their spatial position within the frame are recorded individually and sequentially. When they are played back at normal speed (24 fps in film or 30 fps in video) they produce apparent motion.
2. Do a preliminary test for an animation sequence by creating a series of individual frames such as one animation cycle. Compose pencil drawings for each frame needed to complete a short sequence of actions. Draw the figures and backgrounds on white cards that have an aspect ratio of 4:3. Hold the cards together at the bottom using two fingers of your left hand while rapidly flipping them with your right thumb to simulate the effect of animation and to test the speed of actions you are trying to create. Then, record these cards as single frames of film or video on an animation stand and assess the results.
3. Project individual frames of live action film onto a copy stand or a computer drawing tablet in precise registration. Trace the outlines of the figures within the frame. Record these outlines as individual film or video frames. Use this rotoscoping technique to acquire a feeling for how much movement should take place between each animation frame in a purely imaginary animation sequence.
4. Animate cutout paper figures by placing them on an animation stand and moving them slightly between recordings of individual film or video frames. Vary the speed of movement and evaluate the results.
5. Shoot a series of in-camera special effects, such as slow motion, fast motion, reverse motion, pixillation, fade-outs, fade-ins, and split screens.
6. Digitize a short video sequence, divide it into separate clips, and then image process each clip using a variety of transitions, filters, and superimpositions/keys/mattes using a digital nonlinear editing or special effects program.

Additional Readings

Fielding, Raymond. *The Technique of Special Effects Cinematography,* 4th ed. Boston: Focal Press, 1985.

Halas, John. *Film Animation: A Simplified Approach.* Paris: UNESCO, 1976.

Hoffer, Thomas, W. *Animation: A Reference Guide.* Westport, CT: Greenwood Press, 1981.

Laybourne, Kit. *The Animation Book.* New York: Crown Publishers, 1979.

Levitan, Eli L. *Electronic Imaging Techniques.* New York: Van Nostrand Reinhold, 1977.

Madsen, Roy. *Animated Film: Concepts, Methods, Uses.* New York: Pitman, 1969.

McCarthy, Robert E. *Secrets of Hollywood Special Effects.* Boston: Focal Press, 1992.

Miller, Dan. *Cinema Secrets, Special Effects.* London: Apple Press, 1990.

Perisic, Zoran. *The Animation Stand.* New York: Hastings House, 1976.

Wilkie, Bernard. *Creating Special Effects for TV and Video,* 2nd ed. Boston: Focal Press, 1991.

Yager, Tom. *The Multimedia Production Handbook for the PC, Macintosh, and Amiga.* Cambridge: Academic Press, 1993.

14

Distribution and Exhibition

Introduction

In most business operations, production is analogous to manufacturing, distribution to wholesaling, and exhibition to retailing. A distributor acts as a middleman or intermediary between the people who produce something and those who consume it. Exhibiting film, video, audio, and multimedia productions is similar to running a retail store from which individual consumers buy things. In media production, distribution and exhibition are aspects of postproduction, but producers consider them during preproduction as well (Figure 14.1).

The selection of a specific production format or technology and the preparation of a budget must mesh with the anticipated distribution and exhibition technology and outlets. The initial planning for a feature film, for example, may have to consider a wide variety of distribution and exhibition channels, from major theatrical distribution, to network broadcasting, cable, home videocassettes and laser discs, and nontheatrical/educational distribution to college campuses. Even a corporate or institutional in-house production is designed with specific types of exhibition in mind. The final product may be sent out as videocassette copies or presented "live" via satellite on television monitors at various corporate locations.

In Chapter 2, Producing and Production Management, we saw that specific programs must be targeted for specific audiences. In this chapter we will see how a television or film producer attempts to reach that target audience by selecting the best distribution and exhibition channel(s). Specific projects are tailored for specific forms of presentation in the media, such as cable television or theatrical film, as well as for specific target audiences. A consideration of the technology and economics of distribution and exhibition follows logically from the concern for the audience begun in our study of preproduction. Selecting the best channels requires an understanding of media technology and economics.

MOTION PICTURE BUSINESS COMPARED TO RETAIL BUSINESS

MOTION PICTURES	BUSINESS
Producer	Manufacturer
Distributor	Wholesale
Exhibitor	Retail Sales

Figure 14.1 In the motion picture business, the producer is the equivalent of the manufacturer in retail business. The distributor is the equivalent of a wholesaler and the owner of the theatre where the films are played is the equivalent of a retailer.

Technology of Distribution and Exhibition

Broadcasting, Cable, and Satellite

Broadcasters send video and audio signals to home receivers through the airwaves. Local broadcasters use a limited number of available channels in a restricted broadcast signal range to reach viewers. There are basically two different types of broadcast signals: very high frequency (VHF) and ultra high frequency (UHF). While VHF signals are usually stronger and travel farther than UHF signals, neither can be received with much clarity more than 100 miles away from the transmitter tower.

Television signals use up more area of the electromagnetic spectrum than do radio signals since they carry both video and audio information: about 6 megahertz (six million hertz) compared with 10 kilohertz (ten thousand hertz) for AM (amplitude modulation) radio signals and 200 kilohertz for FM (frequency modulation) radio signals. There are far fewer available television channels than radio channels. Television audio information is broadcast as an FM signal, while video information uses a high frequency AM signal. There are more UHF channels available (70 channels from 14 to 83, although the UHF channels above 70 are being phased out and are no longer assigned by the FCC in most locations) than VHF channels (12 channels from 2 to 13) (Figure 14.2).

Broadcast television signals come from a variety of sources. A station can generate a live signal from the studio, or from a remote location in the field, as during a local news broadcast. A prerecorded signal can be played on a videotape playback machine or a direct feed can come from the network, via satellite, or via a telephone line to the station. Whatever its source, an RF (radio frequency) signal is impressed upon a carrier wave so that it can be amplified and transmitted through the air-

THE FREQUENCY SPECTRUM

Frequency	Frequency Uses	Type of Wave
0-10kH	Audio	Sound
10kH-100kH	Experimental, Maritime Navagation & Comm.	Very Low Freq.
100kH-1MH	Maritime &Aviation Navigation &Comm. & Ham	Low Freq.
1 MH-10MH	AM B-cast,Ham, Radio Navigation, Industrial	Medium Freq.
10MH-100MH	Int'lShortwave,Ham,Citizens,Medical,LORAN	High Freq.
100MH-1GH	Aviation,TV B-cast,FM B-cast,FAX, Ham,Wx	Very High Freq.
1GH-10GH	Aviation,STL Microwave,Gov.,TV B-cast, Ham	Ultra High Freq.
10GH-100GH	Gov.,Radio Nav.,Ham, Fixed & Mobile	Super High Freq.
100GH-1TH	Experimental, Government, Ham	Extremely Hi.Freq
1TH-10TH	Industrial Photo, Research	Infrared
10TH-100TH	Heat Waves	Infrared
100TH-1PH	Heat Waves	Infrared
1PH-10PH	Ligh- Heat Waves	Light-Ultraviolet
10PH-100PH	Ionizing Radiation, Medical Research	Ultraviolet
100PH-1EH	Ionizing Radiation, Medical Research	Soft X-rays
1EH-10EH	Ionizing Radiation, Scientific Research	X-rays
10EH-100EH	GammaRays	Hard X-rays
100EH-1 BH	GammaRays	Hard X-rays

The Higher Metric Classifications

KILO	1,000	Thousand
MEGA	1,000,000	Million
GIGA	1,000,000,000	Billion
TERA	1,000,000,000.000	Trillion
PETA	1,000,000,000,000,000	Quadrillion
EXA	1,000,000,000,000,000,000	Quintillion
BRONTO	1,000,000,000,000,000,000,000	Sextillion

Figure 14.2 The frequency spectrum starts with sound and moves through radio frequencies to light and on to gamma rays. As communication and computer engineers develop equipment that deal with higher frequencies and greater amounts of memory, the metric system nomenclature of higher numbers will become more familiar.

waves to home receivers. An *RF signal* interweaves the audio and video information and is then decoded by a television receiver. Usually the stronger the wattage of the carrier wave, the stronger the signal, and the better the television reception will be. The image quality of broadcast television is limited by the fact that a television station's channel space is restricted to a bandwidth of about 6 megahertz. This bandwidth restriction permits only about 350 lines of resolution (more lines of resolution mean better images) in video signals sent to home receivers. By way of comparison, a projected 35mm film image can have 1000 to 1200 lines of resolution.

A home television receiver has two different tuners, one for VHF signals and another for UHF signals. When a specific channel is selected on a tuner, the carrier wave and television signal from a specific station are picked up by the antenna and then the video and audio signals are decoded. A color receiver separates the chrominance channel (red, green, and blue color information) from the luminance channel (black-and-white brightness information). Broadcast television signals are subject to interference from atmospheric conditions, other signals such as CB radios, and poor antenna placements, but they currently reach a larger nationwide viewing audience in the United States than any other means of television distribution. Some local television stations are affiliated with television networks, such as ABC, NBC, and CBS; others, which are mainly in major metropolitan areas, are owned and operated (O&O) by these networks (the number of O&Os being limited by FCC rules), while still others are independent or nonaffiliated. PBS (Public Broadcasting Service) has member stations in local areas (Figure 14.3).

Satellites are relay stations that orbit the globe and make possible instantaneous communication over vast distances. U.S. satellites are positioned in space so that they maintain a constant position and altitude with respect to land masses on the earth. A satellite's antenna receives signals from the Earth's surface and then relays them back to the Earth. A satellite transmission, like a standard microwave signal

SOURCES FOR BROADCAST PROGRAMS

Local station live studio productions

Local station live field (remote) productions

Local live-to-tape productions

Local tape or film series

Independently produced film or tape documentaries

Independently produced film or tape series

Syndicated tape or film specials

Syndicated tape or film series

Animated film or computer specials

Animated film or computer series

Network specials

Network series

Figure 14.3
Broadcast stations must rely on a wide range of sources for their programming. Few stations can produce all of the programming to fill the entire broadcast day without purchasing or leasing programming from a variety of sources.

used for live remote ENG transmissions, requires a direct uninterrupted, line-of-sight path between the transmitter and the receiver. But receiver dishes across a wide area on the Earth's surface are capable of receiving satellite signals if they are properly positioned.

A satellite transmitter or tracking station on the Earth is aimed at the satellite's receiving antenna, to which it sends a signal. A transmitter on the satellite relays this signal to a wide area of possible satellite dishes on the ground. Satellites can be used for transmitting live television signals from overseas as well as for coast-to-coast transmission of news and sporting events. Satellites are also used for transmitting cable television programming across the country to various local cable television operators, who distribute the programming along cable wires to individual homes (Figure 14.4).

Home satellite use is growing. In the past, a large (approximately ten feet in diameter), unsightly analog satellite signal receiver dish needed to be mounted in the yard in order to receive strong, high quality signals. Digital satellite transmis-

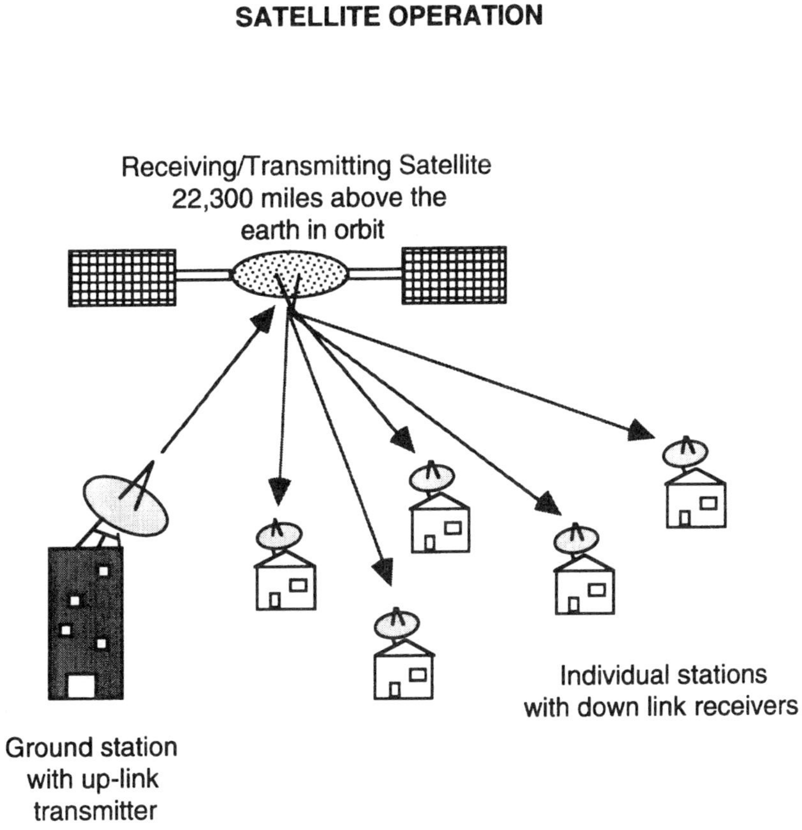

Figure 14.4 A basic satellite system consists of three parts: a ground station that gathers the programming and transmits the signals to an orbiting satellite which then retransmits the signals back to individual stations equipped with down link receivers.

sion has dramatically reduced the size of rooftop-mounted receiver dishes to about two feet in diameter, while dramatically increasing the quality of images and sound to include high-definition television signals and CD quality audio. Regardless of which system, analog or digital, is used, a decoder is needed to receive most services. A dish must be capable of being precisely rotated and positioned, however, to receive signals from more than one satellite.

Cable television distributes television signals from a satellite dish to private homes via coaxial cable (see Figure 14.5). Coaxial cable consists of metal wires encased in plastic and/or metal insulators. The insulation makes it possible to send signals over wide areas with minimal interference and loss of signal. Nonetheless, the signal does decrease in strength as it spreads out from main trunk lines. Amplifiers are strategically located in a community to maintain a relatively constant signal strength as the signal passes along subtrunk lines and drops that carry the signal to individual homes.

Optical fiber trunk lines have significantly reduced signal loss while dramatically increasing information capacity, but it is still quite rare to have optical fiber connections directly to the home. Some cable lines can be directly connected to a television receiver antenna jack, while others require an intermediate decoder and tuner box. The most sophisticated cable systems allow for two-way or interactive communication between the individual subscriber and the cable operator. Two-way communication can be used for opinion polling and obtaining viewer feedback. In addition to television signals, a cable system can be used to transmit information, such as data for home computers, and to serve as a monitoring function for public and private utility companies.

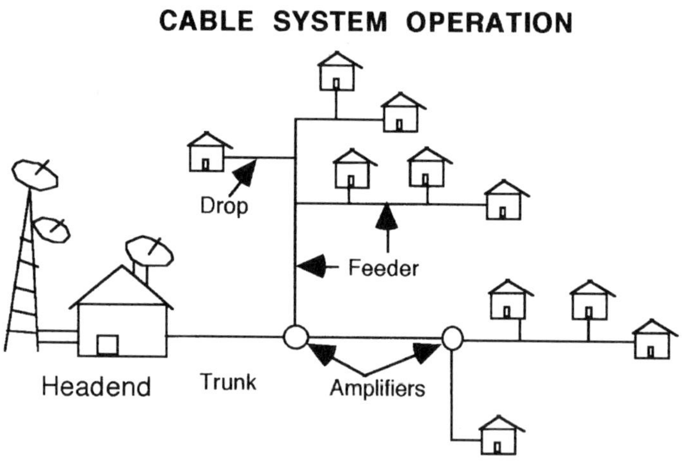

Figure 14.5 A cable system collects broadcast signals from off the air and downlinks program fed by satellites at the headend. At the headend the signals are modulated on to a series of carrier frequencies that are fed down a single cable. From the headend the signal is fed to trunk lines that feed a fairly large area, feeder lines take the signal from the trunk line to feed a smaller area, and then the drop is the final line that runs to the individual subscriber.

High-definition television (HDTV) can produce a high-resolution wide screen video image, which rivals that of film, but HDTV signals require much wider bandwidth than conventional broadcast television signals. Digital satellite and optical fiber systems facilitate the transmission of high-definition television signals to the home, and the use of HDTV for cable and satellite television, if not broadcast television, is developing quite rapidly. Many media productions are using HDTV for production to ensure that they will maintain their marketability as HDTV exhibition increases. Eventually HDTV images may replace film as the preferred theatrical exhibition medium, when high quality large screen HDTV projection devices become readily available.

Theatrical and Nontheatrical

Media productions can be distributed to and exhibited in theaters and educational institutions in addition to being broadcast, cablecast, and transmitted via satellite. Theatrical exhibition requires some form of *large-screen projection*. Electronic projection of large-screen video images is undergoing constant technological improvement and change. While there are obvious projection limitations inherent in broadcast images, as noted earlier, the use of closed-circuit systems and the development of wide-screen HDTV and digital recording is significantly improving the prospects for large-screen electronic projection. Standard television screens are currently made as large as forty inches in diameter.

Most electronic projection systems project three separate colored light beams, for the red, green, and blue components of the signal, onto an enlarged screen, which is usually several feet wide and high. These types of projection systems are commonly used in bars, nightclubs, and video-game arcades, as well as for video projection in homes and institutional settings. Larger screen projection systems have been developed for electronic projection in commercial theaters. These electronic projection systems are often used for the live presentation of boxing matches and other exclusive events. The video transmission from the event itself can be carried across telephone lines or satellite relays as scrambled signals, which can then be picked up exclusively by designated theaters. Eventually a digital system of delivery will be probably used for electronic distribution of theatrical films across the country, once HDTV transmissions and large-screen projection systems are perfected.

While electronic means of projection are constantly improving, film projection maintains a high standard, which large-screen electronic projection attempts to duplicate. A basic film projection system consists of an intermittent film transport, a bright light source, and a highly reflectant screen. The film runs intermittently within the picture aperture or gate area while light passes through each individual frame to illuminate images on a screen. The film movement changes to a smooth, continuous motion over the sound head. Film sound is recorded either optically or magnetically along the edge of the film, and is picked up by a sound head on the projector. The sound is then amplified and sent to a speaker. The most sophisticated feature film sound tracks have six magnetic sound tracks running along the edges of 70mm film prints, and these separate sounds are channeled to different speakers in the film theater so that the spectator is surrounded by multitrack, stereophonic sound.

Dolby Surround Sound and other 360-degree sound systems that envelop the spectator within a theater are widely used for theatrical projection. Dolby and other noise reduction systems are also frequently used with magnetic film projection systems. A noise reduction system such as Dolby or DBX reduces noise and increases the range of sound frequencies (particularly high frequency sound reproduction) by selectively increasing the volume or strength of high frequency sounds during recording and then selectively reducing this strong signal to a normal level during playback.

Different films require slightly different aspect ratios or aperture dimensions in the projector gate. Widescreen films, such as Panavision and CinemaScope, for example, require special film apertures, anamorphic lenses, and wider screens. These aspect ratios often exceed 2:1, that is, the image is more than twice as wide as it is high. Cinerama uses three separate projectors simultaneously to achieve a widescreen effect. Theatrical 35mm projection uses an American widescreen aperture of 1.85:1, while standard 16mm is 1.33:1, as is standard 35mm film shot for television commercials, since this latter ratio corresponds to that of a standard television screen, 4:3 or 1.33:1 (Figure 14.6).

Projectors use a variety of different light sources. The brightest lamps are quartz lamps, HMI lamps, and carbon arc lamps. These light sources are capable of projecting images across wide open areas at drive-ins and large, major hard-top theaters. Carbon arc lamps require special ventilation because they produce noxious fumes, which could quickly asphyxiate the projectionist in a small projection booth. Most multicinemas today use tabletop projectors that run an entire two-hour film without requiring reel changes. These long-run projectors are semiautomatic, but projectionists constantly monitor them during actual operation to prevent damage to the film and to ensure a high-quality image. A single projectionist can monitor several projectors if the images are sent to a group of video monitors. Each projector has a built-in video camera and all the video outputs are sent to the projection booth, where they can be viewed simultaneously by a single projectionist.

Nontheatrical exhibitions often use smaller screens than theatrical exhibitions. Libraries, civic ground, schools, and universities are more likely to use video or 16mm film projectors than 35mm or 70mm conventional or widescreen projectors. The use of any type of film in nontheatrical and educational markets has decreased significantly over the past few decades, however. VHS videocassettes are the most common distribution and exhibition medium, followed by ¾ U-matic videocassettes. Nontheatrical screenings usually involve smaller groups of viewers and significantly less, if any, admission fees than theatrical screenings, reducing the need and demand for high quality, large screen projection.

Home Video, Audio, and Multimedia

An expanding market for film and video material is that of consumer videotapes and videodiscs. Feature films, video albums, and educational or informational programs can be purchased or rented for home or office use. The most commonly used home and office videotape formats are 8mm, Hi-8, ½-inch VHS, and S-VHS. An 8mm videocassette is slightly larger than an audio cassette and has a recording capacity of 120 minutes. Hi-8 uses 8mm width videotape that is capable of storing

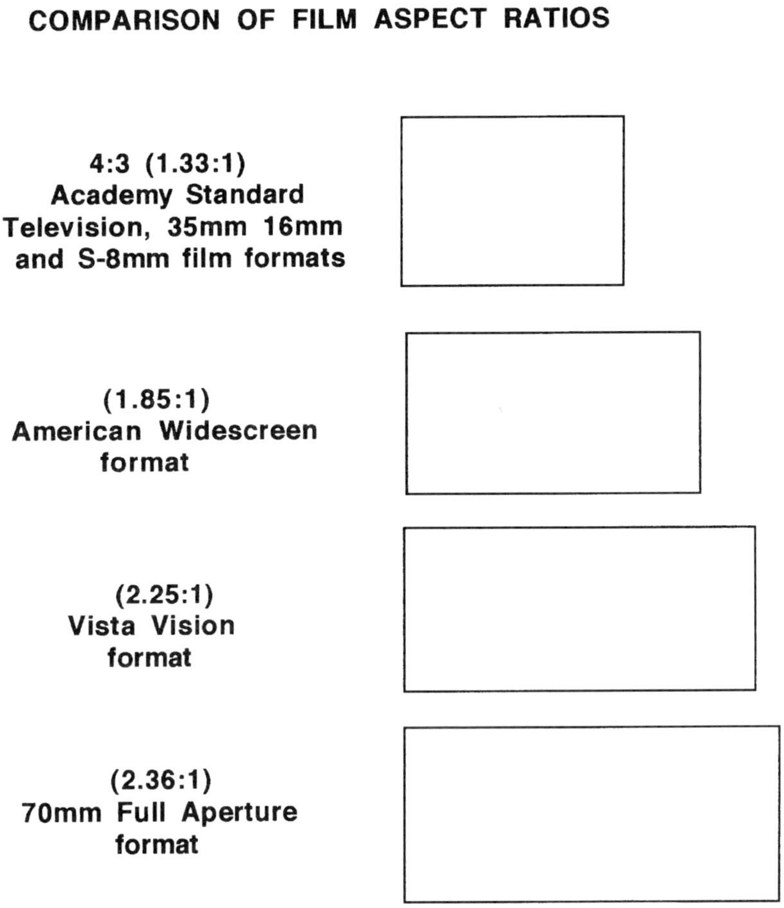

Figure 14.6 Film aspect ratios, or the ratio of the width of the picture projected to the height vary from the Academy standard of 1.33:1 to 70mm full aperture of 2.36:1. The standard television aspect ratio is 1.33:1, but the proposed standard for ATV is 9:6.

more information than 8mm and the tape runs at a faster speed. The image quality of Hi-8 is much higher than that of 8mm. VHS and S-VHS use ½-inch videotape encased in a cassette, and 8mm, Hi8, VHS, and S-VHS videocassette recorders use helical or slant-track scanning of the tape. At slow, low quality playback and recording speeds, a single VHS cassette can record or play back up to eight hours or more of programming (although six hours is more common). Faster recording speeds mean better quality images and sounds.

Videocassettes that record about thirty or sixty minutes of video material at high speed generally have thicker, more durable tape than 120-minute cassettes and are better suited for production purposes. S-VHS is an improved ½-inch consumer format often used for productions not requiring true professional quality. S-VHS is based on the original VHS system but is not downward compatible; this means an S-VHS tape cannot be played on a VHS machine, although a VHS tape can be played on an S-VHS deck. The S-VHS signal is actually a composite system made up of three separate signals that must be carried by three separate cables in order to maintain full S-VHS quality.

Some professional ½-inch equipment (M-II and Betacam SP, as discussed in Chapter 8) use a very high recording speed, which is not compatible with conventional consumer VHS or 8mm. High speed ½-inch video images are of very high broadcast quality, exceeded only by the newer digital formats.

Laser disc technology comes in five basic formats, videodiscs, DVDs CD-ROMs, photo Cds, and audio Cds. A single videotape can hold several hours, a videodisc one hour, and a DVD two hours of NTSC video. Discs are permanent recordings. Like phonograph records, they cannot be erased and re-recorded. Videodiscs are widely used in educational markets. They are two sided and store data in analog rather than digital form so that they can store much more data than a CD-ROM. Analog information stored in a videodisc is not in a form that can easily be used with a computer. A videodisc player usually shows the visual information on an NTSC monitor rather than a computer screen, although a video overlay board can be used to route the playback to a computer screen. DVDs store digital data.

CD-ROM is a very powerful information storage and retrieval medium for certain multimedia applications. CD-ROMs have a fairly high information storage capacity, over 600 Megabytes. They can be used very effectively for multimedia applications that do not require full-screen, full-motion video. The speed at which information can be retrieved is limited, making it difficult to use this digital laser disc technology to record and playback high quality images. The transfer rate for some CD-ROM technology is about 150 kilobytes per second, which is sufficient for digital CD quality music and sound, but the transfer rate needed for noncompressed full-screen, full-motion video is approximately 30 megabytes per second. CD-ROMs can be used effectively for still images and for short-duration, partial-screen, compressed or reduced-motion video segments, as well as CD quality sound.

Photo CDs were introduced by Eastman Kodak for digitizing still images, such as 35mm print negatives and slides. Using a photo CD player, the images can be played on a conventional television set. Since they are compatible with most CD-ROM drives, photo CDs can also be read by computer CD-ROM drives, viewed on a computer monitor, and combined with other digital images and sounds using a digital nonlinear editing or multimedia authoring program.

Laser disc technology, such as videodiscs, CD-ROMs, and photo CDs, does not rely on any physical contact between a stylus and a disc. Instead, a narrow beam of laser light tracks across a rotating metal disc, which is encased in transparent plastic. The laser light passes through small holes in the metal disc to produce video images and two separate stereophonic sound tracks. The plastic casing protects the metal disc. Because there is no physical contact with a stylus, there is virtually no deterioration of the disc with repeated use, as there is with stylus tracking. Laser disc technology is also used by audiophiles in the form of compact discs or CDs. The disadvantage of videodiscs, CD-ROMs, photo CDs, and audio CDs is that they are permanent recordings and therefore cannot be used for temporary storage and retrieval, or be reused.

Recordable CD-ROM technology, CD-R, can be used for temporary or permanent information storage and retrieval. While this recordable and reusable laser technology is relatively expensive, it offers a number of advantages over videodiscs, CD-ROMs, photo CDs, CDs, and hard disks in terms of storage. Recordable CD-Rs are similar in size to CD-ROMs (they usually have a gold bottom compared with the silver bottom of a CD-ROM), but they can also be removed, stored, and replaced, serving as an excellent temporary or permanent storage medium. Their disadvantage is that, like nonrecordable CD-ROMs but unlike videodiscs, information storage and retrieval is relatively slow and thus impedes the display of full-screen, full-motion video. However, they can reproduce limited duration and quality video images and high-quality sounds, and they are quite permanent and wear resistant. Recordable DVDs will be able to record 8 to 18 GB of digital information.

Corporate and In-House

Corporate and in-house media technologies are very diverse. A wide variety of the video, audio, and multimedia systems discussed earlier are used by corporations and in-house units. In addition, closed-circuit television and teleconferencing systems are frequently used for corporate and institutional communications.

A closed-circuit television system interconnects various recording, transmitting, and receiving devices within a single building or building complex. It can be used to send information from a central location to television monitors in various locations or to relay information from one room to another, such as the transmission of a surgical operation from the operating room of a hospital to a classroom in the medical school. Closed-circuit television systems are frequently used in government or educational institutions and businesses, as well as for arrival-departure displays at airports. The signals are carried to various parts of the building by coaxial cable.

Satellite transmission, optical fiber, and traditional wire-based forms of telecommunications are often used for teleconferencing in corporations and government institutions. *Teleconferencing* refers to "live" or instantaneous group interaction that takes place via simultaneous transmission of video, voice, and/or data from several different locations. Digital video, audio, and data telephonic switching and transmission equipment have greatly facilitated teleconferencing. Images and sounds can be digitally compressed and transmitted around the world or within a limited area to facilitate corporate in-house institutional communication using conventional telephone lines, optical fiber lines, and/or satellites.

Economics of Distribution and Exhibition

It is imperative that producers have a basic understanding of the potential markets for a film, television program, or multimedia production. Projects that are initiated without any consideration for, or knowledge of, the economics of distribution and exhibition will rarely if ever reach their target audience. There are many different distribution and exhibition channels, including broadcasting, cable, satellite, theatrical, nontheatrical, home video, audio, multimedia, and corporate and in-house. Each distribution/exhibition channel has different needs, requirements, and economic structures.

Broadcasting, Cable, and Satellite

Commercial broadcasting network television programming in the United States is produced for and by four primary networks: ABC, CBS, NBC, and Fox, and two rapidly growing networks, WB or Warner Bros. Television, and U/PN or United Paramount. News, sports, and most daytime programming is originated by the four primary networks themselves. Most prime-time evening entertainment programming is produced by a limited number of independent producers and production companies.

Network television programming executives rarely take chances on unproven talent. They depend to a great extent on prior success as a guarantee of future success. Executive producers, such as Aaron Spelling and Steven Bochco, have had repeated commercial success and are in a much better negotiating position with the networks than neophyte producers. Although the networks sometimes take a chance on unproven talent, there is usually some compensating factor, such as a presold property that was popular in another media or a major star who is willing to play a lead role. To be seriously considered, a producer must put together an extremely attractive package that guarantees some measure of success in terms of attracting a sizable audience.

The economics of commercial broadcast, cable, and satellite television revolves around the selling of audiences to advertisers. Entertainment programming is an indirect product. It provides revenues to the network or the station only when it attracts a large audience with the right demographic characteristics. The broadcast network, local station, cable channel, local cable operator, or satellite channel sells commercial time to advertisers on the basis of the size of the audience it is able to attract. Some advertisers believe that the most desirable audience in terms of demographics is women from eighteen to thirty-four years of age, since they do the bulk of the buying of commercial products at retail stores. Of course, other demographic groups are also sought for specific products and services, and programming is rarely aimed at just one demographic group (Figure 14.7).

A successful program is one that obtains a relatively high rating and audience share. The rating suggests the percentage of all 80 million-plus television households that are tuned to a specific program. Ratings translate into profit and loss figures, since advertisers are charged for commercial air time on a cost-per-1000 viewers basis. A *share* refers to the percentage of television households actually watching TV at a specific time, called *HUT* (Households Using Television), that are tuned to a specific program. All the shares would add up to 100 percent.

Ratings and shares of television programs are determined by organizations such as A.C. Nielsen and Arbitron, which collect data about what viewers watch by means of diaries kept by viewers or meters attached to home sets. Generally a network program that garners around a thirty percent share is doing quite well. Good ratings can vary from above ten percent in daytime to over twenty percent in prime time. Shows that consistently fail to achieve these ratings or shares are likely to be canceled in midseason or by the next season.

There are, of course, many factors that can affect a show's ratings. Scheduling is a crucial factor. Some time slots and days of the week are simply better than others in terms of ratings. Audience flow is another important factor. The popularity of the shows that precede and follow a specific program directly affects its share and

TELEVISION NETWORK PROGRAM RATINGS

	ABC	CBS	NBC	FOX	U/PN	WB
Mon.	8.1/13	12.0/19	12.7/20	7.3/11	5.0/8	
Tues.	14.0/22	7.6/12	12.7/20	7.3/11	3.0/4	
Wed.	12.1/20	7.4/12	9.8/16	9.2/15		2.9/5
Thurs.	10.5/16	7.4/11	21.2/33	7.2/11		
Fri.	12.6/22	7.0/12	10.0/17	8.6/15		
Sat.	5.3/9	12.8/23	8.5/15	5.8/10		
Sun.	12.5/20	13.8/22	9.7/15	7.5/12		2.7/4
Week Ave.	10.8/18	9.9/16	12.0/19	7.5/12	4.0/6	2.8/4

A typical week of ratings for spring, 1996. Ranking/Share

Figure 14.7 In any one week the number of people or homes watching any one network varies from a share of 4% to 22% (average percentage of TV households using TV at that time). Ranking is a program rating or percentage of all TV households.

ratings, because audiences often stay tuned to the same channel for a long period of time.

From the independent producer's standpoint, the survival of a show for at least five seasons is crucial to financial success. The amount of money that independent producers are given by the network to produce pilots and series episodes rarely covers the complete cost of production. This strategy is known as *deficit financing*. The producer usually signs a contract at the proposal or initial pilot script stage granting a network exclusive rights to the series for at least five years. The contract specifies the year-by-year increase in network payments for each of the years that a series survives. After five years a sufficient number of episodes have usually been produced for the series to go into syndication.

Syndicated programming, often called *stripping*, is marketed to local stations for morning, early afternoon, or early evening broadcast, five days of the week. Independent producers make money from syndication, but they rarely make any revenues from network showings of series. Networks are forbidden by law to directly syndicate their old shows, despite the fact that they would like a share of syndication revenues. Producers take substantial risks in terms of program development, which only pays off if the program goes into syndication. The probability of a show lasting long enough to go into syndication is actually quite low, but the success of a single show can pay for many disasters.

Syndicated programming generally bypasses the major commercial networks. Syndicated programs are broadcast by network-affiliated local television stations during times of the day when there is no network programming, such as late afternoon and early evening. Independent local television stations show syndicated programming during any time slot, including prime time: 8:00 pm to 11:00 pm EST. Affiliates may also broadcast syndicated programming during prime time. Each network pays its affiliated stations a fee for broadcasting network programming, although affiliates in very sparsely populated areas may actually receive no fee other than the free use of the programs as a means to attract or draw viewers for the local commercials that are run during local station breaks between shows. An affiliate can, of course, reject the network programming and substitute syndicated or its own local programming. Some major network affiliates have switched major networks or combined affiliation with one growing network, such as UPC, and one major network, such as NBC. Of course, an affiliated local station that continually rejects its network's programming or also affiliates with a growing network risks losing its primary network affiliate status. However, because of limited television channel space, local affiliates are usually in a strong bargaining position with the networks.

Affiliates and independents have sometimes banded together to partially finance their own entertainment programming. While entertainment programming usually comes to a local station through a network or through an independent syndicator, local news, sports, and public service and information programming is usually produced by the station itself. Local news is one of the most competitive and profitable areas of local TV programming. It is important in terms of both the audience it draws to the local news program itself and the audience drawn to the syndicated programming that surrounds the news. During these non-network time slots, local stations sell commercial time to advertisers who pay relatively high cost-per-thousand prices for commercial time, especially in the top fifty local television markets.

Obviously, the economic conditions of commercial broadcast television make it quite difficult for a small, unproven independent film or television producer to sell a single entertainment or informational program to commercial television stations. Television stations are interested in buying or showing a continuous supply of programming, such as a series or even a miniseries, rather than isolated or individual programs. Local stations will often show independently produced documentaries of local or regional interest during slow or weak time slots, such as Sunday morning or Saturday afternoon, but they will rarely pay much, if anything, for this type of programming. An independent producer would do better to find a corporate or individual sponsor for a single program and then guarantee that sponsor a credit line and a certain amount of exposure during slow or off-hours of commercial broadcasting than to try marketing a speculative program to television stations after it has been produced.

Similar kinds of marketing problems plague an independent producer who hopes to market a single program to cable television. Cable operators are often more interested in filling time slots on a regular basis than in buying isolated programs. Nonetheless, there is greater marketing potential for small, independently produced programming through cable television than through commercial broadcasting. The larger number of cable television channels ensures wider access and a greater ability to *narrowcast,* or to target a small, relatively specialized audience. The economic structure of cable television is quite different from that of commercial broadcasting. The cable operator sells specific channels or packages of channels to individual consumers or subscribers, and the program producer and/or supplier often receives a percentage of the subscription fee or commercial advertising revenues. Some channels are allocated to locally produced programs and provide community access. They are usually available free of charge to anyone who wants to show something of community interest.

Producers can advertise their own programs by publicizing a specific program topic and show time and date in print media. Unlike commercial broadcasters, a cable operator will often accept smaller format, lower quality video recordings, such as material on ¾-inch videotape that is not of broadcast quality. Network broadcasters, of course, usually demand D-2, D-5, 1-inch, or Betacam SP videotapes and 16mm or 35mm films of high quality that meet or exceed NAB (National Association of Broadcasters) standards. Some cable television programming, such as that produced by Turner Broadcasting (superstation WTBS, Atlanta and Cable News Network, CNN, a cable program service), as well as the sports channel ESPN, depends to a significant extent on commercial advertising for its revenues and must meet broadcast standards. Other program channels, such as various movie channels, distribute and sometimes produce expensive entertainment programs and are almost totally dependent on percentages of subscription charges for their revenue.

It is possible to initiate the production and marketing of some cable programs for far less money than is required for commercial broadcasting. Many cable producers are nonunion, and thus can save substantial production costs by paying lower salaries to their personnel. Cable distributors and suppliers have to sell their programming to local cable operators, invest in satellite transmission services, and assume the cost of program advertising. In return, they demand a portion of subscription receipts. It is possible to produce isolated programs on an independent basis for specific cable channels, such as Turner's WTBS, or to produce cable programming speculatively for Arts and Entertainment (A&E) or other cable distributors with greater hope of finding a potential buyer than is the case with commercial broadcasting.

Public television is a noncommercial broadcasting distribution and exhibition channel. In the United States it is partially supported by the Corporation for Public Broadcasting (CPB), which was set up by an act of Congress in 1967 that also authorized funds for its operation. The CPB created the current network of public broadcasting stations. There are basically four types of public broadcasting stations: those owned and operated by colleges and universities, such as stations at the Universities of Houston, Wisconsin, and North Carolina; those owned and operated by school systems, such as that in Cincinnati (only seven percent); those owned and operated by municipal (state) authorities, such as those in Georgia, New Jersey, and Iowa; and those developed and operated by nonprofit corporations, such as stations in Boston, New York, and Chicago.

Public broadcasting is often threatened by inadequate financial support. Federal budget allocations to the CPB are in constant jeopardy. The pursuit of large audiences through popular programming often attracts major corporate sponsors; however, such sponsorship is sometimes criticized on the basis that it gives these corporations power over noncommercial as well as commercial broadcasting. Some critics charge that on-the-air credits are tantamount to advertising and should not be permitted in noncommercial broadcasting. Public television stations frequently raise money through funding drives. The money they collect is used to fund local productions, to purchase national Public Broadcasting Service (PBS) programming (which they have a hand in selecting), and to defray operating costs. PBS is responsive to member stations who are involved in determining which programs will be nationally distributed. This relationship is quite different from that between commercial networks and affiliates, although the extent to which public stations should be controlled by the national network as opposed to local management is an often hotly debated issue.

Public television programming comes from a variety of sources. Some of the programming is at least partially funded by the Corporation for Public Broadcasting and corporate sponsors at the national level and is then distributed through PBS to its member stations. PBS member stations produce much of the programming that is distributed through PBS to other stations. The largest producers of this type of national PBS programming are PBS member stations in Boston; Pittsburgh; Columbia, South Carolina; New York; Washington; Chicago; and Los Angeles. However, member stations usually produce a series of programs on a specific topic rather than single, isolated programs.

Some programming comes from foreign producers, most notably the BBC (British Broadcasting Corporation). Individual stations themselves often produce a certain amount of local or regional public-interest programming, much of which never receives national distribution. At the local or state level, it is sometimes possible for an independent producer to air an individual program on a PBS station or state system. Such programs are often independently funded by other sources, although partial funding can come from a PBS station in return for broadcast rights, usually specifying a specific number of airings over a two- or three-year period. The quality standards of PBS are similar to those of commercial broadcast television.

The subject matter and format of PBS programming can be quite different from commercial broadcast programming, although PBS stations have become increasingly concerned about attracting large audiences, which help to generate public financial support. The length of a half-hour PBS program is currently about twenty-six minutes, compared with about twenty-two minutes for most programs intended for commercial television stations and cable channels.

Commercial spots are short (often fifteen- or thirty-second) television messages that attempt to sell commercial products and services to consumers. The production of network television commercials and national spot sales is largely controlled by major advertising agencies, such as J. Walter Thompson, Leo Burnett, N.W. Ayer, and McCann-Erickson, who contract with production specialists on a bidding basis. The advertising agency usually develops the basic storyline for a commercial in consultation with the client whose product, name, and/or services are being promoted. The advertising agency also develops a storyboard of hand-drawn images to visualize the spot. The director's job is to capture this idea on 35mm film, HDTV, or Betacam SP videotape. Some creative innovation and play with the basic script idea is allowed with a talented director, but the work of production companies is primarily that of technical and aesthetic execution, rather than of developing creative, original ideas.

The production budget for a network commercial is often extremely high, given the relatively short duration of the final product. It is not unusual to spend from half to one million dollars for a single thirty-second network-level spot. The production company must be technically perfect in its execution of the commercial. Sometimes as much as 90,000 feet of 35mm film is shot to produce just 45 feet of final product for a beverage commercial, for example. Major advertisers often contract with a separate individual or company for different aspects of production and postproduction on a commercial, rather than allowing any single production company complete control. Many of the most talented creative producers of network-level commercials work on a freelance basis or have their own production companies.

Local television commercials are often made by a television station or a small production company. Television stations often sell local commercial time to businesses in their area, and then offer to produce the commercial themselves. Small independent production companies sometimes produce the entire commercial for a client, from script to screen. The budgets for locally produced television commercials are quite low compared with network-level commercials. Some are produced on videotape or 16mm film for a few thousand dollars. Only rarely is 35mm film used for the production of local commercials. In the largest local television markets, the production of commercials is handled by major advertising agencies. National spot sales place network-quality spots that are not part of the network schedule on smaller market TV stations. The costs of commercial production represent but a small fraction of the total advertising budget for the promotion of a product, name, or service. Television time costs are usually much higher than production costs, and many other media besides television, such as magazines, newspapers, and radio, may be involved in a particular advertising campaign.

Public service announcements, or *PSAs,* are the least expensive type of commercial. They are usually shown free of charge in the public interest to help promote public service agencies and nonprofit organizations. While PSAs must meet broadcast standards in terms of technical quality, they are often produced in the most economical format possible, such as Hi8, S-VHS, or ¾-inch videotape. PSAs offer an excellent opportunity for neophyte producers to become involved in a serious production, allowing them an opportunity to perfect their technical competence and to experiment with new techniques.

Theatrical and Nontheatrical

Power in the feature film industry is concentrated primarily in distribution. Major distributors, such as Disney, Paramount, Warner Bros., MGM, United Artists, Columbia, Universal, and 20th Century-Fox, receive the bulk of the distribution receipts from feature films. They negotiate with exhibition chains, such as National General, and independent theaters for a split of exhibition receipts. One of the most common splits for a major film is a 90/10 split, which gives ninety percent of the admission receipts to the distributor and ten percent to the exhibitor, above and beyond the latter's fixed operating costs for a specified period of time, such as several weeks. The distributor's percentage decreases gradually over time as the exhibitor's percentage increases. Exhibitors compete with each other for specific films by bidding a specific split and exhibition duration. About fifty percent of the major U.S. distributors' total theatrical receipts come from foreign distribution. Distributors also negotiate with television networks, cable television movie channels, and consumer videotape retailers (Figure 4.18).

RANKING U.S. MOTION PICTURES BY DOMESTIC BOX OFFICE INCOME

RANK	TITLE	RELEASE	RECEIPTS
1.	E. T.: The Extraterrestrial	1982	$339,804,539
2.	Jurassic Park	1993	336,783,914
3.	Forrest Gump	1994	329,691,196
4.	Star Wars	1977	322,740,142
5.	The Lion King	1994	312,774,371
6.	Home Alone	1990	285,761,371
7.	Return of the Jedi	1983	263,734,642
8.	Jaws	1975	260,000,000
9.	Batman	1989	251,188,924
10.	Raiders of the Lost Ark	1981	242,374,454
11.	Ghostbusters	1981	238,600,000
12.	Beverly Hills Cop	1984	234,760,478
13.	The Empire Strikes Back	1980	222,674,266
14.	Mrs. Doubtfire	1993	219,195,051
15.	Ghost	1990	217,631,306
16.	Aladdin	1992	217,350,219
17.	Back to the Future	1985	208,242,016
18.	Terminator 2	1991	204,843,345
19.	Indiana Jones and the Last Crusade	1989	197,171,806
20.	Gone with the Wind	1939	191,749,436

Source: *Compact Variety,* I,1, 1996

Figure 14.8 All-time top grossing Hollywood feature films have earned considerable income from domestic box office receipts.

An average Hollywood-produced feature film today costs over $20 million to produce. The distributor spends about thirty percent more than these production costs for advertising, release prints, and other distribution costs. It is virtually impossible to acquire financial backing for even an average budgeted feature film without a major distributor's endorsement. That endorsement usually requires the involvement of previously proven talent, such as well-known stars and directors, in a dramatic production. The distributor then either puts up the money for a production or provides some sort of guarantee to banks, which then finance the cost of production with a loan. Only rarely are independently produced feature films that do not have initial major distributor endorsement later picked up by major distributors. But major motion pictures are being produced in right-to-work states, especially in the South, to lower production costs by avoiding unions and obtaining considerable state and local cooperation (Figure 14.9).

Low-budget feature films are largely distributed by independent distributors, who do not have as much bargaining power with the largest theater chains and independent theaters as the majors. Of course, a producer can always distribute his or her own film either by negotiating directly with theaters for a split, which is rarely done, or by renting a theater, doing some local advertising, and then receiving any and all gate receipts, a technique known as *four-walling.*

TOP MOVIES OF 1995

Critics Top 10	10 Top Gross	Top 10 VCR Sales	Top 10 VCR Rental
Crumb	Batman Forever	The Lion King	Forrest Gump
Toy Story	Apollo 13	Forrest Gump	True Lies
Apollo 13	Toy Story	Cinderella	Shawshank Redemption
Babe	Pocahontas	Batman Forever	The Mask
Bridges of Madison Co.	Ace Ventura: When Nature Calls	The Mask	Legends of the Fall
A Little Princess	Casper	The Santa Clause	The Specialist
The American President	Die Hard with a Vengence	Casper	The River Wild
Nixon	Goldeneye	Angels in the Outfield	Little Rascals
Before Sunrise	Crimson Tide	The Crow	Outbreak
Il Postino	Waterworld	Apollo 13	Disclosure

Figure 14.9 The calculation of actual dollars earned by motion pictures is a very complex and often mistrusted process. One of the most telling figures is actual box office receipts, but that may not be a fair judgment of a film popularity because some films are shown in many theaters, other relatively few. Also the calculation should be adjusted to today's dollars which would make many films of many years ago appear to have earned much more than their actual income of the time when they were exhibited.

Producers negotiate with distributors for a percentage of the distribution receipts. A producer can demand a certain percentage of either the gross receipts or the net receipts (after the distributor has subtracted certain fixed costs), or sell the film outright to the distributor. Obviously a producer who is able to negotiate a percentage of the gross receipts is in a strong bargaining position. The producer must consider a number of factors before deciding on a specific plan, such as the true earning potential of the film, the length of time before real receipts will be received during which interest on loans must be paid, the reliability of distributor accounting, and the hidden costs of production and distribution.

An increasingly important area of negotiations is ancillary rights and commercial tie-ins, such as toys and T-shirts. Receipts from markets in addition to commercial theaters, such as network and cable television, must be considered. Musical records, books, posters, dolls, toys, clothing, and games that are offshoots of a successful film can make huge profits. Sometimes an especially popular movie star will demand either a large initial payment of several million dollars or a percentage of the gross distribution receipts. The involvement of major stars directly affects not only the production budget but also the producer's negotiations with the distributor and the banks.

The producer and financial backers of a feature film understand that film production is an extremely risky business. Few feature films earn a substantial profit, and most of those that do either are produced on an extremely tight budget for somewhat more smaller domestic and foreign markets or are extremely high-budget films heavily promoted by major distributors. In both of these cases, the successful commercial producer understands the target audience and designs a film and budget that are realistic in terms of audience expectations, preferences, and size.

The term *nontheatrical* refers to films and videos that are shown in places other than commercial film theaters. Nontheatrical films and videos are shown by colleges and universities, other educational institutions, civic groups, and other organizations. They are not always exhibited for profit, but often as a cultural or informational service. While nontheatrical exhibition is usually a nonprofit undertaking, nontheatrical distribution is largely a commercial business. Feature films, for example, are rented to various groups, institutions, and individuals in 16mm film and various video formats for public showing. Renting these works for public showing is often far more expensive than purchasing a home videotape or disc copy, but videotapes and discs, which can be rented or purchased in retail stores, are strictly intended for individual, home use. Higher royalties are demanded for public showings of these films and videos when they are rented from commercial, nontheatrical distributors.

Nontheatrical distribution is not limited to feature films. Individual film and video artists, documentary producers, and producers of other short informational and educational materials often have their work distributed by a nontheatrical distributor. Nontheatrical distributors who make a profit pass on a certain percentage of their gross receipts to producers. Other distributors are cooperatively organized by independent producers and artists themselves. The New York Filmmaker's Cooperative, for example, passes on a greater share of distribution receipts to individual artists, and keeps only a small percentage of rentals or sales for its own operating costs.

Many commercial nontheatrical distributors, such as Pyramid Films, distribute successful short films. Many of the short subjects they distribute have previously won major awards, such as Academy Awards or major festival awards. One of the best means for beginning producers and directors to find good distributors for short works is to win awards at major festivals and contests. A nontheatrical distributor will often offer winners of major awards the opportunity to use the distributor's promotional and advertising services for a major percentage of the distribution receipts or offer an outright payment for exclusive distribution rights. These short films are then distributed individually to nonprofit institutions; as packages of shorts to cable television services, such as HBO (Home Box Office); and to colleges and universities. Nontheatrical distributors actively seek projects that have rather specialized audiences or limited markets, since they do not always have to distribute these works through mass media channels such as commercial broadcasting or commercial film theaters.

Home Video, Audio, and Multimedia

An expanding market for film and video productions includes home videotapes and videodiscs, audio CDs, and various forms of multimedia, including CD-ROMs. These products are rented and sold to individual consumers. Feature films, popular music with accompanying video images, and informational and educational materials can be marketed in this manner. The individual consumer buys a tape or disc and shows it on their own player or computer and monitor. Most entertainment films and videos currently being sold as commercial products were initially produced for distribution to commercial theaters, network television, or cable television. As more consumers possess their own players, more programming will be designed for initial sale to consumers, just like records, books, and computer games in retail stores. Rental and sale of home videotapes has been a rapidly expanding market for entertainment programming for some time. In fact, 1985 was the first year that videotape sales of Hollywood products equaled domestic feature-film distribution receipts from theaters.

The rental and sale of videocassettes is an area that can be easily exploited by smaller producers because many videotape rental and sales outlets are operated as small businesses and distribution is not as tightly controlled as is the theatrical outlet for feature films. Advertising expenses can be substantial, however, and these must be born by the producer who wants to sell videotapes to rental outlets and individual consumers. Most Hollywood films have already had a great deal of publicity and have generated much public interest prior to their availability as videocassettes.

Programming designed specifically for the home videocassette and videodisc market differs in many important respects from programming designed primarily for theatrical distribution. The production of programming for small-screen exhibition raises a number of aesthetic problems. Composition within the frame in a small-screen format must keep key information in the essential area of a TV receiver. Important details cannot be presented on the fringes of the screen, as in a wide-screen feature film production designed primarily for theatrical release. Close-ups are used much more frequently for small-screen productions, and wide vistas and panoramic shots are kept to a minimum. The pacing of entertainment programming intended for television and videocassette distribution is often faster and more action packed to hold the audience's attention.

At present using laser disc technology, such as videodiscs and CD-ROMs, for mastering is still fairly expensive initially, although the cost of mass duplication is relatively low. Initial recordings and editing are not done on disc. Videotapes or film recordings are made, edited, and then duplicated on disc, creating a master pressing or copy from which individual disc copies are made. Because the cost of this master runs quite high ($10,000 or more), it is only economical to use this technology when a large number of copies are needed. The high information capacity, relative permanence, and durability of discs make them an ideal information storage and retrieval medium. The low cost of producing numerous copies once the master disc is made makes the disc an excellent means of distributing promotional materials to salespeople or consumers in retail stores throughout the country. When a large volume of discs are made from the same master, the cost can be as low as $1 to $2 per disc.

In terms of direct sales to consumers, the main advantage offered by the sale of a product (rather than the sale of a seat in a theater or time on commercial television) and the relatively low cost of making multiple video copies is that films and videotapes can be made for and marketed to specialized demographic groups. Distribution channels are not constrained by limited channels of access, as they are in the case of network television and commercial film theaters, where a product must be marketed to a mass, heterogeneous audience. Individual copies can be manufactured and sold to smaller groups of consumers, just as popular rock, country, soul, and classical music can be marketed by the recording industry to smaller groups of people. Individual discs and videotapes can sell for anywhere from about $10 to $100, depending on the size of the market and the cost of production. As the consumer market expands, independent producers will undoubtedly proliferate and videotape and disc production may become as decentralized as production in the audio recording industry or music business.

Consumer marketing of multimedia products is made somewhat complex by virtue of the diversity of standards in terms of hardware, such as Mac versus PC platforms (a problem that plagued the consumer videocassette rental business early on, when both beta and VHS were fairly common), and the diversity of distribution channels, such as computer retail store sales versus catalogue sales (more Mac-based software and CD-ROMs are marketed via the latter than the former channel, for example). Many CD-ROMs, of course, can be used on both platforms. Publishers finance and market multimedia products, while distributors manage the flow of the product of the publisher to the customer.

Publishers coordinate printing, duplication, and packaging, as well as marketing. Marketing usually involves promotions and advertising, as well as sales. Focus groups may provide responses concerning what potential consumers want and what prices they are willing to pay. Products may then be test marketed in specific locations before they are mass marketed across the country. Different pathways to the consumer constitute the distribution channels, such as retail chain stores and catalogue sales. While the distribution of multimedia products is not as concentrated in the hands of a few major companies as is the case with feature films and network television broadcasting, nonetheless major multimedia publishers are emerging who have distinct advantages in terms of access to capital and distribution channels as well as other means necessary to successfully mass market CD-ROMs and other multimedia technologies to consumers.

Hollywood's involvement in multimedia, for example, has been stimulated by the fact that the videogame business currently generates about the same revenues as the box-office portion of the film industry, that is over $5 billion per year, and the videogame business is expected to more than double in the next few years. A number of CD-ROMs and interactive videogames have been produced that carry the same titles as Hollywood motion pictures, giving viewers an opportunity to further their involvement with their favorite plots and characters using multimedia. Interactive multimedia divisions of major studios attempt to establish connections between computer games and movies, although important differences still exist between these media. For example, successful interactive multimedia products usually focus upon the user, rather than a Hollywood actor, as the star.

The probability of succeeding in either medium with a particular product remains relatively low, since only about 6 CD-ROM titles out of every 200 are financially successful. Success and name recognition in one medium can carry over to another. Mass market CD-ROM production costs average about $500,000 compared with about $20 million for a Hollywood feature film, and Hollywood distributors spend as much as thirty percent of their total budgets on advertising and distribution, which can translate into significant name recognition for a multimedia product. However, few hit videogames have appeared that are based upon Hollywood films. Some multimedia firms have joined forces with television and music companies to produce arty, experimental stories that draw name recognition from rock groups and successful television programs. A number of other multimedia publishers have focused upon developing CD-ROMs or videogames as an independent art form, relying upon imaginative graphics, animation, and sounds to stimulate the user's involvement and interaction with unique multimedia worlds and characters.

Corporate and In-House

The overwhelming majority of production in the United States is done by corporations and institutions within house. This is one of the largest and fastest growing areas of possible employment in production. According to Department of Labor statistics, roughly 193,000 people in this country make their living in broadcast television, while 235,000 people make their living in nonbroadcast television, most of which consists of corporate and institutional production done within house. In the 1980s, for example, the largest growth in sales of video equipment came from the industrial/business/institutional market, not the broadcast market.

In-house production by corporations, government agencies, and educational institutions constitutes a special type of distribution and exhibition channel. Much corporate video production is designed to train and motivate employees, to communicate with employees scattered all over the country or around the world, or to communicate with customers and clients. Different kinds of information can be represented in a more entertaining fashion than might be the case with a brochure or other publication. Sales representatives can be trained in the latest techniques and strategies for selling products. Corporate productions often demonstrate these techniques through dramatizations. Some corporations use videotape facilities to record executive speeches and sales meetings, so that corporate information can be widely disseminated.

Specific products are often advertised and demonstrated in automobile showrooms or department stores using videotapes produced within house. Hospitals and educational institutions often produce programs that are helpful to patients and students. Healthcare information is often disseminated via closed-circuit television or by a mobile VCR unit that can be moved from room to room. Special diets, medications, and surgical procedures that a patient is about to undergo can be clarified and explained better and more efficiently on videotape than in person.

One of the fastest growing areas of in-house production is the production of instructional videotapes and computer interactive videotapes and videodiscs for corporate or institutional training. Videotapes can help students learn an incredible range of tasks at their own individual rate, using a student-controlled VCR; an interactive video unit, which consists of a computer and a VCR or videodisc player controlled by the computer; or an interactive computer with a CD-ROM. The viewer's response can be recorded on a touch pad that controls the operation of the computer and the rate at which new information or questions are presented.

An in-house production unit has varying degrees and types of accountability. The production unit may be directly accountable to management in a corporation in terms of its production budgets and production management. Government agencies and educational units are usually accountable to government or academic administrators. Since the programming that is produced is usually aimed at an internal audience or a specialized audience outside the institution, the means of assessing program success are sometimes quite informal, although sophisticated research into program effectiveness is often done by major corporations. Policy is sometimes controlled by a few individuals. There is usually a specific message to tell, and communication usually takes place in a one-way direction down the hierarchy, although programming ideas sometimes originate from employee, patient, or student suggestions.

Most in-house production units produce videotapes or CD-ROMs that can be played at a time and place that is convenient for the recipient of the information. The in-house producer often has all of the facilities needed to produce a completed product and to internally distribute and exhibit it. Medical schools, telephone companies, and public utilities, as well as government agencies, may have completely outfitted video production units with state-of-the-art equipment, such as digital formats, Betacam SP, or 1-inch helical videotape recording and editing equipment, as well as high quality video cameras, lighting, and sound equipment. Small companies and agencies may only have a single Hi8, ½-inch S-VHS camcorder, or a ¾ U-matic deck and single-tube or chip camera, a VCR with a monitor, and no sophisticated production or editing facilities.

Individual project production costs are often kept low by having producers, directors, and technical support people on staff who can serve a variety of functions. Personnel who work in corporate or institutional production often have to be more flexible and have a broader range of skills than those who work in a particular broadcast television position. The staff for a in-house production unit is generally quite small. New personnel may be expected to work with slides, audiotape, and film on occasion, as well as videotape. Production costs are usually kept to a minimum as well by using the most economical medium to communicate a specific message. If motion is not essential, a slide and tape show may be a more economical and effective means of presenting the material. Technical information and statistics might be communicated more effectively and inexpensively by writing and illustrating a brochure or a pamphlet. Regardless of the specific medium that is eventually selected, basic writing and production skills are essential qualifications for anyone pursuing a career in the rapidly expanding area of corporate and institutional in-house production.

Summary

The final stage of postproduction is known as distribution and exhibition. In film and video production exhibitors function somewhat like retail stores by selling or showing film and television products to audiences, while in audio and multimedia production products are often marketed directly via retail and catalogue sales.

Broadcasting, cable, satellite, theatrical and nontheatrical, home videocassette, audio, multimedia, and corporate and institutional each represent different distribution and exhibition channels and different means of reaching target audiences. The selection of one of these channels affects the use of various film, video, audio, and multimedia production, postproduction, and distribution/exhibition technologies and formats.

Distribution and exhibition can be divided into two general areas: technology and economics. Distribution and exhibition channels can be differentiated on the basis of the specific technology they use. Media producers need to be familiar with the technology used by different distribution and exhibition channels, so that they can tailor the production to specific technological requirements. They also need to be acquainted with the financial basis or economic structures under which each different channel functions. A producer must understand the financial exigencies of any potential distributor and funding source so that a realistic budget and estimate of market potential can be made.

Broadcasting refers to the transmission of television and radio signals through the airwaves. A television or radio signal is impressed upon a powerful carrier wave and sent from a transmitter tower to an individual receiver's antenna. The receiver separates the television signal from its carrier wave, and then decodes the separate luminance and chrominance aspects of the video signal. There are a limited number of channels available for television broadcasters. Broadcast television signals also have a limited range. Satellites are relay stations that orbit the globe and allow television signals to be transmitted across wide distances, even around the world.

Cable television distributes video transmissions, often received via satellite dish, to individual homes by way of coaxial cables. Amplifiers are needed at regular intervals to maintain a consistently strong signal throughout all of the trunk, subtrunk, and drop lines in a community. Individual subscribers either have a decoder box or a direct cable connection to their television set. High-definition television (HDTV) provides a wide-screen television image that rivals the clarity, sharpness, and detail of 35mm film (about 1200 lines of resolution). HDTV offers the prospect of providing high quality television images, which will someday be used by large-screen electronic projection systems in commercial theaters and private homes.

Theatrical exhibition requires some form of large-screen projection. While electronic means of projection are constantly improving, film projection maintains a high standard, which large-screen electronic projection attempts to duplicate. A basic film projection system consists of an intermittent film transport, a bright light source, and a highly reflectant screen. Film projectors move a continuous reel of film past a light source. An intermittent movement is used at the picture gate or aperture. When the shutter is closed, the film advances, and when the shutter is open, a single frame is projected on the screen. A standard film projector runs at a speed of 24 frames per second. Nontheatrical exhibitions, such as screenings at libraries, civic groups, schools, and universities, often use smaller screens than theatrical exhibitions. Nontheatrical screenings usually involve smaller groups of viewers and significantly less, if any, admission fees than theatrical screening, reducing the need and demand for high-quality, large-screen projection.

A number of media products are designed or marketed for home use. An expanding market for film and video material is that of consumer or home videotapes and videodiscs. Laser disc technology comes in five basic formats: videodiscs, DVDs, CD-ROMs, photo CDs, and audio CDs. Videodiscs are two sided and store data in analog rather than digital form for display on an NTSC monitor rather than a computer screen. CD-ROMs can be used effectively for still images and for short-duration, partial-screen, compressed or reduced-motion video segments, as well as CD quality sound. Photo CDs can also be read by computer CD-ROM drives, viewed on a computer monitor, and combined with other digital images and sounds using a digital nonlinear editing or multimedia authoring program. Recordable CD-ROM technology, CD-R, can be used for temporary or permanent information storage and retrieval. DVDs store from 8 to 18 GB of digital information.

Corporate and in-house media technologies are very diverse. A closed-circuit television system interconnects various recording, transmitting, and receiving devices within a single building or building complex. Teleconferencing refers to "live" or instantaneous group interaction that takes place via simultaneous transmission of video, voice, and/or data from several different locations.

Producers need to be familiar with the economics of broadcasting, cable, satellite, theatrical, nontheatrical, home videocassette, videodisc, and multimedia, and corporate and in-house distribution and exhibition. Commercial broadcasters sell audiences to advertisers. Programming is useful to the extent that it draws a large audience with specific demographic characteristics, such as women from eighteen to thirty-four years of age, to commercials aired during a broadcast. Scheduling is a key factor in the success of a program, as is the ability of a series to survive at least five seasons so that it can go into syndication. Local television stations also sell audiences to advertisers. Network affiliate stations are paid a fee to carry network programming, but local stations, especially in the largest regional markets, make a considerable amount of money from selling commercial time for local and syndicated programming.

Syndicated programming consists of reruns of old network series, movies, and other non-network programming. Local stations rent this material from syndicators, who pay a portion of their distribution receipts to producers. Local stations also produce much of their own programming for news, sports, and public affairs. From an economic standpoint, a local news program is an important part of a local station's operations in terms of garnering an audience on which it can base its cost-per-thousand charges to advertisers. It is quite risky for an independent to speculatively produce programming for network or local television broadcasters.

Public television is partially supported by the Corporation for Public Broadcasting and contributions from corporations, foundations, endowments, and individuals. PBS programming is produced largely by member stations, although some programming is purchased from foreign producers, such as the BBC. Member stations produce their own regional programming as well as programming of national interest that is distributed through PBS. Stations obtain funding from telethons, as well as government and private foundation grants. Individual stations pay for programming distributed by PBS. PBS stations rarely seek independently produced programming on a single-program basis, although they sometimes broadcast individual programs of regional interest if they meet broadcast standards in terms of technical, aesthetic, and ethical quality.

Cable television offers a somewhat better potential market for independent, small-scale productions. However, most cable operators are interested in filling time with continuing series, rather than with isolated individual programs. Cable suppliers either purchase or produce their own programming. Suppliers then try to sell commercial time to advertisers and/or receive a percentage of the subscription fee charged individual subscribers by the cable operator. Unlike network television producers, most cable producers and production personnel do not belong to unions, and production costs are often somewhat lower.

Commercials are brief messages used on commercial television to sell products, names, and services to consumers. At the national and major local market levels, they are usually produced on 35mm film by production specialists for advertising agencies. At the local level, they are produced by local stations themselves and by small independent producers. Public service announcements (PSAs) are noncommercial messages broadcast free of charge.

Economic power in the theatrical feature film industry resides in the major distributors, such as Paramount, Warner Bros., MGM, United Artists, Columbia, Universal, and 20th Century-Fox. An average feature film distributed by the majors costs above $20 million. About thirty percent more is spent on advertising and distribution costs. The major producers financially back the films they agree to distribute. Independent distributors rarely reach the same number or type of theaters as major distributors. Nontheatrical film refers to the distribution and exhibition of films in places other than commercial theaters. Commercial nontheatrical distributors rent films to colleges, universities, and other institutions. Noncommercial nontheatrical distributors are sometimes cooperatively organized by filmmakers themselves or by educational institutions and foundations. Nontheatrical distribution provides a means for producers of short subject films and videotapes to reach an audience and to receive a return on their production investment.

Videocassettes, videodiscs, and multimedia products are often marketed to individual customers for home use. They are also used for corporate communications. While it is relatively expensive to produce a master disc from which copies can be made, it is relatively inexpensive to make individual discs. Discs and videotapes can be designed for and marketed to relatively small demographic groups. Consumer marketing of multimedia products is made somewhat complex by virtue of the diversity of standards in terms of hardware. Hollywood's involvement in multimedia has been stimulated by the fact that the videogame business currently generates about the same revenues as the box-office portion of the film industry. Interactive multimedia divisions of major studios attempt to establish connections between computer games and movies, although important differences still exist between these media.

In-house production refers to the production of programming by an organization for itself. In-house production units exist in industry, government, and education, and collectively they represent the largest producer of video programming in the United States. A production unit usually maintains a sufficient staff and supply of equipment to produce a videotape or film completely in house. In-house production units use the most economical and efficient medium to communicate with employees, patients, students, and other groups. In some cases videotape, film, or multimedia will be used, but in others a slide and tape show or a brochure will suffice.

Exercises

1. Make a list of all the potential distribution and exhibition outlets for a specific production project. Then prioritize this list by arranging the potential distribution/exhibition outlets in a hierarchy from most to least important in terms of the funding sources or your own expectations and potential returns on production investments. Determine the ideal production, editing, and distribution medium (film, video, multimedia, etc.) and format(s) (16mm, VHS, CD-ROM, etc.) for the most important outlet(s).

Calculate the cost of producing a film, video, or multimedia product using this (or these) format(s). Determine if the potential financial investments and returns from the outlets justify these expenses. If not, determine which medium and format(s) will work most effectively within the desired distribution/exhibition channels without exceeding potential investments and returns.

2. Consider your potential employment in a particular field of media production, such as corporate, public, or commercial television. What will you need to obtain an entry-level position in this field? In what production capacity do you hope to be employed? Investigate the future employment potential of the field within which you hope to work. Is employment expanding or contracting? How many people are currently working in this field?

   Talk to someone who is currently working in this area and find out what it is like. Also talk to a personnel officer or director to find out exactly what he or she is looking for and what specific skills are needed. Request a copy of a résumé from a previously successful applicant for such a position. Study this résumé carefully and compare it with your own.

   Outline a series of production projects and experiences that will help prepare you for this position and demonstrate your ability to perform a particular or wide range of tasks. Finally, when it comes time to actually seek employment, be persistent. Maintain periodic contact with potential employers, such as contacting them in person once a month for several months. When a job becomes available, it pays to be fresh in an employer's mind.

Additional Readings

Apple Computers. *Multimedia Demystified, A Guide to the World of Multimedia from Apple Computer, Inc.* New York: Random House, 1994.

Barnouw, Erik. *The Sponsor.* New York: Oxford University Press, 1978.

Bluem, A. William, and Jason Squire, eds. *The Movie Business.* New York: Hastings House, 1972.

Blum, Richard A. and Richard D. Lindheim. *Inside Television Producing.* Boston: Focal Press, 1991.

Eastman, Susan Tyler, Sydney W. Head, and Lewis Klein, eds. *Broadcast/Cable Programming: Strategies and Practices.* Belmont, CA: Wadsworth, 1985.

Gayeski, Diane M. *Corporate & Instructional Video: Design & Production.* Englewood Cliffs, NJ: Prentice-Hall, 1983.

Kindem, Gorham, ed. *The American Movie Industry: The Business of Motion Pictures.* Carbondale, IL: Southern Illinois University Press, 1982.

Lazarus, Paul N. *The Film Producer: A Handbook for Producing,* 2nd ed. New York: St. Martin's Press, 1992.

Shanks, Bob. *The Cool Fire: How to Make It in Television.* New York: Vintage, 1977.

Squire, Jason, ed. *The Movie Business Book.* Englewood Cliffs, NJ: Prentice-Hall, 1983.

Glossary

ABERRATIONS Disruptions of or imperfections in the light transmission of a lens.

ABOVE-THE-LINE COSTS Production costs relating to producer, director, writers, and stars. See also below-the-line.

A/B ROLL An editing process that uses two separate rolls (cassettes or reels) of tape or film. Each roll contains alternate shots of the sequence, thus enabling the editor to use transitions other than straight cuts between shots.

ACADEMY APERTURE The size of the frame mask in 35mm camera and projectors (1.85:1) as standardized by the Academy of Motion Picture Arts and Sciences.

ACADEMY LEADER A strip of film containing a sequence of numbers indicating the exact number of seconds remaining before the beginning of a film or videotape.

ACCEPTABLE FOCUS The adjustment of the lens so that the important objects are clear and sharp.

ACTUALITY Reporting of a news story on the actual location.

ADAPTATION A relatively faithful translation of a play or piece of literature into a film or television program.

ADDITIVE COLORS The colors used in mixing light and upon which both film and video signals are based: red, blue, and green.

ADI (Area of Dominant Influence) The region covered by ratings of the Arbitron ratings company of one major metropolitan area or area covered by stations covering the same market. Similar to DMA.

ADR (Automatic dialog replacement) A process allowing actors to re-record their lines as they view a playback of their performance.

AERIAL IMAGE Refilming a projected film image. Other images may be combined using mirrors or single-frame film techniques.

AFFILIATE A broadcast station carrying a networks programs, but not owned by that network. See also Owned and Operated.

AFM (American Federation of Musicians) A union that represents performing professional musicians

AFTRA(American Federation of Television and Radio Artists) The union that represents radio and television performers and in some markets directors and associate directors.

ALIASING A noticeable "jagging" of a computer created image cause by a sampling rate that is too low.

ALLIGATOR CLIP A light-mounting device consisting of a spring-held clamp that somewhat resembles the jaws of an alligator.

AMBIENT The prevailing environment; in audio, the background noise present at a location.

AMORTIZATION Depreciation of the value of equipment and facilities over time for tax purposes.

AMPLIFY To increase levels electronically.

AMPLITUDE The instantaneous value of a signal; the electronic equivalent of level or loudness in audio.

ANALOG Electronic signal that is constantly varying in some proportion to either sound, light, or a radio frequency.

ANAMORPHIC Optically squeezed wide-screen film images, which require special lenses for recording and projecting.

ANCHOR, NEWS Newscaster who reads the news in the studio. May or may not have written, covered, or reported the story.

ANCILLARY MARKETS Secondary sales possibilities for a program after it has completed its first run on a network and in the theaters. Also called back-end.

ANGLE OF ACCEPTANCE The angle at which a lens gathers light in front of the camera.

ANIMATION A process of creating the illusion inanimate objects are moving.

ANIMATION STAND The mounting for the animation camera, lights, and the table for shooting animation cels. Sometimes called a rostrum.

ANSWER PRINT The first color-corrected film print returned to the editor from the laboratory to make certain it was printed according to the directions provided.

APERTURE (Iris) The size of the lens opening, measured in f-stops.

ARC Movement of the camera in a semi-circular pattern.

ART DIRECTOR In film and video productions, the person who supervises the overall production design, including sets, props, costumes, settings, and even locations.

ASA The rating of a films ability to reproduce images based on the amount of light required. See also EI and DIN.

ASCII (American Standard Code for Information Interchange) A universal digital standard for reading binary digits to can be read by most all computer operating systems.

ASPECT RATIO The mathematical ratio between the vertical and the horizontal measurements of a frame of video or film.

ASSEMBLE EDIT Sequential arranging of shots in a linear manner. May be accomplished on raw tape without previously recording a control track.

ASSISTANT DIRECTOR In film production, the person who helps the production manager break down the script during preproduction and helps the director keep the talent and crew happy during production.

ASSOCIATE DIRECTOR In video production, the person who relays the director's commands from the control room to the studio floor, keeps accurate time and assists the director as needed.

ASYNCHRONOUS SOUND Sound that does not match its actual or presumed on-screen source.

ATMOSPHERIC EFFECTS Environmental special effects such as fog, rain, snow.

ATR (Audiotape recorder) A tape deck based on an analog linear system of recording audio on a plastic based tape coated with a material that can be magnetized. Generally the tape transport is based on an open reel system.

ATTENUATE To decrease or lower the levels of a signal or parts of a signal.

AUDIO 1) The sound portion of the videotape. 2) Frequencies within the normal hearing range of humans.

AUDIO CONSOLE An audio board through which sounds are channeled, amplified, and mixed during production or post production. See also mixer.

AUDITION 1) An audio circuit designed to allow the operator to hear selected sounds without those sounds being recorded or going on the air. 2) A talent try-out session for directors and producers to watch and listen to prospective performers before casting them in a production.

AURAL Having to do with sound or audio.

AUTOMATIC GAIN CONTROL (AGC) Circuit that maintains the audio or video level within a certain range. Prevents overdriving circuits, which causes distortion, but can increase signal to noise ratio.

AVAILABLE LIGHT Illumination existing at a location.

AXIS OF ACTION (Also 180-degree line) A imaginary line formed by the performers direction of movement or by drawing a line through major stationary objects. Screen directionality will be maintained as long as the cameras do not cross this line.

BACKGROUND LIGHT Light used to illuminate the set or background without lighting subjects in front of the set.

BACK LIGHT Light placed behind the subject, opposite the camera; usually mounted fairly high and controlled with barndoors to prevent light shining directly into the camera lens.

BACKTIME To calculate the start time of a prerecorded sound track so that it will end at a specified time.

BAFFLE A panel designed to absorb or reflect sound.

BALANCED MICROPHONE LINE A mic line that consists of two internal conductors surrounded by insulation and a wrap-around ground mesh.

BALL JOINT The part of the tripod head that can be rotated to level the camera.

BANDWIDTH Amount or volume of information that can be transmitted through a communications link.

BARNDOOR Movable metal flaps attached to lighting fixtures to allow control over the area covered by the light from that lamp.

BARNEY A soft sound insulator placed over a film camera to kill camera noise during synchronous recording.

BARREL A cable adapter designed to connect two cables ending in similar plugs.

BARTER SYNDICATION A system of distributing programs in which the syndicator retains a certain number of commercials slots and markets them, keeping the income.

BASE The shiny side of a piece of film and some tapes. The physical support for either film emulsion or tape oxides.

BASE LIGHT LEVEL The minimum amount of light required to achieve a recording.

BASE MAKEUP Makeup that hides blemishes and creates a consistent overall facial color.

BASS The low frequency end of the audio spectrum.

BELOW THE LINE COSTS Those production costs of the cast and crew and their work with the exception of the producers, director, writers, and stars. See above-the-line costs.

BETACAM ½-inch professional videotape format developed by Sony specifically for use in a camcorders. Has replaced ¾ U-matic as the predominate news gathering video format.

BETACAM SP An improved Sony Betacam format. Uses metal tape but is downward compatible with Betacam.

BETACAM SX Digital Betacam format.

BIAS A high frequency current mixed into a recording circuit which acts as a carrier of the audio to insure a linear response.

BI-DIRECTIONAL Microphone that picks up sound from the front and back but rejects most sound from the sides. The pickup pattern appears in the shape of a figure eight.

BINARY A number in base 2; and either or comparison. Computer systems are binary systems.

BIT The smallest piece of information usable by a computer, either on or off.

BLACK BURST A composite video signal including sync and color signals, but the video level is at black, or minimum.

BLACK LEVEL The normal level for pedestal or video black in a video signal. See also set-up.

BLEED Space beyond the critical or essential area that may be seen on some television receivers but not on others.

BLIMP A hard-shell sound insulator placed over a film camera to deaden camera noise during synchronous sound recording.

BLOCKING Working out talent and camera positions during a rehearsal.

BLOOM The effect seen when a video signal exceeds the capabilities of the system: white areas bleed into darker areas.

BLOOP 1) An audible tone recorded simultaneously with a flash of light for the purpose of synchronizing images and sound during editing. 2) To remove specifics sounds from a sound track.

BLOW UP Print a film on a larger format in an optical printer.

BODY MIC A microphone concealed or hung directly on the body of the performer, sometimes called a lapel or lavalier mic.

BOOM Moveable arm from which a microphone or camera may be suspended to allow for movement to follow the action.

BOOST To raise or increase the level of a signal or portion of the signal.

BOX OFFICE RETURNS The amount of money paid to theaters for tickets purchased by movie goers for specific films.

BNC A type of twist-lock video connector, now the most common for professional equipment.

BREAKDOWN SHEETS A listing of facilities, material, equipment, and personnel needs for production at a specific setting called for in the script, which is filled out during script breakdown.

BRIGHTNESS The intensity of light.

BROAD A type of open-faced fill light, usually rectangular in shape.

BROADBAND CARRIER A high-capacity transmission system used to carry large blocks of information on one cable or carrier; coaxial cable, microwave, optical fiber.

BROADCASTING The sending of video and audio signals by attaching them to a carrier wave of electromagnetic energy which radiates in all directions.

BUBBLE Leveling device mounted on a tripod pan head consisting of a tube containing a liquid with a bubble of air trapped inside. Centering the bubble on a circle or cross-hair indicates that the pan head is level.

BUDGET An itemized list of actual or estimated production costs.

BUFFER A block of memory set aside for temporarily holding data.

BURN A condition caused by exposing camera tubes to excessive light levels. An image is retained on the face of the tube that is the negative of the original subject.

BUS 1) A group of buttons on a video switcher devoted to different sources but sending the chosen signal to a predetermined output: preview, program, or special effects. 2) A wire that carries a series of signals to a common output.

BYTE Eight bits-the standard amount of information used to define a single character.

"C" FORMAT One of three 1-inch helical videotape formats specified by the SMPTE. "C" had become the analog production standard for studios in the United States until the development of digital formats.

CABLE RELEASE A device that allows a film camera to be operated from a distance, often used for exposing single frames.

CAMCORDER Camera-recorder combination. Designed originally for news coverage, but now becoming popular for EFP and other field productions.

CAMEO A lighting technique in which foreground subjects are lit in front of a completely black background.

CAMERA CHAIN A complete video camera unit consisting of: a camera, a power supply, a sync generator, a camera control unit, and an encoder.

CAMERA CONTROL UNIT A series of circuits that provides the signals and controls for operating a video camera.

CAPACITOR An electrical device that can store an electrical charge and alter the flow of electronic signals by changing the electrical current passing through it.

CAPSTAN The rotating shaft which presses against the tape to keep the tape running at a constant speed.

CARBON ARC LIGHT An intense, light at approximately daylight Kelvin temperature emitted by electrically burning carbon rods.

CARDIOID MIC A specialized unidirectional microphone with a heart shaped pickup pattern.

CARTRIDGE A self-contained continuous loop of audiotape or film.

CASE The upper or lower style of letters. Uppercase letters are capital letters; lower-case letters are small letters.

CASSETTE Prepackaged container of either audio, videotape, or film containing a specific length of tape or film stock, a feed reel, and a take-up reel. U-matic, Betacam, VHS, M-ll tape systems and Super-8 film all use cassettes.

CASTING The process of auditioning and selecting performers for a production.

CATHARSIS An element in drama that functions as an emotional release for the audience.

CATHODE RAY TUBE (CRT) A television picture tube.

C-BAND The range of frequencies from 4 to 8 GHz used by many satellite companies.

C-CLAMP An attachment device shaped like a "C" which can be used to secure lighting instruments to the grid or to connect flats and other set pieces.

CD (Compact Disc) A five-inch digital laser disc, generally used for music recordings, but also is used for computer and video recording.

CD-I (Compact Disc Interactive) A large memory CD which can deliver from 2-16 channels of video and/or audio, up to 16 hours of audio, designed to provide the programming for Interactive systems.

CD-ROM (Compact Disk-Read-Only-Memory) A permanently recorded CD disc.

CED One type of video disc.

CEL Short for celluloid. The base material used to draw individual animation frames.

CEL ANIMATION The process of shooting as many as 24 cels per second. Each cel is a drawing on a clear acetate sheet. Cels showing foreground, midground, and background may be layered to give the impression of three-dimensions.

CEMENT SPLICE A device with cutting blades and clamps for welding two pieces of film together with cement. (Often with a warming element.)

CHANGING BAG A light-tight black cloth or plastic bad used to load or unload camera magazines with film wound on cores.

CHANNEL 1) A separate audio signal. 2) A separate broadcast signal.

CHARACTER A single letter, number, or symbol used as a means of describing information in a graphic form.

CHARACTER GENERATOR (CG) Computerized electronic typewriter designed to create titles or any other numeric or alphanumeric graphics for use in video.

CHARGE COUPLED DEVICE (CCD) A solid-state element designed to convert light to electronics; replaced the pickup tubes in video cameras.

CHIAROSCURO LIGHTING Lighting accomplished with high contrast areas and heavy shadows.

CHIP Semiconductor integrated circuit. Depending on design, can replace tubes, resistors, and other electronic components. The most important development for EFP is the light-sensitive chip that replaces the camera tube.

CHROMA KEY A method of combining two or more levels of pictures from more than one source. The process depends on the background behind the foreground subjects being of a solid single color, usually green or blue. A specific type of effects generator ignores the blue or green background so that the foreground subject appears in front of the other signals.

CHROMATIC ABERRATION Visual distortion occurring when different color wavelength bands bend at different angles and intersect at different points behind the lens.

CHROMINANCE (Chroma) The color portion of the video signal.

CHRONOLOGY The timing sequence of events in a story.

CINEMATOGRAPHER Its narrowest definition is the operator or supervisor of a motion-picture camera; over the years it has, to some, included the field of operating a video camera.

CINEMA VÉRITÉ Literally "cinema truth," a style of documentary filmmaking in which the camera runs continuously while recording unstaged events.

CINERAMA A wide-screen film process which used three cameras and three projectors placed side by side.

CLAMPS Locks placed on the end of a rewind spindle on a film editing bench to hold the film reels tight on the spindle.

CLAPSTICK A hinged arm on a board used to make a highly visible and audible reference point at the beginning of a synchronous sound film shot and recorded.

CLEARANCE The process of applying for and receiving permission to use a person's talent, appearance, or property.

CLEAR LEADER Film or tape that has no magnetic or emulsion coating and is thus completely transparent base material.

CLIMAX The decisive point in a drama, where the central conflict becomes so intense that it must be resolved, the central crisis in a drama.

CLOCK TIME 1) The actual time of day. 2)The reference code often used for SMPTE time code recordings.

CLOSED CAPTION A form of teletext designed to permit the hearing impaired to read the dialog and a description of the action of a program. The copy is keyed into a window at the bottom of the frame. A special decoder attached to or built-in to the receiver is necessary to be able to view the copy.

CLOSED CIRCUIT A self-contained wired system as opposed to a broadcast system.

CLOSED SHOP Businesses or industries that require all employees to be members of a guild or a union.

CLOSE UP (CU) Camera framing showing intimate detail. Often a tight head shot.

CLOSURE Psychological perceptual activity that fills in gaps in the visual field.

COAXIAL CABLE A metal cable consisting of a single conductor surrounded by another conductor in the form of a tube designed to carry high frequencies without loss or distortion.

COLOR BARS Electronically generated pattern of precisely specified colors for use in standardizing the operation of video equipment.

COLOR CONTRAST Visible differences between adjacent colors in terms of hue and saturation.

COLOR HARMONY Colors that create a pleasing impression when used or presented together.

COLOR REVERSAL INTERNEGATIVE (CRI) A color reversal print of an original negative which produces another negative to be used to make many prints by saving the original negative from the wear and tear of multiple printing passes.

COLOR TEMPERATURE See Kelvin temperature.

COLOR TIMING The art of setting the best color and density for the printing of each shot in a film.

COMEDY A type of drama characterized by a less serious attitude toward life and an acceptance of its absurdities and incongruities.

COMET-TAILING A lingering after-image of a bright light or reflecting object passing by the camera.

COMMENTATIVE SOUND Sound that has no visible source and which seems to comment on the visual action.

COMMERCIALS Paid brief messages that advertise products, companies, names, and services.

COMMON CARRIER The FCC's classification of transmission systems open to the public use for fees, but the operators are not allowed, within strict limits, to control the content of the messages. Telephone, telegraph, and some satellite systems are regulated as common carriers.

COMPATIBILITY 1)That two systems can operate together. 2) That a tape recorded in one format can be played back in another. 3) That two different types of signals such as NTSC and ATV can be viewed on the same system.

COMPLEMENTARY COLORS Colors on the opposite of the color wheel or when mixed together result in gray.

COMPONENT A signal (often video) in which unique parts are divided and transported or recorded separately. A component video signal may have the luminance and synchronous signals separated.

COMPOSITE A signal (often video) that contains all of the necessary signals in one combined signal. A composite video signal contains both picture and synchronous signals.

COMPOSITE PRINT A single film containing both the picture and sound track.

COMPOSITE SIGNAL A complete video signal including sync pulse.

COMPOSITION The arrangement of visual elements with the frame.

COMPRESSED VIDEO A video signal that has repetitive and redundant portions removed leaving only changes that occur between frames. Allows high frequency video signals to use less memory and bandwidth.

COMPUTER GENERATED IMAGERY (CGI) Images created entirely within a computer system.

COMPUTER GRAPHICS Pictorial images and illustrations created on a computer to be used in video and/or film productions.

CONCAVE The shape of a lens that bends light away from the center of the lens, causing them to diverge from each other.

CONDENSER MIC A transducer that converts sound waves by conductive principle. Requires a built-in amplifier and a power source. Also called *electrostatic* or *capacitor.*

CONFLICT A point of contention, disagreement, or competition in a story.

CONFORMING The final film editing process of actually cutting the original negative into separate rolls and syncing to the sound to be delivered to the laboratory for printing.

CONTACT PRINTER A film printing device in original film is placed in direct emulsion-to-emulsion contact with the copy or print being made from the original.

CONTINGENCY FUND Ten to twenty percent of a budget added to cover any costly delays or unforeseen production problems.

CONTINUITY 1) A depiction of continuous action. 2) Scripts, especially of commercials. 3) See Script supervisor.

CONTRAPUNTAL SOUND Sound that is presented simultaneously with visual images but is unrelated or contradictory in terms of meaning or emotional effect.

CONTRAST RANGE Ability of a camera to distinguish between shades of reflected black and white light: TV, 30:1; film, 100:1; human eye 1000:1.

CONTRAST RATIO The ratio of light measurement between the difference of maximum reflectance and minimum reflectance on a set.

CONTROLLER A specialized computer designed to accurately maintain control over a series of videotape decks during the editing process.

CONTROL TRACK Synchronizing signal recorded onto a videotape to align the heads for proper playback.

CONVERTIBLE CAMERA A video camera that can be used in either portable field productions or mounted with studio accessories for in-studio productions.

CONVEX The shape of a lens that bends light towards the center of the lens so that lights rays converge or intersect at a specific point, beyond which the image is inverted.

COOKY See Cukaloris.

COPY The words on a script.

COPY STAND A flat table with lights that illuminate artwork for an overhead camera.

CORES Plastic wheel upon which film can be rolled: unprocessed film placed on cores must be protected from light and loaded in a camera or magazine in complete darkness.

COSMETIC MAKEUP Facial and body makeup designed to hide imperfections and accentuate a performer's better features.

COSTUME DESIGNER The person who designs and supervises the making of clothing for talent.

COUNTDOWN LEADER A section of film or tape with decreasing sequence of numbers indicating the amount of time remaining before the start of a film or tape.

COUNTER A meter designed to indicate either a position on a reel of tape or film or the amount of tape or film already used. May be calibrated in revolutions, frames, feet, meters, or time.

COUNTERPOINT The simultaneous presentation of two contradictory visual or sound sequences

CPM (Cost per thousand) The cost of exposing viewers to a commercial. Based on ratings of the program in which the commercial is scheduled to run.

CPU (Central Processing Unit) The main circuits that process digital information in a computer.

CRAB DOLLY A four-wheeled camera support on which an operator can sit and operate the camera while it is being moved.

CRADLE The dish on the top of a tripod into which the ball joint of a tripod head or camera mount is placed.

CRANE A relatively large camera mount consisting of a long counterweighted arm on a four-wheeled dolly.

CRAWL Credits or other graphic material moving from the bottom of the frame to the top.

CREDITS Lists of the names and functions of the people who have contributed in some way to a production.

CRISIS An intensification of the central conflict in a drama, usually involving a threat to someone or something.

CRITICAL AREA (ESSENTIAL AREA) Space occupying approximately 80 percent of the center of the video frame. This area will be seen with relative surety by the majority of the television receivers viewing that particular program. The 10 percent border outside of the critical area may not be seen by many receivers.

CROSS FADE A transition in which one sound source fades out at the same rate as another is faded in.

CROSS TALK Signal leakage between two channels.

CRYSTAL OSCILLATORS Small bits of quartz that oscillate at an unchanging rate that can be used to regulate the speed of cameras and recorders.

CRYSTAL SYNC With separate crystal oscillators in the camera and recorder, they will stay in sync without interconnecting cables.

CUE 1) Signal to start talking, moving, or whatever the script calls for. 2) To ready material to be played back or edited by running and stopping a tape, film, record, etc., at a specified spot.

CUKALORIS (Cucaloris) A metal filter with cut-out patterns designed to be placed in front of inside of lamps to throw a pattern or mottled shadows.

CUT (Take) 1)Cue to stop an action, etc. 2) An instantaneous change in picture or sound. "Cut" is considered a film term, "take," a video term, but they have become interchangeable.

CUT-AWAY Close-up shot of an image related to, but not visible in, the wider shot immediately preceding or following it.

CUT-IN Close-up shot of an image visible in the wider shot immediately preceding or following it.

CYCLE Time or distance between peaks of an alternating voltage. Measured in Hertz.

CYCLES-PER-SECOND (CPS) The number of vibrations or successive waves of sound passing a specific point in one second.

CYCLING An animation technique for repeatedly using the same movements of hands and feet or other body parts.

DAILIES A one-light print of the previous day's film shooting for viewing to check the quality of that day's shooting.

DAT (Digital Audio Tape) A series of formats designed to record audio in the digital domain, rather than analog. Formats include R-DAT (rotating-head), S-DAT (stationary head) and others being developed at publication.

DAYLIGHT SPOOL A metal or plastic reel covering the edges of unprocessed film so that it can be loaded into a camera in daylight.

DBS (Direct Broadcast Satellite) A system of relaying television programs from a satellite directly into the home without being retransmitted by the either a cable or TV broadcast station.

DECIBEL (dB) Logarithmic unit of loudness, A dB is $\frac{1}{10}$ of the original unit, the Bel.

DECK In media refers to a machine that plays and/or records audio or video signals.

DEFOCUS To roll the focus ring of a lens so that the image is out of focus.

DEMOGRAPHICS The characteristics of an audience or group of people in terms of age, gender, income, or other social measurements.

DEPTH The illusion of three-dimensionality in visual composition. The "Z" axis.

DEPTH OF FIELD (DOF) The range of distances from the camera within which subjects remain in acceptable focus.

DEVELOPER The chemical solution which brings out the latent image on photographic film.

DIALOGUE Speech between performers, usually seen on camera.

DIAPHRAGM 1) The adjustable opening which varies the aperture size of the lens. 2) The element in a microphone that vibrates according to the pressure waves in the air created by the sound source.

DICHROIC Filters designed to reflect certain colors of light and pass others.

DIFFRACTION Spreading or scattering of light that often occurs around the bald of the iris in the lens.

DIFFUSER Translucent material that breaks up and scatters light from a lighting fixture to soften it.

DIGITAL Binary-based, constant-amplitude signals varying in time. Provides signal recording without noise or distortion.

DIGITAL VIDEO MANIPULATOR (DVM) (Also called a digital effects switcher) A special effects device that uses digital circuits to create unusual images.

DIGITIZE To create a digital equivalent of an analog image by sampling and converting to the binary system.

DIMMER BOARD An electrical control center for lighting that alters the voltage to different circuits in a patch board and thus changes the light intensity of the instruments in those circuits, which also effects the color temperature of the light.

DIN (Deutsche Industrie Normen) The German standards organization. DIN usually refers to a type of plug-jack.

DIRECTOR Commands the creative aspects of a production. In the field, makes creative decisions; in the studio, calls the shots on live productions; and in the editing room, provides opinions.

DISH A parabolic shaped antenna designed to receive satellite or microwave signals.

DISSOLVE Transition of one image fading into and replacing another. If stopped at the midpoint, it is a superimposition. Also called *lap*.

DISTORTION An undesirable change in a signal.

DISTRIBUTION AMPLIFIER (DA) Electronic amplifier designed to feed one signal (audio, video, or pulses) to several different destinations.

DISTRIBUTORS Companies and organizations that rent films to exhibitors and theater owners.

DMA(Designated Market Area) The local ratings area used by the Nielsen Media Research Company. Similar to ADM.

DOCUDRAMAS A type if historical or biographical drama based on actual events of people, but modified for dramatic and aesthetic purposes.

DOCUMENTARY A nonfiction film or videotape that explores a topic in depth with a purpose of making a specific point.

DOLLY 1) Three- or four-wheeled device that serves as a movable camera mount. 2) Movement in toward a subject (dolly in) or back away from a subject (dolly out).

DOUBLE PERF Film with sprocket holes on both sides or edges.

DOUBLE SYSTEM RECORDING Recording synchronized sound on a recorder that is separated from the camera that is recording the matching images.

DOWN LINK Transmission path from a satellite to a ground station. Sometimes used to describe the ground station capable of receiving a satellite signal link. See Up link.

DOWNLOAD The process of transferring electronic information from one source, circuit, or storage medium to another.

DRAMA A sequence of events or actions that tell a story.

DRAMATIC STRUCTURE A combination of various elements that effect the pace at which actions unfold and the emotional response of the audience

DRESS REHEARSAL The final rehearsal or dry run of a production with all costumes, props, and other production units prior to the actual recording.

DUAL-REDUNDANCY Using two if a single element, such as microphones, in case one of them fails during a critical production.

DUB 1) Copying a recorded signal from one medium to another. 2) Replacing or adding voice to a preexisting recording.

DUPE To duplicate, to make a copy of a tape or film or disk.

DUPE NEGATIVE A negative copy of an interpositive which is used to make multiple prints of a negative original film.

DVD (Digital Versatile Disk or Digital Video Disk) A laser disk capable of storing from 8 to 18 GB of digital information, such as a two-hour movie with 8 separate soundtracks and 32 subtitle tracks for international distribution.

DYNAMIC MIC Transducer designed to convert sound to electronics by using an electromagnetic coil attached to a lightweight diaphragm.

DYNAMIC RANGE Loudness range from softest to the loudest that can be reproduced by any system without creating distortion.

EDGE NUMBERS Consecutive reference numbers printed on the edge of a piece of film.

EDIT CONTROL UNIT An electronic device that controls the editing manipulations of videotape recordings.

EDIT CUE A cue that activates an edit at a specific point on the tape.

EDIT DECISION LIST (EDL) List of precise locations of edit points. May be generated manually or by computer.

EDITED MASTER The final product of on-line editing.

EDITOR Tape or film specialist charged with assembling stories from footage and recordings to create the final production.

EFP (Electronic Field Production) Single-camera video production taking place at remote locations from the studio.

EFP UNIT A van containing equipment for a single-camera video recording session at a remote location.

EIAJ (Electronic Industries Association of Japan) Standards setting organization of Japan. At onetime referred to a specific ½-inch open-reel videotape system.

ELECTRET A permanently charged element or capacitor in a condenser mic.

ELECTRONIC NEWS GATHERING (ENG) Process of researching, shooting, and editing materials to visually report on occurrences of interest utilizing video cameras and electronic editing specifically for newscasts.

ELECTRONIC PROJECTION Large-screen video image projection systems, often using multiple monitors or split frames with different images in each frame.

ELLIPSOIDAL A lighting instrument with a mirror reflector in the shape of an ellipse, which produces an intense, harsh spot lighting.

EMULSION The chemical layer containing the light sensitive materials on photography and motion picture film. The makeup of the emulsion determines how sensitive to light the film is and is rated accordingly.

ENCODING Adding additional signals or data such as *time code,* cues of close-caption information to an existing signal or recording.

EQUALIZATION The manipulation of frequencies to correct or compensate for deficiencies in an electronic signal by boosting or attenuating certain frequencies.

EQUAL TIME The FCC's rule requiring stations to sell airtime to all candidates for an office if the sell to any one candidate.

ERASE HEAD A device on a recording machine that is used to align all metal particles on magnetic tape prior to recording and in doing so remove any previously recorded signals.

ESSENTIAL AREA The area of the full frame within which critical information should fall so as to be certain that it will not be cut off by a television receiver. See also Critical area and Safe action area.

ESTABLISHING SHOT (ES) A shot in which the camera is generally located at a sufficient distance from the subject to record their actions in the context of their surroundings thus firmly establishing place, time, and relationships.

EVENT A single activity during an editing session.

EXHIBITORS Film theaters and theater owners.

EXPOSITION A structural element in a drama whereby characters are introduced or settings presented, providing background information and setting a specific mood.

EXPOSURE The presentation of film to light.

EXPOSURE INDEX (IE) A rating of the sensitivity of a specific film stock to light. See also DIN and ASA.

EXPOSURE LATITUDE See Contrast range.

EXTERIOR A setting or location outdoors.

EXTREME CLOSE (ECU or XCU) Tightest framing of a shot in a sequence. For example, just the eyes or hands of a subject.

EXTREME WIDE SHOT (EWS or XWS) Widest shot of a sequence. For example, an entire city block or football stadium.

"F" A type of cable connector for a cable intended to carry a modulated signal or signals. See also RF.

FACILITIES (FAX) Technical equipment, lights, cameras, microphones, studios, editing rooms.

FACSIMILE (FAX) Transmission of information by optical/electronic system through telephone lines.

FADE IN OR OUT A gradual change in signal either from zero to maximum or maximum to zero. Audio, film, or video.

FADER A sliding knob which can be pushed up or down the scale to increase of decrease the audio level.

FADER BAR A movable control for increasing or decreasing the intensity of a video signal on a switcher.

FAST FORWARD A machine operational setting for rapidly advancing tape or film.

FAST MOTION Recording images at a slower speed than normal playback speed so that when played at normal speed the images move faster than normal.

FEDERAL COMMUNICATION COMMISSION (FCC) The federal government agency charged with the supervision and regulation of all electronic communication media in this country.

FEDERAL TRADE COMMISSION (FTC) The federal agency that monitors and oversees trade practices in many industries, including radio and television advertising and industrial market structure and competition.

FEED 1) The part of a recording device that supplies tape or film. 2) A source of video or audio information supplied to a station or studio.

FEEDBACK A continuous sound loop from a microphone through an audio amplifier to a speaker which is picked up by the microphone, creating a loud squeal. Feedback also can occur with recording/playback units that form a continuous loop imitating reverberation.

FIBER OPTICS Glass strands designed to carry communication signals modulated on light waves rather than radio waves.

FIELD One half of a complete television picture. 265.5 lines of the 525 NTSC system occurring once every 6Oth of a second. Two fields make a complete frame.

FIELD GUIDE A transparent sheet that indicates the proper field and spacing for character movement and artwork on an animation stand.

FIELD OF VIEW The exact spatial dimensions of the framed image in front of the camera.

FILL LIGHT Soft, shadowless light used to reduce contrast and lighten shadow areas. Usually placed on the opposite side of the camera from the key light and low enough to remove harsh shadows.

FILM 1) Light sensitive material that is exposed to light in a camera to record visual images. 2) Refers to the whole process of recording, distributing, and viewing images produced by photochemical and mechanical means (excluding video).

FILM PROJECTION The presentation of a film image on a screen by passing light through exposed and processed film in a film projector which is focused by a lens on the screen so that it can be viewed.

FILM PROJECTOR A device that can play back a completed film and project it on screen while amplifying the accompanying record sound track.

FILM STOCK The unexposed film described in terms of format, sensitivity, process, and graininess.

FILM-TO-VIDEO TRANSFER Duplicating a film to video through a telecine or flying spot scanner.

FILM VIEWER A device that projects a film image during the editing process.

FILTER 1) A colored or textured semi-opaque element placed between the subject or lens and the focal plane of the camera. 2) A series of electronic elements used to equalized signals.

FINE GRAIN A film stock with small particles that reproduce at a high level of resolution.

FISHPOLE Handheld expandable mic boom.

FIXING Placing film in a chemical solution that permanently "sets" the developed image as part of the process.

FLAG An opaque piece of material hung between a light and subject or set to control light or throw a shadow.

FLASH FRAME An unwanted frame between two edited shots.

FLATBED A horizontal film editing machine.

FLATS Relatively lightweight background sections that can be lashed together to create a continuous wall in a studio.

FLOODLIGHTS Lighting instruments without lenses which have reflectors and diffusers to spread and soften the light it emits.

FLOOR MANAGER (FM) The director's representative on the studio floor who relays commands to the talent and crew during live or multiple camera video production.

FLOOR PLAN A scale drawing of the studio used in planning scenery design and construction, lighting, and camera and performer blocking.

FLOOR STANDS Three-legged poles that can be raised and lowered, to which lighting instruments and flags can be mounted.

FLOPPY DISK A flat, flexible magnetic medium designed to store and physically transfer computer data.

FLUIDHEAD A camera mount filled with a fluid which helps the operator create smooth camera pans and tilts.

FLUORESCENT LIGHT Light produced by a fluorescent lamp which creates a soft light that does not produce a specific Kelvin temperature.

FLUTTER An audio distortion caused by short and rapid variations in the speed of the reproducer.

FM (Frequency Modulation) Audio broadcasting with a wide frequency range and much freedom from noise.

FOCAL DISTANCE The distance of the subject from the focal plane of the camera.

FOCAL LENGTH The distance from the optical center of a lens to its focal point.

FOCAL PLANE The area behind a convex lens at which the light rays form an inverted image.

FOCUS RING The ring on the barrel of a lens that allows the focus to be changed.

FOOTAGE AND FRAME COUNTER A device that indicates the elapsed tape or film length and duration in feet, frames or minutes, seconds, and frames.

FOOTCANDLE A basic unit of light intensity, theoretically the amount of light from one candle that falls on a one square foot board one foot away from the candle.

FORMAT 1) A rough outline of a script, often used for newscasts and documentaries. The format is the blueprint for the program, not the word-for-word script. 2) A specific type or size of film, audiotape, videotape, or digital medium. Typical film formats are 70mm, 35mm, 16mm, or S-8. Analog audiotapes are usually described by the width of the tape: ¼″, ½″, 1″, 2″. Digital formats may be set by the electronics, not the size of the tape. There are over 20 different analog and digital videotape formats.

FOUR WALLING A means by which an independent film producer can distribute and exhibit his or her own film by renting out a theater for a fixed fee.

FRAME 1) Complete video picture, made up of two 262.5 line interlaced scanned fields. There are 30 frames a second in the NTSC system. 2) The outline of the available area in which to compose a video picture. Today's NTSC standard is a frame 3 units high by 4 units wide frame.

FRAME STORE A digital memory device that scans and stores a complete video frame in order to produce some special effects.

FRANCHISE A license granted to a cable TV, DBS, or telephone company by a civic unit (city, county) to provide electronic communication services to that unit's citizens.

FREEZE FRAME Holding the same frame of video or film so that motion is completely stopped.

FREQUENCY Number of complete cycles an electrical signal makes in one second. Measured in hertz, Hz.

FREQUENCY DISTORTION An unequal reproduction or elimination of some frequencies.

FREQUENCY RESPONSE A measurement of a piece of equipment's ability to reproduce a signal of varying frequencies.

FRESNEL A spotlight equipped with a stepped lens that easily controls and concentrates light.

F-STOP A measurement of the size of opening that allows light to pass through an iris or aperture.

FULL COAT A film stock completely coated with magnetic recording medium designed to record one or more individual tracks of sound. The recording is kept in sync with the picture by the sprockets and recording speed matching that of the picture.

FULL-PAGE SCRIPT A script format organized around scenes, in which both the visual and audio information appear in the same paragraphs.

FULL SHOT (FS) An extremely wide shot that takes in the entire setting of a scene or sequence. See also WS, ES.

FUNCTIONAL Referring to sets or lighting. Designed for a specific purpose to serve the needs of the production.

GAFFER Senior electrician on a crew.

GAFFER'S TAPE A strong gray-colored tape used for securing lights and light mounting devices, among many other objects.

GAIN The amount of amplitude of an electronic signal. Usually measured in dB.

GANG SYNCHRONIZER Several wheels or hubs with sprocketed teeth that hold different reels of film in exact registration frame for frame as they are moved back and forth.

GAP The small distance between the poles of tape heads, usually measured in microns.

GATE The area of the film camera or projector where the film is exposed to light.

GELS Flexible sheets of transparent colored plastic used to create colored light or alter the color temperature of a light source.

GENERAL PURPOSE INTERFACE (GPI) An electronic device controlled by remotely activated electronic switches. With GPI a computer can control a large number of different components from one location.

GENERATION Each level of copies of a medium. The original is the first generation, the next copy is the second generation, and so on. In analog systems each generation adds additional degeneration of the signal.

GENLOCK The process of tying to different synchronous systems together so that a smooth transition may be made between to the two. Also necessary when converting computer signals to video and vice versa.

GENRE A type of programming; i.e., western, comedy.

GIGAHERTZ A measurement of frequency, 1 billion hertz.

GIRAFFE Small mic boom mounted on a tripod on wheels usually designed for limited mic movement.

GOBO 1) In video, a set piece that allows a camera to shoot through it, such as a window. 2) In audio, a movable sound reflector board. 3) In film, a movable free standing pattern cut-out similar to a cookie. 4) On stage, the equivalent of a cookie.

GRAININESS The degree to which grains or crystals of silver halide are visible in a film stock after development and projection.

GRAPHICS A design consisting of shapes and/or colors to produce an object of some significance.

GRAPHICS GENERATOR A digital unit designed to create and combine pictures with type. Sometimes called a *paint box.*

GRAY SCALE A multiple step reflectance intensity scale for the evaluation of a picture. Generally a ten-step scale is used for television between video white and video black.

GRID A system of pipes hanging from the ceiling of a studio design to mount lighting instruments.

GRIP A stagehand, a crew person who moves sets, props, dollies. The head stagehand is the key grip.

GROSS DISTRIBUTOR RENTAL RECEIPTS The total amount of money paid to motion picture distributors by theater owners for the rental of a particular film.

GUILLOTINE SPLICER A film tape splicer that uses unperforated tape which it cuts off and perforates in a downward movement of the handle.

GUN A part of a picture and a camera tube that shoots a stream of electronics at the face plate of the tube.

HANDHELD CARDS Illustrations that a performer holds up to a camera during a production.

HANGING MICROPHONE A microphone suspended from the ceiling or grid.

HARD COPY Generally refers to a printed copy on paper of a computer output, rather than a floppy disk.

HARD LIGHT Direct light that creates harsh shadows.

HARDWARE Mechanical, electronic, or magnetic equipment rather than software—the material recorded or computer programs.

HARMONIC DISTORTION Distortion of the primary signal by harmonics of the primary signal, usually caused by over modulation.

HARMONICS Sounds that are exactly one or more octaves above or below a specific sound frequency.

HARMONY The combined effect of playing several consonant tones simultaneously.

HEAD A pan head supports the camera and is designed to allow both horizontal and vertical movement of the camera.

HEADEND The cable companies central control center where incoming signals from off the air, satellites, and other sources are distributed to output lines to the subscribers.

HEAD LEADERS The beginning leaders placed on film for editing and projection purposes.

HEADPHONES Small audio transducers mounted on a frame to wear over the head to feed sound to the ears of the wearer.

HEADROOM 1) The space above the head of a person in the frame. 2) The amount of level that a piece of equipment handle above the normal 100% modulation without causing distortion.

HELICAL Videotape with multiple recording heads that records information in long slanting tracks; each track records one field of information.

HERTZ (Hz) Measurement of frequency. Number of complete cycles completed in 1 second.

Hi 8 A semiprofessional 8mm videotape format developed by Sony for the "prosumer" market.

HIGH ANGLE SHOT A shot in which the camera is placed high above the subject, tending to reduce its size and importance.

HIGH DEFINITION TELEVISION (HDTV) One of several subcategories of Advanced TV (ATV). Attempt at creating a video system nearly equal to 35mm film in resolution and aspect ratio.

HIGH HAT A minimal platform designed to mount a pan head allowing for shots close to the ground or to mount the camera on a car, boat, or airplane.

HIGH KEY LIGHTING A brightly lit, low contrast scene created by equal intensities of key and fill light and a low key-to-fill ratio. Also called *Notan.*

HITCHHIKER A spider on wheels.

HMI (Halide Metal Iodine) A high-intensity, high color temperature light produced by an energy efficient HMI lamp.

HOOK A dramatic device that grabs the audience's attention and secures their involvement in the story.

HORIZONTAL BLANKING The period of time in a video signal when the electron beam is shut off while the scan returns to start the next line.

HORIZONTAL SYNC The part of the video signal that keeps all of the equipment synchronized.

HOT SPLICER A cement splicer with a built-in heating element.

HUE A specific wavelength band of light, such as red, green, or blue.

HUM Low frequency noise in audio or video equipment usually induced by alternating power lines or stray magnetic fields.

HUT (Homes Using Television) A means ratings companies use to compare audiences for programs by listing the number of TV sets in use at any one time.

HYPERCARDIOD An extremely directional microphone pickup pattern.

IATSE (International Alliance of Theatrical Stage Employees) A union that represents stagehands, projectionists, and many other crafts of the television and film industry.

IBEW (International Brotherhood of Electrical Workers) A union that represents crew member in many markets.

ICON A graphic symbol.

IFB (Interruptable Feedback) A communication circuit that allows the director or associate director to talk to television performers while they are on the air.

ILLUSTRATIONS Stationary visual images such as charts and still photographs.

IMAGE ORTHICON (I0) An early black and white video camera tube. The development of the I0 opened the way for reasonably mobile studio and remote cameras.

IMAGE PERSPECTIVE The apparent depth of the image and the spatial relationships of objects.

IMAGE TONALITY The overall appearance of the image in terms of its apparent contrast and color.

IMPEDANCE Apparent AC resistance to current flowing in a circuit. Measured in Ohms.

IN-CAMERA EDITING Shooting a sequence of shots on film or videotape so that they do not have to be edited in post production.

INCANDESCENT LIGHT Inert-gas-filled electric lamp emitting light and heat from a glowing filament. A typical lamp is the tungsten-halogen lamp used in most production instruments as well as the standard household light bulb.

INCIDENTAL CHARACTERS Minor background figures in a story who often add texture, interest, and depth.

INCIDENT LIGHT Illumination from a light source. Measured in foot candles or Lux by pointing the light meter at the light source.

INCIDENT METER READING A light meter reading of the intensity of light falling on the subject.

INDEPENDENT A producer, distributor, director, writer, or station that is not affiliated with a network or national company.

IN-HOUSE A production unit that creates programming for the organization or institution of which it is a part.

IN POINT Starting point of an edit.

INPUT Signal entering a system or an electrical unit.

INSERT A recording of specific actions in a scene to be inserted into a master shot, usually CUs.

INSERT EDIT Assembling a videotape production by adding video and audio signals to tape stock that already has had control track recorded on it. Insert edits also can be made over existing edited tape.

INSTRUCTIONAL PROGRAMS Educational films or videotapes designed as teaching aids for the public, students, or employees.

INTERACTIVE MEDIA Communication systems that permit two-way interaction between electronic stations (video monitors, computers). May depend on stored programs such as games or shopping networks.

INTERCUTTING A relatively rapid alternation between two or more different shots.

INTERIOR Setting or location inside of a building or structure.

INTERLACE SCANNING The method of combining two fields of scan lines into one frame.

INTERNEGATIVE A copy of the A and B roll film rolls onto a single negative film which can be used for printing multiple positive release prints.

INTERNET A public computer network, originally developed by the military, now linking home, education, science, and business computers.

INTERPOLATION An animation technique in computer graphics which allows the animator to compose the first and last frames of an action sequence from which the computer then generates the images in between.

INTERPOSITIVE A print using negative stock of the original negative which then creates a positive image.

INTRO Abbreviation for introduction.

INVERSE SQUARE LAW A mathematical analysis of changes in alternating energy. The amount of energy is inversely proportionate to the change in distance. The formula is easily applied to calculating lighting and audio levels.

IPS (Inches Per Second) Method of measuring the speed of tape, film, or other longitudinal medium.

IRIS See Aperture.

ISO See Exposure index.

ISOLATED CAMERA A camera that feeds its own videotape recorder as well as being available for live shots in a multiple camera production such as an athletic event.

ITFS (Instructional Television Fixed Service) A microwave video delivery system licensed to educational institutions.

JACK A receptacle for plugs usually mounted on equipment or walls of a studio or control room.

JARGON Terminology and slang of a particular field.

JINGLES Music and lyrics used in commercials which are quickly associated with the product advertised.

JOY STICK A level on a video switcher or computer which allows the operator to select specific placement of a wipe, key, cursor, or other special effect or operation.

JUMP CUT Any one of several types of poor edits that either break continuity or may be disturbing to the audience.

KELVIN TEMPERATURE Measurement of the relative color of light. Indicated as degrees Kelvin; the higher the temperature, the bluer the light, the lower the temperature, the redder the light.

KEY Process of combining two or more images without the background image bleeding through the foreground image (chroma key).

KEY LIGHT Apparent main source of light. Usually from one bright light above and to one side of the camera.

KEY-TO-BACK RATIO A comparison between the amount of light on the subject from the backlight as compared to the amount of light on the subject from the key light.

KEY-TO-FILL RATIO A comparison between the amount of light on the subject from the key light as compared to the amount of light from a combination of key and fill lights.

KICKER A light focused from the side on the subject or on a particular section of the set.

KILL To turn off: light, camera, or audio feed.

KILOHERTZ A measurement of alternating energy; 1000 hertz.

KINESCOPE A film recording of a live or taped video production, now replaced by tape-to-film transfers.

KU-BAND The range of frequencies between 11 and 14 GHertz increasingly used by communication satellite companies.

LAB REPORT See Camera report.

LAG That characteristic of a camera tube in which a picture trails its own images as the camera moves. Lag increases with the age of the tube.

LASER DISC A type of video or audio recording made by a laser disc scanning minute holes in a metal disc encased in a plastic covering.

LAVALIER (Lav) Microphone worn around the neck. Also sometimes called a lapel mic when clipped to a tie or front of the clothing.

LAYBACK The process of rerecording a track in sync after it has been modified. Usually refers to audio tracks after sweetening.

LAYOVER Transferring the edited sound track to a multitrack recorder for final sweetening.

LEAD STORY The most important story of a newscast, usually the first story in the newscast.

LEGAL RELEASE A statement releasing a producer from future legal action, signed by non-professional people appearing in, or providing materials for a production.

LEITMOTIFS Musical themes associated with specific characters in a production.

LENS Glass or plastic designed to focus and concentrate light on a surface to form an image.

LENS CAP Opaque covering to slip over the end of a lens to protect the surface from damage and to protect the image device from excessive light.

LENS COATING A substance placed on the surfaces of a lens to reduce the reflection of lighting entering the lens which increases the light transmission of that lens. Also used to protect the lens from moisture, scratches, and dirt.

LENS HOOD A device for shading the camera lens from direct sunlight or from artificial light set opposite the camera.

LEVEL 1)Relative amplitude or intensity. Used to indicate light, audio, video, and other electronic signals. 2) Aligned with the horizon.

LIBRARY EFFECTS Sound effects catalogued and accessible in a prerecorded form on computer discs, CDs, audio tape, or vinyl discs.

LIGHT Electromagnetic energy which stimulates receptors in the eyes.

LIGHT EMITTING DIODE (LED) A solid-state component that emits light when a small voltage is applied. Useful as a level or operating condition indicator.

LIGHTING DIRECTOR In video production the person who designs and supervises the lighting setup.

LIGHTING INSTRUMENT The housing within which a light source or lamp is enclosed.

LIGHTING PLOT A scale outline of a lighting setup on gridded paper which represents the studio floor, providing an overhead view of the relationship of lighting instruments to sets and actors.

LIGHT METER (Exposure meter) Instrument used to measure the intensity of light. May be calculated in foot candles, Lux, or f-stops.

LINE LEVEL Signal amplified enough to feed down a line without fear of degradation. A microphone level is lower than line level; speaker level is higher.

LIP-SYNC The process of matching the movement of performer's mouths with the words they are speaking.

LIST MANAGEMENT The process of making alterations, trims, or shifting of segments in editing decisions in a computerized editing system.

LIVE ON TAPE A multiple camera video production recording as if it were live, but allowing for some post production.

LOAD To transfer date or information to an analog or digital storage device.

LOCATION Area or site of a production. Usually refers to sites away from studios.

LOG Listing of shots as they are recorded on tape.

LONGITUDINAL Lengthwise, in media refers to the method of recording audio and control track signals.

LOOPING The process of rerecording audio during postproduction. Also now called *Automatic Dialogue Replacement (ADR).*

LOUDNESS Perceived intensity of audio. Depends on the intensity and saturation of the sound, as well as the sensitivity of the listener to a range of frequencies.

LOUDNESS DISTORTION Sound signal disruption caused by over modulation.

LOW ANGLE SHOT A shot in which the camera is placed closer to the floor than a normal camera height. This angle tends to exaggerate the size and importance of the subject.

LOW IMPEDANCE A type of electrical signal created by most professional microphones and some playback equipment.

LOW KEY LIGHTING A lighting aesthetic characterized by pools of light and harsh shadow areas created by minimal fill and a high key-to-fill ratio. Also called *Chiaroscuro.*

LPTV (Low Power TV) Television stations licensed by the FCC to broadcast using limited power to cover areas or markets not served by major market TV stations.

LUMINAIRE See Lighting instrument.

LUMINANCE The brightness component of a video signal.

LUX European measurement of light intensity. There are approximately 10 Lux to 1 foot candle.

MAG TRACK Short for magnetic sound film track.

MAJOR DISTRIBUTORS (Studios) The largest film distributors who receive the bulk of the distribution receipts from their films: Disney, Warner Bros., Twentieth Century Fox, Universal, and Paramount.

MAJOR MARKET One of the top 100 metro areas in number of TV households.

MASTER The final product of an audio or video editing session.

MASTER CONTROL The room to which all video and audio signals of various productions studios are fed for distribution, broadcasting, or recording.

MASTER SHOT Extended wide shot establishing the scene and often running the entire length of the sequence. Intended to be broken down in the editing process.

MASTER TAPE The final result of an editing session.

MATTE (Traveling or Stationary) An opaque covering over the lens of a camera to allow for re-exposure over the covered area later in film, or in video to determine an irregular shape for a special effect.

MATTE SHOTS Combinations of different images in the same frame.

MECHANICAL INTERLOCK A physical connection between different machines or portions of machines that causes them to run at the same speed when driven by the same motor.

MEDIUM CLOSE UP (MCU) Relative average framing for a shot. Often framed from the waist up.

MEDIUM SHOT (MS) Wider than an MCU, often framed head to toe.

MELODY A series of musical notes or tones that create a structured unit or order.

METAMORPHOSIS An animation technique in which one figure is gradually transformed into another figure of an entirely different shape.

METRONOME A device used by musicians to provide a regular beat or rhythm.

M FORMAT (M-II, Recam) Panasonic's professional ½-inch format. Originally sold by RCA as Recam, then upgraded to M-l. Now competing with Sony's BetacamSP.

MICROPHONE An transducer that converts sound waves into comparable fluctuations of electrical current.

MICROPHONE BOOM A long pole to which a microphone is attached so that it can be held just outside of the camera frame.

MICROWAVE 1)High-frequency carrier for both audio and video signals. Operates only a line-of-sight path. 2) Oven for heating the crews lunch.

MIC LEVELS The lower electrical signal strength of a microphone output as compared to line levels of amplified signals.

MIL A unit of measurement (.001) used to designate tape thickness.

MINIATURE A three-dimensional replica of a set or prop to be used as a substitute for a full-sized construction. Also called *models.*

MINI-PLUG (118-inch) Audio connector designed for small equipment. Scaled down version of ¼-inch phone plug.

MIRROR SHOTS 1) The use of two mirrors to make a large periscope that can be used for overhead video camera shots. 2) A partial mirror can be used to combine two film scenes in one take.

MIRROR SHUTTER A reflective coating on the front of a shutter that intermittently deflects all the light to a reflex viewfinder as the film is advanced in the camera.

MIXER A piece of electronic equipment designed to combine several signals. Usually refers to an audio board or console.

MIX LOG SHEET A list of all volume changes, transitions, and equalization changes for a sound mix.

MMDS (Multichannel Multipoint Distribution Service) A video delivery system using line-of-sight microwave with four or more channels operated by a single company. Often called "wireless cable," similar to ITFS.

MODEL See Miniature.

MODELING Highlighting the appearance of a textured surface through the use of shadows.

MODULATOR An electronic component designed to impress one signal on another, usually of a higher frequency.

MOIRÉ EFFECT A distracting vibration of visual images caused by the interaction of narrow stripes in the design of the material being recorded.

MONAURAL (Mono) A single track of audio.

MONITOR 1) To listen to or watch audio or videotapes or off-air programs. 2) Device used to view video signals. Much like a TV receiver, but is usually much higher quality and generally does not have an RF section for off the-air monitoring.

MONOCHROME Black and white film or video.

MOTIF Imagery which is repeatedly used in an artistic work to add depth and symbolism.

MOTION CONTROL A computer controlled system for camera or object movements to match other exposures of background scenes for keying in video or double exposure in film.

MORGUE Library, reference files, storage for used scripts, tapes, maps, and other reference material.

MOS 1) Metal oxide semiconductor. A type of camera chip that replaces the camera tube. 2) A film term indicating a shot was recorded silent, or as the early German film directors said, "Mit out sound."

MSO (Multiple System Operator) A cable company that owns and operates more than one cable system.

MULTI-CAMERA PRODUCTION The use of several film or video cameras to record the same action simultaneously from different viewpoints.

MULTIPLANE ANIMATION Animation shot on an animation stand that holds several levels of cels separated so they may be lit and moved individually. Invented by Ub Iwerks for Walt Disney.

MULTI-TRACK An audio tape recording with from two to sixty-four separate tracks recorded on the same audiotape.

MUNSELL COLOR WHEEL A three-dimensional model of colors which shows different color samples by hue, brightness, and saturation.

MUSIC LIBRARIES Collections of musical recordings that require a minimum royalty payment for use on media productions.

NABET (National Association of Broadcast Employees and Technicians) A union that represents crew members and in some markets everyone at an operation.

NARRATE To tell a story or provide a commentary on events.

NARRATION A verbal commentary on the events taking place within a fiction or nonfiction media production.

NARRATIVE A story that is told or narrated by someone.

NARROWCASTING Aiming programs at a specific non-mass market.

NATIONAL ASSOCIATION OF BROADCASTERS (NAB) Professional organization of radio and television broadcasters.

NAT SOUND Ambient sound that exists on location recorded as a story happens. Often used as background for a VO. Sometimes called *wild sound.*

NATURALISTIC LIGHTING Lighting that appears to come from a known or presumed actual sources in the setting or location.

NEEDLE DROP FEES The payment of music or sound effects fees according to the number of times the cut is used rather than a yearly fee.

NEGATIVE A type of film that produces a reversed brightness image when developed.

NEGATIVE/POSITIVE PROCESS A means of producing projectable film images in two steps by first exposing and developing negative film and then printing that negative film on negative stock to produce a positive print.

NET DISTRIBUTOR RENTALS The amount of money a distributor receives from theater rentals of films minus the distributor's own costs.

NETWORK A company distributing programs to stations interconnected but not owned by the network. The FCC defines a network if it distributes at least 15 hours of programming a week to at least 25 affiliates in at least 10 states. Today there are six television networks: ABC, CBS, FOX, NBC, Universal/Paramount, and Warners.

NEILSEN RATINGS Television audience information researched by the A.C. Neilsen Company, consisting of shares, ratings, and demographics.

NEUTRAL DENSITY A type of filter that decreases light passage without changing the color value of the light.

NEWSFILM Before small camcorders became practical in the late 1970s, all news stories were shot on 16mm film, edited and then projected on a film chain.

NOISE Any undesirable additions to a signal.

NOISE REDUCTION The elimination or diminishing of audio noise by means of signal processing devices.

NONFICTION The depiction, description, or presentation of actual, unstaged events.

NONREFLEX A camera that has a separate viewfinder as opposed to one that allows the operator to look directly through the objective lens.

NONTHEATRICAL FILMS Films that are not produced for or shown in commercial theaters. Today direct-to-video films can gross more than a major motion picture.

NORMAL LENS A lens that presents an image perspective that approximates the vision of a monocular (single eye) human. A mid-range focal length.

NOTAN A lighting style similar to Japanese watercolors: high key, few shadows, evenly lit.

NTSC (National Television Standards Committee) 1) The organization charged with setting the television standard in the United States in the early days of television. 2) The television standard now in use in North America, much of South America, and Japan.

NTSC COLOR STANDARD The television standard first used in the United States for color TV transmission. This standard uses 525 interlaced lines scanned at the rate of 60 fields-30 frames per second.

OBJECTIVE LENS The lens on a camera that is used to record the images.

OFF-CAMERA MICROPHONE A microphone that is invisible to the audience.

OFF-LINE Using the lowest quality and cost editing system suitable for a particular project.

OFF-SCREEN SOUND A sound coming from a location not viewed by the audience.

OMNIDIRECTIONAL Microphone pickup pattern that covers 360 degrees around the mic.

OMNISCIENT POINT OF VIEW In literature a narrative written in the third as opposed to the first person. In media productions a story told from a relatively objective perspective or camera viewpoint.

ON-CAMERA MICROPHONES Microphones visible to the audience.

ON-LINE Using the highest quality and cost editing system suitable for a particular project.

ON-SCREEN SOUND Sound emanating from a source clearly seen by the audience.

OPAQUE BLACK LEADER Film leader that is coated with an opaque layer so that light can not pass through it. Used in conforming process to separate shots on the "A" and "B" rolls and as leader before and after the beginning and ending of the film.

OPEN MIC The instruction from the director to the audio operator to bring the pot or faded up on a particular mic.

OPERATOR Person whose main responsibility is to operate equipment, as contrasted with technicians, whose main responsibility it is to install, repair, and maintain equipment and engineers, whose main responsibility it is to research, design, and construct equipment.

OPTICAL DISK A laser recording medium for digital, video and/or audio information. A vast amount of data may be stored in a relatively small space and can be designed to record once or record many times. CDs and videodisks are examples of optical disks.

OPTICAL PRINTER A device consisting of a projector aimed at a camera which can be used to create special effects.

OPTICAL SOUND Sound recorded optically on the edge of film where variations in intensity are recorded as variations in density or the width of the film exposure.

OPTICS-OPTICAL Having to do with lenses or other light-carrying components of a video or film system.

OSCILLOSCOPE Test equipment used to visualize a time factor system such as a video signal. Shows a technician what the picture looks like electronically. Also may be used to analyze audio or other signals. See also Waveform monitor.

OUT-POINT The end point of an edit.

OUTPUT Signal leaving a system or electrical unit.

OUT-TAKES Recorded shots that are discarded entirely and do not appear in the final edited version of a media production.

OVEREXPOSURE Excessive exposure of film or video camera to light so that the quality of the image suffers and appears as washed out or overly bright.

OVERHEAD SHOT A shot from a camera which is placed directly overhead. This shot can be duplicated with the use of two mirrors. See Mirror shot.

OVER MODULATION Adjusting the sound intensity so high that it exceeds the limits of the equipment causing distortion.

OVER SCHEDULE A production that has exceeded the time limitations specified in the production schedule.

OVER-THE-SHOULDER SHOT (OS) A shot in which the camera is placed behind and to one side of a subject so that the shoulder of that subject is visible in the foreground and the face or body of another subject is in the background.

OWNED AND OPERATED A station actually owned by one of the networks. See also Affiliate.

OXIDE One type of metal coating used on magnetic tape and discs.

PACE A subjective impression of the speed of sounds or visuals.

PACKAGE A marketable combination of production elements such as well known stars, director, writers, and creative staff.

PAL (PHASE ALTERNATING LINE) A color television standard used in England and many other countries around the world. It is based on a 625 interlaced line, 25 frames per second system. It is not compatible with the US NTSC standard.

PALETTE A variety of colors.

PAN Horizontal movement of camera, short for panorama.

PANHEAD Mechanism designed to firmly hold a camera on top of a tripod, pedestal, or boom while allowing for smooth, easily controlled movement of the camera horizontally (pan) and vertically (tilt). May be mechanical, fluid, geared, or counter-balanced.

PANSCAN A system of converting wide screen motion pictures to the 3 x 4 television scan area. A print is made by panning across the film, centering on the most important areas of characters.

PARABOLIC MIC A focused, concave, reflective, bowl-shaped surface with a mic mounted at the point of focus. Used to pick up specific sounds at a distance. Commonly used during sporting events.

PARALLAX The discrepancy between the framed image in an objective lens and the image in a separate viewfinder in a nonreflex camera.

PARALLEL SOUND Sounds that compliment or have a supporting effect on the visual.

PATCH BAY A panel with wires connected to equipment in a control room to allow for flexibility in distributing signals to and from amplifiers and mixers. Also called *patch board* or *patch panel.*

PATCH CORD A short cable with plugs on each end designed to interconnect equipment wired to a patch bay.

PAUSE A mode or function on a recorder or player that holds the medium in position without stopping, but preventing an advance.

PAY CABLE Cable programming channels that must be paid above the amount for the basic service.

PEAK PROGRAM METER (PPM) A standard device for measuring sound intensity of loudness. It measures the peaks rather than the average as is measured in a VU meter.

PEDESTAL 1) Electronic calibration between blanking and black level. 2) Hydraulic, compressed air, or counter-balanced studio camera mount. Designed to permit the camera to be raised straight up or down effortlessly and smoothly.

PENCIL TEST A film shot of simple sketches of an animation production to check timing and other aspects of the production

PERAMBULATOR A large, wheeled, platform-mounted boom that a mic boom operator rides. Capable of swinging a mic over a large area.

PERFORATIONS (Perfs) The sprocket holes at the sides of film or full coat. Single perf-sprockets on one side only, double perf-sprockets on both sides.

PERSISTENCE OF VISION A physical/psychological phenomenon of sight that allows a series of still images to create the illusion of motion. One of the phenomenon upon which animation, motion pictures, and television appear to move.

PERSPECTIVE The illusion of spatial distance in a two-dimensional medium.

PHANTOM POWER 48 volts required by condenser mic preamplifiers located in the mic. If the mic does not carry its own battery power, may be supplied through the mic line by the mixer or recorder.

PHASE The relationship of two signals differing in time but on a common path.

PHASING PROBLEMS The cancellation of certain frequencies caused by placing microphones too close together when they are picking up the same source.

PHI PHENOMENON The illusion of apparent motion from rapidly flashing stationary lights and objects used in the animation process.

PHOTOELECTRIC CELL The transducer in a light meter of film projector that converts light energy into an electronic signal.

PHOTOFLOOD Lamp with self-contained reflectors that do not require a lighting instrument.

PHOTOGRAPHER Originally, a person taking still photographs. In some markets term was applied to news cinematographers and even today sometimes is applied to videographers.

PHOTOGRAPHIC FILM A light-sensitive material, consisting of silver halide particles attached to a flexible support base that yields visual images after proper exposure to light and chemical development.

PHOSPHORS Light-emitting optoelectronic semi-conductors inside a video picture tube.

PICKUP PATTERN The area or space surrounding a microphone within which the sensitivity to sound is the greatest.

PICKUP TUBE A device that converts light entering a video camera through the lens into electrical signals. Now replaced by solid state chips.

PILOTONE A particular type of sync signal used in synchronous film recording.

PISTOL GRIP A hand-held camera mount.

PITCH The perception of, or human response to, different sound frequencies.

PIXEL A single element of a computer or television picture. Picture resolution may be measured by the number of pixels in a set space.

PIXILLATION A system of single frame animation that records only a portion of a live action, creating a floating or jerky movement of subjects.

PLASTIC ANIMATION Animating three-dimensional objects.

PLATES The platters on a flatbed film editing machine that feed and take up film and tracks.

PLAYBACK The mode or machine operational setting for viewing or listening to a prerecorded signal.

PLAYBACK HEAD A magnetic device capable of transforming magnetic changes on a prerecorded tape into electronic signals.

PLOSIVE SOUNDS Sounds made by the human voice that tend to "pop" a microphone. Sounds beginning with the letters "p" and "b" among others.

PLOT A scale drawing of the location of a shoot.

PLUG A mechanical connector fastened to the end of a cable. Designed to mate with a matching jack mounted on equipment or on the wall.

PLUMBICON A type of video pickup tube, one of the last developed before being replaced by chips.

POINT OF ATTACK The beginning of a drama which usually generates interest and excitement.

POINT OF VIEW (POV) A camera angle giving the impression of the view of someone in the scene.

POLARIZER FILTER A glass or plastic filter that reduces glare when properly adjusted over a camera lens and/or lights on an animation or copy stand.

POOL FEED A common video or audio feed to supply more than one operation. Commonly set up for such restricted coverage as presidential appearances or in times of extremes emergencies or tragedies.

PORTABLE LIGHTING KIT A self-contained lighting unit for field production consisting of several lighting fixtures, stand, filters, accessories, and cables.

POSITIVE A type of visual image that reproduces the brightness of the original scene when it is processed or played back.

POST PRODUCTION The final stage of the production process, during which recorded images and sounds are edited and the production completed for distribution.

POT Short for potentiometer, a variable resistor used to change the voltage of an audio or video signal.

POWER AMPLIFIER An electronic circuit designed to amplify signals to a high enough level to power speakers or transmit signals over long lines.

POWER PACK Batteries used to power a piece of portable equipment.

PPV (Pay Per View) A cable service paid for on an individual program basis rather than on a monthly basis.

PREAMPLIFIER (Preamp) Electronic circuit designed to amplify weak signal to usable level without introducing noise or distortion.

PREBLACK The process of recording either a black video signal or color bars with a control track on videotape stock in preparation for insert editing which requires control track prerecorded on the tape.

PREPRODUCTION The preparatory stage of production planning prior to actual recording sounds and visual images.

PREROLL The amount of time needed in advance of making an edit or starting a film, audio, or videotape for playback or editing.

PRESSURE PLATE The surface inside a film camera that keeps the film flat in the gate at the aperture.

PREVIEW To view an image source without sending it to its assigned destination.

PRIMARY COLORS The basic colors used in lighting and filters: Red, green, and blue.

PRIME LENS A fixed focal length lens.

PRIME TIME In general practice, the television broadcast evening hours programmed by the networks between 8-11 PM for the east and west coast, and 6-10 PM for the midwest and mountain states.

PRINCIPAL CHARACTERS Friends and foils of the central character(s).

PRINTING The process of making a copy of a film.

PRINT THROUGH A signal that has bled through from one layer of recording tape to the next.

PRINT-THROUGH EDGE NUMBERS Numbers from the original film that are printed through to the workprint by using an edge light during the printing process.

PRISM A glass or plastic block shaped to transmit or reflect light into different paths.

PRODUCER Person in charge of a specific program.

PRODUCTION The stage of the production process during which production materials and equipment are set up and sounds and images are actually recorded.

PRODUCTION DESIGN The coordination of scenic design and other artistic aspects of production such as lighting.

PRODUCTION DESIGNER The crew person who heads the production design team.

PRODUCTION MANAGER In feature-film production, the person who breaks down the script into its component parts for budgeting and scheduling and who supervises the allocation and use of studio and location facilities.

PROGRAM 1) To set a function of a pot, fader, or other control. 2) A complete production package ready to be broadcast or distributed.

PROMPTER Device used to provide the talent with the copy as they sit on camera. Can be copy handheld beside the camera or a signal fed to a monitor mounted with mirrors to project the copy in front of the camera lens so the anchor can look directly into the camera. This signal may be coming from a black-and-white camera shooting pages of the script or from a signal fed directly from a computer.

PROPERTIES (Props) Functional set furnishings that play a part in a video or film program.

PROPOSAL A concise summary of a project intended as a sales tool to accurately describe a production and to sell a sponsor on funding.

PROSTHETIC MAKEUP Makeup and devices designed to transform the appearance of a performer's face or body through temporary "plastic surgery."

PROSUMER A category of producer and equipment that falls below that of a professional but at a higher level than a consumer.

PROXIMITY EFFECT A change in the audio pickup by moving the source too close to the microphone, can be used to give the appearance of lowering the human voice.

PSA (Public Service Announcement) A non-commercial radio or TV spot.

PUBLIC ADDRESS (PA) Sound reinforcing system designed to feed sound to an audience assembled in a large room or other space.

PULLDOWN CLAW The square pin that grabs each sprocket hole of a film in the gate to advance a single frame in the aperture for exposure.

PURE TONE A single sound frequency.

QUADRAPLEX (Quad) First practical professional videotape format. Used 2-inch tape pulled across four heads to achieve a high quality signal. No longer manufactured.

QUARTER INCH PLUG (Phone) Audio connector used for many years for high-impedance signals. Still used in some consumer equipment and patch panels.

QUARTZ LIGHT A tungsten light source consisting of a tungsten filament, a quartz housing, and halogen gas.

RADIO MICROPHONE (Wireless mic) A microphone connected to a small FM transmitter worn by the performer broadcasting a short distance to a receiver connected to the audio mixer. This allows the performer to operate with trailing wires.

RASTER The complete sequence of lines that make up the field of lines creating a video picture.

RATING Estimated percentage of TV households tuned to the same program at any one time.

RAW STOCK Unexposed film, video, or audiotape that has not been recorded.

RCA The American corporation that promoted the NTSC video system, the developer of many early television inventions, and the original owner of NBC radio and television.

RCA PLUG (Phono) Audio and video connector designed originally for use only with the RCA 45 rpm record player. Now used as consumer audio and video connector. Some professional equipment uses this plug for line level audio. Not to be confused with the phone (¼-inch plug).

REACTION SHOT Close-up of a character's reaction to events.

REALISTIC LIGHTING Lighting that conforms to the audience's conventional expectations of how a scene should appear in "real" life.

REALISTIC SETS Sets designed to represent a specific or general type of place with which an audience is presumed to have some familiarity, usually filled with "naturalistic" details.

REAR PROJECTION A projection of a slide or film on a screen behind the performers on a set.

RECEIVER A television or radio set capable of decoding a broadcast signal.

RECORDING HEAD A magnetic device that transforms electronic signals into changes in a magnetic field so that sounds and pictures can be recorded on tape.

RECORD MODE A machine operational setting for recording pictures and/or sound.

REDUCTION A transfer of film to a smaller format on an optical printer.

REEL-TO-REEL RECORDER A device that can record and/or playback sounds on an open reel of tape.

REFERENCE WHITE A white card or large white object in the frame that can be used for white balancing or the proper color adjustment of a video camera.

REFLECTED LIGHT Illumination entering a lens reflected from an object. Measured with a reflected light meter pointing at the object from the camera.

REFLECTED READING A light meter reading of the intensity of light reflected from the subject and/or background.

REFLECTION A bouncing back of light from an object.

REFLECTOR A flat or curved surface that light can be bounced off to create indirect light on a set or location.

REFLEX A type of camera that allows the operator to look directly through the objective lens.

REFRACTION Light changing direction as it passes through transparent surfaces.

REGISTRATION The alignment of either electronic or physical components of a system. Especially important in tube cameras.

REGISTRATION PIN A device on some film cameras that holds the film steady while a frame is being exposed to light at the aperture.

RELEASE 1) Legal document allowing the videographer to use the image and/or voice of a subject. 2) Public relations copy.

RELEASE PRINT A final copy of a film with sound track that are distributed and exhibited.

REMOTE PRODUCTION A video production performed outside of the studio.

REMOTE VAN A large video production semi-trailer containing a virtual studio control room and all of the equipment normally in a video studio for high level coverage of sports and entertainment events.

REPORTER A newsperson who is responsible for researching, gathering, and writing news stories. May or may not appear on camera or in the studio.

RESEARCH The process of investigating and uncovering sources of information about prospective video or film audiences and/or the facts necessary to write a script.

RESIDUALS Payment made to performers for repeat uses of programs and commercials in which they appear.

RESOLUTION 1) Ability of a system to reproduce fine detail. In video there are limits imposed by the NTSC video system. 2) Overcoming the central conflict in a drama and fulfilling the goals and motivations that have stimulated the dramatic action.

RESPONSE CURVE A graph of the sensitivity of a piece of audio equipment to different frequencies.

REVERBERATION The delay between direct and indirect sounds.

REVERBERATION UNIT A signal processing device that can create sound reverberation or echo.

REVERSAL PROCESS A means of producing projectable film images in a single step by using a type of film stock and development process that produces positive images from a single exposure and development.

REVERSE-ANGLE SHOT A shot which the camera faces in exactly the opposite direction from the previous shot.

REWINDS Rotating spindles on a film editing bench used to advance and rewind the film.

RF (Radio Frequency) 1) Those frequencies above the aural frequencies. 2) A type of plug attached to a cable designed to carry a modulated signal.

RHYTHM The beat or tempo of music or editing which affects the perception of speed or pace.

RIBBON MIC A transducer utilizing a thin gold or silver corrugated ribbon suspended between the poles of a magnet to create an electrical output.

RIGHT-TO-WORK LAWS State statutes prohibiting unions from enforcing closed shops or requiring union membership of all employees covered in a contract.

RISERS Hollow rectangular boxes or platforms to be placed on the studio floor to raise a portion of the set.

ROSTRUM A movable table on which artwork is placed on an animation stand for precise framing and movement from one cel to another.

ROTOSCOPE A means of producing life-like animation by filming a subject moving and then projecting each frame under a transparent drawing board and tracing the subject's position.

ROUGH CUT The initial selection and ordering of shots and scenes in a production.

ROYALTY FEES Money paid to composers, authors, and performers for the use of copyrighted materials.

RUB-ON LETTERS Individual letters that can be transferred to any flat surface to make titles by rubbing on the plastic sheet holding the letters.

RUNDOWN SHEET A basic outline of a program which simply indicates the time and order of specific segments. See also Format sheet.

RUNNING TIME Actual program length or duration of a program.

SAFE ACTION AREA The approximate 90% of the television scanned area that can be reproduced on most home television receivers. Compare this to critical or essential area.

SAG (Screen Actors Guild) The union that represents most film performers.

SANDBAG A bag filled with sand used to steady lamp stands or other set pieces.

SATELLITE Geostationary orbiting space platform with transponders to pick up signals from the Earth and retransmit the signals back down to Earth in a pattern, called a *footprint*, that covers a large area of the Earth.

SATURATION Intensity of a signal, either audio or video, but especially used as the third of three characteristics of a color video signal.

SCA (Subsidiary Communication Authorization) FCC gives permission for a company to use subcarriers on existing channels for audio or data transmission.

SCALE The apparent size of objects within the frame

SCAN LINE A horizontal line of phosphors in a television receiver or video monitor or optoelectronic semiconductors in a pickup tube.

SCANNING AREA The full field of view picked up by the video camera pickup tube.

SCENE A series of related shots, usually in the same time and location.

SCENE SCRIPT A full script without individual shots indicated.

SCENIC ARTISTS Craftsmen who compose detailed sketches, drawings, and set layouts.

SCENIC DESIGN Overall artistic control and coordination of sets, props, costumes, and makeup.

SCENIC DESIGNER In video production, the person who supervises the overall production design, including props and costumes.

SCOOP A lighting instrument with an open bowl reflector that produces soft floodlight.

SCORE Music composed for a specific film or videotape.

SCOUTING REPORT A complete report of the facilities available and the equipment needed for a location production at a specific site. Also *site survey.*

SCRAMBLING Modifying a video signal so it can not be received with out the proper decoder. Pay cable channels are scrambled.

SCREEN A non diffusion scrim.

SCREEN DIRECTIONALITY The left-to-right movement and placement of objects in successive two-dimensional images or shots.

SCRIM A metallic or fabric filter placed over a lighting instrument to diffuse and soften the light.

SCRIPT Complete manuscript of all audio copy and video instructions of a program.

SCRIPT BREAKDOWN Reorganizing the script in terms of specific settings so that production can be scheduled and an accurate estimate of the budget made in terms of equipment and personnel needs at each setting and each scheduled day of shooting.

SCRIPT CONTINUITY The dictates of the script in terms of temporal and spatial details that must be maintained during production.

SCRIPT OUTLINE A semi-scripted format in which only a portion of videotape or live television program is fully scripted, such as the opening and closing segments if other elements are to be ad-libbed. See also *format* and *rundown sheet.*

SCRIPT SUPERVISOR The person who maintains continuity in performer actions and prop placements from shot-to-shot and ensures that every scene in the script has been recorded.

SCRIPTWRITING The process of creating a written outline for a videotape, live television program, audio production, or film.

SEARCH A function on a videotape recorder that allows a specific point on the videotape to be found by moving the tape very slowly.

SEARCH-AND-CUE FUNCTION A machine operational setting that allows a playback machine to search for specific cues on a prerecorded tape.

SEG (Screen Extras Guild) The union that represents extras, or performers who do not speak on camera or have specific actions.

SEGMENT A portion of a program or spot.

SECAM (SEQUENTIAL COLOUR AVEC MEMOIRE) The color television system developed by the French and in use around the world in many countries.

SEGUE The immediate replacement of one sound source with another.

SELECTIVE FOCUS Utilizing depth of field to direct the viewer's attention to certain areas of the scene by varying those elements in and out of focus.

SELF-BLIMPED A film camera that is completely sound insulated for synchronous sound recording.

SEL SYNC An internal means of synchronization within an audiotape, which can be used to record consecutive sound tracks in synchronization with each other.

SEMI-SCRIPTED A partial description or outline of a videotape, live television program, audio production, or film.

SEPARATION LIGHT A general lighting term that includes back lights and kickers, which both help to separate foreground subjects and backgrounds.

SEQUENCE Individual shots edited into scenes, and individual scenes edited together to make a story.

SERVO CAPSTAN A capstan with an accurate motor that varies the speed of the playback to maintain proper synchronization between a video recorder and playback machine.

SET DESIGNER In large-scale productions, the person who does the actual drawing of set floor plans and elevations and layouts and supervises the construction of sets.

SET FURNISHINGS Furniture and props that fill out a set.

SETTINGS Specific exterior and interior places and locations specified in a script.

SET UP Assemble equipment and people in preparation for rehearsing a production.

SET-UP Same as pedestal and black level; electronic calibration between blanking and black level.

SHADING Adjusting the brightness level, light sensitivity, and color of a video camera.

SHADOW MASK A series of windows or aperture deflectors inside a television picture tube which prevent electrons from each gun from striking the wrong color light-emitting phosphors.

SHARE Estimated percentage of HUTs watching a specific program at one time.

SHARPNESS A rating of the edge clarity and focus of images reproduced in video or film production.

SHOCK-MOUNTED MICROPHONE A microphone designed to minimize all vibrations and noise except those inherent in sound waves.

SHOOTING RATIO The ratio of material recorded during production to that which is actually used in the final edited version.

SHOOTING SCRIPT A script complete in all details, including specific shot descriptions.

SHOT One continuous roll of the recorder or camera. The smallest unit of a script.

SHOTGUN Ultra-unidirectional microphone designed to pick up sound at a distance by excluding unwanted sound from the sides of the mic.

SHOT SHEET A listing of all shots in the order they are to be made, regardless of their order in the script.

SHOULDER HARNESS A body brace used as a camera mount.

SHUTTER An opaque device in a film camera that rapidly opens and closes to expose the film to light.

SHUTTLE Movement of videotape back and forth while searching for edit points. Usually done at speeds faster or slower than real time.

SIGNAL LEVEL The signal strength of the electrical current from recording and playback equipment.

SIGNAL PROCESSING Manipulation of the electrical sound signal.

SIGNAL-TO-NOISE RATIO (S/N Ratio) The mathematical ratio between the noise level in a signal to the program level. The higher the ratio, the better the signal.

SINGLE-CAMERA PRODUCTION The use of a single video or film camera to record a videotape or film in segments.

SINGLE PERF Film with sprocket holes on only one side or edge.

SINGLE-SYSTEM RECORDING Recording a synchronous sound track within the camera on the same roll of film as the pictures.

SITE SURVEY A detailed listing of all the information needed to shoot on location at a certain site.

SKEW Tension adjustment during videotape playback. Visible as a "bending" at the extreme top or bottom of the picture.

SKYLIGHT Indirect sunlight which has a higher color temperature than direct sunlight.

SLANT TRACK See Helical Scan.

SLATE Several frames identifying the shot, tape, or film reel number, or other logging information. Usually recorded at the beginning of the tape.

SLIDES Still photographic transparencies which can be projected.

SLIDING TRACK An overhead light grid to which lighting instruments are attached so that they slide into position along the track.

SLIPPING Moving a track (usually audio) forward or backward in relationship to the picture or visual.

SLO-MO DISC RECORDER A video recorder that records live-action images on a rotating disc so that they can be played back in slow motion, such as for game analysis in a sports broadcast.

SLOW MOTION Recording images at a faster speed than the normal playback speed.

SLUG An Identifying name for a news story. Usually only one or two words.

SMATV (Satellite Master Antenna Television) A "private" cable system. Often used by apartment or hotel complexes to serve all of their units.

SMEARING See Comet-tailing.

SMPTE (SOCIETY OF MOTION PICTURE AND TELEVISION ENGINEERS) Professional society of members predominately interested in the technical side of motion pictures, radio, and television. The official organization for setting technical standards in this country.

SMPTE TIME CODE A binary code accurately setting hours, minutes, seconds, and frames used to synchronized audio, video, and film media.

SOFT CUT A very rapid dissolve.

SOFT LIGHT Indirect, diffused light that minimizes shadows.

SOFTLIGHTS Large light fixtures that emits a well-diffused light over a broad area.

SOFTWARE Material recorded on audio, video, and/or computer media. Contrast with hardware.

SOFT WIPE A slight superimposition at the point two images intersect during a wipe from one to the other.

SOLARIZATION A technique that drains the normal color from a visual image and replaces it with artificially controlled colors.

SOP (Standard Operating Procedure) Predetermined methods of completing tasks. Often set by corporate or upper management policy.

SOUND AMPLITUDE The intensity and height of a sound pressure wave.

SOUND EFFECTS Sounds that are matched to their supposed visual sources during postproduction editing.

SOUND FIDELITY The accuracy or illusion of reality inherent in a sound recording.

SOUND FREQUENCY The rapidity with which air molecules move back and forth in direct relation to the vibrations of the sound source.

SOUND INTENSITY The amplitude of a sound wave, which is perceived as a specific loudness level.

SOUND-ON-FILM (SOF) See Single-system recording.

SOUND PERSPECTIVE An enhanced perception of distance achieved through the use of different volume levels for near and far sounds.

SOUND PRESSURE WAVE The compression and expansion of air molecules in response to the vibrations of a sound source.

SOUND TEST A test setting of the sound level prior to actual recording.

SOUND UP AND UNDER Instruction to cut the sound in at its proper level and then fade it down to a lower level, where it is still audible but less prominent.

SOUND VELOCITY The speed of a sound pressure wave.

SOURCE MUSIC Music that comes from a source within the actual scene portrayed on screen.

SPACERS Small wheels used to fill the gaps between take-up reels on a film editing bench so that their spacing matches the spacing of the individual hubs or wheels in a gang synchronizer.

SPATIAL DISTORTION An aural imbalance during stereophonic playback or recording which results from a faulty positioning of the sound source.

SPECIAL EFFECTS GENERATOR Electronic device usually installed in the video switcher, which is used to produce wipes, split screens, and inserts.

SPEED OF ACTION The speed of the movement of objects within the frame.

SPIDER An adjustable device into which the spurs of a tripod are placed on a flat, hard surface.

SPLICING Physically cutting and cementing magnetic tape or film while editing.

SPLIT An agreed-upon division of box office receipts between exhibitors and film distributors.

SPLIT-BEAM A reflex viewing system in which mirrors between the lens and the viewfinder eyepiece continuously deflect about 18 percent to 20 percent of the light.

SPLIT EDIT An edit made in which the audio and video are assigned separate in or outpoints so that the signals do not start or stop at the same point in time.

SPLIT-PAGE SCRIPT A script that has the visual specification on the left side of the page and the corresponding audio specifications on the right side.

SPLIT SCREEN A special video effect in which one image occupies a portion of the frame and another image occupies the remaining portion.

SPLITTER BOX Device used to feed an input signal to more than one output. Commonly used at news conferences to avoid a jumble of microphones by splitting the feed from one mic to all those covering the event.

SPOT EFFECTS Specific sound effects created expressly for a videotape, live television program, or film in a sound studio.

SPOTLIGHTS Lighting instruments with lenses that sharply focus the light they emit, producing intense, harsh lighting.

SPOT METER A light meter designed to read a very small area of reflected light.

SPOT READING A light-meter reading of the intensity of the light reflected by the subject in a very narrow area as determined by the angle of acceptance of the spot meter.

SPREADER See Spider.

SPROCKET HOLES The perforations in a piece of film which allow it to be advanced or driven through a camera or projector.

SPROCKET TEETH Metal teeth which drive a piece of film through a camera, projector, or editing device by engaging the sprocket holes.

SPUN GLASS A flexible light diffuser made out of fiberglass.

SPURS Points on the end of a tripod, which can be stuck into soft ground.

SQUASHING AND STRETCHING Animation techniques that exaggerate and caricature motions by accentuating the initial and ending movements of an action, such as running or jumping, to make them seem more active.

STAGE MANAGER The person who supervises the use of studio space, such as the setup and breaking down of sets and props on the studio floor. See Floor Manager.

STAND MICROPHONE A microphone designed to be secured to a mic stand, which can be raised or lowered to conform to the height of the speaker.

STEADICAM A servostabilizer camera mount attached to the operator's body to minimize camera vibrations when the operator moves with the camera.

STEREOPHONIC SOUND Separation of sounds coming from the right and the left during recording and playback which preserves the directionality of sound sources.

STINGERS Short phrases of music, usually characterized by a rapidly descending scale or series of notes, used as punctuation devices.

STOP MOTION Filming or taping subjects one or two frames at a time.

STORYBOARD A series of drawings indicating each shot and accompanying audio in a production.

STORY TIME The supposed historical time of events presented in a television program or film.

STRIKE 1) A command and action to tear down sets, pack up equipment and clear an area following a production. 2) A work stoppage action of a labor dispute.

STRINGERS Freelance reporters and/or video/cinematographers who are paid by the story or are retained by a news operation but not on full-time staff.

STRIP LIGHTS A series of lights connected in a straight line.

STUDIO A controlled, indoor production environment designed expressly for video, audio, or film recording.

STUDIO PRODUCTION The recording of audio, video, or film images inside a controlled production environment.

STYLIZED LIGHTING Lighting that is intended to achieve a special kind of emotional effect or abstract design through nonnaturalistic patterns of light.

STYLIZED SETS Abstract, imaginative settings that reflect an artistic style or give external form to an interior state of mind, such as a specific character's subjective state of mind.

SUBJECTIVE POINT OF VIEW A story told from the perspective of a specific character or participant in the action.

SUBJECTIVE SHOT A presentation of images supposedly dreamed, imagined, recollected, or perceived in an abnormal state of mind by a character or participant in a videotape or film.

SUBPOENA An order of the court to appear as a witness. May include an order to release sources, notes, and/or original and edited recordings.

SUBTITLES Titles placed in the bottom third of the video or film frame that clarify the image or present the spoken dialogue in written form.

SUBTRACTIVE COLOR The process of using color-absorbing filters to subtract specific wavelengths of light from a white light source and produce the various colors of the visible spectrum.

SUPERCARDIOID A highly directional microphone pickup pattern.

SUPERIMPOSITIONS (Supers) Two or more simultaneously fed video signals, stopping a dissolve at the halfway point.

SUPERSTATION A local television station whose signal is satellite delivered to cable systems across the company. WTBS of Atlanta and WGN of Chicago are such stations.

SWEETENING The process of equalizing, setting levels and mixing voices, music, and sound effects into a master audio recording.

SWISH PAN A rapid horizontal movement of the camera while recording. May be used as a transition device.

SWITCHER 1) In multicamera or postproduction, a device used to change video sources feeding the recording tape deck. 2) The person operating the video switcher.

SYMMETRY The degree to which composition within a camera frame is balanced.

SYNC GENERATOR An electronic device which produces various synchronizing signals necessary for the operation of the video recording system.

SYNC HEAD An additional recording head on a synchronous sound recorder, used for recording the sync signal.

SYNCHRONOUS (Sync) Signals locked in proper alignment with each other; sound and picture locked together, all the various video signals in their proper relationship to each other.

SYNCHRONOUS SOUND RECORDER A device capable of recording sounds in synchronization with the images recorded by a film camera.

SYNC SIGNAL A regular wave of electrical current, which can be used as a speed reference for sound and picture synchronization.

SYNDICATED PROGRAMMING Commercial television programs and films that are distributed directly to local television stations, bypassing the major television networks.

TAKES Individual shots of a single action. There may be several takes of the same shot in single-camera productions, from which one will be selected for use in the final edited version.

TAKEUP The part of a recording device that collects the tape or film.

TALENT Anyone who appears on camera or before the microphone.

TALK-BACK SYSTEM An intercom system in a television studio, used for communication between the creative staff in the control room and the crew on the studio floor.

TALLY LIGHT A light on the top of a video camera which informs the talent and crew which of several cameras has been selected for recording or transmission at a particular time.

TAPE SPLICER A device with a cutting blade and guide for combining different pieces of film or audiotape with transparent tape.

TECHNICAL DIRECTOR (TD) In video production, the person who operates the switcher at the commands of the director.

TELECINE An optical/electronic system of transferring film to videotape. Once called film chain.

TELEPHOTO Long focal-length lens.

TELETEXT Text and graphics broadcast along with a TV signal for especially equipped TV receivers.

TELEVISION The electronic transmission and reception of visual images of moving and stationary objects, usually with accompanying sound.

TELEVISION QUOTIENT (TV-Q) A popularity index of television performers, which is sometimes used to ensure success and aid casting decisions.

TEMPORAL CONTINUITY A continuous flow of events without any apparent gaps in time.

TENT An opaque sheet of material suspended over a subject to diffuse and soften the light.

TEXTURE The roughness or smoothness of a surface.

THEATRICAL FILMS Films produced for commercial theaters.

THEME 1) A central concept, idea, or symbolic meaning in a story. 2) A repeated melody in a symphony or other long musical composition.

THREE-OR-FOUR POINT LIGHTING A basic lighting technique that helps create an illusion of three-dimensionality by separating the subject from the background, using key, fill, and separation light.

THREE SHOT A camera setup in which three subjects appear in the same frame.

THREE-TO-ONE RULE To avoid phasing problems, two or more microphones used simultaneously should be place at least three times as far apart as their subject-to-mic distances.

THROUGH THE LENS (TTL) A type of light meter that measures the amount of light actually coming through the lens of a camera.

TILT A vertical pivoting of a camera.

TILT SHOT A camera shot accomplished by moving the camera up and down on a swivel or tilting device.

TIMBRE See Tonality.

TIME BASE CORRECTOR (TBC) Electronic device used to lock together signals with dissimilar sync. Also may be used to correct for phase, level, and pedestal errors in original recordings.

TIME CODE Time based address recorded on videotape to allow for precise editing. SMPTE time code is one most universally used at present.

TITLES Lettering recorded within the visual frame that identifies the visual images or adds additional text to the videotape, live television program, or film.

TITLE SEQUENCE See Credit sequence.

TONALITY The particular quality or unique characteristics of a musical instrument or voice.

TOPIC RESEARCH The process of gathering accurate information about a prospective program's subject matter.

TRACK A separate tape path.

TRACKING 1) Aligning playback heads on a VCR with the original pattern of video recorded on tape. 2) Movement of a camera to the left or right, usually while mounted on a set of tracks for maximum smoothness and control.

TRAGEDY A type of drama that has a serious tone and often focuses on the misfortunes and problems of life.

TRANSDUCER Any device used to convert any form of energy to another form: a camera transduces light to video; a microphone transduces sound to electronics; a speaker transduces electronics to sound.

TRANSFER A copy of a recording in which the format is changed.

TRANSFORMER Magnetic voltage- or impedance-changing device.

TRANSITION DEVICES Various means of changing from one shot to another to suggest changes of time and/or place.

TRANSPONDER A satellite section that receives and retransmits a signal or series of signals on a single frequency.

TRANSVERSE TRACK See Quadruplex.

TRAVELING MATTE A film matte that moves across the image to create special effects.

TREATMENT A narrative description of a production. It should read more like a novel than a script since it is intended for a nonmedia person.

TREBLE High frequencies of the audio band.

TRIANGLE See Spider.

TRIM IN/OUT The process of making small adjustments in the in and out points of edits.

TRIPOD Three-legged portable camera support.

TRUCKING SHOT A shot in which the camera moves from side to side on a wheeled dolly.

T-STOP Unit of light transmission for a lens based on actual tests of light transmission.

TUNGSTEN LIGHT Relatively efficient gas-filled light source of approximately 32,000 degree Kelvin temperature.

TVRO (Television Receive Only) A satellite downlink system that can not uplink a signal. Home satellite receivers are TVROs.

TYLER MOUNT A helicopter or airplane camera mount that reduce vibration.

TWO-SHOT A camera shot including two subjects.

UHF (Ultra High Frequency) 1) Frequency band for television broad-casting channels 14 through 69. 2) An older, large, threaded type of video connector.

ULTRACARDIOID The most directional (narrowest) microphone pickup pattern available, sometimes called a shotgun microphone.

ULTRAVIOLET LIGHT Invisible light that has a shorter wavelength than visible light but can nonetheless affect film and is present in outdoor shadow areas.

U-MATIC ¾-inch videotape format created by Sony in the early 1970s that revolutionized video news gathering. Has been upgraded by a compatible U-matic SP format.

UNBALANCED MICROPHONE LINE A mic cable consisting of a single conductor that is less well insulated than a balanced line and thus more susceptible to cable noise.

UNIDIRECTIONAL Microphone pickup pattern from a single direction. Comes in a variety of degrees of pickup angle, from cardioid to super unidirectional (shotgun).

UNION AND GUILD CONTRACTS Agreements regarding salaries, working conditions, etc., made between various craft, trade, and talent unions or guilds and television, audio, and film producers.

UNSCALED LAYOUT A bird's-eye view of the studio and set giving a rough approximation of the material that must be constructed.

UP LINK Transmission path from an Earth-based station up to a satellite. Sometimes used to describe the ground station capable of sending a satellite signal. See Down link.

UPRIGHT A vertically arranged film editing machine.

VARIABLE FOCAL LENGTH LENS (Zoom) A lens that can have its focal length changed while in use.

VARIABLE SPEED MOTOR An electric drive motor whose speed can be varied and controlled.

VECTORSCOPE Electronic test equipment designed to show the color aspects of the video signal.

VERTICAL BLANKING The period of time that the television electron beam is shut off, while the beam jumps from the bottom of one field or frame to the top of another.

VERTICAL INTERVAL TIME CODE (VITC) Time address recorded within the vertical interval blanking instead of on a separate linear track.

VERTICAL SYNC A portion of a television signal that controls the rate of vertical scanning and blanking.

VHF (Very High Frequency) The frequency spectrum includes television channels 2 through 13.

VHS, S-VHS JVC-developed consumer VCR system, VHS stands for Video Home System. "S" in S-VHS stands for "separate" since it is a semicompatible component recording system, rather than a composite system.

VIDEO 1) Picture portion of an electronic visual system. 2) All inclusive term for electronic visual reproduction systems; includes television, cablevision, corporate media, and video recording.

VIDEOCASSETTE A self-contained set of reels with videotape.

VIDEOCASSETTE RECORDER (VCR) A machine that can record video and audio signals on cassettes of videotape.

VIDEODISK An optical disk loaded with video and audio material, most often motion pictures or training tapes/films.

VIDEO ENGINEER In video production, the person who adjusts or shades the cameras for optimal recording and monitors the videotape recording equipment.

VIDEOGRAPHER The proper term for the operator of a video camera.

VIDEO METERS Meters on a videotape recorder that indicate the strength of the video portion of the television signal.

VIDEO NOISE Static or unwanted light in a video image.

VIDEO SYNTHESIZER A device that allows an artist to manipulate the analog or digital signal of a video image so that colors and shapes can be creatively altered for special effects.

VIDEOTAPE Magnetic substance coated, plastic based tape used for recording video and audio signals.

VIDEOTAPE EDITING UNIT An electronic editing system consisting of a playback VTR or VCR, a recorder, and an editing control unit.

VIDEOTAPE RECORDER (VTR) A device that records audio and video signals on open reels of tape rather than closed cassettes.

VIDEOTEX An interactive computer graphics database that may be accessed through a modem, cable television, or other lines of electronic communication.

VIDEO-TO-FILM TRANSFER Copying a videotape on film once called kinescoping.

VIDICON A type of video camera tube that replaced the Image Orthicon. It was lighter, smaller, and more durable and provided higher resolution.

VIEWFINDER The miniature video monitor mounted on the camera so the operator can see what is framed by the camera.

VISUAL The video portion of the program.

VISUALIZATION The creative process of transforming a script into a sequence of visual images and sounds.

VISUAL STYLE The particular approach taken by a director to the visual presentation of events in a videotape, live television program, or film, including the selection of specific camera placements, movements, and types of shots.

VOICE OVER (VO) Story that uses continuous visuals, accompanied by the voice of an unseen narrator.

VOLTS An electronic measurement of the pressure available at a power source. In North America the standard is 110-120 V.

VOLUME The measurable loudness of a sound signal.

VOLUME UNIT (VU) Measurement of audio level. Indicates the average of the sound level, not the peak.

VU METER The volume unit meter which indicates the relative levels of sounds passing through a sound system.

WATTS Measurement of power used in a piece of electrical or electronic equipment.

WAVEFORM MONITOR An electronic measuring tool; both oscilloscopes and vectorscopes are waveform monitors.

WAVELENGTH The distance between the crest or valleys of each successive wave of energy in light or sound.

WEDGE Plate fastened to the bottom of a camera that allows it to be quickly mounted to a tripod equipped with a matched slot.

WHITE BALANCE Electronic matching of the camera circuits to the color temperature of the light source.

WHITE LEVEL (Gain) Level of maximum voltage in a video signal.

WIDE ANGLE A lens with a relatively short focal length and wide field of view.

WILD SOUND Ambient background sound. See Nat sound.

WIND NOISE Unwanted sound caused by air blowing over the pickup elements of a microphone.

WINDOW DUPE A copy of a videotape that has the SMPTE time code recorded so that it is visible in a "window" for viewing, for logging, or locating specific points on the tape during the editing process.

WIND SCREEN A plastic foam covering placed over a microphone to inhibit wind noise.

WIPE Electronic special effects transition that allows one image to be replaced by another with a moving line separating the two pictures. Stopping a wipe in mid-movement creates a split-screen.

WORK PRINT An edited master recording video or film used in off-line or preliminary editing stages.

WOW An audio distortion caused by a change in speed of either the record or playback equipment.

WRATTEN A series of filters originally designed for photography but adapted for use in cinematography, videography.

X-AXIS The plane running horizontally to the camera.

XLR PLUG Professional audio connector that allows for three conductors plus a shielded ground. Special types of multi-pin XLRs are used for headsets and battery power connectors.

Y-AXIS The plane running vertically to the camera.

YELLOW-INK EDGE NUMBERS Edge numbers printed by a laboratory on the film as opposed to edge numbers place there by the film manufacturer.

Y SIGNAL See Luminance.

Z-AXIS The plane running away/toward the camera.

ZERO START The beginning point of SMPTE time code on a videotape recording.

ZOOM See Variable focal length lens.

Index